APPROPRIATING SHAKESPEARE

Richard Marius

Feb.

OTHER BOOKS BY BRIAN VICKERS

As author

Francis Bacon and Renaissance Prose (Cambridge, 1968)
The Artistry of Shakespeare's Prose (London, 1968, 1976)
Classical Rhetoric in English Poetry (London, 1970; Carbondale, Ill., 1989)
Towards Greek Tragedy (London, 1973)
In Defence of Rhetoric (Oxford, 1988, 1989)
Returning to Shakespeare (London, 1989)

As editor and contributor

The World of Jonathan Swift (Oxford, 1968)
Rhetoric Revalued (Binghamton, NY, 1982)
Occult and Scientific Mentalities in the Renaissance (Cambridge, 1984)
Arbeit, Musse, Meditation. Studies in the Vita activa and Vita contemplativa
(Zürich, 1985; 1991)

As editor

Henry Mackenzie, 'The Man of Feeling' (Oxford, 1967, 1987)
Shakespeare: The Critical Heritage, 1623–1801, 6 vols (London and Boston, 1974–81)
Public and Private Life in the Seventeenth Century: The Mackenzie-Evelyn Debate (Delmar, NY, 1986)
English Science, Bacon to Newton (Cambridge, 1987)

APPROPRIATING SHAKESPEARE

Contemporary Critical Quarrels

BRIAN VICKERS

YALE UNIVERSITY PRESS
NEW HAVEN AND LONDON · 1993

Set in Goudy Old Style by Best-set Typesetter Ltd., Hong Kong
Printed and bound in Great Britain by Biddles Ltd., Guildford and Kings Lynn

Library of Congress Cataloging-in-Publication Data

Vickers, Brian.
  Appropriating Shakespeare: contemporary critical quarrels / by
Brian Vickers.
    p. cm.
  Includes bibliographical references and index.
  ISBN 0–300–05415–7 (hbk.)
  ISBN 0–300–06105–6 (pbk.)
  1. Shakespeare, William, 1564–1616—Criticism and interpretation—
History—20th century. 2. Literature, Modern—History and
criticism—Theory, etc. 3. Literary quarrels—History—20th
century. 4. Criticism—History—20th century. I. Title.
PR2970.V5 1993
822.3'3—dc20   92–38549
                                                    CIP

A catalogue record for this book is available from the British Library.

For Sabine

But now I was the lord
Of this fair mansion. . . .

Contents

Preface

We are in the business of elucidation, which eschews a number of procedures on grounds of inefficiency: histrionic rejection (*No! never again!*), compulsive recantation (*No, no, we don't believe that now*), or polite evasion (*Oh, don't let's talk in those terms*). The only way to cast off a dogma is to expose its shortcomings.

Vincent Descombes[1]

Anyone who has kept even half an eye on Shakespeare studies over the last twenty years will have noticed the emergence of several different groups of critics presenting a more or less coherent programme for interpreting his plays, and disputing the competence of rival groups. The reader (and soon, no doubt, theatregoer) who basically wants to learn about *Hamlet*, say, as interpreted by contemporary critics, not only has the problem of a vast annual output of secondary criticism — a situation that surveyors of the field have been (rather pointlessly) deploring for decades — but is now faced with the competing claims of four or five different critical schools. There are the psychocritics, the senior group, so to speak, still deriving from Freud but now drawing on Lacan and other (mainly French) neo-Freudians. Equally venerable are the Marxists, who can also draw on the great upheaval in Marxist studies from Lukács to Adorno and beyond. There are the feminists, the most aggressive development in recent times, the New Historicists and Cultural Materialists (two eclectic groups with their individual mixtures of Foucault, Althusser, Hayden White, Clifford Geertz, Raymond Williams, and others), and so on.

Once upon a time the student of Shakespeare could read a wide range of books and articles devoted primarily to interpreting the plays in a modern critical-analytical way, with varying emphases on their historical context. There were a few obviously political or ideological critics — the Freudian Ernest Jones, the Marxist Arnold Kettle, the Christian Roy Battenhouse — but otherwise criticism was essentially literary, concerned with the plays' structure, language, moral values, theatrical history. Such interpretative work, not identified with any particular school or ideology, is still being produced, indeed perhaps the majority of Shakespeare critics are independents, following no specific line. But the works and writers that have attracted most attention in the literary market-place — publishers' advertisements in professional journals and reviews, displays at conferences, special panels at academic meetings — have been those belonging to the

four or five groups competing to achieve a leading profile. To take a
realistic — not cynical — view of the contemporary critical scene is to
notice a great amount of pushing and shoving for attention, commercial
promotion, indeed self-promotion, by forming or supporting a group,
praising other members of it, denigrating rival groups. The new word to
describe such calculated promotional activities is hype, and by means of a
joint commercialising and politicising of literary studies some of these
groups have established their own publishing channels in the form of
journals or book series. As Denis Donoghue recently observed, once a
group of literary theorists has been established, usually focused on some
founding father, on whom critical essays are written 'in a spirit mostly
parasitic but occasionally revisionist',

> the next requirement is a journal in which these essays may be published,
> the theorists taking care to quote only their fellow communicants. The
> aim of this procedure is to give the impression that the entire field of
> discourse has now been appropriated by the commune.[2]

The key-word is 'appropriated': as Frank Lentricchia (in *After the New
Criticism*) glosses the term, in the work of Foucault and others 'appropriation' means 'the interested, self-aggrandizing, social possession of systems of
discourse' (Lentricchia 1980, p. 138).

Each of the groups involved in this struggle for attention is attempting to
appropriate Shakespeare for its own ideology or critical theory. The great
change in — so far mainly English-speaking — culture over recent years
has been this division of the field of criticism into clearly-labelled competing groups, each with its preferred journals, founding mythology,
terminology, and other codes of reference. Those who do not belong to
any group risk being 'marginalized' — dismissed, ignored. In a recent
history of American criticism over the last fifty years everyone is classified
into schools or types of criticism, and those who have been independent of
such groups — critics as diverse as Hugh Kenner, Richard Poirier, John
Hollander — are simply omitted.[3] As Frank Kermode has noted, today
'critics are most admired when associated with a particular creed or
method', and ambitious American university departments will hire one or
more duly-labelled experts in deconstruction, feminism, Marxism, and so
on. In such conditions critics are only recognisable if they have labels
attached:

> Critics of idiosyncratic talent — often, on a sustainable view of the
> matter, the best critics — are left out, while a large number of prac-
> titioners, by adherence to this or that doctrine forming part of many-
> sided theory, achieve a place in the story. (Kermode 1989, p. 41)

Perhaps in time the deficiencies of a situation which cannot classify truly
original critics like Kenneth Burke, R.P. Blackmur, William Empson, will
lead to its own discrediting. The critic surely counts more than the label.

This 'fetishisation' of the label — to borrow a neo-Marxist term — has been taken over and consolidated by publishers, who find it convenient to divide up quarterly and annual catalogues into the same four or five categories. (What they do with books that do not fit, or whether they will even publish such books, are moot points.) When it comes to classifying the criticism of the past, a period of time which stretches back to Aristotle, the same group-labels — none of them more than fifty years old — are applied. A publisher has recently launched a series called 'Case Studies in Contemporary Criticism', which will reprint the text of classic works 'together with 5 critical essays representing 5 contemporary critical approaches: psychoanalytical, reader response, feminist, deconstructionist and new historicist'. (The first reactions from carefully selected members of the profession are predictably enthusiastic: 'splendidly useful, authoritative . . . immensely useful': Prof. J. Hillis Miller.)[4]

Other forms of criticism, or critics who belong to no school, offer real difficulties to classifiers and cataloguers. So the invaluable *International Bibliography* published by the MLA (Modern Language Association of America), having decided a few years ago to subdivide its category 'literary criticism', emerged with no less than twenty-five labels. The 1989 edition distinguishes 'General Criticism' (101 items, of which 32 refer to Paul de Man's wartime anti-semitic journalism), 'Deconstructionist Criticism' (36: of which another 16 deal with de Man's links with the Nazis), 'Feminist Criticism' (29), 'Sociological Criticism' (20), 'New Historicism' (15), 'Psychoanalytic Criticism' (12), 'Historical Criticism' (12), 'Reader-Response Criticism' (11), 'Hermeneutic Criticism' (11), and 'Marxist Criticism' (10). Schools of criticism achieving between 5 and 10 mentions include 'Semiotic, Linguistic, New Criticism, Literary History, Poststructuralist'. Less than 5 mentions were scored by 'Postmodernist, Structuralist, Philosophical, Rhetorical, Phenomenological, Archetypal, Formalist, Contextualist, and Impressionistic' criticism.

But we are only half way. There follow 'Literary Theory' (97 items), 'Semiotic Literary Theory' (70), 'Deconstructionist Literary Theory' (57), 'Feminist Literary Theory' (34), 'Narrative Theory' (28 — which could easily be broken down into all the categories so far mentioned), 'Reader-Response Theory' (24), 'Philosophical Literary Theory' (23), 'Psychoanalytic Literary Theory' (18), 'Marxist Literary Theory' (18), 'Linguistic Literary Theory' (16), 'Hermeneutic Literary Theory' (15), 'Poststructuralist Literary Theory' (14), 'Rhetorical Literary Theory' (11), and 'Reception Theory' (10). Less than 10 mentions were scored by 'Postmodernist, Structuralist, Sociological, Psychological, and Social Realist' Literary Theories.

The Bibliographers go on to genres, but we can stop there, numbed as we are by the amount of writing pouring out each year — although the MLA Bibliography is in many (especially European) areas notoriously incomplete — and by the proliferation of labels, groups, schools, the unstoppable process of specialisation and fragmentation in literary studies.

The situation in Shakespeare studies reflects this general pattern of well-defined groups competing with each other for the reader's attention, allegiance, and purchasing power. The annual bibliography of *Shakespeare Quarterly* now also classifies criticism into categories, and without going into detail we can see the same groups consolidating themselves. Among the newer key-words in the annual index are: 'allusion, colonialism, culture, deconstruction, discourse, eroticism, female characteristics, feminism, gender, historicism, ideology, Judaism, literary theory, male characteristics, mimesis, naming, patriarchy, post-structuralism, power, psychoanalysis, psychology, reception, representation, self-reflexiveness, sexuality, structuralism, subversion, theatricality, transvestism'.

At one level, of course, it is right and proper that Shakespeare criticism should, albeit belatedly, reflect the general current of ideas. Considering that specialists in Shakespearian and Elizabethan drama have all too regularly constituted their subject as a self-contained enclave, cut off even from broader studies of Renaissance literature and history, any outside influence might be thought an improvement. But unfortunately the fragmentation and consolidation into individual and rival groups has meant that critics have adopted the theory, method, and terminology of whichever group has won their allegiance as templates with which to interpret Shakespeare. Instead of a critical model opening up a field to fresh enquiry, these approaches effectively close it down, recasting it in their own images. As the following studies will show, each group has a specific ideology, a self-serving aim of proving the validity of their own approach by their readings of the text. Shakespeare's plays, for so long the primary focus of the critic's and scholar's attention, are now secondary, subordinated to the imperialism and self-advancement of the particular group.

That seems to me a regrettable state of affairs, and this book aims to analyse and evaluate the current situation. The conclusion I reach, very simply put, is that Shakespeare critics have aligned themselves too easily with a number of attitudes deriving from the upheaval of received opinion brought about in Paris during the late 1960s. A homogeneous group of intellectuals associated with structuralism and post-structuralism (Lévi-Strauss, Lacan, Barthes, Althusser, Foucault, Derrida) rejected several traditional principles of philosophy and literary criticism: the notion of a subject or individual producing language and making sense of the world by a free, intentional act; the notion of an author as the originator of a literary work; the idea of language as a medium by which human beings reliably communicate with each other (despite misunderstandings, which can usually be overcome); the notion that an argument, or larger systems of thought, should be built up by coherent reasoning, citing evidence; the sense of history as having been made by human actors in a sequence of actions and reactions which can be chronicled and interpreted by language but remain independent of it. These concepts were rejected in vigorous, often violent polemics, convincing some people that a new, alternative critical theory had emerged.

It was hard, in the late 1960s, not to be influenced by the critical upheaval emerging from Paris. Like many others, I bought and read Lévi-Strauss, Lacan and Foucault when they appeared,[5] and although disappointed by semiology as developed by Barthes (based on a pre-semantic or non-semantic concept of the sign), I feel that the late A.J. Greimas (whose semiology rested on the notion of discourse as constitutive of meaning) produced more valuable work, on which others can build,[6] and I believe that narratology (in the wake of Propp, Greimas, Genette and others) has much to offer. That said, taking stock of this whole iconoclastic movement from an independent position a quarter of a century later, any claims that it produced a coherent literary theory seem unfounded. The adversarial mode that it thrived on was essentially negative, destructive. As one recent commentator puts it, post-structuralism (the latest stage of structuralism) is to be regarded as 'a movement of protest against capitalism, science, Western metaphysics, patriarchy and of anything else that the theorists dislike', rather than as a current of ideas producing 'serious theories about literature or culture' (Jackson 1991, p. xi).[7] Paradoxically, given its largely combative nature (its real goal being to attack the systems of ideas which then held place, interpreted as instruments of power and repression, rather than develop a more sensitive or perceptive approach to literature), Theory was elevated to the status of a separate, self-contained literary activity, and Vincent Descombes recalls 'the weighty and rather arrogant tone adopted in the sixties to talk about *theory* (always in the singular)' (Descombes 1986, p. 82). Thirty years later the arrogance seems even less justified, and it becomes increasingly important to resist the notion of theory as a self-fulfilling enterprise. While I accept that theoretical activity can be pursued independently of practical criticism, or detailed analyses of literary texts, that it need not always lead into those activities, I regard theory in the same terms as the sociologist W.G. Runciman, as a concept describing 'a body of ideas . . . within which an explanatory hypothesis which is demonstrably in accordance with the evidence is itself provisionally explicable'. Even under that 'relaxed definition', as he calls it, setting aside the notion of laws which would apply to theory in the natural sciences, 'a theory must still be held to be testable', for 'two rival theories can in principle be tested against each other given the appropriate set of observations' (Runciman 1983, pp. 150–51). Despite its claims to be an autonomous activity, literary theory — if it is to justify that title — must concern itself with the 'evidence', or 'set of observations' deriving from the study of literary texts — in this case Shakespeare's plays.

In the first two chapters I offer a historical description and evaluation of this iconoclastic movement, a history of its anti-theories. In studying the individual groups of Shakespeare critics, I found time and again that their underlying ideas, assumptions, even methods derived from that rhetorically powerful and influential group working in Paris between 1950 and 1980. (Lévi-Strauss and Derrida are alive as I write, but I think it would be agreed that their influential work appeared some time ago.) I thought a general account of that movement as a whole was needed before examining the various schools of Shakespeare criticism, so that the reader could identify the main body of ideas from which they derive. This attempt to sketch in a phase of contemporary intellectual history takes up most of the first two chapters, divided (for convenience, although they are not easily separable) into language and literary theory respectively. In Chapter 1 I trace the diminution, indeed virtual disabling of language which was brought about by that group of Paris intellectuals citing as their authority 'the founder of modern linguistics', Ferdinand de Saussure. As I show, his system, although incomplete and existing only from students' reports, reveals traces of a much wider concept of language as a social medium. His editors and commentators, anxious to boost the status of linguistics as an autonomous scientific discipline, over-emphasised his discussion of the self-contained nature of the linguistic system, and played down his complementary approach to language as a social phenomenon. In the French tradition from Lévi-Strauss to Derrida, Saussure was fragmented and misread, used first to legitimise the elevation of language as the model for all the human sciences (an idea that he had explicitly denied), and then to enable a progressive diminution of language as being incapable of the reliable expression of meaning, useless as a tool of human communication.

This disabling of language has gone so far, and has been so often uncritically endorsed by literary critics (including Shakespearians) that I felt provoked to outline a counter-argument, drawing on contemporary linguistics and philosophy of language to defend some of the key attributes of natural languages — reference, meaning, intention — so categorically rejected. To do so, I refer to the work of contemporary linguists and philosophers more in the spirit of an interested amateur than of someone claiming expertise, and I have not pursued the more difficult, and often controversial developments in the philosophy of language represented by the work of W.V. Quine, Hilary Putnam, Donald Davidson, Michael Dummett and others.[8] Considering that too many literary critics have allowed the issue to go by default, I thought it worth trying to suggest (in non-technical terms) a reasoned case for an alternative to Derrida, Lacan, Barthes, and Foucault, each of whom presents a negative or nihilistic view of language. In order to show that this opposed view is not remote from either ordinary life or literature, I have added a specimen analysis of *Othello* in the light of recent developments in speech-act theory and pragmatics, applying the notions of intentionality and implicature to characters in drama, conceived as able to speak and act by their own free will. I should, perhaps, apologise for the length of this chapter, but I hope readers will agree that an issue of such fundamental importance to all literary criticism deserves detailed discussion.

In Chapter 2 I move on to literary theory, outlining the iconoclasts' claims for what are now clichés of the scene, 'The Death of the Author' and 'The Impossibility of Interpretation', and giving a reasoned response to them. I draw on a wide range of contemporary literary theory to make the case for the author creating, and critics interpreting, works of literature as intentional acts, opposing the Barthes-Foucault notions of 'discourse' or 'textuality' produced and circulated anonymously. In mentioning other, more coherent approaches to interpretation and to the much-maligned concept of *mimesis*, I draw on some recent work on representation and make-believe which, I think, opens up this topic in an important new direction. I also briefly touch on the need to approach Elizabethan drama as a genre involving a set of non-naturalistic conventions which demand (now, as then) the spectator's active imaginative participation. Here again I tie the discussion to Shakespeare, reverting to *Othello* to argue that the many changes from the sources that give coherence to that play can only be understood as the intentional act of an author responsible for his creation. I should underline the obvious point that I am not engaging in biographical speculation about Shakespeare's views or attitudes outside the plays, as some critics do (the New Historicist Greenblatt, for instance), but am addressing the demonstrable evidence of his shaping power behind the play-text. I also try to reconstruct the historical reality of a dramatist working in a theatre where authors frequently collaborated, and where some notion of a collective aesthetic must be entertained in order to account for their ability to produce unified literary works. Any notion of a depersonalised discourse performing these acts is anachronistic and in any case impossible. It is a 'truism that action, thought and feeling can be attributed only to individuals and not to the collectivities constituted by them' (Runciman 1983, p. 30) — let alone some anonymous 'discursive practice'.

Throughout this chapter, also, I deliberately cite a number of contemporary theorists in literature, philosophy, and aesthetics, to show that a vigorous discussion is taking place in many different ways in several countries known to me. (What I don't know will of course be equally evident.) The fact is that some publishers and self-styled practitioners have applied the term 'Contemporary Literary Theory' to a small group of derivative critics who are not at all representative of the richly varied work currently being produced (for this reason I call it Current Literary Theory, recalling that currents can flow in small areas of a larger stream, and do not go on for ever). Much of the inheritance of the 1960s avant-garde is now exhausted, still (or perhaps, all the more) vociferous, but not having developed or transcended the limitations that have become so glaringly evident over the years.

Some of the historians of literature and philosophy whose negative evaluation of this once-new movement I draw on — John Searle, Edward Said, Denis Donoghue, M.H. Abrams, Frederick Crews, Christopher Butler, John M. Ellis, Raymond Tallis — may be familiar to literary critics. But their objections are shared and extended by a formidable group of scholars of several different countries and backgrounds outside Anglo-American literary criticism: J.G. Merquior (Brazil: anthropology), Manfred Frank (Germany: hermeneutics), Sebastiano Timpanaro (Italy: classical philology; Marxism), Vincent Descombes (France: philosophy), Thomas Pavel (France: literary theory), and four English scholars, Perry Anderson and E.P. Thompson (history; Marxism), Simon Clarke (sociology), and Peter Dews (German and French philosophy). One of the stock weapons of the iconoclasts' attack on extant literary criticism has been its supposed indifference to new ideas. In fact, as I show in several places, it is the so-called avant-garde that has cut itself off from a number of important new developments, remaining locked in the configurations of 1960s Paris. Exponents of the once-new wave simply conceal any criticisms of their leaders: Fredric Jameson's self-proclaimed Marxist theory of literature, based on Althusser, draws a discreet veil over the devastating response by Marxists to Althusser's distortions of Marx; Malcolm Bowie dismisses those who demonstrate Lacan's ignorance or misunderstanding of contemporary linguistics as simply unqualified to comment.[9] It will be interesting to see whether defenders of the 1960s avant-garde in the 1990s will manage to dismiss this group of critics quite so easily. The cumulative impact of those iconoclastic theories has been damaging to literature, and I hope that my assemblage of a wide range of counter-criticism will have an appropriately deterrent, or liberating effect.

The main chapters (3 to 7) devoted to Shakespeare criticism are self-explanatory, I think. In each of them I describe the theoretical basis for each school of critics — deconstructionist, feminist, new historicist, psychoanalytical, Marxist, Christian — and then evaluate its effects on their reading of the plays. All of them, I argue, distort the text as experienced in the theatre or in private reading to make it fit their critical theories or ideologies. In the Epilogue I show that the self-conscious development of separate critical schools has led to an unpleasant intolerance towards all other approaches, resulting in a 'demonisation' of rivals, who are labelled, proscribed, and dismissed without further argument. I also return to an issue discussed in the first two chapters to show how this iconoclastic attack on all previous systems produced in turn new systems that tried to become self-sufficient, protected from outside evaluation.

*   *   *

My thanks are due, first of all, to Alan Hollinghurst of the *Times Literary Supplement*, who in 1987 sent me two dozen new books on Shakespeare to review, making me realise just what a state of quarrelsome fragmentation and spurious innovation had been reached.[10] When I had written what I thought to be the body of a book (an earlier version of Chapters 3 to 7 as represented here), Robert Baldock of Yale University Press took the not uncontroversial step of accepting it for publication. (Other publishers, one must sadly say, who have invested heavily in what they think is a bold new wave of criticism, would not have taken it on.) He commissioned two readers, whose separate reports caused me to rethink many sections, encouraging me to toughen up my arguments and to develop a reasoned alternative to the critical approaches which I found wanting. My wish to draw on contemporary linguistics, philosophy of language, and literary theory resulted in my adding Chapters 1 and 2, delaying delivery of the manuscript for another year. (It also made me omit, because of length, two ancillary chapters on the current state of textual theory and practice in Shakespeare editing, which may yet see the light of day.) I think the delay was worth it, and personally found the constructive work on these two chapters more rewarding than the largely critical analyses I had to perform in the five chapters on the competing schools of interpretation. Still, to draw attention to false directions in literary criticism is also a positive act.

I owe a great deal, then, to these two readers, whose identity I was happily able to discover. One was Professor Richard Levin (State University of New York, Stony Brook), whose critical analyses of current trends in the interpretation of Elizabethan drama I had known and admired for many years (see bibliography). The other was Dr David Daniell (University College, London), a specialist in Elizabethan drama, who also brought to bear his knowledge of recent critical developments, accumulated in contributing the Shakespeare chapter to *The Year's Work in English Studies*. Both scholars produced cogent and constructive criticism which was of great help. Professor Levin kindly agreed to read the whole of the revised version, putting me (and the reader) even more in his debt. At a late stage Professor A.D. Nuttall (New College, Oxford) read the first two chapters, on linguistic and literary theory, making some penetrating and helpful criticisms. None of these colleagues should be thought to endorse any of my evaluations of specific schools or critics.

In preparing the text for publication I have had the sterling help of my assistant Dr Margrit Soland, who obtained many out-of-the-way books from libraries here and abroad, typed and made sense of innumerable versions and revisions, prepared the index and helped correct proofs. As a copy-editor I was privileged to work with an old friend, Peter Barnes, classicist and publisher, who made many welcome suggestions.

My greatest debt is to my wife, who put up with both my long absences from the family and, worse still, my even longer monologues about what I had been doing. Her patience and support almost never gave way, and to her I dedicate these first-fruits, 'the *hau* of the gift'.

PART I

CRITICAL THEORIES

CHAPTER ONE

The Diminution of Language: Saussure to Derrida

Nothing can be understood, we must realise, that has not been reduced to language. It follows that language is necessarily the right instrument for describing, conceptualising, interpreting nature as much as human experience, therefore this union of nature and experience which is called society. It is thanks to this power of transmuting experience into signs and of ordering things into categories that language can take as its object any order of givens, including its own nature.

Emile Benveniste[1]

To some readers it may seem strange to begin a book about Shakespeare with the history of linguistics. To others, who know how often the names Derrida, Foucault and Lacan recur in some areas of contemporary Shakespeare criticism, the strangeness will consist in starting as far back as Ferdinand de Saussure (1857–1913). I have three reasons for doing so. First, to reflect the generally acknowledged role of Saussure as not only 'the father of modern linguistics' but also the founder of structuralism, a methodology which spread from linguistics to anthropology (Lévi-Strauss), semiology (Barthes), and literary criticism in the 1960s and 1970s. Secondly, by invoking structuralism I am also suggesting that the work of Derrida, Foucault, and Lacan is in fact a neo-structuralism, continuing some aspects of that movement even though ostensibly rejecting others.[2] Thirdly, and more drastically, I shall argue that many ideas and attitudes in current literary theory have derived from the particular linguistic (and, later, anti-linguistic) models of structuralism and neo-structuralism, and are for that reason irrelevant and inapplicable to works of literature.

Since this book is about Shakespeare in our time, it must concern itself with the influences that have shaped contemporary literary theory. The critical system of any age is a mixture of concepts, each having a different genealogy, product of a particular situation, evolving out of a previous system or reacting against it. I agree with Marc Angenot that 'we usually don't know how notions and paradigms are being parachuted, borrowed, or recycled in our fields of research', especially in 'those blurred, fuzzy sectors of knowledge made out of conflictual traditions, as literary studies are . . .' (Angenot 1984, pp. 150–1). The history of literary criticism, like the history of ideas, is often a record of conflicting practices defined on an oppositional basis. To understand these practices we need to know what they are reacting against, and why. The brief account that follows will be partly historical, partly analytical, but also evaluative. I intend not only to outline some of the factors that have formed the contemporary critical scene, but also to evaluate their claims for serious attention.

SAUSSURE: LANGUAGE, SYSTEM, REALITY

Saussure's *Cours de linguistique générale*[3] is widely recognized as a key work in modern linguistics, one of those stimulating books that can be regularly re-read. Yet it is an incomplete and in many respects incoherent and enigmatic book, never intended by its author for publication, put together from the copious notes taken by some of the dozen or so students who attended the three lecture-courses that Saussure gave on this subject at the University of Geneva in 1907, 1908–9, and 1910–11. Saussure, who had made his name as a linguist with a brilliant *Mémoire sur le système primitif des voyelles dans les langues indo-européennes* (1875), only gave this course as a replacement for a colleague who was ill, and while he covered a lot of ground he only concentrated his thinking on those topics that interested him. We know from his correspondence that he felt deeply dissatisfied with the current state of terminology in linguistics, which seemed to him sloppy and unscientific.[4] Much of his most penetrating work was addressed to redefining the nature of 'the linguistic sign', as he called it (reluctantly conceding that 'the word' was a rough equivalent: CLG, pp. 154, 158). The editors who published their version of his lectures took this to be his major idea and drastically re-arranged the sequence of his exposition in order to highlight it.[5] They also took great liberties with the text, curtly summarizing the lecture notes in some places, and in others adding comments or interpretations of their own. The most notorious insertion was the book's concluding words restating 'the fundamental idea of this lecture course: *the true and unique subject of linguistics is language considered in itself and for itself*' (CLG, p. 317) — words invented by the editors.[6]

That single instance typifies the slant given to Saussure's work by its first editors and commentators. In a sense, of course, the Saussure who remains 'an important figure' in 'twentieth-century linguistics . . . European philosophy and the human sciences' (Holdcroft 1991, p. 4) is Saussure as published in 1916, and the manuscripts that exist in Geneva cannot affect this tradition. But the emphasis given by the interpreters has brought to undue prominence the idea that Saussure was concerned with language purely as a self-contained system, unrelated to reality, society, or anything outside itself. In Rudolf Engler's useful *Lexique de la terminologie Saussurienne*, for instance, which pursues the (often fluctuating) meaning of key terms in great detail, there is simply no entry for 'collectivité', 'social', 'société', as if these terms were unimportant to Saussure. But in fact he conceived of language as the fundamental mode of communication between human beings living in society. Saussure deploys three terms to describe the phenomenon of language, *langage*, *langue*, and *parole* (since they are notoriously difficult to translate I shall retain the French forms). His definition (registered more clearly in the manuscript notes than in the edited text) links all three: '*langue* is an ensemble of necessary conventions adopted by the social group to allow individuals use of the faculty of *langage*. . . . By *parole* we describe the act of the individual realising his faculty [of *langage*] by means of the social convention which is *langue*' (*CLG*, p. 25 and p. 419 n. 63). According to Saussure, *langue* is 'the receptive and co-ordinative part' of language, which exists as a deposit or storehouse in the brains of those individuals forming a language community in a virtual state, ready to be drawn on and activated by *parole*. *Langue* is variously described as a 'produit social', a 'cristallisation sociale', a 'fait social', and a 'lien social' that unites the members of a language group (*CLG*, pp. 25, 29, 30, 420 n. 64).

For Saussure (resembling in this point Durkheim), *langue*, like society, is something pre-existing into which the individual is born. But each person then develops *parole*, 'an individual activity deriving from the will and the intelligence'. *Parole* describes both the 'combinations through which the speaking subject uses the code of *langue* in order to express his personal thoughts', and also the 'psycho-physical mechanism which allows him to exteriorise these combinations' (*CLG*, pp. 30–31, 423 n. 67). *Parole* is both the action of communicating and the particular results of that communication, the linguistic utterance (spoken or written). While emphasising that *langue* and *parole* are interdependent, Saussure gives the priority to *parole*, for the speech-act which 'associates an idea to a verbal image' must precede *langue* (*CLG*, p. 37). This sequence is rather vague, and it is not clear whether Saussure means 'priority' in the Aristotelian sense of the prior, hence determining element, or whether he is speculating about the genesis of language as a social act. A recent, philosophically oriented study has argued that *parole* is needed to explain 'how the social crystallisation of *langue* occurs', namely 'those systematic features of language *use* which make face-to-face communication possible' (Holdcroft 1991, pp. 32–33). And in fact the introduction to the *Cours* includes a diagram illustrating 'the circuit of *parole*', in which two individuals are represented facing each other, their communication being shown by arrows running from mouth to ear and back again, this process through the vocal-auditory channels being discussed in terms of physiology and psychology (*CLG*, pp. 27–29). These individuals, of whom only the head and shoulders are visible, represent the 'sujets parlants', the speaking subjects for whom '*langue* is a system of signs expressing ideas' or thoughts (*CLG*, pp. 30, 33). The primary use of language is in communication, then, and — as two recent commentators agree — for Saussure 'face-to-face oral communication is the relevant norm' (Harris 1987, pp. 25, 106, 198–9, 204, 210–16; Holdcroft 1991, pp. 25, 152).

It is essential to realise that Saussure's theory of language implies an interplay between, on the one hand, the speaking subject, articulating thought in what I can only describe as the intentional act of *parole* (since whoever wishes to communicate his ideas must have an intention); and, on the other, the community or '*masse parlante*' (CLG, pp. 112–13), which shares *langue* as 'a sum of impressions deposited in each brain, like a dictionary' common to all, put into action by the individual's will (CLG, p. 38). All this is implied by his distinction between *langue* and *parole*. But it is not coherently developed, and the text as printed leaves out key connecting arguments. In the edited text there is no proper discussion of what is meant by a social institution (Harris 1987, pp. 8, 225, 228–9), although in the recently-recovered lecture notes we can see that Saussure had further thoughts on this topic.[7] On the crucial issue of how language communicates in society, Saussure invokes the '*fait social*' that 'a sort of medium exists between all the individuals linked by *langage*', namely that 'all will reproduce — not exactly of course, but approximately — the same signs linked to the same concepts' (CLG, p. 29). Unfortunately, in what is perhaps the most serious lacuna in the book, Saussure never pursued the question of how this process of mutual understanding works, leaving out all consideration of semantics, the study of meaning. When he says that *langue*, the 'social dimension of *langage*', 'only exists by virtue of a sort of contract exchanged by the members of the community' (CLG, p. 31), we may assume that what they exchange involves signification, but how this process works we are never told. As Roy Harris observes, the role that Saussure assigns to *langue* in the speech circuit 'demands uniformity between speaker and hearer: otherwise communication breaks down. But the account given of *la langue* as a social product of *parole* does not yield uniformity' (Harris 1987, p. 198). Saussure gives two accounts of *langue*, one as 'a communal average', the other as 'a communal aggregate' (CLG, pp. 29, 30), which are not the same thing, and in any case 'neither offers any guarantee that speaker and hearer operate with identical cognitive systems for the purpose of *parole*' (Harris 1987, p. 199). If we want to know just how signs receive 'the collective ratification of the linguistic community' there are only vague remarks, the key questions being passed over (*ibid.*, p. 211). Yet it is obvious, as Harris puts it, that 'unless the system is the same for *all* its users, it can hardly yield for them a uniform identification of linguistic signs' (p. 233).

The silence over the interaction between individual and collectivity as regards the meaning and understanding of speech acts exposes the partial, incomplete nature of Saussure's lectures on linguistics. But it also high-lights both Saussure's historical position and his method. Historically, he was in opposition to many trends in nineteenth-century linguistics, especially the nomenclaturists who understood language to be 'a list of terms correspondent to the same number of things'. Saussure illustrates this theory with two diagrams, one of a tree, alongside it the word 'Arbor', another of a horse, labelled 'Equus' (*CLG*, p. 97), before dismissing it with some brief and unclear remarks (Harris 1987, pp. 56–9). His opposed theory would remove any link with 'things' or the outside world by describing the linguistic unit as a double-sided psychological entity, formed by the association in our brain of two terms: 'The linguistic sign unites not a thing and a name, but a concept and a sound-image' (*CLG*, pp. 97–8). The '*image acoustique*' is a configuration of sounds as perceived mentally, that is, with the inner ear rather than the outer. In his later lectures Saussure replaced '*concept*' with '*signifié*' and '*image acoustique*' with '*signifiant*' (*CLG*, p. 99), his students recording the following diagrams:

Saussure always emphasised that the linguistic sign was an abstract category used for theoretical discussion, and that the terms *signifié and signifiant* were abstractions, not really existing entities. The dominant partner, as he consistently emphasised, is the signified, the concept, for the vocal sound 'is only the instrument of thought, and does not exist for itself'; *langue* is '*pensée organisée* dans la matière phonique' (*CLG*, pp. 24, 155; my italics). Two of Saussure's best commentators agree that the 'concepts' are 'the prime movers in the activity which occupies the speech circuit' (Harris 1987, p. 213), and that it is 'only by means of an *interpretation*, whose initiator is thought (consciousness, the individual)', that discourse (*parole*) can appear as 'something meaningful and conscious' (Frank 1989, p. 283). Yet, while giving thought the initiating role within the formation of the linguistic sign, Saussure compared *langue*, in a famous analogy,

> to a sheet of paper, where thought is the front and sound the back: you cannot cut the front without at the same time cutting the back. Just the same in *langue*, we can separate neither the sound from the thought nor the thought from the sound: we could only do so by a process of abstraction which would result in either a pure psychology or a pure phonology. (*CLG*, p. 157)

What we must remember as we read the structuralists and their successors is that for Saussure the linguistic sign was a unity, indivisible. It is typical of his method that this central idea should be formulated as a binary category, like other key distinctions, diachronic/synchronic, syntagmatic/paradigmatic. . . . Such binary oppositions add force, and seeming clarity to his discourse. On closer analysis, however, they can be seen to conceal inconsistencies and confusion.

One notoriously unsatisfactory passage is Saussure's attempt to define the linguistic sign purely and solely in terms internal to the language-system, avoiding all reference to an extra-linguistic reality. In the *Cours* we read that the constituent parts of the linguistic sign, signified and signifier, are defined not by any 'positive' feature or 'content' but by their differences from other concepts or acoustic images, respectively (*CLG*, p. 162). Saussure then draws the paradoxical (and none too satisfactory) conclusion that in *langue* — at the level of the sign and its constituent halves, be it always noted — '*there are only differences*', conceptual for the signified, acoustic for the signifier (p. 166). Each formation is given individual identity by being differentiated from other possible formations. However, Saussure held, once the two halves unite to form a sign the result is 'a positive fact', something actually existing, and signs are no longer abstractions but material objects (*CLG*, p. 144). At this stage, then, in comparing 'signs — positive terms — with each other, we can no longer speak of difference, but of oppositions' (p. 167). This sequence has been judged one of the most obscure parts of Saussure's theory (Holdcroft 1991, p. 130), in which his desire to see language as a self-contained system blinded him to the other implications of his categories, namely that signifiers have actual values in themselves.[8] The wider issue, obviously enough, is that while Saussure's own terminology implies that the word as a 'positive fact' has a 'content', which we might imagine to be its meaning, his attempt to produce a system-internal definition of the linguistic sign totally ignored the relationship between language and reality (including language as a part of reality), and suspended all discussion of meaning. I shall return to this issue.

Continuing his definition of the linguistic sign, Saussure has two far-reaching arguments to make. First that it is '*arbitraire*' or '*inmotivé*' (*CLG*, pp. 100–1), secondly that it is '*linéaire*' (*CLG*, p. 103). By arbitrary he means that the link between signified and signifier made for each linguistic sign existing in *la langue* (and ratified over a period of time by the linguistic community recognising its existence and differentiating it from other signs), does not derive from the psychological, physiological, acoustic, or logical nature of the things denoted by it (*CLG*, p. 426 n. 70). In explicit opposition to some widely-shared nineteenth-century theories that the link between a word and its meaning is not arbitrary but motivated,[9] Saussure insisted that the relationship within the linguistic sign was neither inherent nor immanent in the physical properties of the word, but arbitrary, depending on social convention, the endorsement of a specific association by the 'language group'. The problems that this concept of the sign's arbitrariness have given rise to derive, as Simon Clarke has shown, from Saussure having two quite different, conflicting views of language and of linguistics. 'The dominant view is the mentalist one according to which a language is a psychological reality, seated in the brain, and the linguist explores psychological connections.' The other view, clearly implied by his notion of *langue* and *parole*, 'is that language is a collective institution, and so a social reality, and the linguist therefore explores functional connections.' Although the psychological approach is concerned with the way in which the individual learns and uses a language, even from this point of view

> the sign is not arbitrary... The meaning of the sound 'tree' for a particular individual is not determined only by its relations with other linguistic sounds: its contrast with 'bush', 'house', 'sky', 'pole', etc. It is also determined by all the previous uses of the sign that the individual has encountered: the trees to which it has been applied, the contexts within which it has been uttered. (Clarke 1981, p. 123)

(And those 'trees', I add, include metaphorical ones, such as shoe-trees, tree-diagrams in linguistics text-books.) When we hear or read a word, Clarke adds, 'the psychological connections it establishes contemporaneously refer to a whole series of past linguistic events' (*ibid.*). Even if we accept Saussure's idea that language 'names the concepts that divide up sensations', giving order to what would otherwise be a 'sense-engendered chaos', Wendell Harris comments, we must realise that 'the flow of sensation is divided up by concepts (signifieds) according to human purposes. Signifieds make distinctions, distinctions are made where useful, usefulness depends on purpose. We distinguish between mist, drizzle, and rain (in English) because it is useful to be able to do so' (Harris 1988, p. 7). Saussure kept his distance from all theories of reality as far as he possibly could, but the dangers of so doing while developing a theory of language are all too evident.

Returning to Saussure's conception of the linguistic sign, the second characteristic he emphasised was its linearity. By linear he means that the signifier, or phonetic image, 'being by nature auditory, unfolds itself solely in time', having an extent or span which is measurable in one dimension, like a line. Whereas [the meaning of] visual signifiers, such as nautical signals, can be grasped instantly, auditory signifiers can only [be understood] one after the other, unfolding in time like a chain (*CLG*, p. 103). In that summary I have added the two passages in square brackets to bring out the element that Saussure seems to be always deliberately suppressing, the fact that signifiers of either kind are produced by human beings for other beings with — one can only assume — the intention to communicate some thought or meaning. Roy Harris draws attention to 'Saussure's deliberate exclusion of the fact that the *prima facie* reason for the existence of the linguistic sign *arbor* is that speakers feel some social necessity or desirability for a word referring to trees (and, similarly, of other "names" for "things")...'(Harris 1987, p. 63). That is truly a massive exclusion of language's ability to refer to external reality (not just objects but persons, events, processes, ideas, words), which many philosophers and linguists regard as fundamental both to language and to human beings' ability to live together in social groups. In a later part of this chapter we will see an impressive unanimity among contemporary linguists and philosophers as to the crucial role of reference in language.

For Saussure language's external dimension is meant to be ignored or suspended for the purposes of defining both the linguistic sign, and *langue* itself, as a system formed out of self-contained units. This is his goal, but reality is constantly breaking in. Sebastiano Timpanaro (a classical philologist) has shown that Saussure's desire to defend the scientific status of linguistics against some nineteenth-century theories of the subjective nature of language led him into over-emphasising *langue* as a self-contained system (Timpanaro 1975, pp. 138–50). Nonetheless, a conception of language's instrumental value in communication can be seen in Saussure, both in the published text and in the manuscript notes (pp. 151–3). The most notorious example of Saussure's linking of language with reality, despite all his efforts to the contrary, is his claim that the arbitrariness of the sign is 'proved by differences between languages and even by the existence of different languages: the signified "ox" has its signifier *b-ö-f* on one side of the border and *o-k-s* (*Ochs*) on the other side' (*CLG*, p. 100). This example (from an early lecture) has been attacked as a 'blatantly nomenclaturist argument' (e.g., Harris 1987, p. 65), but Timpanaro (among others) replies that Saussure is not arguing that language is '*reducible* to a naming-process', and that this 'much deprecated example of *boeuf-Ochs* is elementary — and as such far from definitive — but it is not at all erroneous. To reject it one would have to believe that there is a "French way of conceiving ox" which is completely different from a "German way" of conveiving it...' (pp. 154–5), which might be rather difficult. Timpanaro notes the survival of this conception of language as a tool for human exchange as one of several 'waverings' in Saussure's system (pp. 155–8). Two recent detailed analyses have revealed many more inconsistencies.[10]

Saussure's attempt to treat language as an entirely self-contained system imposed considerable strain on his argument, but he still did not manage to exclude all reference to the reality which uses language. Another instance of this would be his concept of the linearity of the sign, which, Harris shows, implies that *langue* is put to work on the time-axis that we all share (p. 76), thus admitting 'an involvement of linguistic structure with the structure of the external world', however much the principle of arbitrariness would deny it (p. 77). Again, Saussure's account of linguistic change sees the passage of time allowing social forces to be brought to bear on language (p. 84: *CLG*, pp. 112–13), so admitting both historical and socio-logical criteria. While challenging the exclusively historical orientation of nineteenth-century linguistics with his important assertion of the need for language to be studied synchronically (at a given point in time), Saussure also discussed diachrony (linguistic change over time) as deriving essentially from *parole* (*CLG*, p. 138). As Harris observes, since 'contact between individuals is what ensures diachronic succession', and since 'the world of Saussurean linguistics is a world of face-to-face interaction', then each individual act of *parole* occurs in a context definable in terms of space as well as time, so that Saussure in effect acknowledged the spatio-temporal dimension which has been so important in recent linguistic theories (CLG, pp. 138, 143; Harris 1987, p. 106; Lyons 1977, pp. 80, 570, 636–8).

The sequence in which Saussure's argument for an internalist notion of language explicitly reaches out to the external world, but in a most confusing way, is the chapter on 'linguistic value' (CLG, pp. 155–69), where finally we might expect to find a discussion of meaning. In the two lexica to Saussure (Godel 1957, pp. 280–1; Engler 1968, pp. 52–3) we find that 'valeur' is indeed defined as 'sens, signification', in some contexts, but has a bewilderingly fluctuating sense elsewhere. Saussure insists that *langue* 'can only be a system of pure values', as already explained by the arbitrary linkage of ideas and sounds, and that on any other account 'the notion of value would lose something of its character [that is, as Saussure conceives it!] since it would contain an element imposed from outside' (CLG, pp. 155, 157). Everything that we need in order to define language can be found within it. Saussure's crucial claim, which became the structuralists' first principle, is that value derives not from the sign itself but from the place the sign occupies in the total system. Saussure supports his claim for 'pure values', internally determined, first by the image of an amorphous plane of ideas lying parallel to an amorphous plane of sounds. The linguistic sign is formed by an arbitrary slice across the two planes, making a single unit in which one signifier is linked with one signified (CLG, pp. 155–7; Harris 1987, pp. 119–20; Holdcroft 1991, pp. 112–15). This serves well to support his conception of the arbitrary sign, but it is hard to see how it can explain the process of signification.

Saussure then introduces a second analogy, in which a word is compared to a coin having a determinate value, such as a five-franc piece, which 'can be exchanged for a fixed quantity of some different commodity, such as bread', but which 'can also be compared with a similar value in the same monetary system, for instance a one-franc piece, or a coin from another system (a dollar, etc.)' (CLG, pp. 159–60). Saussure then argues that in the same way 'a word can be exchanged for something different: an idea; or, on the other hand, it can be compared with something of the same nature: another word' (p. 160). So, *volens nolens*, Saussure has got himself out into the real world, where commodities have price-levels set in currencies, and where, as he himself observes, the English can say 'sheep' for the animal and 'mutton' for its meat, while the French have to use the same word, *mouton* for both (*ibid.*). But a close analysis of Saussure's economics analogy will show that it does not work, either on its stated terms, to define language as a self-contained system (Holdcroft 1991, pp. 108–12, 130–33), or within his own distinction between *parole* and *langue*. For coins as 'objects actually exchanged in commercial transactions' would be items of *parole*, but 'coins as units in a system of currency' would be items of *langue*. The former can indeed be exchanged for various commodities, but the latter cannot be exchanged for anything, being part of a 'virtual' store or treasury (Harris 1987, pp. 120–3). Saussure's claim that *langue* 'can only be a system of pure values' (*CLG*, p. 155) does not explain what happens when people exchange words, since linguistic transactions are quite different from commercial transactions. Furthermore, items of currency (gold coins, say) can have an intrinsic value, unlike words; economic values vary continuously, unlike *langue*, which he frequently describes as fixed; and 'values are subordinate to transactions, and not the other way round' (Harris 1987, pp. 121–2, 222, 231).

I dwell on this unfortunate analogy because any discussion of 'sens, signification, fonction' brings us to a central feature of language, which post-structuralism, a tradition claiming to derive from Saussure has, over the last thirty years, increasingly denied. The failure of Saussure's arguments at this point is instructive, it seems to me, for any theory of language, especially if that theory is then adopted as the norm for criticising works of literature. As Roy Harris has argued, 'every linguistic theory presupposes a theory of communication', for a theory provides, more or less adequately, 'the conceptual underpinnings' needed to analyse 'how an interactive social activity like language works' (p. 204). Saussure's basic theory is that of face-to-face oral communication, based on a rather limited concept of the speech-circuit as a 'two-track rectilinear model', a plausible model to start with, but unable to deal with 'the dynamic or developmental aspects of speech communication' (pp. 213–18). The circuit model attracts Saussure because it supports his holistic notion of *langue* as a fixed code in which the connection between signified and signifier is determined from 'inside', not 'outside' (p. 220). Inside there are only signs, but with his economic metaphor Saussure in effect acknowledged a 'contact' between language and some structures 'outside' it (pp. 220–1). Yet, as Harris rightly observes, to develop that admission would ultimately 'bind linguistics hand and foot in dependence on social anthropology' (pp. 219–20).

It is this uneasy position, partly claiming language as self-contained, partly acknowledging its social nature as the interplay between *langue* and *parole*, that makes the *Cours* a fascinating but frustrating work. According to Saussure, linguistic innovations are made at the level of the individual's *parole*, while they are ratified by the collectivity at the level of *langue*: but Saussure never shows what 'collective ratification amounts to' (p. 225). Although he insists that *langue* is a social institution, that idea amounts to little, Harris points out, 'if the institution cannot provide the most basic of social requirements, which are those of communication' between its members. A monetary system, analogously, could hardly be treated 'as a social institution if it failed to provide the members of society with a means of buying and selling things'. Here Saussure has allowed his theory of communication as face-to-face oral exchange to be simply pushed into the background, as incommensurable with a theory of pure value. But the consequence is, that 'once language and communication become theoretically divorced, the key Saussurean concept of *valeur* is itself rendered vacuous...' (p. 230). His system does couple language and communication, but it starts linguistic theory from the wrong end. Harris's final judgment deserves attention:

> Saussurean linguistics begins by focussing upon the properties of the linguistic sign in the abstract, and hoping that somehow at the social end, where signs are put to everyday use, everything will work out satisfactorily in terms of communicational corollaries. Unfortunately, it does not work out at all. (p. 230)

It might have worked out had Saussure developed all the implications of the economic analogy, but this, like so much else in the *Cours*, was hinted at only, one of many brilliant and provocative ideas thrown out in passing but neither developed nor co-ordinated with other parts of the system.

Saussure must have been a marvellously stimulating lecturer. Although poorly-edited, the *Cours* still provokes high praise, 'one of the most impressive intellectual landmarks of modern thought', as Harris judges it, 'one of the most penetrating books I have read', in the words of A.H. Gardiner, but 'also one of the most obscure' (Harris 1987, pp. 237, 1). Even my brief account shows its inadequacy as anything approaching a complete treatment of language, and its faults had an inevitable effect on its followers and imitators. The fact that Saussure regards *langue* 'as basically a store of signs with their grammatical properties, that is, a store of word-like elements', Noam Chomsky observed, meant that he was 'quite unable to come to grips with the recursive processes underlying sentence formation', the system of generative rules which produce the '"rule-governed creativity"... involved in the ordinary everyday use of language' (Chomsky 1964, p. 23). Chomsky argues that Saussure's 'conception of *langue* as an inventory of elements', and his 'preoccupation with systems of elements rather than the systems of rules which were the focus of attention in traditional grammar', had a damaging effect in turn on structural linguistics (*ibid.*, pp. 23–4, 75–111). Insofar as it encouraged the neglect of syntax, that seems a fair comment, and certainly the new direction given to linguistics by transformational grammar was salutary, although not without its problems, too. At all events, we can agree with Thomas Pavel's observation on the ironically bad timing by which, in the late 1950s, 'structuralism, whose decrepit models were rejected by linguistics, was selected as the starting point for a revolution in French epistemology' just when the work of Chomsky and his associates was about to revolutionise the subject (Pavel 1989, p. 131).

Saussure cannot be blamed for what his so-called followers did to his ideas, of course, but the limitations of structuralism derive in part from its taking over Saussure's system and reducing its scope still further. As a model for a general theory of language, the *Cours* itself is severely limited, unless one is willing to make the kind of reconstruction attempted here, working out the implications of language as an activity in human society over time in order to complement the brilliant but incoherent passages focussing on the sign as a self-contained unit. But those whose use of Saussure attracted the greatest attention in the world of letters — setting aside the exegesis of professional linguists like Benveniste, Hjelmslev, Emile Buyssens, Tullio de Mauro, Robert Godel, Rudolf Engler — did not bother to reconstruct, or even cite, Saussure's concepts of *langue* and *parole*, diachronic change, or the nature of the 'masse parlante'. The many confusions that have resulted, Wendell Harris points out, all derive from 'the tendency to think of *langue* as existing, like Plato's Ideas, quite insulated from the daily experience of men and women' (Harris 1988, p. 7). But the fact is that 'words do not remain suspended in the system of *langue*; they are used in particular contexts by human beings' (p. 8). Modifying Saussure's terms by introducing the notions of meaning and purpose, Harris concludes that '*langue* is the abstraction that explains the possibility of meaning in language; dicourse (*parole*) expresses meaning' (p. 158). Those writers who seized on Saussure in the 1950s and 60s as the harbinger of a revolution in the human sciences simply ignored such considerations. They focussed exclusively on language as a self-contained entity, the sign as a unit emerging out of a system of differences, with its mutually determining elements. Not content with this reduction of scope, they went on to fragment Saussure's system into its component parts, misreading and destroying his ideas in ways which still dominate contemporary critical theory, and Shakespeare interpretation. The history of Saussure's reception in our time is one of almost continuous distortion, as summed up in the title of Raymond Tallis's indignant account of the movement that calls itself 'Post-Saussurean Literary Theory': *Not Saussure* (1988).

STRUCTURALISM: FRACTURING THE SIGN

Although venerated as inaugurating modern linguistics, Saussure's system was broken up and re-used for drastically different purposes. Just as Greek temples were vandalised, their stones re-used for building a Byzantine basilica or a medieval abattoir, so the *Cours de linguistique générale* has been decomposed into units to be re-used ad lib. For the Prague school (Troubetzkoy, Jakobson) it represented a model for a more scientific approach to language as a sound-system (phonemics), with the dichotomy between *langue* and *parole* enabling a new distinction between phonology and phonetics (Timpanaro 1975, pp. 160–1). In fact, as Simon Clarke has shown, that group of linguists started from Husserlian phenomenology, seeing language as 'an intentional object whose structure is an expression of its function as an instrument of human communication', so breaking with Saussure's mentalism by conveiving language not as an object but as an instrument, 'a socially defined code' (Clarke 1981, pp. 146–51). Unfortunately, their research turned into a formalism that ignored questions of communication and meaning, studying the sound system of language as 'a series of functional distinctions, a structure of distinctive relations' that could be studied without reference to extrinsic meaning (*ibid.*, pp. 151–2). This approach is legitimate if understood as a temporary abstraction from language, made for methodological reasons, since 'in any particular context one phoneme will be opposed to others not as a whole, but only by those phonetic features that define its functional distinctiveness' (p. 153). Yet, as Clarke observes, 'the analysis of the sound system cannot in fact be carried out in complete abstraction from meaning: since the phoneme is a functional concept and not a substantive acoustic reality the identity of one phoneme and its difference from others can only be defined functionally, by reference to identity and difference of meaning' (p. 154). In studying phonology the Prague linguists were isolating functional wholes below the level of linguistic meaning, assuming that 'the meaning of the elements of the system is given unproblematically'. The peculiar nature of phonology, however, is that 'only reference to the intentions and understanding of native speakers can establish which phonological distinctions are meaningful, but once the units have been identified in this way the system can be analyzed without reference to meaning' (pp. 173–4). Thus while phonology appears to fulfil the positivist dream of an objective system which itself produces meaning, closer inspection shows that here again the language-user creates meaning.

The Prague linguists were in the end true to the spirit of Saussure's system, we might say, moving away from a phenomenology rooted in the subject to a formalism with pretensions to a scientific status. For the Danish school (Brøndal, Hjelmslev) the *Cours* also encouraged the treatment of language as a self-contained system at a highly abstract level, becoming almost 'an algebra of language', expunging semantics from linguistics, and even abandoning the term linguistics (apparently contaminated by its links with sociology and psychology) for the more scientistic term 'glossematics'. As Timpanaro justly comments, 'while the links between linguistics and everything that has an empirical and naturalistic quality about it' were severed, no care was taken to distinguish linguistics from a 'formalistic epistemology based on *a priori* models' (Timpanaro 1975, pp. 158–62). Self-generated systems replaced the study of language as a mode of social communication.

That comment is particularly relevant to Lévi-Strauss, who took over from the Prague school some of the main principles of the structuralism he promoted in the 1950s and 60s. As Simon Clarke has shown in his outstanding study of that movement, Lévi-Strauss (who met Jakobson in New York in 1942) welcomed Prague phonology as providing 'a reduction of the sound system to a purely formal structure in which the significance of different sounds is reduced to their relations with other sounds within the system' (Clarke 1981, p. 152). Building on the formalist aspect of phonology, and ignoring the fact that phonemic distinctions derive from the user's intentionality to communicate meaning, Lévi-Strauss claimed in 1963 that the '"phonological revolution"' in structural linguistics had consisted of '"the discovery that meaning is always the result of a combination of elements which are not themselves significant... in my perspective meaning is always reducible. In other words, behind all meaning there is a non-meaning..."' (cit. ibid., p. 198). But the analogy is false, for once those elements are combined a meaning is produced, which is not 'reducible' in any simple sense to its component parts. The important idea of Lévi-Strauss was that of a combination of elements within a system obeying laws immanent to that system, and expressing 'an absolute and objective meaning', independent of any content or individual subject, indeed imposing its laws 'on the individual with the force of the unconscious' (pp. 115, 125).

For Lévi-Strauss Saussure was one of several sources that could be used to establish the humanities on a positivistic, scientist basis. Another was cybernetics, whose goal of a rigorous mathematical study of communication systems, he claimed, had already been fulfilled by Prague school phonology (Lévi-Strauss 1963, pp. 55–6, 277–323). Lévi-Strauss invented structuralist anthropology as a science, and extended its methods to semiotics, applying to both the notions of system and code, a joint inheritance from Prague linguistics and cybernetics. His imposing scientist claims had an enormous effect on the other leaders of French thought who emerged in the 1960s, and who continue to influence literary theory, and hence Shakespeare criticism, to this day: Lacan, Althusser, Barthes, Foucault. His influence took several forms, which I shall summarise briefly: the licence to fragment Saussure's categories; the erection of language as a model for all the human sciences; the rejection of historicism and empiricism; the denial of the subject; the evolution of a system derived from a priori principles and subjectivism; treating analogies as if they were concepts, or even physical laws; privileging the unconscious mind as a determining influence not just on individual behaviour but on human society as a whole; and treating literary texts in arbitrary and schematic terms. Much commentary on Lévi-Strauss exists,[11] which I shall draw on to give a skeleton outline of the progression from structuralism to post-structuralism to current literary theory, as it affects Shakespeare studies now.

For an example of the a priori assertion, couched in the binary form so popular in structuralism, together with the fragmenting of Saussure, I refer to the introduction that Lévi-Strauss wrote to the reissue (in 1950) of some

anthropological classics by Marcel Mauss, where he defined the anthropologist's goal as being 'to reduce phenomena in the social world to their
underlying symbol system', for 'symbols are more real than that which they
symbolise, the signifier precedes and determines the signified' (Lévi-Strauss
1950, pp. xxxi–xxxii). That fragmentation of Saussure's unified linguistic
sign was to be prophetic of French avant-garde thought over the next
twenty years, with its privileging of the signifier (acoustic image) over
the signified (concept). Lévi-Strauss went on to sunder the two terms
definitively, inventing the notion of a 'floating signifier', still in vogue in
Current Literary Theory (see my account of Garber in Chapter 5). He
claimed to have discovered 'a fundamental opposition in the human mind'
between symbolism, which he believed to be discontinuous, and cognition
(*connaissance*), which is continuous (p. xlvii). Boldly reconstructing 'la
condition humaine', Lévi-Strauss hypothesised that

> since its origin mankind possesses a totality of the signifier which it has
> great difficulty in assigning to a signified, given as such without being
> known. There is always an inadequacy between the two, only reabsorb-
> able by divine understanding, and which results in an excess of the
> signifier compared to the signifieds on which it can settle. (p. xlix)

In effect Lévi-Strauss was inventing an allegory of the birth of language in
which humanity suddenly received (or invented) language as a system
complete in itself. Thus, as one commentator glosses this passage, in the
beginning man 'could say everything that his language authorised him to
say, . . . yet he had nothing to say (for lack of any knowledge, for lack of a
signified). The inadequacy of signifier to signified was at that moment
complete; the entire realm of the signifier was floating . . .' (Descombes
1981, p. 96). That account only makes clearer the artificial nature of Lévi-
Strauss's notion of the sudden appearance of language with a tremendous
number of items (Pope, atomic bomb, divine right of kings) which must
have been meaningless for centuries. Even if we accepted that extraordinary
idea, since knowledge has in the meantime caught up, then the two parts
of the sign must cohere, and nothing now 'floats'.

This wilful destruction of Saussure's unified linguistic sign was made in
order to support the theory that man, attempting to understand the world,
'always has a surplus of signification (which he distributes between things
according to the laws of symbolic thought . . .)' (Lévi-Strauss 1950,
p. xlix). Thus, Lévi-Strauss reasons, notions like *mana* in symbolic thought
represent 'this floating *signifier*', earlier described as 'an indeterminate significatory value . . . whose sole function it is to fill a gap between signifier
and signified' (*ibid.*, p. xliv). Since Lévi-Strauss is operating a vast and
exclusive dichotomy between symbolic thought and cognition, he must
now argue that this 'floating' or indeterminate signifier is the mark of 'all
art, all poetry, all mythic and aesthetic invention', as opposed to scientific
knowledge (p. xlix). It is hard to know why Lévi-Strauss should have

wanted to ruin Saussure's unified concept in this way. A 'signifier' having 'an indeterminate significatory value' is already a nonsense, since the two halves of the linguistic sign are mutually determining, and to describe such a category as 'floating', able to 'fill a gap between signifier and signified', is to heap confusion on confusion. A binary category has no need of another party: three is definitely a crowd. Although influential in the 1960s, recent comments on Lévi-Strauss's theory have been critical. Anthropologists have taken issue with his concept of symbolism, indeed Dan Sperber has forcefully argued the opposite case, that symbolism is indeed a cognitive system (Sperber 1975). Vincent Descombes has commented on the confused speculation which collapses the distinction between human linguistic potential and its actualisation, offering what I would call an aetiological myth to justify a semiological explanation of 'the gap between the sudden acquisition of language and the laborious acquisition of knowledge' (Descombes 1986, p. 174). As a philosopher, Descombes judges that 'this little fable does much to illuminate the bizarre side' of Lévi-Strauss's conception of language, which he patiently dismantles (pp. 175–7). To the Marxist critic Perry Anderson, this 'improbable thesis' of a 'permanent "superabundance of the signifier, relative to the signified on which it can pose itself"', could only lead to a 'gradual megalomania of the signifier' (Anderson 1983, pp. 45–6).

By shifting the priority, or leading power, from the signified to the signifier, Lévi-Strauss in fact reversed Saussure's hierarchy, in which thought (la pensée, le concept) determined the 'slice' of acoustic matter to which it united itself (CLG, pp. 24, 155). He also ignored Saussure's whole emphasis on the arbitrariness of the linguistic sign (although he was to insist on it subsequently) by positing the faculty of human knowledge choosing 'in the ensemble of the signifier and in the ensemble of the signified, those parts which offer among themselves the most satisfying relations of mutual conformity' (Lévi-Strauss 1950, pp. xlvii–xlviii). Any such criterion of convenance governing a deliberate choice is totally foreign to Saussure. Lévi-Strauss's largest, and most influential distortion of Saussure, though, was to make language, and by extension structural linguistics, the basic model for all the human sciences. Saussure insisted, both in the published text of the Cours and in his lecture-notes, that language was an institution 'without analogue', a 'pure institution' founded on the arbitrariness of the sign, whereas 'other institutions — customs, laws, etc. — are all based, in varying degrees, on the natural relationships of things'. Just as Saussure's concept of the arbitrary nature of the sign distinguished it from the symbol, where 'there is the rudiment of a natural link between signified and signifier' (as in a pair of scales symbolising justice) — another point ignored by Lévi-Strauss — so the unique nature of language made it unsuitable as an analogy for any other institution. As one of the unpublished notes put it, 'we are profoundly convinced that whoever sets foot on the terrain of langue can tell himself that he has been abandoned by all the analogies of heaven and earth'.[12]

Lévi-Strauss was responsible for the development in structural anthropology and in semiotics of the notion of language as a privileged model for
all the 'sciences humaines', a notion which was passed off as Saussurian
but was in fact the exact opposite. As Timpanaro points out, Saussure
was 'very far from using the conventional and "systematic" character of
language as a model which can be freely applied to all the other sciences',
for he emphasised 'very strongly the non-conventionality (i.e. the lesser
conventionality) of everything in life and human society which is not
language' (Timpanaro 1975, pp. 156–8). Anderson agrees, that 'Saussure's
whole effort, ignored by his borrowers, was to emphasise the *singularity* of
language, everything that separated it from other social practices or forms',
and he notes the irony that Saussure himself 'warned against exactly the
abusive analogies and extrapolations from his own domain that have been
so unstoppable in the past decades' (Anderson 1983, pp. 42–3). It is not
just a question of being true to a predecessor or not (although the question
of honesty does arise if you invoke his authority while in fact saying the
opposite). The fact is that Saussure warned against such a privileging of
language with good reason. The analogies are deceiving, and a science
based on them rests on hollow foundations.

In Lévi-Strauss's hands, furthermore, analogy regularly transformed itself
into identity. A properly scientific study of reciprocity in anthropological
terms, he claimed, could be achieved 'only by treating marriage regulations
and kinship systems as a kind of language', for 'the rules of kinship and
marriage serve to insure the circulation of women between groups, just as
economic rules serve to insure the circulation of goods and services, and
linguistic rules the circulation of messages' (Lévi-Strauss 1963, pp. 61, 83).
Francis Bacon once divided people into those who could only see resemblances, those who could only see differences, and those who could see
both:[13] Lévi-Strauss comes in the first group. But many critics have found
this supposed analogy 'extremely misleading', as Simon Clarke put it, since
'linguistic rules have nothing whatever to do with the circulation of
messages, they are concerned with the *constitution* of messages' (Clarke
1981, p. 161). This is to confuse, as the structuralists and their followers
often did, linguistics as a system with language in use. Perry Anderson
forcefully objected to Lévi-Strauss's 'intrepid generalization' of this analogy
to '*all* the major structures of society' as ignoring crucial differences, indeed
the analogies 'give way on the smallest critical inspection'. Kinship cannot
be compared to language, for 'no speaker alienates vocabulary to any
interlocutor, but can freely reutilize every word "given"' as many times as
he wants, whereas 'wives are not recuperable by their fathers after their
weddings'. And in the economy exchange describes only a small area of
activity: 'production and property are always prior' (Anderson 1983, pp.
42–3). As Timpanaro judges, such analogies 'distort Saussure's concept of
the "sign" and turn it simply into a term indicating a relationship between
similar things', whereas for Saussure it was also 'a relationship between a
similar and a *dissimilar* thing' (Timpanaro 1975, p. 183). Having thus

'taken away all specificity from the concept of the sign', Lévi-Strauss was able to lump many human activities together as analogous to some linguistic entity (*ibid.*, p. 184).

Lévi-Strauss established the programme for structuralism of what Anderson calls the '*exorbitation*' or 'absolutization of language' (Anderson 1983, pp. 40, 45), which was to affect, in different ways, all the Parisian iconoclasts. Anderson, whose penetrating critique of structuralism and its successors ought to be required reading wherever Current Literary Theory is taught, describes the second operation inaugurated by Lévi-Strauss as 'the *attenuation of truth*', caused by language being 'taken as an all-purpose model outside the domain of verbal communication itself. For the condition of its conversion into a portable paradigm was its closure into a self-sufficient system, no longer moored to any extra-linguistic reality' (*ibid.*, p. 45). This stage can be seen in Lévi-Strauss's reproaching other anthropologists for falling into a 'confusion resulting from too much acquaintance . . . with concrete and empirical data' (Lévi-Strauss 1963, p. 70), for to him, as Simon Clarke has shown, 'the object of any science is an ideal object, not to be confused with any particular empirical object'. Kinship theory as he practised it was not to be limited to the conscious representations of kinship systems reported by particular individuals, for these 'may fail to correspond to the deeper, unconscious reality of the system' (Clarke 1981, p. 102). Lévi-Strauss took over Freud's concept of the unconscious but reduced it to 'a purely formal structuring capacity, defined by the universal unconscious, an absolute object' (p. 27). His theories of kinship scorned empirical verification, reducing the kinship systems of actually existing societies 'to abstract models that are supposedly located in the unconscious and supposedly underlie and give meaning to the systems that are observed on the ground' (p. 54). But the overwhelming objection to this whole line of thought must be that since the unconscious is inaccessible it cannot possibly acquire an objective meaning. When Lévi-Strauss claimed that both kinship systems and language are 'systems of meaning constituted by the unconscious' (p. 159), he cut himself free of any appeal to observed behaviour in favour of some ideal model to which he alone had access. Indeed in 1953 he declared that '"in my mind models are real, and I would even say that they are the only reality. They are certainly not abstractions, . . . but they do not correspond to the concrete reality of empirical observation. It is necessary, in order to reach the model which is the true reality, to transcend this concrete-appearing reality"' (*cit. ibid.*, p. 165).

As we have known since Plato's polemical use of such dichotomies as appearance and reality, any thinker who claims a privileged knowledge of a true reality is setting himself off from the rest of mankind. Over and above the details of Lévi-Strauss's arguments, I believe, his great influence on French intellectuals of the 1960s was in the massive self-confidence with which he pronounced his idiosyncratic theories to be absolute laws. The most notorious example of this 'ériger en lois ses impressions personnelles', at the same time a total rejection of empiricism, was his claim that since his subject-matter was the human nature that existed beneath the diversity of cultures, then '"it is in the last resort immaterial whether in this book [*Mythologiques* I, 1964] the thought processes of the South American Indian take shape through the medium of my thought, or whether mine take place through the medium of theirs"' (*cit. ibid.*, p. 216). Recent commentators have not been amused by Lévi-Strauss elevating his own theories to the status of objective mental operations characterising mankind at large (Timpanaro 1975, pp. 171–4; Anderson 1983, p. 47). His contempt for empiricism was shared by Althusser, Barthes, Foucault (in some modes), and Derrida.

The third major move within structuralism Anderson describes as 'the *randomization of history*. For once the linguistic model becomes a general paradigm in the human sciences, the notion of ascertainable cause' begins to weaken (Anderson 1983, p. 48). This stage is represented by Lévi-Strauss's rejection of historicism (*ibid.*, pp. 37, 49–50), and leads directly to Foucault.

*   *   *

While agreeing with Anderson's masterly summary, the orientation of this book leads me to focus on the first stage he describes, the absolutisation of language. I would extend his critique in a different direction, however, for what strikes me about the course of structuralism is that the fragmentation of Saussure led in the event to a diminution of language. The fact that this homogeneous group of French intellectuals reduced literary enquiry to the nature of the sign (while the rest of the world was pursuing any number of other topics in linguistics) produced (or expressed) a dissatisfaction or disillusionment with language. It was detached from meaning, but then proclaimed unable to mean. That property was first removed, then denied.

The process began with Lacan, who made language the dominant factor in his supposedly neo-Freudian psychoanalysis. Lévi-Strauss's fragmentation of Saussure was known to all French intellectuals, and Lacan — while giving the conventional praise to Saussure's distinction between the signified and signifier as a founding feature of the human sciences in our time (e.g., Lacan 1966, pp. 467, 497) — took it a stage further. Setting out the relationship between the constituent halves as an algorithm, S/s, that is, 'signifier over signified, the "over" corresponding to the line separating the two levels' (p. 497), Lacan claimed that the line separating the two terms represents 'a barrier resisting signification' (p. 497), as if meaning were somehow blocked by the separation of the two levels and would be enabled by their merging or fusion. The result would, however, be a reification of the sign, exactly what Saussure rejected. Lacan then attacked what he called 'the illusion that the signifier fulfils the function of representing the signified . . .' (p. 498). But Saussure never claimed that the signifier's function was to *represent* the signified: the two terms united to form the linguistic sign, which itself signifies as a complete unit. Lacan went on to claim that 'the signifier does not have to justify its existence in the name of any kind of signification whatsoever' (*ibid.*), emulating Lévi-Strauss in liberating it from the sign, and asserting that in any case 'the signifier . . . anticipates on meaning by unfolding its dimension' first (p. 502). But in fact we perceive the meaning of a word simultaneously with its shape: consciousness does not work on two dislocated axes. Lacan did everything he could to break up Saussure's unified sign, claiming that the signifier intrudes into the signified, that the terms cannot be separated (which would destroy his own theories), and/or that the relationship between them is unstable (pp. 498–503).[14] Referring to Saussure's diagram representing the two levels of undifferentiated thoughts and indeterminate sounds as running in parallel — before being cut up to form stable units in which each signifier corresponds to a signified (*CLG*, pp. 155–7) — Lacan, on the contrary, proclaimed 'an incessant sliding of the signified under the signifier' (Lacan 1966, p. 502).[15] From Lévi-Strauss's *flottant* to Lacan's *glissement*, the linguistic sign was de-stabilised, and, as ever in structuralism, the signifier (the acoustic image? — the word? — the meaning of a statement?) emerged triumphant, displacing the concept. Indeed, in Lacan's work 'the supremacy of the signifier' became a fixed point, as the copious entries in the analytical index to *Ecrits* show (*ibid.*, p. 895).

Lacan emulated Lévi-Strauss not only by praising Saussure while distorting him but by making language the privileged model for another human science, psychoanalysis. His most famous version of 'our doctrine of the signifier', as he liked to call it, was that 'the unconscious is structured like a language' (*ibid.*, p. 594), a slogan that was repeated through the sixties and seventies as if it held the key to some deeper revelation. In the eighties, however, sceptical readers were able to see its deficiencies. Vincent Descombes pointed out that Lacan, although still using the term from Saussure, had in fact 'abandoned Saussurean signifiers (whose signified is a concept)' in favour of a quite different conception of them, as signifiers 'whose signified is the meaning of a statement'. This radical change meant that language was now tacitly understood 'in the sense of discourse. All Lacanian formulas take the manifestation of the unconscious to be speech (*des paroles*). "The dream has the structure of a sentence"'; or, '"The symptom is itself structured as a language"' (Descombes 1986, p. 179). As Descombes observes, 'the *structure of language* invoked in all these Lacanian edicts has thus nothing to do with the system constituted by a language'. Lacan's 'signifiers' refer to 'speech, statements', but Saussure's theory of the linguistic sign's arbitrary nature 'applies to words, not to sentences' (*ibid.*). As can now be seen, the system builders of the sixties often made such silent redefinitions of terms for strategic goals. Lacan wished to assert the

So what?

fundamental ambiguity of language as a system of signifiers, and so he conceived of the signifier as inherently unstable, yielding no fixed meaning 'but something else between the lines' (*ibid.*, p. 180–1). This concept (like Lévi-Strauss's claimed access to 'the true reality') has the great advantage of giving its user complete freedom in interpretation, but Descombes dismisses it as 'a piece of sophistry'. A word can have 'various potential meanings', he observes, but they are not 'latent in each one of its uses'. We can say that a word 'has different meanings in different contexts but not that it has different meanings in a single context', for the speaker selects the one he wants, and gives a word 'the meaning it has in that particular use' (p. 181). (This characteristic of language, that while it gives its users great freedom it also sets constraints, imposing the need to choose and to organise the material chosen according to rules of grammar and syntax, is one that the sixties avant-garde frequently fretted over, as we shall see.) For Lacan the symptoms to be analysed were signifiers having a plurality of meanings but all expressing desire, that desire which, as he put it, was '"produced" by man, '"an animal at the mercy of language"' (p. 182). Descombes subjects Lacan's 'grammar of the object of desire' (an innovation pungently rejected by Lévi-Strauss)[16] to a devastating philosophical analysis (pp. 182–7), revealing 'irremediable confusion', 'fanciful' explanations, incoherent argument, and a 'sleight of hand' in juggling terms. I should like to underline particularly Lacan's perverse inversion of the age-old conception (going back to Isocrates and Cicero) of mankind as being singled out from the animals by having the power of speech: now man is 'an animal at the mercy of language'. And of Lacanian analysts.[17]

In Lacan language is absolutised, isolated, but then fragmented, disabled. The analogy between language and the unconscious, unsuitable in so many respects,[18] turns into an identity, only to bring unfulfilment. As Perry Anderson summarises Lacan's 'doctrine', the unconscious is not merely 'structured "like" a language, . . . it is language as such that forms the alienating domain of the unconscious, as the Symbolic Order that institutes the unsurpassable and irreconcilable Other and therewith, at the same stroke, desire and its repression down through the chain of signifiers' (Anderson 1983, pp. 41–2). Two other commentators draw attention to the categorical way in which Lacan cut language off from reality. 'Lacanian theory merely duplicates, partially and passively . . . accepts a situation in which language is no longer a tool for appropriating social reality, but an alienated and alienating system . . . ; a situation in which language has become separated from reference and denotation' (McDonnell and Robins 1980, p. 200). They illustrate their point with a quotation from Lacan's address to the Rome congress of psychoanalysts in 1953:

Let me therefore say precisely what Language signifies and what it communicates: it is neither signal, nor sign, nor even sign of the thing in so far as the thing is an exterior reality. The relation between signifier and signified is entirely enclosed in the order of Language itself, which completely conditions its two terms. (*cit.* p. 200)

As always, Lacan uses Saussure's categories but dislocates their function, subverts his system and with it language itself. According to a recent admiring exponent of Lacan, where Saussure saw signifier and signified as interrelated, 'Lacan sees signifiers as interacting among themselves and escaping from the signifieds, leaving the subject signifying "something entirely different from what it says"'. Language thus both forms and deforms the subject, who tries to communicate with other people ('the Other', as Lacan negatively reifies the human community) but can only do so at a high cost, 'namely the acceptance of the "Castration" which is the inevitable by-product of being subject to language and its prohibitions'.[19] (Lacan's phallocentrism is all too evident.)

For a final comment on this blank view of language as alienated and alienating I turn to Peter Dews, who has recently produced a lucid and helpful account of Lacan (Dews 1987, pp. 45–108). Dews brings out clearly the effect of Lévi-Strauss's determinist science (*ibid.*, pp. 74–7) on Lacan, which resulted in Lacan adopting a new fatalism about the possibility of human communication, diagnosing an irremovable wall between the speaker and the person spoken to. The speaking subject, Lacan concluded, always attempts 'to discover a confirming image, a reinforcement of his or her own ego in the response of the other', but in so doing only expresses its own 'powerlessness', for 'our preconceptions can never be replaced by a definitive grasp of who the other subject truly is' (Dews 1987, p. 78). Since our understanding relies on the interpretation of meaning, which is never 100% certain, there is always, as Lacan puts it, ' "a possible dissimulation" ' — a morally charged term implying an intention to deceive. But of course, no communication system could rule out deliberate deception, and the human use of language to lie (which does of course mean that it *can* communicate truth) should not be blamed on language. From this negative position, and once again in opposition to all other theories over the last two thousand years of language as the medium for communication, Lacan describes it as an insuperable obstacle dividing human beings: ' "The subject is separated from the Others, the true Others, by the wall of language" ' (*ibid.*). The subject desires to be known, to be recognised, but the 'semantic uncertainty' of language 'produces an endless reflexive movement of speech endeavouring to grasp its own meaning. "Language", Lacan remarks, "is constituted in such a way as to found us in the Other, while radically preventing us from understanding him" ' (p. 79). All understanding implies meaning, obviously enough, but that possibility is denied, *a priori*, in Lacan's system. ' "The meaning of meaning in *my* practice" ', Lacan states, ' "can be grasped in the fact that it runs away: in the sense of something leaking from a barrel . . ." ' (pp. 80–1). What began as absolutisation of language, then, ends in something like its disablement. If your only conception of language is the narrowest version of Saussure, then once you begin to dislocate and fragment the sign, meaning may also disappear, and with it the whole possibility of conversation or human exchange.

*   *   *

A similar reversal can be traced in the career of Roland Barthes. As is most visible in his *Eléments de sémiologie* (1964; English tr. 1967), and *Essais critiques* (1964; English tr. 1972), Barthes began as a disciple of Lévi-Strauss, sharing his ambition to produce a scientific study of culture based on the linguistic model. Just as Lévi-Strauss had applied the Prague structuralists' phonology together with cybernetics to anthropology, creating a kind of semiology which would classify cultural products and activities (food, cooking, dress) and help to discover the cultural code that determined social behaviour (Pettit 1975, pp. 76–7), so Barthes took Hjelmslev's more rigorous version of Saussure to found a semiotics that would be applicable to fashion, motor-cars, Japanese wrestling, or anything else. The elasticity of the method, however, was achieved at the cost of meaning: to use an old category, form could be studied, content ignored. In his early essay on 'Le mythe, aujourd'hui', written in September 1956, familiar with Lévi-Strauss's work and having just read Saussure for the first time,[20] Barthes wrote: 'Semiology is a science of forms, because it studies meanings (*significations*) independently of their content' (Barthes 1957, p. 196). In his little primer on semiology (a studiously academic and rather disappointing work) Barthes repeated that the 'classification of the linguistic signifieds' is a 'fundamental' operation in semiology, 'since it amounts to isolating the *form* from the content' or meaning (Barthes 1967, p. 44). He also informed his readers 'that according to some linguists, the signifieds are not a part of linguistics, which is concerned only with signifiers, and that semantic classification lies outside the field of linguistics' (*ibid.*, p. 45). This rigid demarcation of interests would dismiss the question of meaning altogether, relegated to some other non-linguistic discipline (which, though?). Defining the sign in 1962, Barthes assigned it three relations: an 'interior' one, uniting signifier and signified, and two 'exterior' relations, a virtual one linking it to the 'reservoir of other signs', and an actual one, linking it to 'other signs in the discourse preceding or succeeding it' (Barthes 1972, p. 205). Any links with external reality have been abandoned.

It is often remarked that structuralism tended to isolate 'the signifier as such, as an object of study, from what it signified' (Jameson 1972, p. 111). Semiology inherited the structuralists' privileging of the signifier, yet, as the anthropologist Dan Sperber has observed, false expectations can be aroused by the terms used. For although semiologists borrowed linguistic terminology, they did not in fact treat symbols 'as signs. The symbolic signifier, freed from the signified, is no longer a real signifier except by a dubious metaphor . . .' (Sperber 1975, p. 52). The fact that Lévi-Strauss (like Lacan) continued to use Saussure's terminology, describing symbolic phenomena as 'signifiers', makes us assume that 'the investigation is into an underlying code which pairs these signifiers with their "signifieds". Yet, if the reader begins looking for the signifieds, he soon realizes that the underlying code relates signifiers to other signifiers: there *are* no signifieds. Everything is meaningful, nothing is meant'. Lévi-Strauss is really concerned with the question how — how 'natural and social phenomena lend themselves to intellectual elaboration' (Sperber 1979, p. 28). Somehow this is to be settled by studying signifiers in the way Barthes recommended for semiology, as forms lacking content. Sperber concludes that whereas for Saussure the question 'How do symbols mean?' still implied the question 'What do they mean?', Barthes and the semiologists influenced by him, making a radical break with tradition,

> have completely left aside the what-question, and have studied not at all 'How do symbols mean?', but rather 'How do symbols work?' In this study they have established, all unknowing, that symbols work without meaning. Modern semiology . . . has refuted the principles on which it is founded. (Sperber 1975, pp. 51–2)

This deliberate avoidance of the meaning of social symbol-systems may account for the disappointing development of a semiology which bases itself on a pre-semantic notion of the sign (rather than discourse, a human activity of meaning), its failure to achieve the scientific status to which it aspired.[21]

Barthes, ignoring (like Lévi-Strauss) Saussure's warnings against taking language as a model for other institutions, attempted to apply Saussurian principles to objects existing and circulating in the real world, not to discover what these objects signified, but how they circulated. The fact that semiology does not feel 'bound to give the meaning of signs', Descombes observes, poses the awkward problem of whether 'it would be able to provide meanings?' As he shows, some followers of semiology accepted the rather absurd belief 'that signs can signify without signifying anything in particular'. Thus they took something to be a sign by 'crediting it with a determinate meaning that is unknown to' them, a charitable but illogical act, for in terms of linguistic philosophy 'an indefinite sense would not really be a sense at all' (Descombes 1986, pp. 150–1; Wittgenstein 1958, §99). The very concept of a sign implies transitivity — it is always a 'sign of' something — so to use the concept while denying its transitivity deliberately defeats language. Barthes obviously never faced this whole problematic. Answering a *Tel Quel* questionnaire in 1961, he recorded that 'ideas and themes interest me less than the way society takes possession of them in order to make them the substance of a certain number of signifying systems' (Barthes 1972, p. 151). But how could you study them without knowing *what* the system signified, and *how* it did so? Barthes defined 'the goal of structuralist activity' in 1963 as being 'to reconstruct an "object" in such a way as to manifest thereby the rules of functioning (the "functions" of this object)' (*ibid.*, p. 214). This concern with 'how things circulate' persists in Current Literary Theory, whether in the New Historicist Greenblatt's vague notion of the 'circulation of social energy' (Chapter 4), or the Cultural Materialists' interest — also drawing on Foucault's concept of discourse — in how ideologies are disseminated (Chapter 7). In all these writings, unfortunately, the question of meaning is ignored, as if signs could be taken for granted as having some significance, without enquiring what. But as the philosopher Nelson Goodman reminds us, 'a symbol system . . . embraces both the symbols and their interpretations' (Goodman 1976, p. 40 note). 'A symbol system consists of a symbol scheme correlated with a field of reference', a process of denotation which, as far as language is concerned, can cover a system where words are correlated 'with their pronunciations, as well as a system where words are correlated with what they apply to or name' (*ibid.*, pp. 143–4). In Barthesian semiotics the symbol system exists on its own, shorn off from any level with which it could be correlated.

To the rigorous abstractionism of Hjelmslev's semiotics Barthes added another would-be scientific model, also concerned with function, not meaning: cybernetics (again following Lévi-Strauss). Structuralism's 'new category of the object', he enthused in 1963, was 'the *functional*, thereby joining a whole scientific complex which is being developed around information theory and research', which would show 'how meaning is possible' (p. 218). This development might suggest that Barthes had adopted the speech-act orientation of Wittgenstein and J.L. Austin, according to which function is meaning, the meaning of a word is its use. But once again Barthes was using a transitive term while depriving it of its object. For him, evidently, things just 'function', as in one of Tinguely's creations. As Barthes said in 1961,

> fashion and literature are . . . homeostatic systems, that is, systems whose function is not to communicate an objective, exterior *signified* which pre-exists the system, but merely to create an equilibrum of operations, a signification in movement. . . . Fashion and literature signify strongly . . . but . . . they signify 'nothing', their being is in the signifying, not in what is signified. (p. 152)

In 1960 Barthes described literature as 'at bottom a tautological activity, like that of those cybernetic machines constructed for themselves (Ashby's homeostat): the author is a man who radically absorbs the world's *why* in a *how to write*' (p. 144). Theatre, too, is 'a kind of cybernetic machine' (p. 201).

This interest in 'the formal nature of signifying systems', where 'the use of a code always implies the repetition of a limited number of signs' (p. 191 note), was a further stage in the fragmenting of the Saussurian sign begun in 1950 by Lévi-Strauss's assertion that 'the signifier always precedes the signified'. In applying communications theory to sign systems, however, as Vincent Descombes has shown, semiology took over several assumptions which are alien to natural languages (Descombes 1981, pp. 92–103). First, by 'preceding' the message, the code defines all the situations in which it can be used (p. 93). In terms of semiology this has the drastic consequence that

> The signifier precedes the signified. Language is in no sense a medium, a means of expression, a mediation between interior and exterior; for the code precedes the message. There is not, therefore, any lived-through situation . . . to express. . . . The message is not the expression of an experience;

but rather the expression of the possibilities and limitations of the code (p. 95). Secondly, the code is independent of the message, which implies that 'the phenomenon of communication is studied from the point of view of the receiver', since the communications engineer is primarily concerned with what emerges at the exit of the channel (p. 93). Therefore 'the analysis of the material process of communication favours the receiver', and minimises the role of the emitter (p. 94). Thirdly, in communications theory the code is independent of the emitter, which means that 'by fixing what can be said, the code defines and patterns the situations capable of being signalled' (pp. 93–4). For semiology this means that 'the subject submits to the law of the signifier' (p. 97). Thus 'the code, and not its emitter, decides what shall and shall not be pertinent. If language is a code, it is language which speaks each time that the speaking subject delivers a remark . . .' (p. 98). It follows that the meaning of the message is not the meaning of experience but 'the meaning that experience can receive in a discourse which articulates it according to a certain code . . .'. Man's need to express himself in speech 'subjugates him to the signifier' (ibid.). This is a subjugation to the communication system similar to that ascribed, as we shall see, by Foucault to the 'episteme'.

The adoption of a code model, however unsuitable for language, undoubtedly accounts for some of the artificial and extreme attitudes towards natural language developed in the hothouse of Parisian thought in the 1960s.[22] The sense of language existing outside human agency, of man being 'subjugated to the signifier', expressed in Lacan's image of man as 'an animal at the mercy of language', recurs in Barthes. In 1963 he announced his vision of 'the new man of structuralism' as one who listens to 'the shudder of an enormous machine which is humanity tirelessly undertaking to create meaning', who believes that 'this fabrication of meaning is more important . . . than the meanings themselves', and who 'knows that it will suffice that a new language rise out of history, a new language which speaks *him* in his turn, for his task to be done' (Barthes 1972, pp. 219–20). What the 'new language' of literary criticism should look like Barthes showed in his *S/Z* (1970; English tr. 1974), an elaborate commentary on Balzac's short novella *Sarrasine*, in which the notion of code emerged as a master-concept.[23] The ideal text that Barthes begins by celebrating would be plural and infinite: 'the codes it mobilizes *extend as far as the eye can reach*, they are indeterminable' (Barthes 1974, pp. 5–6). But so is the reader, for 'this "I" which approaches the text is already itself a plurality of other texts, of codes which are infinite or, more precisely, lost (whose origin is lost)' (*ibid.*, p. 10). Structural analysis should 'abandon no site of the signifier without endeavouring to ascertain the code or codes' involved (p. 12), an injunction which Barthes carried out by itemising five codes at work in Balzac's text, the hermeneutic, the semic, the proairetic, the referential, and the symbolic (pp. 18–21, 261–3). As always the emphasis is not on what is meant but how it (whatever that 'it' is!) means, which Barthes describes through a metaphor, 'the weaving of voices': 'The five codes create a kind of network, a *topos* through which the entire text passes . . .'. Yet, unwilling to seem too definite (Barthes is divided between making highly schematic analyses and parodying schematism), he denies any effort to structure a code, emphasising rather 'the multivalence of the text, its partial reversibility', with the code as only 'a perspective of quotations, a mirage of structures . . .' (p. 20).

This whole depersonalised system, 'the most exhaustive attempt to read fiction without positing an author who might be disclosed there in his freedom' (Donoghue 1981, p. 167), follows the essays by Barthes and Foucault in 1968–9 announcing 'The Death of the Author' (an episode discussed in the next Chapter). While shifting attention, as Descombes observed, to the receiver rather than the emitter of the signal, the emphasis on codes was also meant to break the constraints on language and interpretation which Paris intellectuals of this period found so oppressive. They tried to escape from the constraints and conventions of language by deploying a simple rhetoric of 'liberating' or 'freeing' the text, setting the pulsating terms 'plural' or 'arbitrary', full of glamour and the promise of freedom, against the limited and limiting concepts 'singular' or 'determinate'. So in *S/Z* Barthes invoked a Nietzschean goal of interpretation as revealing the plural meanings of a text, stating that

> To interpret a text is not to give it a [single] . . . meaning, but on the contrary to appreciate what more or less *plural* constitutes it. Let us first posit the image of a triumphant plural, unimpoverished by any constraint of representation (of imitation). In this ideal text, the net-works are many and interact, without any one of them being able to surpass the rest; this text is a galaxy of signifiers, not a structure of signifieds; it has no beginning; it is reversible; . . . the codes it mobilizes

... are indeterminable ...; the systems of meaning can take over this absolutely plural text, but their number is never closed, based as it is on the infinity of language. (Barthes 1974, pp. 5–6)

The metaphor of a 'galaxy of signifiers' opposed to 'a structure of signifieds' is rhetorically made to seem attractive, but it is incoherent, inasmuch as the terms are interdependent, and a collection of signifiers having no signified would be an impossibility. As for the assertion that the number of meanings 'is never closed', Descombes objects that 'the "infinity of language" is here posited on the basis of an *a priori* reasoning upon the nature of the sign: a text is made up of signs; each of these signs can carry an infinity of meanings by virtue of the infinity of contexts in which it can be placed; a text is therefore "plural". This argument is unfortunately sophistical' (Descombes 1986, p. 7). As with Lacan's sophistries, the decisive counter-argument is that a sign may have several meanings, but this depends on how it is used, and it does not imply that the sign '*has* several meanings in each use', since the choice of one automatically excludes the others. For '*potentially to say* is not yet *to say*', and 'to play with the possibilities of play is not yet to make a move in the game' — which involves a choice. Critics desiring a plural text, Descombes judges, are 'like a player who hankers to play every possible move in one move', or like a child who imagines that a limited sum of money can satisfy an infinite number of desires (pp. 7–8).

Unrealistic, Utopian perhaps, the desire to be free from the constraints of language was shared by many in this etiolated tradition descending from Saussure. Language, the unquestioned model for all the human sciences, having been redefined in increasingly fragmented and depersonalised terms, was ultimately unable to meet the demands placed on it. In an interview of 1963 Barthes referred to the 'myth which makes language "the best and worst of things"', and concluded that 'language has become at once a problem and a model' (Barthes 1972, pp. 275–6). The core problem was meaning, the fact that an individual speaker is free to communicate his thoughts on any topic he wishes. That basic property of language was retained by Saussure, we recall, both in the form of the linguistic sign conveying the speaker's 'concept, idée', and in the distinction between *langue* and *parole*, with all its implications for language as an interpersonal and social medium. The strange fact about the steadily diminished and fragmented version of the Saussurian sign, as we follow its career through the 60s and 70s, was that somehow it was still connected with meaning, as if the semiotic-cybernetic abstractionism could not manage to kill off this traditional property of language. At all events, language and meaning came increasingly to be seen as a burden, a liability. In *Roland Barthes par Roland Barthes* (1975; English tr. 1977) Barthes said of himself: 'Evidently he dreams of a world which would be *exempt from meaning* (as one is from military service)'. Yet, Barthes wrote, 'for him, it is not a question of

recovering a pre-meaning . . . but rather to imagine a post-meaning . . .'
(Barthes 1977, p. 87), another wistfully Utopian fantasy.

The culminating point for Barthes of this difficulty with language and
meaning was the inaugural lecture he gave on being appointed to the 'chair
of literary semiology' at the Collège de France in 1977. In it he defined the
revolutionary goal of the intellectual as being to attack power, especially as
embodied in a trans-social organism that has fettered mankind since the
beginning. What is this constraining power? Religion? The class-system?
Morality? No, 'language [*langage*] — or, to be more precise, its necessary
expression, the language [*langue*] we speak and write'. We do not notice
the insidious power of language, Barthes claimed,

> because we forget that all speech is a classification, and that all classifi-
> cations are oppressive. . . . Jakobson has shown that a speech-system is
> defined less by what it permits us to say than by what it compels us to
> say. In French . . . I am obliged to posit myself first as subject before
> stating the action which will henceforth be no more than my attribute:
> what I do is merely the consequence and consecution of what I am. In
> the same way, I must always choose between masculine and feminine,
> for the neuter and the dual [forms] are forbidden me. In the same way, I
> must indicate my relation to the other person by resorting to either *tu* or
> *vous*; social or affective suspension is denied me. Thus, by its very
> structure my language implies an inevitable relation of alienation. To
> speak, and . . . to utter a discourse is not . . . to communicate; it is to
> subjugate. . . . (*ibid.*, p. 460)

Language, then, 'is neither reactionary nor progressive; it is quite simply
fascist;[24] for fascism does not prevent speech, it compels speech', since
'once uttered, even in the subject's deepest privacy, speech enters the
service of power' (p. 461). There are two 'inevitable' categories in speech,
Barthes argued, 'the authority of assertion, and gregariousness of repetition.
. . . Once I speak, these two categories unite in me; I am both master and
slave' (*ibid.*). The only path open to the intellectual, therefore, is 'to cheat
with speech, to cheat speech', an evasion or 'imposture which allows us
to understand speech *outside the bounds of power*, in the splendor of a
permanent revolution of language, I for one call *literature*' (p. 462).

This reads like an attempt finally to annihilate Saussure. The individual's
'executive power', through *parole*, to activate the system of *langue*, that
'social link', in order to communicate his thoughts — this is turned upside
down, the individual now not controlling, but controlled by, language, an
instrument used — by whom? for what end? — against him. There is more
than a suspicion of paranoia here (a detail worthy of *1984* is that 'even in
the subject's deepest privacy', in a diary or interior monologue, say, his
language is in the service of power).[25] But perhaps Barthes, in rebelling
against language, was rebelling not so much against its classificatory powers
as against the reality it classifies and differentiates. If only one could be

neither masculine nor feminine, neither speaking subject nor addressee, but just a fluid entity enjoying 'social or affective suspension', a floating signifier in an undifferentiated mass of . . . bodies? — But as soon as we work out the consequences of these longings we realise that they would destroy individuality, wipe out consciousness and humanity.

*   *   *

Barthes, like other intellectuals of the Paris 60s, was dissatisfied with Saussure's linguistics — in the one-sided, structuralist version of language as a self-contained system — but was either unwilling or unable to conceive of any other. Instead of turning to Wittgenstein, ordinary language philosophy, speech-act theory, transformational grammar, or, above all, semantics, which was developing in several interesting directions in the 1960s and 70s, this influential group stuck with a notion of language as reduced to the linguistic sign and fretted at its limitations. Michel Foucault's synthesis of the available models in French culture drew more on philosophy and science (Dumézil, Canghuilem, Hippolyte, Lévi-Strauss) than on linguistics, but for him too the Saussurian categories were a hindrance. In *Naissance de la clinique* (1963) he had objected against 'the things said' having to be 'treated exclusively in accordance with the play of signifier and signified', and proposed that the ' "facts of discourse [be] treated not as autonomous nuclei of multiple significations, but as events" ', events that came together to form a system (*cit.* White 1979, p. 88) — as it were, without any human agency. In an interview in 1969 Foucault declared that he felt 'ecstatic' over the use of signs 'in their modality of signs, and not in their capacity to transmit meaning' (*cit.* Timpanaro 1975, pp. 184–5). The burden of meaning was one of the themes in the inaugural lecture that he, too, gave at the Collège de France, *L'Ordre du discours* (1971; English tr. 1972). Here Foucault attacked the traditional view in which the 'speaking subject' (in Saussure's terms) 'indicates the field of meanings . . . in which propositions . . . ultimately find their foundation. In this relationship with meaning, the founding subject has signs, marks, tracks, letters at his disposal' (Foucault 1972, pp. 227–8). For most people this would be a normal description of one phase of linguistic activity, although obviously much more is involved (as I shall suggest later in this chapter). But Foucault complained that 'this exchange, this writing, this reading never involve anything but signs. Discourse thus nullifies itself, in reality, in placing itself at the disposal of the signifier' (p. 228). The conclusion could only be 'to abolish the sovereignty of the signifier' (p. 229). This was a much more radical remedy.

Foucault's most sustained attack on language came in *L'Archéologie du savoir* (1969; English tr. 1972). Evidently already influenced by Lacan and Derrida, Foucault made another of those categorical, *a priori* assertions so popular in French intellectual discourse at this time, objecting that the 'signifying' structure of language always refers back to something else; objects are designated by it; meaning is intended by it; the subject is referred back to it by a number of signs even if he is not himself present in them. Language always seems to be inhabited by the other, the elsewhere, the distant; it is hollowed by absence. Is it not the locus in which something other than itself appears, does not its own existence seem to be dissipated in this function? (Foucault 1972, p. 111)

In this pessimistic view, language as a means of communication is irredeemably flawed, for 'men's discourse is perpetually undermined from within by the contradiction of their desires, the influence that they have been subjected to, or the conditions in which they live' (p. 149), because 'contradiction is always anterior to discourse, and because it can never . . . entirely escape it' (p. 151). Given such a negative, Lacanian-deterministic view, Foucault urged mankind to simply 'ignore' the whole power of language 'to designate, to name, to show, to reveal, to be the place of meaning or truth, and, instead, turn one's attention to the moment — which is at once solidified, caught up in the play of the "signifier" and the "signified" — that determines its unique and limited existence'. We must 'suspend, not only the point of view of the "signified" (we are used to this by now), but also that of the "signifier" . . .' (p. 111).

Foucault's remedy for the unreliability of language as traditionally conceived was another dose of scientism, his new notion of discourse. Echoing the move of Barthesian semiology from 'what is said' to 'how it is said', Foucault defined the 'discursive practices' he would study as a form of linguistic activity from which human agency was virtually eliminated. Systematically rejecting all previous human attributes (his book is in effect one expanded polemical dichotomy: 'not that old, regressive, anthropomorphic system but this new, progressive, dehumanised system'), Foucault elaborated his new world of words around a series of scientistic metaphors, taking the lead from Lévi-Strauss. Studying the history of concepts (or 'objects of discourse') we should 'map the first *surfaces* of their emergence' (p. 41), 'analyse the *grids of specification*' (p. 42), locate the 'planes of differentiation in which the objects of discourse may appear' (p. 43). Rather than concerning ourselves with meaning or reference, we should try 'to determine according to what schemata (of series, simultaneous groupings, linear or reciprocal modification) the statements may be linked to one another in a type of discourse' (p. 60). We should also 'determine the possible *points of diffraction* of discourse', whether '*points of incompatibility*' or '*points of equivalence*' (p. 65). This scientistic terminology reaches such a density that if the referent were withheld, it would be hard to guess which discipline could be described in terms of 'isomorphism . . . transference . . . proximities, symmetries or analogies . . . to describe the field of vectors and of differential receptivity (of permeability and impermeability) that has been a condition of historical possibility for the interplay of exchanges' (p. 161). Foucault was in fact talking about language and the history of ideas in this numbingly abstract jargon, a style that continues to influence Shakespeare criticism, whether New Historicist or Cultural Materialist (Chapters 4 and 7 below). This would-be scientific terminology marks Foucault's debt to positivism, which constituted indeed one of the poles of his thought. Descombes has shown Foucault's debt to 'the French positivist school' by his tracing 'the evolution of concepts and thought . . . in the various states of different disciplines'. But he points out that Foucault's 'positivist notion of *fact*' coexists uneasily with the nihilism of Nietzsche 'when he proclaims the disarray of positivism: "no facts, only interpretations"' (Descombes 1981, pp. 110–17).

The depersonalisation involved in Foucault's concept of discourse is not accidental, but reflects another key element in structuralist thought deriving from Lévi-Strauss, the attack on the subject. Reacting against existentialism and phenomenology, which postulated an individual subject not just perceiving but giving meaning to the world, Lévi-Strauss erected the concept of structure in opposition to the subject (Anderson 1983, pp. 33–54). Ethnographic analysis, Lévi-Strauss believed, especially myth, could reveal the 'anonymous' or 'objectified thought' which lay beneath human diversity. His deeper purpose, he wrote in 1971 (perhaps reciprocally influenced by Foucault), was '"to reduce the subject to the insubstantial place or space where anonymous thought can develop"', relegating the subject to the background '"so as to allow free play to this anonymous deployment of discourse"' (*cit*. Frank 1989, p. 53). The so-called 'anti-humanism' that Lévi-Strauss unleashed was taken up by most French intellectuals, but by no-one more thoroughly than Foucault, who welcomed Lévi-Strauss for having pronounced 'the death of the subject in the advent of structures', and proclaimed in 1966 the ultimate extinction of mankind (Ferry and Renaut 1985, pp. 138–47). Foucault subsequently resented being labelled a structuralist, and indeed developed in several different directions, but that part of his work which continues to influence Current Literary Theory, and some areas of Shakespeare studies, is, if not 'for' structure, certainly 'against' the subject. Widening to the linguistic domain what was originally a philosophical objection, Foucault conceived of the subject as 'dispersed' into an 'anonymity' by the 'discursive practice', those 'rules of formation' that operate 'in discourse itself . . . according to a sort of unifying anonymity on all individuals', the 'enunciative domain' being 'an anonymous field whose configuration defines the possible position of speaking subjects' (Foucault 1972, pp. 50–53, 63, 122). Anyone tempted to use such terminology in the 1990s should take careful stock of what it entails.

Rejecting any notion of the speaking subject as someone 'who, in speaking, exercises his sovereign freedom' (p. 122), the one feature that all theories of language since the Greeks have taken as basic, Foucault erected with one hand anonymity, and with the other determinism:

I shall abandon any attempt . . . to see discourse as a phenomenon of expression — the verbal translation of a previously established synthesis; instead, I shall look for a field of regularity for various positions of subjectivity. Thus conceived, discourse is not the majestically unfolding manifestation of a thinking, knowing, speaking subject, but, on the contrary, a totality, in which the dispersion of the subject and his discontinuity with himself may be determined. (pp. 54–5)

(We note in passing those *a priori* and totalising assertions of the subject's dispersion and discontinuity.) Discursive practice, as Foucault conceived it, is 'a body of anonymous, historical rules, always determined in the time and space that have defined', for a given area, 'the conditions of operation of the enunciative function' (p. 117). The apotheosis of this concept of 'a body of anonymous, historical rules' was Foucault's postulation of the existence of an *episteme*, that is, 'the total set of relations that unite, at a given period, the discursive practices'. The *episteme* is in effect

a world view, a slice of history common to all branches of knowledge, which imposes on each one the same norms and postulates, . . . a certain structure of thought that the men of a particular period cannot escape — a great body of legislation written once and for all by some anonymous hand. (p. 191)

It is hard to imagine that the flight from the subject, the flight from language, could reach any more extreme point. As Simon Clarke has shown, Foucault's neo-positivism resulted in a 'philosophy of the concept', in which 'human individuals become simply the instruments of an impersonal thought, the "problematic", "episteme" or "discourse" that they live out. Both reality and the subject become constructs of the concept, having no independent existence, so there is no escape from the tyranny of the concept' (Clarke 1981, p. 88).

Paradoxically, although he dismissed any notion of the speaking subject exercising 'his sovereign freedom', this whole critique of extant attitudes to language, knowledge and history was the product of Foucault's own 'unifying function' as a 'thinking, knowing' subject, 'majestically' expressing his discomfort with the whole Western tradition in a regular series of first-person utterances (e.g., pp. 15, 31, 37, 80). But while he may have 'included himself out' (in Sam Goldwyn's celebrated phrase), Foucault's attack on the traditional concepts of language, thought, and knowledge was the culmination, in one direction, of that unease with language as a constricting factor on human behaviour that we have already seen in Lacan and Barthes. But a negating reaction can end up with a state worse than that negated, for in fleeing from the subject Foucault also had to abandon the notions of selection, invention, originality (all excoriated at one point or another), and therefore freedom. Although, like every other French intellectual of his day, he constantly asserted the need to free oneself from previous systems of thought (e.g., pp. 14, 16, 17, 26, 29, 121, 203), the end point reached by his concept of *episteme* is a terrible determinism, a single 'slice of history common to all branches of knowledge', imposing 'on each one the same norms and postulates', and which no one can escape. That is as totalising and deterministic a conception as one could possibly imagine, but lacking empirical evidence for any period of history known to me.[26] It is beyond belief that only one 'structure of thought' could rule at any given time (rather like the much mocked notion of a single 'Elizabethan world-view'), and that it could impose itself equally on optics and musicology, say, or mathematics and hermeneutics. Foucault seems to have given in to the desire to erect a model of domination and subordination which would remove human agency, but which ends up destroying human responsibility. If we are all imposed on by the *episteme* then no one can be responsible for their words, thoughts, or deeds. To place language ('hollowed absence') outside human agency is to negate not only the notion of human interchange but also ethics, and with it society. Communication would have no function, other than to demonstrate the points of diffraction of discourse, or 'the *temporal vectors of derivation*' (p. 169).

NEO-STRUCTURALISM: EMPTYING THE SYSTEM

Foucault represents one line of development for structuralism's thinned-down notion of language as a self-contained system: the denial of individual meaning, the 'dispersion' of the subject into 'discontinuity', the reification of discourse as an anonymous 'totality' which imposes itself on the individual, determining his utterances and, presumably, his thinking. A quite different way out of structuralism's linguistic cul-de-sac was taken by Jacques Derrida, who attached discontinuity not to the subject but to discourse, diagnosing in language itself a whole series of gaps, uncertainties and postponements which make it unable to represent reality or human experience in any reliable fashion. Derrida's career runs parallel with all the other French 60s intellectuals discussed in the previous section, and my postponement of him till now was partly artificial but at the same time acknowledging that his development of the structural legacy reached a more extreme point than those contemporaries whom he also outlived. For many readers today neo-structuralism (also known as post-structuralism, or deconstruction) *is* literary theory, and literary theory *is* Derrida (cf. Ellis 1989, p. 18). Some of his admirers regard Derrida as a truly original, revolutionary figure, as if sprung fully-grown from Minerva's head. But Derrida's mental equipment, his assumptions and attitudes, were formed by the same forces that shaped Barthes, Foucault, and many more. With a rather different philosophical background than the others — the key figures now are Husserl, Nietzsche, Heidegger[27] — but frequently invoking Saussure, Derrida developed that inheritance in his own distinctive manner. But he, too, knew Lévi-Strauss's essay on Marcel Mauss, quoting from it in the paper he gave at the conference organised at Baltimore in 1966 to publicise in America the advent of structuralism. Derrida quoted precisely the passages where Lévi-Strauss destroyed Saussure's unified system with his notion of a 'floating signifier', and he also acknowledged his debt to Lévi-Strauss for the concept of a 'supplement', which was to loom so largely in Derrida's own idiosyncratic terminology (Derrida 1978, pp. 289–92).

But this paper, 'Structure, sign and play in the discourse of the human sciences', also marked Derrida's rejection of structuralism. His tactic was, first to accuse Lévi-Strauss and others of using the term 'structure' in such a way as to imply that structures have a centre, a fixed presence or origin (Derrida 1978, pp. 278–80). Subsequently, however, Derrida congratulated Lévi-Strauss for his 'stated abandonment of all reference to a *centre*, to a *subject*, to a privileged *reference*, to an origin . . .' (p. 286). Whether or not this self-contradiction was merely a way of placating a distinguished predecessor, the first accusation was allowed to stand, and by the end of the essay Lévi-Strauss had been rejected, along with structure, for a 'Nietzschean . . . joyous affirmation of the play of the world . . .' ['le jeu du monde'] (p. 292). Like Barthes, Derrida invoked Nietzsche as a talisman for the rhetorical (or Utopian) vision of a future for language and thought beyond all constraints of good and evil, truth or lies ('a world of signs without fault, without truth'). Derrida's polemics were based on the recognition, as Perry Anderson puts it, that 'the supposition of any stable structure' postulated a subject distinct from it, an autonomy which Derrida set out to liquidate, in so doing, however, not 'purifying' the structure but '*destructuring*' it.

> For once structures were freed from any subject at all, delivered over totally to their own play, they would lose what *defines* them as structures — that is, any objective coordinates of organization at all. Structurality, for Derrida, is . . . play [which] now knows no boundaries of any sort — it is 'absolute chance', 'genetic indetermination', 'the seminal adventure of the trace'. Structure therewith capsizes into its antithesis, and post-structuralism proper is born, or what can be defined as a subjectivism without a subject. (Anderson 1983, p. 54)

As Anderson acutely observes, structure and subject are interdependent categories, so that to attack the latter would eventually subvert the former, the result being 'a finally unbridled subjectivity' (*ibid.*). This is in effect the philosophical position that Derrida incorporates, the irony being that his subjectivism has become dogma.

Another way of describing Derrida's intervention would be to say that he took over structuralism's etiolated version of Saussurian linguistics, and ruined it from within. In formulating his own system in the 1960s he regularly attacked Saussure, in the process severely misrepresenting what the *Cours de linguistique générale* says, as a number of critics have protested.[28] Derrida was equally unscrupulous — the distortions are so persistent, in the context of specific reference to Saussure's text, that they cannot be the result of accident or deficient memory — in reporting Saussure's discussion of *différence*. In the *Cours*, we recall, Saussure declared that the constituent parts of the linguistic sign could be defined only in terms of differences, distinctions from other possible formations, conceptual for the signified, acoustic for the signifier. When it came to the complete sign, however, we are at the level of positive terms, no longer abstract categories like signified and signifier, but words or lexemes, material objects actually existing. Derrida ignored Saussure's careful (albeit ultimately obscure and unsatisfactory) distinction between the constituent parts (abstractions) and the whole linguistic sign (an entity), and took *différence* to be a defining characteristic of language as a whole in Saussure's system. Having attributed an altogether spurious generality to Saussure's concept, Derrida then announced that he would adopt Saussure's *différence* but bend it to form his coinage *différance*, which supposedly contains both senses of 'différer' in French, namely 'to differ' and 'to defer'. Embarrassing though it might be for him to admit it, the fact that Derrida had to change the word exactly proves Saussure's point that each linguistic sign is a unique correlation of a distinct signified with a distinct signifier, so that change at one level must result in change at the other (*CLG*, p. 167).

In focussing mainly on this neologism, *différance*, which has been described as 'Derrida's master-concept' (Spivak 1976, p. xliii), I want to side-step the problem that Derrida poses to his commentators through constantly returning to something he said earlier, rephrasing it, redefining it in terms of another idea he has subsequently had, linking it with a new term he has invented, an always expanding chain of neologisms (*trace, dissémination, marque, écriture, archi-écriture, supplément, pharmakon . . .*), which give the impression 'both prolific and mysterious', as two French critics put it, that 'we are sharing step by step in the birth and development of some original enterprise' (Ferry and Renaut 1985, p. 168). But in fact, as many independent readers of Derrida have discovered after some wasted weeks, or months, the chain leads nowhere, back into itself, generating a further need for exegesis, which leads to . . . further exegesis. Derrida's repeated redefining of the terms of discussion means that anyone trying to expound his work risks getting caught in an exegetical web, a hermeneutic process where all points are mutually and endlessly redefinable, and which has the effect on his expositors of them reproducing the nature, and especially the indeterminability, of the Derridian texts they are trying to explicate. The result of this endlessly weaving web of self-reference is that Derrida has, over the last twenty-five years, put into circulation a huge vocabulary or conglomerate of interrelated ideas and attitudes, which constitute an empire of discourse, over which he rules unchallenged (since he can always correct his hermeneuts). To discuss his theories you are virtually compelled to use his terminology, and once you are inside his system you have no external purchase on it, no means of judging it in independent terms.

The point at issue here is an important one for the evaluation of any thought-system, and merits discussion. As we shall have occasion to observe several times in the course of this book, one of the striking characteristics of the various systems built up by this powerful group of thinkers, Lévi-Strauss, Foucault, Lacan, Derrida, Althusser, was that they were complete in themselves, self-validating. Polemically destroying their predecessors' concepts and categories, developing their own terminology and methodology, ignoring the conventions of rational analysis (often invoking unconscious or irrational elements), mocking empiricism and dispensing with the very notion of evidence, they each created a system that was self-confirming, immune to external testing. As Ernest Gellner, a penetrating thinker in many fields (philosophy, anthropology, sociology) puts it, commenting on Freudianism, the first and in many ways the model for all subsequent self-validating systems: 'the first principle of the study of any belief system is that its ideas and terms must be stated in terms other than its own', for 'concepts, like feelings and desires, have their cunning', and only by restating them in other terms can 'we hope to lay bare the devices they employ to make their impact' (Gellner 1985, p. 5). Many ideologies, Gellner shows, are in effect 'bilingual', operating 'simultaneously . . . within a language in which they alone absolutely define the facts and norms, and another more public and neutral language within which they adopt a more modest stance and can be called to account' (p. 50). Derrida's method of practical criticism, a 'double-dealing', as M.H. Abrams calls it, uses two languages in just this way, as we shall see in Chapter 3. Derrida's theory, however, is conceived in the first, closed language, an agglomerate of special terms which effectively evades accountability. For, as Gellner points out,

> the testability of an assertion depends in a great part on whether the terms occurring in it have a meaning that is (a) reasonably precise and fixed, and (b) independent of the theory that is being tested, and of the guild of those committed to it. (p. 182)

The impregnability of Derrida's position depends on the fact that his assertions are never testable, because the terms he uses are never precise (indeed, he denies that language is capable of determinate meaning), refer always to other terms, and are part and parcel of the theory. We cannot get outside them, rephrase them independently, and so we cannot subject them to critical analysis and evaluation. They, like Derrida's system, must be accepted or rejected wholesale.

With this important proviso in mind, I return to Derrida's invented term *différance*, which attempted to combine two meanings, to differ and to defer. The role that the second sense has in his neologistic philosophy can be seen *in nuce* in this next passage, where he invokes 'classical semiology' (which can only refer to Saussure) and its supposed deficiencies:

> The sign is usually said to be put in place of the thing itself, the present thing, 'thing' here standing equally for meaning or referent. The sign represents the present in its absence. . . . When we cannot grasp or show the thing, state the present, the being-present, when the present cannot be presented, we signify, we go through the detour of the sign. . . . The sign, in this sense, is deferred presence. . . . [The] circulation of signs defers the moment in which we can encounter the thing itself, make it ours, consume or expend it, touch it, see it, intuit its presence. (Derrida 1982, p. 9)

Setting aside the rhetorical repetitions, evidently intended to dazzle and confuse (one of many sequences where Derrida reduces argument to the level of a three-card trick),[29] the strangest point in that passage introducing the key notion of 'deferral' is the crude concept of language behind it, a pre- and indeed anti-Saussurian reduction of language to the dichotomy of 'words' and 'things'. Derrida reifies the exchange of meaning as the first step to disqualifying or denying it. He is trying to dazzle us into thinking that language can never make meanings or referents 'present', *in the same way as words can never make things appear*. But whoever thought that language could or should do that? The concept of 'presence' is irrelevant here. A linguistic utterance can refer to, or denote, people or things that may be present, or absent, in an actual speech situation involving two or more participants: all that matters in either case is whether the utterance identifies them correctly first time round, or only after further clarification. But an utterance can also refer to, or denote, concepts such as 'beauty', or 'justice', or 'deconstruction', that are never either present or absent.

What Derrida is doing is to use the etiolated Saussurian categories as passed down through structuralism but then attempt to destroy them by a series of *a priori* denials. (There is never any discussion of alternatives, never any hint that a vast domain of language exists beyond the carefully delimited area at which Derrida is now gnawing away.) So he attacks Saussure's notion of the concept on the grounds that

> the signified concept is never present in and of itself, in a sufficient presence that would refer only to itself. Essentially and lawfully, every concept is inscribed in a chain or in a system within which it refers to the other, to other concepts. . . . (*ibid.*, p. 11)

But concepts do not 'refer' to other concepts; they are differentiated from them, within the sign, by each being associated with a distinct phonic image, and they can also denote, or refer to entities in the outside world.

Having travestied that part of Saussure's thought, Derrida went on to sabotage his crucial distinction between *langue* (the social) and *parole* (the individual) by invoking the 'speaking subject' yet then perversely aligning it with *langue*, not with *parole*, to which it belongs. (Wendell Harris has also observed that the basic deconstructionist strategy 'lies in conflating that which may be said of a word regarded under the aspect of *langue* [with] that which is true of it under the aspect of *parole*': Harris 1988, p. 25.) In fact Derrida never mentions *parole*, writes as if this part of the dichotomy does not exist, and by this omission manages to reduce the speaking subject to a passive condition (like Lacan and Foucault, but for a different end). Quoting a passage from Saussure, Derrida takes it as proving that the subject 'is inscribed in language, is a "function" of language' (*ibid.*, p. 15). But this is exactly the opposite of what Saussure says, namely that *langue* is 'not a function of the speaking subject', and *parole* is 'an individual act involving will-power and intelligence' (*CLG*, p. 30). To leave out such key ideas does indeed destroy the system you purport to be describing.

I insist, albeit very briefly, on these gross inaccuracies, among many others, in order to show, once and for all, that the reputation enjoyed by Derrida for careful reading of texts — and extended to deconstruction, the practical criticism modelled on him — is an illusion. One loyal exegete claims that 'Derrida's method of deconstructive reading is laboriously textual' (Spivak 1976, p. 318 note 19), another that his criticism offers 'a patient and minutely philological "explication de texte"' (Miller 1976b, p. 336). This would be a remarkable achievement, since Derrida has supposedly shown that there is no determinate object to which one can be true. I think that there are determinate objects such as texts, which can be interpreted faithfully (subject always to discussion, never apodictically or categorically definite), and from that position I must say that Derrida's reading of Saussure is biassed, fragmentary, wilfully ignoring crucial stages of the argument, misrepresenting others, and soaking the remnant in his own terminology until it begins to dissolve and can be reconstituted in the form he wants to give it.

This high-handed treatment of the authors discussed is another characteristic of the 60s system-builders, sometimes euphemistically described as 'strong misreading'. Lévi-Strauss misrepresented the Prague structuralists on several important points, Foucault regularly distorted what nineteenth-century linguists actually said, while Althusser's version of Marx is virtually unrecognisable.[30] Derrida energetically continued his distorting destruction of Saussure (while simultaneously accusing him of contradiction), postulating the existence of '*a concept signified in and of itself*, a concept simply present to thought, independent of a relationship to language, that is of a relationship to a system of signifiers', and suggesting that in fact 'every signified is also in the position of a signifier' (Derrida 1981, pp. 19–20). As every reader of the *Cours* will recognise, these ideas are wholly foreign to Saussure, would indeed be impossibilities in his system. By reducing it to confusion, 'de-structuring' it, as he had done to Lévi-Strauss, Derrida accomplishes what is known as an 'immanent' critique, ruining a system from within (Descombes 1986, pp. 2–3).

Another tactic — also well known in philosophical polemics since the time of Lactantius, at least — is to play off one authority against another. So in order to strengthen his attack on the Saussurian signified concept as never being 'present in and of itself', Derrida fused it with a term derived from Edmund Husserl, the 'transcendental signified', in order to argue that language is incapable of 'presence'.[31] Modern commentators would agree with Derrida, as Descombes puts it, that 'the Husserlian requirement for the signified object to be present in order to fulfill the signifying intention is unjustifiable . . .' (Descombes 1986, p. 63). But Derrida went on to argue that any 'statement of perception already states not only presence, but absence', parasitically depending on Husserl's concept while ostensibly refuting it. In Derrida's own words, ' "the absence of . . . the subject of the intuition . . . is *required* by the general structure of signification . . . It is radically required: the total absence of the subject and object of a statement . . ." ' (cit. *ibid.*, p. 64). Descombes comments that 'the Husserlian requirement for the intuitive presence of named objects was arbitrary, but the complementary demand for the absence of these same concepts seems equally unjustified' (*ibid.*, p. 65). All Derrida has done is to turn Husserl's proposition upside down, and Descombes easily shows that while the issue of absence or presence may affect both the meaning and the truth of a statement, it cannot be collapsed into this dramatic and exclusive opposition (pp. 65–6). Raymond Tallis has also objected that Derrida jumps from one extreme position to another, taking 'the impossibility of Husserlian *metaphysical* presence to imply the impossibility of presence *tout court*', that is, 'ordinary presence meant in the ordinary sense' (Tallis 1988, p. 205). Refusing to accept that 'in ordinary experience, presence (to) and self-presence are not absolute but matters of degree', Derrida insisted on taking presence as 'all-or-nothing, non-graded. And since presence is an unachievable absolute, it must be nothing' (*ibid.*, p. 208). Manipulating an argument by forcing it into extreme opposites, denying alternatives, is an easy but hollow procedure common to all the self-validating systems which continue to influence literary theory.

Derrida needed to postulate the absence of a signified, since he wished to deny language any possibility of meaning, any way of referring outside itself. In his 1966 lecture he proclaimed that at some (unlocated) point in time, a 'rupture' took place in the notion of structure, at which time 'language invaded the universal problematic'. This was

the moment when, in the absence of a center or origin, everything became discourse . . . that is to say, a system in which the central signified, the original or transcendental signified, is never absolutely present outside a system of differences. The absence of the transcendental signified extends the domain and play of signification infinitely. (p. 280)

Derrida, for whom the word 'metaphysics' is simply 'shorthand for any science of presence' (Spivak 1976, p. xxi), in this way set Saussure against Husserl, proclaiming that 'the metaphysics of presence is shaken with the help of the concept of *sign*'. But he then himself undermined Saussure, asserting that since 'there is no transcendental or privileged signified' then 'one must reject even the concept and word "sign" itself — which is precisely what cannot be done' (p. 281). Derrida went on to juggle Saussure's terms around ('we cannot' risk 'erasing difference in the self-identity of a signified reducing its signifier into itself or . . . simply expelling its signifier outside itself . . .', and so on; p. 281), a process which did not advance the discussion, nor was of course meant to. Then he transferred his wish-fulfilling diagnosis of a mythical moment of rupture to another set of enemies, claiming that it had also '*dislocated*' the whole of 'European culture', including metaphysics, and 'forced [it] to stop considering itself as the culture of reference' (p. 282).

It will be clear by now that Derrida postulated the existence of a transcendental signified or Divine Terminus merely in order to deny its presence. That may seem a perverse act, but he did so in order to link it to language, once again attempting to deprive language of its basic property of meaning. His claim may be restated as an informal syllogism: language can only signify determinately if it has a reliable centre or origin, the 'transcendental signified'; but it doesn't; so it can't. Once upon a time, though, it did, and — emulating Lévi-Strauss in inventing mythical narratives of human pre-history — Derrida imagines a prelapsarian state in which man experienced 'full presence', the 'transcendental signified' being there to be consumed, expended, touched, known. This may sound as if Derrida conceived of his absent centre as a real thing, with all the implications of essentialism, and indeed in an interview he once described 'the transcendental signified' as 'that which *in and of itself, in its essence*, would refer to no signifier, would exceed the chain of signs' (Derrida 1981, pp. 19–20; emphases mine). Derrida, of course, regularly denounced essentialism, but in these utterances several commentators have detected a nostalgia for absolute certainty.[32] More important, it seems to me, is to state that no adequate evidence has ever been given for the presence or absence of a transcendental signified, or its necessity to language. We can simply deconstruct Derrida's metaphysical, pseudo-historical structure by affirming that language signifies constantly, from moment to moment, as I write these words and you read them, without any need of an absolute presence to validate it. As John Searle has written,

> the Husserlian project of a transcendental grounding for science, language, and common sense is a failure. But . . . this doesn't threaten science, language, or common sense in the least. As Wittgenstein says, it leaves everything exactly as it is. The only 'foundation', for example, that language has or needs is that people are biologically, psychologically, and socially constituted so that they succeed in using it

to state truths, to give and obey orders, to express their feelings and attitudes. . . . (Searle 1983, p. 78)

Language is much more than a system of differences, formally defined. Meaning inheres in each linguistic sign, subject to the normal hazards of ambiguity or misunderstanding, hazards which can be overcome, as linguists and philosophers in our time have repeatedly emphasised. Meaning is fully realised in language through the joint operations of semantics, grammar and syntax, vital linguistic elements which, since Saussure and the structuralists ignored them, continue to be ignored by the post-structuralists and deconstructionists, with increasingly fatal consequences. It is no accident that this whole movement has not been taken seriously by either linguists or philosophers of language.

Without going into further detail, I think it can be reasonably stated that all of Derrida's deductions from these false premises are equally false. His attack on Saussure (and indeed the whole Western philosophical tradition since Plato) for privileging speech over writing, an error denounced by Derrida as 'phonocentrism' or 'logocentrism', has been judged wholly misguided, either as a historical or analytical claim.[33] As for his notion of *différance*, to which he gives quite positive attributes while simultaneously denying that it is a concept, or even a word (a notoriously specious claim, as is often observed: Said 1983, p. 210; Nuttall 1983, p. 43; Jackson 1991, pp. 175, 189), it supposedly generates verbal signs but 'defers' the 'presence' of what they signify through a never-ending process of substitution. His notion of the endless 'deferral' of meaning has been taken over uncritically by so many literary critics that it seems worth observing that nothing in linguistics would support it, since the various operations that the brain performs in processing language are remarkably swift. Noam Chomsky described the understanding of an utterance as, in part, 'a process of constructing an internal representation (a "percept") of its full structural description', and saw no reason 'to doubt that the full apparatus of the generative grammar that represents the hearer's linguistic competence is brought to bear immediately in carrying out this task' (Chomsky 1964, p. 112). Other linguists have observed that 'the sentences of a natural language can be parsed. We do it all the time. Furthermore, we do it very fast', this being 'one of the most important, and most neglected facts about natural languages: parsing is easy and quick' (*cit.* Newmeyer 1988, p. 10). And a literary critic adds that 'to the literate, print is instantaneously transparent: the mind intuits the word in the token so swiftly . . .' (Nuttall 1983, p. 85).

Derrida's theory of deferral cites no empirical evidence, and once again a spatialised metaphor substitutes for argument.[34] He simply asserts that 'no element can function as a sign without referring to another element . . . of the chain or system' which 'itself is not simply present', and exists only as a 'trace' of something which — to spell out the semantic implications of his metaphor — must have been there once, but has since moved on some-where else: out of sight, out of mind (Derrida 1981, p. 26). The metaphor of a chain of discourse had already been used by Lacan to argue that any meaning can only be sustained by reference to another meaning (Lacan 1966, p. 498). Derrida, begging the question by his metaphor of meaning somehow being passed along a chain (notice the rhetorically loaded impli-cations: away from both speaker and addressee, out of their reach or control, not precipitating itself at any of the links), is in effect denying meaning altogether, emptying the system. This is to produce an 'anti-hermeneutics' in which the non-presence of the sign would prohibit sig-nification at any point, now or later. The philosopher Manfred Frank judges this 'an absurdity that could be maintained only by going contrary to the experience of speaking and understanding' (Frank 1989, p. 432), with which many ordinary readers will agree.

But the point is that Derrida, like Barthes, Foucault and Lacan, nowhere invoked our normal, everyday experience of speaking and understanding. What this generation of French intellectuals gave us — tirelessly publicising their ideas, writing and speaking at great length, and thus showing an untiring faith in the powers of language to persuade, impose, deceive, confuse, convince — were mere assertions, not even theories about language. Their assertions did not derive from the analysis of grammar, syntax, speech acts, utterances, or any other form of discourse. With a token reference to 'the founder of modern linguistics' they took a system that was at best fragmentary, needing good will and an effort of reconstruc-tion to see how Saussure might have bridged the gaps between the various stages in his argument, and fragmented it still further. As early as 1968 Roland Barthes identified 'the major concern of modernism' as being 'the disintegration of the sign', and could assume general agreement that 'the goal today is to empty the sign . . .' (Barthes 1982, p. 116). That term indeed became deprived of all meaning by the frequency and the looseness with which it was used. Descombes complains that many post-1960 'obser-vations about the concept of sign or about language are so general as to remain indeterminate; as soon as the analysis of language begins, it will compel us to replace this notion of the sign with others: simple and complex signs, signs that are propositional or constitutive of the proposi-tion, designative or descriptive signs, and so on' (Descombes 1986, p. 63). In the notorious utterance of Derrida, for instance, 'from the moment there is meaning there is nothing but signs' (Derrida 1976, p. 50), we can see that the reductive form of his proposition attempted to relegate the concept of the sign to an inferior position (by contrast with what, one wonders). As Derrida provocatively (but wrongly) added, 'We think only in signs. Which amounts to ruining the notion of the sign . . .' (ibid.). Having reduced language to the sign, and then emptied that of meaning, the structuralists and their followers were free to assign any significance they wished to the original categories. The result was a terminological free-for-all. As Marc Angenot has observed, 'the *signifier* was perseveringly confused with the material signal, with the phonation, with the word considered apart from its meaning, with the libidinal investment in speech', and much else,[35] while 'the *signified* was indifferently taken for meaning, message, psychological or ontological reference, class of empirical objects, nonverbal reality', and so on (Angenot 1989, p. 158). Both terms constantly recur in Current Literary Theory, and hence in Shakespeare studies, bearing an indeterminable meaning, allowing their users unlimited free play. They now serve as a substitute for thinking, vague gestures that lend a spurious patina of expertise to a discussion.

The result of this whole process has been the attempt to set up an absolute barrier between language and whatever we might describe as physical or psychological reality, or to reverse the relationship between them. Foucault described the task of his new 'archaeology of knowledge' as consisting 'of not — of no longer — treating discourses as groups of signs (signifying elements referring to contents or representations) but as practices that systematically form the objects of which they speak' (Foucault 1972, p. 49). Language does not represent reality: it forms reality. The same idea was expressed in a notorious pronouncement of Lacan: 'it is the world of words that creates the world of things' (Lacan 1966, p. 276).

The most celebrated of these utterances come from Derrida's *Grammatology*, where he offered a justification of his theories by describing critical reading as producing a 'signifying structure' that will not simply reproduce 'the conscious, voluntary, intentional relationship that the writer institutes' in language (we note that Derrida's own writing displays intention). Derrida's form of reading believes that 'it cannot legitimately transgress the text toward something other than it, toward a referent (a reality that is metaphysical, historical, psychobiographical, etc.) or toward a signified outside the text whose content could take place, could have taken place outside of language, that is . . . , outside of writing in general'. Derrida's argument naturally depends on us accepting his other principles concerning 'the absence of the referent or the transcendental signified' in language, in general. If those are accepted, Derrida claimed, then we can see that '*There is nothing outside of the text*' (Derrida 1976, p. 158: '*il n'y a pas de hors-texte*'). That is, he added,

> beyond and behind what one believes can be circumscribed as Rousseau's text, there has never been anything but writing; there have never been anything but supplements, substitutive significations which could only come forth in a chain of differential references, the 'real' supervening, and being added only while taking on meaning from a trace. . . . And thus to infinity . . . . what opens meaning and language is writing as the disappearance of natural presence. (*ibid.*, p. 159)

In that extraordinary series of reductive sophisms ('never anything but . . . only . . . only') we reach the ultimate legacy of Saussure in Derrida's hands, the effacement of natural reality by *écriture*. As Perry Anderson comments, while rejecting 'the notion of language as a stable system of objectification', with this 'truly imperial decree' Derrida 'radicalized its pretensions as a *universal* suzerain of the modern world' (Anderson 1983, p. 42). This would be 'the wearisome condition of humanity', to apply Fulke Greville's Calvinist belief, 'Born under one law, to another bound', mankind condemned to use language but unable ever to actualise their thought or meaning in it.

Most followers of Derrida quote this passage as if they have just played a super-trump, annihilating all opposition, decisively changing the direction of human history. Few bother to scrutinise it as an argument. One who has done so is Vincent Descombes, who glosses Derrida's paradox as meaning that 'the *referent* of the text cannot be considered to be independent from it, since it cannot be identified independent of it'. Had there been anything outside the text, so the argument goes, 'it would have been the *referent*' — but obviously, and by definition, the referent is 'something found "in the text", in that the referent will be *whatever the text refers to*'. Descombes judges the principle 'hollow', for it merely says that we can only discover what the text purports to speak of by reading it, and by looking 'in' the text we find what there is 'outside' it.

> In a frivolous sense, it is true that whatever is 'outside the text' must nevertheless be included 'within the text'. But the problem is to know whether what is described as *the referent*, when found 'within the text', still appears in the form of a referent posited by (and *only* by) the text when considered as it is 'outside the text'. If this were so, there would be no difference between fiction and nonfiction. The real would only be an *effect of language*, as the delightful phrase goes. But this remains to be proved, to say the least. (Descombes 1986, pp. 8–9)

Put very briefly, that sceptical analysis cuts the ground from under all Derridians' feet. We can leave them, hanging over a void of their own making.

*   *   *

If this brief survey has achieved anything, it will, I hope, have shown how these notorious denials of the possibility of language to refer to reality all derive from the fracturing of Saussure's notion of the linguistic sign. It seems appropriate, then, to end this section by referring to a recent study by Luce Irigaray evaluating schizophrenia in Saussurian terms, one symptom being the patient's inability to make a coherent connection between signifier and signified.[36] The schizophrenic is in the unfortunate state of being unable to make sense of the signifier, the phonic part of the sign:

... he is affected by the 'sounds' whose 'concepts' remain hidden from him, veiled. From this state derives his relation, simultaneously fascinated and painful, to signifiers, which he repeats, transforms, severs, fractures, spells out, re-works . . . , as if he wanted at one and the same time to destroy them and to reclaim their power for his own use. (cit. Calvet 1975, pp. 100–101)

That sounds uncannily like our group of French critics of language, certainly not schizophrenic, whose work still influences Current Literary Theory. The difference, though, is that schizophrenics fragment the sign involuntarily, as a result of a psychic disturbance, in the language that they speak. Our band of four intellectuals fragment the sign deliberately, 'being in their right wits and good judgments', but only in the language that they talk about — la langue — not the language that they speak (la parole). That discrepancy between a metalanguage that displays coherence while claiming that the object language is incoherent may stand as an ironic comment on the artificiality and futility of this whole tradition, which ought by now to be seen for what it is, a dead-end.

REDEEMING LANGUAGE: REFERENCE, MEANING, INTENTION

We want to establish an order in our knowledge of the use of language: an order with a particular end in view; one out of many possible orders; not the order.   Wittgenstein[37]

Anyone coming afresh to the distortions of Saussure, and the resulting diminution of language emanating from the Paris of the 60s might wonder how such a theory could have had any impact on literary critics, or continue to do so a quarter of a century later.[38] I cannot answer that question, which would be an interesting problem in the sociology of knowledge, taste, and fashion. I can only suggest that on such topics the literary critic is at a disadvantage, knowing little about either linguistics or philosophy, neighbour disciplines which are assumed to have their own concerns, sometimes forbiddingly technical. Never having reflected on language as it is used in ordinary life, some literary critics are extremely vulnerable when Modern Masters like Lacan, Barthes, Foucault or Derrida appear, with all the kudos of a supposedly avant-garde, high-powered intellectual movement, expressing themselves forcefully, and ruthlessly demolishing a series of outdated paradigms — or so it seems. What the gullible literary person never realises is that the real issues are elsewhere, that the iconoclasts addressed a few (in some cases illusory) targets, and that many interesting alternative approaches exist once we get outside this narrow and ever-diminishing focus. There is no need to follow Lacan into seeing meaning as incommunicable, or desire as unrealisable; or Barthes with language as fascist, compelling its users to define or declare themselves; or Foucault, with his depersonalised circuit of discourse determining subjects' 'insertions' into it; or Derrida with his complacency about infinitely deferred meaning. These may have posed as liberating systems in 1968, but it is from them, now, that we need to be liberated.

The first position to set down in this brief counter-statement (by a literary critic who is at least open to linguistics and philosophy, while not pretending expertise in either), is that language is not a self-contained system, an abstract model that can be studied purely in its own terms. Language is *used* by human beings for a remarkably wide range of purposes. *Used!?* If we adopt John Searle's distinction that linguistics 'attempts to describe the actual structures — phonological, syntactical, and semantic — of natural human languages', whereas the philosophy of language studies 'certain general features of language, such as reference, truth, meaning, and necessity' (Searle 1969, p. 4), both disciplines agree that language is the central instrument for personal knowledge and social intercourse. In his excellent introduction to the subject, *Spreading the Word. Groundings in the Philosophy of Language*, Simon Blackburn starts with the simple proposition that a speaker 'uses the language' to 'put himself into various relations with the world. He can describe it, ask questions about it, put himself under obligation to act in it in different ways, offer metaphors, images, jokes, about what it is like'. So the philosophy of language is concerned with a triangle of elements:

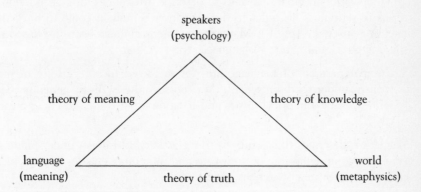

The philosopher's task is 'to obtain some stable conception of this triangle of speaker, language, and world', a conception that has varied at different points in history (Blackburn 1984, p. 3). The ancient Greeks wanted 'to establish by metaphysical enquiry some features of the world, of reality'. A later European tradition, from Descartes to Kant, concentrated on 'the individual, with his particular capacities for experiencing and reasoning', believing that the nature of his mind determined 'what kind of language this individual can intelligibly speak' (p. 41). In our time the so-called 'linguistic turn' has focussed attention on the nature of language itself, giving it 'considerable autonomy, and even sovereignty over the other elements of the triangle', now subordinated to it (p. 5). Some moderns believe that both metaphysics (the study of the 'world' element) and epistemology (the nature of perception and the theory of truth) have been destroyed, leaving only the theory of meaning. Forgetting these other axes of relationship, Blackburn observes, 'causes distorted history of philosophy', making it impossible to appreciate philosophers of the past, who had a quite different perspective (p. 6). If that comment applies to some modern philosophies of language, how much more parochial seems the iconoclasm of the 60s, which would destroy meaning altogether — not so much a 'linguistic turn' (for the worse) as a total voiding of language.

Blackburn's wide-ranging and detailed argument develops from some basic principles which run counter to the iconoclasts' dogma, starting with the speaking subject they so often derided, the individual. 'The person who has mastered a language *understands* its sentences and the terms used to make them up. He gives them a meaning, and members of his linguistic community do the same' (p. 7). For Blackburn it is self-evident that language exists for the communication of meaning: 'understanding the sentences of a language is knowing what they are used to say — which thoughts or questions or commands or wishes they express...' (*ibid.*). In order to study meaning philosophers and linguists consider both the functions of language and functions within language. So the discipline known as 'compositional semantics' aims to describe 'the functioning of individual terms in sentences' in order to discover 'how sentences come to have the meanings they do' (p. 10). Many recent theorists have been impressed by the compositional nature of language, the fact that

> Competent users of language are not restricted to a repertoire of previously understood sentences. We possess the skill to generate new sentences meaning new things and to know what these sentences mean. (p. 10)

Blackburn describes this ability as the 'elasticity' of human understanding, since our comprehension 'of the words and the syntax enables us to identify the meaning of new sentences' (*ibid.*).

The two linguistic elements noted there, words and syntax, have been assigned varying importance by modern linguists. Blackburn argues that 'semantics precedes syntax', for 'a complete lexicon and syntax of a language cannot be given before we have any grip on the interpretation its sentences bear' (p. 25).[39] A compositional semantics, then, will locate 'which features of a sentence are responsible for its meaning, and the rules whereby those features (notably words in various positions) yield the meaning' (p. 26). Developing his discussion of the nature of linguistic knowledge or competence, Blackburn takes issue with Noam Chomsky's theory that the language-learning ability in mankind depends on 'an innate "universal grammar", or biological inheritance' of linguistic categories and the rules governing their combinations (p. 28). Chomsky based his theory on the claim that children learning a language overcame a 'poverty of stimulus'. The fact that 'after a relatively small "exposure" to examples', to vocabulary and syntactical rules, a child is able to master an enormous and complex system, Chomsky argued, could only be explained in terms of an innate cognitive structure. But several philosophers have challenged the empirical observation from which Chomsky began. Gilbert Ryle pointed out that the infant is not 'a solitary thinker, unfostered and alone', trying out hypotheses 'about which noises count as sentences amongst the strangers around him'. Rather than such laboratory isolation, the infant 'is helped, encouraged, guided, taught, trained; he models sayings on those of others, practises, impersonates, invents', learning by doing (pp. 28–9).

As for Chomsky's 'innateness' argument, Blackburn replies to it (in terms that apply equally to the claims of some current literary theorists that language is an affair of the unconscious) by insisting that 'the rules of semantics and syntax of our language should be conceived not as hidden', but as intelligible, open to view. They are discoverable 'by reflection upon the purposes for which we use language and the means we have naturally developed to serve those purposes' (p. 30). One inescapable fact about language, conveniently ignored by Derrida (although he naturally makes use of this resource) is that 'in communication we are extremely skilled at selecting and organizing exactly the meaning-determining features which result in our messages communicating what we want' (p. 34). On reflection, then, Blackburn argues, it is unsurprising that 'a child's needs and training' should cause it to conform to the rules of its native language, 'since those rules mark not meaningless and arbitrary restrictions on patterns of combination of terms, but natural consequences of the need to communicate' (p. 30). A child is born into what William James described as a world of '"a blooming, buzzing confusion"' to the senses, out of which 'patterns begin to separate and order begins to form: we begin our acquaintance with sounds, tastes, colours, shapes, and with the reliable recurrent things which make up the landscape we live in' (p. 56). We become familiar with things and learn to appreciate not only 'what words actually mean' but also what they could mean.

> Acquiring the concept needs learning that there are things which persist in time, which have various clusters of properties, and it requires becoming able to distinguish those terms from others on the basis of these properties. Without this knowledge terms cannot be understood.

Given this learning process we must 'think of the language as itself growing, in its semantic powers, as the infant increases his appreciation of the world, and his ability to cope with it' (*ibid.*). The 'functional organization'

of language, so to speak, itself 'grows, adapts, and changes with an appreciation of the world' (p. 57).

Simon Blackburn's brief critique of Chomsky touched on some of the
major issues in the philosophy of language that his work brought to
prominence. Simon Clarke made a more extended analysis which is helpful
in exposing the deficiencies of any formalist system that tries to avoid
the centrality of meaning. As Clarke shows, Chomsky sought to 'isolate
language as an object from meaning and from context', making a 'neo-
positivist separation of syntax from semantics and pragmatics' which allowed
him to 'isolate language as a scientific object and so to consider it without
reference to the communicative intentions of speakers' or to 'any extrinsic
meaning' (Clarke 1981, pp. 135–6, 173). In this way he reduced language
to a set of sentence-forms: but 'a set of grammatical sentences, divorced
from the context in which they serve a linguistic function, do not constitute a language' (p. 141). For if we ignore both their meaning and their
function within the 'human interaction of communicating meaning' then
we are left with a purely formal abstraction that cannot explain how
and why language is used (*ibid.*). Chomsky's theory was based on an
idiosyncratic conception both of language and human psychology. He
regarded language as 'a mechanical model that derives sentences by the
automatic application of rules', and took over mathematical logic as an
appropriate analytical tool (pp. 141–2). As for psychology, Chomsky's
distinction between linguistic competence and performance was a purely
formal model constructed on purely formal criteria, positing the existence
of 'innate mental structures', man's linguistic ability being 'a simple formal
mechanism rooted in the brain' (pp. 168–71).

Chomsky's conception of language-learning reveals the obvious consequences of ignoring meaning and linguistic function. Like the be-
haviourists, he regards language-learning as a 'discovery procedure by
which the mind analyses the formal properties of a linguistic input without
any reference to meaning or to context', so depriving 'the language learner
of a large proportion of the information on the basis of which the language
is learned' (p. 169). Clarke's reply is to urge that language be seen
as 'a social product and as one aspect of the relationship between social
individuals', making it unnecessary to posit 'the existence of complex
innate mental structures' as the means of access to language. Rather, we
should appreciate the role of language in communicating meanings:

> The moment at which a child starts to learn a language is not the
> moment at which its mental capacities mature, it is the moment at
> which it comes to grasp the social function of language and to internalize
> this knowledge in the form of an intention to communicate meanings.
> The child can then make use of a whole range of non-linguistic informa-
> tion to guide it in learning the language. (p. 171)

Chomsky's theory, avoiding any notion of human interaction, represents
'an extremely impoverished conception of language that puts into the

mind what it has taken out of the context within which language is used'
(p. 172).

The formalism that Chomsky espoused has obvious parallels with the
systems of Saussure and Lévi-Strauss in not recognising that 'language is
above all a means of communication of meaning from one subject to
another' (p. 181), and in presenting meaning as somehow 'intrinsic to an
objective system'. To which Clarke makes the crucial objection that

> Meaning can only be a relationship between a subject and something
> external to that subject: cultural and linguistic meanings can only
> be meanings for someone, recoverable only through the conscious
> apprehension of those meanings. (p. 175)

Language and culture are not meaningful objects in themselves, 'they are
the objective *instruments* by means of which meanings are expressed and
communicated' (p. 176). Against the positivism and spurious objectivism
of Chomsky and Lévi-Strauss Clarke invokes phenomenology, which sees
language not as 'an object but as a "gesture" by which the subject signifies
the world. Language cannot therefore be dissociated from its ideal aim (to
say something) and its real reference (to say it about something). Language
cannot be reduced either to the subject (thought, consciousness, the mind,
or whatever) or to the object (the natural world) because it is language
that mediates the relationship between the two, not only relating subject to the world, but also keeping a distance between them' (*ibid.*). It
follows that cultural products can only be understood by reference to the
intentionality that gives them significance; that semantics must be able to
relate language to some extra-linguistic reality and to 'the intentionality of
people who mean'; and that the meaning of a linguistic utterance has both
'an intersubjective reality' for the subjects experiencing it and 'a social and
historical unity', shared by the individuals who form a speech community
(pp. 176–82). 'Thus the study of linguistic semantics can never be a
formal discipline', but must consider 'the social and historical conditions
within which the world is experienced and signified by social subjects'
(p. 182).

*   *   *

The approaches of Blackburn and Clarke overlap in their conception
of language as an intentional activity communicating meaning between
individual speakers. This I take to be the fundamental position, from
which we can see the shallowness of either formalist systems or theories of
linguistic dysfunctioning. Both writers touch on the child's acquisition of
language, a topic of such importance to our understanding of its function
in the adult, social world that I should like to give it more extended
treatment, drawing on M.A.K. Halliday's admirable study, *Learning How to
Mean. Explorations in the Development of Language*. Halliday presents an
intensive study of a child's linguistic development between the ages of nine

months and two years, relating his observations to a functional theory of language, which also sees linguistic structures as existing to serve particular human needs, above all, to convey meaning (Halliday 1975, pp. 5, 16). Halliday consciously avoided the limited approach of both cognitive psychology, which 'assumes that the only function of language is ideational', and of social anthropology, which sees it as purely 'interpersonal', since the two approaches are complementary (pp. 107–8). In the ideational mode 'the speaker expresses his experience of the phenomena of the external world, and of the internal world of his own consciousness' (p. 17). In the interpersonal mode he 'participates in the speech situation', adopting a role or set of roles, expressing his own judgments and attitudes, so affecting, and being affected by, the other actors. In addition to these two dimensions, embodying the individual as observer and as participant, linguistics recognises a third element, which Halliday describes as 'the *textual* function', language's ability to create a text, through which the speaker can 'make what he says operational' in the speech context, as distinct from being 'merely citational, like lists of words in a dictionary, or sentences in a grammar book' (*ibid.*).

Halliday's basic orientation is through semantics, understood as 'the totality of meaning in language, whether such meaning is encoded in the form of vocabulary or not' (p. 9). From this functional point of view, 'as soon as there are meaningful expressions there is language', the fact that a child can express a considerable range of meanings before it 'has any words or structures at all' proving that it already has a linguistic system (p. 6). Halliday shows that to begin with, a child invents its own system of sounds, with coherent patterns of expressive intonations, subsequently adopting adult language (pp. 14–15, 22–6, 61–2, 66–7). In this early phase its language is limited to two levels, 'the *content* and the *expression*, or the meaning and the sound', the latter being 'a system of vocal postures, including the two components of articulation and intonation', while the meaning or content level takes the form of specific linguistic functions (pp. 12–13). Halliday distinguished six fundamental meaning-functions in child language: instrumental (for satisfying material needs), regulatory (controlling behaviour), interactional (interacting with the people close to him), personal (expressing personal feelings), heuristic (exploring the world around him), and imaginative (creating his own environment, 'a world initially of pure sound', later 'one of story and make-believe'; pp. 18–20, 42–3, 63, 79, 82–5). In this early phase a child creates its own language in order to satisfy 'those needs which exist independently of language', essential features of human life at all times and in all cultures (pp. 32, 66, 121). All these functions persist in adult life, needless to say, but in more complex states and combinations.

The child's proto-language already has the two requirements of a linguistic system, a constant relation between content and expression (systematicity), and a coherent link between that element and function.

But, as Halliday emphasises, there are only these two levels, linked in this way: 'there is no system of content as such, in abstraction from the context of situation' (p. 15). Language is instrumental, within a social context, but even when the child begins to adopt the language of adults several essential elements are lacking. One crucial function, only developed late, is the informative, 'the idea that language can be used as a means of communicating information', independently of the child's personal needs or social interaction (p. 21). This is a harder concept for the child to grasp since, unlike the other functions, referring to extra-linguistic contexts, 'served by and realized in language, but . . . not defined by language' (p. 31), the informative function is 'purely intrinsic', 'definable solely by reference to language' (p. 21). Mastering this more complex concept, Halliday suggests, depends on the child progressing beyond the simple two-level content-expression system, in which it is either in the ideational or in the interpersonal mode — observer *or* participant, never both at once — to the beginnings of an adult system, in which a third level is acquired, allowing him a plurifunctional role, both observer and participant (pp. 47, 52–4, 77–8). This third level is that of 'linguistic "form" (syntax, morphology, vocabulary) intermediate between content and the expression' (p. 38), where meanings are no longer output directly as sounds but coded as ' "words-and-structures", i.e. lexico-grammatical units' (p. 48). Reaching this level is crucial in allowing the child to use language beyond its immediate personal context:

> The direct dependence of a speech instance on the perceptual environment disappears the moment he introduces the third level into his system, the lexico-grammatical level of words and structures, since this provides him with an abstract ('formal') level of coding which intervenes between content (the level of reference to the situation) and output. (p. 142)

Once the child is able to use language at this more abstract level, learning word-meanings and grammatical structures, recognising the informative function of language, it can begin to make the fundamental transition to adult language, taking part in dialogue. 'Dialogue involves the adoption of roles which are social roles of a new and special kind, namely those which are defined by language itself' (p. 30). The roles involved in dialogue 'exist only in and through language, as roles in the communication process — speaker, addressee, respondent, questioner, persuader and the like'. The importance of these communicative roles is that 'they serve both as a channel and as a model for social interaction' (p. 48). This more abstract role of language, over and above its instrumental features, allows the child to develop still further what Halliday defines as *mathesis*, the function of language in learning about his social and material environment by such processes as 'observation, recall, and prediction' (pp. 27–8, 42–3, 54, 75, 86, 106), and also to extend the pragmatic or interpersonal function of language, opening the way to the adult linguistic systems of transitivity and mood. 'Transitivity expresses the speaker's experience of process in the external world', involving the categories of participants and circumstances, while 'mood expresses his structuring of the speech situations' in such forms as 'indicative, declarative and interrogative, imperative' (pp. 72, 104, 106–8). In these developments, both ideational and interpersonal, language becomes for the child

> an effective channel of social learning, a means of participating in and receiving the culture. Meanings are expressed as verbal interaction in social contexts; this is the essential condition for the transmission of culture. . . . (p. 50)

As sociolinguists have shown, a child's socialisation process is deeply marked by the linguistic context in which it grows up.

The special values of Halliday's account of a child's 'learning to mean' for my argument is that he brings out so clearly the multiple functions of language in both individual development and social relations. After the negative, dysfunctioning notion of language put about by the Parisian system-breakers it is salutary to follow his exposition of the process by which a child becomes integrated into the linguistic community. Once it has progressed to the stage of using language as a symbol system independent of his immediate environment, the child begins to construct what Halliday calls 'a social semiotic, a model of the culture of which he is himself a member' (p. 66), understanding the social system as 'a system of meaning relations' (pp. 10, 79). This development involves both major linguistic processes, ideational and interpersonal, interacting on each other (p. 106), for language and culture are interdependent, both 'in the sense that a child constructs a reality for himself largely through language, but also in the more fundamental sense that language is itself part of this reality. The linguistic system is part of the social system' (p. 120). In effect, the child is learning 'one semiotic system, the culture', while simultaneously 'learning the means of learning it — a second semiotic system, the language, which is the intermediary in which the first one is encoded' (p. 122). Where the semiotics of Barthes separated sign from meaning and deprived the individual subject of any power or agency with regard to the system, Halliday draws attention to the semantic properties of language, seeing its 'meaning potential' as 'realizing a higher level system of relations, that of the social semiotic', with the individual language user not just transmitting the social semiotic but also 'constantly modifying and reshaping it' (p. 60). Since the social system 'is a system of meanings, it is constituted out of innumerable acts of meaning which shape and determine the system' (p. 121). As against Lacan and others who see mankind as trapped by language we can set Halliday's assertion that

> We are not the prisoners of our cultural semiotic; we can all learn to move outside it. But this requires a positive act of semiotic reconstruc-

tion. We are socialized within it, and our meaning potential is derived from it. (p. 140)

(Indeed, the fact that Barthes, Foucault and others were able to challenge their cultural semiotic so violently proves that the individual has freedom and creativity.)

In developing the ideational and interpersonal dimensions of language the child is involved in a cognitive process, but one which takes place in contexts of social interaction. This interactive process 'takes the form of the continued exchange of meanings between the self and others' (pp. 139–40). If the act of meaning is a social act, the form it results in is what Halliday calls 'text' or 'texture', the 'relevance function of language, whereby the meanings derived from the other functional components relate to the environment' and finally become operational (pp. 111, 128). The texture of discourse involves, first, 'structuring the parts in an appropriate way and joining them together', activating both grammatical structure (in more technical linguistic terms, 'the theme and information systems of the clause, expressed through word order, nominalizations', intonation and other forms of emphasis), and cohesion (the 'various anaphoric relations of reference, substitution, ellipsis, conjunction and collocation'). Secondly, the texture of discourse is adjusted to the speech context and to such genres as narrative and dialogue (pp. 111–12).

Two other essential properties of text, as Halliday shows, are meaning — a text is 'made of meanings, and encoded in wordings, soundings and spellings' — and choice. 'A text represents a selection within numerous sets of options', which have the potentiality of being selected. 'Text is "what is meant" — presupposing a background of what might have been meant but was not' (pp. 123–4). A text, in the sense of a speech utterance, is 'a semantic structure that is formed out of a continuous process of choice' among innumerable semantic options, by means of which speakers actualise the 'meaning potential' of the semantic system within which they move. So, to return for a last time to the child learning to speak, everything he says is interpreted by those who interact with him in everyday life as 'a pattern of selection within the meanings that make up his semantic system at that time'. This explains why 'the mother understands everything the child says, much of which [is] unintelligible to those outside the circuit of his daily life' (p. 124). Only she knows the child's meaning potential, the range of semantic choices open to him. As it develops its mastery of language those able to understand it increase, as the child progresses towards 'the sharing of meanings, which is the distinctive characteristic of social man in his mature state' (p. 36).

*   *   *

I have summarised Halliday's lucid and tightly-argued book in some detail not only for its own contribution to our understanding of how a child learns how to mean, but also because it represents an open-minded attitude towards several important developments in modern linguistics. Halliday draws on Peter Berger and Thomas Luckmann, *The Social Construction of Reality* (1967); on Basil Bernstein's *Class, Codes and Control* (1971, 1973); on anthropological linguistics, from Malinowski and Firth to Kenneth Pike and Dell Hymes; as well as on the large literature concerning children's acquisition of language.[40] His book opens up many approaches, some of which I shall take up in more detail. As against the Parisian *maîtres*, who saw language as wholly deterministic and rushed to pursue the 'free play of the signifier' or a *jeu sans règles*, many linguists and philosophers of language emphasise the co-existence of linguistic rules and free choice. In his comprehensive study of semantics the linguist John Lyons declares 'one of the most fundamental principles of semantics' to be that 'meaning, or meaningfulness, implies choice', the 'selection between alternatives' in the linguistic repertoire (Lyons 1977, p. 33). Emile Benveniste, a notable student of Indo–European languages, also emphasised the rich possibilities of choice that exist in language, 'the great variety of expressions available for uttering, as we say "the same idea"'. Expressing our thoughts in language involves an interplay between free choice and rules:

> When thought passes into words it submits to the constraint of the laws governing their organization. In the utterance of a thought there is, of necessity, a subtle mixture of freedom in expressing an idea and constraint in the form of its utterance, which is the condition of all actualisation in language. (Benveniste 1966, p. 227)

After those fashionable theories of linguistic determinism and alienation, it is good to be reminded of the freedom and responsibility that the language user has, drawing on a system that allows him unlimited creativity provided that he submits himself, in turn, to its rules.

The individual language user, the speaking subject, was proscribed by the adversarial 60s originally on philosophical grounds, a veto subsequently recast in linguistic terms. Nothing in modern linguistics or philosophy of language supports this proscription, indeed both disciplines have shown that language contains built-in elements that are there solely in order to allow human beings to register the presence of other human beings as taking part in a speech exchange, or to describe human action in the world, or to represent our view of external reality. M.A.K. Halliday pointed out in an introduction to 'Language structure and language function' that 'the grammar of every language comprises sets of options representing broad categories' of processes: actions, events, states, relations, and the persons, objects and abstractions associated with them. These are the transitivity functions (briefly described in his later work on language acquisition), involving 'an "actor", a "process" and a "goal"' (Halliday 1970, p. 146). These functions can be subdivided further, for 'systematic distinctions in the grammar' represent such differentiations in actual human interchange as actor, patient, and beneficiary (p. 147). The way in which language is structured around the modalities of human behaviour can be seen from the fact that

> The three main types of transitivity role — process, participant, circumstance — correspond, by and large, to the three major word (or word group) classes found in most languages: verb, noun, adverb. In English, typically, processes are expressed by verbal groups, participants by nominal groups and circumstances by adverbial groups — the last often in the form of prepositional phrases. (p. 149)

These distinctions are not arbitrary, but show how language is modelled on, and models, human acts and actors. Halliday's analysis of clause types shows how language can integrate 'a number of roles in a single complex element of structure' (p. 152). It is hard to imagine that language could ever be depersonalised.

*   *   *

The philosopher Stuart Hampshire, in his classic *Thought and Action*, had earlier developed a similar conception of language as 'a means of singling out, and directing attention to, certain elements of experience and reality as subjects which can be referred to again and again. A language must provide a means of differentiating, of dividing, reality into the pieces and segments which are to be constant subjects of reference' (Hampshire 1959, p. 11). In order to describe the phenomena of persistence and change we need criteria of identity and individuation, for we can only conceive of reality as 'consisting of persisting things of different types and kinds . . .' (pp. 16–17). Any language that is 'fit for statement-making' must be able to distinguish 'between a thing and its changing properties' (p. 18), to register the difference between 'is' and 'seems' (p. 45). Perception of things and their properties presupposes a perceiver, who cannot but refer to himself as a 'persisting object' among other objects, having at each point a distinct perspective of the other objects (including persons) around him, as they have of him (pp. 30–41). The existence of the perceiving subject has fundamental consequences for language. Verb tenses, 'as indications of the temporal relation between an utterance and the topic of the utterance, could not be interpreted without the possibility of a reference to a persisting thing, which might be either the speaking subject, or the subject of the statement' (p. 30). Another fundamental property of language, as Hampshire showed, is that speakers should be able to discriminate one person from another; once they can do this they can also discriminate objects in the external world from each other (p. 57). A language which could not discriminate between persons would be one in which 'pronouns would have no sense', where a speaker's description of his own sensations would be meaningless to anyone else 'and would involve no possible intersubjective comparison. A language without the possibility of communication would be a language at vanishing-point' (p. 58). Admirers of Lacan should reflect on that.

audience

For Hampshire, as for the great majority of philosophers and linguists, 'the structure of language, as we know it, is built upon the fact that each speaker speaks to an actual or potential hearer, marking the point of view in space and time from which he speaks' through 'devices of attachment, such as pronouns, demonstratives and tenses' (p. 58). The most important of all these referential devices, the nucleus on which the others depend, is the first person singular, the centre from which we make any spatial or temporal reference (p. 87). Here philosophy rejoins linguistics, for in three celebrated essays Emile Benveniste described the personal relations implied in verb forms, in pronouns and relationship, and in subjectivity in general.[41] Benveniste showed that the verb and the pronoun are the only types of word subordinated to the category of the person. In all languages that possess a verb, conjugated forms are divided into three categories — whether of person (first, second, third) or number (singular, plural, dual) — and three only (Benveniste 1966, pp. 225–6). A linguistic theory of the person in verb forms can only be established by marking the oppositions that differentiate persons in real life, as the Arabic grammarians recognised in their definition of the first person as 'he who speaks', the second as 'he to whom one speaks', and the third as 'he who is absent' (pp. 227–8). Concerning the first two persons, Benveniste wrote,

> there is implied both a person and a discourse about this person. 'I' designates he who speaks and at the same time implies an utterance on the part of 'I': saying 'I', I cannot not talk about myself. In the second person, 'you' is necessarily designated by 'I' and cannot be conceived of outside a situation laid down on the part of 'I'; and, at the same time, 'I' utters something as the predicate of 'you'. (p. 228)

The third-person predicate, however, is uttered outside the 'I — you' relationship, and could be described as the verbal form which 'expresses the *non-person*' (*ibid.*), there being a real disparity between the first two persons and the third. In Indo-European languages the third person has been made to conform to the other two 'for reasons of symmetry and because all verbal forms in Indo-European tend to emphasise the index of the subject, the only form that it can show' (p. 230). Subjectivity, we might say, is built into our language.

Personal pronouns have other important characteristics in the human-speaking dimension of language. For one thing, they are unique: 'the "I" which speaks, the "you" to whom "I" addresses itself are each time unique. But "he" can be an infinity of subjects — or none', for 'the "third person" is the only one by which *a thing* can be verbally predicted'. Secondly, pronouns are reversible: 'he who "I" defines as "you" thinks of himself and can invert himself into "I", and "I" (me) becomes a "you". No such relationship is possible between one of these two persons' and he/it, which stands outside this interpersonal relationship (*ibid.*). The interchange between 'I' and 'you' (and between 'I', 'you' and 'thou', significant in Shakespeare's plays and poems), expresses the fact that pronouns are 'a reality of speech' only (p. 252).[42] Whereas 'every use of a noun refers to a constant and "objective" notion', either virtual or actual (*ibid.*), pronominal forms refer not to reality but to 'the enunciation, each time unique, that contains them' (p. 254). The basic function of pronouns, then, is to 'solve the problem of intersubjective communication' by constituting a class of 'empty' signs which 'become "full" as soon as a speaker assumes them in each instance of discourse'. These 'shifters', as some linguists call them, bridge the gap between *langue* and *parole*, for 'each speaker puts the whole system of language to his own use' in discourse — that is, a verbal communication which implies partners in a dialogue (p. 258). Contrary to his iconoclastic contemporaries, Benveniste concluded: 'It is in and through language that man constitutes himself as *subject*, because language alone founds in reality, in *his* reality . . . the concept of "ego"'. Subjectivity, understood as the speaker's capacity to pose as the subject of discourse, presupposes 'a psychic unity which transcends the totality of all the lived experiences that it brings together', but also implies dialogue (p. 260). It is significant that no known language lacks personal pronouns (p. 261).

As we can already see, to form an adequate conception of language we must often contradict what that group of Paris intellectuals laid down. Benveniste's observation that 'A language that cannot express the person would be inconceivable' (*ibid.*), might not negate Foucault's own practice of writing, where the 'I' is constantly asserting itself, but it would play havoc with his theory of the impersonality of 'discourse'. When Stuart Hampshire recorded, in the late 1950s, that 'philosophers have in the last twenty years carefully studied the use of referring expressions and have tried to show why they are indispensable to the use of language, and to the expression of any kind of thought that is not wholly abstract and formal' (Hampshire 1959, p. 200), and when Simon Blackburn described the 'great glory' of analytical philosophy since Frege as being its work on 'the problems of classifying and understanding the various ways we have of referring to the world around us' (Blackburn 1984, p. 302), we realise just how much the sixties iconoclasts isolated themselves from contemporary linguistics and philosophy. Lacan, Barthes, Foucault, Derrida, all denied that language could refer to a reality constituted of other people, or to the natural world, human artefacts, or mental processes. As Descombes put it, their 'doctrine of the emancipated signifier prides itself on having dispelled the illusion that language is composed of pointers to things' (Descombes 1986, p. 188). Language can do far more than this, of course, but this is one of its unalienable powers, as we can see if we imagine the alternative. Sebastiano Timpanaro did so, concluding that if one wishes to maintain that language *has no nomenclatural features at all*, i.e. that it does not refer back to any sensory-conceptual experience which is distinguishable from language itself (even though incapable of developing without the aid of language as a tool) and represents a common point of reference for those who speak different languages, then one arrives at two possible conclusions, both equally unacceptable: either language becomes a *système pour le système* which has no meaning and serves no purpose,

or else languages are said to be untranslatable since each derives from a different conception of the world (Timpanaro 1975, p. 154). It seems to me that the Parisian system-breakers came dangerously close to that first dead-end, at any rate as far as their discussions of an object-language was concerned. (Their own meta-language, as ever, escaped all limitations.)

To re-establish some rational grounds for the semanticity of language, its ability to convey meaning — not necessarily linked to the external environment (Lyons 1977, pp. 79, 118) — I draw on that outstanding survey of modern semantics by John Lyons, who begins his discussion of the meaning property of language by introducing another triadic scheme, the 'triangle of signification':

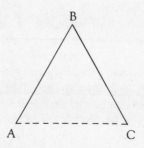

Here A is the sign, or lexeme; B the concept; and C the significatum, 'whatever it is that a sign stands for' (pp. 95–6). The dotted line AC shows that the relation 'between a lexeme (A) and its significatum (C) is indirect, being mediated by a concept (B)'. The two continuous lines AB and BC represent 'more basic relationships' (p. 97). This triangular structure is a great improvement on Saussure's binary system, in which the sign is the composite entity AB (pp. 98, 101), suspending the dimension of external reality altogether. If, as the triangle of signification suggests, 'words signify things by means of mediating concepts', then we can call 'the object that is signified by a word' the significatum, and the mediating concept the signification. So we can say that what a word signifies directly (the link AB in the triangle) is its signification, and what it signifies indirectly (the link AC) is its significatum (p. 110). Lyons uses 'concept' in

*Concepts=
universals*

two senses, purely 'mental concepts', internally existing, and 'objective concepts', i.e. 'the postulated extramental entities that were apprehended by the mind in its knowledge and perception of the external world' (p. 111). For instance, in the process of language-learning we can correlate pattern-recognition and concept-formation: 'Before a child can be said to have learned the meaning of the word "table" (i.e. to have formed the concept associated with the word "table"), he must be able to recognize that there are certain objects, of various shapes and sizes, that are correctly referred to as tables and other objects that are not' (p. 16). Vincent Descombes pithily defines 'this mental capacity known as the concept' as 'the capacity to make signifying use of a word' (Descombes 1986, p. 167).

The distinction that Lyons makes between direct and indirect significa-tion finds its counterpart in his distinction between reference and denota-tion, processes that Derrida *et Cie.* wish to deny. By reference, Lyons argues, we understand the relationship between a 'referring expression — typically a proper name, a definite noun-phrase or a pronoun' — and what that expression stands for in a particular speech situation. The reference is successful if, used 'in accordance with the rules of the language-system' it enables the hearer 'to pick out the actual referent from the class of potential referents' (Lyons 1977, pp. 174, 177, 180). Reference, then, is 'an utterance-bound relation' that does not refer in the first instance outside the language-system (p. 208). Denotation, by contrast, refers to the relationship that holds between a 'lexeme and persons, things, places, properties, processes and activities external to the language-system', a relationship that holds 'independently of particular occasions of utterance' (pp. 207–208). In order to show how external reality enters into the substance of language itself, Lyons sets out to re-define the parts of speech in semantic terms (pp. 438–52), classifying afresh 'the ontological categories . . . which comprise persons, things, actions (including events and processes) and qualities' (p. 442). Lyons makes the working assump-tion that 'there exists in the external world a variety of entities of various kinds (persons, animals, plants, etc.)', which are in fact distinguished as individual physical objects by 'the lexical and grammatical structures of particular languages' (pp. 110, 442).

Acknowledging a debt to P.F. Strawson's *Individuals* (1959), Lyons proposes a triple classification of reality as mediated in language. What he calls 'first-order entities' are physical objects, within which 'persons occupy a privileged position', the distinction between persons and non-personal entities being 'lexicalized or grammaticalized, in various ways, in many, and perhaps all, languages' (p. 442). Language individualises persons more strongly than animals, animals more than things, but all members of this class are seen as 'relatively constant as to their perceptual properties', being clearly located in space and time (p. 443), subject to our normal expecta-tions that 'the same person cannot be in two different places at the same time' (pp. 444–5). They are in that sense unique, neither substitutable nor duplicable. Second-order entities are 'events, processes, states-of-affairs, etc., which, in English, are said to occur or take place, rather than to exist' (p. 442). These can be located in space and time, but not in the definite way that first-order entities can. The same event — 'arrival', 'death', 'marriage' — 'can occur or be occurring in several different places, not only at different times, but at the same time' (p. 444). But all second-order entities are observable and all, 'unless they are instantaneous events, have a temporal duration' (p. 445). By contrast, the third order or degree covers 'such abstract entities as propositions', which are unobservable and cannot be located in space or time (p. 443). 'Third-order entities are such that "true", rather than "real", is more naturally predicated of them; they can be reasons, but not causes . . .'. This class of entities can also 'function as the objects of such so-called propositional attitudes as belief, expectation and judgement' (p. 445).

The advantage of this classification is that parts of speech can now be defined not in purely linguistic terms but as being related to the class of entities involved. Nominals — that is, 'referring expressions' which 'are invested with reference by the utterer' — can be distinguished as first-order and so forth 'in terms of their characteristic referential function. Proper names, pronouns and descriptive noun-phrases that are used, characteristically, to refer to first-order entities may be described as first-order nominals' (pp. 445–6). Lyons suggests that 'no language will have second-order or third-order nouns that does not also have first-order nouns' (p. 447). In other words, the higher levels of abstraction in linguistic categories rest on a classification of persons, animals, objects and other actually-existing entities, a hierarchical or pyramid-like structure from the more to the less concrete. Categories within language thus form a coherent system which corresponds to categories in physical and psychological reality. Let me underline the fact that neither Lyons, nor anyone else in modern linguistics, is arguing that the only possible use of a language is nomenclature. Anyone who thinks that, as Descombes observes, must believe that 'we are describing a language when we describe the construction of nomenclature in that language'. But such a view 'is based upon a confusion of logical categories: the words of a vocabulary are part of the language, whereas assigning those words to things belongs to the use of language' (Descombes 1986, p. 162).

My point is simply that language contains within itself a whole repertoire of categories for classifying reality, so that when Derrida asserts that it cannot represent reality he is blinding himself to the observable properties of the medium while investing years of his life, and an untold expenditure of energy (not without acquiring 'symbolic' and other forms of capital) in arguing a clever but empty paradox. One result of Lyons's discussion is that we can now more accurately describe neo-structuralist theories of language as being parasitic on a system which they attempt to deny. Derrida, for instance, depends on the existence of third-order nominals, as successfully mediated by language, such concepts as 'deconstruction', 'deferral', 'logocentrism', the 'transcendental signified', and all the other special terms he has invented. But he uses them, perversely enough, in order to deny the power of first- or second-order nominals to refer to their respective categories of entities, whether clearly fixed in spatiotemporal terms or not. This is to rely on the referential and analytical functions of language while claiming that they do not exist. As I have already suggested, this is more than just a 'technical foul', but must undermine Derrida's theory itself. Of the many similar comments I select A.D. Nuttall's judgment that Derrida 'accepts a conclusion so disabling that he cannot even enunciate it without violating it (since to enunciate is to *mean*)' (Nuttall 1983, p. 35).

John Lyons distinguished direct and indirect signification, reference being 'utterance-bound' as against denotation, which refers outside the language-system and is independent of the utterance. Both options are covered in normal usage by the term meaning, the major property of language which the adversarial 60s tried to discredit. For all other students of language meaning is central: as Benveniste put it, 'Before anything else, language signifies, that is its primordial characteristic and original vocation, transcending and explaining all the functions that it ensures in the human domain' (Benveniste 1974, p. 217). At this point semantics, the study of meaning in communication, 'the domain of language in use and action' becomes a crucial source of knowledge, for 'only the semantic function of language allows the integration of society and its adaptation to the world, and in consequence the co-ordination of thought and the development of consciousness' (*ibid.*, p. 224). Roland Barthes, we recall, rejected semantics because its classifications lay 'outside the field of linguistics', as if one could make a neat distinction between language and a world outside. To which a philosopher, Vincent Descombes, asserts the principle we have seen expressed by the linguist, M.A.K. Halliday, namely that

> there is no face-to-face relationship between the language (English, for instance) and the world. Things are not 'extra-linguistic', as if they were outside the world, for the language is a thing in the world. Languages exist because there are people to speak them. (Descombes 1986, p. 153)

And to reiterate the case against all the *a priori* attitudes embodied in those iconoclastic systems — systems, oddly enough, claiming the dysfunctioning of language — I cite a linguist's principle that 'only through the study of language in use are all the functions of language, and therefore all components of meaning, brought into focus' (Halliday 1970, p. 145).

*   *   *

The study of meaning in contemporary linguistics leads into semantics, currently developing in several interesting directions (Ladusaw 1988), and into pragmatics, ' "the science of the relation of signs to their interpreters" '

(Horn 1988, p. 116). The latter seems to me more immediately applicable
to literary criticism, and I shall return to it when I touch on speech-act
theory and implicature. Within the main area of literary interpretation,
the topic that will concern us more closely in Chapter 2, some essential
principles were set out by E.D. Hirsch, Jr., in his study of *Validity in
Interpretation*. Hirsch based his whole discussion of meaning on the two-
sided nature of language exchanged between author and reader, recognising
that 'meaning is an affair of consciousness not of words', since any word
sequence can represent more than one meaning (Hirsch 1967, p. 4). The
element ignored by the Parisian iconoclasts in their discussion of an
object-language, while constantly assumed in their meta-language, is that
meanings conveyed in verbal utterances are 'sharable', and that the very
fact of writing implies a belief in the 'accessibility of . . . verbal meaning'
(p. 18). Few people, wrote Hirsch in 1967, innocent of what had been
going on in Baltimore the previous year, would 'be so eccentric as to deny
the sharability of meaning. To whom and to what purpose would they
address their denial?' (p. 40). Since the communication of meaning between author and reader is 'an affair of consciousness and not of physical
signs or things', Hirsch continued, then 'the meanings . . . actualized by
the reader are either shared with the author or belong to the reader alone'
(p. 23). Even in the latter, extreme case, 'any construction of a text still
constitutes a meaning that must have an author — though he be merely
the critic himself' (p. 27). Subjective meanings are constructed, like all
others.

Verbal meaning essentially involves 'the determining will' of author
and/or interpreter, but the norms of language both influence and limit
their wills, for language is 'a controlling factor that sets limits to possible
verbal meanings' (pp. 27–8). While recognising the constraining effect of
linguistic norms, Hirsch, like so many constructive thinkers, emphasises
that '"the norms of language" are not a uniform set of restrictions, requirements, and patterns of expectation, but an immense number of different
ground rules that vary greatly' according to the type of utterance (p. 30),
always assuming that meaning can be shared (p. 31). The principle
of sharability involves two other crucial features, reproducibility and
determinacy:

> Reproducibility is a quality of verbal meaning that makes interpretation
> possible: if meaning were not reproducible, it could not be actualized by
> someone else and therefore could not be understood or interpreted.
> Determinacy, on the other hand, is a quality of meaning required in
> order that there be something to reproduce. Determinacy is a necessary
> attribute of any sharable meaning, since an indeterminacy cannot be
> shared: if a meaning were indeterminate, it would have no boundaries,
> no self-identity, and therefore could have no identity with a meaning
> entertained by someone else. (p. 44)

Of course, many verbal meanings are imprecise and ambiguous, but even ambiguity 'has a boundary like any other verbal meaning' (*ibid.*). Derrida, we might say, depends on his readers being able to share his meaning, while denying the principle of determinacy that makes this possible.

The criterion of determinacy also involves the notion of human will, for 'a determinate verbal meaning requires a determining will' (p. 46). The fact is that 'unless one particular complex of meanings is *willed* (no matter how "rich" and "various" it might be), there would be no distinction between what an author does mean by a word sequence and what he could mean by it' (p. 47). Will is the crucial factor on both sides of communication, in a process that once again involves both restrictions and free choice. As M.A.K. Halliday also emphasised, 'an author's verbal meaning is limited by linguistic possibilities but is determined by his actualizing and specifying some of those possibilities. Correspondingly, the verbal meaning that an interpreter construes is determined by his act of will, limited by those same possibilities' (*ibid.*). Hirsch rejected the notion sometimes advanced of there being an obvious distinction between primary and secondary meanings, for 'no meaning represented by a verbal sign is manifest; all meanings must be construed . . .' (p. 61). Even the term context, so often invoked in linguistics as a natural 'given', implies not only the speaker's words in their 'entire physical, psychological, social and historical milieu' (p. 86), but also 'a construed notion of the whole meaning narrow enough to determine the meaning of a part' yet at the same time flexible enough 'to signify those givens in the milieu which will help us to conceive the right notion of the whole' (p. 87). Recreating the context is a resource open to control by the reader or listener, for — to restate a principle constantly ignored by the 60s critics of language — 'understanding requires an active construction of meaning and is not simply given by the text' (p. 134). It follows that understanding is an autonomous act, which 'occurs entirely within the terms and proprieties of the text's own language and the shared realities which that language embraces', those 'shared realities and conventions — concrete and social as well as linguistic — which are required in order to construe meaning' (p. 134). For Derrida to say that 'as soon as there is meaning, there are only signs', is to remain sublimely unaware of how language works.

One feature that Hirsch particularly emphasised was the importance of the speaker's will or intention in conveying meaning, which is always conscious, for it 'involves not merely choices and goals, but *voluntary* choices and goals' (p. 52). All the linguists and philosophers I have read agree that the use of language is a free act performed by the individual actualising the expressive possibilities of the system, an act in which the notion of intentionality takes on major importance. To discover meaning, Wittgenstein wrote in *Philosophical Investigations* (1945; English tr. 1953), we must examine purpose, the speaker's intention. 'Look at the sentence as an instrument, and at its sense as its employment' (Wittgenstein 1958,

§421). 'Language is an instrument. Its concepts are instruments' (§569).
Language expresses personal interests, is closely connected with interpersonal behaviour, and implies the intention to approach another person.
'Yes: meaning something is like going up to someone' (§457). For the
linguist Benveniste the semantic expression par excellence is the sentence,
and within it the key element is 'the intention, that which the speaker
wants to say, the actualisation of his thought in language' (Benveniste
1974, p. 225). The semiotics of Barthes limited its concerns to the sign,
internal to language and effectively presemantic, but this is not enough. As
soon as we reach the level of the sentence, 'we are connected to things
outside language', for the meaning of a sentence implies reference to the
situation of discourse and the attitude of the speaker (*ibid.*).

For John Lyons, similarly, 'the important point is that meaning and
understanding are correlative, and both involve intentionality: the
meaning of an utterance necessarily involves the sender's communicative
intention'. As speech act theorists (such as Paul Grice and John Searle)
have shown, the receiver needs to recognise 'the sender's communicative
intention' (Lyons 1977, pp. 732–5), the fact that he intends an act of
communication to take place. For the philosopher Stuart Hampshire, with
his scrupulously argued account of the individual as a self-moving object in
a world of objects (Hampshire 1959, p. 45), 'aware of his own identity as a
thing alongside other things' (p. 64), the power of 'intentional movement'
is the primary factor giving us a sense of being in the world (p. 69), with a
continuity of experience (pp. 72–3). Consciousness itself is a continuous
state of 'acting and moving with intent', a constant 'flow of intention into
action', suspended only in sleep (pp. 78–85). The fact that 'men have a
language adequate to express their intentions' is a fundamental factor
not just in the development of individuality (p. 89) but also in the
maintenance of civil society, for 'every convention or rule that I accept is
an intention that I declare' (p. 99). Accepting social norms is a free
intentional act. As Hampshire observes,

> The often quoted fact that human beings are essentially thinking, and
> therefore symbol-using animals is a special case of the fact that they are
> essentially intentional animals. (p. 135)

Intention produces the wish to communicate; symbols permit its expression.

If we regard meaning as 'an intentional object', like 'anything else
that consciousness is averted to', E.D. Hirsch writes, then 'an unlimited
number of different intentional acts can intend the same verbal meaning'
(Hirsch 1957, p. 38). It follows that any intentional act can be misunderstood, that the conventions of language can fail to make plain
the intention that lies behind it. From the speaker's point of view, as
Wittgenstein pointed out, an inexact command can still work perfectly
well, for 'no *single* idea of exactness has been laid down' (Wittgenstein
1958, §88), and the notion that one could solve ambiguities in language by

having fixed rules is an illusion. 'A rule stands there like a sign-post. — Does the sign-post leave no doubt open about the way I have to go?' (§85): Obviously not! It may be true that a word or name does not have 'a fixed and unequivocal use for me in all possible cases', Wittgenstein conceded, but added: 'is it not the case that I have, so to speak, a whole series of props in readiness, and am ready to lean on one if another should be taken from under me and vice versa?' (§79). From the listener's side, Stuart Hampshire observes,

> It is a condition of the meaningful use of language with a definite reference to reality that a part of the user's intention in making the statement is not unambiguously expressed in the form of words that he uses. Something always remains to be elicited by further questioning, or to be inferred from the context of utterance, if the statement has a definite intended reference. (Hampshire 1959, pp. 202–3)

Socrates

As so many contemporary thinkers on language emphasise, the act of comprehension involves inference, the process by which the hearer construes the speaker's intention. One reason why we can understand other people's thought, Hampshire writes, is that 'it comes to light in statements of intention accompanying or preceding visible behaviour' (p. 206). The knowledge that another man does or does not 'follow the same habits and conventions of thought as we do, together with observation of his behaviour, gives us the basis of analogy, and the rule of inference' enables us to form a reasonably accurate impression of his thoughts and intentions. Where a Derrida or a Lacan jumps from the possibility of misunderstanding to the impossibility of understanding, Hampshire's argument arrives at the opposite conclusion:

> Within a single society of men who have learnt to enter into the common conventions of behaviour and expression that are the background of a common language, systematic misunderstanding is virtually impossible. (p. 207)

!!

Indeed, I would add, it is only in the carefully constructed but highly artificial form of farce that misunderstanding can be made to persist over any length of time, a dysfunctioning that we find amusing precisely because it is so abnormal. (There is more to Feydeau than this, needless to say.)

The growing recognition of intentionality as a key factor in language has led to a new interest in the 'context of utterance' and what Hampshire calls 'the common conventions of behaviour and expression' basic to any shared language. David Lewis has helpfully defined convention as ' "a regularity . . . which benefits each member of a group" ' (cit. Blackburn 1984, p. 119), such as everyone agreeing to drive on the left or stop at red lights. Linguistic conventions are established over time, seldom as a conscious agreement, Blackburn reminds us, indeed conventions in language are usually non-overt, requiring 'complicated and even technical description, which ordinary speakers will not be aware of' (*ibid.*, p. 122). Speech-act theory, with its basic principle that the fundamental unit of communication is not a sentence but the issuing of an utterance in a speech situation, has shed much light on these conventions. The outstanding work so far has been the late Paul Grice's William James Lectures (Harvard, 1967), on *Logic and Conversation*, published posthumously in 1989.[43] Grice started from the recognition that natural languages freely use 'many inferences and arguments', an unsystematic logic which in effect proposes a set of general 'conditions governing conversation' (Grice 1989, pp. 23–4). By conversation he implies talk, ordinary language, yet seeing it as 'a special case or variety of purposive, indeed rational, behavior . . .' (p. 28).

Grice's analysis focusses on what he calls 'implicature', the process by which a speaker can imply (here, 'implicate') something other than, or in addition to, what he overtly says (pp. 24–5). What is said is 'closely related to the conventional meaning of the words (the sentence) . . . uttered', for the full identification of which we need, as usual, to know the context of utterance (p. 25). But what is implied, 'conversational implicatures' as Grice calls them, is understood according to the general nature of talk exchanges, which are not random and undirected but rather 'cooperative efforts' in which each participant recognises 'a common purpose or set of purposes, or at least a mutually accepted direction' (p. 26). For instance, unmotivated changes of the subject under discussion, random observations unrelated to the issue or speakers, lengthy and uninvited disquisitions, cryptic or obscure comments, all these would be instantly recognised as violating what Grice calls the 'Cooperative Principle' underlying all human exchanges. He develops this principle, borrowing from Kant 'the categories Quantity, Quality, Relation, and Manner', to formulate a set of maxims felt to be operative in normal conversation.

The category of Quantity, first of all, 'relates to the quantity of information to be provided', and Grice suggests that we observe it in effect by obeying 'the following maxims:

1. Make your contribution as informative as is required (for the current purposes of the exchange).
2. Do not make your contribution more informative than is required.' (p. 26)

The second category, Quality, relates to whether the information offered is genuine or spurious, and under it falls what Grice calls 'a supermaxim — "Try to make your contribution one that is true" — and two more specific maxims:

1. Do not say what you believe to be false.
2. Do not say that for which you lack adequate evidence.' (p. 27)

Under the category of Relation Grice places 'a single maxim, namely, "Be relevant"', while observing that the issues involved here are much more complex than that terse formulation would suggest. Finally, in the category of Manner, which, unlike the previous categories, relates not to what is said but how it is said, Grice includes 'the supermaxim — "Be perspicuous" — and various maxims such as:

1. Avoid obscurity of expression.
2. Avoid ambiguity.
3. Be brief (avoid unnecessary prolixity).
4. Be orderly.'   (*ibid.*)

Grice's analysis in fact reconstructs the norms of conversation (descriptively, not prescriptively), which are shown to have potentially great effect on the lives of those involved. Being prolix, say, is far less serious than telling a lie (his first maxim of Quality). Indeed Grice suggests that this maxim is of an importance far exceeding the others, and that all conversational maxims 'come into operation only on the assumption that this maxim of Quality is satisfied' (*ibid.*). That is, we assume that all the people involved in a talk-exchange are passing on neither lies nor fantasies but what they believe to be truths. Like Lyons, Grice gives less importance to language as the 'exchange of information', for obviously our talk also involves 'influencing or directing the actions of others' (p. 28). Most conversational exchanges observe these maxims silently, as norms, but those taking part can recognise when they are violated. A speaker may 'quietly and unostentatiously' violate a maxim, and 'in some cases he will be liable to mislead' other people (p. 30) — without them noticing it, so to speak. Or he may visibly opt out, making it plain 'that he is unwilling to cooperate in the way the maxim requires. He may say, for example, *I cannot say more; my lips are sealed*'. Or, although willing to observe the maxims, he may be faced by a clash between them, wanting to 'Be as informative as is required' while not violating the injunction 'Have adequate evidence for what you say'. (So he might fulfil his hearer's desire for information by enlarging or embroidering his story, as in the closing scene of Conrad's *Heart of Darkness*, where Marlow unwillingly lies in order to tell Kurtz's intended what she wants to hear.) Or, finally, a speaker may 'flout a maxim, . . . may blatantly fail to fulfill it', talking at great length on an irrelevant topic, say, or promising information but failing to provide it. This raises what Grice calls 'a minor problem' for the hearer, namely how to reconcile the speaker's behaviour with the supposition that he is otherwise observing the Cooperative Principle (*ibid.*) — and, I add, provoking the further question, if not, why not?

A great virtue of Grice's account, and one that makes it particularly valuable for understanding talk-exchanges not only in real life but also in drama and prose fiction, is that he is able to reconstruct in realistic psychological terms the process by which conversational implicature is recognised. I shall shortly make use of it for a fresh account of intentionality and implicature in *Othello*, but first I want to return to pragmatics, '"the study of linguistic acts and the contexts in which they are performed"' (*cit.*

Horn 1988, p. 116), and to a recent work that illuminates the related process of inference. In *Relevance, Communication and Cognition* (1986), Dan Sperber and Deirdre Wilson, building on Grice's work, have developed an inferential model for language, according to which 'communication is achieved by producing and interpreting evidence' (p. 2). Opposing the code-model of semiotics, they see the process of understanding as an *'inferential process'*, starting from a set of premises and resulting in 'a set of conclusions which follow logically from, or are at least warranted by, the premises' (pp. 12–13). In many crucial areas successful communication depends on inference. When it comes to clearing up ambiguity, for instance, or recovering the attitudes held by the speaker, the force given to an utterance by a particular speech-act, or distinguishing between literal and figurative meanings, in all such cases the hearer must infer the intended sense. If the speaker's representation of his thought is incomplete or ambiguous, the hearer (a charitable hearer, I would add), assuming that the speaker is obeying the Cooperative Principle and maxims, 'can eliminate any thoughts that are incompatible with this purpose', until he reaches the right one (p. 34). Grice's model also explains 'how utterances can convey not just explicit but also implicit thoughts'. In a question and answer sequence, where 'the explicit content' of an answer does not directly respond to the question, and cannot therefore be relevant as it stands, the questioner infers another conclusion from it (Sperber and Wilson 1986, pp. 34–5, with examples). This may seem a long-winded account, but anyone who observes conversational exchanges in real life will verify the speed with which the brain can rule out alternative interpretations — 'rightly or wrongly', we must add, as a corrective to their rather idealised linguistic model. It is generally accepted that 'ordinary utterance comprehension is almost instantaneous' (Derrida's theory of deferral remains completely idiosyncratic), and that human beings can control more than one technique of inference (*ibid.*, pp. 66–7, 73, 83). Procedures of inference, therefore, 'work well enough in everyday affairs' (p. 70): the 'looseness' of language does not prevent us from being able to use it effectively.

A key concept in understanding communication, once again, is the context of utterance. Linguists usually mean by it the immediate speech situation, but Sperber and Wilson widen it to describe 'a psychological construct, a subset of the hearer's assumptions about the world', including 'expectations about the future, scientific hypotheses or religious beliefs', general cultural assumptions, and 'beliefs about the mental state of the speaker' (pp. 15–16). In this wider conception context is no longer something static but incremental, for 'the context used in interpreting a given utterance generally contains information derived from immediately preceding utterances' (p. 16). As human interaction continues we learn more, and have to integrate more of what we have learned. Misinterpretations can occur, since these mechanisms 'make successful communication

probable, but do not guarantee it' (p. 17). The possibility of misunderstanding, however, does not make the system worthless (as Lacan deduced),
indeed it assumes that there can be a correct understanding. Misunderstanding merely shows that the wrong context has been invoked, and
should be replaced with the correct one. An adequately shared context
not only filters out inappropriate interpretations but 'provides premises
without which the implicature cannot be inferred at all' (p. 37). The
whole comprehension process depends on what Sperber and Wilson call a
'contextual effect':

> As a discourse proceeds, the hearer retrieves or constructs and then
> processes a number of assumptions. These form a gradually changing
> background against which new information is processed. Interpreting
> an utterance involves more than merely identifying the assumption
> explicitly expressed: it crucially involves working out the consequences
> of adding this assumption to a set of assumptions that have themselves
> already been processed. (p. 118)

That is a most helpful description of human interaction in language,
responsive (unlike Saussure's simple two-track circuit) to the dynamic
process in which we absorb new information and relate it — modifying,
supporting, transforming — to information already received. The hearer is
constantly making 'an interpretive assumption about the speaker's informative intention' (pp. 230–1), and although various interpretations are
possible, in a normal speech context the hearer can usually know what the
speaker must have intended. 'Linguistic communication is the strongest
possible form of communication: it introduces an element of explicitness
where non-verbal communication can never be more than implicit'
(p. 175).

That affirmation of the power of language to communicate is one shared
by linguists and philosophers of language, however diverse their background. It should by now be clear that the main developments of both
disciplines in the last thirty years have taken quite different, often explicitly
opposed directions to those views emanating from Paris in the 1960s. As
Vincent Descombes comments, 'the doctrine of the emancipated signifier'
was so popular in those days because it seemed to support 'the notion of an
autonomous language', by the adoption of which 'linguistics became free of
anthropology (envisaged . . . as a key to the sum of human activity as
a whole)' (Descombes 1986, pp. 187–8). One linguist, Roy Harris, as
we have seen, felt that to acknowledge the links between language and
the outside world would ultimately 'bind linguistics hand and foot in
dependence on social anthropology' (Harris 1987, pp. 219–20). But many
people — setting aside the emotive metaphor of 'bind' — would willingly
accept that a philosophy of language might resemble an anthropology, or,
as Wittgenstein described his project, a 'natural history' or unsystematic
record of observed behaviour: 'What we are supplying are really remarks on

the natural history of human beings' (Wittgenstein 1958, §415), since 'Commanding, questioning, recounting, chatting, are as much part of our natural history as walking, eating, drinking, playing' (§25). One philosopher who would certainly accept such a connection would be Stuart Hampshire, concluding that

> The different uses of language have ultimately to be understood as acts of communication, and therefore as parts of different forms of social life. The setting and context of use must be illustrated with a wealth of concrete detail before the lines of division in language are understood. Philosophy as linguistic analysis is therefore unwillingly lured into a kind of descriptive anthropology. The principle of individuation, by which one use of language is distinguished from another, has to be founded upon some division of human powers and activities that is external to language itself. (Hampshire 1959, pp. 223–4)

Words alone are not 'a certain good'.

A TEST CASE FOR LANGUAGE THEORY: *OTHELLO*

'It is not words that shakes me thus'. (4.1.41)

Any theory of language has at least a possible application to literature. Its usefulness will depend on the level at which it operates, whether above or below the semantic water-line, so to speak. The analysis of phonemes or syntactical patterns abstracted from the context-of-utterance will yield results for linguistics, no doubt, but with no interest to a literary student. Studies of vocabulary in terms of etymology, equally, will be of little relevance unless it can be shown that a particular character, say, was consistently given words of one specific kind, thus differentiated from the other people in that novel or play. The two essential attributes of any theory of language, if it is to illuminate works of literature, are that it should be able to cope with meaning and that it should respect the context-of-utterance, namely the fact that in literature, as in life, words are spoken by specific characters on specific occasions for specific purposes. The structuralists and their followers wrote as if literature could be discussed in the same (negative) terms as language, assuming, as Barthes put it, that 'literature is never anything but language', or, more provocatively, that 'structurally, literature is only a parasitical object of language, . . . only language, and a second language at that, a parasitical meaning which can only connote reality, not denote it' (Barthes 1972, pp. 159, 266–7). Against such reductivism we can set the forthright statement of Ezra Pound, that 'the medium of drama is not words, but persons moving about on stage using words'.[44] The unit of analysis in drama is the utterance of individual characters; in a novel, in addition, it is the discourse of the narrator. The point of reference in drama is not 'the play', as many critics suppose. The play is the aesthetic whole that contains and organises these utterances, by representing an action, that is, a sequence of human behaviour. But we ought not to reify the play by ascribing agency to it. Agency belongs to the characters, who are presented as self-moving, self-willed, and thus coming into relationship with other characters having complementary, or conflicting values, desires and goals. Out of their interplay the dramatist builds a determinate literary work.

It will be instantly obvious that drama, in this description — which I take to be non-controversial, generally accepted — is unlikely to respond to structuralist approaches if, as is usually the case, they ignore the meaning of individual utterances or indeed the existence of separate characters. If 'the play' is erected as the reference point, ignoring the individual characters, structuralist analysis will easily discover a series of operative dichotomies, such as nature/culture, heaven/hell, civilised/savage. To take *Othello* as an example, it would be easy to find similar dichotomies, such as black/white, Christian/pagan, angel/devil, native/stranger, military virtues/ social breeding, and so on. But these dichotomies are not operative in the play as a whole — *by* the play, as Lévi-Strauss might put it — they are deployed by individual characters for individual ends. In the opening scenes many of these binary pairs are applied to Othello's clandestine marriage to Desdemona, and applied — such being the highly goal-directed nature of speech in drama, concentrating a decisive series of changes in several people's lives into two or three hours' performing time — by, or on behalf of the distressed father, Brabantio, who rejects the marriage as abnormal, distasteful by his standards.

The agent of notification to Brabantio is Iago, making use of Roderigo, a disappointed suitor for Desdemona, and presenting the union in the worst possible light:

> Even now, now, very now, an old black ram
> Is tupping your white ewe. (1.1.89–90)

These negative judgments on Othello all make use of a basic dichotomy between normal and abnormal. To Iago (in hiding) Othello is 'the devil' (92); to Roderigo, rejected Venetian, he is 'an extravagant and wheeling stranger / Of here and everywhere' (137–8). To Brabantio, unable to understand why his daughter should have eloped, Othello's capturing her cannot be the result of open, non-coercive wooing. He must have used 'charms' (1.1.172), 'bound' her 'in chains of magic' (1.2.65), deceived her through his knowledge of the occult, 'arts inhibited and out of warrant' (1.2.73–9). These implied oppositions between legal and illegal, white and black ('the sooty bosom / Of such a thing as thou': 1.2.70–1), natural and unnatural, are given full expression in Brabantio's accusation before the senators that Desdemona has been made to 'err / Against all rules of

nature' (1.3.101), and that only witchcraft could cause 'nature so pre-
posterously to err' (60–4), only the 'practices of cunning hell' could make
her 'fall in love with what she feared to look on!' (96–102). These
and other dichotomies are used by Brabantio intentionally, to express
his particular opinion and anger. Othello, in his defence, also uses
binary oppositions, setting his 'rude . . . speech' against 'the soft phrase of
peace', his many years' experience in 'the tented field' against his complete
ignorance of 'this great world' of Venetian society (1.3.82–7), and describing Desdemona's reaction to his life-narrative as a complementary, not
opposed feeling:

> She gave me for my pains a world of sighs . . .
> She loved me for the dangers I had passed,
> And I loved her that she did pity them   (1.3.158–68)

A structuralist who ascribed these dichotomies to the play, ignoring the
characters, would simply destroy drama as a representation of human
interaction. If it is not that, it is nothing.

A neo-structuralist, convinced that language cannot communicate,
would have a hard time with this, or indeed any play. Apart from some
very recent drama, which looks as if it has been directly influenced by neo-
structuralist theory (some plays by Botho Strauss, for instance), the very
nature of drama presupposes a highly condensed series of verbal exchanges
between characters who understand each other as quickly as we do in real
life. Of course, some understand less than what is meant — Agamemnon
doesn't see the sinister implications of Clytemnestra welcoming his home-
coming, neither in words nor deeds (the unrolling of a blood-coloured
carpet for him to walk on, into the house of Atreus),[45] and Claudius
can hardly understand Hamlet's ambivalent witticisms (nor do most
theatregoers). But otherwise in all Western drama, at least, language
thrives on the characters' instant understanding of each other's speech
acts. As for the neo-structuralists' fracturing the sign, proliferating signifiers
without signifieds, one reason why I have chosen Othello as a test-case is
that such an event actually occurs here (uniquely in Shakespeare). It
happens as Iago evasively describes what Cassio is alleged to have said
about his alleged affair (both alleged by Iago, we recall) with Desdemona:

IAGO.   Faith, that he did. — I know not what he did.
OTHELLO.   What? what?
IAGO.   Lie —
OTHELLO.   With her?
IAGO.   With her, on her; what you will.
OTHELLO.   Lie with her! lie on her! — We say lie on her, when they
    belie her. — Lie with her! 'Zounds, that's fulsome! Handkerchief —
    confessions — handkerchief!   (4.1.31ff)

There indeed the signifier splits up into multiple signifieds, for Shakespeare
(as for Luce Irigaray in her account of schizophrenia) the symptom of

collapse into incoherence and mental chaos. But this collapse is not a property of language as such, it being an extremely rare event, marked on the stylistic register by Othello dropping down into prose (the conventional medium for madmen, real or pretended, in Elizabethan drama), and reverting to verse when he awakes from his trance (line 60). The key comment on Othello's fracturing the linguistic sign is Iago's remark as he loses consciousness: 'Work on, / My medicine, work!' (44–5). Othello's collapse is the result of Iago's intentional behaviour, not an attribute of language *per se*.

My thesis is that only those theories of language fit drama which allow for the characters behaving as intentional agents. The philosophy of language that studies speech acts, the branch of linguistics known as pragmatics, these are, it seems to me, potentially valuable linguistic approaches to drama since they recognise the autonomy of the speaking subject, and analyse the conventions of communication as a social process. The linguistic models so far developed are inadequate in one major respect, however, in basing themselves on a norm that presupposes honest communication, the intention to inform or state a personal opinion in a spirit of open co-operation. This norm is certainly observed in drama, and perhaps a majority of the speech acts in Shakespeare are of this kind. Yet Shakespeare and his contemporary dramatists, in that hot-bed of linguistic development in English literature between the 1570s and 1630s, derived much entertainment (and meaning) from the violations of these norms. Grice's injunctions not to make your contribution more informative than is required, and to be brief and orderly, are conspicuously ignored by the garrulous (Polonius, Shallow), or by an accused person pleading extenuating circumstances (Hotspur in *1 Henry IV* explaining why he had not delivered his prisoners to the King, as promised, distracted by the King's emissary, 'perfumed like a milliner', / 'And telling me the sovereignest thing on earth / Was parmaceti for an inward bruise'), or by the politicians in *Troilus and Cressida*, at once devious and pompous. Verbal comedy in Shakespeare and his contemporaries derives much of its resources from the thoroughgoing violation of the Gricean injunctions to avoid obscurity, irrelevance, ambiguity, and disorder. We think of any number of clowns (Speed, Gobbo, Lavatche, Feste), of Mrs Quickly (in *Merry Wives*), of Dogberry and Verges, of the artisans in *Midsummer Night's Dream*, and the whole lower plot of *Love's Labour's Lost*, that walking catalogue of all the vices in communication then known to man.

In Shakespeare's tragedies many of the most decisive uses of language also represent violations, but more serious ones, of such ethical norms as honesty, sincerity, accountability: the opening scenes in *King Lear*, with the flattery or fawning competition of Goneril and Regan, set against Cordelia's refusal to share their debasement of the Cooperative Principle; the varying modes of hypocrisy in Claudius and Macbeth; the lessons in political lying that Volumnia gives her son. Limiting ourselves to *Othello*, we can see that Iago observes Grice's Cooperative Principle and maxims

when it suits his purpose — which is sinister enough: in Blake's pregnant
rhyme,

> A truth that's told with bad intent
> Beats all the lies man can invent.

— but also that he willingly and constantly violates them, showing great
resource and inventiveness in so doing. If we imagine Iago reading through
Grice's list, all the maxims governing social exchange take on a distinctly
ironic tinge: 'Make your contribution as informative as is required'; 'Do not
say what you believe to be false', or 'for which you lack adequate evidence';
'Avoid obscurity of expression'; 'Avoid ambiguity'. Iago is well aware
that honest, socially responsible persons observe these conventions, and
that they assume — unless and until they receive contrary evidence — that
those they converse with do so too. Grice's fundamental idea, 'that the
very act of communicating creates expectations which it then exploits'
(Sperber and Wilson 1986, p. 37), is one that Iago realised long ago.

*   *   *

The intentionality governing all of Iago's behaviour, in words as in deeds,
is hatred for Othello. This is the first thing we learn about Iago:

RODERIGO.   Thou toldst me thou didst hold him in thy hate.
IAGO.   Despise me if I do not.   (1.1.7f)

Iago's resentment at being passed over for promotion (the first, but not the
only motive he gives for hating Othello), makes him in no way 'affined /
To love the Moor' (39f): rather 'I do hate him as I do hell-pains' (155). If
he follows Othello, it is only 'to serve my turn upon him' (42). The fact
that the audience knows Iago's true feelings from the outset means that we
regard all his dealings with Othello from that point on as instances of
hypocrisy.[46] Iago demonstrates a remarkably convincing exterior in his
professions of love and loyalty, false declarations that become all the more
painful to us as his plots develop, since we alone know that Iago is actually
destroying Othello — preparing to 'poison his delight', as he had urged
Roderigo, throw 'vexation' on his 'joy' (1.1.69ff). This technique of divided
knowledge, where we share confidences from one or more characters that
are hidden from the other people in the play, is a resource only available to
drama (and opera) among the literary genres, and it is one that Shakespeare
used frequently and consciously.[47] It is developed, characteristically,
through two structural devices unique to drama, the soliloquy and the
aside, which put us in direct contact with a character while the action is
proceeding. If the character is passive, acted on rather than acting, such as
Cordelia in the opening scene of King Lear, the asides arouse concern in
the audience, pathos, but hardly involve us in the action. If the character
is forceful, however, as are Iago, Richard III, Macbeth, direct address

to the audience involves us immediately with the full range of their intentions, before, during, and after their execution. As I have observed elsewhere,[48] this involvement leads to an intimacy which we would willingly avoid, if we could. There is no-one in the world whose confidence I would rather less share than Iago's.

Iago's confidences to us, either in soliloquy or aside, are illocutionary acts, taking two main forms. There are plain statements of fact — 'Thus do I ever make my fool my purse'; 'I hate the Moor. . . . He holds me well . . .', characteristically in the present tense. From these he derives statements of intention cast in the future tense: 'The better shall my purpose work on him. . . .' Already ominous in soliloquy, Iago is even more frightening in the asides he speaks while Cassio is courteously entertaining Desdemona, waiting for Othello to arrive on Cyprus:

> He takes her by the palm. Ay, well said, whisper. With as little a web as this will I ensnare as great a fly as Cassio. Ay, smile upon her, do; I will gyve thee in thine own courtship.   (2.1.166ff)

This is frightening because the prediction accompanies the action, and as we alone know how completely concealed Iago's real motives are, and how resourceful he is in pretence, we sense the future implicit in the present. All of Iago's soliloquies juxtapose in this way illocutionary, present-tense statements of his observations, generalisations about the people whom he has been studying — 'For 'tis most easy / Th'inclining Desdemona to subdue / In any honest suit'; 'His soul is so enfettered to her love . . .'; 'When devils will the blackest sins put on, / They do suggest at first with heavenly shows' (2.3.330ff); 'Trifles light as air / Are to the jealous confirmations strong . . . / The Moor already changes with my poison' (3.3.324ff) — with future-tense announcements of his intended manipulations, sometimes deductions from the previously-expressed statements — 'I'll pour this pestilence into his ear . . . So will I turn her virtue into pitch' (2.3.349ff); 'Not poppy, nor mandragora, / . . . Shall ever medicine thee to that sweet sleep / Which thou owedst yesterday' (3.3.333ff). Step by step Iago extends his control over both present and future, a control predicted in the soliloquies, performed in the action following.

The peculiar nature of Iago's intentionality is that it is completely hidden both from the people who are the objects of his hatred — Othello, Cassio — and from the instruments through whom he fulfils his wish to destroy them — Roderigo (who suspects he is being used, but never realises to what extent), and Desdemona. The intentionality he expresses directly to them is one of love and readiness to help on all possible occasions. To Roderigo he professes 'love' (1.3.306), loyalty: 'Thou art sure of me' (1.3.360f), and the desire to help him achieve his desires (2.1.270f). To Cassio — whom he has just made drunk, involved in a brawl, and had cashiered — he says 'I think you think I love you' (2.3.304), an illocutionary act with two embedded phrases marking the remarkable gap

in awareness between Cassio's implied utterance ('I think Iago loves me')
and Iago's ('I hate, but pretend to love him'), the repetition of 'think'
making it clear how much Iago depends on the image he has created of an
honest, loving friend. Iago's affirmations of goodwill to Cassio become
almost effusive: 'I protest, in the sincerity of love and honest kindness'
(320). To Desdemona Iago feigns concern and sympathy after Othello's
violent accusations, but he must be gloating inwardly: 'What is your
pleasure, madam? How is't with you?'; 'What's the matter, lady?'; 'What
name, fair lady?'; 'Why, did he so?'; 'Do not weep, do not weep. Alas the
day!'; 'Beshrew him for't! / How comes this trick upon him?'; 'Go in, and
weep not; all things shall be well' (4.2.111–172). A linguistic analysis that
did not attend to context and intentionality could find no evil in these
utterances.

To Othello, Iago punctuates the terrible scene where he plants the first
jealous suspicion with protestations of love: 'My lord, you know I love you'
(3.3.119); '— now I shall have reason / To show the love and duty that I
bear you . . .' (195ff); 'I humbly do beseech you of your pardon / For too
much loving you' (214f). Since we alone have known from the beginning
that Iago only serves for his own gain, when we see him professing to
observe the Cooperative Principle and maxims, we alone know to what
degree he is perverting them. The climax of this silent perversion of trust
is the apparent concern Iago shows to Othello that his insinuation of
Desdemona's betrayal 'hath a little dashed your spirits' — which we know
to be a covert expression of triumph — followed with an audacious allusion
to the fact that, notwithstanding the catastrophic nature of the allegation,
Othello will still infer from it that Iago loves him:

> I hope you will consider what is spoke
> Came from my love.   (218f)

The 'hope' (which can also mean 'think') is a mere flourish, for Iago knows
that he has the supreme skill of being able to make vice appear virtuous,
virtue vicious, at will.

The function of these affirmations of love by Iago is to set up a context-
of-utterance in which the hearer in the play will infer two propositions: (a)
Iago is honest and reliable; (b) Iago is concerned for my welfare; leading to
the conclusion (c) I should follow his advice. Roderigo silently accepts
this conclusion, regularly overwhelmed by Iago's persuasiveness, but both
Cassio and Othello spontaneously express these deluded inferences just
after Iago has left them: 'I never knew / A Florentine more kind and
honest' (3.1.39f); 'This honest creature doubtless / Sees and knows
more, much more, than he unfolds' (3.3.244f); 'This fellow's of exceeding
honesty, / And knows all qualities, with a learned spirit, / Of human
dealings' (260ff). These normal people are truth-tellers, and expect others
to tell the truth, a naïve belief, perhaps, but without it language and
communication could not get off the ground. (Imagine the lengths you

would have to go if you suspected universal dissimulation: where could you ever place certainty and trust? You would end up in the paranoid state of Master Ford.) Judged by the deceivers, however, the truth-tellers are easy prey. As the rogue Autolycus says, 'what a fool Honesty is! And Trust, his sworn brother, a very simple gentleman!' (*The Winter's Tale*, 4.4.597f); or as Iago confides,

> The Moor is of a free and open nature
> That thinks men honest that but seem to be so,
> And will as tenderly be led by th'nose
> As asses are.   (1.3.397ff)

Othello, like the other normal but naïve people in the play, naturally assumes that Iago is observing the conventions of honesty and sincerity that we expect from human interchange, and Iago can exploit these assumptions. This proves the justice of Alasdair MacIntyre's observation that lies are parasitic on truth.[49] As MacIntyre puts it, language can only exist if there are shared rules, 'of such a kind that an intention to say that what is, is can always be presumed.' If someone tells us that it is raining, we have to assume that he is reporting an observed event, in order for him to communicate with us.

> But this presumption, necessary for language to be meaningful, is only possible where truth telling is the socially accepted and recognized norm. Indeed, lying itself is only possible where and on the assumption that men expect the truth to be told. . . . Thus the recognition of a norm of truth telling and of a virtue of honesty seems written into the concept of society. (p. 77)

The further point to be drawn is that 'although the liar vindicates in his practice the existence of the very norm which his practice violates', this shows that norms may be descriptive (as Grice argued) but are certainly not prescriptive, since they cannot provide 'a guide how to live' (p. 96). The gap that Iago exploits is between the observation that this is how most people behave, so making society possible, and the belief that everyone behaves like this all the time. The fact is that 'not only different individual choices but very different codes of honesty lie within the range of possibilities open to us' (*ibid.*). Outward behaviour is not a reliable guide to a person's true intentions. As Iago mockingly says, 'Men should be what they seem' (3.3.129). The awful fascination of these scenes derives from Iago's knowing control over people's inferences, his ability to present a situation, and himself, in such a light that others draw exactly the conclusions he wants. After the drunken brawl he has engineered to destroy Cassio's career, Iago rebukes the quarrellers for lacking 'all sense of place and duty' (both violated chiefly by him), and easily gulls Othello with his simulated concern:

Honest Iago, that look'st dead with grieving,
Speak who began this; on thy love I charge thee.   (2.3.162ff)

Iago makes an evasive speech, as if wanting to disobey the maxim of Quantity ('make your contribution as informative as is required') in order to protect Cassio. He is pressed again by Othello — 'Iago, who began't?' — at which point Montano, hurt in the scuffle, intervenes to warn Iago not to 'deliver more or less than truth'. Iago's evasiveness thus creates an implicature from which Montano infers that Iago will be biassed in favour of his colleague, Cassio. Iago can then pretend to affirm Cassio's innocence — 'to speak the truth / Shall nothing wrong him' — while ending his apparently neutral speech, purged of all visible emotion, with an apologia for Cassio — he 'did some little wrong to' Montano, but 'men are men'. This apparent excuse is, both in intention and in take-up, an indictment. So Othello takes it:

I know, Iago,
Thy honesty and love doth mince this matter,
Making it light to Cassio.   (2.3.213ff)

Othello believes that that inference is of his own making, but Iago controlled it throughout.

The most brilliant extended sequence of manipulated inference is the long scene where Iago undermines Othello's trust in Desdemona, Cassio, and even his own perception of reality (3.3.92–481). Here speech-act theory, together with pragmatics as developed by Sperber and Wilson, can be helpful. In Grice's theory, when the Cooperative Principle and maxims are violated, 'hearers are expected to make any additional assumptions needed to dispose of the violation' (Sperber and Wilson 1986, p. 35), those implicatures that, I suggested, a charitable hearer will make. At the beginning of the scene Iago and Othello enter, seeing Cassio hastily leaving Desdemona ('I am very ill at ease'), whom he has been petitioning to intercede with Othello. Iago instantly expresses a reaction, but refuses to clarify it:

IAGO.   Ha! I like not that.
OTHELLO.   What dost thou say?
IAGO.   Nothing, my lord; or if — I know not what.   (3.3.35ff)

Not completing an utterance is the well-known rhetorical device *aposiopesis* (or *reticentia*), which Quintilian described as a mode of arousing suspicion in the judge by indicating 'that our meaning is other than our words seem to imply', in effect an implicature which the hearer turns into an inference, as if he had discovered the hidden meaning. As the advocate withholds completion of his utterance, Quintilian observed, the judge is 'led to seek out the secret which he would not perhaps believe if he heard it openly stated, and to believe in that which he thinks he has found out for himself'. The Spanish Renaissance rhetorician Vives extended this account of the involuntary cooperation produced by this figure, describing *reticentia* as being particularly effective 'among men of suspicious natures, who go to great lengths to see sinister conjectures everywhere'.[50] In case Othello has not made the precisely damaging inference that Iago wants, he puts the idea explicitly into the open:

IAGO.   Cassio, my lord! No, sure, I cannot think it,
    That he would steal away so guilty-like,
    Seeing you coming.
OTHELLO.   I do believe 'twas he.

By pretending to doubt his own senses, Iago has made Othello confirm the fact (Cassio's hasty departure) together with the implication (he must be guilty).

Explicit here, for much of the following sequence Iago gives only the vaguest reactions. Once Desdemona has been dismissed, having for fifty lines pleaded on behalf of Cassio, Iago asks Othello whether Cassio knew of his love for Desdemona — 'But for a satisfaction of my thought; / No further harm' (3.3.97–8), as if that were not harm enough. Receiving confirmation that Cassio 'went between' them when they were courting, Iago makes an apparently noncommittal comment: 'Indeed!' This is a bait designed to provoke Othello to an irritable demand for information:

OTHELLO.   Indeed? ay, indeed. Discern'st thou aught in that?
    Is he not honest?
IAGO.   Honest, my lord?
OTHELLO.   Honest? ay, honest.
IAGO.   My lord, for aught I know.
OTHELLO.   What dost thou think?
IAGO.   Think, my lord?   (101ff)

By refusing to enlarge on his reaction to Cassio having gone 'a-wooing with' Othello, denying to do so four times over, Iago is now blatantly flouting Grice's first maxim of Quantity, to make one's contribution as informative as is required. This patent refusal, on top of the insinuations already planted about Cassio's guilty-seeming departure, can only make Othello impatient to know more:

        Think, my lord! Alas, thou echo'st me,
        As if there were some monster in thy thought
        Too hideous to be shown. Thou dost mean something:
        I heard thee say even now, thou likedst not that,
        When Cassio left my wife. What didst not like?
        And when I told thee he was of my counsel
        In my whole course of wooing, thou criedst 'Indeed!'
        And didst contract and purse thy brain together,

As if thou then hadst shut up in thy brain
Some horrible conceit.   (110ff)

The figure *reticentia* does its work: Othello is made to draw the desired
inference as if it were his own discovery. Classical rhetoric and modern
speech-act theory are at one in describing the process by which an unscrupulous speaker can violate the conventions of speech exchange in
order to plant suspicion in the hearer's mind. This blatant violation of the
expectation that speakers will exchange information freely leads Othello to
think that Iago is concealing information that could be peculiarly damaging to him, Othello. This is the implicature (perfectly described by Grice,
if in rather technical terms),[51] to which Iago's evasiveness directs Othello,
since it is the only possible explanation why someone should behave in
such a way who otherwise has impeccable credentials for 'cooperative
efforts' in conversation (restoring to the word its additional, older sense of
'social interchange'). Othello appeals for Iago to play the game, take
part in the Cooperative Principle governing human communication, even
making it a test of his love and loyalty:

OTHELLO.   If thou dost love me,
   Show me thy thought.
IAGO.   My lord, you know I love you.
OTHELLO.   I think thou dost;
   And for I know thou'rt full of love, and honest,
   And weigh'st thy words before thou giv'st them breath,
   Therefore these stops of thine fright me the more:
   For such things in a false disloyal knave
   Are tricks of custom; but in a man that's just
   They're close dilations, working from the heart
   That passion cannot rule.   (117ff)

That is a text-book definition of the normal expectation, in a truth-
loving community, that a clear heart speaks with a clear tongue, and that
whoever hesitates to speak (these 'stops' are the uncompleted utterances of
aposiopesis) must have something awful to hide.

   In appealing to Iago, 'Show me thy thought', Othello is requesting what
linguists call 'ostensive behaviour' or 'ostension', 'behaviour which makes
manifest an intention' to show something (Sperber and Wilson 1986,
p. 49). In a normal speech context 'ostensive behaviour provides evidence
of one's thoughts' in a deliberate act of communication, which intentionally
points out that information is waiting to be picked up (*ibid.*, p. 50). All
interpretation, as we know, depends on a context, and on what Sperber
and Wilson call the individual's 'cognitive environment', the set of facts
that are 'manifest' to him (that is, 'perceptible or inferable'), such that he
is capable of 'representing it mentally and accepting its representation as
true or probably true' (p. 39). By insinuating that (a) he has thoughts

but (b) that he is concealing them — thoughts that Othello assumes (as intended) to convey some unpleasant facts about Desdemona and Cassio — Iago begins to modify the context in which Othello lives, that 'psychological construct, a subset of the hearer's assumptions about the world', as it has been defined (pp. 15–16). By seeming to withhold the truth, apparently unable for once to obey the maxims of Quantity ('be informative'), Iago is all the time violating the maxim of Quality, that fundamental principle of human communication, not to say what you believe to be false. Iago does not yet do anything as obvious, or incriminating as that, but by seeming to withhold information that he could impart he drives Othello to desperation. Othello is made to beg for these withheld 'facts', as if his life and happiness depended on them.

> I prithee, speak to me as to thy thinkings,
> As thou dost ruminate, and give thy worst of thoughts
> The worst of words.   (133ff)

Othello gives to 'thoughts' the sense of 'justified deductions from observation', the honest man's end of a spectrum which, as we know, really involves the other end, that of 'malicious and groundless fantasies'. Iago ignores this appeal to reveal the full extent of his 'thoughts' (which in effect gives him *carte blanche* for lying), despite Othello's insistent reiterations: 'Thou dost conspire against thy friend. . . . / If thou but think'st him wronged and mak'st his ear / A stranger to thy thoughts' (145–8) — 'I'll know thy thoughts!' (164). Not yet satisfied that he has sufficiently disturbed Othello, Iago takes refuge in a form of metacommunication, discussing what effect it would have to 'Utter my thoughts', supposing they were 'vile and false . . . . uncleanly apprehensions', supposing he were 'vicious in any guess', since 'oft my jealousy / Shapes faults that are not' (139ff). Iago's extraordinary admission of the insubstantiality of his fantasies cannot be understood by Othello, desperate for information and unable to consider what truth-criteria are involved.

Iago's transparent violation of the Cooperative Principle has a series of effects not yet considered by the philosophers and linguists who have based their theories on normal, straightforward communication.[52] Othello's rising frustration at this blatant withholding of information — 'What dost thou mean?' (157) — raises his passion to a point where he is particularly vulnerable, off balance, open to insinuation, unable to rationally weigh the issues involved. Exploiting this state, Iago launches on a twenty-line disquisition, in a sententious and verbose manner that recalls Polonius, or perhaps the set speeches of that arch manipulator Ulysses (compare his disquisition to Achilles: 'Time hath, my lord, a wallet at his back', with Iago here: 'Good name in man and woman, dear my lord, / Is the immediate jewel of their souls'). By starting with Reputation, and going on to Jealousy, as if repeating *sententiae* from some commonplace book, Iago appears to be digressing from the point (thus visibly violating further conversational norms), so that when he describes the agonies of life to one 'Who dotes, yet doubts, suspects, yet fondly loves!', Othello can offer the brief but detached comment, 'O misery!', a general observation that (he thinks) does not apply to him. Iago then pointedly repeats his account of the suffering of the jealous man, who 'ever fears he shall be poor', but Othello still confidently brushes it aside, sure that he will never be con-cerned with 'such exsufflicate and blown surmise / Matching thy inference' (183ff). This is a comment both on the style of Iago's speech here ('full of air, inflated') and its insubstantiated allegation. Dismissing its relevance to him, Othello is driven to make the crucial counter-affirmation, that Desdemona's social graces only enhance her virtue, and that despite his 'own weak merits' he has no 'fear or doubt of her revolt; / For she had eyes and chose me' (186ff).

This is an important stage in Iago's manipulation, for he has now managed to tie all his seemingly irrelevant disquisitions on Reputation, Jealousy, and Cuckoldry directly to Othello's relationship with Desdemona. Further, he has made Othello utter a positive statement of the context in which he lives, those 'assumptions about the world . . . . expectations about the future', general beliefs about himself and those nearest and dearest to him. This is the context that Iago can now eagerly and directly attack:

> I am glad of it; for now I shall have reason
> To show the love and duty that I bear you
> With franker spirit. Therefore, as I am bound,
> Receive it from me. I speak not yet of proof.
> Look to your wife; observe her well with Cassio. . . .   (195ff)

There it is, finally out, the direct statement that, for over a hundred lines, Iago has been hinting at, alluding to, but never making. These are the 'thoughts' Othello has begged for, longed to share, and as Iago adds detail to what he himself describes as his 'inference' Othello 'receives' his loyal lieutenant's gift with a dulled, crushed spirit — 'Dost thou say so?'; 'I am bound to thee for ever'. Iago first calls in question 'our country disposition', the tricks of the women of Venice (notorious for its courtesans) in deceiv-ing their husbands; then Desdemona's known ability to 'deceive her father, marrying you', uncanny that one 'so young could give out such a seeming . . .' (203ff). Having made these two points Iago breaks off '— but I am much to blame; I humbly beseech you of your pardon / For too much loving you'. This self-interruption (aposiopesis again) seems to show Iago's concern for Othello, further expressed in his injunctions that his superior should 'consider what is spoke' a sign of love, and 'not to strain my speech / To grosser issues nor to larger reach / Than to suspicion' (a telling insinuation), which would give his 'speech . . . such vile success / As my thoughts aimed not at'. The continuum that Iago affirms between thought and speech as an index of love would indeed be a norm for sincerity in communication if he were not — so visibly to us, invisible to Othello — relentlessly perverting it.

What Iago does in this amazingly concentrated sequence is to unsettle Othello's cognitive environment, place in Othello's head the same uncertainties (about Cassio; about Desdemona; about women in general) that Iago has himself professed. Compare these two utterances:

1.   IAGO.   For Michael Cassio,
    I dare be sworn I think that he is honest.
    OTHELLO.   I think so too.   (127ff)

2.   OTHELLO.   I do not think but Desdemona's honest.
    IAGO.   Long live she so! and long live you to think so!   (227ff)

The first is a complete lie, cunningly deflating the profession of certainty ('I dare be sworn . . . that he is honest') with the all-embracing doubt of 'I think'. Othello's utterance is more contorted syntactically, a double negative which amounts, eventually, reluctantly, to affirming a belief in Desdemona's honesty (here having the additional sense of 'chastity'), only to be undermined by Iago's divisive distinction between being honest, and being thought to be. The linguists' general proposition that 'when you communicate, your intention is to alter the cognitive environment of your addressee' (Sperber and Wilson 1986, p. 46) is true in a very special sense for Iago: for alter read destroy.

The cognitive process, Sperber and Wilson argue in terms that may now seem rather naïve, is 'aimed at improving the individual's knowledge of the world' (p. 47), and involves an ongoing absorption and adjustment to new information. When 'interconnected new and old items of information are used together as premises in an inference process, further new information can be derived', in what they call 'a multiplication effect' (p. 48). Where Grice had defined the basic conversational implicature as depending, amongst other things, on 'all relevant items . . . of background knowledge' being 'available to both participants' (Grice 1989, p. 31), their version allows for the dynamics of a developing talk-exchange, in which the added new information creates a 'gradually changing background'. Within this shifting context interpretation has not only to identify 'the assumption explicitly expressed' but to work out 'the consequences of adding this assumption' to what has already been communicated (Sperber and Wilson 1986, p. 118). This process can be observed in almost test-case conditions in this scene, as each item of 'information' introduced by Iago — lies, slanders, insinuations — forces Othello to adjust his image of the world he lives in. The assumptions, beliefs, and expectations created by and fulfilled in his relationship with Desdemona — 'O my soul's joy!' as he exclaimed at their reunion in Cyprus,

> My soul hath her content so absolute
> That not another comfort like to this
> Succeeds in unknown fate . . .   (2.1.179ff)

are undermined one by one. The collapse of his private world — 'when I love thee not, / Chaos is come again' (3.3.91ff) — initiates the collapse of the public world:

> O now, for ever
> Farewell the tranquil mind! farewell content!
> Farewell the plumèd troops and the big wars
> That make ambition vitue!   (3.3.349ff)

In both worlds, 'Othello's occupation's gone'.

The multiplication effect, which accounts for the speed with which this scene develops, undermines Othello's trust in Desdemona, Cassio, his own perception of the world, even — as a desperate last gesture, invoking the unthinkable to mark the stage of crisis he has reached — his trust in Iago. After that fateful and fortuitous interlude when Othello leaves the scene with Desdemona, she having dropped the handkerchief which passes from Emilia to Iago, Othello returns in visible distress, poisoned by Iago's 'dangerous conceits', and greeting him as if he were a witch — 'Avaunt! be gone!' Othello resents Iago's agency in having destroyed those 'perceptible or inferable' facts that constituted his cognitive environment:

> thou hast set me on the rack:
> I swear 'tis better to be much abused
> Than but to know't a little.   (3.3.337ff)

Where Othello had earlier appealed, in the heroic confidence of innocence, for Iago to 'give thy worst of thoughts the worst of words', wiser now, he would have preferred the completely unheroic state of an ignorant cuckold's complicity: Desdemona could have indulged in any vile behaviour, 'So I had nothing known'. Iago, having destroyed the context of his existence, is not just resented but threatened:

> If thou dost slander her and torture me,
> Never pray more: abandon all remorse.   (370f)

Yet Othello clings to him as the one sure point in his world — 'Nay, stay; thou shouldst be honest' (are supposed or reputed to be) — before including Iago, too, in his uncertainty:

> By the world,
> I think my wife to be honest, and think she is not;
> I think that thou art just, and think thou art not:
> I'll have some proof.   (385ff)

'Villain', he has said, 'be sure thou prove my love a whore; / . . . give me the ocular proof'; 'Make me to see't . . .' (361ff).

Othello has long since lost any grasp on a reality independent of, or different to the cognitive environment that Iago has constructed for him. In asking for 'ocular proof' he shows himself ready to accept any ostensive behaviour on Iago's part without bothering to check its truth-conditions, happy with any figment that will put him out of this debilitating uncertainty. Iago's fictitious story — the product of 'honesty and love', he calls it — of Cassio's erotic dream of a clandestine love affair with Desdemona, with Iago as unwilling surrogate, is psychologically plausible (someone in that situation would indeed say 'let us be wary, let us hide our loves'), and marvellously graphic, convincing in its physical detail. It is yet more 'information', driving the multiplication effect up several more degrees until Othello reaches the deciding point of vowing revenge, joined by Iago in a hideous parody of love and service (3.3.455ff). In a sense Othello sees what he wants to see: but Iago has made him want to see it. The recipient of ostensive behaviour has to decode it, make inferences that relate it to what he already knows. Iago's genius is to set up situations in which Othello can make only the one inference expected of him. What is normally an intentional act of interpretation has been totally controlled by the hands of the manipulator.

Shakespeare's most brilliant, and most deliberate development of the inferential process implicit in human communication is the overhearing scene, after Othello has recovered from his collapse into madness. That fit was induced by Iago's insinuations about Cassio's 'lying' with Desdemona, a studied indirectness which he maintains by not answering Othello's direct question — 'Did he confess it?' — but giving a vague account of the millions of men who nightly 'draw with you' in being cuckolded. Iago's insinuations now have a tremendous effect on Othello's distraught mind, which has had one image of the world destroyed and is rapidly building another, prefabricated out of Iago's 'uncleanly apprehensions'. Having made Cassio withdraw for a while, Iago has Othello 'encave' himself, telling him to observe 'the gibes, and notable scorns' on Cassio's face:

> For I will make him tell the tale anew
> Where, how, how oft, how long ago and when

— a passage reminiscent of the training in rhetoric of asking yourself '*quis, quid, ubi*' and so forth in order to fill out the *copia* or stuff of your discourse: only Iago is using it sadistically, his verbosity postponing the delayed predicate —

> He hath and is again to cope your wife.
> I say, but mark his gestures.   (4.1.81ff)

As Iago well knows, gestures are inherently ambivalent, lacking the element of explicitness that language gives, thus offering more liberty for misinterpretation. To the audience he says, in another direct address cast in the future tense — by now we believe him capable of achieving any plan

— that he will in fact question Cassio about Bianca, a topic which always puts Cassio into 'an excess of laughter':

> As he shall smile, Othello shall go mad;
> And his unbookish jealousy must construe
> Poor Cassio's smiles, gestures, and light behaviours,
> Quite in the wrong.   (100ff)

The key word is 'construe', making Othello a schoolboy again, haltingly translating, guided by his teacher, making out the sense of a strange text according to his knowledge of grammatical rules. Earlier in this sequence Iago had described his own 'critical' nature in a series of self-accusations to suggest that perhaps his innate suspiciousness 'Shapes faults that are not'. Exploiting the normal reaction in talk-exchange, when one person offers the other a negative account of himself, a gesture of openness and good intent which the other person is meant to dismiss, Iago had urged Othello to 'take no notice' of

> one that so imperfectly conceits,
> . . . nor build yourself a trouble
> Out of his scattering and unsure observance.   (3.3.148ff)

That was a clever prediction, we realise in retrospect, of what Othello would do. Rejecting that false self-image, Othello has in effect accepted Iago's supposed 'observation' of Cassio and Desdemona, precisely built himself his own trouble out of these carefully scattered pieces of disinformation, organised them into a new cognitive set that destroys his whole world. He has really 'construed' both text and subtext along the invisible lines that Iago has laid down. So, in a bizarre reversal of the earlier scene where Iago had spied on Cassio's courtesy with Desdemona, giving us his obscene commentary in asides, now Othello spies on Cassio in an equally harmless context and gives us *his* commentary in asides, apparently triumphant but actually hopelessly deluded:

> Look how he laughs already!   (109)
> Now he denies it faintly, and laughs it out.   (112)
> Now he importunes him to tell it o'er.
> Go to, well said, well said . . .   (114)
> Iago beckons me; now he begins the story . . .   (131)
> Now he tells how she plucked him to my chamber. O, I see that
> nose of yours, but not that dog I shall throw it to. (140ff)

His ostension successful — to use the term in a far more complex sense than the linguistic model envisaged — Iago exultantly checks that his dupe has seen, and inferred, as intended:

> IAGO.   Did you perceive how he laughed at his vice?
> OTHELLO.   O Iago!

IAGO.   And did you see the handkerchief?
OTHELLO.   Was that mine?
IAGO.   Yours, by this hand . . .   (4.1.170ff)

While accepting the value of speech-act philosophy in its task of reconstructing the norms of social intercourse, and while drawing on pragmatics for its analysis of the process of interpretation, we see that these
models are much simpler than Shakespeare's. The remarkable fact about
this sustained perversion of the co-operation basic to all human communication is that while Iago hides his devices from Othello he displays
them openly to us. As A.D. Nuttall has suggested,[53] these scenes 'constitute
a spectacularly successful act of communication between Shakespeare and
the auditor/reader. We read off falsity as falsity, correctly.' As he adds,
Iago's deceptions derive mostly from his skills in simulation and dissimulation, but in addition 'Othello is especially disposed to trust Iago because
the other breathes an atmosphere of male, soldierly shrewdness, a world
which Othello feels he has successfully made his own', unlike the domestic
world of marriage or the social world of Venice. This is a valuable point, I
think, since it reminds us that understanding requires the existence both of
language and of a context of interpretation. The context here, within the
play's action, is military life, with its institutional attitudes valuing action
over contemplation, direct confrontation rather than deviousness. Iago is
so fatal to Othello precisely because he shares this context, knows what its
assumptions are, in which ways it can be put under pressure or exploited.
Iago's understanding of how honest people rely on the conventions of
truth-telling in communication is so sharp that he can insert himself into
them with perfect decorum yet violate them in every respect, in order to
fulfil his intentions of deceiving and destroying. When Othello, in his mad
fit, says 'It is not words that shakes me thus', he is saying more than he
knows. On the surface, it is only words, verbal structures having no
correspondence to reality; but on a deeper level the words express Iago's
intentionality. This is what 'shakes' him and everyone else in this play, an
intentionality that cannot bear not to fulfil itself in all its perverted energy
and resourcefulness. It is a fitting, if belated irony that Iago's plots are
exposed, his plans thwarted, by the freely expressed conflicting intentions
and values of a person that he had exploited and ignored: his wife.

CHAPTER TWO

Creator and Interpreters

Don't take it as a matter of course, but as a remarkable fact, that pictures and fictitious narratives give us pleasure, occupy our minds.

Wittgenstein[1]

The negative view of language that emerged in French thought during the 1960s and 70s was the culmination of one strand in the general upheaval of attitudes which characterised those years — in some areas, for some thinkers. Certainly that upheaval left its mark on the human sciences (theories of language, literature, philosophy, politics, anthropology), and some of its effects on Shakespeare studies can now be seen. But to anyone who uses libraries and bookshops, keeps an eye on publisher's lists, reads newspapers and journals (other than those of a specific party or group), talks to fellow-teachers and students — to such a person observing the whole spectrum of current intellectual activity it will be clear that the so-called 'critical revolution' was the work of a small group of writers, and has been followed up by a relatively small group of readers and publicists. The great majority of scholars, critics, book-reviewers, journalists, general readers, teachers, and students have remained unaffected by the forward march of critical theory, as it has advanced from Paris to Baltimore, and from New Haven to Cardiff.

The proportionally small number of people involved is not an argument for ignoring the various challenges to accepted attitudes, or for dismissing them with the response 'empty vessels make the most noise'. Ignoring the things you don't like won't make them go away, and refusal to take part in debate with theories that challenge your own merely exposes you to the charge that you cannot defend your theories, either because you're unaware that you have any, or because they are so feeble or contradictory as to be indefensible. (This charge now applies, in fact, to the exponents of Lacan, Derrida, Althusser *et Cie.*, who regularly ignore or dismiss any criticism as 'ignorant' or 'reactionary'.) In this chapter I want to give a reasoned defence of a theory of literature which has survived the 1960s revolt, and will continue to do so, since it actually functions as a theory, being derived from the object studied and having a genuine explanatory role. It has also produced some powerful analytical work from a number of different fields in recent years (philosophy of art, literary history, speech-act theory, discourse analysis), with an impressive convergence of thinking on the major issues of meaning, intention, interpretation, representation. The gap between this tradition, developing fruitfully in several directions, and the anti-systems, locked in their 60s configuration, grows wider every month.

On the one hand are those who see a work of literature as an organisation of words set down by an author at a specific point in time according to the expectations of a particular literary convention. (He may, of course, subvert these conventions, as Sterne does in *Tristram Shandy*, but to appreciate that novelist's wit we still need to know what he was subverting.) In fictional works, which give a representation of human beings interacting in situations and in ways not unlike life as we know it, our involvement is with the characters conceived of within their 'possible worlds'[2] as free agents, responsible for their own actions, towards whom we express reactions which are both ethical and emotional (love, hate, fear, disgust). To those who share this conception of a writer creating fictional worlds which can touch our emotions and moral feelings, reading works of literature is both an enjoyable and a serious activity to which they are prepared to devote a great deal of time, energy, substance. They believe that the experience will enrich but also disturb their lives, provoke them to reconsider human situations and reactions — including their own — and not necessarily leave them in a state of reassurance.[3] Works of art, this type of theorising holds, have a finite form, are delimited in time and structure, the best of them possessing a completeness which can be emotionally satisfying on a formal plane, although the feelings aroused during our experience of it may live on after the work is over. *Tristan und Isolde* produces in me a feeling of loss and waste that persists long after the performance ends; *Die Meistersinger* arouses a sense of euphoria even before it begins. These personal observations, trivial to everyone else, are meant to make the point that our experience of a work of art is complicated, involving aesthetic, ethical, psychological, philosophical responses.

On the other side are the exponents of 'radical literary theory', as they still call it, who reject virtually every concept or category that I have just used. The author as such does not exist, any more than the subject (individual) does. There can be no distinction between works of literature or other written forms since all are texts, all manifest the operation of textuality, which both shapes and constrains utterances. Discourse is an impersonal circulation of language, subject to contestation and appropriated by interested power groups. Language cannot refer to reality, works of literature by definition suffer from the same limitation. If *mimesis* or representation is rejected, then the notion of character must go, too. As Denis Donoghue defined 'graphireading', his name for the school of Derrida, Barthes and de Man, the exemplary stance is to 'put under the greatest possible stress such words as these: self, subject, author, imagination, story, history, and reference' (Donoghue 1981, p. 200).

Anyone who has followed these developments in contemporary literary theory is entitled to ask, 'What, then, are we left with?' The answer would seem to be: a collection of negativities, of positions or principles negated, evacuated, destroyed. No replacements have been erected, since no one 'at the cutting edge' of radical theory believes that any ground can be discovered on which firm theoretical structures can be built. John Ellis's account of the peculiarity of deconstruction, that it attacks accepted models without attempting to replace them, indeed preserves them as if to validate its own success (Ellis 1989, pp. 70–74) — a David, cast in lead, standing on the heads of a hundred Goliaths — can be applied to Current Literary Theory in general. It has rejected the extant system but has no replacement for it. In that sense it reminds me of Nietzsche's definition of the philosophical nihilist as one who 'is convinced that all that happens is meaningless and in vain; and that there ought not to be anything meaningless and in vain'.[4] So, in this interregnum, seated on the bare ground surrounded by ruins of his own making, the contemporary theorist may experience a sense of triumph, but may also be wondering what on earth to do next.

The situation in advanced literary theory today, if one were to accept all the radical proposals put forward by all the interest groups, would be a bit like the seventeenth-century response to Copernicus' destruction of a geocentric universe. As Donne described it in his *First Anniversary* (1611), the 'new Philosophy calls all in doubt', and men frantically seek new worlds in the universe because

> they see that this
> Is crumbled out againe to his Atomis.
> 'Tis all in pieces, all cohaerence gone;
> All just supply, and all Relation. . . .[5]

The attacks on established critical theory since the 1960s, however, do not amount to a Copernican revolution, for they offer no alternative model to replace what they have attacked. Theirs is an anti-system, wanting to annihilate every accepted notion, destroying whatever coherence the previous system had. But it does not constitute a true revolution of ideas, as Thomas Kuhn has described it, which depends on maintaining an 'essential tension' between the accepted consensus and those areas in which innovation is being pursued.[6] The successful scientist, Kuhn writes, 'must simultaneously display the characteristics of the traditionalist and of the iconoclast' (p. 227), for it is not violent opposition but 'the continuing attempt to elucidate a currently received tradition' which finally produces 'one of those shifts in fundamental theory' that make a scientific revolution possible. The accepted consensus arises out of a convergence of ideas and attitudes which defines a problem and focusses the energy of thought on it in a concerted way. Paradoxical though it may seem, 'work within a well-defined and deeply ingrained tradition seems more productive of tradition-shattering novelties than work in which no similarly convergent standards are involved' (p. 234). In the purely iconoclastic criticism that has reigned in some areas since the 1960s all traditions have been swept contemptuously aside, leaving not so much a *tabula rasa* as a ruin, or a ground so thoroughly devastated that (it is hoped) no one will build there again.

Yet, for all its polemical energy, the iconoclasts' attack on extant literary theory is both merely negative and poorly argued, indeed its success has come from readers being persuaded to accept polemic rather than argument, and to naïvely trust the polemicist. The uncritical acceptance of their anti-theories has derived from the credulity of their audience, its readiness to take at face value the iconoclast's description of the position that he is attacking. For instance, the reception of Derrida's work, Peter Dews observes, has been 'marked by an astonishingly casual and unquestioning acceptance of certain extremely condensed — not to say sloganistic — characterisations of the history of Western thought, as if this history could be dismissed through its reduction to a set of perfunctory dualisms' (Dews 1987, p. xv). The hundreds of articles that unquestioningly reproduce Derrida's polemic manifest a striking (sophisticated and well-informed though it imagines itself to be) credulity, which believes that just because a position has been questioned, the questioner must have a case, the position must have a weakness. So Frank Lentricchia observes that intentionality is 'a category long under attack in modern critical theory' (Lentricchia 1983, p. 115) — but, he might have added, one that has also had some powerful and cogent support from philosophers, linguists, and literary critics. Janel Mueller, introducing a special issue of *Modern Philology*, and therefore professionally obliged to demonstrate an awareness of current trends, records her feeling that many 'presuppositions about language use and language users . . . are deeply discredited at present. . . . In the wake of two decades of intense theorising', she feels, an atmosphere of 'skepticism' has been produced, largely by deconstruction, which is 'radically skeptical' with its 'aporias and indeterminacies . . .'.[7] But to many people unpersuaded by its programme or methods, deconstruction has displaced nothing, although it has certainly placed its most successful exponents in tenured positions. Universities that are anxious not to appear outmoded have no option but to give place to those who accuse them of being so. The fact that deconstructionist critics have jobs speaks much for the catholicity (or vulnerability) of the departments that have hired them, but it hardly means that language and its users are now being institutionally discredited, too.

In some ways the conquest has been too easy. Those who have been willing to concede crucial philosophical positions to their critics have had little notion of the meaning or value of what they abandoned. Those with a superficial knowledge are easily impressed, and easily converted. The vogue for post-structuralist theory had faded in France by the 1970s, giving way to the rise of 'nouvelle philosophie', a new interest in Kant, and a revival of phenomenology and hermeneutics, so bitterly traduced and travestied by the structuralists and their successors (Dews 1987, pp. xii–xiii), but it persists in America, especially. In 1986 Julia Kristeva, long-time associate of Philippe Sollers and the *Tel Quel* group, one of the most intelligent and knowledgeable survivors of that generation, commented on the continuing naïve acceptance in America of the polemical successes claimed by deconstruction:

> 'In America, the so-called deconstructionists think that, because ethics and history belong to metaphysics and because metaphysics is criticized by Heidegger or his French followers, ethics and history no longer exist.'

Lecturing in America, she added, '"somebody in the audience always asks why I speak about ethics and history when those notions already have been deconstructed. Not even the most dogmatic French deconstructionists ask such questions"' (*cit.* Lehman 1991, pp. 55–6).

Lest I be accused of anti-Americanism, let me take an example from nearer home to show that we ought not simply to believe iconoclasts when they claim to have destroyed some monument or other. F.R. Leavis, who disliked the largely unthinking endorsement of Milton in the 1920s as a major English poet, took 'the few critical asides' of T.S. Eliot and 'an acute page or two' by Middleton Murry as having constituted a decisive blow to his reputation, and began his chapter on Milton in *Revaluations* (1936) with the coolly triumphant words: 'Milton's dislodgement, in the past decade, after his two centuries of predominance, was effected with remarkably little fuss.' In the same year T.S. Eliot published a polemical essay on Milton, accusing him of 'having done damage to the English language from which it has not wholly recovered', and the dislodgement seemed complete. However, in 1947 Eliot publicly recanted,[8] and the status of Milton as a major English poet — on rather different grounds than those held by Robert Bridges, needless to say — now seems beyond question. Current Literary Theorists who think they have totally demolished character, or representation, or the author, may be surprised if they look again, to see that life goes on undisturbed by their intervention.

DESTRUCTIVE CRITICAL THEORIES

> I went to the Garden of Love
> And saw what I never had seen:
> A Chapel was built in the midst,
> Where I used to play on the green.
>
> And the gates of this Chapel were shut,
> And Thou shalt not, writ over the door —
> And Priests in black gowns were walking their rounds,
> And binding with briars my joys & desires.   Blake[9]

The 'intellectual origins' of European literary theory in the 1960s, Edward Said observes, were 'insurrectionary. The traditional university, the hegemony of determinism and positivism, the reification of ideological bourgeois "humanism", the rigid barriers between academic specialities', these were some of the targets which unified literary theory in attacking the status quo (Said 1983, p. 3). Similarly, Luc Ferry and Alain Renaut's study of La pensée 68, while denying that French philosophy of the 1960s can be summed up under that title, nevertheless presents May 1968 as the catalyst which precipitated many of the issues in that adversarial mode which continues to absorb so-called radical theorists in the 1990s. These include anti-humanism, which pronounced the 'death of man', and claimed that the autonomy of the subject was illusory; the theme of the end of philosophy; the dissolution of the idea of truth; the historicisation and relativisation of all categories, and a denial of universal values (Ferry and Renaut 1985, pp. 11–103). The thrust of this reaction against established ideas, established figures, was violently oppositional, not just qualifying but dismissing altogether previously respected figures in French thought: Descartes, Sartre, Merleau-Ponty. While historically understand-able, precisely its nature as a French reaction ought to have limited its value and relevance in other cultures. If, rejecting their own tradition, and rushing to find new authority figures in Marx, Nietzsche, Freud, Heidegger, one school of French thinkers reduced itself to 'the hyperbolic repetition of German philosophy' (ibid., p. 46), that is a reaction that English, German, or Italian philosophers, who start with other traditions, would find it hard to share. A philosopher who has never taken the Cartesian cogito as the centre and circumference of philosophical enquiry will hardly need to reject the concept of a subject so violently.

We must reconstruct the French cultural context to understand the forms that this reaction took, forms that are still at work (long after they have disappeared in France) in the English-speaking world. The extraordinary intellectual energies produced in Paris, which made it for so long the goal of all forward-looking intellectuals, were in many respects autocentric, preoccupied with their own traditions and not well informed of others. The fact that Derrida, for instance, oriented himself so strongly to domesticating German philosophy in France, meant that he was largely unaware of the developments in linguistics and the philosophy of language in America and England. As John Ellis has shown, ignorance of this tradition led to Derridian deconstruction presenting as an original critique (as of linguistic essentialism, for instance) a position which had long been worked out, with more detail and cogency, in the Anglo-Saxon world (Ellis 1989, pp. 37–8, 42–4, 142). The fact that so many English-speaking literary critics have taken Derrida's claims to innovation and iconoclasm at face value, in ignorance of their own native traditions, can only be explained by an uncritical acceptance of 'the new' which ranks in its passivity with the medieval deference to the auctoritas of virtually any written record. Ellis also observes that some of the literary targets that Barthes and others attacked were specifically French phenomena, such as the notion of an objective literary history as presented by an authority figure like Gustave Lanson (*ibid.*, pp. 83–6; Barthes 1972, pp. 256–7). One could add that a standardised national examination system (the Baccalauréat, Agrégation, CAPES), can only encourage a centralised corpus of authoritiative interpretations. But English and American critics, who have never been confronted with this degree of regimentation, hardly need to attack it so violently.

Understandable within a French context in the 1960s, many of the polemics of radical literary theory as translated into the Anglo-American world of the 1970s and 80s ('Say, heart, what doth the future bring?'), look distinctly odd. Their targets seem unreal, straw men, opinions that have been manufactured only to be attacked, only to have something to attack. One form taken by this polemic was to erect a binary opposition, in which category I represented some absurdly stupid or superficial point of view, to be mocked with withering scorn, and replaced by category II, in all respects superior, and which was recommended without being subjected to critical enquiry. This is an ancient debating technique, already brought to a high peak by Plato, as Chaïm Perelman, restorer of a rhetoric based on philosophical argumentation, showed so well.[10] In all such oppositions, as between 'appearance' (Term *I*) and 'reality' (Term *II*), it is the second term that provides the criterion, the unexamined norm to which value is attached in order to devalue the opposed pole (*I*), here seen as 'merely illusion and error' (pp. 416–17). But in fact the dichotomy begs a number of questions ('appearance' is in many ways a less problematic concept than 'reality'). All these dichotomies are meant to be accepted at face value, and those who use such pairs introduce them not as terms open to dis-cussion but as data, 'instruments that make it possible to structure the discourse in a manner that *appears objective*' (p. 422; my italics). But in fact they are designed to weight the discussion and to put one's interlocutor in the wrong. 'For in argumentation, what one person terms appearance is generally what was reality to someone else, or was confused with reality' (p. 424), so that to introduce the concept of error is 'to assert that there is a rule', which one's opponent is either ignorant of or has broken knowingly (p. 425). All such binary oppositions ultimately express the simple attitude of 'I'm right, you're wrong'.

The most persistent users of these excluding dichotomies have been the deconstructionists. Derrida deployed many such oppositions in order to privilege his own ideas and disqualify his opponents'. In *Of Grammatology*, for instance, he set 'linearity' in language in the disfavoured pole *I*, opposing itself (note the cunning formulation) to 'pluridimensionality': who would not prefer the latter? What Derrida mockingly described as linear thought (Term *I*, triumphing in the Enlightenment and in modern science) 'paralyses' and 'reduces' history; its pluridimensional converse (Term *II*) defeats successivity (Derrida 1976, pp. 85–7). At the end of his 1966 attack on structuralism Derrida placed in the inauspicious, left-hand category Rousseau (and by implication, Lévi-Strauss), nostalgia, guilt, origin, presence, man, humanism, metaphysics, ontotheology — the whole Derridian 'hit list'. (This mode of itemising what you hate resembles the *tabellae defixionum* or curse-tablets which practitioners of magic in classical antiquity employed to bring disaster on their enemies, inscribing their ill-wish on a sheet of lead and burying it in some gloomy spot, near graves and water.) On the other, right-hand or pre-eminent side, winging their way into the sun, their wings tinged with gold, Derrida placed Nietzsche (and by implication, Derrida too), play, and 'a world of signs . . . without origin' (Derrida 1978, p. 292). As several commentators observe, Derrida's dismissal of logocentrism as an illusion was intended to put all of Western philosophy into the Platonist dustbin, his system alone perceiving the true reality (Pavel 1989, p. 15; Butler 1984, p. 64). These claims to superior certainty can also take the form of crudely branding any system other than deconstruction as 'naïve objectivism' (Dews 1987, p. 11). Derrida's whole attack on the referential dimension of language as having only a secondary and derivative status emerged from his strategic handling of 'a simple opposition between identity and difference'. Yet, Peter Dews counters, 'nothing obliges us to accept Derrida's initial dichotomy', which would result in the perceived world being reduced to 'no more than a system of traces' (*ibid.*, p. 115). Dews sets us an example of independence, that crucial position in all serious intellectual exchange, it seems to me, of refusing to accept the terms in which an argument is framed if the effect will be to drive us into a corner. Coercive dichotomies are intended to do just that, trap you in a cul-de-sac from which you can only yearn after the illusory vista on the other side.

I draw attention to this sophistic trick since Current Literary Theory has made great use of it, paradoxical though it may seem, to call in question the possibility of interpretation. As M.H. Abrams was the first to point out, Derrida made absurdly high demands on the terms traditionally used 'to analyze the workings of language — terms such as *communication, context, intention, meaning*' — demanding that 'in order to communicate "a determinate content, an identifiable meaning", each of these words must signify a concept "that is unique, univocal, rigorously controllable"', and so forth. Abrams made the essential objection, that no words can meet 'these criteria of absolute fixity, purity and singularity', since language does not work like that. The 'finite set of words' in language, and the 'finite set of regularities' governing them, can, however, generate 'an unlimited variety of utterances adaptable to an unlimited diversity of circumstances . . .' (Abrams 1979, pp. 275–6). Instead of examining the actual workings of language, 'Derrida's all-or-none principle admits of no alternative: failing to meet absolute criteria which language cannot satisfy without ceasing to do its work, all spoken and written utterances . . . are deconstructable into semantic indeterminacy' (*ibid.*, p. 276). Several critics have commented on Derrida's habitual either-or, all-my-way-or-no-way type of argument,[11] which has resulted in one of the strangest developments in modern literary theory, the idea that since no interpretation can be single and un-ambivalent, there can be no interpretation. This claim, if it were true, would mean the collapse of all the varying critical approaches to literature, and indeed of literary theory as a whole. Although it has often been refuted, since the critical avant-garde maintains a protective silence over criticism that devastates its foundations, the counter-arguments may be worth rehearsing again.

Followers of Derrida have made great play with this false opposition, typically collapsing the poles into one shocking, attention-catching formula combining assertion and denial (this is another rhetorical figure, *synoeciosis*). So Paul de Man declared that 'Interpretation is nothing but the possibility of error' (de Man 1971, p. 141), a statement to which, Wendell Harris replied, 'the appropriate analogue would be that "food is nothing but the possibility of poison"' (Harris 1988, p. 160). In a later book de Man asserted that 'any narrative is primarily the allegory of its own reading' but at once added, 'the allegory of reading narrates the impossibility of reading' (de Man 1979, pp. 76–7). Whatever form the assertion took in de Man, its negation followed hard on its heels: 'allegorical narratives tell the story of the failure to read' (p. 205); 'the allegory of unreadability begins by making its pretext highly readable' (p. 216). In this book de Man's insistence on the collapse not just of reading but of meaning and reference reached an obsessive degree.[12] Less obsessively, but equally categorically, J. Hillis Miller asserted without exception that 'all reading is misreading' (Miller 1976c, p. 98), and that 'any reading can be shown to be a misreading on evidence drawn from the text itself' (Miller 1976b, p. 333). The contradiction within these positions — that we know that all reading is misreading from the evidence of Miller's own text, which claims to be the true reading — has not bothered this school of theorists. One of the most provocative-seeming statements in this line was Miller's claim that Shelley's *The Triumph of Life*

> can never be reduced to any 'univocal' reading . . . The poem, like all texts, is 'unreadable', if by 'readable' one means a single, definitive interpretation. (Miller 1979, p. 226)

To which Gerald Graff rightly objected that 'the concept of a "single" interpretation could not be legitimately maintained by anybody since it is nonsensical: there are no units for segmentary interpretations' into 'one' or 'many'. And since no one claims that a 'definitive' reading is possible, to parody such dogmatism by 'merely placing the prefix *un-* before the word' gets us nowhere: 'a third possibility is needed' (Graff 1980, p. 421), that vast 'excluded middle' ground so often ignored by contemporary critics.

As for the claim, parroted by so many popularisers of deconstruction, that 'all interpretation is misinterpretation', John Ellis has produced a definitive demolition, which I shall not attempt to summarise (Ellis 1989, pp. 97–112). But I select and endorse one point, that it is precisely the 'categorical form of the assertion [that] dooms it', making it either trivial or false:

> For example: either interpretation is never final (trivial) or it is always suspect to the same degree (false); either bias is a constant problem to watch in interpretation (trivial) or bias is always damaging to the same degree or in the same way (false). All the important theoretical issues involved in interpretation require . . . making distinctions between different cases. . . .

But any chance of contributing to the necessary process of differentiation is destroyed from the outset by 'the grandiose form of the categorical claim'. For Ellis the appropriate judgement on this proposition 'is not that it is wrong but that it is *empty*', having no 'theoretical content' (pp. 107–8). That judgement applies to many of the sweeping assertions made by current literary theory, seemingly exception-free, on closer inspection found to be hollow. Yet, as their reception proves, the confidence conveyed can be rhetorically effective in capturing and hypnotising the unwary reader. As Ernest Gellner has observed of Freudian psychoanalytic theory,

> Sheer confident assertion, in a world . . . in which no one of any sense has any grounds to be confident of either certainty or doubt, makes a certain impact. . . . The fact that the confidence is devoid of visible means of support hardly seems to diminish its authority. In fact, were its means of support visible, they could be subject to evaluation; and the assertion would have . . . conceded its own ordinary, human status — making its own contentions arguable, negotiable. . . . But bare, brazen, unnegotiated assertion, if skilfully presented, can have a kind of stark authority. (Gellner 1985, pp. 42–3)

Despite the deconstructionists' frequent assertions of scepticism and doubt, the mode they use to communicate their critique is just this dogmatic assertiveness. As we know so well from other contexts in life, outside the rarefied discourse of literary theory, not everyone who asserts their views confidently deserves to be believed.

THE 'DEATH OF THE AUTHOR' THESIS

Among the inherited notions that the 1960s iconoclasts tried to destroy was the figure of the author. They attacked not the existence of actual authors, such as 'Barthes', 'Foucault', 'Derrida', and 'Lacan', but the critical practice of invoking an author by working back from a book to the mind and hands that conceived it. They wished to disqualify such a move, stigmatise it as irrelevant to the true experience of reading. Two brief essays by Roland Barthes ('The death of the author') and Michel Foucault

('What is an author?'), published, appropriately enough, in 1968–69, document this attempt to banish the author from critical discourse. Both essays are much cited to this day, and are frequently reprinted in under-graduate anthologies of 'Modern Criticism and Theory' (e.g., Lodge 1988). Both typify, it seems to me, the simplifications and unargued assertions vitiating so much recent literary theory.

On one point we can agree with Barthes, in his complaint that the image of literature 'in ordinary culture is tyrannically centred on the author, his person, his life, his tastes, his passions', as we see from much literary journalism, interviews, television book-programmes (Barthes 1968a, p. 143). It is true that some journalists (fortunately, perhaps) do not go beyond this superficial concern with writers' lives. But at the same time serious discussion of literature has been going on in Europe and America for centuries, and it is simply false of Barthes to say that 'the *explanation* of a work is always sought in the man or woman who produced it'. The remedy, in any case, would be to direct readers away from literary tittle-tattle to more responsible criticism. For Barthes, however, the vulgarisation of critical discourse that he diagnosed became the pretext for abandoning the author altogether. He invoked Mallarmé as the first writer 'to substitute language itself' in place of the author, and he asserted that 'it is language which speaks, not the author; to write is . . . to reach that point where only language acts, "performs", and not "me"' (p. 143).

Displacing responsibility from the author to language itself seems now a rather desperate way of countering the journalistic tendency to bio-graphical gossip. Barthes attempted to justify it by briefly invoking linguistics, claiming that 'the whole of the enunciation is an empty pro-cess', not needing 'the person of the interlocutors', for '*I* is nothing other than the instance saying *I*', that is, 'a "subject", not a "person"' (p. 145). Barthes was referring to the verbal category known as 'shifters' (or 'indexicals'), the personal pronouns *I* and *you*, for instance, which shift between the speakers engaged in conversation. But, as linguists always observe, shifters are essentially markers which serve as 'a function from context to individual by assigning values to variables for speaker, hearer, time and place of utterance, style or register, purpose of speech act', and so forth, a sequence in which the subject is in no sense 'empty'.[13] Barthes then switched his linguistic authorities, from Jakobson and Benveniste to Austin and Searle, claiming that in the modern age '*writing* can no longer designate an operation of recording, notation, representation', but is limited to what speech-act theorists classify as 'performative, a rare verbal form . . . in which the enunciation has no other content (contains no other proposition) than the act by which it is uttered . . .' (pp. 145–6). This is a savagely reductive conception of writing, but it is of course a travesty of speech-act theory, which distinguished a whole range of verbal actions, including all kinds of content and performing many different functions in conversation and society.[14]

Already we can see how these swiftly produced iconoclastic pronouncements collapsed complex issues into conveniently simple forms, skated over vital distinctions. The quickness of the hand is meant to deceive the eye. Barthes then employed the coercive dichotomy, offering a choice between two extreme positions as if these constituted all that could be thought or said, leaving out the many interesting and practicable alternatives in the middle ground. So Barthes declared:

> We know now that a text is not a line of words releasing a single 'theological' meaning (the 'message' of the Author-God) but a multidimensional space in which a variety of writings, none of them original, blend and clash. (p. 146)

There we are offered the 'choice' between the Ten Commandments, say, and a kind of soup or wash of texts deprived of originators or indeed originality. The first pole is unreal, to start with, for it is hard to imagine any text having a single meaning. To then parody the notion of an 'Author-God' by labelling such a meaning 'theological' only reminds us that in fact a vast amount of exegesis, quite properly, has been expended on sacred texts in many religions. The second pole of the opposition is the most drastic conceivable alternative, abolishing authors and even the notion of a creatively original work. As one critic has observed, 'the assumption that the context of discourse is nothing but other discourse . . . seals language off from all extralinguistic experience' (Harris 1988, p. 58): but it is only an assumption. In place of reality, authors, and creative work Barthes offers us 'multi-dimensional space', an impressive-sounding but tautologous concept (space is by definition pluri-dimensional, until delimited). The reader who wishes to preserve the power of thinking and independent judgement can only say at this point 'No: I refuse these alternatives. Give me a bigger range of choice.'

But Barthes, instead, pressed on with his preferred option, defining the text — any text, it would seem, produced anywhere at any time by any person — as 'a tissue of quotations drawn from the innumerable centres of culture'. This is to insinuate a further extreme but unargued claim, that a text is really made up out of other texts. Barthes then explicitly denied the writer — any writer — the very possibility of creativity: 'the writer can only imitate a gesture that is always anterior, never original. His only power is to mix writings', those produced by earlier writers, all of whom suffered from the same mistaken idea, each thinking he could '*express himself*'. However, Barthes belittlingly added, the 'inner "thing"' thus expressed 'is itself *only* a ready-formed dictionary, its words *only* explainable through other words, and so on indefinitely . . .' (p. 146; my italics). Such a ruthlessly reductive form of argument — a variant on Derrida's chain of signs stretching meaninglessly to infinity — would deny the possibility of a work of literature having an autonomous and determinate meaning at any stage of communication (however trivial). In this way it would lay waste any possibility of individual expression, and ultimately, perhaps, of individual experience. But of course it is ignorant of the simple but fundamental property of language described by M.A.K. Halliday as its 'textual function', language's ability to create a text through which the speaker can 'make what he says operational' in the speech context, as distinct from being 'merely citational, like lists of words in a dictionary' (Halliday 1975, p. 17).

Not really concerned with reflecting how language works, Barthes continued his polemic with an unholy alliance between Oscar Wilde's crisp paradox, that life imitates art, and Derrida's différance, to produce the dismissive statement that 'life never does more than imitate the book, and the book itself is only a tissue of signs, an imitation that is lost, infinitely deferred' (p. 147; my italics). By this mode of argument (if it deserves to be given that name) any book can be reduced to a tissue of quotations from other books — a notion popularised about this time as 'intertextuality' — and writers can be similarly reduced to conduits transmitting each others' ideas. Indeed, Barthes actually brought all writers down to the level of two of the most hopelessly unoriginal characters in the whole of European literature, 'Bouvard et Pécuchet, those eternal copyists', Flaubert's devastating and extreme parody of people utterly lacking invention, originality, persistence, or judgement. With this massively reductive account of authors and texts, Barthes wished to destroy critics, too, and with them the whole possibility of interpretation:

> Once the Author is removed, the claim to decipher a text becomes quite futile. To give a text an Author is to impose a limit on that text, to furnish it with a final signified, to close the writing. Such a conception suits criticism very well . . . (p. 147)

By abolishing the author Barthes hoped to put the critic out of business, setting in motion a 'truly revolutionary' or 'anti-theological' activity, that of 'refusing to assign a "secret", an ultimate meaning', since 'to refuse to fix meaning is, in the end, to refuse God and his hypostases — reason, science, law'. In 1968 everything could be rejected — verbally, at least.

The iconoclast's mind and pen range so swiftly over his targets in seven short pages that the reader barely has time to voice an objection. But should we feel like taking Barthes seriously as a figure from the culture of a rapidly fading era then we would have to say that 'to give a text an Author' — to pursue his fiction that it doesn't otherwise have one — is in no sense to 'impose a limit' on it, or close it off. This is precisely the point at which the reading experience begins, when the book that has been created by its author — shaped over a period of time by an incomputable series of artistic decisions, each choice involving many rejections — becomes available to its audience. Competence in reading varies enormously, obviously enough, along a spectrum ranging from the brilliantly perceptive to the crassly unaware. To Barthes, however, the reader was simply a focal point in which the 'multiple writings' that make up the text cohere — in 'the reader', he insisted, 'not, as was hitherto said, the author' ('hitherto' meaning 'in the whole of literary criticism until me'). The reader, however (in the orthodoxy of that time), turns out to be not a person but 'the space on which all the quotations that make up a writing are inscribed', a remarkably passive, depersonalised, and incoherent series of metaphors. (It will be difficult to 'inscribe' quotations on a 'space', since you would have nothing solid to write on.) Pursuing his ruthlessly reductive argument to its ultimate position, Barthes issued another prohibition ('Thou shalt not, writ over the door'). The writer's relationship with the reader

> cannot any longer be personal: the reader is without history, biography, psychology; he is simply that *someone* who holds together in a single field all the traces by which the written text is constituted. (p. 148)

Barthes ended his devastation of the whole tradition of literary criticism since Aristotle with another facile dichotomy: now 'we know that to give writing its future . . . the birth of the reader must be at the cost of the death of the Author' (*ibid.*). But who or what is this reader, slouching towards Paris to be born, 'without history, biography, psychology'? Here the recommended pole of the dichotomy seems to be wholly unreal, another consequence of that violent rejection by French intellectuals of the 1960s of what they derisively dubbed 'humanism'. Readers of a future age will be neither men nor women but androids, holding 'in a single field' (three-dimensional metaphor) the 'traces' or 'quotations' that constitute a text, written, presumably, on air.

*   *   *

Michel Foucault's treatment of this topic was more substantial, and included a historical dimension lacking in Barthes. However, like many of Foucault's essays in history, it was a highly personal interpretation which (knowingly or otherwise) simply ignored most of the counter-evidence. As a French historian of philosophy puts it, 'Foucault's historical works elude discussion, in that the gist of their argument remains indeterminate', belonging 'properly to the genre of fiction' (Descombes 1981, pp. 116–17). Foucault began by claiming that in pre-modern times, as in the Middle Ages, 'texts that we today call "literary" . . . were accepted, put into circulation, and valorised without any question about the identity of their author; their anonymity caused no difficulties . . .'. Texts that we would call scientific, however, were 'accepted as "true" only when marked with the name of their author' (Foucault 1969, pp. 202–203). Texts 'really began to have authors', he claimed, when 'authors became subject to punishment', their discourses having been 'transgressive', a point which Foucault did not specify but which the surrounding argument would put in the seventeenth and eighteenth centuries (*ibid.*). But this account is insufficient at every point. Writers in ancient Rome, to go no further back, are regularly described as having published their work at a specific date, and their names were firmly attached to their poems or histories. If we want an instance of a writer being punished for transgressing social, religious, or political norms then we can cite Ovid, banished by Augustus to the Black Sea in 8 AD for some still unknown offence. As for the Middle Ages, many texts remain anonymous, but they were still identified by their putative place of origin, the poet 'of Paris' or 'of Vienna', say. And there was no such distinction between literary and scientific texts as Foucault claims. Anyone familiar with medieval books of alchemy or astrology will know that equally fictitious or garbled names were attached as authors, especially in the textually hazardous Greco-Arabic-Latin transmission process (such as 'Picatrix').

The history, in other words, was invented in such a way as to support another thesis, involving one of Foucault's gross contrasts between past and present.[15] Following Barthes, it seems (although so many of these ideas were common property in 1960s Paris that they can hardly be individually assigned), Foucault celebrated contemporary writing (écriture) for having 'freed itself from the dimension of expression. Referring only to itself', écriture is 'an interplay of signs' which 'unfolds like a game', and so on (pp. 198–9). Having erected a completely mythical picture of imaginative literature as breaking with any notion of reference to a human world, real or imaginary, Foucault complained that 'modern literary criticism' still relied on the concept of an author to explain the 'presence of certain events in a work', to provide 'the principle of a certain unity of writing' which ignored contradictions in order to identify 'a particular source of expression' (p. 204). Critics practising such archaic procedures, Foucault objected, 'try to give this intelligible being' of an author 'a realistic status by discerning, in the individual', such qualities as motive, creativity, design. But, he asserted, 'these aspects of an individual which we designate as making him an author are only a projection . . . of the operations that we [we who? we critics? we readers?] force texts to undergo, the connections that we make, . . . the continuities that we recognize . . .' (p. 203). Now, it seems, it is the reader who makes or fashions the author. Foucault wished to deny future critics any such focal point, so — like many writers of his generation reacting against the phenomenology of Sartre and Merleau-Ponty — he went on to attack the notion of 'an originating subject', the by now (Paris, 1969) sufficiently discredited idea that a 'free subject' could 'activate the rules of a language from within and thus give rise to the designs which are properly its own' (p. 209). This idea being anathema, Foucault expressed the hope that 'as our society changes, . . . the author-function will disappear' (p. 210), proposing that the future critic (he or she still exists, then!) displace attention from the writer or creator to the 'type of discourse', thus 'depriving the subject . . . of its role as originator' and treating it (him? her? human gender seems to have disappeared) as 'a variable and complex function of discourse'. This pseudo-mathematical description (like the scientistic metaphors in Barthes, 'a multi-dimensional space', 'a tissue of signs', 'a single field') would replace the human attributes of language, reading and writing, with a de-humanised but completely vague entity or process. But, we must object, where does 'discourse' come from? Who produces or consumes it? Where (or what) are the readers? Who *recognises* it, even, so allowing it to circulate? This is a non-world, of non-beings, in which some unspecifiable agent(s) produce non-works in a form — 'discourse' — which remains an abstract and privileged category, never defined and never called in question.

In line with the whole oppositional thrust of the iconoclastic literary theory of the 60s, Foucault saw 'the traditional idea of the author' as a concept which needed to be 'entirely reversed'. Where previously the author had been considered 'the genial creator of a work', now 'the truth is quite the contrary', and — like Barthes — Foucault could only express it in negatives:

> the author is not an indefinite source of significations which fill a work; the author does not precede the works, he is a certain functional principle by which, in our culture, one limits, excludes, and chooses; in short, by which one impedes the free circulation, the free manipulation, the free composition, decomposition, and recomposition of fiction. (p. 209)

Foucault was a much tougher-minded writer than Barthes, who seems intellectually light-weight in comparison (if both more sensitive and more interesting in the long run), but this argument is no better founded. It is to create another unreal pole of a dichotomy to say that the author is 'not an indefinite source of significations', since no one with any sense would ever think he could be. A book is by definition a finite object, the product of choices and exclusions, whose range of meanings may be wide but is still limited. Significations are in any case produced by the reader. Secondly, Foucault's claim that 'the author does not precede the works' (typical, as we have seen, of the structuralists' rejection of language-as-expression for language-as-code), would imply that works of literature were self-authoring, acts of 'spontaneous creation', as it were, and that 'fiction' could circulate, compose, or even decompose, without any agent intervening. This is obviously absurd. And it is the height of paradox, verging on un-meaning, to say that the concept of the author 'impedes the free circulation . . . of fiction'. Various things, we can imagine, would impede the circulation of fiction or any other form of writing: totalitarian censorship, a paper-shortage, an electricity break-down. But surely the truth is 'quite the contrary': it is authors (and publishers, and readers) who create circulation in the first place. Readers thirty or more years later must judge for themselves whether they wish to take over this collection of ideas; to me they seem senseless, the mere product of a wish to reject or negate an existing system of concepts, carried to the absolute limit regardless of the incoherence that results. The whole case is built on a simple adversarial rhetoric, on one side 'impede, limit, exclude', on the other 'free . . . free . . . free'.

Foucault's treatment of these topics in *L'Archéologie du savoir* (1969) covered some of the same ground, defining the book as a multiple and fluid entity, 'caught up in a system of references to other books . . . : it is a node within a network', having an undecideable essence (Foucault 1972, pp. 23–5). The only unity that a book or an author's *oeuvre* can have is 'rhetorical' (pp. 116, 135), a term that Foucault intended as derogatory, and he ascribed to himself 'methodological rigour' in setting aside both these 'traditional unities' (p. 79). In this fuller discussion Foucault seemed at times willing to concede the notion of a subject or writer: 'As we know, there can be no signs without someone, or at least something [*sic*], to emit them. For a series of signs to exist, there must — in accordance with the system of causality — be an "author" or a transmitting authority' (p. 92). Experienced readers of Foucault will at once realise that if this is the case then any 'system of causality' will have to be abandoned, and indeed a few pages later this apparent concession is withdrawn. The speaking subject or author is now 'not in fact the cause, origin, or starting-point' of a sentence or larger discourse. That role 'is a particular, vacant place that may in fact be filled by different individuals', and 'instead of . . . maintaining itself as such throughout a text, a book, or an *oeuvre*, this place varies — or rather it is variable enough to be able either to persevere, unchanging, through several sentences, or to alter with each one' (p. 95). Yet, in inverting the *status quo ante* by a theoretical statement which constitutes itself by negation, Foucault once again lost all sense of reality. Where can we find a book in which the author changes with every sentence, or even after several sentences? This may happen in that party-game where the players write in turn a sentence or episode of a story on a piece of paper which is folded up before being passed on to the next, but it is hard to imagine any other instance. Theorising in a vacuum risks becoming ridiculous, and inverting a previous system does not necessarily produce a usable alternative.

In their iconoclastic phase Foucault and Barthes were ready to privilege their own highly artificial and synthetic notions of language *over and against* — so to speak, however unnatural it may seem — works of literature. In *S/Z* (1970) Barthes could dismissively describe the author as 'that somewhat decrepit deity of the old criticism' (Barthes 1974, p. 211), discredited all of two years earlier, and obviously fading fast. In an essay entitled 'From Work to Text' Barthes declared that recently a change had taken place 'in our conception of language and, consequently, of the literary work which owes at least its phenomenal existence to this same language' (Barthes 1971, p. 155). Thanks to the 'sliding or overturning of former categories', we could now contemplate 'a new object, . . . the *Text*' (p. 156). Barthes described this object by a series of propositions in which he attempted to ascribe all manner of positive attributes to the Text and to free it of any negative ones. Thus — negative pole — a mere 'work' (of literature, say) would be 'a fragment of substance, occupying a part of the space of books (in a library for example)', able to be displayed, seen, held in the hand (pp. 156–7). Transcending such mundane attributes, 'the Text' — positive pole — would be 'a methodological field', 'a process of demonstration', which 'only exists in the movement of a discourse', or rather, 'is experienced only in an activity of production' (p. 157). This extremely abstract concept seems to be another definition by negatives, its coherence lying only in its systematic contradiction of the dichotomy's other and lower pole. Whereas 'the work' is fathered by the author, and modern society has belatedly recognised the laws of copyright (Barthes's debt to Foucault is evident, as are other borrowings from Lacan and Derrida), 'the Text . . . reads without the inscription of the Father', can be 'read without the guarantee of its father' (p. 161). Having rejected God and his hypostases in the previous essay, Barthes now rejects the father, complementary acts in a culture based on Nietzsche and Freud.

*   *   *

Although given specific forms by Barthes and Foucault, with characteristically different emphases, the death of the author thesis was really the extension of another *locus communis* in French thought deriving from structuralism, the rejection of the subject as a locus of experience and evaluation which persisted in philosophy, in varying forms, from Descartes to phenomenology. In that comprehensively iconoclastic reaction led by Lévi-Strauss (who dismissed the work of Sartre and Merleau-Ponty as 'shopgirl's philosophy', too concerned with 'private preoccupations', whereas the philosopher's true mission was 'to understand being in relation to itself, and not in relation to oneself'),[16] the standpoint of subjective consciousness was subjected to withering attacks, being travestied and trivialised in the process (Dews 1987, pp. xii–xiv). Lévi-Strauss announced in 1962 — so 'unloosing the slogan of the decade' (Anderson 1983, p. 37) — that 'the ultimate goal of the human sciences [is] not to constitute but to dissolve man',[17] studying instead the 'anonymous thought' found in myth, that type of discourse from which, by definition, the subject of the enunciation has been eliminated. We have already seen how often Foucault's *Archéologie du savoir* invoked the state of anonymity as the norm for discourse. The widespread nature of what Luc Ferry and Alain Renaut call '*l'antihumanisme contemporain*' has been recognised and well documented,[18] and there is no need here to rehearse the movement from Foucault's prediction (in the late '60s) of the imminent disappearance of man, to his subsequent turn-round, less than a decade later, in which he formed the notion of writing a 'history of the subject', starting with a history of sexuality in six volumes (Ferry and Renaut 1985, pp. 148–57).

Nor do I need to spell out the parallel move in Barthes, from his doctrinaire rejection of the subject as 'a mere effect of language' to his rediscovery of the 'enjoying body [which] is also my *historical subject*' (Barthes 1976, p. 62). Lacan, similarly, attempted to retain the subject while demolishing consciousness, but as Manfred Frank's searching critique has shown, this attempt already presupposes consciousness (Frank 1989, pp. 287–316). Derrida, also, uttered the by now conventional diatribe against man and humanism (Ferry and Renaut 1985, pp. 19, 172–4), and in his later work went to flamboyant lengths to deny agency of the texts published under his name, a simultaneously sophisticated and naïve move, as two shrewd commentators observe. The fact that 'it is always a subject which *decides* to efface itself as subject', they add, is a comforting demonstration that 'subjectivity seems strangely capable of resisting the most methodical attempts to liquidate it' (*ibid.*, pp. 192–5). In Althusser too, as Chapter 7 will show, the rejected subject came back like a boomerang.

One result of this euthanasia of the subject might seem to be the paradoxical survival of thought in the void left by its disappearance (Frank 1989, p. 189). But every time the subject was abolished something had to be erected in its place, usually 'the instatement of the symbolic system itself, self-enacting and self-perpetuating, as a kind of meta-subject' (Dews 1987, p. 77). We may well ask 'whether the idea of a grounded centre of meaning . . . is overcome by excluding subjectivity as the unifying centre . . . or whether it reappears in disguised form' (Frank 1989, p. 53). In Lévi-Strauss the alternative to subjectivity was 'objectified thought and its mechanisms', or '*l'esprit humain*', a vast abstraction which was postulated by Lévi-Strauss as a speaking subject and puzzled over by everyone else. For Foucault's *Archéologie* (echoing Derrida), the goal was to redeploy the history of thought 'in an anonymity on which no transcendental constitution would impose the form of subject', and so 'to cleanse it of all transcendental narcissism', thus freeing history from 'that circle of the lost origin . . .' (Foucault 1972, p. 203). In the *Discourse on Language* (1971) Foucault rejected the four notions that, he claimed, had hitherto 'dominated the history of ideas', namely 'signification, originality, unity, creation', preferring to place himself in a newly submissive position in which

the fundamental notions *now imposed upon us* are no longer those of consciousness and continuity (with their correlative problems of liberty and causality), nor are they those of sign and structure. They are notions, rather, of events and of series, with the group of notions linked to these, regularity, randomness, dependance, transformation. . . .[19] (Foucault 1972, p. 230; my italics)

Yet, despite Foucault's repeated rejection of the notions of meaning and sign (not to mention the far more radical rejection here of liberty and causality — this is truly to bind yourself to what he calls 'the rich uncertainty of disorder': *ibid.*, p. 76), it has been conclusively shown that Foucault's system 'appeals constantly to a theory of meaning', and accepts 'the inescapability of the world of signs' (Frank 1989, p. 386). As Schiller wrote, not all are free who mock their chains.

The concepts which were most often promoted to executive authority in place of the deposed and discredited subject and author were 'language' and 'textuality'. As historians of modern critical theory have noted (e.g., Fischer 1985, pp. 51–4, 64–6), many of its exponents quote with satisfaction pronouncements by Heidegger, for instance, that '"language itself speaks" and that we are that which is spoken by it', or by Gadamer that '"it is less true that the subject speaks language, than that it is what is spoken by language"' (*cit.* Frank 1989, pp. 6, 97). For Foucault, as we have seen, our interest in language should be 'at the level of the "it is said"...' (Foucault 1972, p. 122), a similar preference for the neutral or passive form. De Man, loyally passing on to American readers a decade later the news from Paris, asserted that 'we do not "possess" language in the same way that we can be said to possess natural properties. It would be just as proper or improper to say that "we" are a property of language...' (de Man 1979, p. 162).

This fashion of attributing to language the powers of agency, choice, or even deliberate inconsistency and incoherence, is a form of determinism which writers of many different persuasions have rejected. Wendell Harris, recording the tendency of some theorists to invoke Saussure while giving *langue* the completely un-Saussurian connotations of a Platonic ideal, outside daily human experience yet capable of acting on it, objected that 'language cannot *act* at all: it exists only as understood and used by human minds' (Harris 1988, p. 7). There may indeed be 'constant change within *langue*', but such change is brought about 'by human activity acting on language', not by 'language somehow acting on itself' (p. 8). Commenting on the move in French thought from Lévi-Strauss's notorious claim that '"myths operate in men's minds, without their being aware of the fact"' (*à leur insu*), to the wider view that language itself speaks, Harris writes that 'such hyperbolical statements result from speaking of discourse [*parole*] as if it were *langue*, and of reifying the abstraction of *langue*...' (p. 58). E.P. Thompson, discussing Althusser, identified behind his pseudo-Marxist categories the fashionable 60s 'notions of men and women (*except*, of course, select intellectuals), not thinking or acting, but being *thought* and being *performed*' (Thompson 1978, p. 148). Althusser, he objects (as we now know, this was a common tactic of the 60s system-builders), 'offers us a pseudo-choice: either we must say that there are no rules but only a swarm of "individuals", or we must say that the rules *game* the players', however absurd that formulation. In the jargon of structuralism, which denies that 'men and women remain as subjects of their history', the passive voice rules:

we are *structured* by social relations, *spoken* by pre-given linguistic structures, *thought* by ideologies, *dreamed* by myths, *gendered* by patriarchal sexual norms, *bonded* by affective obligations, *cultured* by *mentalités*, and *acted* by history's script. None of these ideas is, in origin, absurd, and some rest upon substantial additions to knowledge. But all slip, at a certain point, from sense to absurdity, and, in their sum, all arrive at a common terminus of unfreedom. (*ibid.*, p. 153)

For Thompson structuralism was 'the ultimate product of self-alienated reason . . . in which all human projects, endeavours, institutions, and even culture itself, appear to stand *outside* of men, to stand *against* men, as objective things, as the "Other" which, in its own turn, moves men around as things' (*ibid.*). Much of his polemic against Althusser and 'The Poverty of Theory' is directed against such determinism, and to restoring a concept of human beings as actively involved in making their history.

E.P. Thompson is an English left-wing historian; Manfred Frank a German philosopher of the hermeneutic school, equally outraged by deterministic systems which attempt to destroy 'the idea that the subject chooses its interpretation of the world sovereignly and by virtue of its own autarchy'. His response is a robust denial: 'On the contrary, language is no fate; it is spoken by *us*, and we are able to critically "question" it at any time'. Language is a virtuality, not a determinism forcing itself on individual language users (Frank 1989, pp. 6, 97). Indeed, the linguistic form that the determinists choose betrays the need for an alternative agency:

> Even the reified statement 'Language speaks itself', or even the systems-theoretical statement about the 'self-reflexivity of systems' has to employ reflexive pronouns that then hypostatize what was earlier considered a characteristic of the speaking subject as a characteristic of language or of the system itself. The subject that is crossed out in the position of the individual recurs in the position of a subject of the universal. (*ibid.*, p. 11)

Frank shows that the same recoil recurs, *à leur insu*, in those writers trying to erase the subject, a conclusion reached by many historians of structuralism and after.[20]

Textuality, the other substitute for the subject or author, has been elevated by some theorists to a kind of universal status, the mode-of-existence for all written communication, a concept intended to level out any distinction between literature and non-literature, and inevitably resulting in a dehumanising of discourse (Abrams 1979, pp. 269–70). Edward Said has bitterly criticised the post-structuralists' isolation of textuality from 'the circumstances, the events, the physical senses that made it possible and render it intelligible as the result of human work' (Said 1983, p. 4). Literary theory in the 1960s and 70s, he complains, abandoned the world and 'the existential actualities of human life, politics, societies, and events' in its search for aporias and paradoxes (*ibid.*, pp. 4–5), promoting a false idea of 'the limitlessness of interpretation' within a 'textual universe which has no connection with actuality'. But texts are in the world, Said rejoins, and 'place themselves . . . by soliciting the world's attention. Moreover, their manner of doing this is to place restraints upon what can be done with them interpretively' (*ibid.*, pp. 39–40). As his discussion of three modern writers shows, each conceives 'the text as supported by a discursive situation involving speaker and audience' (p. 40). Said's critique receives strong and independent support from the philosopher Peter Lamarque, performing a witty 'analytical autopsy' of 'The Death of the Author' thesis. Lamarque takes issue with the ideal shared by Barthes and Foucault, as indeed by so many writers in their milieu, of a notional 'free circulation' of discourse, of an *écriture* that is authorless, 'lacking in determinate meaning, . . . free of interpretative constraints'. Barthes's idea of 'a text as an explosion of unconstrained meaning', Lamarque writes, 'without origin and without purpose, is a theoretician's fiction' bearing no relation to the actual function of language.

> Writing, like speech, or any language 'performed', is inevitably, and properly conceived as purposive. To use language as meaningful discourse is to perform speech acts; to understand discourse is, minimally, to grasp what speech acts are performed. Barthes's view of *écriture* and of texts tries to abstract language from the very function that gives it life. (Lamarque 1990, p. 330)

Similarly with Foucault's belief that there is an intrinsic merit in the 'proliferation of meaning' without consideration of context or purpose, to which the appropriate vernacular reply might be that here again, 'more means less'. The whole concept of the death of the author has been finally put to rest by Seán Burke.[21]

As the iconoclasm of the French 1960s spread to the English-speaking world over the next decade, the pioneering cultural importers spreading the news of the author's demise eagerly applied it to the greatest of authors. J. Hillis Miller, having swallowed Derrida's claim that since the context surrounding a speech act 'can nowhere be fully identified or fully controlled' (as if that extremely formulated objection automatically implied that meaning could not be communicated), concluded that 'the uncertainty of context' dissolves other certainties, including

> the concept of authorizing authorship, or indeed of selfhood generally in the sense of an ultimate generative source for any act of language. There is not any 'Shakespeare himself'. 'Shakespeare' is an effect of the text, which depersonalizes, disunifies. (Miller 1977, p. 59)

Although Miller jocularly retracted the absolute implications of that statement (saying that the works of Shakespeare 'must have been written by a committee of geniuses'), it was soon taken up by other critics anxious to emulate the iconoclasm, producing a trend in Shakespeare studies that Richard Levin has analysed in a penetrating essay, 'The Poetics and Politics of Bardicide' (Levin 1990). The debts to Barthes and Foucault are embarrassingly obvious in such pronouncements (by Catherine Belsey in 1980) that ' "The Death of the Author . . . means the liberation of the text", allowing criticism "to release possible meanings" in the text, as if they were imprisoned there' (*cit.* Levin 1990, p. 502), or in similar calls by Jean Howard and Terry Eagleton to 'break free' from previous critical practices that 'still inhibit' us, in order to achieve 'the liberation of Shakespeare'. The general influence of the French iconoclasts is seen in Kathleen McLuskie's pronouncement in 1985 that 'she will be "refusing to construct an author behind the plays and paying attention instead to the . . . strategies which construct the plays' meanings" ' (p. 493). In effect, as Levin shows, the 'text' is given a 'new status as authorial surrogate', and acquires 'a repertoire of new activities', such as having 'a project' — 'the equivalent of the rejected concept of authorial intention, now introjected into the text' (p. 492). Readers familiar with Renaissance Latin tags may recall the much-quoted remark of Horace, *Naturam expelles furca, tamen usque recurret* (*Epistles*, I.x.24: 'You may drive out nature with a pitch-fork, yet she'll constantly return'). The text now 'has strategies' of its own, 'displaces' some issues, 'conceals' others, 'is silent' here, 'offers an imaginary resolution' there. It even 'gets nervous', as Levin wittily puts it, for 'with the Death of the Author the text acquires human emotions, as well as purposes', with *The Tempest* supposedly expressing guilt at promoting colonialism (p. 496 — a claim I discuss in Chapter 7).

The shift of emphasis from Author to Text has, in the end, achieved very little. The critics analysed by Levin belong mostly to the Marxist, feminist, and neo-Freudian schools, all of whom go about their business as before. The Marxists find the text concealing 'the contradictions in its own ideological project' (p. 493), but they are easily able to validate their own 'conceptions of ideology and class conflict' (p. 501). The neo-Freudian feminists talk less of concealment than of '*repression* or *suppression*, which is now attributed not to individual characters but to the text itself', often in the form of a 'feminine or maternal "subtext" that conflicts with, and often exposes the true nature of, the dominant patriarchy . . .' (p. 494). In other words, the text reveals 'precisely what the critics want to find there' (p. 497), and even though they have 'personified, reified, mystified, hypostatized, alterized, and demonized' the text (p. 498), these critics have just reasserted the validity of their own conceptual system. Far from liberating them to new readings, 'the same one meaning' is found over and over within the various schools. As Levin shows, independently endorsing the philosophically-oriented critiques by Manfred Frank and Peter Dews,

The rejection of the Author Function is not just a negation, the removal of a constraint, since it creates a hermeneutic vacuum that must be filled by something else that replaces authorial intention as the determinant of meaning. (p. 502)

Each school proposes its own 'universal law . . . that dictates what one must look for, and must find, in every play. The Death of the Author, then, has left these critics not more but less free . . .' (ibid.).

That judgment applies to many facets of iconoclastic literary theory since the 1960s, where a promised liberation has produced rather different effects. In another popular formulation, a 'system' was toppled and replaced by a 'game', which might seem a harmless enough move. Yet, as John Ellis has observed of Derrida's introduction of the wholly alien concept of 'play' into his account of Saussure's notion of difference, the idea of a 'limitless, indefinite play of differences' merely reduces Saussure, and language itself, to meaninglessness:

If terms can play (a) indiscriminately against all other terms and (b) endlessly and indeterminately rather than specifically, the result would be nothing — no specific contrasts that generate meaning, no significant differences forming systems, nothing identifiable or recognizable to anyone, hence no communication and no meaning at all. (Ellis 1989, p. 54)

By returning us 'from the finite system of a language to the infinite — to what there was before a language coalesced "arbitrary" decisions to reduce it to a finite system', Derrida 'has abolished language, not redefined it' (ibid.; also pp. 52–6, 61, 118–19). In opposition to, and perhaps ignorance of, the whole Chomskyan revolution in seeing language as rule-bound, a system of permitted and forbidden combinations that nevertheless allows the speaking subject full creativity, Derrida and his followers offer us their image of a game without rules, which, if taken literally (none of them ever did, of course), could only result in aimless or purposeless behaviour. The 'repressive' forces of language were attacked, to be replaced by 'the free play of signifiers', words without meaning, utterances without purpose, in theory at least indistinguishable from nonsense or babble. The rhetoric of liberation produced not an alternative and superior — more egalitarian, less coercive — system, but nothing, a vacuum.

READERS, AUTHORS, INTERPRETATIONS

My work shall not be an utter failure because it has the solid basis of a definite intention — first: and next because it is not an endless analysis of affected sentiments but in its essence it is action . . . action observed, felt and interpreted with an absolute truth to my sensations (which are the basis of art in literature).

Joseph Conrad[22]

In order to rescue the notion of interpretation from the depths to which some iconoclasts wish to consign it, one might begin with a counter-assertion, that 'all interpretations are provisional'. That is, interpretation is an activity performed by the subject experiencing a work of literature and resulting in a considered judgement which hopes to possess some good qualities — to be coherent, do justice to as many of the work's facets as it reasonably can within the time or space available, illuminate qualities not immediately visible or not properly seen by other interpreters — but never claims to be definitive. In this respect interpretation resembles perception itself, as Ernest Gellner defines it, which is never 'the innocent encounter of a pure mind with a naked object, and therefore capable of serving as an untainted foundation for an edifice of knowledge'. Perception is, rather, 'the encounter with some given element . . . by a corpus of knowledge acquired up to that time, but open to revision in future' (Gellner 1985, p. 91). An interpretation may contribute to an ongoing discussion but it does not attempt to end that discussion. Interpretation implies choice on two levels, as Christopher Butler has said: the text 'has multiple implications amongst which the interpreter chooses, and . . . the interpreter can also choose amongst' competing critical approaches (Butler 1984, p. x). The 'object of interpretation', another writer observes, 'is no automatic given, but a task that the interpreter sets himself. He decides what he wants to actualize', and which norm for interpretation he will use, in a 'free social and ethical act' (Hirsch 1967, pp. 25–6).

Interpretation may offer a choice of methods, but as a process it is unavoidable, starting with the simplest verbal exchanges, or reading how-ever elementary texts. Meaning is not something automatically given, conveyed without loss or surplus between transmitter and receiver. As E.D. Hirsch puts it, 'no meaning represented by a verbal sign is manifest; all meanings must be construed . . .' (Hirsch 1967, p. 61). Understanding is not always certain, interpretation never complete, since both depend, in Manfred Frank's words, on 'the hermeneutical imagination of the recipient'. For this reason 'interpretations of chains of signs or expressions can be *motivated*, but not . . . "mechanized"'. Abandoning 'the illusion of a primordially given, self-identical meaning of a text', we must recognise that 'already the signs that are interwoven *in* the utterance (or in *the* text) exist, i.e., acquire the status of signs, only by virtue of an interpretation' (Frank 1989, p. 442). The attribution of meaning, then, is not a definite or finite process but depends on, is subject to, 'the life experience, perspective, world-view, and linguistic competence of different speakers'. This does not mean that words or utterances have no meaning, however, only that

meaning is not objectively (i.e., extracommunicatively) decidable. In other words, meaning has to prove itself over and over again in social praxis (and without a final judicial authority to which it might appeal).

'To interpret' means nothing other than this. Something whose objective meaning (if there were such a meaning independent of communication) were known would not have to be interpreted. Only the fact that we can never *entirely* understand each other . . . makes it possible that we understand each other. (*ibid.*, p. 444)

The fact that interpretations remain without a final criterion, equally, does not mean that they 'are arbitrary or cannot be assimilated (*nicht nachvollziebar*). Interpretive hypotheses are always motivated . . .' (*ibid.*, p. 445).

Frank writes as an exponent of hermeneutical philosophy, which resembles phenomenology in basing itself 'on the side of the speaking subject', seeing 'speech as one means among others of corporal expression'. As several scholars remind us, phenomenology defined speech as 'a gesture, that is, a manner of "being in the world" through the body proper', a world in which the subject's linguistic or other gesture ' "delineates his own meaning" ' (Descombes 1981, p. 97). This emphasis on the interplay between speaker and hearer is in profound opposition to structuralist semiology, which, as we know, concerned itself solely with the receiver and with the code as something independent of human users (*ibid.*, pp. 92–100). While semiology has faded, its limitations all too evident, phenomenology and hermeneutics continue to develop, and remain of great value to anyone concerned with literature since they also take as axiomatic the existence of author, text, and reader in a communication cycle, with language as essentially a medium for the expression of meaning. A fruitful link between hermeneutics and literary criticism was made by E.D. Hirsch in his classic study of *Validity in Interpretation*, which I drew on in Chapter 1 for its analysis of meaning as involving such qualities as sharability, determinacy, and reproducibility. Hirsch made a useful distinction between 'meaning' and 'significance': '*Meaning* is that which is represented by a text; it is what the author meant by his use of a particular sign sequence; it is what the signs represent. *Significance*, on the other hand, names a relationship between that meaning and a person, or a conception, or a situation, or indeed anything imaginable' (Hirsch 1967, p. 8). Although an author wills a specific meaning in a conscious act, he 'almost always means more than he is aware of meaning, since he cannot explicitly pay attention to all the aspects of his meaning' (p. 48). Hirsch conceives of meaning as 'a willed' or 'shared type', an entity that has a boundary, and is therefore determinate and sharable, but which 'can always be represented by more than one instance', since its 'determining characteristics are common to all instances of the type' (pp. 49–50, 65). The author wills a meaning-type, but since it can contain a bundle of sub-meanings the reader is able to discover other meanings, including future ones.

As for significance, that is 'always "meaning-to", never "meaning-in".

Significance always entails a relationship between what is in a man's verbal meaning and what is outside it' (p. 63). Interpretation, then, must begin by understanding a text 'on its own terms', must be 'intrinsic' in that sense (p. 113). Such understanding is 'a *construction* of meaning', the necessary preliminary to interpretation, here defined as 'an *explanation* of meaning' (p. 136). Whereas understanding is 'cast only in its own terms', interpretation 'nearly always involves . . . discussing meaning in terms that are not native to the original text' (pp. 135–6), using 'categories and concepts' that are not necessarily found in the literary work (p. 136). The challenge to the interpreter, obviously enough, is to produce an interpretation which develops its own concepts and categories while remaining true to the meaning of the text. Invoking Husserl's concept of 'a "horizon", which may be defined as a system of typical expectations and probabilities', so that the 'explicit meanings' of a verbal intention 'are components in a total meaning which is bounded by a horizon' (p. 221), Hirsch defines the interpreter's aim as being 'to posit the author's horizon and carefully exclude his own accidental associations' (p. 222). This is an important point, given the anachronistic nature of much current Shakespeare criticism, from the imposition of modern socio-political expectations down to lexical misunderstandings (e.g. the misreadings of 'grope' and 'finger' discussed in Chapter 6 below).

One purpose of Hirsch's book, he writes, is to 'encourage a degree of methodological self-consciousness' (p. 169), particularly concerning the goal of interpretation. Unlike the natural sciences, with their claims for certainty, the aim of literary criticism is to achieve nothing higher than 'consensus — the winning of firmly grounded agreement that one set of conclusions is more probable than others' (p. ix). In interpretation 'certainty is always unattainable' (p. 164), and what the interpreter offers is an 'interpretive hypothesis', amounting to 'a probability judgment that is supported by evidence' (pp. 174–5, 180). All the interpretations of Shakespeare that I offer in this book are of this nature, citing evidence to support a hypothesis in the hope of reaching not certainty but a greater degree of probability than other interpretations discussed here. The interpreter's goal 'is simply this', Hirsch writes, 'to show that a given reading is more probable than others', and he suggests four criteria that must be met (p. 236). First 'the criterion of *legitimacy*', that is, a given reading should be possible 'within the public norms of the *langue* in which the text was composed'. Secondly, '*correspondence*: the reading must account for each linguistic component in the text', and can be judged improbable if it 'arbitrarily ignores . . . or inadequately accounts for them'. Thirdly, '*generic appropriateness*', not confusing a scientific essay with casual conversation, say. The final and decisive criterion is 'plausibility or *coherence*', which depends on 'the nature of the total meaning under consideration' (p. 237). Here again the argument concerns the most probable reading, and the interpreter must base his argument on a wide range of evidence: the work's date or period, its genre, the attitude of 'the speaking subject' (pp. 237–44). The goal of interpretation, appropriate to the humanities, is not verification but validation, which is always provisional, subject to revision, capable of improvement (pp. 170–1).

To return, strengthened by Hirsch's example, to the iconoclasts' dismissal of all interpretation as misinterpretation, we can now see the movement from interpretation to criticism as a rational activity. Any competent critic ought to be able to justify his behaviour, to give a coherent account of the assumptions about literature which he has brought to bear on a poem, novel, or play. He should be able to account for the kind of method he has used, and the relationship between the initial assumptions, the method, and the judgments that result. We all know that, from the basic nature of perception up to carefully constructed arguments, the assumptions that we make control what we are able to see, and that the type of question we ask will open up one issue but close off others. Some critics cannot or will not discuss any of these matters, as F.R. Leavis notoriously refused René Wellek's challenge to do so, a refusal that I have always taken as a sign of weakness.[23] To me it seems reasonable to expect a critic to be aware of both critical principles and practice, just as we expect him to be able to provide evidence for his interpretation. Reference to the text is crucial in arguments which aspire to probability, since a rival interpretation will either cite other passages or submit the passages already cited to a different interpretation. I am not making the naïve suggestion that reference to the text will automatically settle a dispute (as Leavis did so unfortunately in his attack on Bradley's interpretation of *Othello*),[24] merely reiterating the point that interpretation is a two-way activity between text and reader, and that an interpretative construct can win more, or less agreement at various points in history, but will never be final, or definitive.

The starting point for interpretation until very recently has been the assumption that a literary work constitutes, or at least aspires to be a unity, a coherent whole. This idea, too, fell into disfavour among Paris iconoclasts. Roland Barthes, restlessness embodied, was one of the first to abandon the notion of literature as a coherent activity. In an essay of 1955 he praised a novel by Robbe-Grillet as existing 'in that very narrow zone . . . where literature unavailingly tries to destroy itself, and apprehends itself in one and the same movement, destroying and destroyed' (Barthes 1972, p. 57). Never slow to widen a judgment on one writer to embrace the whole of a period (a trick imitated by de Man), Barthes pronounced that 'in our present social circumstances . . . literature can exist only as the figure of its own problem, self-pursuing, self-scourging' (*ibid.*, p. 58). Over the last hundred years, Barthes repeated in 1959, from Flaubert to Robbe-Grillet, an 'interrogation' had been going on 'in that asymptotic zone where literature appears to destroy itself as a language object without destroying itself as a metalanguage, and where the metalanguage's quest is

defined at the last possible moment as a new language object' (p. 98).
Here, as so often, Barthes reduces literature to the level of language, 'a
language, subject, like any other, to logical distinction' (p. 97), before
disabling it in one or other key function.

In his essays of the early 1960s the main literary function that Barthes
attacked was meaning. Literature, he declared in 1960, 'is at bottom a
tautological activity', a 'narcissistic activity' that starts by interrogating the
world but 'becomes its own end': 'the author rediscovers the world' in his
writing but in a process of 'perpetual inconclusiveness', an 'alien world'
which literature represents 'as a question — never, finally, as an answer'
(pp. 144–5). The influence of structuralism, and its imperialistic aggression towards other theories of language, is evident in the generalising
deduction that follows: 'Language is neither an instrument nor a vehicle:
it is a structure' (p. 145). Lévi-Strauss, with his penchant for binary
categories, may have inspired the dichotomy Barthes then made between
author and writer. The non-creative 'writer' (Term I) 'is a "transitive"
man, he posits a goal (to give evidence, to explain, to instruct), of which
language is merely a means . . . an instrument of communication'. The
'writer' uses language in institutions which are not primarily concerned
with language: 'the university, scientific and scholarly research, politics,
etc.', using language naïvely to resolve an ambiguity, making it 'a simple
vehicle, its nature as . . . merchandise transferred to the project of which it
is instrument'. The 'author', by contrast (Term II), novelist, poet or
dramatist, 'knows that his language, intransitive by choice and by labor,
inaugurates an ambiguity', offering itself as a question, 'a monumental
silence to be deciphered' (pp. 147–8). Transitivity, that fundamental
property of language (as Halliday defined it) to convey 'the experience of
process in the external world', with its basic categories of actor, process,
goal, is thus granted the critic but denied the creative writer: 'for the
author, to *write* is an intransitive verb' (p. 145); or again, 'to write is either
to project or to terminate, but never to "express"; between beginning and
end, a link is missing, which may yet pass for essential, the link of the
work itself' (p. xiii). True to type as iconoclast (Derrida learned from
him), Barthes only used the metaphor of a communicative link in order to
subvert it: 'The texts which follow are like the links of a chain of meaning,
but this chain is unattached' (p. xi).

Developing his hostility towards the notions of literature as either a
coherent and meaningful utterance or as a representation of reality, its
language never able to function as 'a vehicle of "thought"', doctrine or
evidence ('by identifying himself with language, the author loses all claim
to truth': *ibid.*), Barthes increasingly saw literature as a non-meaning, non-
communication. The 'entire art' of Robbe-Grillet, he declared in 1962,
consists in 'disappointing meaning precisely when he makes it possible' (p.
200). Jumping to generalisation again, Barthes affirmed that 'all literature'
posed the question, 'what does the world signify?', but it merely recorded

'this question minus its answer' (p. 202), and he looked forward to the day
when it would 'be possible to describe all literature as the art of disappointment, of frustration' (p. 203). In formulae that de Man was to take over,
Barthes stated that literature 'at one and the same time designates and
keeps silent' (p. 204); the literary work 'offers itself to the reader as an
avowed signifying system yet withholds itself from him as a signified object'
(p. 259). Diagnosing in 1963 this fundamental split between purpose and
effect — denying transitivity — Barthes saw the functioning of literature to
be a 'disappointment of meaning', 'undermining . . . assured meanings' yet
providing no alternatives, 'simultaneously an insistent proposition of
meaning and a stubbornly fugitive meaning' (*ibid.*). All literature, from
Horace to Prévert, is both 'the institution and the "disappointment" of
meaning, . . . a system of meaning at once posited and unfulfilled' (p. 269).

Basing himself on the *nouveau roman* of Robbe-Grillet — his Parisian
parochialism nowhere more glaring when we consider what a powerful
instrument the novel became at this time in Latin America for the representation and criticism of social and political reality — Barthes developed
his theory of the dysfunctioning of literature as a source of meaning by
such categorical assertions, not attempting anything like detailed analysis,
relying on formulae and slogans. Whether, in wishing to frustrate one of
the traditional attributes of literature, Barthes was original or merely a
symptom of a climatic shift, must await a more detailed history. But his
image of literature as in some basic way divided against itself was embodied
by others at this time in methods of interpretation designed to demonstrate
the incoherence of all texts. One such was Derrida's technique of deconstruction (to be considered in Chapter 3). Another was the Freudian
fashion in Paris of the 50s and 60s, from Lacan and Derrida to the
Althusserian Macherey (see Chapter 7), of applying the psychoanalytic
method of 'symptomatic reading', which looks for absences or contradictions that undermine a patient's utterance or a literary work's apparent
meaning. Yet, as several commentators observe, the *soi-disant* avant-garde's
search for incoherence is an *a priori* expectation which is somewhat perverse. As John Reichert has judged, the search for incoherence in texts is
as odd as if one were to choose 'one hypothesis over another on the ground
of its greater inconsistency', or because it accounted for 'fewer of the facts
that we want to explain', or was 'unnecessarily complicated' (*cit.* Harris
1988, p. 70). This is to deny the possibility of interpretation from the
outset.

More damagingly, even, the expectation of incoherence runs counter to
literary theory historically considered, which regularly emphasised the need
for a writer to unify his work in style, subject-matter, and construction. To
give only one example, the opening of Horace's *Ars poetica*, a key text in
European literary theory from the fifteenth to the eighteenth centuries,
considered the ridiculous idea of a painter producing a picture which combined 'a horse's neck with a human head', clothing 'a miscellaneous

collection with various kinds of feathers, so that what started out at the top as a beautiful woman ended in a hideously ugly fish'. Horace argued from this analogy that 'a book whose different features are made up at random like a sick man's dreams, with no unified form to have a head or tail, is exactly like that picture' (1–8). In Renaissance literary theory the demand for unity was met by the complementary demand for variety: but no-one before 1960 expected incoherence! This is another iconoclastic attitude whose date is out.

The process of reading resembles the general mental operation of trying to make sense of the reality perceived by our senses. As several studies of reading have shown, in this activity the mind tries to find cohesion in a text, is prepared to make numerous redefinitions of what it has read in order to achieve that goal, and only when frustrated recognises incoherence (Butler 1984, pp. 4–6; Harris 1988, pp. 50–51, 68–70). The linguistic criteria for cohesiveness, syntactical and lexical, are not enough, as Wendell Harris has shown in his book *Interpretive Acts. In Search of Meaning*. There must also be an internal coherence relating 'the content of the sentences which make up the discourse' to each other, according to conventional patterns of organisation. However, that internal coherence turns out to be 'inseparable from intelligible relationships to external patterns of organization and sets of experientially understood relationships' (Harris 1988, p. 53).

Harris draws on discourse analysis, which began to develop in the 1970s and 80s (another new development in the humanities ignored by Current Literary Theory, clinging to its relics of 60s Paris), for the insight that understanding an utterance presupposes 'knowledge and a process that is interactional, situational, and strategic'. The hearer or reader takes into consideration the situation in which discourse appears, assumes intentions and purposes in the utterer, and reaches understanding 'by means of tentative interpretations that are matched and rematched against experiential knowledge' (*ibid.*, pp. 53–4). Harris's discussion extends the account of implicature and inference that I gave in Chapter 1 into the area of literary interpretation. The author's intentions, he argues, are important, whatever the post-structuralist dogma about their absence from the text. 'Of course authors are not present in their texts, but all sorts of clues as to their intentions are', so that 'to try to regard a text as embodying no authorial intent requires us to regard it as having no author at all', a pretence that cannot be maintained for long (p. 60). The criteria which the reader uses for judging the probably applicable contexts which the author intends are 'consistency' and 'unity', which Harris subsumes under the term 'consonance' (p. 68). Both speech-act theory and discourse analysis, he shows, converge in agreement on some fundamental principles, namely that

interpretation requires the assumption of (1) knowledge, both immediate and general, shared between the formulator of the discourse and the interpreter, (2) that the formulator intends a meaning that is to be understood within that shared context, and (3) that the pursuit of coherence (consonance) is essential to the pursuit of meaning. (pp. 54–5)

Drawing on the well-established fact that 'readers will always seek some explanation for the total pattern of a work, or indeed of any set of words that they believe to be intended as a connected utterance' (p. 69), Harris invokes Grice's Co-operative Principle to suggest that in reading 'we seek a consistent interpretation because we assume that we and the author share certain assumptions about the communication of meaning' (p. 70). Harris agrees with Hirsch that all interpretation of the author's intention rests on probability, not certainty (pp. 91, 160), and concedes, with Grice, that we may fail 'to recognize a crucial instance of implicature because we do not possess certain elements of knowledge or awareness that the author expected'. However, he points out, 'the direction in which implicatures are resolved is often indicated by *several* elements of the surrounding context', and a misinterpretation at one stage can be corrected in the light of further reading (p. 71). It is a common experience that a later passage in a book helps us to grasp something that we had not properly understood before.

Developing the principle that '*all uses of language require interpretation, and interpretation is possible only within shared contexts*' (p. 72), Wendell Harris argues that 'the most pervasive dimension of context' is a 'knowledge of reality', which interpreters often take for granted (p. 78). The most 'pedestrian of situations', as he puts it, such as cashing a cheque or filling up a car, 'carries with it a congeries of presuppositions and related bits of knowledge' (p. 110). We bring all our knowledge of the operation of the world with us to the reading of literature, and 'unless we are told otherwise, we interpret discourse on the assumption that the world is the world we know' (*ibid.*). Attacking eleven currently fashionable fallacies in literary theory (pp. 162–3), Harris lays down as a first interpretive principle that all discourse assumes the existence of 'a "brute" reality', even though 'we can never get outside or beyond that interaction of sense reports, language, and experience we call thought' (p. 157). It is true that 'our conceptualization of reality is a fabric of conventions, but these conventions have been called into being by the interaction of human purpose and an insistent physical reality' (*ibid.*). The conventionalities so developed cannot simply be detached as such from reality, or used to deny the existence of reality.

Another important principle, arising from this (and one which recalls Halliday's account of a child's language-learning), is that 'words are always used (uttered or written) in relation to a set of contexts' which can be described in or influenced by language, 'but most of which require the existence of extralinguistic objects, feelings, and institutions' (p. 158). Since discourse 'occurs in a complicated and interactive environment or context', then, as we know from speech-act theory and pragmatics, meaning depends on a context assumed by the author and reconstructed by the reader. The expectation of consonance turns out to be functional in the whole communication of meaning (which means that the iconoclasts' preference for incoherence is actually parasitic on meaning as communicated). As Harris puts it,

> That authors intend consonance of discourse as the means of expressing their intended meanings and that readers will attempt to discover the intended meaning by seeking consonance in their reconstructions can only be assumptions, but they are constitutive assumptions: they constitute the possibility of meaning by defining it. (*ibid.*)

Harris deduces from his argument two basic principles for interpretation. First, 'that an author's intended meaning *can* be understood with reasonable probability and accuracy, but only through knowledge of as much of the context assumed by the author as possible' — which means that 'interpretation requires knowledge of historical events, cultural attitudes, linguistic usages, and biographical fact' (p. 168). The unthinking anachronism of much current Shakespeare criticism stands condemned. Secondly, 'that multiple analyses of any discourse are not only possible but may be of great value' (p. 169). There can be no single, correct interpretation, however vociferous its proponents may be.

The way in which we seek for, and discover, cohesion in literary texts has been well described by the Danish scholar S.H. Olsen in a book called *The Structure of Literary Understanding*. (I am deliberately quoting a wide range of contemporary literary theories to show that Current Literary Theory, as commonly defined by some of its exponents, and by some of their publishers, is a limited, derivative undertaking which has already closed down most of the interesting and complex issues.) Olsen argues that reading a literary work involves the ability to recognise formal features — episodes involving contrasts or parallels — and to judge how they affect the work's overall meaning and our response to it (Olsen 1978, p. 14). The experienced reader tries to discover the structure of a complex work by dividing it into parts and interrelating these parts or segments into a pattern. His aim in singling out a segment is 'to determine the *artistic significance* or *purpose* he believes this passage to have in the context of the work' (*ibid.*, p. 82). Interpreting a text, we place each segment into one or more descriptive categories, gradually interrelating the descriptions by a 'process of *redescription*' which ultimately produces an 'explanatory grid of concepts', covering the whole work and relating different parts to each other (*ibid.*, p. 83). Although that may sound forbiddingly technical, redescription is in fact the activity all readers perform to make sense of a literary work, from a brief lyric to a large novel: 'the construction of a web of concepts which the reader uses to interpret the work is a necessary condition of getting aesthetic satisfaction from it' (*ibid.*, p. 89) — or not, as the case may be.

Olsen suggests five criteria (overlapping with Hirsch's four) by which we can 'judge interpretations: completeness, correctness, comprehensiveness, consistency, and discrimination' (p. 126). Anyone who compares different critical accounts of a novel or play will see that some can be remarkably comprehensive, leaving out relatively little of the text, showing how the parts cohere; others deal with a small segment, or from a limited viewpoint. Although Olsen speaks of evaluating interpretations he believes that evaluating a literary work is a separate activity, a 'second-order judgement', made only as a recommendation (p. 168). To me, however, the act of description already implies a process of evaluation, since the very terms that we use to analyse works of literature are not value-free (and are none the worse for that). Still, I welcome his emphasis in a later book (optimistically entitled *The End of Literary Theory*), in opposition to the dehumanising systems of Foucault and others, that 'literary practice is a human practice defining and serving human goals and purposes. Evaluation, both in the form of appreciation and . . . value-judgements, is at the heart of this practice' (Olsen 1987, p. 155).

In defending the possibility of interpretation Olsen joins an increasing number of contemporary thinkers who accept the notion of human intentionality as fundamental. In his version of speech-act theory a work of literature is the result of 'intentional behaviour . . . directed at some response in the receiver', who attributes an intention to the producer (Olsen 1978, p. 5). An intentional (or 'purposive') theory stresses 'the central role of the reader's/author's attitude, feelings or intentions in a description of the aesthetic properties of a literary work' (*ibid.*, pp. 6–7). Conceiving a novel or play as the product of intentional action does not involve us in trying to discover the writer's intentions other than those discernible by the very existence of the work (p. 49). Rather, the concept of intentionality brings with it the notion of literature as an institution — an ongoing social activity — depending on 'a framework of assumptions, concepts and practices' which the reader applies to literary texts, whether aware of them or not. Where some people today think of theory as a self-sustaining activity unrelated to the experience of reading, Olsen sees the function of literary theory as being 'to provide an account of the logic of these practices and judgements which the reader makes about the literary work' (p. 23). Since, according to speech-act theory, utterances are purposive, intended to have consequences (pp. 50–4), the author of a literary work commits himself to having certain aesthetic intentions, as realised in the literary work,[25] which 'differs from other texts in its capacity to fill a certain role in a community of readers: a role defined by concepts and practices which the readers master' (p. 82). The role played by literature is to be 'a cultural value', experienced for its own sake (Olsen 1987, p. 26). Whereas a speech-utterance aims at the primary effect of securing uptake only as a means to a further effect, a literary work is 'a text where the interest is only in interpretation and not in use' (*ibid.*, p. 39).

While I agree that works of literature are meant to be enjoyed, are different in kind from factual hand-books, say, and have uses prescribed by the community (a point well argued in Ellis 1974), I shall argue in the next section that their primary function is to make possible the games of make-believe that we perform as readers.

Olsen's account of interpretation, like those cited earlier by Manfred Frank, E.D. Hirsch, and Wendell Harris, preserves the separate categories of author, reader, and text. Indeed, it is hard to see how the discussion of literature, or any human product could take place if we did not distinguish the artificer from the artefact, the artist from his public. Olsen even uses at one point the word 'aesthetic', which, like several concepts deemed undesirable, old-fashioned ('bourgeois', 'humanist', or whatever), has been stigmatised and rejected.[26] But unless you wish to deny that *King Lear* or the *Missa Solemnis* are works of art created by their (paid) composers to be seen and heard (by a paying audience), and that they provide experiences differing in kind (and degree) from those conveyed by a view of the Mont Blanc or the Grand Canyon, the term 'aesthetic' is unavoidable and harmless. It can become harmful when barriers are erected around works of art in order to deny, for instance, the continuity between our cognitive and emotional responses to them and to life. But the theory I shall be outlining here refuses any such separation. The term aesthetic, as I use it, describes some specific properties of works of art and our experience of them, but does not exclude consideration of their ethical, rhetorical, political or any other properties. Rather, it interrelates with, and complements those considerations. I share Olsen's view that the reader's response to a literary work involves an imaginative reconstruction of it, expressed in a vocabulary which is not specialised (as are those of law, economics, chess) but open, continuous with life: 'literary aesthetic argument' uses 'terms which have an established use in other spheres of life'. We describe Hamlet with the same terms we 'would use to describe a real human being', and we impute 'motives, mental states, and emotions to characters' in literature as in real life (Olsen 1987, pp. 16–17). There cannot be a separate, non-human conceptual system to describe literature.

Aesthetic theories need not erect a barrier between art and life, nor retreat behind it into self-absorption. Nelson Goodman, a distinguished philosopher of the arts, argues that aesthetic theories must include both the art-work and its appreciators. As he puts it in *Languages of Art*, 'since the exercise, training and development of our powers of discriminating among works of art are plainly aesthetic activities, the aesthetic properties of a picture include not only those found by looking at it but also those that determine how it is to be looked at' (Goodman 1976, pp. 111–12). Subsequently Goodman attacks (in similar terms to Gellner's rejection of the naïve idea of perception) the erroneous tradition which sees the aesthetic attitude as 'passive contemplation of the immediately given, direct apprehension of what is presented, uncontaminated by any conceptualization'. Goodman's whole work argues the contrary view, that we have to read the painting as well as the poem, and that aesthetic experience is dynamic rather than static. It involves making delicate discriminations and discerning subtle relationships, identifying symbol systems and characters within these systems and what these characters denote and exemplify, interpreting works and reorganizing the world in terms of works and works in terms of the world. Much of our experience and many of our skills are brought to bear and may be transformed by the encounter. The aesthetic 'attitude' is restless, searching, testing — is less attitude than action: creation and re-creation. (pp. 241-2)

Goodman's theory of art emphasises the dynamic inter-relation of the art-work and the person experiencing, an exchange that takes place in, uses the same terms as, normal life. The idea that 'aesthetic experience is distinguished . . . by a special emotion', he comments, is one that 'can be dropped on the waste-pile of "dormitive virtue" explanations' (p. 243). The spectator or viewer's response involves both the mind and the feelings. Rejecting attempts (such as those of Lévi-Strauss) to distinguish science from art in terms of cognitive as opposed to emotive satisfactions, as if knowing and feeling were separate activities, Goodman argues that both aesthetic and scientific experience are 'fundamentally cognitive' (pp. 243-5). Certainly works of art offer an emotional experience in a way that scientific discourse and practice rarely do, but aesthetic experience is not 'a sort of emotional bath or orgy'. The continuity he has been arguing between art and life here undergoes a reversal, in his claim that the emotions involved in aesthetic experience are 'reversed in polarity. We welcome some works that arouse emotions we normally shun. Negative emotions of fear, hatred, disgust may become positive when occasioned by a play or painting' (pp. 245-6). Goodman's crucial argument, I believe, is that 'in aesthetic experience the *emotions function cognitively*' (p. 248). We apprehend a work of art through the feelings as well as through the senses, and using our emotions cognitively involves 'discriminating and relating them in order to gauge and grasp the work and integrate it with the rest of our experience and the world' (*ibid.*). Our emotions combine 'with one another and with other means of knowing' (p. 249), for 'in aesthetic experience, emotion positive or negative is a mode of sensitivity to a work' (p. 250). Knowledge and feeling work together.

Our experience of *Othello* or *King Lear*, then, is not the palliative-therapeutic notion of *catharsis* (p. 246) — in any case a doubtful inter-pretation of Aristotle's *Poetics*[27] — but a heightening of feeling which makes us perceive both the play and the human actions it represents, more intensely. So it is perfectly legitimate for an interpreter to report on his feelings, as Dr. Johnson did so memorably as he completed annotating the scene (5.2) where Othello kills Desdemona — 'I am glad that I have ended my revisal of this dreadful scene. It is not to be endured'.[28] Inded, his emotional reactions have shaped the interpreter's experience of the play throughout. If Johnson's reaction is normal, then we may be surprised how few contemporary critics report their feelings, or even acknowledge that they have any. Nor will we find them discussing the fact that, over time, an interpreter's or appreciator's response can change. Critics of other persuasions regularly observe that the appreciation of the arts is an ability that has to be acquired, and that readers (can, at least) learn from critics (Butler 1984, p. 33; Olsen 1978, p. 21). In learning, in reading and re-reading complex literary works, we come to see and feel some things more clearly, more strongly. As Goodman puts it,

> where there is density in the symbol system, familiarity is never com-plete and final; another look may always disclose significant new subtleties. Moreover, what we read from and learn through a symbol varies with what we bring to it. Not only do we discover through our symbols but we understand and reappraise our symbols progressively in the light of our growing experience. (p. 260)

Awareness of this dimension is wholly lacking in Current Literary Theory.

Goodman's argument makes the appreciator's response to a picture or play an integral part of that work's existence. While welcoming that emphasis, the intentionalist notion of interpretation, as I understand it, will not lose sight of the artist's prime responsibility for the work that makes such experience possible. Another distinguished philosopher of aesthetics, Richard Wollheim, in *Art and its Objects* (1968; rev. 1980), has attacked the tendency to give primacy to the spectator and to ignore 'the aims or intentions of the artist'. This has the damaging consequence that 'once the artist is not accorded at least equality with the spectator, he ends up by dropping out of the picture altogether' (Wollheim 1980, p. 228). Wollheim insists on keeping a balance between artist and spectator, arguing that 'it is always the artist who . . . shapes the forms that bear his name'. These forms are not created out of nothing but from 'inside a continuing activity or enterprise', with its own repertoire, offering both constraints and opportunities, and thereby providing within the framework of an agreed system 'occasions, inconceivable outside it, for invention and audacity' (pp. 124–5). The artist's intentions, Wollheim argues, are realised in the art-work, but there can never be a complete correspondence between the artist's activity and the spectator's reaction. In a remark which links up with E.D. Hirsch's notion of verbal meaning as a willed type which the author intends, but whose sub-meanings he cannot control, Wollheim observes that 'the spectator will always understand more than the artist intended, and the artist will always have intended more than any single spectator understands . . .' (p. 119). Both roles must be emphasised equally, then, for creation and interpretation are reciprocal activities. Quoting Valéry, Wollheim writes that 'the artist is active, but so also is the spectator, and the spectator's activity consists in interpretation. "A creator", Valéry puts it, "is one who makes others create"' (p. 87).

Yet the interpreter's 'creation' is not free and indeterminate, as Current

Literary Theory would wish, but is subject to constraints, limits, as is that of the artist himself. These limits are in fact set by the artist, in the complex process of selection and rejection which has given his work its distinctive shape, content, style. As Christopher Butler has argued, all texts 'construct situations which control a great deal of what it is plausible to say in interpretations', for they all 'implicitly select an area of experience with which to deal' (Butler 1984, p. 46). That proposition would be anathema to exponents of rule-free play, as would its corollary, that the situations constructed by an author 'are part of the mimetic commitments of the text. They thus relate to the ways in which we think about the world' (*ibid.*), the process Nelson Goodman described as integrating the work of art 'with the rest of our experience and the world', by interpretation 'reorganizing the world in terms of works and works in terms of the world'. One of many vital elements ignored in recent literary theory is that shared knowledge of life as lived in specific places at specific times which an author depends on his reader having, or being willing to acquire. If you once reflect how much you need to know about human society in order to understand *Measure for Measure* — what justice is, or authority, or power, or corruption, the responsibility of the magistrate, the vulnerability of the woman in an informal marriage-contract sworn *de futuro*, the professions of whore, criminal, executioner — then you may agree that that play is as it is, to begin with, because Shakespeare has chosen these situations, and the issues they raise, and rejected everything else. As that small example shows, more needs to be said about mimesis, and how the author shapes his text.

REFERENCE, REPRESENTATION, MAKE-BELIEVE

And let us, ciphers to this great account,
On your imaginary forces work. . . .
Piece out our imperfections with your thoughts;
Into a thousand parts divide one man,
And make imaginary puissance.
Think, when we talk of horses, that you see them,
Printing their proud hoofs i'th'receiving earth.
For 'tis your thoughts that now must deck our kings . . .

Henry V, Prol. Act 1, 15ff.

It was only to be expected that the iconoclastic movement of the mid-1960s, having denied that language could reliably convey meaning about or reference to the world we live in, would sooner or later extend that veto, embargo, prohibition — since this, too, is an attempt to deter people from thinking differently — to literature. A convenient starting-point for this polemic might be 1968, again, and another essay by Roland Barthes, called 'L'effet du réel', which argued that description in literary texts was included purely for aesthetic ends and could not denote reality. To think otherwise was to indulge 'the *referential illusion*'.[29] From that time on, we can say, and for all would-be avant-garde or post-whatever critics, any notion that a drama, novel, or poem could or should be seen as (among other things) representing human life was to be rejected with scorn. With another of those easy but empty polemical dichotomies, the literary text was said to be *not at all a representation of reality* but instead *a self-contained system of signs or codes*. As structuralism gave way to post-structuralism, the positive, privileged pole of that dichotomy was replaced by a new formula, *a self-contained system calling its own existence in question by its unfulfillable desire to refer outside itself*. I shall be discussing deconstructive literary theory, and its catastrophic effects on the interpretation of Shakespeare — deliberately catastrophic, demonstrating the workings of human intentionality at its most intransigent — in the next chapter. Here I want to review some arguments against representation, and some of those for it, in order to outline a new theory which moves the discussion in a different and more fruitful direction.

In the 1960s attack on mimesis we find the same sloppy, self-serving modes of argument that underwrite so much of Current Literary Theory, unjustified assertions, facile dichotomies that privilege one pole and dismiss the other, mockery of competing views. One exponent of post-structuralism, as A.D. Nuttall points out, 'proposes without a tremor that we cease to pretend that the ordinary world is real: "First, there is the socially given text, that which is taken as 'the real world'"'. Notice that [he] places inverted commas around *the real world* but none around *text*. The traditional relation of object and representative is silently reversed' (Nuttall 1983, p. 10). Robert Alter, discussing 'Mimesis and the motive for fiction', noted that in the iconoclastic theories of the '60s 'the attack on mimesis ultimately depends on defining experience out of existence' (Alter 1978, p. 233). Where 'previous epistemologies talked about data of experience or objects of knowledge', the structuralists and their successors only discuss signs, codes, texts, and intertextuality, in a deliberate exclusion (as we saw in Chapter 1) of language as a medium for expression. And whereas 'intertextuality' originally referred to the practice of literary allusion, that secondary process of *imitatio* (as it was called in the Renaissance to distinguish it from the primary process of *mimesis*, which drew on human life not on books), and to the conscious use of models implied by the whole notion of genre, now, Alter suggests, 'intertextuality' replaces 'the old-fashioned notion of verisimilitude'. In the once-new Paris theories, since the real world is itself only 'something we construe, a shifting constellation of texts we decode', then intertextuality can serve as an all-purpose, freshly-minted, but 'ultimately casuistic' term (*ibid.*, pp. 233–4).

This attempt 'to exorcise the other-than-literary presence of the real world by reducing everything to text' is one of two 'complementary strategies' that Alter diagnoses in the iconoclasts' attack on mimesis (*ibid.*, p. 234). The other — building yet again, we see, on their travesty of Saussure — is to present the literary text as

> a collocation of arbitrary signs that can be joined together only on the basis of internal principles of coherence even as they pretend to be determined by objects outside themselves to which they supposedly refer. In this view, reality, whatever it may be, is inaccessible to the literary text because of the text's very constitution. (*ibid.*)

Here the pseudo-Saussurian inheritance, even in such an intelligent critic as Gérard Genette,[30] appears in the claim that since the linguistic sign is arbitrary then '"the motivation of the sign, and particularly of the 'word', is a typical case of realist illusion"'. With the term 'motivation' Genette was referring to the Russian Formalists' analysis of narrative elements and their internal functioning, which they used to rule out any discussion of a novel's relation to the society it portrays. Alter is disturbed by the 'either-or rigidity' of Genette's formulation, but as we now know, this technique of privileging your own case and disqualifying every other is the foundation method of the so-called literary theories that we have inherited from the 60s.

Alter's reply to '*the linguistic fallacy*' of post-structuralist theory, which assumes a total coherence between its view of language and its view of literature, is to argue that the word 'tiger', for instance, may be a conventional and arbitrary sign, but that we know the difference between a tiger in a poem by Borges, one in a painting, and one in reality. The fact that the same perceptual apparatus and cognitive processes are involved in our recognition both of the image and the real thing does not mean that we can't tell them apart (pp. 235–7). This may seem an elementary reply, but after all, the mistakes made by Current Literary Theory are often elementary.[31] As I showed in Chapter 1, philosophers and linguists have, independently of each other, built up a model of reality to serve as the framework for analysing how language can reliably refer to the world of persons, animals, objects, processes, and abstract categories such as mimesis. Since literature uses language there is no reason why it cannot refer to imagined worlds, animals, objects and categories, which may behave like those with which we are familiar, or may not. In refuting the iconoclasts' notion of language we must also refute their view of literature. As Alter says, this 'tendency to see literature as closed-circuit poesis rather than mimesis' would have disastrous effects on the novel, to which an untold number of readers since the seventeenth century have turned in order to 'enter into' the experience of fictional characters, 'testing our perceptions of reality against the absorbing details of their invented worlds' (*ibid.*, p. 237).

Against the Literary Theorists' coercive and reductive 'not mimesis but poesis' we must assert a non-coercive 'both'/'and', truly 'freeing' ourselves from a new and oppressive critical system. Christopher Butler, rejecting 'useless discussion' concerning the ' "pseudo-statement" nature of literature', argues that interpreters of a text can either relate it to the world or concentrate on its 'internal thematics':

> There is ultimately no logically coherent or reasonable way of legislating in favour of one of these modes of interpretation to the permanent detriment of the other. What is at issue is the pragmatic ends which interpretation may serve . . . (Butler 1984, p. 54)

And in fact, nearly all forms of interpretation outside the self-sufficient post-structuralist camp 'inevitably move to and fro between the two' (*ibid.*). Thomas Pavel similarly attacks these excluding dichotomies: '*Madame Bovary* is *both* a conventional narrative structure textualized with the help of a set of equally conventional discursive procedures *and* a description of provincial boredom in mid-nineteenth-century France' (Pavel 1989, p. 119). Since Formalists have tried to 'conjure away the referential properties of realist texts', hoping to reduce them to 'a combination of purely formal characteristics', Pavel finds it necessary to restate the legitimacy of mimesis as a critical category for discussing literature, and to make the challenging counter-assertion that we should 'start out from the primacy of reference and representation to which narrative structures and discourse techniques are subordinate' (*ibid.*, p. 111).

The concept of mimesis can be presented crudely, as the iconoclasts have shown all too easily, but it can also form the basis of a flexible and sensitive theory of literature. Those wishing to travesty it frequently pick out some previous exponent (Aristotle, Sidney) or period (the neoclassic critics), and summarise their views inaccurately and sarcastically. Aristotle is taken to task for implying that literature imitates reality as if that were a given and the writer passively transcribed it.[32] For late twentieth-century critics aware of the degree of interpretation involved in perception these are obviously primitive notions. But Aristotle in fact said that a drama was the *mimêsis* of a human action involving words, music, and all the other resources of theatrical presentation. According to the *Poetics*,[33] 'the objects of this *mimêsis* are people doing things' (48al), interacting, as we might put it, in the pursuit of shared or conflicting goals. The word translated there as 'doing', *prattontas*, means for Aristotle 'people performing responsible and characterizable actions', for, as he puts it later, 'tragedy is a *mimêsis* of an action; action implies people engaged in it; these people must have some definite moral and intellectual values' (49b36ff). Thus the dramatist's *mimêsis* of character inevitably 'makes plain the nature of the moral choices the personages make' (50b8ff). Aristotle firmly places the dramatist's mimetic act in the realm of recognisable human behaviour having both an intellectual and an ethical dimension: a definition that can still stand. As Aristotle knew better than anyone (see his two books on ethics, and the

masterly treatise on rhetoric), 'moral choices' involve disagreement and
discussion, so that there can be nothing passive about the literary presentation of human behaviour. The dramatist, involved in the story being
dramatised, cannot help making judgments about the issues concerned.
And far from literature having the purely mechanical role of transcribing
events as they had happened, that was the nature and limitation, according
to Aristotle (deploying one of the original Greek evaluative dichotomies),
of history rather than poetry: 'the one tells us what happened and the other
the sort of thing that would happen'. History tells us 'what Alcibiades did
or what happened to him', poetry tells us 'what sort of man would,
probably or necessarily, say or do what sort of thing' (51b3ff), the picture
it presents being 'an investigation of moral possibilities' (as Margaret
Hubbard notes in her admirable translation).

This distinction between poetry and history on the grounds of generality
had a vast influence in the Renaissance,[34] and is one of the main supports
of Sidney's *Apology for Poetry*, accounting for the poet's superiority over
both historians and philosophers. All human arts are based on nature,
Sidney writes,[35] but 'Only the poet, . . . lifted up with the vigour of his
own invention, doth grow in effect another nature, in making things either
better than Nature bringeth forth, or quite anew . . .' (p. 100). In a
memorable image, Sidney describes how the poet 'goeth hand in hand with
Nature, not enclosed within the narrow warrant of her gifts, but freely
ranging only within the zodiac of his own wit' (*ibid.*). These famous lines
have recently been interpreted by Howard Felperin, a born-again deconstructionist, who comments on that final image (the zodiac as the circle
through which the world moves) in purely Derridian terms:

> poetry, that is, is an autonomous, generative, and self-enclosed system.
> To the extent that the two, poetry and nature, are heterogeneous, they
> are clearly incommensurate. If poetic language is orphic [a misplaced late
> twentieth-century concept, never used by Sidney] and autonomous, it
> can never quite be referential; if it is referential, it cannot be completely
> autonomous and orphic. (Felperin 1990, p. 48)

Reading through Derridian spectacles is not necessarily good for the eye-
sight. Sidney in fact states that although the poet is not bound by *mimêsis*,
can freely invent, he is still walking hand in hand with nature, and his
subject-matter is still the *prattontas*, people doing things. Any gulf between
poetry and nature is created by Felperin, who predictably goes on to accuse
Sidney of 'self-contradiction', for 'to make something "better" than nature
is not the same thing as . . . "other" than nature', thus making Sidney
prove a deconstructionist thesis, namely 'the potential frustration of representation by the self-enclosure of the formal systems that mediate it'
(p. 49).

But Sidney wrote not 'other than nature' but 'another nature', that is, a
new nature, having all the properties of the world and human life as we

know them. Representation is not frustrated in Sidney's theory of poetry but enabled, gloriously so, above all other forms of writing. Felperin's final attempt to insert a deconstructionist fissure into Sidney's concept of 'a paradise lost than can be represented but not regained through poetic language, "figured forth" but not literally delivered' (*ibid.*), reveals the same elementary error as his master's voice. The most that *any* linguistic utterance can do is to 'figure forth'. Only magicians, and frustrated Derridians, believe that language could 'literally deliver' an idea or state, as if it could arise from off this page and we could enter into it. Such a confusion between the actual and the represented is amusing when we find characters in films (Buster Keaton's *Spite Marriage*, or Woody Allen's *The Purple Rose of Cairo*) who can walk into and out of the screen. But such a confusion coming from professional philosophers and literary critics, and then being used to discredit language and literature, is absurd and debilitating. As A.D. Nuttall has observed, the effect of Derrida's 'complaisant nihilism' on his followers is 'strangely enervating' (Nuttall 1983, p. 28). It removes personal initiative, encloses criticism within its wholly determined 'zodiac', where, as Alter puts it, the effect of 'insisting, for book after book, that the novel is a self-referential system of signs in which the real interest is in the way language calls attention to its own predicament', is to 'make all novels, from *Eugénie Grandet* to *A Hundred Years of Solitude*, sound tediously alike' (Alter 1978, pp. 237–8).

Mimêsis, like any other concept or category, can be trivialised. Some neo-classical critics succeeded in reducing it to a mechanical criterion. In the seventeenth century Aristotle's system became broken up into rules, which then took on a prescriptive nature, intended to legislate how drama should be written now and in future. Plays were evaluated under separate Aristotelian categories: plot (or fable), characters, thought, style, in each case appealing to the criteria of probability or correctness that then applied. Throughout the dominant period of neoclassicism (well into the nineteenth century), many critics also applied this prescriptive system retrospectively, without any awareness of anachronism, and Shakespeare in particular was found guilty of having violated rules that he could not possibly have known, including those involved with *mimêsis*.[36] The neo-classic system, like many others, subordinated individual aesthetic criteria to general notions of decorum and convention, as defined by polite society. The nature to be represented in literature was always selective, with clearly defined rules and exclusions (as it still is today). These governed both specific genres and the forms of life that could be represented, so that kings should behave in a king-like manner, comedy should not be mingled with tragedy, and so forth.

These criteria derived jointly from life and literature, but in his claim that reality is a mere 'effect' produced by literary means Barthes asserted that neoclassical literary theory *opposed* 'the "real" . . . to the "vraisemblable"', and forbade any 'contamination of the "vraisemblable" by the real' (Barthes 1982, p. 15). This is a specious claim, which derives, as A.D. Nuttall has shown, from a misreading of the single seventeenth-century text cited to prove it (Nuttall 1983, pp. 57–9). For that period, as for the following century at least, J.E. Spingarn's description of Hobbes's literary theory remains the norm: '"the subject-matter of poetry is, then, the manners of men; its method is that of verisimilitude, or resemblance to the actual conditions of life"' (cit. ibid., p. 59). That neo-classic criteria of probability derived from their own 'conditions of life' can be seen very clearly in Thomas Rymer's vicious attack on Othello in A Short View of Tragedy (1693). Rymer invoked not only the literary criterion of genre for defining tragedy and judging Shakespeare incapable of it (in the coarsest possible manner), but he also appealed to social and indeed racist attitudes. With a fine disregard for history (remarkable considering that he became Historiographer Royal in 1693), Rymer found Shakespeare guilty of im-probability in his fable by fancying that the Venetians would 'set a Negro to be their General, or trust a Moor to defend them against the Turk. With us a Black-amoor might rise to be a Trumpeteer. . . . With us a Moor might marry some little drab, or Small-coal Wench . . .', and so forth.[37] Rymer could indict Shakespeare for violating probability by reference to the actual conditions of life, but other critics writing at the same time and using the same system could defend him from the charge.[38] This disagreement shows that no critical category (before post-structuralism, at least) is so rigid that it denies individual variations in its use, but it also shows that the concept of mimesis is always governed by conventions, social and/or artistic.

Any attempt to represent reality must submit itself to the conventions of the medium it uses. As E.H. Gombrich showed in Art and Illusion,[39] spectators of a painting bring with them a set of conventional expectations: there is no innocent eye. Yet, Gombrich argued, artistic conventions are far from arbitrary, being determined by the psychological constraints of visual perception. Resemblance constitutes a condition of representation, and artistic conventions have been introduced or regularly challenged in the name of a more accurate resemblance. In the same way mimesis in literature submits itself to the conventions of the age and culture in which the writer works. In the novel, as Robert Alter puts it, 'mimesis is never a direct reproduction of reality but rather a way of eliciting in the mind of the reader — through complex chains of verbal indicators — the illusion of persons, places, situations, events, and institutions convincingly like the ones we encounter outside the sphere of reading' (Alter 1978, p. 238). At the same time we accept, often unquestioningly, the conventions of the novel genre. We accept that the chapters of a novel can be numbered in sequence, and that between two successive chapters the action can stay in the same place and time, or shift to a new place, at the same or any other time, involving the same or (up to a point) any other characters. We accept that the narrative can be told by one omniscient narrator, by a first-person actor in the narrative, or even by two first-person actors alternately (as in *Bleak House*). We accept that the main narrator can draw on eye-witnesses and other agents to fill out the narrative, as Conrad's Marlow does in *Lord Jim*, and also that the result may be to shed not more light but more uncertainty on the main character and his actions. We even accept the so-called 'self-conscious novel', which keeps the reader constantly aware of being engaged in reading an act of representation. This may seem an extreme case where literary conventions push against the process of representation, but I agree with Alter that such works involve not so much the abandonment of mimesis as 'an enormous complication and sophistication of it: mimesis is enacted as its problematics are explored' (*ibid*., p. 239).[40]

The need to recognise that specific conventions govern the representation of reality in a given genre at a given time is particularly pressing for Elizabethan and Jacobean drama. The fact that there has been a continuous tradition of theatrical performance in England since the Middle Ages (even during the Civil War) means that the theatregoer — and, until recently, the critic — may be influenced in his attitude to older drama by the conventions and production practices of the contemporary theatre. The more remote the drama, the more likely we are to misunderstand it. (The 'theatre of cruelty' already seems remote.) One of the great break-throughs in modern drama criticism was the conscious and constructive attack, in the 1920s and 30s, on Victorian attitudes to Elizabethan drama, attitudes formed by an alien, naturalistic tradition, as seen in such a typical figure as William Archer. It was constructive inasmuch as the scholar-critics involved, notably E.E. Stoll and Muriel Bradbrook, went back to Elizabethan drama to define the conventions that then applied. In Bradbrook's suggestive definition, convention is 'an agreement between writers and readers, whereby the artist is allowed to limit and simplify his material in order to secure greater concentration through a control of the distribution of emphasis'.[41] Conventions vary from genre to genre, each arousing and fulfilling the expectations proper to itself, a process which, as Wendell Harris has observed, 'implies participation by the reader', who is invited to read a text in a certain way. The 'recognition that we are reading a poem leads us to attend more carefully to the sounds of words, the relations between them, the associations that accompany them, and the precision of their choice' (Harris 1988, p. 96). Since, in David Lewis's helpful formulation, a convention is 'a regularity . . . which benefits each member of a group' (*cit*. Blackburn 1984, p. 119), it is essential to discover what agreements are made by the group participating in the experience of drama, a genre more dependent than any other on those involved — actors and audience — simultaneously observing a whole range of conventions. And since, in any medium, conventions are usually silently observed, it needs an act of historical reconstruction to recall those operating in the past. It is important not to lose sight of the conventions of Renaissance drama as scholars have retrieved them, especially at the present time, when any piece of scholarship or criticism more than twenty years old risks being automatically and unthinkingly treated as obsolete. Erroneously naturalistic expectations continually crop up in Shakespeare criticism, as with Greenblatt on *King Lear* (Chapter 4), the psychocritics Nevo and Stockholder (Chapter 5), or any number of feminists (Chapter 6), who express disapproval of characters on the simple everyday grounds that 'people ought not to behave like that'. These are wholly inappropriate criteria.

The scholars who recovered Elizabethan theatrical conventions were able to show that Renaissance drama was symbolic rather than naturalistic, that it relied on broad imaginative effects, not minutely observed detail. Frank appeals to the audience's cooperation were intended to overcome the deficiencies of representation, and a study of the theatrical props owned by the impresario Philip Henslowe — 'one rock', 'one cage', 'one tomb', 'one Hell mouth', 'one bedstead', 'two steeples & one chime of bells', 'one golden fleece', 'one lion's skin', 'a robe for to go invisible'[42] — reveals an odd mixture of the schematically suggestive and the faithfully realistic. The actors' costumes were gorgeous, costing the company much more than the play text. Dramatists received between £3 and £6, while Henslowe paid 'over £38 for taffetas, velvets and gowns for *Cardinal Wolsey*' alone (Chillington 1980, pp. 448–9, 452). Costumes were also much sought after, as we see from the list of items that Henslowe records as 'Gone and lost': 'one orange tawny satin doublet, laid thick with gold lace'; 'one blue taffeta suit'; 'one pair of carnation satin Venetians [breeches], laid with gold lace'; 'Harry the Fifth's velvet gown'. In the Elizabethan playhouse real swords were used, pistols and cannons were set off, bells rung, candles lit, food and drink consumed, all devices to aid the faculty of make-believe on which all representational works of fiction depend. Not that every invitation to 'pretend' needed elaborate helps. In the scene where Falstaff and Hal act out an imaginary confrontation between Hal and his father, the King, they seize whatever props are to hand:

> FALSTAFF.   This chair shall be my state, this dagger my sceptre, and this cushion my crown. . . . Give me a cup of sack to make my eyes look red, that it may be thought I have wept. . . . (*1 Henry IV*, 2.4.374ff)

And when the artisans in *Midsummer Night's Dream* prepare their production outdoors, they transform the natural setting into a theatre: 'here's a marvellous convenient place for our rehearsal. This green plot shall be our stage, this hawthorn brake our tiring-house . . .' (3.1.2ff).

Conventions applied not only to costumes and settings, to time and place (where the flexibility they used seemed scandalously irregular to neo-classical critics), but also to the representation of human behaviour. Characterisation was often a question of types and roles: the melancholic lover, the quarrelsome braggart, the dignified king. Two obvious influences here were the classification of human types in ethics, rhetoric, and medicine (physiognomy, humours theory),[43] and the sheer volume of plays that companies produced and performed. In the forty weeks between October 1596 and July 1597, for instance, 'the Admiral's Men at the Rose gave 184 performances of thirty different plays', fifteen of which were marked by Henslowe as 'new', a frequency of about two new plays per month (Chillington 1980, p. 446). Actors learning a new part every two weeks, while continuing to perform a dozen old ones, do not have time to construct elaborately naturalistic interpretations, any more than the dramatists involved in joint authorship could provide them with psychologically detailed roles. For the period 1590 to 1642, in which we know the authorship details of about 1,100 plays, anything from a third to a half of them 'incorporated the writing at some date of more than one man. In the case of the 282 plays mentioned in Henslowe's diary . . . nearly two-thirds' were joint-authored (Bentley 1986, p. 199). In some cases, as Carol Chillington has argued for *Sir Thomas More*, collaborators 'distributed the work by looking at a plot outline and selecting episodes that appealed to them'. Her breakdown of its eighteen scenes suggests a collaboration between Anthony Munday, Henry Chettle, Thomas Heywood, Thomas Dekker, and John Webster, with an almost communal revision process (Chillington 1980, pp. 461–9). That play was unusual in several respects, and ran into trouble with the censor Edmund Tilney. With other companies, it seems, a more common division of labour was for writers to compose whole acts (Bentley 1986, pp. 227–34), even though their styles were noticeably different. In at least a dozen plays on which Massinger and Fletcher collaborated 'they obviously divided the first two acts between them and the style of neither appears in the other's act' (*ibid.*, p. 232 note). Whichever form collaboration took, different authors would necessarily create parts of the same personage, so that characterisation could only have been carried out using conventions as a kind of short-hand.

It is a well-known convention in Elizabethan drama, for instance, that a slanderer is usually believed. This may be thought to derive from the highly-compressed nature of the performing-time, but it is just as much a convention in early prose-fiction (such as the romance), and indeed the novel. It is a way of making things happen, and the psychology concerned is not so much unlike life — do official denials always dispel newspaper rumours or malicious report? — for us to reject it as 'artificial'. Conventions were often subsumed under the criterion of verisimilitude in Renaissance literary theory, but this drew, in turn, on attitudes applying in the real world. To an age that conceived women as the weaker sex on medical, ethical, and legal grounds,[44] it was inevitable that a literary theorist like Giraldi Cinthio should lay down a rule that 'young girls should be shown as shamefast and timid, matrons as chaste and solicitous' (Doran 1954, p. 221). The convention of women's weakness, as Madeleine Doran notes, was 'observed in at least one way in English drama. Women, even good women, generally yield quickly and easily to persuasion'. Queen

Anne in *Richard III* (in an episode invented by Shakespeare) would be a familiar instance of this rule. Yet against it we must set some 'striking exceptions', such as Isabella in *Measure for Measure*, which 'gain force through our awareness of the convention. Isabella's resistance to Angelo is a sign of superior strength and nobility of character, not of prudishness, as modern readers are likely to feel' (*ibid.*). Another noteworthy exception is Marina in *Pericles*, sold as a prostitute but having so much power in eloquence that she can shame her customer Lysimachus, and turn him into a husband. This transformation, which is all the more remarkable given the wide-spread Renaissance belief that women need not be taught rhetoric, since they take no part in public life,[45] shows that conventions may be a type of shortcut that enable dramatists to achieve many effects quickly, but do not constrain them.

The relationship between convention and representation is variable, flexible. Yet the iconoclastic, formalistic criticism since the 1960s has produced what A.D. Nuttall describes as the 'curiously uncritical yet metaphysically radical' theory by which realism itself is said to be 'a tissue of conventions and therefore has nothing to do with reality'. Striking though this idea may seem on first reading,

> The truth is almost exactly converse. All reference to reality (including pointing with the finger) is conventionally ordered. Language is an immensely rich system of conventions and is the best means we have of referring to the real. (Nuttall 1983, p. 53)

In rejecting previous theories the radical critics have again used the yes/no, all-or-nothing claim. But no one of any sense is claiming that representational works of art present life 'exactly as it is'. The writer of realistic fiction, such as George Eliot, does not wish 'to dupe her readers into supposing that her books are factually true . . . She does however implicitly claim probability for her stories', suggesting no more than that 'such events do occur in real life' (*ibid.*, pp. 54–5). Representational art, Nuttall writes, does not 'transcribe actualities; it offers variously quickening hypothetical cases. And these must be answerable to reality or they will not succeed' (*ibid.*, p. 77). The reality of people and things to which the writer refers is conventionally represented, and thus 'it is never possible in a finite work to exhaust reality; always we receive a selection only . . .' (*ibid.*, p. 182). That restatement of a fundamental truth can be linked with what we must now probably call the 'rehabilitation' of the author, who made that selection from reality in the first place. A novelist's control over his material is total, including the power to falsify history, as Zola did in *Germinal*, making the mining industry look far worse than it was at that time (Butler 1984, p. 57).[46] Yet no text guarantees a relationship between itself and the world. That relationship is always hypothetical, and the estimate of the degree to which a text may or may not resemble the external world is made by the interpreter, drawing according to his lights on the interpretative conventions that govern the existing conceptions of the 'vraisemblance' (*ibid.*, pp. 53–4). What is involved is not merely the meaning of the text so much as 'its significance and hence use to us' (p. 57).

*   *   *

What use are texts? What do we do with novels and plays while reading or watching them? What role is played by their representation of reality in our experience of them? An attractive answer to these questions has recently been provided by Kendall Walton: *Mimesis as Make-Believe*.[47] This thoughtful and wide-ranging study links up with a number of positions adopted here and in other recent literary theory, starting from the inadequacy of a purely linguistic model, which has produced so many 'distortions' when applied to novels, paintings, theatre and film (Walton 1990, p. 5). The approach through language has too often focussed on literal, non-fictional discourse, with works of fiction then seen as 'deviant' or 'parasitic'. However, Walton argues, fiction is something positive, special, not just language stripped of its normative functions (p. 78). Works of fiction 'are not *necessarily* vehicles of assertion or of any other illocutionary acts' (pp. 76, 81), so that speech-act theories alone cannot explain them, nor is their goal 'communication' in the sense of imparting information (p. 89). Walton expresses the view of every philosophically-aware person in not believing that 'reality is a realm of things-in-themselves independent of sentient observers, nor that to be true is somehow to picture or mirror this objective reality', since notions of truth and false-hood are notoriously culture-dependent (p. 99). But equally he rejects the extreme deduction, put about by the 1960s iconoclasts, that discourse creates reality: 'the insight that facts are not "brute" . . . is a far cry from collapsing the distinction' and arguing that everything is fiction (p. 100). Walton judges the notions of truth and reality 'so central to our thinking' as to be 'inseparable from the subject matter of any investigation of human institutions. An investigator cannot dispense with the very thing he is investigating' (p. 101). Representation concerns precisely 'the difference between truth and fictionality, the possibility of propositions' being true but not fictional, or fictional but not true', and how these differences affect 'our personal and social experience' (*ibid.*). Actual objects of representation may indeed exist 'independently of the works that represent them' (p. 127), but the key issue is not the accuracy of the representation.

The core of Walton's theory is that all representations have in common 'a role in *make-believe*', which can be explained in terms of imagination and participation (p. 4). Whereas some theories of fiction have made an unfortunate separation between aesthetic and metaphysical approaches, his theory unifies them by basing itself on make-believe (p. 6). 'There is nothing distinctively "aesthetic" about make-believe itself', Walton argues, 'and works of art are neither the sole nor the primary instances of representation in our sense', for children's games of pretending will do just as well. Since I have been arguing that the primacy of human behaviour as represented in fictional works means that our response to them cannot take some special aesthetic form, but must involve the same feelings and the same language that we would use in real life, I welcome Walton's theory as allowing us 'to see representationality in the arts as continuous with other familiar human institutions and activities rather than something unique requiring its own special explanations' (p. 7). To understand 'paintings, plays, films, and novels', he writes, in words that will horrify the critical avant-garde, 'we must look first at dolls, hobbyhorses, toy trucks, and teddy bears' (p. 11). Just as these toys function as 'props' in games of make-believe, so do representational works of art, which permit 'indefinitely many' games of make-believe, 'played by different appreciators on different occasions' (p. 51). Imaginings resemble day-dreams, being mental events which are not disconnected but woven together into a continuous sequence (pp. 13–17). Yet neither are they 'free-floating fantasies': 'most imaginings are in one way or another dependent on or aimed at or anchored in the real world' (p. 21), and many imaginings are about real things (p. 25).

One strength of Walton's theory is that — unlike those who invoke 'jeu' as a desirable state freed from all constraints — it takes the notion of game seriously, and follows out the implications of the model, to which certain conditions apply. When something is true in a game of make-believe, Walton suggests, the proposition is '*fictional*, and the fact that it is fictional is a *fictional truth*', true in the world of fiction, not necessarily outside it (p. 35). The props provided by representational works of art, created by and for human beings, 'function only in a social, or at least human, setting' (p. 38). As in any game of make-believe, some rules must apply. The work of art needs 'a certain convention, understanding, agreement' from its players (*ibid.*), most importantly 'the acceptance rule' by which we agree to take part in the game world (p. 44). Imaginings (like language, I add, and like the creation and interpretation of art works) are not 'free, unregulated', but 'constrained also; some are proper, appropriate in certain contexts, and others not'. So, 'a fictional truth consists in there being a prescription or mandate in some context to imagine something' (p. 39). The person participating, while bound by some rules of context, is free both to share and enlarge the game or dream: 'the body of propositions fictional in the dream is to be filled out in certain natural or obvious ways, preserving the coherence of the whole' (p. 46). The artist need not define everything.

Walton's theory is based on the fundamental point, often lost sight of in iconoclastic anti-theories, that works of art exist in order to be appreciated, and that the appreciator's experience involves him or her in participation. 'Appreciation of representational works of art is primarily a matter of participation' (p. 213), for it is chiefly by imagining ourselves facing certain situations that we come to terms with our own feelings, or can understand other people's (p. 34). By taking part in a game of make-believe we consider its 'rules or principles of generation' as applying to us, too (p. 209), so that participants in games of make-believe 'are thus props, objects, and imaginers all three'. They prescribe imaginings, which are in some way both about themselves and addressed to themselves, even though they concern a character on a stage or in a novel. The participant takes part in the game by imagining about himself 'in a first-person manner . . . he imagines this *from the inside*' (p. 212), and so he achieves 'a kind of empathy with the characters, an ability to look at things more purely from their points of view' (p. 237). This notion of first-person participation, as if we were on speaking terms with the characters, helps account for the fact that we often

> seem to be in *psychological* contact with characters, sometimes even intimate with them. We have epistemological access to fictional worlds. . . . Often we are privy to characters' most private thoughts and feelings. And we respond to what we know, apparently, in many of the ways in which we respond to what we know about the real world. (pp. 191–2)

Our involvement can take quite intense forms: 'fictional characters cause real people to shed tears, lose sleep, laugh, and scream' (p. 192). 'Fictionally one may fear for someone else, if not for oneself' (p. 250) — both, I would suggest.[48] It is not so much that 'appreciators lose touch with reality when they are immersed in a work of fiction' (p. 241), as that most of us (Don Quixote excepted) have the ability to live in two worlds simultaneously, and can tell the difference between them. As in life, our responses to characters in literature can be complex, a mixture of attraction and resistance, anger and respect, sympathy and resentment (p. 253).

While applauding this whole direction in Walton's argument, I would add the qualification that although our involvement with fictional characters resembles similar feelings for people in real life, it is both more pronounced and more explicit. It may only be once or twice in real life (if we're lucky) that we are ever confronted with the totality of devastation that we feel when participating in *The Trojan Women* or *King Lear*. It is very seldom in life that we see a crucial issue facing us as unavoidably as Cordelia does, or experience a sense of uncertainty as totally as Othello, undermined by Iago. When I read *Middlemarch* I can share the crucial stages in the lives of Dorothea or Lydgate, the decisive decisions or encounters that will shape their whole beings, with a clarity and coherence that my own life seldom brings. In life we pass through crises sometimes without knowing it: never in literature. In that sense the games of make-believe that we play are unrealistic. Literature makes an artful selection from life, speeded up, brought to a crisis and resolution, within the bounds of the time it takes to watch a play or read a novel, the whole represented experience being subjected to rational explanation. (Even works that do not clarify the main characters' situation or life in general make it clear that they have reasons for not doing so.) We understand works of literature far better than we understand our own lives, and they form satisfying wholes, aesthetic and ethical and intellectual unities, in a way that life seldom does. (This is a potential source of danger, too.) But I agree with Walton that the illusion of life is created for our participation, and that 'we don't just observe fictional worlds from without. We live in them', experiencing what the characters experience. We know that these worlds are fictional, but '*from inside* they seem actual . . . and our presence in them . . . gives us a sense of intimacy' (p. 273).

That participation, that sense of intimacy, is shaped and controlled by the artists who create and/or perform the art work, the author, actors, producer, lighting-engineer, camera-man, editor, all with their experience of guiding make-believe. As Walton puts it, 'creators of props can predict how their creations will be used, and so can direct people's imaginings by designing props appropriately' (p. 53). If fiction-making is the activity of constructing the props to be used in games of make-believe (p. 88), then, I suggest, study of that shaping activity may help us to understand better the work that has been constructed, why it takes one form rather than another, what modes of imagining it directs, and why. If it is true that 'representations do not just present us with a collection of fictional truths; they order and arrange them for us, focusing on some more than others' (p. 149), then the selection and forms are the author's doing, and to a lesser extent the performers'. Walton concedes that 'much of what is fictional in appreciators' games is determined by the work appreciated and by the artist responsible for it' (p. 228), just as with a painting 'the artist's choice' has a decisive effect on the viewer's visual games of make-believe (pp. 318–27). We 'are *not* free to play any game we like with a given prop' (p. 303). While make-believe functions equally well in literature and the representational arts, a particular strength of literature is that 'words are well suited for use in make-believe' since they come 'with built-in semantic and syntactic properties', so an author can combine them 'to prescribe imaginings' in quite precise, or delimited ways (p. 353). The Derridian 'indeterminacy of language' thesis receives no support here, either.

Kendall Walton's study of mimesis as make-believe made me concede at once its main argument, as if it were something I had always thought, but never got round to formulating. It is perfectly symptomatic, as he points out, that many discussions of fiction, visual or verbal, never mention make-believe, pretence or imagining, so deeply are we immersed in it (pp. 388, 390). Yet, while retaining our awareness of the difference between it and reality, we must remain 'sensitive to the fictional world':

> Appreciation and criticism, participation and observation, are not very separate. . . . The critic usually cannot get very far in describing the world of a work unless she allows herself to be caught up in the spirit of pretense to some extent, as appreciators are. . . . (p. 394)

Interpretation presupposes participation, for understanding a work of art is not possible unless we have first taken it in, taken part in it as an organised whole. The main weakness of many Shakespeare critics writing today is that, intent on practising the type of interpretation of the school to which they belong, they tend to lose all notion of experiencing or interpreting a play as a whole.

While Walton's book obviously does not solve all the problems concerning mimesis in literature, his view of representation as a collaborative activity between author, actor, and audience seems to me a great improvement on anything yet produced.[49] His account of the relation between the art-work and the audience's involvement with it needs to be supplemented with the theory I have outlined above recognising the relevance of the author's intentions towards both the art-work and the audience. The two approaches are complementary, and if properly integrated open the way for a coherent approach to literature as a totality. Given the element of convention involved in representation and make-believe, a suitable conclusion to this section might be a passage from Borges' story 'Everything and Nothing', with its tribute to Shakespeare. Here Borges describes the dramatist coming to London as a young man and finding

> the profession to which he was predestined, that of the actor, who on a stage plays at being another before a gathering of people who play at taking him for that other person.[50]

SHAKESPEARE AT WORK: THE AUTHOR
TRANSFORMS HIS SOURCES

> ... it is pleasant to see great works in their seminal state, pregnant with latent possibilities of excellence; ... to trace their gradual growth and expansion, and to observe how they are sometimes suddenly advanced by accidental hints, and sometimes slowly improved by steady meditation.   Samuel Johnson[51]

Dr. Johnson's comments on Milton's sketches for *Paradise Lost* come from a work which the proponents of Current Literary Theory would deter anyone today from emulating, *The Lives of the Poets*. Johnson was himself a poet, a professional writer in several genres, and his remarks on the unpredictable growth of literary works doubtless derive from his own experience and from studying many authors and many books over a long literary life. Some of our contemporaries, content to discuss literary theory without reference to concrete examples of authors creating and revising their works, have been able to take the Barthes-Foucault attacks on the concept of an author as constituting an unquestionable principle of post-modern aesthetics. Having accepted all its implications for a dehumanising of the reader (a mere focal point, a three-dimensional space on which traces of the passage of a text have been left), a reduction of all written works to an undifferentiatable mess of *écriture* and intertextuality, and a depersonalisation of language to a discourse lacking agents — this fortunate few must find the literary criticism of a previous age, or of any school other than their own, unreadable, incomprehensible. What is this thing called an author? What are these 'works', let alone 'great works'? How can they be 'advanced' or 'improved' by human agency? Presumably such readers imagine intertextuality washing over texts at various intervals in time, adding a character here, deleting one there, changing motives, altering beginnings and endings, filling out the background of the representation of a given society at a given time with the relevant historical, geographical, social, economic, and cultural detail. Can discourse do all these things? How remarkable!

Such might well be the reflections of a very naïve reader brought up on a curriculum limited entirely to the iconoclasts of the 60s and their imitators of the 70s and 80s. It may seem only a pleasantry to imagine the effects of an education confined to such a canon, but a growing number of commentators disenchanted with iconoclasm are beginning to realize the effects such a School of Criticism and Theory would have on its pupils. I do not raise this as a real possibility, since I find it hard to believe that any teacher could so effectively close off all alternative approaches, and I dislike the sensationalising of intellectual issues, that arousal of anxiety or fear of the enemy as a means of rallying the forces of good sense against the threat from outside. Such polarisation and demonising are in fact the techniques used by the ideological schools of criticism which I shall be discussing shortly, and to emulate them would be to risk reducing literary criticism to a no-man's-land.

My aim in outlining the possible consequences of an exclusive diet of iconoclastic literary theory is to show that its rejection of so many fundamental concepts and categories would leave us with no way of discussing individual writers, or individual works. It would also make it impossible to think about a writer's development, from *The Comedy of Errors* to *The Winter's Tale*, say, or from *Titus Andronicus* to *King Lear*. Shakespeare's output covers a period of twenty to twenty-five years at the most, which would amount to a single 'episteme' of Foucault (since only one episteme is supposed to operate in any given period). Therefore, unless they are really going to ascribe everything to intertextuality, exponents of a depersonalised theory of literature would have no way of accounting for the differences between Shakespeare's early attempts — by no means negligible, on any criteria — and the masterpieces of his maturity. But since their literary theory couldn't detect such differences in the first place, having abandoned the concept of character, and rejected as 'formalism' a critical concern with plot, structure, poetry, prose, rhetoric or any approach other than that approved by their ideological camp, then presumably they would not be disturbed at the inadequacy of their theory here; indeed they could hardly recognise it.

To readers of another persuasion, however, it makes a lot more sense to think of the author as the controlling consciousness that draws on a lot of varied material, his own or other people's experience, often recorded in books (histories, biographies, other poems, other novels, other plays), organising it into a new literary work by the processes of selection, omission, amplification, and invention. To use sources as an aid or framework for individual creation has been the common practice of many writers in many cultures at many times. For some the recollection of their reading may be unconscious, as J. Livingston Lowes claimed for *Kubla Khan*.[52] For others we have abundant evidence of what they read and how they used it. Modern scholars have reconstructed George Eliot's 'Quarry for *Middlemarch*' and other notebooks.[53] We are extremely well informed as to what Joyce read and how he used it in *Ulysses* and *Finnegans Wake*,[54] or just what Wagner did to his sources for *Der Ring des Nibelungen*.[55] Joseph Conrad, accused in 1898 by a reader in Singapore of displaying in *Almayer's Folly* a 'complete ignorance of Malays and their habits and customs', defended himself in a letter to his publisher, William Blackwood:

> Well I never did set up as an authority on Malaysia. I looked for a medium in which to express myself. I am inexact and ignorant no doubt (most of us are) but I don't think I sinned so recklessly. Curiously enough all the details about the little characteristic acts and customs which they hold up as proof [of ignorance] I have taken out (to be safe) from undoubted sources — dull, wise books. It is rather staggering to find myself so far astray.[56]

One writer who specialised in reading 'dull, stupid books' was Flaubert, who for some thirty years kept a notebook (which he called 'un sottisier') in which he entered specimens of human stupidity. He then decided to use this material for a novel, originally to be called *Les Deux Cloportes* (*The Two Woodlice*), which became *Bouvard et Pécuchet*, unfinished at his death in 1880, and which bears the evidence of his having read, and taken notes from, some 1,500 books.[57] Flaubert may be a special case in this novel, but it remains quite normal for writers to research their works. The contemporary Peruvian author, Mario Vargas Llosa, based his novel *La Guerra del Fin del Mundo* (1981), set in late nineteenth-century Brazil during a millenarian uprising, on a novel, *Os sertões* by the Brazilian Euclides da Cunha, and on several historical accounts. Comparison between the sources and the novel reveals all kinds of transformations.[58]

*   *   *

Shakespeare is no different from other writers in using sources and re-shaping them to express his own conception of a story and the issues raised by it. We know a great deal about his life, and although documentary evidence is lacking on this point it has long been evident that the range of his knowledge of classical authors, myths, and customs can only be accounted for by assuming that he had a normal grammar-school education. The sixteenth-century grammar school had a limited and essentially literary curriculum, based on acquiring a working knowledge of Latin grammar, rhetoric, and compositional forms, but it instilled its teaching with formidable thoroughness.[59] There can be no doubt that Shakespeare had been through the normal training in verse and prose composition, and could read Terence, Caesar, Ovid, and some Virgil in the original. When it came to collecting materials for a play, Shakespeare used two major sources in English, Holinshed's *Chronicles of England, Scotlande and Irelande*, and North's English version (via Amyot's French) of Plutarch's *Parallel Lives of the Greeks and Romans*. Other translations he is known to have used include Chapman's Homer, Holland's Pliny, and Florio's Montaigne. With Ovid's *Metamorphoses*, a popular school text that he had studied in Latin, he regularly used Arthur Golding's English version. Yet at some points he went back to the Latin, and translated more exactly (Muir 1961, pp. 3–4). There is ample evidence that Shakespeare had 'read Latin works of which there was no translation — two plays by Plautus, Buchanan, Leslie, some of Livy . . .' (*ibid.*, p. 4), and he certainly knew enough French[60] and Italian[61] to be able to refer to sources in those languages if a story interested him. The full extent of his reading can now be studied in Geoffrey Bullough's magnificent collection, *Narrative and Dramatic Sources of Shakespeare*, which reprints sources and analogues, both definite and possible, with full critical discussion.[62]

Source-study can help us to reconstruct the process by which Shakespeare formed a play. Given that any literary work is an intentional product, by comparing the finished play to its sources we can deduce something of the author's intentions towards that work by considering what he included, omitted, changed. Throughout the time he spent reading, planning, and writing a play, usually between three and nine months (given his responsibility for at least thirty-seven plays over a period of about twenty years), we can think of Shakespeare performing a sustained exercise of discrimination. As Susanne Langer wrote,

> Art, and especially dramatic art, is full of compromises, for one possible effect is usually bought at the expense of another; not all ideas and devices that occur to the poet are co-possible. Every decision involves a rejection.[63]

This tissue of choices and rejections is governed by an aesthetic, a conception of drama which, consciously or otherwise, guided the process of invention, transformation, and integration by which a play became unified and complete in itself. Like other Elizabethan dramatists, Shakespeare had a working notion of plot in drama as implying a completed unit of action.

Perhaps they knew some of the commonplaces of classical literary theory, which itself derived from a discipline they certainly knew at first hand, rhetoric (the major document being Horace's *Ars poetica*).[64] The period in which they worked had in any case seen an enormous explosion of literary theory, most of it written in the universal language of Latin.[65] Another influence was from Latin drama, for the plays of Plautus and Terence were staples of every grammar school throughout Europe, both for their Latin and their improving doctrine, while Seneca's tragedies attracted many would-be actors and dramatists.[66] Schools and colleges regularly performed their own plays in Latin and English, pieces which, whatever their other faults, did not lack knowledge of classical models and the appropriate decorum.[67] Despite some pseudo-Marxist attempts to fence Elizabethan drama within the confines of 'popular culture', the dramatists were — by the standard of their contemporaries, and even more by ours — well-educated men, often keen to display their knowledge. Some had a University education (Marlowe, Lyly, Greene, Peele), but the output of those who had 'only' been to grammar school (the 'only' typifies the unconscious imposition of our social experience on to theirs) proves that they could cope with quite demanding Latin texts, while autodidacts like Jonson and Chapman were as knowledgeable as any professional writer in Europe. The English Renaissance, as J.W. Binns has recently shown, was open to international neo-Latin culture in ways that many modern scholars could not emulate.[68]

Elizabethan and Jacobean drama constitutes an almost unique phenomenon, a medium in which highly and lowly educated people could take part in the invention, performance, and enjoyment of works that drew on a great deal of literary and historical knowledge while including an immediately comprehensible, and often enthralling presentation of human behaviour. As the output of plays and the number of dramatists increased, actors and theatregoers grew in proportion, and conventions governing the writing of tragedy and comedy, already familiar from classical models, became widely accepted (Doran 1954, pp. 55–7, 85–8, 105–11, 217–20). The conventions of such newer genres as the chronicle play and tragicomedy had to be worked out, often in the face of disapproval from the more classically-minded, such as Sidney and Jonson. Without digressing into literary or theatrical history, we can simply affirm that all writers faced the problem of synthesising their literary and historical sources, which could be vast and diffuse, into the 'two-hour traffic of the stage'. They could all say, with the chorus in *Henry V*, 'we'll digest / Th'abuse of distance, force a play' (2, Prol. 31–2). They must all have had some notion of how much 'stuff', *copia*, was needed to fill a play, give it a satisfactory body and extent. Since, as we have seen, dramatists regularly collaborated on plays, with as many as five involved in an agreed division of labour[69] (something like 'story conferences' must have been regular events at the Globe or Swan), then they must have had some shared aesthetic principles for drama.[70] When Hamlet asks the First Player to recite the speech of 'Priam's slaughter' from 'an excellent play, well digested in the scenes, set down with as much modesty as cunning' (2.2.439–40), he is drawing on criteria for both structure and style, and when he rebukes those clowns who speak 'more than is set down for them' and 'themselves laugh too, though in the mean time some necessary question of the play be then to be consider'd' (3.2.38–43), he is appealing to a concept of dramatic focus as against digression and dissipation. The Elizabethan dramatists' working criteria for the composition of a play must have concerned the form, extent, and above all finality of the fable. 'Tragedies end with deaths, comedies with weddings, history plays with coronations or peace-treaties' — such a rule of thumb might be a starting point. As Thomas Heywood put it, in his *Apology for Actors* (1612: paraphrasing the fourth-century grammarian Evanthius in his commentary on Terence), 'Comedies begin in trouble, and end in peace; tragedies begin in calms, and end in tempest' (Doran 1954, pp. 106–107). While comedy dealt with the private affairs of citizens, especially love, ending with a happy solution to all problems (*ibid.*, pp. 107–108), 'ruin in tragedy meant death' (p. 118).

Shakespeare clearly had a concept of final unity. All his comedies end with weddings, sometimes multiple, having overcome any number of obstacles. The one exception is called, precisely, *Love's Labour's Lost*, in which, as Berowne complains of the year's penitence imposed on the lovers before they can renew their suit,

> Our wooing doth not end like an old play;
> Jack hath not Jill. These ladies' courtesy
> Might well have made our sport a comedy.
> KING.   Come, sir, it wants a twelvemonth and a day,
> And then 'twill end.
> BEROWNE.   That's too long for a play.   (5.2.870ff)

The chronicle material that Shakespeare used was all 'too long for a play', and anyone interested can see for themselves how he went about his task of cutting and re-shaping. Not that he read slowly, word-by-word: Matthew W. Black, looking at his shaping of *Richard II* from Holinshed, thinks he can trace Shakespeare's eye skipping as it read, first sifting the summaries in the marginal notes.[71]

If the chronicles are inherently shapeless, by definition inclusive rather than selective, much of the narrative material, whether verse or prose, that Shakespeare used for the histories and comedies is too drawn-out for the stage, being designed for sixteenth-century readers, who either read slowly or liked their money's worth in bulk at least. Adaptation of prose-fiction for drama carried its own problems, as has been shown.[72] Verse sources needed the same drastic handling. The events narrated in Arthur Brooke's *Romeus and Juliet* take nine months, in Shakespeare's play only a day or two, a reduction of time with a corresponding growth of intensity. Adapting Chaucer's *Troilus and Criseyde*, with its long-drawn and marvellously subtle account of a love affair building from desire to fruition to betrayal, Shakespeare starts late in the sequence and compresses the lovers' whole union and separation into half-a-dozen scenes, interwoven with the war material derived from the medieval chronicles of Troy and Chapman's *Iliad*.[73] The sudden parting forced on Troilus and Cressida is as much a shock to the audience as it is to them.

Dramatic unity, as Shakespeare practised it, referred not to the two lesser unities of place and time (although already formulated as prescriptive literary theory in the neoclassicism of Castelvetro), but to the major criterion of unified action. Two principles that he seems to have observed were that the deaths of characters, when relevant to the action, had to be contained within it; and that all characters should be integrally related either to the main or subplot, and ideally to both. Not all deaths were relevant to the action as Shakespeare conceived it. In Greene's *Pandosto*, his source for *The Winter's Tale*, the main character Pandosto (Leontes), having failed to recognise his sixteen-year old daughter Fawnia (Perdita), lusts after her, attempting her chastity with threats of force. This is one of several titillating scenes in his sources that, as Alfred Harbage showed, Shakespeare (unlike some dramatists) deliberately omitted.[74] Greene ends his novel, after the reunion of Leontes and Polixenes, and the wedding of Florizel and Perdita, by making Leontes commit suicide in self-disgust. Shakespeare keeps Leontes alive since he has kept the slandered wife alive (in Greene Bellaria really dies), in order to end his play with the recognition and reunion scenes so essential to the genre of Greek romance, on which he had long drawn. The continuity of life and love are proper to comedy, so Leontes lives.

In the sources Shakespeare used for his tragedies the main characters often live on in the rhythms of real life. For *Hamlet* he used the *Histoires Tragiques* of Belleforest (1576, 1582; not yet translated), in which the hero successfully revenges himself on his uncle, murderer of his father, and is crowned King. Subsequently he evades being killed by Hermutrude, Queen of Scotland, who has slain all her previous suitors but falls in love with Hamlet and 'marries' him. (He is already married, but his first wife doesn't object.) A wishfulfilling hero, not unlike the Trickster in many folktales and myths, this Hamlet is only killed a long time later, by another man, in a different quarrel (Bullough VII: 6–9). His death is 'outside' the events of the main plot, and unrelated to it, typical enough for chronicle material but of no use to Shakespeare's conception of tragedy. The source for *King Lear*, Geoffrey of Monmouth's *Historia regium Britanniae*, also has several unrelated climaxes. Lear divides his kingdom among his three daughters but disinherits Cordelia for not flattering him. Discovering the ingratitude of Goneril and Regan, Lear goes to Cordelia (who has married the King of Gaul), is well received, and is helped to regain his throne. Three years later he dies. Cordelia then becomes Queen and rules for another five years. Then her late sisters' sons depose her and put her in prison, where she kills herself (Bullough VII: 272–3, 311–16). This is the version retold in the *Mirror for Magistrates* and *The Faerie Queene*, both known to Shakespeare (*ibid.*: 274–6, 323–34), but he also knew *The True Chronicle Historie of King Leir and his Three Daughters* (1594; publ. 1605). The anonymous author of this play made the obvious decision over dramatising the chronicle, cutting it off at the point where Lear is restored to his throne and apologises to Cordelia and to his good counsellor for the wrongs he has done them (*ibid.*: 276–83, 287–98, 337–402), a happy end that Nahum Tate was to revive so successfully.

In *Hamlet* and *King Lear* Shakespeare reshaped his source material to give a tragic ending, and in both cases he did so by a remarkable demonstration of an author's shaping power, which Current Literary Theory would be wholly unable to describe. He attached a second level of plot to the main action, then intertwining the two to create many significant parallels and contrasts before making them collide destructively. Multiple plots are a well-known feature of Renaissance drama,[75] and the problem that English dramatists set themselves was not 'just the conversion of one story into a play, but the combining of two or three stories' into a coherent whole (Doran 1954, p. 298). In some plays the levels of plot run in parallel, without impinging on each other, in others unity is attempted by a contrast of tones, with the comic action parodying the serious one (*ibid.*, pp. 289–91). The great classical model for the skilful interrelation of double plots was Terence (p. 277), and contemporary Italian critics introduced the concept of a '"favola intrecciata", in which all lines . . . lead into and out of a central knot' (p. 301). As a budding author Shakespeare had outdone Plautus' *Menaechmi* in *The Comedy of Errors*, involving not one but two pairs of identical twins, developing the master-servant convention in ways that contemporary Italian comedians might have envied,[76] and inserting an episode from Plautus' *Amphitruo* for good measure. In the later comedies we can see him learning from Lyly, as G.K. Hunter showed in a classic study,[77] setting up several parallel strands of action before intertwining them, achieving deliberate effects of symmetry and repetition (Bullough VIII: 355–61).

The ability to intertwine plots presupposes that they have something in common, similarities of subject or theme which allow the dramatist to create meaningful juxtapositions. To the main plot of *Hamlet*, involving a father murdered and a son seeking revenge, Shakespeare added a subplot where another father is murdered. Hamlet, having killed Polonius (a deed which drives Ophelia to madness and suicide), becomes in turn the object of Laertes' revenge. That parallelism in the private world is echoed by one in the public realm, with Fortinbras trying to achieve compensation for the death of his father and the loss of his heritage not by covert revenge but by open military action. Shakespeare makes the parallels and contrasts between these three avenging sons explicit, in Hamlet's comparison between himself and Fortinbras (4.4.32–66), and in his resemblance to Laertes: 'by the image of my cause I see / The portraiture of his' (5.2.75–8), adding a fourth one in the Player's speech describing Pyrrhus killing Priam (2.2.448–518). The two major plot-levels are then made to cross destructively as Laertes, now the instrument of Claudius, kills Hamlet and is killed in turn by him. Having finally refused covert revenge Hamlet is able openly to kill Claudius in retribution, and without planning. Significantly, it is Fortinbras, the only character remaining outside the revenge action, who survives. In *King Lear* the sub-plot again parallels situation and theme. Shakespeare took a striking instance of filial ingratitude from Sidney's *Arcadia*, the story of the Paphlagonian king, who rejected his good son, Leonatus, trusted his bastard son Plexirtus, only to be blinded by him and cast out. (In the source the good son returns to nurse his father, defeating the bastard's murder-attempt, yet then pardons the evil son, who lives on to wreak more evil.) Shakespeare, having set up a remarkable resonance between the mad Lear and blinded Gloucester, brings the two plots together, once again with a destructive effect. Edmund is linked to Goneril and Regan by a web of lust and rivalry which makes one daughter kill the other and then herself, while he has the third hanged, so causing Lear's death. Edmund is himself killed by Edgar, a justified revenge and the logical consequence of Shakespeare's conception of tragedy as a disaster deriving from human conflicts in a strict pattern of cause and effect. In this play he not only makes the two plots echo and cross each other destructively, but also allows the blinding of Gloucester to create a whole sequence of imagery relating to sight and blindness in the main plot (Bullough VIII: 395–6).

*   *   *

The central problems facing the dramatist, Madeleine Doran observed in her pioneering study of form in Elizabethan drama, were 'how to get concentration, and how to achieve organic structure', requiring a successful 'fusion between story and characters' (Doran 1954, pp. 265, 250). The last play in which I want to explore, in rather more detail, Shakespeare's deliberate and controlled transformation of his sources is *Othello*, usually regarded as having a single plot and a single source, the *Hecatommithi* or 'Hundred Tales' of Giraldi Cinthio (1565; not translated). In fact, there is evidence that Shakespeare did some well-directed background reading for a plot-element that he added to the play, the Turkish military threat. Cinthio has no mention of the Turks, but Shakespeare was well aware of the danger they represented in the Mediterranean in the sixteenth century. Just as in *King Lear*, where he drew on a recent exposure of a Jesuit pretence to exorcise demons, Samuel Harsnett's *Declaration of Egregious Popish Impostures* (1603), to give Edgar in his feigned madness the authentic jargon of devils,[78] for information about the Venetian-Turkish wars Shakespeare consulted a recent book (the play was written in 1603–04), Richard Knolles's *History of the Turks* (1603), alongside two older authorities. Having assembled these background sources (Muir 1961, pp. 128–9; Bullough VII: 211–14, 262–5), Shakespeare then wholly integrated them into his plot. (It is always a surprise to start from a play you know well, then to compare the sources and find borrowings which you could never have suspected, so seamlessly are they absorbed.) News of the Turkish fleet sailing towards Cyprus reaches Othello just after Iago has told him of Brabantio's anger at Desdemona's elopement, beginning that interplay between private and public life that is to run through the whole play. Cassio reports that the Council of Venice is in emergency session, having 'hotly called for' Othello, and sent three search-parties to find him (1.2.34ff). Othello is prevented from going there at once by Brabantio's angry arrival, but the news of this urgent business of state in turn means that Brabantio has to accompany Othello to the council-chamber in order to lay a formal accusation of seducing his daughter by magical arts. In this invented episode of a man defending himself against the charge of witch-craft (for which Shakespeare drew on classical models),[79] Othello is allowed to demonstrate that dignity and imperturbability in the face of danger or misfortune which belonged to the classical virtue of fortitude, and which was his settled characteristic before Iago destroyed him. ('Is this the nature / Whom passion could not shake?', as Lodovico subsequently asks in amazement: 4.1.265ff.) Shakespeare invented not only the accusa-tion and self-defence, but added several details in this scene to show Othello's high standing as a servant of the state: the fact that the Duke welcomes him so warmly — 'Valiant Othello, we must straight employ you / Against the general enemy Ottoman' (1.3.48) — and justifies appointing him governor of Cyprus in place of Montano as having a superior reputation (221ff); the readiness with which the Duke accepts Othello's request to allow Desdemona to go with him (275ff). The picture that Shakespeare creates of Othello in Venice is of a man who has triumphantly overcome all obstacles in both public and private life.

Having introduced the Turkish threat to motivate Othello's despatch to Cyprus, Shakespeare dispels it with the same creative freedom by calling up a storm to destroy their fleet (2.1.1–32). But he then makes the storm serve several dramatic functions. Not only Cassio but the whole population of Cyprus expresses anxiety for Othello's safety (2.1.53–4), showing their dependence on him. Shakespeare's placing of Desdemona and the other Venetians in a second ship, which arrives first, puts Desdemona in the temporary care of Cassio and Iago (2.1.83–179), a situation immediately used to display Iago's sinister abilities in improvising witty (and misogynist) verses, and to reveal the true depth of his hatred of Cassio ('Yet again your fingers to your lips? Would they were clyster-pipes for your sake!'). The foregrounding of Iago for the audience in asides and soliloquies sets up a

double action by which Shakespeare can both celebrate Othello's reunion
with Desdemona and undermine it. Othello's sense of having attained the
highest degree of human happiness seems immediately vulnerable given
Iago's aside to us: 'O, you are well tuned now! But I'll set down the pegs
that make this music, as honest as I am'. On the outer level of events, the
public rejoicing ordered by Othello to mark the 'perdition of the Turkish
fleet' (2.2) allows a scene of drinking and revelry, which Iago can exploit
to make Cassio drunk and to foment the fatal quarrel that has him
cashiered (2.3.12–145), which in turn . . . and so on. Shakespeare not
only invented the Turkish threat and the storm, he tied them into the plot
at several levels in order to define and display the human beings involved
and the relations between them, so stable now, so suddenly changed. If we
look at his source, we find Cinthio reporting only that 'the Venetian lords
made a change in the forces that they used to maintain in Cyprus; and they
chose the Moor as Commandant of the soldiers whom they sent there'
(Bullough VII: 242). There is no crisis, no Turkish threat, and no storm.
Having been persuaded by Disdemona to let her accompany him, Cinthio's
moor 'embarked in the galley with his lady and all his train, . . . and with a
sea of the utmost tranquillity arrived safely in Cyprus' (243).
    Already by this point in the play Shakespeare has articulated many of
the important issues, matters never touched on in Cinthio's narrative.
Where the source gives Disdemona some 'relatives' who try to dissuade her,
Shakespeare invented the disapproving father, ready to welcome Othello
into his house to entertain his daughter, but not to have 'the sooty bosom /
Of such a thing as you' for a son-in-law. Either the awareness that her
father will not give his permission, or Othello's impending despatch to the
Cyprus wars, makes Desdemona elope rather than try to marry him openly.
But while proving her love for Othello, their tricking Brabantio with a
secret marriage gives Iago one of his most vicious insinuations about her:

> She that so young could give out such a seeming,
> To seal her father's eyes up close as oak,
> He thought 'twas witchcraft. . . .   (3.3.208ff)

Brabantio in fact accused Othello of witchcraft, but Iago cunningly
leaves the imputation open, as if referring to Desdemona. Iago can make
such insinuations without being refuted because Othello obviously does
not know Desdemona well. Whereas the Moor in the source has served
Venice for an unspecified period, living a happy and stable marriage with
Disdemona for some time before leaving Venice, Shakespeare's Othello has
only been in Venice for nine months, having seen uninterrupted military
service until then. He is truly a stranger in 'this great world' (1.3.83ff),
and only just married. Indeed, the urgency of his despatch to fight the
Turks means that their marriage cannot be consummated on their wedding
night (1.3.221–8, 298–300), but has to await their safe arrival on Cyprus
(2.2.6–7; 2.3.8–11, 15–18). Even then, the consummation is interrupted

by the drunken brawl that Iago has instigated (2.3.246–53). The fact that Othello is unfamiliar with Venetian society, and can have no deep knowledge of Desdemona, these are two crucial changes to the source, making Othello unusually vulnerable to Iago's attack. As so often in the tragedies, Shakespeare takes great pains to place his characters in a context where their personal qualities can only bring them greater sufferings.

In adapting Cinthio Shakespeare is pursuing several goals simultaneously, the most important being to give Iago greater prominence. Having argued in Chapter 1 that Iago's destructive intentionality is the decisive element energising the plot, I find it fascinating to see the ways in which Shakespeare adapted the source to establish Iago's supremacy. Cinthio gave a concentrated account of Iago's hypocrisy which provided a useful character-outline:

> The Moor had in his company an Ensign of handsome presence but the most scoundrelly nature in the world. He was in high favour with the Moor, who had no suspicion of his wickedness; for although he had the basest of minds, he . . . cloaked the vileness hidden in his heart with high-sounding and noble words. . . . (243)

That passage gives us the 'honest' Iago, the hypocrite whose true nature is never suspected. Shakespeare then had to dramatise his powers of dissimulation, make them plausible by showing how Iago transmits a positive image of himself of everyone he meets, in quick succession: Othello, the Venetian Council, Cassio, Montano, Desdemona, Lodovico. The only people who know something of his true nature are Roderigo and Emilia, but neither can disclose it, his wife out of loyalty, Roderigo since he is Iago's accomplice or dupe. One decisive change made by Shakespeare which at first seems to reduce Iago's importance concerns the 'love-triangle'. In the source we read how

> The wicked Ensign, taking no account of the faith he had pledged to his wife, and of the friendship, loyalty and obligations he owed the Moor, fell ardently in love with Disdemona, and bent all his thoughts to see if he could manage to enjoy her. . . . (243–4)

Afraid that the Moor 'might straightway kill him' if he wooed her openly, the Ensign attempted to communicate his desires to her 'deviously', but she did not respond. The Ensign then thinks that he has failed because Disdemona is 'in love with the Corporal' (Cassio), a good friend and frequent visitor to the Moor's house. His desire frustrated,

> the love which he had felt for the Lady now changed to the bitterest hate, and he gave himself up to studying how to bring it about that, once the Corporal were killed, if he himself could not enjoy the Lady, then the Moor should not have her either. (244)

So he decides to accuse her to the Moor of adultery with the Corporal.

The Iago of the source primarily hates Desdemona, because she has not reciprocated his desire; in the second place he hates Cassio, whom he suspects Desdemona of loving; and only as an afterthought does he attempt to harm Othello, the one man for sure who enjoys her favour. Shakespeare eliminates the motif of Iago loving Desdemona, apart from one reference — 'The Moor [will] prove to Desdemona / A most dear husband. Now, I do love her too . . .' (2.2.282ff) — a remark which, in isolation, and considering all his other stated motives, can only seem gratuitous. Given that this Iago no longer loves Desdemona, there is no occasion for hatred, indeed he expresses (in his own person) unforced admiration for her beauty and virtue. As for Iago's feelings towards Cassio, Shakespeare makes two crucial changes. First, Iago resents Cassio not because Desdemona loves him (Shakespeare transferred that motive to Roderigo), but because Cassio has been promoted over Iago's head — or so he claims (1.1.8–40). Yet the terms in which Iago vilifies Cassio ('a great arithmetician . . . bookish theoric') make it clear that Cassio is one of that new breed of soldiers in the sixteenth century with a knowledge of military science and technology, while Iago can only claim the old sweat's seniority as grounds for promotion. Further, the trust in Cassio shown by Othello, whose professional judgment is otherwise endorsed by everybody (including Iago), and by the Venetians who appoint Cassio to govern Cyprus (4.1.235ff), proves that Iago's criticisms of Cassio's soldiership are not justified — but therefore all the more bitter. Secondly, Shakespeare makes Iago jealous of Cassio as a lover, not with Desdemona but (improbable though it seems) with Emilia ('For I fear Cassio with my night-cap too': 2.1.301). Both changes give Iago more powerful and (presumably) longer-standing motives, in public as well as private life, to hate and harm Cassio than his putative success with Desdemona.

The biggest change of all concerns Iago's attitude towards Othello. In the source the Ensign accuses Disdemona of adultery in order to harm her and the Corporal, using the Moor to bring about their destruction. Shakespeare reverses this motivation. From the first few moments of the play, as we saw in Chapter 1, Iago expresses his consuming hatred of Othello: 'Despise me if I do not' hate him, he tells Roderigo (1.1.8), making a real litany of his malice: 'I have told thee often, and I re-tell thee again and again, I hate the Moor' (1.3.362ff). To Roderigo, we notice, Iago justifies his hatred purely with motives from his public life, the career-soldier passed over for an upstart. To the audience 'in private', however, he admits another motive, from his private life:

> I hate the Moor;
> And it is thought abroad that 'twixt my sheets
> He's done my office. (1.3.384ff)

Again he tells us, 'I do suspect the lusty Moor / Hath leaped into my seat', so that he must have 'revenge', be 'evened with him, wife for wife'

(2.1.289ff). This is a completely new, obviously irrational but therefore all the more powerful motive for hatred. These several changes intertwine public and private domains to achieve a maximum friction. Where the source gave the Ensign a purely sexual motivation for hating the Corporal, Shakespeare has invented the fact of Cassio being promoted at Iago's expense, so giving an additional reason for resentment but then redirecting it away from the woman towards the two men. Uninterested in Desdemona, Iago evidently believes that Cassio and Othello have destroyed both his public career and his marriage, by seducing Emilia. (As critics have long observed, this makes Iago the truly jealous man, displaying both misogyny and paranoia.) To achieve revenge on Cassio Iago gets him dismissed, just fails to murder him, and has Bianca arrested as an accomplice, nearly ruining both Cassio's career and his sole personal relationship. By destroying Othello's private life Iago destroys his public one, too, as Othello recognises in that anguished word-play concluding his formal renunciation: 'Othello's occupation's gone' (3.3.359). The desire to harm Othello, an afterthought in Cinthio, becomes for Shakespeare's Iago the driving force in all his deeds, but always covert: hiding in the dark while slandering him to Brabantio (1.1.68–160), producing those destructive predictions in his asides when Othello greets Desdemona (2.1.166–198), and when he manipulates Cassio's appearance to Othello (4.1.93–172). The hatred is expressed most of all, as we alone know, in the many soliloquies, only equalled in number among Shakespeare's characters by Richard III and Hamlet; but distinguished from them by a single-minded focus on hatred and destruction. Our view of Iago is so complete that it is easy to forget how little anyone else knows about him.

In Acts I and II Shakespeare created a dramatic structure of his own, only beginning to draw on Cinthio closely in Act III, for Iago's insinuation of Desdemona's adultery.[80] By then Shakespeare has so transformed the nature of Iago's intentionality that his manipulation of Othello is put to a wholly different purpose, and is in any case carried through with a psychological intensity that Cinthio never approaches. Given this fundamental change of motive it was only to be expected that Iago should now play a larger role. But what is surprising when we read Cinthio for the first time is to see how many times Shakespeare invented new, or adapted extant material in order to link it to Iago's controlling design. The most striking invention in connection with Iago is Roderigo. In Cinthio the Ensign performs his slanders to the Moor single-handed, and he himself attacks the Corporal in the dark, managing to cut off his leg but not kill him (Bullough VII:249). Iago has far more ambitious plans, involving the destruction of Cassio, Othello, and Desdemona ('out of her own goodness make the net / That shall enmesh them all': 2.3.353f). So Shakespeare invents Roderigo as an accomplice to do the visible dirty work, slandering Othello to Brabantio, picking a quarrel with the drunken Cassio, and undertaking his murder. Since this 'gull'd Gentleman', as the Folio *dramatis personae* describes him, would hardly agree to such evil deeds unless he stood to benefit from them, Shakespeare makes Roderigo hopelessly in love with Desdemona. Roderigo the suitor has for some time been the familiar gull for Iago, who has pretended to act as go-between, demanding money to advance his affairs. (As Kenneth Muir noted, this relationship echoes that of Toby Belch in *Twelfth Night*, exploiting Aguecheek while purportedly furthering his suit to Olivia: Muir 1961, p. 131.)

Roderigo is more than a cipher, however, for Shakespeare uses him to reveal more facets of Iago's character. The oscillation of hope and despair that the unsuccessful suitor experiences means that Iago must periodically cheer him up, encouraging his aspirations by describing both Othello and Desdemona as attracted by sensual appetite only, a denigration so far from the truth as to show Roderigo's pathetic gullibility, as well as Iago's talents for defamation (1.3.341–59; 2.1.215–57; 2.3.362–74; 4.2.174–245). Shakespeare creates Roderigo and lets him act to fulfil his desires; but what seems to him freedom is, we see, a terrible dependence on a ruthless exploiter. 'Thus do I ever make my fool my purse' (1.3.381) is Iago's first comment on Roderigo, and he punctuates his manipulation with equally contemptuous metaphors — 'a snipe' (1.3.383), 'this poor trash of Venice, whom I leash / For his quick hunting' (2.1.297–8), 'this young quat' (5.1.11). 'O inhuman dog!' are Roderigo's dying words (5.1.62), yet we wonder at his self-deception in thinking that Iago would treat him more kindly than he does other people.

The scenes with Roderigo were designed by Shakespeare to have another important function, that of showing us how Iago manages to convince his dupes that he loves them and acts only on their behalf. Iago does the same thing with Cassio, first in public, that cunning pretence of loyalty to his comrade in which he seems to be trying to suppress the truth about his drunken quarrel (2.3.173–245) — Shakespeare invented the drunkenness — then in private, when he offers Cassio sympathy and advice (2.3.254–328). In this sequence, too, Shakespeare adapts his source to show the action being controlled by Iago, as if everything that happens takes place at his bidding. In Cinthio Cassio's dismissal is a brief incident with which Iago has no connection: 'Not long after, the Moor deprived the Corporal of his rank for having drawn his sword and wounded a soldier while on guard-duty' (Bullough VII: 244). In Shakespeare the plot is devised, partly controlled, and finally exploited by Iago in a development that, for once, he had not forecast in the regular briefings he gives us. All that he told us was: 'I'll have our Michael Cassio on the hip, / . . . Make the Moor thank me, love me, and reward me' (2.1.299ff). Having achieved both goals Iago then deftly improvises a new stage of pretence, consoling Cassio and giving him 'probal' advice: 'I'll tell you what you shall do. Our general's wife is now the general. . . . Confess yourself freely to her; importune her help to put you in your place again' (2.3.307ff). This invention, too, shows Iago both directing events and predicting their outcome. In the sources

Disdemona, grieved by the Corporal's loss of rank, on her own initiative 'tried many times to reconcile the Moor with him' (244), without the Corporal asking her to intercede. By persuading Cassio to petition Desdemona, knowing that she will gladly act in a good cause, Iago sees that he can set up a chain-reaction in which, while

> she for him pleads strongly to the Moor,
> I'll pour this pestilence into his ear,
> That she repeals him for her body's lust;
> And by how much she strives to do him good,
> She shall undo her credit with the Moor.
> So will I turn her virtue into pitch . . .

(2.3.346ff)

In this way Iago establishes a linked intercession, Cassio → Desdemona → Othello, in the realm of Cassio's public life, his military career, which he can then present to Othello as displaying the relationship Cassio ↔ Desdemona, in the private, erotic sphere. Neither Cassio nor Desdemona ever realise how Iago misrepresents their innocent concerns.

Having carefully constructed this series of plots, all coined by Iago, Shakespeare inserts them into the next stages of Cinthio's narration, which is a straightforward sequence of action and reaction. In the source it is the Moor who reports to the Ensign that 'his wife importuned him so much for the Corporal', and only then does the Ensign, in response, insinuate that she does so out of love for the Corporal. The Moor then openly confronts Disdemona with his suspicion, and she affirms her innocence while not managing to remove the Moor's suspicion (Bullough VII: 244–6). Shakespeare takes over several details in Iago's slandering of Desdemona and Cassio but adapts them to a narrative quite different in kind, since all the suspicions now emanate from Iago. By his devious insinuations Iago has created so much distrust that Othello cannot ask his wife direct questions, since he no longer believes that she would reply truthfully. Iago's intentionality in manipulation and destruction is given its climactic expression with the handkerchief. In the source the Corporal, having found Disdemona's handkerchief in his lodgings (where the Ensign had placed it), goes to their house to return it. He knocks on the door, but the Moor has unexpectedly returned, and the Corporal, 'fearing that he might come down and attack him, fled without answering'. The Moor opens the door, finds nobody there, and angrily asks his wife who it was. She does not know, but the Moor is convinced that it was the Corporal (247). Shakespeare uses this incident, yet brings it forward to the beginning of the insinuation scene, and allows Iago to initiate mistrust that Cassio 'would steal away so guilty-like, / Seeing you coming' (3.3.35ff). That gives Iago the all-important opening move for his duping and destroying of Othello. These scenes (3.3.93–481; 4.1), which I have already discussed in terms of Iago's perversion of the principles governing human intercourse, seem completely convincing within the highly concentrated form of drama, since Shakespeare has invented virtually the whole of Acts I and II in order to show Iago successfully manipulating, one after the other, every one to whom he addressed himself. In Cinthio, given the normal rhythms of prose narrative, the arousing of the Moor's jealousy to the point where he wants to kill both Disdemona and the Corporal takes weeks. In reducing the time-scale of his source Shakespeare vastly increased both its intensity and the plausibility of Iago as the supreme deceiver.

While consistently tying events to Iago, Shakespeare makes another change which apparently reduces Iago's involvement, this time concerning his acquisition of the handkerchief. In the source the Ensign, using his three-year old daughter as a decoy, himself steals the handkerchief from Disdemona, and plants it in the Corporal's lodgings (246–7). In Shakespeare Desdemona drops it, Emilia picks it up and, all the loyal wife — 'I nothing but to please his fantasy' — gives it to her husband (3.3.292–322). Although Iago's plot prospers here by accident rather than design, as every reader of Machiavelli knows, *fortuna* smiles on those who display *virtù*. In any case, the more important result achieved by this change is that Emilia unknowingly becomes the accomplice of Iago in his whole plan to destroy Othello and Desdemona. By humouring her husband's wishes here she provides Othello with the 'ocular proof' he has desired, the clinching detail to justify him executing his wife. Although that is a terrible service she performed, the fact that Emilia can reveal to Othello after the murder that it was she who found and gave the handkerchief to Iago provides undeniable proof, now, of Desdemona's innocence and Iago's guilt (5.2.216–35). Critics who object to this trivial piece of linen have seldom noticed that Shakespeare's plotting involved Emilia with the handkerchief for the crucial evidence she could supply later. Emilia is the mute but surely uncomfortable witness in three scenes to the sufferings Desdemona endures for having lost this all-precious love token: Othello's cross-questioning her (3.4), the scene where he calls her a whore (4.2), and the scene following, where she helps to get Desdemona ready for bed. Emilia's crime is still venial, for she cannot know what Iago and Othello intend. Wifely obedience is another virtue that Iago can exploit. In the source the Ensign's wife was not involved in stealing the handkerchief, but otherwise she 'knew everything (for her husband had wished to use her as an instrument in causing the Lady's death, but she had never been willing to consent) . . .' (248). This detail makes her a much more serious accomplice to the crime, but she escapes punishment.

The tragic catastrophe in Cinthio is sensational, sordid, and anti-climactic. The Moor conceals the Ensign in a closet in his bedroom, and when Disdemona gets out of bed in the night to investigate a noise the Ensign kills her with three blows from a sand-filled sock. 'Then, placing her in the bed, and breaking her skull, he and the Moor made the ceiling fall', so that Disdemona's death is put down to accident (250–51). The Moor, 'who had loved the Lady more than his life', is inconsolable after her death, and begins to loathe the Ensign, openly expressing his hostility. The Ensign then goes to the Corporal, who now has a wooden leg, and persuades him to return to Venice, where he alleges that it was the Moor who cut off his leg and murdered Disdemona. The Corporal duly denounces the Moor to the Signoria, who bring him back from Cyprus for trial, but despite torture 'he denied everything so firmly' that no admission could be extorted from him. The Moor was released from prison but condemned to exile, 'in which he was finally slain by Disdemona's relatives, as he richly deserved'. The Ensign returned to his country and to his evil ways, made another false accusation, was arrested and tortured on evidence 'so fiercely that his inner organs were ruptured', and he died miserably. 'Thus did God avenge the innocence of Disdemona. And all these events were told' by the Ensign's wife, the sole survivor (251–2), the accomplice kept alive to be their narrator.

That sequence is typical of much of the source material Shakespeare used, in that a series of disasters is spread over a great period of time and only loosely related to the main events of the story. By having the Ensign murder Disdemona Cinthio allows him to fulfil his revenge on her for not reciprocating his love — a motive of which both Disdemona and the Moor remain ignorant to the end, so denying them recognition of the cause that destroys them. The Moor's attempt to deny responsibility for Disdemona's murder deprives him of any ethical dimension, and his being killed by Disdemona's relatives introduces an outside element into the plot, quite unprepared for. The Ensign's death 'in another country', for an unrelated quarrel with an unnamed figure, completes the dislocation in Cinthio of action from consequence. In *Othello* the fates of all these characters are interrelated, derive organically from the destructive designs of Iago and their virtual realisation, were it not for the intervention of Emilia. Most important for the tragedy, Shakespeare gives Othello the feeling of responsibility for his deluded actions which makes him accuse and destroy himself in a mixture of disgust and remorse. His ethical sense finally gives him tragic stature.

The credit for this coherent and meaningful transformation of the diffuse source lies neither with intertextuality nor discourse, but with the author. In order to appreciate Shakespeare's decisive intervention in this story we have simply to reverse Foucault's scheme and reclaim all the things he discarded. The author is indeed 'the unifying principle in a particular group of writings . . ., lying at the origins of their significance, as the seat of their coherence'. It is he 'who implants, into the troublesome language of fiction, its unities, its coherences, its links with reality' (Foucault 1972, pp. 221–2). Far from rejecting them, we shall continue to use the four notions that have dominated the history of ideas, 'signification, originality, unity, creation', and we shall continue to concern ourselves with 'the point of creation, the unity of a work, . . . the mark of individual originality and the infinite wealth of hidden meanings' (p. 230). The meanings are indeed multiple, but not hidden: they are open to all who read or see these plays performed.

PART II

CRITICAL PRACTICES

CHAPTER THREE

Deconstruction: Undermining, Overreaching

As a mode of textual theory and analysis, contemporary *deconstruction* subverts almost everything in the tradition, putting in question received ideas of the sign and language, the text, the context, the author, the reader, the role of history, the work of interpretation, and the forms of critical writing.   V. Leitch[1]

> Let it work,
> For 'tis the sport to have the enginer
> Hoist with his own petar, an't shall go hard
> But I will delve one yard below their mines,
> And blow them at the moon.   *Hamlet*, 3.4.205–9

I

The term deconstruction was coined by Derrida in the 1960s, and to a generation of critics who have been brought up to identify that term, with all its vague connotations of subverting existing order, with Derrida himself, it evidently seems as if he had originated all the critical attitudes that are conveniently summed up in the first epigraph above. One of my concerns in this book is to restore some order into the history of contemporary literary theory, to identify sets of attitudes and beliefs while also tracing their filiation, the thinkers or groups who formulated them at a specific time for a specific purpose. Because it is so recent, contemporary attitudes are sometimes thought not to have any history, just existing as the expression of some profound need in our situation, here and now. In fact, the conglomerate of subversive attitudes identified in that quotation all go back to the structuralism of Lévi-Strauss and Barthes, to the Paris of the 1950s and 60s.

Since then, of course, deconstruction has been institutionalised, largely in America, has been taken up by a number of prominent academics, has been a source of bitter controversy and even journalistic scandal following the revelation that one of its leading advocates, Paul de Man, had written pro-Nazi journalism during the second world war. My dissatisfaction with deconstruction long antedated these disclosures and has been unaffected by them, although the ways in which some of its proponents reacted to these unpleasant truths showed a sad lack of balance and integrity. (Anyone who doubts this should read David Lehman's thoroughly documented history of the episode.)[2]

Although strikingly successful in American universities, moving within a decade 'from an anti-establishment insurgency to an entrenched institutional power' (Lehman 1991, p. 53) — a success which seems to its more radical exponents to show the academy's sinister ability to absorb, and so neutralise whatever challenges it — deconstruction has been very sharply evaluated by a formidable array of literary critics and historians of criticism. These include, in the first phase, between 1977 and 1984, M.H. Abrams, in three trenchant essays,[3] Gerald Graff in his book *Literature Against Itself* and other review essays,[4] Denis Donoghue in his book *Ferocious Alphabets* and in some essay-reviews,[5] and — in many ways its most devastating critic — the philosopher of language John Searle in two celebrated (or notorious) essays.[6] So far all the critics of deconstruction were either American or working in America. The solitary full-length English study in this period was Christopher Butler's *Interpretation, Deconstruction, and Ideology,*[7] which was particularly helpful in not only evaluating deconstruction but in outlining some reasoned alternative approaches to language and literature.

All these writers were critical of deconstruction from the outset. In others we can trace a movement from excited acceptance to a rather sour disappointment. Frank Lentricchia, in *After the New Criticism* (1980), accepted without demur almost all the theories of Derrida and Foucault, but attacked their American disciples.[8] In *Criticism and Social Change* (1983), however, deconstruction itself is attacked as 'that passive kind of conservatism called quietism', and de Man is found chiefly guilty in that both his mode of reading and his attitude to politics produce a sense of paralysis that encourages resigned acceptance of the political and social status quo. Later, in *Ariel and the Police* (1988), Lentricchia made a very sharp analysis of 'Michel Foucault's Fantasy for Humanists', including some sardonic comments on the so-called American 'New Historicism'. Edward Said's enthusiastic espousal of the new continental critics in 1971 gave way to a rather ambivalent view in 1978, culminating in substantial disillusionment by 1983.[9] Finally, in the second half of the decade, four complementary book-length studies appeared, by Michael Fischer, Wendell V. Harris, Raymond Tallis, and John M. Ellis, which between them delivered some decisive blows.[10]

At the same time critiques of deconstruction were being produced by writers working in the history of contemporary thought. These include a number of books that I have drawn on in my first two chapters. Two Marxist critics made penetrating evaluations of structuralism and post-structuralism while defending a materialist concept of history and society in the face of the French 1960s elevation of language to a suzerainty in human knowledge. Sebastiano Timpanaro, in *Sul Materialismo* (1970; English tr. 1975) wrote a long essay on 'Structuralism and its Successors'

(Timpanaro 1975, pp. 135–219), giving perceptive accounts of Saussure, Lévi-Strauss, Chomsky, and Althusser, while Perry Anderson, in his Wellek lectures, *In the Tracks of Historical Materialism* (1983), made a brief evaluation of the debate over 'Structure and Subject' (pp. 32–55) which combines remarkable insight with trenchant criticism.[11] The philosopher and historian of philosophy Vincent Descombes, in *Le Même et l'autre: quarante-cinq ans de philosophie française 1933–1978* (1979; English tr. 1981) and *Grammaire d'Objets en tous genres* (1983; English tr. 1986), made some patient, witty, but highly critical evaluations of Lévi-Strauss, Barthes, Foucault, and Derrida.[12] Simon Clarke, an English sociologist, in *The Foundations of Structuralism. A Critique of Lévi-Strauss and the Structuralist Movement*, produced one of the best studies of that movement in any language, while J.G. Merquior, a Brazilian who studied anthropology with Lévi-Strauss for several years, wrote from first-hand experience *A Critique of Structuralist and Post-Structuralist Thought*, the sub-title of a book called *From Prague to Paris*, and a shorter but extremely acute study of Foucault.[13] The hermeneutic philosopher Manfred Frank, in *Was ist Neostrukturalismus?* (1984; tr. 1989), evaluated this French movement from a German viewpoint, avowedly working for a rapprochement between the two traditions: the cumulative effect of his book, however, is rather devastating for the philosophical reputations of Derrida, Lacan, and Foucault.[14] An English critic, Peter Dews, with a rare and refreshingly wide first-hand knowledge of continental philosophy, in *Logics of Disintegration. Post-structuralist Thought and the Claims of Critical Theory*, gave a no less devastating evaluation of the philosophical and political incoherences of this movement, judged to have already lost its vitality ('no longer . . . a living force in France': Dews 1987, p. xii).[15] Finally (from my knowledge, that is), Thomas G. Pavel, with a detailed knowledge of contemporary linguistics and French philosophy, described *Le Mirage linguistique* (1988), translated as *The Feud of Language. A History of Structuralist Thought*,[16] which begins 'My generation witnessed the rise and, one might safely add, the *fall* of one of the most influential yet perplexing trends in this century — French structuralism and poststructuralism' (Pavel 1989, p. 1). News of the fall has yet to reach some places.

I have briefly listed these studies to show that deconstruction has been much discussed as a theoretical system, and that the balance of opinion has shifted, I believe decisively, to the critical side. My own evaluation of its theories of language and literature in the first two chapters was certainly not encouraging. In this chapter I want to analyse its value when used for practical criticism, especially when applied to Shakespeare. Originally, however, deconstruction was not intended as literary criticism. The goals of deconstruction, as defined by Derrida, were philosophical. They were directed in particular against metaphysics, but were enlarged to attack what Derrida denounced as the 'logocentrism' of 'the whole of Western philosophy since Plato'. Many of Derrida's exponents in America have echoed this resounding phrase. Thus J. Hillis Miller: 'A deconstructionist is not a parasite but a patricide. He is a bad son demolishing beyond hope and repair the machine of Western metaphysics' (Miller 1979, p. 251). (Parricide or Luddite?) Actually, as Vincent Descombes has shown, all that deconstruction can 'undermine' are the 'descriptive ambitions' of phenomenology, in particular 'Husserlian descriptions', that is, merely 'the descriptive facade of phenomenology' (Descombes 1986, p. 62). Phenomenology has survived; one doubts if deconstruction will.

At times, it sounds as if deconstructionists are trying to emulate Herostratus, who set out to become the most famous man in the world by destroying the temple of Artemis at Ephesus. (He at least succeeded.) But although its first orientation was against philosophy, deconstruction has been taken up neither by philosophers, nor linguists — a significant rejection, as John Searle observed (Searle 1983, pp. 78–9) — but by literary critics. Deconstruction may have attracted them initially with its scepticism about language, but they accepted without demur Derrida's claim that all the weaknesses he diagnosed in language must, perforce, hold for literature. An older type of philosophical approach to language would treat it as primarily propositional, having a truth-content that could be analysed by conventional means. A more recent school would analyse actual language-usage. Derrida, however, scorned both logical analysis and empirical observation, merely proclaiming in his uniquely evasive style that language could not convey a single determinate meaning. As we have seen, he depends on semantics while simultaneously rejecting it, invoking the identification of meaning only to deny that it can ever be identified with certainty. So the deconstructionist following Derrida's lead will locate key words in the text he reads, draw attention to their ambivalence or indeterminacy, and thereby not just 'call that text into question' but — always as ever also already — language itself.[17] This is a rather easy activity, as Wendell Harris observes: 'if one surveys either an extended text or several texts by the same author, it is almost always possible, by lifting out sentences from here and there, to show that an author has used the same word in incompatible senses' (Harris 1988, p. 145). But I have a more pressing objection to this procedure, which obviously assumes from the outset that the coherence of literary works stands or falls on the referential firmness of its organising concepts. This might well be true of certain philosophical works (Hobbes's Leviathan, for instance, with its scrupulous care over accurate definitions), but it cannot be true of works of literature, which do not rely on language in this way. As we saw in Chapter 2, novels and plays are representations of human behaviour, their language embodies the utterances and actions of the characters involved, and, in fiction, those of the narrator. These words and utterances do not have a propositional value, and cannot be analysed as if belonging to philosophical discourse. If ambivalence is found, then, as we know from the work of William Empson and the New Criticism, that can produce an enrichment of their literary substance. A different, functionally or rhetorically oriented approach, might want to enquire whether the ambivalences were intended by any of the characters, and if so, who used them, and for what purpose. Ambivalence in itself is not particularly damaging, being an unavoidable feature of human communication, as we saw in Chapter 1, and which can usually be cleared up by further speech acts. To Derrida's followers, however, ambivalence in a literary work is neither a virtue nor a facet of character, but proof of the innate weakness of language.

Forcefully uttered and endlessly repeated, the deconstructionist campaign is rather naïve, to start with, in assuming (despite their rejection of objectivity) that ambivalence is an objectively detectable or absolute quality of a word or phrase. Detecting ambiguity is not an objective, automatic reflex of the reader or listener, but is itself an interpretive act, and one which depends on lexical knowledge, subject to historical evidence. Most of the so-called 'New Criticism' of the 1940s and 50s, with its concern with ambiguity in older literary texts, would have been impossible without the existence of the Oxford English Dictionary 'on Historical Principles', which made a pioneering attempt (the inevitable limitations of which are becoming apparent)[18] to identify the date at which a particular sense of a word came into, and went out of, usage. Accurate lexical knowledge tells us what meanings were available at any stage of history, and is an important tool in the history of ideas.[19] But the critic using it still has to show its relevance in the text under discussion, and the interpretive acts that follow are subject, of course, to argument and counter-argument — Empson being a notorious example. The sense of any word is governed by its context, syntactically defined and delimited.[20] Not all possible meanings are simultaneously present. It is therefore rather simple-minded of deconstructionists to imagine that the detection of ambivalences, however frequent, in any way threatens language, or philosophy, or literature, for detecting them is not an innocent act. Deconstruction begs the question it sets out to prove, and offers no independent evaluation of the evidence.

A 'deconstructive reading', then, is one bent on locating ambivalence or indeterminacy in a text, and drawing the most absolute conclusions from it. As Edward Said describes the method, 'What each of Derrida's works tries to do is to reveal the entame — tear, incision — in every one of the solid structures built up by philosophy, an entame already inscribed in written language itself by its persistent desire to point outside itself . . .' (Said 1983, p. 207). Derrida has claimed that a text, insofar as it relies on words having '"a double, contradictory, undecidable value, . . . plays a double scene upon a double stage"' (cit. ibid., p. 206). So he evolved a notion of 'écriture double' which derives, in Said's words, from the 'undecideable fold (pli) [sic!] in his work between the description of a text, which he deconstructs, and the enactment of a new one, with which his reader must now reckon' (Said 1983, pp. 185–6). However, as M.H. Abrams showed in two classic analyses, this process involves Derrida in an ongoing contradiction, making him 'on principle a double-dealer in language, working ambidextrously with two semantic orders — the standard and the deconstructed'. That is, in deconstructing what he describes as 'logocentric' language Derrida 'assumes the stance that this language works, that he can adequately understand what other speakers and writers mean' (Abrams 1979, p. 277). This is to concede a point that he will subsequently deny.

Developing his account of how Derrida first construes, according to normal uses of language, but then deconstructs what he has construed, Abrams helpfully distinguishes 'reading$_1$', in which Derrida makes out 'the determinate meanings of the sentences he cites', from 'reading$_2$', which — Derrida claims — 'disseminates' (disintegrates) those meanings (Abrams 1986, p. 304). Thus, in *Of Grammatology*, Derrida performs readings of selected passages from Rousseau's *Essay on the Origin of Language* in which he first 'construes these passages as conveying determinate meanings', attributes the authorship to an individual named Rousseau, happily reporting 'what "Rousseau affirms . . . unambiguously", or what "Rousseau says"' here and elsewhere (*ibid.*, p. 305). Then Derrida finds 'strata, or "strands" in Rousseau's text which, *when read determinately*, turn out to be mutually contradictory', and instead of concluding (as readers not bent on forcing this thesis might do) that Rousseau's arguments are incoherent, he takes this fact as proving the existence of what he calls logocentrism (p. 306; my italics). So, practising a 'determinate reading', he 'repeatedly uncovers an opposition of meanings between what Rousseau "wishes to say" and what "he says without wishing to say it"' (p. 307) — Paul de Man quickly absorbed this trick — in particular the 'duplicitous word *supplement*', one of the Janus-faced terms in which Derrida delights (p. 308).

This double-reading produces two texts which are left, so to speak, standing side by side. Derrida emphasises that the deconstructive reading$_2$ 'does not cancel the role of intention' or the other conventions that 'operate in a determinate reading of a limited text, but merely "reinscribes" them . . . in an alternative system of *différance*' as 'no more than "effects" of the differential play' (*ibid.*, pp. 310, 312). This is a considerably less violent and imperialistic goal for deconstruction than other pronouncements of Derrida. But it is still based on a strangely 'deliberate anomaly', as Abrams shows:

> He cannot demonstrate the impossibility of a standard reading except by going through the stage of manifesting its possibility; a text must be read determinately in order to be disseminated into an undecidability that never strikes completely free of its initial determination; deconstruction can only subvert the meanings of a text that has always already been construed. (p. 310)

This is a penetrating diagnosis of the most damaging contradiction at the heart of deconstruction, that it is parasitic on a system which it violently assaults yet never transcends. The limitations of this subversive but conservative approach have been well exposed by John Ellis, who shows that Derrida's refusal to work out an alternative to the attitudes he attacks under the name of logocentrism (a bogus concept, in any case), negates any forward movement, preserving the status quo but also the deconstructionist's assertions of superiority to that which he has denounced (Ellis 1989, pp. 29–30, 41, 70–71, 80–81). Derrida, we may conclude, remains the *enfant terrible*, cocking a snook at his predecessors, demonstrating a precocious cleverness but unconcerned to provide a coherent alternative to the system he mocks, and finally embodying many of its faults in his own construct, inverted, negated, but still preserved.

II

The philosopher who has had the vanity of the logos revealed to him will not rest until he has made the empty labyrinths echo his discovery.

Thomas Pavel[21]

Most of the Shakespeare critics who have so far flirted with deconstruction owe their knowledge of it not to Derrida's sibylline texts but to the writings of Paul de Man and his friend and disciple J. Hillis Miller, who jointly played the main role in institutionalising deconstruction within American universities.[22] The literature discussing both writers is already vast; all I need to do here is to indicate the ways in which they domesticated Derrida, made him reusable, reduced his endless self-exegesis to a set of easily graspable attitudes, in short, a method.

De Man's debts to structuralism and its successor are evident. He believed that 'contemporary literary theory comes into its own in such events as the application of Saussurian linguistics to literary texts' (de Man 1986, p. 8): that is, after Lévi-Strauss and Barthes. He loyally followed those leaders in fragmenting the sign in order to deny its power to function, affirming — there is never any attempt at argument — a deep-rooted 'discrepancy . . . in everyday language, . . . the impossibility of making the actual expression coincide with what has to be expressed, of making the actual sign coincide with what it signifies' (de Man 1971, p. 11). It is 'the distinctive curse of all language', de Man announced, that the simplest wish cannot be expressed 'without hiding behind a screen of language that constitutes a world of intricate intersubjective relationships, all of them potentially inauthentic', for — and here the debt to Lacan becomes obvious — 'the other is always free to make what he wants differ from what he says he wants' (*ibid.*). The 'task of structuralist literary critics', then, naturally desiring to 'eliminate the constitutive subject' of discourse, is 'to show that the discrepancy between sign and meaning (*signifiant* and *signifié*)' — another misreading of Saussure — 'prevails in literature in the same manner as in everyday language' (p. 12). De Man in effect aligned himself with structuralism with this assertion:

> For the statement about language that sign and meaning can never coincide, is what is precisely taken for granted in the kind of language we call literary. Literature, unlike everyday language, begins on the far side of this knowledge; it is the only form of language free from the fallacy of unmediated expression. (p. 17)

But, as several critics have pointed out,[23] this confuses Saussure's categories while making an assertion that depends, for its understanding, on its own refutation — for if sign and meaning 'never' coincide, how can we even understand what de Man has written? In a later book de Man freely distorts Saussure in the vein of Lévi-Strauss, Lacan, Barthes, and others, in phrases like 'the seductive plays of the signifier', or 'a free signifier', or 'the arbitrary power play of the signifier' (de Man 1979a, pp. 207, 288, 296). A German critic complained that these were 'Unbegriffe' ('nonsense concepts'), quite falsely attributed to Saussure, and that de Man not only split off the signifier, destroying its function, but also reified it, thus turning an 'epistemological distinction' into 'an ontological, substantial one' (*cit.* Ellis 1989, p. 65). But in so doing he was only following a pattern established in France for over three decades.

Given this by now traditional background of questioning the sign, de Man set out to undermine works of literature insofar as they depend on language. In his interpretation of Shelley's *The Triumph of Life* — an interpretation that distorts the poem's obvious meaning by a combination of selective quotation and misreading[24] — de Man asserts, with a deadly seriousness quite different to Derrida's cheerful insouciance,[25] the impotence of language. Developing an obscure theory about 'the figurality of all signification', which is somehow 'posited by an arbitrary act of language', reified now into an agent of unquestionable power — language's 'positing power' being both arbitrary and inexorable (de Man 1979b, p. 62) — de Man then asserts that we human beings

> impose, in our turn, on the senseless power of propositional language the authority of sense and meaning. But this is radically inconsistent: language posits and language means (since it articulates) but language cannot posit meaning; it can only reiterate (or reflect) it in its re-confirmed falsehood. (p. 64)

I find this sequence (and I am not alone)[26] deeply confused but typical of much of de Man's thinking in obeying obscure patterns of flow and counter-flow, a simultaneous asserting and negating, always turning against itself. Shelley's poem is unfinished, a fragment, to de Man an accident but also a profound if obscure allegory: 'this mutilated textual model exposes the wound of a fracture that lies hidden in all texts' (p. 67).

All texts are fractured; the act of criticism consists in reading them until we locate their fissures. But this is *la condition humaine*, too, for literary criticism merely imitates life — or rather, death. Shelley's poem, one amazingly nihilistic sentence affirms,

> warns us that nothing, whether deed, word, thought, or text, ever happens in relation, positive or negative, to anything that precedes, follows or exists elsewhere, but only as a random event whose power, like the power of death, is due to the randomness of its occurrence. (p. 69)

This fascination with nothingness pervades de Man's writing. In reading Proust, where other critics he quotes describe the '"powerful unity"' of *A la recherche du temps perdu*, or the 'solidity of the text', de Man closes his specimen analysis of a passage from the novel — a reading several times refuted[27] — on a typically unresolved note:

> The question remains whether by thus allowing the text to deconstruct its own metaphor one recaptures the actual movement of the novel and comes closer to the *negative epistemology* that would reveal its *hidden meaning*. Is this novel the allegorical narrative of its own *deconstruction*? (de Man 1979a, p. 72; my italics)

The italicised words there bring out the peculiarly inverted or divided form that reading takes in de Man's theory. As observant readers will have noticed, a hidden meaning is after all a meaning, and to invoke a negative is also to make it parasitic on the positive. Commenting on Rilke (the actual occasions for de Man's comments soon become irrelevant, mere pretexts), de Man categorically asserts that 'only negative experiences can be poetically useful' (*ibid.*, p. 50). In Nietzsche, he affirms, the concept of representation 'functions . . . with a negative value-emphasis' (p. 94), and 'the negative thrust of the deconstruction remains unimpaired' (pp. 125–6). At one point in Rousseau (the ostensible subject) the language of passion is restored by the 'unproblematic figurality of the metaphor' — whatever that might mean — 'albeit in the form of a negative power that prevents any specific meaning from coming into being' (p. 198). The language of this book is dense with images of the 'vertiginous' (p. 10), the 'whirlpool' (p. 203), elimination (p. 32), annihilation (p. 37), failure (pp. 147, 205), meanings that fight each other (p. 76), selves that 'remain confronted in a paralyzing inequality' (p. 185), states in which something 'undoes' itself (pp. 161, 173, 187), or is subverted (p. 269), or reduced to impotence (p. 294). R.M. Adams, for many years a colleague of de Man, recalls 'the intense interior dialectic that went into his thought, as well as the dark negativity that kept him from bringing that dialectic to unequivocal conclusions'.[28] That sense of paralysis seems to lie very deep. To me it recalls James Thomson's *The City of Dreadful Night* (1874), presided over by a Queen — 'Melencolia', in Dürer's engraving — whose presence emanates 'A sense more tragic than defeat and blight':

> The sense that every struggle brings defeat
> Because Fate holds no prize to crown success;
> That all the oracles are dumb or cheat
> Because they have no secret to express;
> That none can pierce the vast black veil uncertain
> Because there is no light beyond the curtain;
> That all is vanity and nothingness.

Her subjects often 'gaze up to her there', to drink 'renewed assurance / And confirmation of the old despair' (part XXI).

De Man may have had good reasons for his 'dark negativity', and I shall not pursue them. What disturbs me is that his enormous reputation in the 1970s and 80s has influenced many teachers and students, including Shakespearians, and is likely to go on doing so, such being the conservative nature of institutionalised literary practices. These readers take from de Man a critical model in which literature is found to be riven by fissures, aporias (doubts, uncertainties). In an essay on Rousseau, for instance, de Man identifies the meanings of Rousseau's texts as 'ethical, religious, or eudaimonic', but then declares that 'each of these thematic categories is torn apart by the aporia that constitutes it, thus making the categories effective to the precise extent that they eliminate the value system in which their classification is grounded' (de Man 1979a, p. 247). That is a typical de Man sequence, detecting a profound and contradictory split ('torn apart by [what] constitutes it'), then resting happily in its consequences — 'from fissure to impasse', as it were. As a result of his reading of Proust, he claims with some satisfaction, we 'end up in a mode of negative assurance that is highly productive of critical discourse' (*ibid.*, p. 137). The role of the deconstructive critic is to frustrate, to spoil, to deny authors and texts fulfilment: 'again and again', it has been said, de Man 'deprives writers of the goals for which they appear to be striving' (Butler 1984, p. 71). Transitivity, that fundamental property of language rejected by Barthes, is assumed never to have existed. In his first book, *Blindness & Insight* (1971), rapidly reprocessing Derrida's exposition (in 1967) of the discrepancy between what Rousseau 'wishes to say' and 'what he says without wishing to say it', de Man diagnosed in a whole group of contemporary critics 'a paradoxical discrepancy' between their general statements about literature and their interpretations; 'their findings about the structure of texts contradict' their general conceptions (de Man 1971, p. ix). In an essay called 'The Rhetoric of Blindness: Jacques Derrida's Reading of Rousseau', de Man was inspired by Derrida's example (but also Lacan, who described the subject as signifying 'something entirely different from what it says'), to find Lukács, Blanchot, Poulet, and the American

New Critics as a group all 'curiously doomed to say something quite different from what they meant to say', their critical stance being 'defeated by their own critical results' (pp. 105–106, e.g.). Not just critics, above all texts are made to negate themselves, to disclose their fissures, as deconstruction successfully reveals what de Man claimed to be the 'hidden articulations and fragmentations within assumedly monadic totalities' (de Man 1979, p. 249). There again critical theory has had to erect a straw man to topple, since few if any readers have imagined that a literary work was a 'monadic totality'.

De Man practised an extremely negative form of criticism, but his literary theory still depended on the ancient and honourable concept of *mimesis*, the representation of human existence. When coupled with his nihilism, however, this requirement gave literature the difficult task of representing nothingness. Commenting on a letter by Rousseau describing the 'unexplainable void' that he felt as a result of having unfulfillable desires, de Man (emulating Barthes in such moves) suddenly leaps from describing Rousseau's idiosyncratic consciousness to making a general and categorical statement about literature:

> here, the consciousness . . . consists of the presence of a nothingness.
> Poetic language names this void with ever-renewed understanding and,
> like Rousseau's longing, it never tires of naming it again. This persistent
> naming is what we call literature. (de Man 1971, p. 18)

Not only poetry, but 'the work of fiction', too, 'invents fictional subjects to create the illusion of the reality of others' — note the unargued assumption behind that binary category of illusion and reality — simply in order 'to avoid facing "the nothingness of human matters"' (*ibid.*). Imitation, then, is of the void, and the 'imaginary source of fiction' only shows that 'the human self has experienced the void within itself and the invented fiction, far from filling the void, asserts itself as pure nothingness, *our* nothingness . . .' (p. 19). De Man regularly took over an extreme position from an individual writer and made an absolute, categorical literary-critical or philosophical law out of it. Thus Mallarmé's poetry expresses 'a persistent negative movement that resides in being. We try to protect ourselves against this negative power by inventing stratagems, ruses of language . . .', but 'the existence of these strategies reveals the supremacy of the negative power they are trying to circumvent' (p. 73). Literature is not only the space of 'negative knowledge about the reliability of linguistic utterance', he wrote in 1982, but even of its own 'aesthetic function': 'Literature involves the voiding, rather than the affirmation, of aesthetic categories' (de Man 1986, p. 10). This recurring imagery of the void defines the 'moralistic nihilism' often noted in de Man (e.g., Lehman 1991, p. 201), and to me it recalls Schopenhauer.[29] Increasingly de Man made propaganda for deconstruction as being the mode of criticism perfectly suited to express the sense of impasse, hollowness, void and darkness that his work expressed during the 1970s. In *Allegories of Reading* there are many statements of the negation and self-negation involved in deconstructive criticism (e.g., pp. 125, 187, 205, 212, 234, 235, 242, 243, 249), but the prize specimen must be this account of Rousseau's *Julie*, as read by de Man:

> The readability of the first part is obscured by a more radical indeterminacy that projects its shadow backwards and forwards over the entire text. Deconstructions of figural texts engender lucid narratives which produce, in their turn and as it were within their own texture, a darkness more redoubtable than the error they dispel. (de Man 1979a, p. 217)

Such a model for criticism hardly seems auspicious for Shakespeare. Woe betide any writer approached with these expectations of fissure and *Finsternis*!

De Man is occasionally criticised for having taken Derrida's thought and 'reduced it for practical purposes to a series of formulas and a method' (McFadden 1981, p. 338). However, credit (or blame) for the routinisation of Derridian theory within the university is equally due to J. Hillis Miller, who has crusaded tirelessly on behalf of deconstruction, and used many opportunities — including the prestigious lecture given as President of the Modern Language Association — to press the claims of deconstruction as a form of reading to be taught in both the undergraduate and graduate curricula.[30] Miller stands to de Man in much the same relationship as Quintilian, the school-teacher, stood to Cicero, the man of public affairs. De Man, you feel, really lived with a void, confronted nothingness as an existential fact, yet felt comforted to have 'confirmation of the old despair' regularly provided by literature. Miller, by contrast, has not lived in the abyss, but knows how to expound it as a technique in literary criticism. The formulaic phrase he did so much to popularise (Lentricchia 1980, pp. 162, 179), the *mise en abyme* which the deconstructionist discovers being performed by textuality, is for him a literary-critical manoeuvre rather than a psychological experience. Although in one place Miller clearly echoes de Man in describing how the deconstructive method can lead us to glimpse the abyss itself in a 'vertigo of the underlying nothingness' (Miller 1976a, pp. 11–12), that is a rare excursion into nihilism. Otherwise Miller's gaze is comfortably fixed on the fissures he claims to find in texts, not to what may lie behind them.

Miller's writing professes its indebtedness to both Derrida and de Man, taking over the assertiveness of both. The categorical assertion has become a trade-mark of deconstructionists, who can be seen both 'undermining' works of literature while 'overreaching' in their own arguments. Their hyperbolical affirmations remind me of George Puttenham's anglicising of the rhetorical figure *hyperbole* as the 'Over reacher', that is, 'when we speake in the superlative and beyond the limites of credit'.[31] Where the earlier Hillis Miller, author of a number of studies of poetry and fiction which I recall with gratitude from my undergraduate days,[32] combined sensitive reading and argument supported by reference to the text, the later Miller makes *ex cathedra* pronouncements (in a newly provocative manner oddly untypical of such a courteous critic), which are *a priori* statements of faith in deconstruction rather than reasoned argument. In his later writings we frequently find an enormous gap between the claims he is making and the text cited in support. His interpretation of Wordsworth's 'A slumber did my spirit seal', for instance, has been accused of wilfully misreading and negating the poem, treating it as an allegory of the non-functioning of the *logos*, and violating his own professed method in order to drag in irrelevant lexical information not only from outside the poem but from outside the English language, or any cultural context that one could reasonably ascribe to Wordsworth. The myth of deconstructionist critics as responsible close readers of a text will not survive the examination of what Derrida did to Saussure, de Man to Shelley, or Miller to Wordsworth and Pater, among others.[33]

Hillis Miller, in his later career, has been more influential as a theorist than a practical critic (reversing his earlier skills), yet having said this we must qualify what weight we give to the word 'theory'. If we mean by it a patient exploration of the nature of language, literary form, genres, the reading process, the workings of evaluation, a sustained analysis which takes into account alternative views, then we will be disappointed. We find, rather, a large number of essays, published in all the leading 'theory' journals, which re-affirm the deconstructionist credo in the light of one or more texts, briefly alluded to rather than analysed, forming the kind of utterance sometimes called a 'position statement'. It is statement rather than argument, affirmation rather than enquiry, even if delivered in an elegant and lucid style distinct from either Derrida's trapeze-work or de Man's burrowing into the darkness. It is usually easy to understand what Hillis Miller is saying, and his utterances are eminently quotable: but, we must ask, what good are they as a model for readers of literary texts, in particular drama?

Miller frequently reiterates the motifs of fissure, negation, especially self-negation, taken from his two heroes. But he vacillates uneasily between attributing this divisive quality to the texts themselves or to the activity of the deconstructionist critic.[34] Sometimes the text is said to subvert, or deconstruct itself. (However many times I read this claim, it still seems to me unproven. By what independent criteria, outside the deconstructor's negative hermeneutics, could a text of any length or complexity negate itself? What would the evidence for such a claim look like?) Nietzsche is cited as the model for this topos (Miller 1979, p. 229), but it is obviously Derrida who lies behind the pronouncement of 'a regular law which can be demonstrated, . . . the self-subversion of all the great texts of Western metaphysics from Plato onwards' (*ibid.*, p. 228). Miller asserts as a categorical fact about literature that 'the text performs on itself the act of deconstruction without any help from the critic. The text expresses its own aporia' (Miller 1975, p. 31). Another borrowing from Derrida, the presence of incompatible meanings in a text, is now said to reveal 'the heterogeneity of a text (and so its vulnerability to deconstruction) . . . the fact that it says two entirely incompatible things at the same time' (Miller 1975, p. 30). In another place, however, it is 'deconstructive criticism' that uncovers an 'oscillation' in literary texts (a revealingly scientist metaphor), in which 'two genuine insights into literature in general inhibit, subvert, and undercut one another', such oppositions as 'idealism and scepticism', or a referentiality which does not refer, or 'performatives which do not perform' (Miller 1979, p. 252). So, the impatient reader might object, who does the deconstructing, the text or the critic?

Several abruptly categorical assertions locate the act of negation in the text itself: 'Any literary text . . . already misreads itself' (Miller 1976b, p. 333); 'every literary text performs . . . its own self-dismantling' (ibid., p. 330). Other, longer sequences, situate the critic in a dramatic encounter with the text, often described as a labyrinth. The writings of Walter Pater, for instance

> are at once open to interpretation and ultimately indecipherable, unreadable. His texts lead the critic deeper and deeper into a labyrinth until he confronts a final aporia. . . . Only by going all the way into the labyrinth, following the thread of a given clue, can the critic reach the blind alley, vacant of any Minotaur, that impasse which is the end point of interpretation. (Miller 1976c, p. 112)

As M.H. Abrams rightly observes, that passage implies that 'the deconstructive critic's act of interpretation has a beginning and an end; that it begins as an intentional, goal-orientated quest; and that this quest is to end in an impasse' (Abrams 1977, p. 248). It is, in effect, a perfect account of the progress of so many of de Man's essays; except that de Man always knew that the goal was an impasse.

Miller's favourite metaphor of the labyrinth gives deconstructionist activity a narrative line, rather like an episode from a medieval or Renaissance chivalric epic, say, 'The Quest for the Impasse'. It can also be combined with the root metaphor of 'deconstruction' itself — which Derrida derived from Heidegger's Destruktion of the metaphysics of ontology[35] — leading to deconstruction being conceived of as the dismantling of a structure, or even, as in this instance, a building:

> The deconstructive critic seeks to find, by this process of retracing [each textual labyrinth], the element in the system studied which is alogical, the thread in the text in question which will unravel it all, or the loose stone which will pull down the whole building. The deconstruction, rather, annihilates the ground on which the building stands by showing that the text has already annihilated that ground, knowingly or

unknowingly. Deconstruction is not a dismantling of the structure of a text but a demonstration that it has already dismantled itself. (Miller 1976b, p. 341)

Such a clinical description has lost any of de Man's nihilist undertones, and is oddly reassuring in its assurance that the method will work. To misapply a Biblical text: 'seek and ye shall find, knock and' — the whole structure will magically collapse. I am reminded of Astolfo, the English paladin in Ariosto's *Orlando Furioso*, who has only to blow his magic horn — 'to which he always resorted in desperate situations' — to set the earth quaking and strike terror into all oppressors. Thanks to its help Astolfo destroys the enchanted palace of the evil magician Atlas, driving away its wicked spirits before 'smashing everything. . . . The palace dissolved into smoke and mist':

> e di strugger quello incanto vago,
> . . . fece fraccasso,
> . . . e si sciolse il palazzo in fumo e in nebbia.[36]

But Astolfo can distinguish between good and evil, helpers and harmers: J. Hillis Miller's horn brings down all texts indifferently.

If that brief account, using their own words, may serve as an adequate outline of de Man and Hillis Miller as re-workers of the Derridian heritage, then we can now answer the question, what use is deconstruction as a model for literary criticism. My answer, and that of a number of other independent observers (we are not dealing here with assertions and counter-assertions by rival groupies, each bent on advancing their own school), has to be: not much. Deconstruction might be a useful propaedeutic exercise in philosophy classes, like the training in Renaissance logic and rhetoric courses in how to identify and refute sophisms. But as a model for literary criticism it is seriously defective. For one thing, the critic always knows in advance what he will find. Gerald Graff has shown that Hillis Miller's reading of Dickens's *Sketches by Boz*, 'for all its heavy documentation, . . . rests not on textual evidence from the work itself but on a theory that tells him in advance what this evidence must be evidence *for*'. Since Miller 'forecloses the very possibility of language's referring to the world', he 'can read all texts without fail as self-deconstructing' — that is, calling attention to 'their inability to refer to external reality' — and so 'the method he employs establishes his case by default' (Graff 1979, pp. 176–7). This is to make life very easy for yourself, perhaps one of the attractions of this school of criticism. As M.H. Abrams says, 'the deconstructive method works, because it can't help working, it's a can't-fail enterprise', but — or 'alas' — one in which the critic finds that all 'the texts to which he applies his strategies . . . reduce to one thing and one thing only' (Abrams 1977, p. 241). As Miller himself admits, each deconstructive reading, 'performed on *any literary, philosophical, or critical text* . . . reaches, in the particular way

the given text allows it, the "same" moment of an aporia. . . . The reading
comes back again and again, with different texts, to the "same" impasse'
(Miller 1975, p. 30; my italics).

To the deconstructionist, this security, the guarantee of arriving where
you aimed at, may be reassuring, and pedagogically useful; to others it will
seem frightfully monotonous. Surely there must be something wrong with a
critical method that produces the same reading of every text it comes
upon? It 'reduces', or 'dissolves' its objects in the same way that the bath
which Dr. Crippen filled with sulphuric acid dissolved his victims' bodies,
bone, flesh, organs, all to the same indeterminate flux (textuality?).
Abrams comments that the first few such readings may produce the desired
feeling of vertigo, the 'uncanny *frisson* at teetering on the brink of the
abyss', but the excitement will soon be 'dulled by its expected and invariable
recurrence' (Abrams 1977, p. 249; Abrams 1986, p. 332). The fact
that anyone can use the method — as Miller assures us, the 'ultimate
justification for this mode of criticism . . . is that it works' (Miller 1979,
p. 252) — that anyone can reduce *Middlemarch*, *King Lear*, or 'any literary,
philosophical, or critical text' to a pile of rubble, or dispel it *'in fumo e in
nebbia'*, is not, to my mind, a recommendation. It may satisfy the critic's
desire for power, especially as a surrogate for political action,[37] but its
effect on works of literature, and on the whole practice of criticism, seems
potentially disastrous.

III

Shakespearians were rather late in noticing the deconstructive revolution.
The first reference to it in the analytical index to *Shakespeare Quarterly*'s
annual bibliography was for 1985 (vol. 37, p. 890): by 1987 there were
eight references (vol. 39, p. 940). If slow in catching on, those promoting the deconstruction of Shakespeare have also been rather parochial,
ignorant of the vigorous and wide-ranging debates it has provoked. In 1985
Terence Hawkes, a solidly established middle-man for the cultural avant-
garde (editor of the Methuen (now Routledge) New Accents series, editor
of the journal *Textual Practice*), expounding 'new critical approaches' in a
widely sold student handbook, could declare that 'the implications' of
deconstruction for the Shakespearian critic 'are vast'.[38] It means, Hawkes
announces, that we must abandon 'Bradley's notion of reading poetry as a
pathway to the final "presence" of the author's mind. Bradley's sense of the
capacity of the text to reveal "character" is also doomed by it' (p. 292).
The fact that Hawkes keeps dragging in Bradley, whose book on the
tragedies dates back to 1904, shows again how modern critical theory needs
straw men, however ancient, against whom to measure its superiority.
Against Bradley, and twenty years after Derrida, Hawkes sets out the new
dogma with effusive, not to say, pompous emphasis:

Precisely because of its tropes, its metaphors, its images, language cannot be reduced to a series of unified, graspable, 'readable' and authorially validated meanings. *It certainly cannot accurately depict character.* Texts are never accurate or finished or concluded. They are endlessly, like language itself, in free play . . . , referring to other texts, other uses of language, rather than to a limited range of referents imposed from outside themselves. The kind of reduced 'readability' presupposed by 'old' Shakespearian criticism is not genuinely available. As Hillis Miller puts it, all texts are unreadable, if by 'readable' one means a single definitive interpretation. (p. 292; my italics)

There we meet many of the familiar characteristics of deconstruction: the categorical assertions (Precisely . . . cannot . . . certainly cannot . . . are never . . . not genuinely . . . all . . . unreadable), the proliferation of inverted commas to mark suspected words or concepts, the caricature of opposed critical practices in an attempt to legitimate its own (the 'old' criticism is rebuked for being reductive, while deconstruction is about to impose on texts a degree of reduction undreamed of till now), and above all the false oppositions. We are offered the choice, either the 'free play' of language or 'a limited range of referents imposed from outside themselves'. But what does this phrase actually describe? How *can* 'referents' be 'imposed' on texts 'from outside themselves'? And who would ever be so silly as to attempt it? Texts are actually built out of referents, utterances that discriminate one character from another, one motive from another, one social group, institution, or landscape from another. If language could not perform these functions, life, let alone literature, would be impossible. Finally Hawkes gives us, once again, the old threadbare alternative (the excluded middle yawning open, with all the other possibilities inviting discussion) of either 'unreadable' texts or 'a single definitive interpretation'. This is presented as a dilemma, but it has long lost its horns. As for the sentence I have italicised, it totally misses the point that the complexities of human behaviour — for which 'character' is the starting-concept in literature — can only be adequately registered in language. No other medium of comparable accuracy or subtlety exists. Music and dance can achieve remarkably powerful presentations of character in their own media, but it can only be analysed, criticised, reflected on in language.

Coming to the actual critical practice of deconstructing Shakespeare, Hawkes predicts it demonstrating that

no such limited 'readability' exists. By running the readability film backwards, by unpicking or 'deconstructing' the carefully woven strands which make up the text's sense-making surface, by focusing attention on its contradictory features which the writer — unwittingly — is unable to control . . .

the deconstructive critic will show that literature privileges the free play of language over meaning. As Geoffrey Hartman expresses it, deconstruction . . . recognizes that words offer, not the restriction of presence, but the freedom of 'a certain absence or indeterminacy of meaning'.

The fact that Hawkes quotes Miller and Hartman but none of the twenty or more critiques of deconstruction available at the time he wrote means either that he was ignorant of them or else deliberately disdained to acknowledge them. Readers of this guide (republished unaltered in 1991) deserve better. They also deserve some more appropriate literary model than Hawkes's horrible metaphor of a 'readability film', as if the experience of drama could be fragmented into various mechanised processes (and surely, spooling backwards would only reverse the reading, not prove that reading is impossible?). The other metaphor of 'unpicking the carefully woven strands' of meaning gives an unintentionally appropriate account of deconstruction as a process which deliberately destroys the integrity of texts, breaks up precisely those areas where meanings are located, creating fissures or voids which it then claims were inherent. This new mode is then set against its ancient and purely mythical rivals, 'logocentric or incarnationist' views of language, in order to collapse into Hartman's equally vacuous claims that the text has a 'potentially endless proliferation of meaning', and that 'writing covertly resists its own reduction to unitary "meaning"' — resists, that is, until the deconstructionist imposes his greater weight to prise open the text, reveal or create the gaps euphemistically known as 'aporias'. And this is called 'freedom'.

Hawkes was writing, as he pointed out, before the deconstruction of Shakespeare had really got going, but his account of what it would look like turns out to be uncannily accurate (or would be uncanny if the critical method were not so predictable). From what must probably be described as the 'first wave' of criticism since then I have picked out a number of essays published in two collections, Alternative Shakespeares (1985),[39] and Shakespeare and Deconstruction (1988),[40] together with Howard Felperin's collected essays announcing his conversion to deconstruction, The Uses of the Canon (1990).[41] My selection is intended to be representative, not definitive, and may be premature. But certain trends are already visible: loyalty to the founding fathers, especially the American clan; studious avoidance of the ever-increasing number of critiques of deconstruction (either in ignorance or self-protective knowledge); and the assumption, with no historical discussion, that this idiosyncratic late twentieth-century critical theory is an appropriate tool for discussing drama, and particularly drama written some four centuries ago. The assumption seems to be: 'these famous contemporary critics say that language and reference undermine themselves and all works of literature: let us see how we can apply their ideas to Shakespeare'. Or, as an actual editor of Shakespeare and Deconstruction puts it, 'Attempting to link a current literary critical theory

with the greatest English writer seemed a goal worthy in and of itself'
(Atkins and Bergeron 1988, p. vii). But handsome is as handsome does.

Shakespearian deconstructionists inherit a system, in the language of
antiquarian booksellers, 'with all faults'. They, too, find themselves caught
in false oppositions, as between single readings/infinitely multiple and
indeterminate ones; rigidly bound and determinate/wholly free and un-
restrained interpretation; viciously subjective/aridly objective; and so on.
An interesting example is Howard Felperin. In his preface Felperin re-
erects on the one hand that straw man of modern critical theory, pressed
into service again but always reliable, 'the pseudo-objective "facts" of an
older historical empiricism' (Felperin 1990, p. vii) — who are these
purveyors of facts? Where can their graves be found? On the other, he puts
the 'new "conventionalist" historical hermeneutics consisting only of
"texts" and "discourses"' (he is just as profligate with quotation marks as
Hawkes, often for obscure reasons). This second pole may seem the
promised land to post-structuralists, but Felperin finds it unsettling, since it
offers 'nothing solid to fall back on when its "knowledge" is relativized'.
(What, exactly, is the force of the inverted commas around 'knowledge'? Is
this now a dubious concept, in need of decontamination? If so, good night
all human intellectual pursuits!) Despite the ontological nostalgia for 'something solid to fall back on' — like Derrida's 'transcendental signified' —
Felperin must know that there never was any such comforting support.
Literary judgments and interpretations have always been personal, not
merely subjective but intersubjective — that is, open to discussion,
counter-argument, appeal to a text, amendment. Felperin's dilemma,
caught between 'interpretive realism' and the 'opposed and no less vitiating charge of interpretive relativism', is imaginary, though much sought
after by deconstructionists. ('Comfortable impasse to rent, near all main
services; good view of the abyss'.) All that he can think of doing is to
acknowledge the impasse, even if that means 'revisiting . . . the dreaded
state of aporia[42] now and again . . .', and admit 'the incapacity of my
readings to tell the truth about the texts they take up' by foregrounding
'their [sc. his readings'] "writerly" play' (pp. viii–ix), a limp — perhaps
designedly exemplary? — admission of failure.

The deconstructionists' false oppositions do not always result in self-
paralysis. They can be invoked to dismiss other readings, legitimise their
own, or even suggest that their work, while manifesting 'writerly play',
has somehow come into being independently of the reading process. So
Felperin 'comes out' with this statement:

What a deconstructionist like myself . . . increasingly values is the
resistance the great text throws up against my efforts to impose my
preconceptions upon it, to make it say what I want to hear. I confess I
have come to enjoy being led by the text, by its train of signifiers, in
directions I could not have predicted and might not initially have

wanted to go — even if the outcome of being led, indeed 'read', in this
way is to end up in the state of aporia without a visa. (p. x)

This passage deploys another specious antithesis, between an active and a
passive reading, leading or being led by. But the act of reading involves
an active energising of the system of signs and meanings embodied in
writing, and no reader can abandon his or her minimum responsibility for
intellectual involvement. To allegorise the text as somehow 'reading' you is
merely to push the problem on to another plane, where it is harder to
reach — in plain language, a cop-out.

In taking over deconstructionist concepts and methods Shakespeare
critics further the domestication of an originally disruptive system. Paul de
Man gave the impression of really having confronted the void, but the
academic impresarios hail his achievement in terms more appropriate to a
guided tour: he 'led the way in revealing the power of figural language to
mask the abyss over which human being constantly hovers' (Atkins 1988,
p. 9: I am reminded of a Victorian's comment on Carlyle: he 'led [us] all
out into the desert and . . . left [us] there').[43] The deconstructive *frisson*,
that sense of teetering on the edge of a huge abyss, has wholly disappeared
as Gary Waller cheerfully sets about 'Decentering the Bard'. Deconstruction, he reports, has 'most successfully attacked' the notion of the unified
text, showing that 'texts are always riddled by abysses, closed only by
repression' — as if a writer 'repressed' his novel or poem by pronouncing it
completed, or a critic-reader 'repressed' it by ending his commentary —
there being, 'as Derrida puts it, no texts, only an infinite textuality always
on the move' (Waller 1988, p. 32). On the move, easy rider, Waller
promises a 'peculiar excitement' in deconstructing Shakespeare, running
together in one breath a whole series of one time radical propositions, now
just part of the scene viewed from the driver's seat. The bardic deconstructor will inevitably focus on

> the disruptiveness of textuality, on the infinite deferral of meaning, on
> the real emptiness of language and the insistence that textual practices
> always operate in contradiction to their own intended existence. (p. 22)

Waller's list turns these originally anarchic ideas into glib counters, showing an easy, comfortable acceptance of the deconstructive goal, to make
'his plays unravel our (and Shakespeare's) attempts to fix meaning in
words' (p. 23). This is, after all, only being true to the 'inherent deconstructive nature of the Shakespearean script' itself, for as every student
knows, 'as the text ravels itself together at one end, it is always unravelling
at the other . . .' (pp. 34–5). Where the generation of Derrida had to
detonate or undermine, and that of Hawkes had to unpick the text, the
latest metaphors give a much easier role to the critic: just sit back and let
the text unwind for you. Penelope is invisibly at work.

The sense we have here of a once-flourishing intellectual movement being increasingly diluted while being transmitted down the cultural hierarchy is confirmed by these critics' treatment of Saussure. In Hawkes's allusions to 'the free play of language over meaning', to the endless 'free play of differences', and to 'referents imposed from outside', we find an uncritical endorsement of Derrida which extends to Derrida's attack on, and perversion of Saussure (but Hawkes has been often enough rebuked for misreading Saussure).[44] In Felperin we find the same distortions in his account of being 'led by the text's train of signifiers' (Felperin 1990, p. x), and in a later definition of language as a 'self-contained system of arbitrary signs' (p. 51). Catherine Belsey begins her essay on 'Disrupting sexual difference' with the bold statement: 'Meaning, Saussure argued, is an effect of difference' (Belsey 1985, p. 166). But no, he said that the relations between the signified (concept) and other signifieds, just like that between the signifier (sound-image) and other signifiers, was established differentially; whole signs were distinguished by opposition; and he said almost nothing about meaning.

What is new, and depressing about Shakespearians appropriating Saussure in the 1980s and 90s is that his ideas are not only reified and torn out of context but are vulgarised, treated in a literal-minded way. Thus Geraldo U. de Sousa, starting an essay on *Richard II* with the easy-to-use slogan of Derrida — 'from the moment that there is meaning there are nothing but signs' — invokes Saussure's 'radical view' of the linguistic sign 'as a two-faced structure containing the signified and the signifier, which, however, can never be contemporaneous' (De Sousa 1988, p. 173). Once past the inept formulation 'two-faced' (recalling Iago's god Janus), the reader is left wondering what on earth the critic means by 'never . . . contemporaneous', since everything Saussure says implies that their mental association is simultaneous. (The linearity of the sign means that it, like language in general, unrolls in time, but comprehension moves with it.) Perhaps de Sousa has, as a Derridian might say, 'spatialised' the sign, or 'subjected it to deconstructive violence'. Equally bizarre is Jonathan Goldberg's comment on the fact that in *King Lear* Dover Cliff is mentioned only by Edgar (disguised as Poor Tom, as Gloucester contemplates suicide). To Goldberg this absence is significant:

> The refusal to allow the word *Dover* to arrive at the place it (apparently) names, the failure, in other words, for signifier to reach signified — the failure of the sign — establishes the place that *Dover* occupies in the text. It is the place of illusion. . . . (Goldberg 1988, p. 247)

This is to literalise an abstract concept to the point of some primitive form of drama, in which actual signs were hung up giving the theatrical location.

Not only is Saussure falsified and de Man tamed, but Derrida's endlessly self-explicating system is trivialised, as in Gary Waller's fateful proposal to apply deconstruction to the very performance of drama. Waller sees theatrical production as 'the quintessential deconstructive act — unravelling not only a tyrannous origin' — Shakespeare is now a 'tyrant' since he wrote or originated the play! — 'but undoing its own action as it proceeds' (p. 28): just watch it unravel! Waller quotes from an undergraduate text-book that he has joint-authored, which tells students that ' "there is, in one sense, [1] no such thing as a Shakespeare play — at least there is [2] no original meaning or [3] single authentic way" of producing it. . . . The Shakespearean text is [4] a script that decomposes as it is performed' (p. 27; my numbering). Those four assertions mimic the deconstructive categorically-assertive style but expose its emptiness: who would ever claim that there *was* an 'original meaning' or 'single authentic way'? The door that they are trying to batter down does not exist; their enemies are ghosts, manufactured simpletons. (As for the text 'decomposing', as if it were organic matter, the falseness of the metaphor displays the vagueness of thought.) But Waller joins hands with another Derridian (David Macdonald) to labour the point of these fatal reversals:

the play is there in the beginning to be done, one [*sic*] once it is per-formed or read, it is undone. Productions are 'struck'; sets and costumes are 'deconstructed'. The cast departs, lines are forgotten. The work of art disappears, and all of this deconstructive activity appears as an essential method and mode of the art form.

To which Waller adds: 'there is no performance or reading that can capture the absent origin; presence is something that tantalizes but can never be materialized' (Waller 1988, p. 28).

It is not difficult to spot the faults of logic in that argument, which makes drama and theatre meaningless by leaving out altogether the per-formance, the actor's art, and the audience's reactions (not to mention all the begged questions of an 'absent origin'). Loyal Derridians will have been more disturbed at the banalisation of the master's ideas that has taken place, for whatever he meant by 'presence' and 'absence' it was certainly nothing as literal-minded as Waller's conceptions (ideology, he tells us later, is an 'ever-changing absence': p. 39). Just as Saussure's concept of the sign was literalised, so Derrida's distortion of Saussure (in which the 'play of the signifier' results in an infinite 'deferral' of meaning) is reified and banalised. Messrs Waller and Macdonald join forces to suggest that

the Derridean category of 'deferral' is at the necessarily absent heart of *Hamlet*, in which the hero, 'putting off until later what is presently impossible', may be said to deconstruct the possibility of himself attain-ing full presence. Thus the traditional reading of *Hamlet* as a tragedy of delay may be related to deconstructive deferral. (p. 26)

And thus the antiquated Romantic theory of Hamlet as a man who could not make up his mind — now due to his 'decentered presence' — is given a new lease of life by being dressed in a hand-me-down Paris outfit of the 1960s.

That absurdly literal-minded understanding of what Derrida meant by *différance* is matched by G. Douglas Atkins, who derives from James Calderwood's book on *Hamlet* (which got it in turn from René Girard) the insight that the play's hero has to overcome 'the evaporation of differences and the consequent blurring of identities' created by Claudius's usurpation (Atkins 1988, pp. 10–11). (We can only be puzzled as to what sense of 'difference' is implied here — abstract? concrete? somewhere in between?) Says Atkins (says Calderwood [says Girard]): Hamlet's solution to his crisis lies in overcoming 'torturous [*sic*] self-difference' to achieve identity. 'Hamlet must, in other words, establish his legitimate difference from Claudius (and Laertes), rather than, by proclaiming his difference, merely ensure his doubleness'. (If readers wait a while, the sense of blur will disappear.) Atkins catches one of his authorities out, seeing that Girard 'acknowledges . . . that "differences never really disappear" . . . an admission that effectively deconstructs his argument' (p. 12). What that does to Atkins's argument we can only wonder. He goes on to use the term 'difference' in this literalising fashion another twenty times in the next two pages, before taking refuge in a still greater authority, albeit at two removes, Barbara Johnson's exposition of Derrida's notion of *différance*. Atkins concludes with a crassly literal-minded summary of Derrida that will have all true devotees groaning in frustration:

> It is precisely this notion of *différance* that opens up important, if vertiginous, new vistas for understanding the *relationship* between entities, whether they be supposed oppositions such as time/space, body/soul . . . ; the differences between peoples, for example Christians/Jews; or even the way one person is situated vis-à-vis another. (pp. 14–15)

By now Derrida's term has completely lost its distinctive, idiosyncratic meaning (whatever it was).

*   *   *

Although Shakespearian deconstructionists treat Derrida and his sources in a banalisingly literal way, they faithfully follow him in reducing everything to the level of language. G. Douglas Atkins claims that deconstructionists read with 'closeness and rigor', 'attending closely to tropes or to concepts, following the de Manian or the Derridian emphasis' by 'intensely pressuring texts' (Atkins 1988, p. 6). But this claim, as we have seen, is mythical. Deconstructionists only read selectively, small texts or small bits of texts, only those bits that will allow them to exercise their method or prove its assumptions. Shakespearian deconstructionists, although perhaps old-fashioned in preserving the notion of 'texts', specific poems, plays, or genres (not yet willing to collapse everything Shakespeare wrote into undifferentiated 'textuality'), within the text discussed dutifully focus on language as a Derridian, non-functioning system. Gary Waller, for instance, declares that Shakespeare's *Sonnets*, 'like the Petrarchan lyric generally, . . . articulate the frustration of language's indeterminacy. The desire for signification leads only to a lack, as trope piles on trope, ending inevitably in the repressive silence or frustration of closure' (*ibid.*, p. 25). An innocent reader faced with those statements would never imagine that Shakespeare's *Sonnets* are not at all like the Petrarchan lyric; that they are remarkably eloquent and inventive, handling a limited range of subject-matter in always changing forms; that their language is highly significant and determinate (if it were not, it could hardly use a trope, which by definition involves the turning of a word to another signification); that they actually use tropes less frequently than rhetorical schemes or figures;[45] and that since the standard English sonnet is a fourteen-line poem it regularly reaches 'closure', which represents, however, neither 'repression' nor 'frustration' but the literary convention of prescribed forms. (Have the deconstructionists really no other way of dealing with fixed literary forms than to protest about closure? That seems an extraordinarily primitive category choice, 'endless play' or 'premature enforced close-down'.)

Waller's description of the *Sonnets* as articulating 'language's indeterminacy' is, of course, just another glib recycling of the clichés of 'post-structuralist criticism', but it is representative of what Derridian methods do to works of literature. To return to Geraldo U. de Sousa on *Richard II* for a moment, is to find another critic literalising Saussure and Derrida while bringing all issues down to language. To the characters in the play, he writes, 'the king — a power broker — is a sign that depends on the play of differences in order to signify'. A sign, not a person, Richard is still able to exert his rule: however, 'when the king wields his power in an arbitrary way, the political and linguistic equilibrum collapses' (de Sousa 1988, pp. 176–7). But if the sign is arbitrary in the first place, we might ask, caught between reifying the sign and de-reifying the person, what's the difference? When this happens in a play, apparently, 'signifier and signified break apart', as witnessed by the Welsh captain's list of omens:

> The bay-trees in our country are all wither'd,
> And meteors fright the fixed stars of heaven. . . .
> These signs forerun the death or fall of kings.   (2.4.7ff)

To most readers of the play so far these signs have been perfectly clear omens of unnatural disasters, but de Sousa claims they 'have lost their usual meanings. No longer meaning the death and fall of kings, *because the king is still alive*, these signs fluctuate haphazardly . . .' (p. 178; my italics). This is an extraordinarily myopic comment, ignoring the immediately following speech by Salisbury ('Ah, Richard! . . . I see thy glory like a shooting star . . .'), and indeed the whole movement of the play through its second half, in which all the omens are validated. De Sousa's comment is, once again, linguistic, not dramatic: 'ironically [in what way?], the play establishes that the sign, however arbitrary it may be, is the only way to signification'. This is surely a truism on any count, and a strangely thin and abstract judgment on a play. Once you reduce characters to signs ('the king, the sign of signs, proves himself to be a sign breaker'), you soon reach allegory. De Sousa shortly takes this final step to abstraction, saying that 'if . . . York *stands for* the feudal system, John of Gaunt ironically [in what way?] *speaks for* the ideology of the Divine Substitute' (p. 179; my italics).

This is an easy, but fatal step in deconstructionist reading, from seeing drama as language only, to seeing it as in some way allegorical. A prime instance of this reduction of drama to allegory is an often-cited essay by J. Hillis Miller, 'Ariachne's Broken Woof' (Miller 1977), which takes its title from the scene in *Troilus and Cressida* (5.2) where Troilus, having managed to get into the Greek camp, has seen Cressida (who has been swapped for the return of a Trojan prisoner, Antenor) meet alone for the first time her new wooer, Diomedes. It is obviously a painful experience for Troilus, and once the spied-on couple has left he releases his feelings in sixty lines of highly rhetorical, contorted, Latinate language (using such rare words as 'recordation, credence, esperance, attest, deceptious, calumniate, bi-fold, perdition, conduce, inseparate, orifex, constring'd . . .'). Striking a rather affected pose — 'Was Cressid here? . . . She was not, sure. . . . Rather think this not Cressid. . . . No, this is Diomed's Cressida' — he tries to refuse to believe his eyes, only to come back to the contradiction between what he has seen and what he had believed Cressida to be:

> This is, and is not, Cressid.
> Within my soul there doth conduce a fight
> Of this strange nature, that a thing inseparate   152
> Divides more wider than the sky and earth,
> And yet the spacious breadth of this division
> Admits no orifex for a point as subtle
> As Ariachne's broken woof to enter.   (5.2.150ff)

Editorial opinion is divided as to the meaning of the 'thing inseparate' (line 152): David Bevington's edition glosses it as 'Cressida, an indivisible entity'; Hillis Miller states that it 'is Troilus's soul' (Miller 1977, p. 53). No great critical issue is at stake here, the real crux being 'Ariachne'. Most contemporary editors see it as an odd spelling for Arachne, another of those unfortunate humans in classical myth who challenged a god in some skill. This one engaged Athene in a weaving contest, which ended in the goddess becoming angry, tearing up Arachne's work, and turning her into a spider. But Miller, in company with many commentators since the eighteenth century,[46] prefers to see in the spelling a conflation of 'Arachne' with 'Ariadne', another mythological heroine involved with weaving — or at least with a thread, with which she helped Theseus escape from the

Cretan labyrinth. It is perfectly possible, of course, that Shakespeare conflated the two stories, since in some versions at least, each heroine hangs herself. But it could also be a printer's error, or even a deliberate alteration for the sake of the meter. The dominant allusion is obviously to Arachne, since she alone had a woof that was broken,[47] but it may well be that Shakespeare confused the two (as others confuse Plutus and Pluto, or the virgin birth with the immaculate conception). To Miller the deconstructionist, however, all Shakespeare readers can be categorised according to whether they accept the portmanteau form: those that do are 'dialogical', those that don't are 'monological' — 'learned gentlemen', he tells us, but sadly limited (pp. 45–6). This binary opposition is then linked to what Miller has said this speech is all about, namely as showing 'the division of the mind into two when the single narrative line of monologue becomes the doubled line of dialogue. When one *logos* becomes two, . . . all the gatherings or bindings of Western logocentrism are untied or cut' (p. 44). Enter Derrida — but when did he ever leave?

The first of Montaigne's essays has the thoughtful title, 'How, by various ways, one can arrive at the same goal' (Book I, Chap. 1: 'Par divers moyens on arrive à pareille fin'). From whatever remote position the deconstructionist starts, his path will soon join one of Derrida's, and the old targets will be hunted down again. Troilus' speech is said to call in question 'the "whole shebang" of Occidental metaphysics' (p. 47), showing 'that *dialogue, in the sense of a division of one mind against itself*, is ultimately a matter of language or manifests itself as a subversive possibility of language' (*ibid.*; my italics). Troilus' speech explores 'the metaphysical implications of the possibility of dialogue', a word that Miller repeatedly refuses to take in its normal sense of 'speech between two people', but pronounces (against all the etymological evidence, when it suits him) to mean 'the dividing of a single mind against itself'. Thus dialogue, defined in his way, 'puts in question the notions of the mind [a tautology, given the definition: now we see its rhetorical purpose] and of the self and sees them as linguistic fictions, as functions in a system of words without base in the *logos* of any substantial mind. When the monological becomes dialogical, the dialogical loses its *logoi* and becomes alogical' (p. 51). Miller is a great one for citing etymologies (e.g., pp. 53, 57), but in this sequence he has given in to a form of Derridian doublespeak, the assertion-with-denial, which gives with one hand and takes away ('becomes . . . loses', 'dialogical . . . alogical') with the other. Miller has taken this text as a pretext for another crash course in deconstructionist thought-processes. The 'dialogical' form, Ariachne, is said to fit 'the wider context of Occidental discourse . . . in which the coherence of the monological has all along been undermined by the presence within it . . . of that other non-system, . . . the absence of unifying authority' (p. 55). These are familiar elements of deconstructionist belief: what have they got to do with Troilus?

This freewheeling deconstructionist discourse bases itself on one passage in Troilus' speech, but in doing so it ignores the intentionality behind Troilus' words; it ignores the unique dramatic situation — since onstage at this time, having observed Diomedes' encounter with Cressida, are not only Troilus and Ulysses, but also Thersites; and it ignores the fact that we, the audience or readers, have seen Cressida independently of Troilus, and know one or two things about her that he does not. Typically enough for a deconstructionist, Miller ignores the specifically dramatic or theatrical elements of this passage, and treats Troilus' words as if they were contributions to a philosophic debate, about metaphysics or logic, as if Troilus were qualified to talk about these things, as if his words were addressed, with consequence, to an abstract issue, and not the outpourings of immediate suffering.

The take-off point for Miller is Troilus' attempt to link Cressida's betrayal to the forces governing the universe. Using the rhetorical linking-figure *anadiplosis* (in which the last word of one clause becomes the first word of the clause following), Troilus verbally links Cressida to the gods:

> If beauty have a soul, this is not she;
> If souls guide vows, if vows be sanctimonies,
> If sanctimony be the gods' delight,
> If there be rule in unity itself,
> This was not she.   (142ff)

He and Cressida had sworn vows of constancy to each other (3.2.136–193), with Pandarus holding their hands in a mock ceremony of solemnisation — I call it mock, not serious, since Pandarus brings the exchange down to prose and is given a retrospective irony which sounds like a prophecy, an illocutionary act of swearing that, 'if ever you prove false one to another . . . let all pitiful goers-between be call'd to the world's end after my name; call them all Pandars' (195–9: we do, we will). But in retrospect Troilus now sees that prelude to their one and only love-night together as having been some kind of divinely sanctioned ceremony:

> Instance, O instance, strong as Pluto's gates,
> Cressid is mine, tied with the bonds of heaven;
> Instance, O instance, strong as heaven itself,
> The bonds of heaven are slipp'd, dissolv'd, and loos'd,
> And with another knot, five-finger-tied,
> The fractions of her faith, orts of her love,
> The fragments, scraps, the bits and greasy relics
> Of her o'er-eaten faith, are bound to Diomed.   (157ff)

But there never were any 'bonds of heaven'. Pandarus is no priest, and this was no legal ceremony. Cressida's father, Calchas, is a priest, however, a Trojan serving on the Greek side, to whom she is returned in recognition of parental claims (4.5). Troilus invokes canons of legitimacy to which he is in no way entitled.

Miller, however, takes Troilus' attempt to invoke logic ('If there be rule
in unity itself' — the principle that an entity can only be indivisibly equal
to itself) as alluding to 'the basic assumption of monological metaphysics',
now said to be underwriting the whole order of the universe, 'the religious,
metaphysical, or cosmological links binding earth to heaven', and — the
deconstructionist credo — the order of language itself (p. 47). To the
reader or theatregoer aware of Troilus's intentionality, of the pain motivating the eloquence, it is no more surprising that our young hero should
invoke Aristotle on his side than the gods. But Miller takes Troilus'
words
au pied de la lettre, endorsing them while lining up another deconstructionist
target:

> Cressida's faithlessness, the possibility that her original vows to Troilus
> were *not grounded on her substantial self* in its ties to the rest of the
> ethical, political, and cosmic order all the way up to God, puts in
> question that whole order. Cressida's lying makes it possible to conceive
> that the story of that order, as it is told by the reasonable discourse of
> Western metaphysics, is itself a lie . . . (p. 48; my italics)

Derrida's well-known theses return from the ante-room: 'the possibility that
language may be cut off from any source in the mind, human or divine'; 'In
Western metaphysics a linguistic principle has been externalized and made
the basis of the cosmic order, as Christ is the *Logos*, the Word' (p. 49;
what's Christ doing here?). Cressida is at least granted 'a substantial self',
unusually enough after the post-1960s attack on the subject, yet because
her vows were not 'grounded' and she betrayed Troilus, then 'the whole
structure of Western culture is broken, fragmented, doubled and redoubled'
(p. 50), reduced to the nauseating metaphors of scraps and leftovers with
which Troilus ends his harangue, or diatribe, or *vituperatio* (whichever
rhetorical form seems appropriate). Yet, Miller adds, 'out of these fragments a new non-system . . . is created. . . . It is the non-system made of
the remnants of an act of deconstruction, like a meal of distasteful leftovers . . .' (p. 54: for those who have wondered how a work of literature
looks, or tastes, after it has been deconstructed).

Miller's deconstructionist commentary, riding on the back of this
speech, is absurdly overblown, calling up attitudes and positions from the
Derridian repertoire which are simply overlaid on the Shakespearian text
with the flimsiest connection. His concepts of monological, dialogical,
metaphysical and logocentric discourse are forced on the play from outside
(perhaps this is what Hawkes meant by referents being imposed on texts
from outside themselves). More serious, perhaps, he ignores crucial evidence from the text which would call in question all his assumptions,
starting from his passive endorsement of Troilus' utterances as if they were
meant to be taken wholly sympathetically. But Troilus' use of language, as
Shakespeare has been careful — and marvellously inventive — to show

from the beginning of the play, is excessive, exorbitant, anguished in its frustration (1.1.1–110), and agonising just before the fulfilment:

> I am giddy; expectation whirls me round.
> Th'imaginary relish is so sweet
> That it enchants my sense. What will it be,
> When that the wat'ry palates taste indeed
> Love's thrice repured nectar? Death, I fear me . . .
>
> (3.2.7–27)

Aristotle said that the speech of young men was characterised by hyperbole:[48] Troilus exemplifies that figure. In debate among his peers Troilus is nothing but hyperbolic (2.2.25–32, 46–50, 76–83, 199–207), outdoing even Marlowe:

> Why, she is a pearl
> Whose price hath launch'd above a thousand ships.

In flytings with the enemy he is even more reckless (4.4.123ff, 5.4.19f, 5.10.12–32). Shakespeare gives to Ulysses a formal *laudatio* of Troilus: 'a true knight, / Not yet mature, yet matchless. . . . / Not soon provok'd, nor being provok'd soon calm'd' (4.5.96–112), a non-partisan description which must be given some weight.

In the scene where Troilus observes Cressida's conversation with Diomedes, we are not surprised that he should burst out in such fury — 'nor being provok'd soon calm'd'. The excess of hyperbole is rant and bombast, and if those terms would be too harsh for a balanced judgment of Troilus they are still deliberately invoked by Shakespeare in his decision to have onstage throughout this overhearing scene not only Ulysses but Thersites, two reference points that permit a triangulation of our attitudes. Thersites the coarse-mouthed reduces all love to lechery — 'A juggling trick — to be secretly open' — 'How the devil Luxury, with his fat rump and potato-finger, tickles these together! Fry, lechery, fry!' (5.2.25, 57f). We do not simply endorse Thersites' worm's eye view, but Shakespeare's intentional interposition of him as a commentator appealing directly to the audience (in asides and soliloquies), so placing him between the potentially heroic-romantic action and our experience of it, has, cumulatively, a distinctly sobering or disillusioning effect. We never fully accept what Thersites says, but his saying it illuminates the action from an angle that Shakespeare does not want to leave unexplored. So when Troilus strikes his pose of doubting whether he has actually seen Cressida or not (5.2.121–36), Thersites' comment — 'Will a' swagger himself out on's own eyes?' (139) — is coarse, but not wholly unjust. And when Troilus inflates himself for his final bombastic threat of how he will, on the field of battle next day, smash Diomedes' helm bearing Troilus' favour, which Cressida has just given away —

Not the dreadful spout
Which shipmen do the hurricano call,
Constring'd in mass by the almighty sun
Shall dizzy with more clamour Neptune's ear
In his descent than shall my prompted sword
Falling on Diomed.   (172ff)

— Thersites deflates this resounding hyperbole with his unique vulgarity:
'He'll tickle it for his concupy'. The point being that Shakespeare has put
Thersites there for a purpose, a purpose that is certainly not conducive to
sympathy with Troilus. (Hillis Miller never mentions Thersites.)

Even more telling, because more balanced, are the comments of Ulysses,
especially after we have seen his unprompted admiration of Troilus.
Having managed with difficulty to restrain the Trojan from betraying their
hiding place, he is eager to go, but Troilus wishes to stay in order 'To make
a recordation to my soul' of all that he has heard, another self-conscious
pose. After his first speech we move from monologue to dialogue (in the
word's normal sense):

TROILUS.   Was Cressid here?
ULYSSES.   I cannot conjure, Trojan.
TROILUS.   She was not, sure.
ULYSSES.   Most sure she was.
TROILUS.   Why, my negation hath no taste of madness.
ULYSSES.   Nor mine, my lord. Cressid was here but now.
TROILUS.   Let it not be believed for womanhood!
    Think, we had mothers.

Ulysses' cool detachment, his refusal to play along with Troilus' language-
game, the sardonic denial ('I'm no magician'), all this establishes a
perspective from which we can see and judge Troilus's pose-striking. When
Troilus falls into a generalised misogyny — a reaction Shakespeare often
shows as the pique of a man who thinks he has been deceived by a woman
(Ford, Leontes, Posthumus) — 'Think, we had mothers', so showing
himself indeed ready 'to square the general sex / By Cressid's rule', Ulysses
has the absolutely just, and deflating counter:

What hath she done, Prince, that can soil our mothers?

And after Troilus' anguished speech invoking 'the bonds of heaven' only to
collapse into 'greasy relics', Ulysses sarcastically enquires,

May worthy Troilus be half attach'd
With that which here his passion doth express?   (165f)

Even reducing his words to half their import would still leave Troilus
resounding his anger and sense of hurt. A man who, 'being provok'd' is not
'soon calm'd', whose passion, expressing itself in hyperbole and vitupera-

tion, nevertheless claims to have the gods and logic on his side, Troilus is hardly the character I would pick as expressing a philosophic point of view to be taken seriously. Shakespeare, at all events, deliberately places two non-sympathetic commentators to suggest that we should not take Troilus at his own evaluation.

We, as audience or readers, have yet a third point of view by which we can judge Troilus, since we have seen Cressida's reaction to being traded off, like a hostage or prisoner of war. When she receives the news from Pandarus that she is to be handed over to the Greeks (4.2.95–110), her anguish is moving, the accents of a true love that 'admits no qualifying dross' of moderation (4.4.1–10). Troilus does not see her spontaneous reactions in these two scenes, so that his injunctions to her at their parting to be 'true of heart' (4.4.58–97) can seem unloving, unnecessarily suspicious, Polonius-like. (But of course he can also be serving a proleptic function, anticipating the betrayal that is soon to take place.) In the overhearing scene, even, although perforce having to negotiate with Diomedes — being one of the spoils of war, she truly has no choice — Cressida is full of regrets, giving Troilus' sleeve to her new 'guardian' but imagining her first love lying 'thinking on his bed / Of thee and me', bestowing 'memorial dainty kisses' on the glove she has given him (5.2.71–95). She calls herself 'false wench!', wants the sleeve back, resolves to break off with Diomedes — 'I will not keep my word' — and only gives in when he threatens to leave her. After Diomedes has gone, and she is left alone (she thinks), her thoughts are still with Troilus: 'farewell! One eye yet looks on thee: / But with my heart the other eye doth see' (119ff). All told, this is a sympathetic but realistic account of what it means to be traded off like a commodity, subject to the fortunes of war. Shakespeare, who has put Thersites and Ulysses on one side of Troilus, puts Cressida on the other side, these three characters giving us a perspective from which to judge his words. Nothing in Cressida's behaviour as we have seen it would justify Troilus' vituperative reduction of her faith to 'fragments, scraps, . . . bits and greasy relics', truly a 'filthy simile', as one of the interlocutors in a Pope satire objects.

Hillis Miller's distinguished example shows that it is not enough to pick out one passage from a play as the text for a deconstructionist sermon. To do so is to risk endorsing the speaker's intentionality in all its egoism, all its self-justifying appeals to right and wrong, all the incoherences of its self-vindicating arguments. To be fair, Hillis Miller does note Troilus' incoherence, but he fails to see that it should make us qualify the seriousness or sympathy with which we respond. He describes 'Troilus's all-or-nothing rhetoric' as leading to the 'universalizing' statement (misogynistic might be the appropriate epithet), 'Let it not be believed for womanhood!', but he then finds the universalising (and not the misogyny?) 'justified, for if one exception to the law of self-identity can be found', then this law is revealed to be merely 'a human positing' (p. 50). But laws are only ever

human positings, never transcendental absolutes, and neither Troilus'
misogyny nor Cressida's transfer to the Greeks calls in question the law of
self-identity. She is still the same woman; he is still the same eloquent
speaker, excelling in epideictic rhetoric, the branch devoted to praise
(*laus*) and blame (*vituperatio*). Commenting on the 'fractions . . . orts . . .
scraps' sequence of the speech, Miller notes 'the incoherence of the syntax',
but the deconstructionist (as with de Man's concept of poetry) can always
see language in mimetic terms when it suits him. So Miller describes
Troilus' incoherent syntax as enacting 'the fragmentation, the suspension
of logical order', that 'metaphysical order which Cressida's vows to Troilus
implied' (p. 54). Similarly, 'the syntactical and figurative incoherence
of Troilus's speech' forms an anacoluthon which is present not only in
grammar, but also — *mimesis* again! — in 'the anacoluthon of Troilus's
divided mind, the narrative discontinuity of the entire play, and so on up
to the immense anacoluthon of Western literature, philosophy, and history
as a "whole"' (p. 56). The stylistic pecularities, the 'mind-twisting or
mind-disintegrating' rhetoric of Troilus (pp. 56–7), instead of being taken
— along with many other dramatic emphases pointing in the same direction — as a sign of the speaker's emotional and rational imbalance,
another instance of the hyperbole or verbal excess that has marked him
throughout, these concrete and carefully worked details of language
become grist to the deconstructionist mill, which only attends to those
elements of a play which can fit its theory.

   Miller ends his essay, as he did so many essays in the 1970s, with a
reminder of the Grand Theory: the materials of 'Occidental Culture', as
'this interpretation of one passage in *Troilus and Cressida* has implied, are
fundamentally heterogeneous. They contain both logocentric metaphysics
and its subversion'. Like the closing passages of a Bach fugue, the key notes
recur: 'dialogical not monological . . . ; dialogical heterogeneity . . . ;
Deconstruction . . . attempts to reverse the implicit hierarchy . . . ;
the logocentric as a derived effect of the dialogical . . . ; Deconstruction attempts a . . . displacement of the whole system of Western
metaphysics. . . . That this attempt always fails, so that it has to be performed again and again, interminably . . .' (pp. 59–60). If we wanted one
text to show how deconstructionist doctrine imposes itself on works of
literature in an act of appropriation that ruthlessly picks out those parts
that can be consumed and rejects the rest (as the macho lover parodied(?)
in one of Donne's love-poems says: 'And when hee hath the kernell eate /
Who doth not fling away the shell?'), then Hillis Miller's ingestion and
recycling of Troilus's speech would be the ideal exhibit.

*   *   *

Deconstruction obviously cannot cope with the fundamental nature of
drama as the interaction, concordant and discordant, between characters

who have clearly defined and differentiated goals, values, thought-habits, and styles. Unable to read the words of the characters as utterances designed to achieve a personal goal, or deflect someone else's, they have to twist the drama towards a metaphysical or anti-metaphysical level, or reduce the characters to some abstract principle. So John M. Kopper, expounding 'Subjectivity and the Duplicity of Discourse' in *Troilus and Cressida*, categorically asserts, without even the pretence of discussion, that 'Pandarus is the principle of autology, and Cressida of heterology, of the cleavage inherent in the sign' (Kopper 1988, p. 158; any puns on 'hetaira' and 'cleavage' probably unintended). That binary category (later absorbed into the opposition between tragedy and comedy, and Lacan's 'Symbolic' and 'Imaginary' realms: pp. 161–2) leaves the ordinary reader wondering what other function those characters might have, if any, outside the linguistic domain. Again, this play is said to be really about language (this is truly the 'monological', monocausal slant of deconstruction). Kopper follows Miller, and many more, in discussing Troilus's angry speech on Cressida's betrayal, but finds its main significance to concern the 'understanding of proper names'. That is, he informs us, the 'word "Cressid" should denote one person', and the fact that it does not 'function in this way', calls in question — would you believe it? — the power of language to refer to reality. Kopper is blind to the obvious point in the dramatic context that it does indeed denote one person, but one who has just been seen transferring her allegiance away from the man she swore to love, he being understandably confused about the discrepancy between promise and performance, and indulging in excesses of rhetoric in order to come to terms with it in his own fashion. But for Kopper this complex dramatic situation, reduced to being a purely grammatical (onomastic) phenomenon,

> questions the very possibility that language can be referential. For the denotation of 'Cressid', as philosophers in the Frege tradition could have explained to the anguished Troilus, depends on activation of an amorphous aggregate of connotations, only a majority of which need hold for the members of a society in order for the name to function successfully as 'proper'. (pp. 151–2)

But this learned note is wholly beside the point: what is at issue in Troilus' speech is not a name but a person, a woman and her love — or rather, 'the orts of her love'. Nothing in his speech could undermine language's referential function, in any case. It is precisely through language's power to refer — to Cressida, to the bonds of heaven, to Ariachne's broken woof — that Troilus can express his sense of betrayal.

If Troilus is given low marks for his ignorance of Frege (to my knowledge, the first Shakespearian character to fail this test), he does rather better on the Saussure question. One of the 'persistent themes' of the play, says Kopper, using a strangely old-fashioned concept, 'is the attempt to establish the value of an object'. So, in the Trojans' debate over whether to return Helen to the Greeks, Troilus accepts her 'arbitrary value', and in thus 'rejecting Hector's concept of intrinsic worth, he allies himself with a post-Saussurian attitude towards meaning. While Hector looks for a correspondence between sign and referent', Troilus 'splits the sign into signifier and signified'. This confuses several issues in Saussure, but at least seems to be leading in a new direction. However, Kopper jerks it back to the deconstructionist goal: 'the theme of valuation calls into question language's referential powers, thereby challenging the stability of language as a structure' (pp. 152–3), and so — hey presto! — validating once again the Derridian enterprise. Speeches or scenes in Shakespeare are singled out for comment only when they confirm what the deconstructionist already thinks. Any sense of criticism as discovery, an open-minded engagement with a text, has been lost. Commenting on Troilus' early, pre-coital imagery of Cressida as a 'pearl' in India, with himself as the merchant and Pandarus as 'our convoy' (1.1.94ff), Kopper gratuitously claims that the images recall Pluto's rape of Proserpina. She — allegory again! — 'exemplifies the duplicitous woman', but also, more importantly, 'that ambiguity in language' seen in Troilus' words, 'this is, and is not Cressid'. These words, in turn, show Troilus vainly trying to 'utter the original, absolute difference. Cressida is that difference, and . . . that difference is an unspeakable term' (pp. 159–60: see Derrida *passim*). Odd, then, that Troilus manages to speak it so often, some forty times according to the Concordance.

Unconcerned with what actually happens in them, deconstructionists read Shakespeare's plays in order to confirm their pre-existing theories and to validate their method, with its 'unravelling of the text'. So Kopper, having used two tiny passages in one play to call in question language and reference (is there not a slight discrepancy here?), can proudly assert that in this reading of the play 'I have created a logical confusion that is real and very important' — as if exclaiming '*heureka!*', or '*Quod erat deconstruendum!*' We see what he means by 'logical confusion' in his next sentence, which says that by acknowledging 'the "madness of discourse", Troilus undergoes a rite of initiation which is simultaneously impossible to undergo . . .' (p. 161). This is indeed a way of 'intensely pressurizing texts', or 'opening up' Shakespeare to the presence of the critic.

IV

The reduction of drama, a three-dimensional, two-way experience, first to the level of language and then to the validation of a Derridian theory, seems to be the unavoidable result of deconstruction. Howard Felperin, expounding 'The Deconstruction of Presence in *The Winter's Tale*' (Felperin 1990, pp. 35–55; previously in Parker and Hartman 1985, pp. 3–18), sets out to call in question all the traditionally fixed points in that text, beginning — oddly enough — with the oracle scene (3.2.132ff). Before unwarily following his plunge *in medias res*, it may be helpful to remind ourselves of the dramatic situation at this point. Leontes, having himself urged Hermione to plead with Polixenes to extend his nine-month visit (1.2.27–108), falls into a sudden and irrational fit of jealousy, which has a disastrous outcome. First he convinces himself that the courtly behaviour between his wife and Polixenes is proof of an ongoing adultery (1.2.108– 19, 137–46, 180–6, 216–19); then he suspects Mamillius not to be his legitimate son (1.2.119–36, 187–208); and, putting zero and zero together, reveals his jealous suspicions to his trusted courtier Camillo and tries to suborn him to poison Polixenes (211–349). Overwhelmed by Leontes' insistence, Camillo at first agrees, but as soon as the King has gone he feels revulsion at the plot, reveals it to Polixenes, and they leave the court of Sicilia in haste (351–464). Camillo's horrified disbelief, Polixenes' shock, Hermione's obedient and dignified behaviour on the one hand, and on the other Leontes' manic language, his metaphors running riot, his syntax disintegrating into incoherence — this extreme opposition within the play polarises reactions in a way that isolates Leontes. When he reveals his nasty imaginings to Hermione, accusing her of being an adultress and a traitor before having her put in prison (2.1.33–125), the polarisation is intensified. Leontes is convinced that he is right — 'How blest am I / In my just censure, in my true opinion!' (36–7), while Hermione affirms her innocence in the confident hope that she will be vindicated:

> How this will grieve you,
> When you shall come to clearer knowledge, that
> You thus have publish'd me!

Leontes' reaction is that of a tyrant: whoever speaks in her defence makes himself guilty by so doing (96–105).

Yet, in a reassuring demonstration of solidarity with the innocent party, no-one at Leontes' court is intimidated by him, no-one believes his jealous suspicions, all affirm their belief in Hermione. The First Lord and Antigonus forcefully wager their life and happiness on her innocence and his injustice (2.1.126–72), to which Leontes arrogantly replies that he is not asking their advice but only out of his 'natural goodness' telling them the truth of the matter (161–70). A ruler who rejects his counsellors and accuses everyone else of 'ignorant credulity' is self-isolated. Leontes' authority, however, seems to be crumbling, as we see from the courage of Paulina, Antigonus' wife, in standing up to the King, 'loyal servant' and 'most obedient counsellor' as she is, reaffirming Hermione's innocence, and presenting his new-born and legitimate baby daughter, her face 'the whole matter / And copy of the father' (2.3.26–130). Leontes' reactions are hysterically violent, but impotent. Having wished, at the beginning of this scene, in a speech of paranoid incoherence, to have Hermione 'Given to

the fire' (2.3.7–8), now he threatens Paulina: 'I'll ha'thee burnt' — 'I care
not', she replies, challenging him to produce any evidence to justify
his 'cruel usage' of Hermione other than 'your own weak-hinged fancy'.
Leontes then impotently orders his courtiers to take 'the bastard' child and
'burn it' (131–57). They all refuse to do so, defending Antigonus from the
charge of having provoked Paulina to her attack, and Leontes is reduced to
a peevish accusation, 'You're liars all'. By this point in the play Leontes
has reached a degree of inhumanity that makes him either disgusting or
ridiculous.

Not content with his own suspicions, Leontes reveals that he has sent to
the oracle 'for a greater confirmation' of his imaginings, 'whose spiritual
counsel had / Shall stop, or spur me' (2.1.181–7). After he has made
Antigonus swear on his life to take the 'female bastard' and leave it
in 'some remote and desert place' (2.3.158–92), news arrives that the
messengers sent to Delphos have returned (2.3.193–207; 3.1.1–22). The
imminent disclosure of the oracle's response hangs over the scene in which
Leontes gives Hermione what he calls 'A just and open trial', which, he
thinks, will also clear him of the charge of being tyrannous, and will run its
'due course' for her, 'Even to the guilt or the purgation' (3.2.1–8).
Hermione's dignified and eloquent defence of her integrity and virtue
(22–123) is set against Leontes' snide sneers (54–7) and incoherent
accusations, as he breaks the pretence of impartiality by threatening her
with death (82–91). This is the dramatic situation, totally polarised —
Leontes completely isolated in his manic suspicions and inhuman violence,
everyone else in the play convinced of Hermione's innocence — in which
the oracle's judgment confirms the judgment of the humane party:

'Hermione is chaste, Polixenes blameless, Camillo a true subject,
Leontes a jealous tyrant, his innocent babe truly begotten . . .'. (132–6)

The depths of dishonour and inhumanity to which Leontes' mania has
brought him are displayed by his reaction. Although he has sworn that the
oracle's 'spiritual counsel . . . shall stop, or spur me', and that the trial will
run its course either 'to the guilt or the purgation', now, his destructive impulses unsatisfied, he breaks his word in a gesture of overweening
arrogance:

> There is no truth at all i'th'oracle.
> The sessions shall proceed. This is mere falsehood.   (140–41)

And at that point a messenger brings news that Mamillius, ill with anxiety
over his mother's torment, has died.

Mamillius' death is the shock which brings Leontes back to his senses, to
reason and virtue, and to linguistic coherence. First he interprets his son's
death as a divine indictment of his guilt:

> Apollo's angry, and the heavens themselves
> Do strike at my injustice.   (146–7)

As Hermione faints, and he concernedly orders her to be cared for, the 'clearer knowledge' that she had predicted would come, makes Leontes denounce himself and vindicate everyone he has accused:

> I have too much believ'd mine own suspicion. . . .
>   Apollo, pardon
> My great profaneness 'gainst thine oracle!
> I'll reconcile me to Polixenes,
> New woo my queen, recall the good Camillo,
> Whom I proclaim a man of truth, of mercy . . .

'most humane / And fill'd with honour'. Consideration of Camillo's virtue makes Leontes see his own faults the more clearly, as he sums up the polarisation of reason and madness, good and evil, brought about in these five scenes:

>   How he glisters
>   Through my rust! And how his piety
>   Does my deeds make the blacker!   (151–72)

This full and frank confession vindicates the innocent, condemns the single source of viciousness, so re-establishing Leontes' virtue, which is put to a further test when Paulina brings news of Hermione's death. Leontes accepts Paulina's violent accusations of him (172–214): 'Thou canst not speak too much; I have deserved / All . . .', and orders that on the tomb of Hermione and Mamillius 'shall / The causes of their death appear, unto / Our shame perpetual', undertaking to visit the chapel where they are buried as a 'daily vow' (214–43). In his remorse and self-accusation Leontes regains our respect, although the disasters he has seemingly caused can never be righted.

There, in brief, I have summarised the dramatic structure of the first half of this play, reminding readers of what they already know in order to bring out the coherence and explicitness of Shakespeare's creation. We now see that Leontes was wrong from the first, Hermione and all those sided against him fully justified. Some such reconstruction of the play as an experience (whether in solitary reading or in the company of a theatre audience), as a totally polarised sequence in which we perceive false accusations exposed, true virtue upheld, would seem to me the starting-point for critical discussion. Returning to Howard Felperin, however, we find that a deconstructionist approach must once again ignore the sequential experience of drama, picking out passages here and there in order to disseminate doubt and uncertainty. Felperin begins with the oracle since (I imagine) he sees it as the key pronouncement which authenticates our judgment on Leontes' unjust and inhumane behaviour. And since such an explicit division of guilt and innocence would suit neither the deconstructionist project of seeking incoherence, nor its desire to subsume all texts to its theory of linguistic indeterminacy, he calls the oracle in question. First he argues that the death of Mamillius is not necessarily related to the oracle, and *could* be 'the result of natural rather than supernatural causes', which would of course rupture the link between human and divine (Felperin 1990, pp. 38–41). But the person who most matters in this connection, the man who has called up the oracle as the embodiment of truth and then denied it, certainly sees the death as supernaturally caused. It is most regrettable that Felperin did not think it worth quoting either Leontes' lines affirming his sense of divine punishment (3.2.146–7), or his later prayer to Apollo to pardon his 'great profaneness' against his oracle (153–4). (Ignoring those passages in the play that do not fit your interpretation always seems suspicious when the reader notices it.)

The crucial point in this scene is that Leontes first affirms his belief in the oracle's omniscience and then denies it for not agreeing with him. The resulting religious guilt that Leontes feels should be seen as a recognition of his own blasphemy and arrogance, a deduction within a belief-system to which the modern reader must assent for the duration of the play at least. (Unwillingness to make this elementary suspension of disbelief would render all religious texts incomprehensible, deny any possibility of that imaginative co-operation which is the essence of involvement with works of art, in the absence of which aesthetic criticism becomes futile.) Felperin's motives for wishing to affirm a rationalist, non-religious explanation, denying the oracle the power which Leontes ascribes to it, emerge more clearly in his next 'demystifying' argument, that oracles were commonly seen in Renaissance literature as pagan and thus deceitful (pp. 38–9). But the fact that the witches in the Scottish tragedy are *ambiguous* in their pronouncements to Macbeth does not mean that they lie, and in any case their equivocations are to be seen in the specific context of common attitudes towards witchcraft in classical antiquity and in the Renaissance.[49] Witches are deceitful not because they are pagan but because they are controlled by the power which St. Paul attributes to 'your adversary the devil, [who] as a roaring lion walketh about, seeking whom he may devour' (1 Pet. 5.8).

Felperin then attempts to undermine the reliability of Apollo's oracle further by finding it significant that Apollo does not appear in person to deliver his oracle, especially since there are theophanies in the other late romances, notably *Pericles* and *Cymbeline*. That it is only reported here means that this oracle must be seen to be 'disturbingly difficult to verify or validate', so that 'Shakespeare's divorce of the god's words from the god's presence' leads us to another aporia (pp. 42–3), that abyss over which the deconstructionist comes to a satisfied rest, his task completed — rather like the chasm over which the priest of the Delphic oracle was supposed to sit, absorbing the fumes and illumination that arose from the earth. But if you wish to unravel the text this is a bad place to start. For one thing, no law compels Shakespeare to bring on a god in person every time the text he has written involves a divine communication. In this play, especially, he has a stunning revelation up his sleeve at the very end, in the statue scene, and might reasonably not want to dull that effect by anticipation. For another, as Shakespeare or any other reader of classical texts (such as the Greek romances, newly popular in the Renaissance) would have known, in antiquity oracles were commonly fetched by ambassadors who journeyed to the sacred spot, paid the priests, and returned with the message.[50] No one expected Apollo to turn up in person to answer every query. Not even in Euripides' *Ion*, the most sustained examination of the reliability of oracles in classical drama, does Apollo appear in person: he sends Athene to represent him.[51]

If the oracles totally resist deconstruction, Felperin may do better with the play's language. In the Sicilian court he finds 'slipperiness and ambiguity' everywhere, also 'sexual innuendo', as in Polixenes' courtly statement of his debt of thanks for Leones' hospitality:

> And therefore, like a cipher
> (Yet standing in rich place), I multiply
> With one 'We thank you' many thousands more
> That go before it.   (1.2.6ff)

Rather than seeing 'a sniggering phallic allusion to his "standing-in" for Leontes' (p. 44), this is in fact a common Renaissance metaphor from numbers, and we would need rather more warrant before taking every use of the word 'stand' as referring to an erection.[52] Felperin, in effect, here pursues the standard deconstructionist ploy of generalising a specific feature — the courtly language appropriate to such a milieu, made even more effusively circumlocutory in Shakespeare's late style (compare the poet and painter scenes in *Timon of Athens*, or the penultimate scene (5.2) of courtly dialogue in this play)[53] — into a thematic comment. It now supposedly represents the play's (or the court's) 'loss of verbal innocence' and its (or their) 'discovery of ubiquitous verbal duplicity' (p. 45) — 'ubiquitous', that is, *pace* Derrida and Co., not just in this milieu, but in language as such. Behaviour typical of one character — Leontes' ability, in his jealous fits, to see innuendos everywhere (a mark of extreme psychological imbalance, as in Othello's agonies over the verb 'lie' — 'Lie with her? on her?...') — is depersonalised and allegorised as a feature of language itself. These deconstructionist ploys are especially noticeable in Felperin's commentary on that notoriously difficult soliloquy of Leontes on the subjective reality of jealous feelings:

> Affection! thy intention stabs the centre....
> With what's unreal thou coactive art,
> And fellow'st nothing....   (1.2.138ff)

Felperin could have glossed the key words in their historical context, that is, Renaissance psychology ('Affection: *affectio*, a sudden, unexpected change in mind and body; here, jealousy'; 'intention: intensity'; 'fellow'st nothing': 'you associate yourself with what is non-existent').[54] Read in this

appropriate context we see Leontes simultaneously recognising the actual
insubstantiality of his fears while experiencing their reality in maddeningly
concrete, physiological terms ('I find it . . . to the infection of my brains /
And hard'ning of my brows').

But, true to his *profession de foi déconstructionniste*, Felperin allegorises
this unique and specifically Renaissance conception into a condition
of language *per se*. 'Leontes grasps, as we have begun to grasp' — we
twentieth-century readers, that is, anno Derridae 25 —

> that the instability of meaning and uncertainty of reference he is
> experiencing first-hand — what I have termed linguistic indeterminacy
> — is not a function simply of expression but of interpretation as well. It
> arises . . . out of the radical subjectivity of the listener or interpreter. For
> this reason, it is doubly inescapable, a condition that prevents us from
> ever arriving at certain or complete communication in human affairs,
> not to mention final or definitive interpretations of literary texts. (p. 46)

That passage, which reads rather like a lay sermon, typifies the deconstructionist's subordination of the text discussed to the theory it
supposedly supports. I recall an acute comment, that 'one of the many
difficulties of de Man's work is that his practical criticism is written for the
sake of the theoretical questions it provokes' (Donoghue 1981, p. 172).
Where other critics develop a theory in order to challenge or improve their
practice, the deconstructionist does the opposite. If you like the theory,
you will like the criticism; if you prefer the play, you won't like the theory.

The skeleton of Derrida's system is visibly imposing itself on Shakespeare's
romance. Felperin finds Leontes deluded by 'engrossing subjectivity'
(p. 47), and claims that

> in his very transition . . . from a *poetics of difference* to a *poetics of
> reference*, Leontes enacts in a mad, parodic form a characteristic drift of
> European literary criticism: a superstition of the word that endows it
> with the power to conjure its referent into being. (p. 48; my italics)

Such comments are no longer concerned with the play but with reiterating
the credos of deconstruction. To attribute to Leontes a shift from a 'poetics
of difference' to a 'poetics of reference' — truly, a grandiose achievement
— is to pile on him a weight of pseudo-historical significance which no
literary character could possibly sustain. In any case, since the former
('difference') is copyright Derrida, and the latter ('reference') belongs to
Aristotle, and everyone since, to call this a 'drift' in European criticism is
to run history backwards. And it is completely unfounded to accuse the
standard view of language as capable of reference as being a 'superstition'
that thinks it can 'conjure' a referent into being. This was (and still is, for
all I know), the belief of magicians and other practitioners of the occult,
that words had power over things, against which the standard tradition
vigorously and consciously opposed itself.[55] Deconstructionists typically

misrepresent alternative approaches in order to 'dismantle' them, thus claiming an empirico-rational legitimacy by citing evidence yet at the same time perverting it. What matters is to push on to confirming another point in its credo, the belief that 'in its very nature as representation, as figurative language, the literary text is never really "there" or fully present, and the actions and transactions it generates are always . . . estranged by the linguistic medium in which it has its existence' (p. 51). That de Manian vein of complacent pessimism, the satisfaction of having fissurised drama into two incompatible halves, action and language, shows the habit-forming slide into the abyss — protective in its darkness, all need for decision infinitely deferred or declared impossible, safe from challenge, criticism, or development — to which deconstruction leads. It must be clear to the non-addicted, though, that to accept this fissurising of language from action would destroy drama itself — if that still matters.

This whole regurgitation of the Derrida-de Man anti-*fiat* ('Let it not be!' is their uncreating Word), was notionally sparked off by a Shakespeare play, and Felperin finally returns to it by conceding, to our great surprise, that the sign can still 'refer', can still 'constitute a world of reference . . .' — only to undermine that idea at source:

> Yet this world of reference, as we have begun to see in *The Winter's Tale*, has finally no objective reality or ontological stability, but recedes into an infinite play of signs and deferral of affirmative or authoritative meaning. (p. 51)

— All this, we recall, just because Apollo did not appear in person, and because Leontes suspects his wife of adultery! — After still more deconstructionist dogma ('reference is never quite presence, yet it is not quite absence either'; 'this fall into textual instability') Felperin proceeds to unravel the whole text. *The Winter's Tale* 'dramatizes . . . the precariousness of its own linguistic enterprise', since 'validation is unavailable' for Leontes, there is no 'resting-point for reference repeatedly deferred and finally lost in the precariousness of language and the absence of an authoritative divine voice' (pp. 52–3). Once again we see the levelling, reductive effect of deconstructionist methodology: the special case of Leontes, his remarkable fit of jealousy, the *affectio* that overpowers his psyche and produces what seems to all the people around him (and to himself subsequently) a mental aberration or sickness, and which is rendered in a totally idiosyncratic style, a *ne plus ultra* even for Shakespeare of condensed metaphor, fragmented syntax, and insistent rhetoric — this completely realised idiolect, product of a temporary delusion, is now generalised into the deconstructionist's sentimental pathos of the instabilities of language, the 'endless process of deferral', and what else.

But readers of the play will protest: the validation is not lost! It is given by the horrified reactions of everyone else to Leontes, especially his nearest attendant Camillo; by the oracle's statement; by the death of Mamillius, and the reported death of Hermione; by Leontes' psychological collapse and recovery; and by his sixteen years of remorse. Any critical method which has to blot out ninety percent of the play and to distort the rest to achieve its reading must be regarded with suspicion. Deconstruction, however, has a way of making everything prove its case. Felperin now presents the non-appearance of Apollo, one of the fixed points in his negation of the play, in a favourable — albeit allegorical — light, as showing Shakespeare referring to 'the fallen nature of human speech . . . the condition of secularity within which we all' dwell (p. 53). And where almost every other critic known to me feels the play's ending to be a remarkably warm reunion and reconciliation, Felperin refuses this. The 'linguistic problems foregrounded in the opening act', he tells us sternly, 'are never, because they cannot be, solved' (pp. 53–4) — certainly not in a deconstructionist reading, we concede. He finds Paulina's language 'incommensurate and incompatible with the "nature" it attempts to define', and the 'faith [she] appeals to us to awaken' (this is her injunction to Leontes, not to us, before revealing that the 'statue' is his living wife: 'It is requir'd / You do awake your faith'), merely 'foregrounds' (Felperin's puzzling italics) 'the inescapable mediacy of language, the radical difference between presence and reference, and the ultimate subjectivity of all interpretation'.

That flat tone, the note of tired moralising, is far away from the excitement that deconstruction promised us. Felperin has only sententiousness left, though:

> In sum, the fallen and incorrigible nature of language — of which the casual duplicity of the pun, Shakespeare's fatal Cleopatra, is only the most familiar symptom — paradoxically enables it in Shakespeare's hand to become the perfect medium for defining human reality. (pp. 54–5)

This sequence recycles yet again the deconstructionist repertory of false dichotomies (as if 'interpretation' could be objective), tautology (that language — 'fallen' — is suitable for fallen mankind is hardly surprising), and confusion. The fact that we can pun does not make language 'fallen'! Felperin seems to want an ideal language of non-ambivalence, of single and unmistakable denotation, but there never was such a thing. Deconstructionists commonly accuse their opponents — nous autres — of nostalgia for a language of presence, a 'paradise lost' that can be 'literally delivered' (p. 49). I have yet to come across anyone expressing this wish, apart — of course — from devotees of the occult, with their belief in a linguistic essentialism, where words could have power in the physical world.

Once we have absorbed and classified the deconstructive constituents in Felperin's twenty pages on The Winter's Tale, we might ask ourselves, what have we been reading? Have we learned anything new, or interesting about the play? Or have we learned anything new, or interesting about the critical method? In other forms of criticism a writer can bring something fresh out of a play by using a new approach, or, confronted with what he finds in the play, be forced to revise his critical model. Here, though, and with due respect to Felperin, who shows much more sensitivity to language and literature than most of the critics of this school, his critical method has been imposed like a template on the play and has yielded utterly predictable results. Only a fragment of the text fitted the method, and even that only by ignoring the dramatic and psychological individuality of Leontes' frantic jealousy, and reducing it to the level of language. Everything else in the play had to be ignored, or forcibly adapted, un-ravelled, undermined, or whatever.

*   *   *

By now the sanguine expectations of an impresario summoning Shakespearian deconstructionists together — it 'seemed a goal worthy in and of itself' (Atkins and Bergeron 1988, p. vii) — may appear doubtful. The last effort of this kind I shall examine, Malcolm Evans's exercise in 'Deconstructing Shakespeare's Comedies' (Evans 1985) raises even more doubts. The fissure in Shakespeare that Evans wishes to create, from the first words of his essay, concerns the notion of imitation. He quotes from *Love's Labour's Lost* the disparaging comments of the schoolmaster Holofernes on the sonnet sent by Berowne to Rosaline:

> Here are only numbers ratified, but for the elegancy, facility, and golden cadence of poesy, *caret*. Ovidius Naso was the man. And why indeed 'Naso', but for smelling out the odoriferous flowers of fancy, the jerks of invention? *Imitari* is nothing: so doth the hound his master, the ape his keeper, the tired horse his rider. (4.2.120ff)

Since Shakespeare is parodying the Elizabethan schoolmaster at his most ostentatious (Holofernes, alas for his *auctoritas*, has just misquoted the beginning of Mantuan's first eclogue, an extremely well-known grammar school text, saying *Facile* instead of *Fauste*), to understand this passage it is natural to refer to T.W. Baldwin's massive refutation of the myth that Shakespeare was ignorant of the classics.[56] (His book established beyond doubt that Shakespeare's writing habits were indelibly affected by the humanist methods adopted in English grammar schools during the six-teenth century.)

As Baldwin shows (II, 382), Latin verse-writing in the grammar school was based on two main models, elementary — Mantuan's *Bucolica*, and advanced — Ovid. Schoolboys worked, however, not from the original texts but from a collection of poetical excerpts, such as the *Flores Poëtarum* ('flowers of fancy', as Holofernes calls them, after his stale pun on Naso/nose), which included passages from Ovid, and then graduated to more advanced works in order to further the 'imitation of the best Poets' (II, 386–90). From these handbooks, as Baldwin shows, Shakespeare took the technical term 'ratified', since 'the *ratio* of verse demanded that it be strictly bound in an exact and legitimate number of feet', as laid down by Rudolphus Gualtherus in *De Syllaborum et Carminum Ratione* (London, 1573) — a book bought for Philip Sidney at Shrewsbury School in 1566, aged eleven — who writes, 'numeri autem sine pedum & syllabarum ratione observari non possunt'. The erudite phrase 'ratified' is a deliberate Latinism (II, 392–3), one of several details invented by Shakespeare to display Holofernes' pedantry. Baldwin's detailed analysis of this scene shows that Shakespeare knew enough about the principles of verse-writing 'to enable him to satirize thus intelligently and tellingly the pedantic use of them' (II, 405). Holofernes dismisses Berowne's poem as prosodically correct but lacking 'the jerks of invention', so invoking the standard distinction between mere *imitatio* — 'Imitari is nothing', as he says — and invention, in rhetoric the higher and essential part, thus performing what Erasmus would call a 'laus inventionis, quae praecipua pars est eloquentiae' (407). Of course, in the Renaissance rhetorical system even *inventio* depended on a knowledge of other writers' style and thought, but one that had been properly digested. *Imitatio*, once fully absorbed or metabolised, could lead to the higher stage of invention; but undigested, unpractised, it could only be superficial, resulting at best in pastiche.[57] In Horace's famous diatribe, imitators were a 'slavish herd' (*O imitatores, servum pecus: Epist.* I.xix.19).

In the Renaissance, as in antiquity, literary theory distinguished *mimesis*, the imitation proper to drama as a representation of human action, from *imitatio*, the copying of a verbal model. For a familiar instance of this distinction we can turn to Ben Jonson's notebook on literature (probably compiled with a view to publication as some kind of treatise), *Timber; or Discoveries*, which defines a poet as 'a Maker, or a fainer: His Art, an Art of imitation, or faining; expressing the life of man in fit measures, numbers, and harmony, according to *Aristotle*'. Outlining the qualities needed of a poet, and synthesising a number of sources, Jonson lists these as *ingenium* ('a goodness of naturall wit'), *exercitatio* ('Exercise of those parts, and frequent'), *lectio* ('an exactnesse of Studie, and multiplicity of reading'), and above all *imitatio*, that

> requisite in our *Poet*, or Maker, . . . to bee able to convert the substance, or Ritches of an other *Poet*, to his owne use. To make choise of one excellent man above the rest, and so to follow him, till he grows very Hee: or, so like him, as the Copie may be mistaken for the Pricipall. Not as a Creature that swallowes what it takes in, crude, raw, or indigested; but that . . . hath a Stomacke to concoct, devide, and turne all into nourishment. Not to imitate servilely, as *Horace* saith, . . . but to draw forth out of the best and choisest flowers, with the Bee, and turne all into Honey, worke it into one relish and savour: make our Imitation sweet: observe how the best writers have imitated, and follow them.[58]

Many other passages could be quoted to show that in Renaissance literary theory *imitatio* was a verbal training exercise, essential to a writer's development, which was subsumed under the primary process of *mimesis*. Malcolm Evans, however, unaware of this distinction, explains the passage thus:

> Imitation, the pedant Holofernes suggests, is beneath human dignity. At best *mimesis* is for animals. But elsewhere in Shakespeare's comedies even the hound is in two minds about it. (Evans 1985, p. 67)

This last remark is a reference to the scene in *The Two Gentlemen of Verona* (4.4) where the clown Launce rebukes his dog for misbehaving in public ('when didst thou see me heave up my leg and make water against a gentlewoman's farthingale?'). That is, of course, a completely inappropriate text to serve as an example of *mimesis*, but it is enough for Evans to launch into full deconstructionist flow:

> Already, in these early plays, the status of *mimesis* is problematic. Defined as fit only for animals then spurned even by them, this mimicry in crisis is a gift to deconstruction . . . (p. 68)

But the only 'crisis' here is the misunderstanding caused by Evans confusing *mimesis* with *imitatio*, repeated in his remark that Holofernes' 'insistence that imitation is only for apes, horses, and dogs contravenes Aristotle, for whom *mimesis* is proper . . . only to humanity' (p. 71). This mistaken and spurious opposition means that from the outset Evans's case rests on air.

But the Shakespeare text, as we now know, is only a means by which deconstruction can reassert its own mastery, deploy its own heady idiom. The comedies, Evans writes, are concerned with 'acting, representation and identity' — among other more important things, we might add, such as making the good society, establishing lasting human relationships, properly defining both work and play. But for Evans

> the mirror that reflects deconstruction is always itself divided and already in more than one place — at the site of a mimetic *sign* or action, but also in the *signifier* released in the enactment of acting, the representation on the stage of the process of *mimesis* itself which may, as Holofernes maintains, be no more or less than 'nothing'. (p. 68)

Perhaps the reader would like a briefer or clearer restatement of that point? Read on:

> In the Comedies the *process* of representation is never finally effaced from its *product*, leaving these categories themselves indistinct. This denigration of a 'represented' to which representation must always subordinate itself, or a 'meaning' which can be located beyond the play of signifiers, radically undermines from within those metaphorical constructions through which meaning is constituted. What Derridean deconstruction removes is this 'reassuring certitude, which is itself

beyond the reach of play' (Derrida 1978, p. 279), a certitude designated in metaphysical thought as simultaneously *part* of a total structure but not *of* it — a paradox which calls into question

— but 'enough, no more', I stop there.

What Evans gives us, with considerable *hwyl* (Welsh for 'eloquence' or 'possession'), is a fantasia on Derridian themes in which thought seems to coalesce, categories collapse, the repertory of available phrases being urgently redeployed in a confused tissue of on-going regression. This is much more than a question of style, where *de gustibus est disputandum.* Here thought is forced back on itself. The 'structure proposed by mimesis', Evans continues, 'is a structure only because it has a centre', but 'that centre must also always be outside — in the object or signified on which the structure is grounded', therefore 'in Derrida's terms "the center is not the center" and coherence is constituted in contradiction' (p. 68). Who will offer to make sense of this? John Searle once offered a parody of deconstructive argument (Searle 1983, p. 78), but I am reminded of that great satirist Karl Kraus, who in his journal *Die Fackel* thought it enough to satirise National Socialist newspapers by reprinting excerpts from them.

But in addition to this confusion of thought and language there is the overall incongruity of Derridian methods being employed for *Love's Labour's Lost.* Admittedly, the play includes a grotesque gallery of linguistic oddballs, who have 'been at a great feast of languages, and stol'n the scraps', as Moth judges (5.1.36–7), and it might well be given the subtitle *A Comedy of Grammars.* But the linguistic eccentricities it satirises are not endemic to language itself. They are well-known faults of style according to Renaissance literary theory, reprovingly catalogued by rhetoricians and grammarians in terms that now seem to us (perhaps they always were) as outlandish as the vices they describe. Holofernes is guilty, *inter alia,* of *cacozelia* (affected diction, especially coining fine words out of Latin), *soraismus* (mingling of sundry languages ignorantly or affectedly, what Puttenham calls 'mingle-mangle'), *cacemphaton* (an unpleasing combination of sounds, such as results from excessive alliteration).[59] Evans claims, in effect, that *these linguistic perversions prove Derrida's theory of language right.* Exhibit one is Holofernes' absurdly over-alliterated sonnet beginning 'The preyful Princess pierc'd and prick'd a pretty pleasing pricket', in which, Holofernes announces, he will 'affect the letter' (emphasise the initial letters) 'for it argues facility' — a gross error, evidently, since the 'facility and golden cadence of poesy' celebrated in Ovid is light-years away from his comically turgid doggerel. Evans, though, seizes on this sonnet as exemplifying 'the grammatological spacing of Derridean *différance,* the process in which semantic *differentiation* is caught up in a signified which is endlessly *deferred*' (p. 70). 'Would that it had been', we might feel! Exhibit two is the schoolboy trick by which Moth traps Holofernes into reversing the 'a, b' of his hornbook (the ABC), to declare himself a '*Ba,* most silly sheep' (5.1.46ff). This feeble joke is said by Evans, who obviously lacks any sense of humour or proportion, to reveal 'the randomness and play of what Derrida, in "White Mythology", describes as a "nonsense" which exceeds signification and in which "language is not yet born"' (p. 72). Doubts that Derridians may feel about this positive alignment of the master's theories with Shakespeare's comic anatomies of language perverted will come to a head in exhibit three, Evans' pronouncement that

> Holofernes, who rejects imitation, also shares with Derrida the convic-
> tion that writing, far from being merely supplementary, in fact *precedes*
> speech, even 'thought',[60] and believes that those who refuse to speak
> words as they are written are prisoners of a phonocentric madness. . . .
> (p. 73)

To put Derrida on the same level as this pedant might offend those who know that Holofernes is here being satirised as a linguistic freak precisely for mocking standard pronunciation as practised by those he calls 'rackers of orthography' who pronounce 'doubt' or 'debt' with the 'b' silent. (Let Evans try to sound it!) In the play, at any rate, Holofernes is a laughing-stock, to be pitied, not emulated.

Deference to Derrida may do him an injustice, but it does Shakespeare a greater disservice. Like other deconstructionists, Evans reduces drama to language, and characters to mere signs. Indeed, in his topsy-turvy perspective,

> the figures who speak and gesticulate on stage in the Comedies are
> *much more than imaginary people*. They are literally and ostentatiously
> 'characters' — hieroglyphs, letters, elements in a signifying system which
> flaunts its own abstractions. . . . (p. 72; my italics)

(Only a peculiarly academic mind could imagine that signs in a system which 'flaunts its own abstractions' are '*much more than imaginary people*'.) The loyal following-through of a Derridian paradigm can only reduce and falsify this or any other play. According to Evans, *Love's Labour's Lost*, 'were it not so impenetrable, would already be a classic of Western phonocentrism, ranked alongside Plato's *Phaedrus* . . .'. For here, he claims, 'as in the *Phaedrus*, writing is set against the *presence* and fecundity of speech', that is, in 'the Academe's edict *for* writing and *against* speech' (p. 78).

But this is a wholly false account of what happens in the text. The play begins with the King of Navarre's ill-conceived and soon-exploded attempt to live for three years in withdrawal from society, 'Still and contempla-tive in living art' (1.1.13–14) — that is, practising silence in the *vita contemplativa*, the most austere *ars vivendi*. The statutes that the king proposes includes an edict for this retired community (stricter than Little Gidding, even) prohibiting any woman coming within a mile of the court 'on pain of losing her tongue', and specifying punishments for any man 'seen to talk with a woman' (1.1.122, 129). Typically interested only in language, the deconstructionist fails to notice that the edicts are against 'conversation' in the old sense of intercourse, society, associating with people (especially women, dangerous distractions from chastity and asceticism), and are intended to ensure the courtiers' contemplative isolation. Communication by writing would be equally reprehensible, indeed within a short space of time, as Berowne has predicted, all four courtiers are unmasked having written love-poems to the ladies. The main operative distinction in *Love's Labour's Lost* is missed by Evans, but it is one that all deconstructionists should take to heart, namely the danger of valuing language or book-learning over life. Berowne utters this caveat in the first scene (1.1.59–93) and recurs to it in his remarkable speech ending Act 4, 'Have at you then, affection's men at arms' (4.3.286–362). But in the final scene the tables are turned on him, and as a punishment for his unfeeling verbal games at others' expense Berowne is made to work in a hospital for a year, to cheer 'the speechless sick' with his talk (5.2.841–71). Language, so often misused in this play, is finally put to serious social use, validating the ethos of rhetoric as a support to human virtue that extends from Cicero and Quintilian to Melanchthon, Erasmus, and Vives.

Far be it from me to draw out this moral of setting language against life, but it is symptomatic of deconstruction's narrow range of interests that Malcolm Evans can apparently fail to notice so much else that goes on in Shakespeare's comedies. As a genre, he claims, they resist being related to life, society, human *mores*, or anything else:

> The Comedies confront interpretation with surfaces that are concerned not so much with yielding textual depths as with reflecting other surfaces or deconstructing the surface-depth opposition. (p. 82)

Deconstructionist dogma, we appreciate, does not allow any 'truth about such texts' other than the 'conditional, inscribed in contradiction and absence' (p. 83). To other readers and playgoers, however, it is clear that the comedies have a purpose, that each achieves something in the course of the action, at the very minimum performing a process of selection, choosing some modes of being as likely to create and sustain social harmony, rejecting others as divisive and destructive. It is no accident that at the end of *As You Like It*, Hymen, the god of marriage appears, attended by '*Still music*', to show that 'there is mirth in heaven, / When earthly things made even, / Atone together'. His task is to 'bar confusion, . . . make conclusion / Of these most strange events' (5.4.108ff). The musical harmony reinforces the physical reconciliations and unions performed on stage, with Rosalind — no longer disguised as the boy Ganymed, but a woman again — restoring herself to Duke Senior as a daughter, and to Orlando as a wife-to-be. Both men accept her identity, 'If there be truth in sight', — there is! — and by the same token, 'If sight and shape be true', — they are! — Phebe realises that she can no longer think of wooing

Ganymed, but had better accept Sylvius. Using the same grammatical form, a seeming conditional that in fact describes an actual state, Hymen calls together

> eight that must take hands
> To join in Hymen's bands,
>   If truth holds true contents.   (5.4.128ff)

Ordinary, and even specialist Shakespearians, will add 'it does!', since they instantly perceive the 'If' to be redundant, for Rosalind is really a flesh and blood woman (within the play's fictional world, of course), and the harmony between three of the couples at least (Touchstone and Audrey facing 'foul weather') has been earned.

To Evans as deconstructionist, however, no such positive conclusion is possible. Hymen makes at best

> gestures towards the truth, identical with itself, only to break down in a delirium of wordplays on 'truth', 'holds', 'true' and 'contents' which leaves no centre but tautology, endless supplementation. . . . (pp. 82–3)

That Evans should give such an absurdly false account of the language of this scene ('delirium of wordplays') may show the pressure he is under, and to which he subjects the text, in order to pronounce the deconstructionist's Q.E.D. Once again actual human behaviour is reduced to language, and to a language endlessly working against itself. And here, too, a Derridian significance is discovered in the reduction, for

> This climactic utterance of the Comedies comes, appropriately, from a *deus ex machina* with no serious function to perform but who mirrors the work of one of Derrida's favourite rhetorical devices — also named the 'hymen'. In Derrida, as in Shakespeare, this figure marks the point beyond which interpretation has no jurisdiction: . . . 'the violence of a truth stronger than truth'. . . . This final coincidence completes the conspiratorial work of deconstruction in the Comedies. (p. 83)

Setting aside the question of who has conspired with whom, and also Derrida's wilful claim that 'hymen' has an indeterminable meaning, here is perhaps a fitting point to end this account of the language-fixated, language-fissuring world of deconstruction, that it can imagine that a god who presides at marriages has 'no serious function'.

CHAPTER FOUR

New Historicism: Disaffected Subjects

> He that goeth about to persuade a multitude, that they are not so well governed as they ought to be, shall never want attentive and favourable hearers. . . . And because such as openly reprove supposed disorders of state are taken for principal friends to the common benefit of all, and for men that carry singular freedom of mind; under this fair and plausible colour whatsoever they utter passeth for good and current.
>
> Richard Hooker[1]

After the resolutely ahistorical attitude of deconstruction, its relentless attempt to apply the same sceptical disintegrating reading techniques to texts of all periods, irrespective of context or design, any historical approach to literature may seem welcome. A school of critics practising a 'new historicism' will surely have to accept that language can have a determinate meaning, can refer to a known reality, otherwise it would have to reject all historical documents as equally uncertain. And a 'new' historicism, which promises to avoid the faults of the old one — that is something to which everyone who accepts the historical dimension of human experience can look forward. The mere name of this type of criticism will make many readers favourably disposed towards it from the outset.

But the name itself, to start with, turns out to be extremely vague. Although the phrase was apparently first used in 1980,[2] its vogue as a critical label dates from 1982, when Stephen Greenblatt (as he reports), having 'collected a bunch of essays' for a journal called *Genre*, 'out of a kind of desperation to get the introduction done, . . . wrote that the essays represented something I called a "new historicism"'. Wickedly disclaiming any abilities in self-publicity ('I've never been very good at making up advertising phrases of this kind'), Greenblatt professes to feel 'giddy with amazement' at its success (Greenblatt 1990, p. 146). Greenblatt went on to describe it as a critical 'practice — a practice rather than a doctrine, since as far as I can tell (and I should be the one to know) it's no doctrine at all' (*ibid.*) 'Does this mean', he asks, 'that new historicism is a completely empty term, its relative success due entirely to the felicitous conjunction of two marketable signs: "new" and "ism"?' (*ibid.*, p. 3). His answer is negative, but the opinion is often expressed that it 'remains a phrase without an adequate referent' (Veeser 1989, p. x). Historicism itself is a notoriously loose concept,[3] many things to many people, never properly distinguished from the German term *Historismus* (Thomas 1989, pp. 182–92). To some users it has 'signified reductionism, present-mindedness, and teleology' (Fox-Genovese 1989, p. 215). To others, lexicographers included, it can mean '1. The belief that processes are at work in history that man can do little to alter. 2. The theory that the historian must avoid all value judgments in his study of past periods or former cultures. 3. Veneration of the past or of tradition.' Greenblatt, having made that quotation from the *American Heritage Dictionary*, tries to subvert it: 'Most of the writing labelled new historicist, and certainly my own work, has set itself resolutely against each of these positions' (Greenblatt 1990, p. 164). However, as we shall see, the first of these points does apply, in that version of history put about by Michel Foucault.

Although eluding exact definition, the avowed success of New Historicism means that it has been the subject of intense discussion within its brief life so far (hardly a decade as I pen these words). Seldom, if ever, has a new and relatively small critical movement (its acknowledged practitioners barely reach a dozen) provoked so much heated discussion in so short a time, with so small a body of achieved work. Critics and commentators on New Historicism indeed already outnumber the practitioners,[4] proof again of the latent panic in the contemporary cultural scene, as each 'latest trend' has to be spotted, identified, celebrated, or attacked. Many of the evaluations so far published come from rival groups, feminists, deconstructionists, cultural materialists . . . , each writer anxious to align with, or reject, whatever aspect fits or jibes with their own practice. We are not surprised that a deconstructionist critic should judge New Historicism to be 'a sort of academic media hype mounted against deconstruction' (Spivak 1989, p. 280), with the dispute between the two groups a 'turf battle'. But the suspicion of hype affects even those aligned with this group, such as Louis Montrose, who wryly and deprecatingly refers to it as 'a term appealing to our commodifying cult of the new', representing that 'acceleration in the forgetting of history which seems to characterize an increasingly technocratic and future-oriented academy and society'.[5] In the by now world-wide disease of 'hype' in advertising, the term 'new' is a signal to the consumer that conveys both an invitation and a warning: 'You must buy this model, unless you want to feel superseded'. It is hard not to relate the consumer-industry-induced stigma of owning an out-of-date automobile or hi-fi, last season's model, to the fear of obsolescence so rife in literary critical circles today.[6] This new school has barely come to prominence before the speculations over its waning or demise begin to appear: 'so swiftly do our paradigms now seem to shift' (Felperin 1990, p. 142; Montrose 1989, p. 18).

The hype has not, however, managed to silence some rather severe reactions, which have judged the New Historicism neither new nor historical. Howard Felperin has argued that it is in fact continuous with 'older habits of thought to which it is overtly opposed' (Felperin 1990, p. 143),

and that Greenblatt's early work is not essentially different from that of
E.M.W. Tillyard (pp. 149–50), who has become the unfortunate butt of
avant-garde literary critics. (A rather safe target, which may be attacked
without danger.) 'American New Historicism', he concludes, 'is not all
that "new"', and is 'not genuinely *historical* or seriously political either'
(p. 155). Edward Pechter had also pointed out that Greenblatt's assumption that the literary text is determined by 'its ideological and historical
situation' is in effect the same procedure as Tillyard's,[7] and his analyses of
Greenblatt's essays on *King Lear* and *Henry IV* argue for a continuity of
method (Pechter 1987, pp. 293–4). Elizabeth Fox-Genovese, a social
historian with wider than literary interests, has commented that

> the emphasis on newness bespeaks the central paradox that informs the
> new historicism as a project: Notwithstanding some notable exceptions,
> it is not very historical. It is especially not self-critically or self-reflexively
> historical. (Fox-Genovese 1989, p. 214)

Despite their professedly radical goals, she holds, its practitioners 'implicitly perpetuate the dubious politics of what many are calling our society
of information' (*ibid.*, pp. 220–1). This comment, in turn, endorses
Gerald Graff's diagnosis of the remarkably accelerating rate 'at which a
critical methodology goes from being celebrated as revolutionary to being
condemned as complicitous. Whereas it took several years before one heard
that deconstruction was really an extension of the establishment, it took
only a few months for this charge to be made about the new historicism'
(Graff 1989, pp. 174–5).[8]

What concerns me is not whether a critical approach is new or old, but
how good it is, in particular when applied to Shakespeare. I have cited
some accounts of New Historicism to show that the very identity of this
approach, as well as its value, are at present hotly disputed. Historians of
contemporary culture have the advantages of nearness to their topic, but
they notoriously lack an overview. I shall try to outline some common
attributes of this school, amorphous though it yet seems, well aware that
the landscape may change very quickly. Then I shall discuss some of the
Shakespeare criticism it has produced, as representing at any rate the first
phase of what is claimed to be the 'turn away from the formal, decon-
textualized analysis that dominate[d] new criticism' (Greenblatt 1990,
p. 163). 'New' — such is the paucity of modern critical vocabulary,
referring to a school of criticism flourishing in the 1940s and 50s, which is
sometimes said to have reacted against historical criticism. (I think it could
be shown that most of the 'New Critics' in fact worked inside a historical
framework, and had a far better sense of period and genre than those who
claim to have superseded them.)

I

New Historicism can certainly be distinguished from 'old' (that is, any earlier historical approach or any contemporary one that does not share its stake in Current Literary Theory), in that it is a product of the 1960s upheaval leading to post-structuralism. Not that New Historicists can afford to accept the whole Derridian indeterminacy-of-language-and-meaning thesis, of course: they draw just as much from that particular line as suits them.[9] They also draw on Lacan, occasionally, and on Althusser and his followers discussed in Chapter 7 below. Barthes is cited for the death of the author idea, but not for semiology, nor for his elaborate *Barthes* system of codes. The major acknowledged inspiration is Foucault,[10] and Greenblatt is given to observing in a rather proprietorial manner on the advantages of having had him around Berkeley in the last few years of his life (Greenblatt 1990, pp. 3, 146–7). Greenblatt acknowledges a further debt to 'European (and especially French) anthropological and social theorists' (*ibid.*, pp. 146–7), particularly Pierre Bourdieu, but has also drawn on the American anthropologist Clifford Geertz (*ibid.*, pp. 26, 28–9). The mere recital of these names opens up a vast area of potential influence, which needs to be examined more closely.

The biggest influence, generally recognised, is that of Foucault, in various phases of his work. The earlier Foucault, as we have seen him in *L'Archéologie du savoir* (1969), was preoccupied with discourse as an anonymous, depersonalised system, deprived of a subject or author, circulating through 'sites' of power, appropriation and contestation. His ideas are still dominant in a recent account of 'The Poetics and Politics of Culture' (Montrose 1989). Louis Montrose invokes 'the multiplicity of unstable, variously conjoined and conflicting discourses' in post-structuralist theory (p. 16), claims that New Historicism is 'new' in refusing 'to posit and privilege a unified and autonomous individual — whether an Author or a Work — to be set against a social or literary background' (p. 18); defines it 'as a terminological site of intense debate and critique, of multiple appropriations and contestations within the ideological field of Renaissance studies . . .' (p. 19); sees individuals as enduring a process of '*subjectification* . . . constraining them within — *subjecting them to* — social networks and cultural codes that ultimately exceed their comprehension or control' (p. 21 and note 12, acknowledging a specific debt to Foucault); and so on through a by now familiar litany of Foucauldian jargon, from 'social positionalities', 'shifting conjunctures', and 'conceptual sites within the ideological field from which the dominant can be contested' (p. 22), to 'the ideological analysis of discursive *practices*' (p. 26).

This whole abstract panoply of concepts, formulated by Foucault in the 1960s, attempting to avoid all that he saw as problematic in 'humanist' criticism but merely introducing new and more resistant problems, continues to be invoked by younger critics writing about the Renaissance in the 1990s. Some of them specialise in drama, where — the ordinary reader might feel — the remoteness and inappropriateness of such abstractions would be instantly apparent the moment Iago, Falstaff, or Volpone walked on to the stage. Fox-Genovese's criticism of New Historicists for not being 'self-critically or self-reflexively historical' is justified in that none of them seems to have considered to what extent this eclectic post-structuralist system might be appropriate for Renaissance literature, or just anachronistic. Montrose, who has written some essays on pastoral held up as an example of this school at its best,[11] seems more concerned in this essay to display his awareness of theoretical positions 'now' (pp. 22, 23) — virtually none of the works he cites dates from before 1980. For a critical school so conscious of its orientation vis-à-vis other non-historical approaches, so concerned with redefining, as Fredric Jameson puts it, '"our relationship to the past, . . . our possibility of understanding the latter's monuments, artifacts, and traces"' (cit. Thomas 1989, p. 182), not to have considered whether its own ideology is appropriate to the historical task it aims to perform, is surprising and disappointing.

New Historicism, like so many branches of contemporary criticism, is more interested in present theories than in the past. Hence the influence of Foucault's middle period work on power and knowledge, on discipline and punishment, as he moved from studying hospitals and clinics to prisons — as if the whole of human society consisted of those who devised and administered repressive institutions and those who suffered from them. As many former admirers of Foucault protested, once the direction of his development became clearer, his concept of power was all-embracing but anonymous and passive.[12] He saw its oppressive presence everywhere, yet refused to specify the detail of its working, institutionally or individually, and he explicitly rejected any interest in reforming or transforming power structures.[13] The effect of Foucault's legacy on New Historicism is a curious blend of vagueness (no specific or detailed analyses are attempted, since there are no models to work from), a sense of unidentified oppression verging on paranoia, and the feeling of complicity—exhilarating or disturbing. As several commentators have shown (Graff 1989, p. 169; Pecora 1989, pp. 247, 267), particularly influential on New Historicism was Foucault's insistence that 'knowledge could not avoid its complicity with structures of power in whose language it would have no choice but to speak' (Pecora 1989, p. 267). As Foucault put it in Discipline and Punish, 'there is no power relation without the correlative constitution of a field of knowledge, nor any knowledge that does not presuppose and constitute at the same time power relations' (cit. ibid., p. 276 note 53). Logicians might object that this is to give the terms 'knowledge' and 'power' such a vast application as to be meaningless, but the totalisation of that utterance was precisely its attraction (like other arbitrary pronouncements of Lacan, Derrida, Althusser, de Man, the categorical assertion is rhetorically effective, as we know). As a formula, it resembles Barthes's notion of language as inherently involving one in power relations, even when thought silently or written down privately, and it recalls Derrida's insistence that deconstruction could not escape from the weaknesses of the system that it had to use in order to denounce. All three assertions make everyone guilty, caught in an inescapable double-bind. H. Aram Veeser, editor of an anthology of twenty essays on New Historicism, in an introduction notable neither for clarity nor historical accuracy,[14] lists some 'key assumptions' of New Historicism, two of which have the same linguistic structure: 'every act of unmasking, critique, and opposition uses the tools it condemns and risks falling prey to the practice it exposes' (Veeser 1989, p. xi, nos. 2 and 5). We are trapped in our own systems.

Foucault's ideas on power and complicity lie behind one of the most commented-on features of New Historicist ideology and methodology, the identification of a symbiotic relationship, so to speak, between subversion and containment. That is, certain forces in society attempt to 'subvert' the status quo, which responds by 'containing' them. So the 'Establishment' or 'Government' can be seen as allowing subversion to emerge, simply in order to contain it; or even creating subversion in the first place. Foucault is the explicit source for the belief that the 'dominant authority' itself 'produces elements of apparent subversion or transgression as a means of maintaining its control' (Pechter 1987, pp. 296–7). New Historicists like to see the Elizabethan theatre itself, Walter Cohen observes, as 'a contradictory institution', both an 'extension of authority and a subversion of it, a representation of state power and a contestation of its ideology' (Cohen 1987, pp. 34–5). Their interest in power means that much New Historicist writing has been concerned with the English court, especially that of James I, and with genres that could be directed towards the ruler, such as pastoral and the masque.[15] Although certainly an important factor in English literary and intellectual history, the court has too often been interpreted in glib categories derived from Norbert Elias, or selectively read to echo New Historicist concerns. As J. Leeds Barroll has recently shown, their attempt to 'implicate drama in the whole fabric of the new King's theory, policy and practice', including the claims that James '"wanted the theatrical companies under royal patronage because he believed in the efficacy of theater as an attribute of royal authority"', have absolutely no historical justification (Barroll 1988, pp. 454–5). James in fact expressed the usual moralistic disapproval of actors, and contemporary accounts (setting aside his drinking bouts!) record his attendance at state entertainments without any particular pleasure. Indeed, Barroll's careful documentation proves that over the years James attended fewer and fewer performances, much preferring hunting (*ibid.*, pp. 455–61). The New Historicists, as he puts it, 'constricted by old narratives that tell a traditional story of the drama in a special relationship to the state or to the person of the monarch' — albeit, I add, a story now used to cast suspicion on power and its legitimising processes — have turned their own 'story-making propensities' and 'causal constructs' into supposed facts (pp. 461–3). Barroll's conclusion, which must evoke wide agreement, is that

> the documents . . . do not allow us to infer a narrative in which the monarch as authority-figure views drama as a special and vital medium with potentialities for subversion, or for the enhancement of the royal image. . . . (p. 463)

Bent on creating this myth of royal involvement in the subversion-and-containment pattern, the New Historicists have also overlooked the fact that the impulse to give the drama and masques greater prominence at court derived in fact from women, from Queen Anna of Denmark and the countesses who actually 'sponsored and enacted the masques Ben Jonson is so often said to have written for King James'. Recent, 'patriarchically inclined' criticism focussing on the King has overlooked the 'powerful women' who were 'an obvious source of power and patronage' (pp. 463–4).

Evidently the all-absorbing concern for the 'subversion-and-containment' model can blind one to other important aspects of literary and social history. The deeper problem is that this formula, like Foucault's thesis itself, is so shapeless and undifferentiated as to 'explain' any event. In effect, every play which comes to a coherent conclusion, and ends neither in uproar, nor advocating anarchy or the burning of London, can be said on Foucault's principles to 'enact order' and hence 'support state power' — if you are ready to agree that all events other than riots can be seen as legitimising the state. Cohen fairly objects to the New Historicists' unsystematic handling of Foucault's thesis, their 'failure to specify the necessary and sufficient conditions for either containment or subversion' (Cohen 1987, pp. 35–6), while Jean Howard has made an acute critique of the 'subversion and contestation' model, posing six questions that need to be answered by the critics relying on it (Howard 1986, p. 35). Recently one of their own number has warned that

> the terms in which the problem of ideology has been posed and is now circulating in Renaissance literary studies — namely as an opposition between 'containment' and 'subversion' — are so reductive, polarized, and undynamic as to be of little or no conceptual value. (Montrose 1989, p. 22)

Montrose is obviously right, and we may well agree that a model which allowed for 'collective and individual agency' and for two-way movement would be preferable.

But it is significant that Montrose's misgivings are theoretical, not historical, nor literary-critical. That is, he considers neither the historical appropriateness of the model for Elizabethan and Jacobean society, nor what happens to works of literature when read in these terms. For the first point, without citing a large body of historical evidence, the causes of social unrest in the sixteenth and seventeenth centuries are surely common knowledge: shortage of food, high inflation, worries about the succession, fears of foreign invasion or religious change. The groups most affected by these conditions occasionally uttered their grievances, but were obviously not manipulated into doing so by a hypocritical government. For the second point, the effect of the subversion-containment pattern on New Historicist literary criticism has been to reinforce its general suspicion of authority, and to express solidarity with anyone who challenges it. In their writings 'subversive', 'anarchic', or — in that aestheticisation of disorder mechanically borrowed from Bakhtin — 'carnivalesque' characters, such as the rebel Jack Cade in *2 Henry VI*, Falstaff and Pistol in the *Henry IV* plays, Caliban in *The Tempest*, are sympathised or identified with, those who put them down are booed and hissed. This celebration of subversion (endorsed also by old and new Marxist critics, as we shall see in Chapter 7), often takes the form of old-fashioned character criticism, ignoring both the rationale for civic order and the structure of the play.

The politicisation of New Historicists is widely acknowledged to be the consequence of their having grown up in America during the 1960s. As Catherine Gallagher observes, in the course of a sensitive intellectual and political autobiography of these years, 'the importance of such slogans as "serve the people"' was that '"the people" was a category designed to include oneself and anyone else content to join a decentered coalition of disaffected groups' (Gallagher 1989, p. 40). Identification with marginalised groups in literature of the Renaissance was somehow seen as expressing solidarity with their counterparts today; attacking Henry V or Prospero was the same kind of activity as attacking President Reagan or the White House. Greenblatt declares that

> my own critical practice and that of many others associated with new historicism was decisively shaped by the American 1960s and early 70s, and especially by the opposition to the Vietnam War. Writing that was not engaged, that withheld judgements, that failed to connect the present with the past seemed worthless. Such connection could be made either by analogy or causality; that is, a particular set of historical circumstances could be represented in such a way as to bring out homologies with aspects of the present or, alternatively, those circumstances could be analyzed as the generative forces that led to the modern condition. (Greenblatt 1990, p. 167)

In either mode, he adds, 'value judgments were implicated', for neutrality would be 'itself a political position, a decision to support the official policies in both the state and the academy'. Studying 'the culture of sixteenth-century England', then, was not 'an escape from the turmoil of the present', but 'a mode of relation' between past and present that revealed the 'unsettling historical genealogy of the very judgments I was making' (*ibid.*).

I have quoted that passage at length because it will link up with several issues to be discussed in New Historicist Shakespeare criticism. The first and obvious comment to be made is that such a voluntary acceptance of politicisation and polarisation puts the writer in a state of crisis: as Councillor Mikhulin, the bureaucrat of Tsarist autocracy puts it in *Under Western Eyes*, 'abstention, reserve, in certain situations, come very near to political crime'.[16] The pressure to display political engagement can induce feelings of guilt and fear in the writer who realises that he has not demonstrated in his writing that he is on the 'right' side now, and such felt pressures can make him display his political correctness however unsuitable the topic may be. ('How am I doing? Is this account of Lyly sufficiently politically radical?') It also raises the crucial methodological issue of how we relate to the past, and how we can write history. Here, too, Foucault's influence has been felt, generating a peculiar anomaly, as Lentricchia has shown, by his 'insistence that historians cannot objectively represent the past because they cannot know and therefore put distance between themselves and the circumstances which produced and disciplined them as social beings enmeshed in the practice of a historical *discipline*' (Lentricchia 1988, p. 95; 1989, p. 237). Greenblatt himself recorded 'the "impossibility of fully reconstructing and reentering the culture of the sixteenth century, of leaving behind one's own situation"', in the process bidding 'elegiac farewell', as Lentricchia ironically comments, to such values as 'objectivity, determinacy, and completeness in historical interpretation', while at the same time shifting the apology 'into a subtle claim to virtue' (*ibid.*, pp. 96; 238). It is this sense of superior knowledge, of having seen through the illusions of previous ages, that marks so much of Current Literary Theory. Yet Foucault's model has been anything but liberating. As Brook Thomas points out,

> new historicists have been strongly influenced by Foucault's argument that constructions of the past are inevitably implicated in present networks of power and domination and thus never disinterested. That insight, however, catches new historicists in a seemingly unresolvable contradiction. The authority of a new historicism rests on the faith that knowledge of the past matters for the present. To admit that a history is not an account of how it really was but a present construction intervening into current political debate seems to undermine that authority. (Thomas 1989, p. 201)

At one level there is nothing new in Foucault's argument. Thomas shows that the realisation that 'historians do not objectively and scientifically recover the past but construct it from a present perspective' was generally recognised at the beginning of this century, if not before (*ibid.*, p. 195). Foucault's insistence on history being 'a present construction intervening into current political debate' is new, however, and accounts for the fact that so much New Historical writing cannot ever forget the present and its discontents. What I mean is that while no-one I know (or could take seriously), imagines they can 'fully' re-enter a past culture, or achieve absolute disinterestedness, the goal of reconstructing the past as an imaginative activity based on all kinds of historical evidence — charters, myths, political institutions, religious and social practices, trade-routes, family history, science, music, medicine — does demand at some points the ability to suppress or at least control present attitudes, present expectations. We have to be able, at certain key points, to keep ourselves out of the picture. The relevant concept (which I don't recall ever seeing dis-   *Anachron-* cussed by New Historicists) is anachronism. The crucial distinction has been made by the sociologist W.G. Runciman, namely that it is not 'necessarily illegitimate to apply to other people's behaviour theoretical terms which they neither would nor could have applied to it themselves', since (I add) we cannot forego the enormous development in analytical power that has been achieved in literary, historical, and philosophical writing since the Renaissance. 'It is illegitimate only if the application of such terms assumes that they did when they didn't — as, for instance, imputing a choice to some person in the past in terms that they could never have used themselves (Runciman 1983, p. 14). It seems to me, and others, that New Historicism is often guilty of anachronism,[17] and is seldom able to suspend its own self-awareness as a critical school having an ideology that needs to assert itself, prove its validity as a system. Against this self-centred, self-validating ideology I would set Brook Thomas's paradoxical principle that 'the present has an interest in maintaining a belief in disinterested inquiry into our past' (Thomas 1989, p. 201). To give up that principle would have devastating consequences for historians.

New Historicists' concern with the past can link itself to the present, in Greenblatt's terms, 'either by analogy or causality'. What he did not declare is that in both modes the motive behind the linkage is often an indicting or incriminating one. The Renaissance state, like the modern state, so the argument goes, was built on hypocrisy and oppression; or, the origins of our corrupt society lie in 'early modern England'.[18] This immediate juxtaposition of the sixteenth century (that somewhat delayed English Renaissance) with the twentieth inevitably recalls Jacob Burckhardt's similar linking of fifteenth-century Italy and nineteenth-century Europe. Burckhardt's (re)discovery of the Renaissance was a great act of historical imagination, but it was bought at a price. In linking classical antiquity to the Renaissance he virtually omitted, or downplayed the Middle Ages; and in seeing the Renaissance as the origin of the modern state he left out an embarrassingly large number of intervening historical factors, such as the scientific revolution, the Enlightenment, the Romantic movement, secularisation, urbanisation, the Industrial Revolution, and much else. Those who celebrate Burckhardt as a pioneer are also aware of his shortcomings.[19] Greenblatt is in effect turning the tables on Burckhardt, and those who admire him, by saying: 'yes, the Renaissance is like the modern world: aren't they both awful?' He candidly admits as much in a recent essay, describing 'one of the more irritating qualities' of his literary training (at Yale) to have been 'its relentlessly celebratory character', dedicated to showing that all Elizabethan plays were 'complex wholes', and that 'great works of art were triumphs of resolution . . . , the mature expression of a single artistic intention'. (For the mid-1960s attack on this idea see the discussion of Macherey in Chapter 7.) Greenblatt then accuses his teachers of glibly linking this kind of 'formalism' to social concerns, with 'the artist's psychic integration' seen as 'the triumphant expression of a healthy, integrated community. Accounts of Shakespeare's relation to Elizabethan culture were particularly prone to this air of veneration . . .' (Greenblatt 1990, p. 168).

The fact that Greenblatt suffered from uncritical teachers marketing Renaissance culture with such enthusiastic gush is unfortunate. But his response, thirty years on, is to market another version of the Renaissance as 'like us', disintegrated, decentered. He quotes from an earlier book (*Renaissance Self-Fashioning*, 1980) in which he affirmed, rather portentously, that 'we are situated at the close of the cultural movement initiated in the Renaissance; the places in which our social and psychological world seems to be cracking apart are those structural joints visible when it was first constructed' (*ibid.*, p. 182 note 4). Inasmuch as Greenblatt reverses Burckhardt, he accepts the same telescoped historical model as Burckhardt, with all its faults.[20] Other New Historicists share this desire to display such 'cracks' in the Renaissance world. Thus Montrose complains that the extant critical tradition in English Renaissance studies reveals 'an apparently continuous tradition of religious, social and aesthetic values shared by sixteenth-century poets and twentieth-century critics'. (Let other readers try to count how many modern critics they know of who believe in Protestantism, the thirty-nine articles, the divine right of kings, the supremacy of rhetoric, and the delights of display, . . . my list is short.) In place of these 'idealizations of a Renaissance England at once ebullient and ordered', Montrose invokes 'surviving documentary evidence of Elizabethan religious, economic, social and domestic violence, instability, and heterodoxy' (Montrose 1989, p. 24). Although this is another example of that familiar tactic in Current Literary Theory, erecting a straw man embodying a supposedly ridiculous view and then rushing to the opposite extreme, we can certainly grant Montrose some of his case.

Yet the New Historicist, rooted in his present sense of dislocation, may be projecting these fissures on to the past. Categorical assertions, so far, substitute for detailed analysis or weighing of the evidence on either side. Jean Howard has emphasised the ways in which New Historicism expresses some preoccupations of 'postmodern Culture' — 'self-reflexivity, and a self-consciousness about the tenuous solidity of human identity'. All these concerns are now 'discovered' in the Renaissance (Howard 1986, pp. 16–17). These writers, as she understands them, 'construe the period

in terms reflecting their own sense of living inside a gap in history' (p. 17).
Writing about the Renaissance, the New Historicists *make the period
intelligible by narratives of rupture, tension, and contradiction* (*ibid.*; my italics).
A case in point is *Renaissance Self-Fashioning* (arguably one of the most
unhistorical books in modern times), where Greenblatt professed that in all
the texts he studied he could find '"no moments of pure, unfettered
subjectivity"', the human subject always being '"the ideological product
of the relations of power in a particular society"' (*cit.* Pechter 1987,
p. 300). That is a clear instance of anachronism, for all those categories
derive from Foucault, and the totalising nature of Foucault's assertion
already predetermines the issue. (The power relations being all-pervasive,
it doesn't matter whether you can see them or not.) Another influence on
that book, Howard points out, was 'Lacan's neo-Freudian psychology with
its assumption, not of a unified and autonomous self, but of a provisional
and contradictory self which is the product of discourse' (Howard 1986,
p. 37). It is as if a contemporary student gets the idea that, because this
model of the human psyche now exists, we can re-read Renaissance texts
in its light. But this is to remake the past in our own anachronistic image
with a vengeance, lacking any independent control. It has not realised
the necessity of 'negative instances', as Francis Bacon described them,
counter-indications that invalidate facile inductive arguments based on an
uncritical assemblage of evidence that would prove your case by ignoring
everything else. In that sense I must agree with Howard's criticism of New
Historicism as it exists so far, for 'its failure to reflect on itself', for
suppressing 'any discussion of its own methodology and assumptions. It
assumes answers to the very questions that should be open to debate . . .'
(*ibid.*, p. 31) .

II

The last theoretical issue that needs discussing concerns the relation between literary texts and their context, whether a 'socio-historical site' or a
'cultural system'. The normal distinction in modern literary history has
been between text and context, where the critic reconstructs what he or
she deems to be the relevant background in order to illuminate specific
elements of the literary text. To do this properly demands historical
knowledge, sensitivity to the text, and an awareness of the two-stage
process of interpretation involved. New Historicism also reads texts in this
way, but at times it can treat text and background as of equal importance,
or reverse the emphasis, taking the work of literature as illuminating the
background. There are obvious dangers involved from whatever direction
one comes, as every experienced scholar knows, but since there are no
hard-and-fast rules for historically placing a text, I for one would recom-

mend a state of open-minded scepticism. Most people, I imagine, do the
same, examining the procedure, the arguments and evidence used in a
book or essay, and evaluating them according to their knowledge of the
text and the period. I would never dream of declaring certain procedures
illicit in advance. Some books can totally transform one's notion of the
relevant evidence in historiography. Fernand Braudel's *Histoire de la
Méditerranée* was for me a revelation in the range of evidence it drew on
and the diverse ways it integrated statistics, documents, anecdotes, aspects
of geography, climate, trade patterns, and so much else.

Some aspects of the New Historicist handling of text and historical
evidence do arouse misgivings, however. Howard Felperin describes the
'fundamental and far-reaching' post-structuralist strategy of New Historicism
as being 'its "textualising" of history and culture in the first place, its re-
framing of them as discursive constructs'. Felperin judges this move as
having been 'necessary to open an appeal from the pseudo-objective "facts"
of an older historical empiricism to "texts" and "discourses" now explicitly
political and therefore newly *reconstructible*' (Felperin 1990, p. vii: this
author is as lavish with inverted commas as some men with aftershave).
Once again a literary critic shows himself to be hopelessly out of touch
with wider cultural movements. Felperin is announcing as a recent event
the programmatic rejection of history as an objective discipline that was
made in the mid-1960s by Derrida and Foucault (and pushed to extremes
by de Man) in their desire to attack referentiality, the 'linear model of
history', subjectivity, and other targets popular in those days (Simpson
1988, pp. 725–37). In this, as in so many areas, the iconoclasts used the
tactic of coercive dichotomising, 'as if there were no alternative between
complete self-confidence (all information is objective) and complete
agnosticism (all information is projected or undifferentiated)' (*ibid.*, p.
745). David Simpson, reviewing the various dead-ends into which the 60s
masters led us, calls for a return to the notions of historical evidence and
objectivity (pp. 744–7). The changes he advocates were set out ten years
earlier and much more cogently by a practising historian, E.P. Thompson,
with his concept of historical logic as a 'dialogue between concept and
evidence'. The concept is a series of interrogative hypotheses, the evidence
'"facts" . . . which certainly have a real existence'. But their determinate
properties make 'only certain questions . . . appropriate', and they are, like
history itself, 'necessarily . . . incomplete and imperfect'. Historical enquiry
legitimately uses elaborate theories, but 'each notion, or concept, arises out
of empirical engagements, and however abstract . . . its self-interrogation',
it must be engaged once more 'with the determinate properties of the
evidence . . .'. This whole discussion (Thompson 1978, pp. 38–50) has
a cogency and depth which should convince literary critics that the
'textualisation' of history was an amusing idea that can now be abandoned,
along with flared jeans and flower-pattern shirts.

In traditional enquiry, one historian states, 'the text exists as a function, or articulation, of context' (Fox-Genovese 1989, p. 217). New Historicism sometimes abandons this relationship. As Pecora observes, it 'tries to diminish, or in certain cases to eradicate, distinctions between the "aesthetic object" per se and something called a "historical background", between one kind of "text" and another', seeing the whole of material reality as involved in a process of 'representation' (Pecora 1989, p. 243). Representation is another Foucault-derived concept (Jameson 1972, pp. 191–2), which has been adapted to an eclectic mixture of semiology and anthropology. In some current 'American new historicism', Pecora writes, '"representation has become a code word for the denial that any distinction whatsoever exists between a non-signifying "real" and some realm of cultural production that "reflects", or reflects upon it' (*ibid.*, p. 244) . One consequence of collapsing this distinction is that 'what, for many historians, would be more "basic" categories such as material want and material struggle' are reduced to 'merely culturally constructed sign systems' (*ibid.*). Any notion of social injustice, oppression, or the need for reform also disappears.

The key figure in New Historicist adoption of 'cultural semiotics' is the anthropologist Clifford Geertz, in particular a single essay, 'Thick Description: Toward an Interpretive Theory of Culture', written as a preface to a collection of his writings (Geertz 1973). Geertz applies the term 'thick description' (borrowed from Gilbert Ryle) to characterise the setting of an individual event in its appropriate cultural category. The 'object of ethnography', he writes, is to create 'a stratified hierarchy of meaningful structures' through which significant human communication is 'produced, perceived, and interpreted' (p. 7). Human behaviour is 'symbolic action — action which . . . signifies' (p. 10), and culture 'consists of socially established structures of meaning' (p. 12), 'interworked systems of construable signs' or symbols (p. 14). Culture, then, 'is not a power, something to which social events, behaviors, institutions, or processes can be causally attributed; it is a context, something within which they can be *intelligibly* — that is, *thickly* — described' (p. 14; my italics). Cultural analysis, Geertz emphasises, is always a process of interpretation, concerning what 'specific people say, what they do, what is done by them' (p. 18). I fully accept this approach to culture in terms of socially established structures of meaning, and I agree that 'the important thing about the anthropologist's findings is their complex specificness, their circumstantiality' (p. 25). Both points obviously apply to the study of literature. Although Geertz's own work has been recently attacked on both ideological and methodological grounds,[21] I am perfectly happy to accept his invocation of 'thick description' as the best way of analysing 'the conceptual structures that inform our subjects' acts'.[22]

A proper reconstruction of the 'stratified hierarchy of meaningful structures' is a major undertaking even for pre-industrial or pre-literate societies, and anyone familiar with only a cross-section of modern ethnographical studies — Malinowski on the Trobriand Islanders, Evans-Pritchard on the Nuer, Gregory Bateson on the Naven — knows what a demanding task that can be. To attempt the same for the European Renaissance, with its complex economic structures, varieties of social stratification, elaborate techniques for the acquisition and dissemination of knowledge, would be a worthwhile but massive undertaking, and no-one can blame New Historicists for citing samples only. But the problem is, how to choose such samples, and what status to give them within the society as a whole. Commentators have long complained that the samples chosen are not representative and that they have often been misapplied. (My prior objection would be that the exponents of this method have not even attempted the methodological discussion as to what the 'stratified hierarchy of meaningful structures' would look like, and where the samples would fit.) Where Montrose proposes that New Historicism substitutes 'for the diachronic text of an autonomous literary history the synchronic text of a cultural system' (Montrose 1989, p. 17), Hayden White replies that this reconstituting of 'the historical context' as 'the cultural system' gives offence to historians in that now 'social institutions and practices, including politics, are construed as functions of this system, rather than the reverse' (White 1989, p. 294). New Historicism thus seems to be based on what White calls 'the "culturalist fallacy"', which marks it as a brand of historical idealism', and is 'reductionist in a double sense: it reduces the social to the status of a function of the cultural, and then further reduces the cultural to the status of a text' (ibid.).

The cultural 'samples' that New Historicism brings into the foreground may be chosen at random, although some commentators see a deliberate pattern. To White their concern with the anecdotal reflects a Foucault-inspired interest in the fragmentation of 'dominant codes — social, political, cultural, psychological' (ibid., p. 301). To Lentricchia the 'lengthy citations of bizarre, apparently off-center materials' at the beginning of Greenblatt's essays 'seem to promise what, in theory, new historicism, so hermeneutically savvy, isn't supposed to promise — direct access to history's gritty ground-level texture' (Lentricchia 1988, p. 91; 1989, p. 234). In fact, he argues, the dominant idea is still Foucault's, 'that all social life is organized and controlled down to its oddest and smallest details' (ibid.). Other commentators object that the New Historicists seldom declare what status they are claiming for the 'cultural samples' on display, an opportunistic silence which leaves their readers unable to know what weight to give this anecdotal material. The Marxist critic Walter Cohen has observed that 'New historicists are likely to seize upon something out of the way, obscure, even bizarre: dreams, popular or aristocratic festivals . . . sexual treatises . . . descriptions of clothing, reports on disease', and much else (Cohen 1987, p. 33).[23] These have always figured in traditional historiography, only now they are elevated from the margin to the centre, indeed displace the centre, dispensing with the notion of a coherent structure in politics, society, religion, or any other aspect of Renaissance culture. But the New Historicists' fondness for the 'telling anecdote' or 'overlooked detail' of social history, Cohen objects, rests on the large and unexamined methodological assumption that 'any one aspect of a society is related to any other', and that therefore 'any social practice has at least a potential connection to any theatrical practice' (p. 34). This belief in 'arbitrary connectedness' results, as he shows, in alarming con-tradictions between pronouncements by the same writer. In one essay Greenblatt sees the history play as aristocratic, in another as bourgeois; elsewhere the 'relation between power and subversion is formulated in' contradictory terms'. Power is visible; power is invisible. 'Since each essay [by Greenblatt] pursues a particular issue to a logical extreme' without the constraint of an organising principle, 'contradictions are bound to occur'. Further, the New Historicists' fragmentation of history into a series of uncoordinated episodes encourages the belief that any single episode may be proclaimed fully representative.

The dangers of this elevation of the anecdotal to a central status are clear, encouraging as it does the use of interesting little stories not as ornaments to the text but as load-bearing props in the argument, a role to which they are unsuited. Robert N. Watson, otherwise an effusive admirer of this group, commenting that to begin an essay with a historical anecdote has become 'practically a generic signature of New Historicist studies', and floating the idea of renaming it 'the New Anecdotalist movement', lists some of the risks involved in such a method:

> The historical data may be so fragmentary as to be worthless for char-acterizing the crucial activities of an entire culture; the critic may allow the mere suggestive juxtaposition of specific historical and literary arti-facts to serve in place of any specific explanation of the connections, ignoring all the dangers of the argument by analogy; and the use of an historical rather than a literary excerpt may be exploited to give the essay an aura of being somehow more real and important than 'purely literary' criticism, as if pageants or inquisitions or architecture were legible in objective and ideologically liberating ways that literature itself is not.[24]

Jean Howard also objected to the anecdotal method, for not declaring whether the 'illustrative example' is representative, and if so, on what grounds, statistically, say, or just by one's own authority (Howard 1986, p. 38). Despite their evasiveness on this, as on other major issues, the success of the new anecdotalism clearly means that most readers have been happy to accept the validity and meaningfulness of the anecdotes at face value. (This may, of course, be a comment on current critical and scholarly standards.)

As we can see, some critics have begun to raise the methodological issue of what Howard describes as the 'theoretical aporia' created by New Historicism's discussing 'neither the rationale for the method nor the status of the knowledge produced', thus not allowing others to relate the cultural sample to 'a culture's whole system of signifying practices' (*ibid.*). To me these misgivings in principle are well justified; others may feel that they would prefer to see the method in practice. In which case, as Greenblatt might say, 'consider the following document', the opening of his essay 'Resonance and Wonder':

> In a small glass case in the library of Christ Church, Oxford, there is a round, red priest's hat; a note card identifies it as having belonged to Cardinal Wolsey. . . . [The] note informs us [that] the hat was acquired for Christ Church in the eighteenth century, purchased, we are told, from a company of players. If this miniature history of an artifact is too vague to be of much consequence — I do not know the name of the company of players, or the circumstances in which they acquired their curious stage property, or whether it was ever used, for example, by an actor playing Wolsey in Shakespeare's *Henry VIII* — it nonetheless evokes a vision of cultural production that I find compelling. The peregrinations of Wolsey's hat suggest that cultural artifacts do not stay still, that they exist in time, and that they are bound up with personal and institutional conflicts, negotiations, and appropriations. (Greenblatt 1990, p. 161)

In such a way one can begin a paragraph in the mode of Hazlitt or Charles Lamb, and end up sounding like Foucault.

Unfortunately, as Anne Barton has pointed out, almost every detail in this anecdote is wrong:

> A wide-brimmed cardinal's hat . . . can indeed be viewed under glass in Christ Church library. The note accompanying it, however, provides information rather different from that Greenblatt attributes to it. It explains that the hat was found in the Great Wardrobe by Bishop Burnet (who died in 1715) when he was Clerk of the Closet. Burnet's son left it to his housekeeper, from whom it passed to the Dowager Countess of Albermarle's butler, and then to the countess herself, who in 1776 presented it to Horace Walpole. Described in the Strawberry Hill sale of 1842 as Wolsey's, the hat was bought by the actor Charles Kean, who is said to have worn it more than once when playing Wolsey in *Henry VIII*. Kean died in 1868. It was after the death of his only child, a Mrs. Logie, that various members of Christ Church purchased it, for the sum of sixty-three pounds. This note card is known to have been in place for at least a quarter of a century. (Barton 1991, p. 51)

That cautionary tale, displaying what Barton describes as 'Greenblatt's tendency to handle historical circumstances approximately', shows that anecdotal history may express neither a Foucauldian interest in fragmented codes nor the nitty-gritty of history but a mixture of dilettantism and carelessness. The open-minded scepticism I have recommended must include a readiness to check all sources.

III

Turning finally to New Historicist Shakespeare criticism, I shall limit this discussion to the essays by Greenblatt, who coined the term and is widely regarded as its outstanding practitioner, and I shall focus on two characteristic aspects, the juxtaposition of literary texts with unusual contextual material, and the use of both to indict government past and present, all structures of legitimacy. This is what he described himself as doing, linking 'the Renaissance . . . to the present both analogically and causally'. Both modes might appear to be historical, or diachronic, but a prior methodological point that needs discussion is the effect of the New Historicists substituting 'the synchronic text of a cultural system' for the diachronic approach of conventional history (Montrose 1989, p. 17). In this mode they follow the orientation of semiology after Barthes, which — as we saw in Chapter 1 — was concerned not with what signs mean but how they function, or how they circulate within a society. In 1988 Greenblatt collected four previously published essays to make a book called *Shakespearean Negotiations. The Circulation of Social Energy in Renaissance England*, adding a new essay justifying his concept of 'the circulation of social energy' (Greenblatt 1988, pp. 1–20), in which he tries to offer 'insight into the half-hidden cultural transactions through which great works of art are empowered' (p. 4). But any notion that these might be produced by authors in an intentional act of creation disappears into a generalised and depersonalised idea of circulation, 'moving certain things — principally ordinary language but also metaphors, ceremonies, dances . . . from one culturally demarcated zone to another' (p. 7). This is obviously a restatement of Foucault's account of the circulation of discourse, and Greenblatt acknowledges his debt to *L'Usage des plaisirs* for the term 'dynamic circulation' (p. 12). Updated perhaps, the Barthes-Foucault emphasis on the system of transactions still ignores the crucial issue of meaning, as well as agency. If we are to write a history of cultural transactions we need to ask who instigates this 'circulation' (if we must keep this inherently vague and all-encompassing term), and why; also what it meant at each stage, and what it means now.

The new term here is energy, for which Greenblatt acknowledges a debt to the French anthropologist Pierre Bourdieu. Checking the work cited, we find Bourdieu using the term 'social energy' in discussing what he calls 'symbolic capital', that is, the standing that a person or group achieves in the eyes of peers by such tactics as 'amassing food only to lavish it on others', or by conspicuous purchases to indicate often illusory wealth in store. The result of such attempts to preserve domination is an 'endless reconversion of economic capital into symbolic capital, at the cost of a wastage of social energy . . .'.[25] Greenblatt uses Bourdieu's concept, but attempts to improve on it (or 'historicise' it) by referring to the OED and noting (Greenblatt 1988, p. 5) that the word 'energy' entered English through Elizabethan rhetoric, with George Puttenham drawing on a tradition going back to Aristotle.[26] However, this attempt to provide a historical context is badly informed, for in classical rhetoric *energeia* denotes the forcefulness or 'vivacity' imparted to language by the proper use of rhetorical tropes and figures, especially metaphor. Sidney calls it 'forcibleness', through which a writer can arouse passion, and Scaliger identifies it with rhetorical *efficacia*, that is, *vis orationis repraesentantis rem excellenti modo*.[27] To Bourdieu, as to most people using the term, energy obviously implies a finite and ultimately quantifiable resource, and Greenblatt admits that 'the term implies something measurable' (p. 6). Yet by invoking rhetoric he in fact confuses mensurability with performance, and treats content as form. As a result he is reduced to defining social energy not in terms of resources which may be 'wasted' (although evaluation of that topic could only be made once one had discussed its purpose, function, and success), nor even as forcefulness, but merely as a process of relocation within 'culturally demarcated' zones.

For readers who might be getting restive at the absence of definition or localisation Greenblatt asks, 'what then is the social energy that is being circulated?' and answers — 'in a sense the question is absurd' — that 'everything produced by the society can circulate', such as 'power, charisma, sexual excitement, collective dreams, wonder, desire, anxiety, religious awe . . .' (p. 19). But this is indeed obvious. Whereas Bourdieu gives a rigorous account of actual exchange processes in a closely-studied society, including a critique of the terms in which such processes have been hitherto described, Greenblatt offers a loose, all-inclusive but nothing-defining term which, Matthew Arnold-like, he attempts to legitimise by rhetorical repetition (pp. 19–20). My point is that the synchronic, pseudo-semiological, pseudo-anthropological interest in cultural systems or (more recently) 'cultural artifacts' (Greenblatt 1990, p. 161), is so vaguely conceived, so lacking in methodological reflection, as to risk declining to a magpie-like collecting of objects that glitter and catch the eye. To anyone who has learned from modern ethnography, there is a vast gulf between that detailed, vigorous, conceptually self-aware exploration of other cultures, and the New Historicists' all too frequent anthologising of the unusual. Whoever is ambitious, in Greenblatt's words, 'to erase all boundaries separating cultural studies into narrowly specialised compartments' (*ibid.*, p. 4), needs to take seriously the analytical and historiographical standards that apply in each discipline.

As an example of Greenblatt's placing of literary texts in social contexts let us take an essay that begins 'far from the Renaissance, with a narrative

of social practice first published in the *American Baptist Magazine* of 1831'
(p. 80). Why not, if it can link up convincingly with the literary work?
The 'social practice' (another portentous phrase) here invoked is actually
an individual action by the Rev. Francis Wayland, a Baptist minister and
early president of Brown University, recording how he disciplined his
15–month old son, an 'unusually self willed' boy, who had started crying
one day when his father took him from the arms of his nurse, and angrily
thrown away a piece of bread his father offered him. Convinced of 'the
necessity of subduing his temper', Wayland kept the boy in solitude and
periodically offered him food, provided that he accepted both it and his
father in a welcoming way. Having 'fasted thirty-six hours', as Wayland
misdescribes his enforced withdrawal of food and love, the boy 'was now
truly an object of pity'. Unmoved, though, Wayland persisted in his
'course of discipline' until his son's will was completely broken, and he
'repeatedly kissed me, and would do so whenever I *commanded*. He would
kiss any one when I *directed* him . . .', and finally came to love his father
more than anyone else (pp. 80–82; my italics). This is a chilling narrative,
particularly in Wayland's unawareness of the incongruity of such words as
'commanded' and 'directed'. To anyone familiar with the boisterous and
unpredictable energies of children at this age (as I write this my youngest
daughter is 15 months old, as it happens), the scene can be vividly
imagined, in all its cruelty.

For Greenblatt, scourge of twentieth-century complacency, it would be
'a mistake' to imagine that we today have freed ourselves from such
'primitive disciplinary pathology'. We have not; but then, we also know
where it comes from, for

> Wayland's struggle is . . . the sophisticated product of a long historical
> process whose roots lie at least partly in early modern England, the
> England of Shakespeare's *King Lear*. (p. 82)

Wayland's demands 'that his son take food directly from him and come to
him voluntarily' are, Greenblatt suggests, a 'bourgeoisified version of the
love test with which Shakespeare's play opens' (*ibid.*). Everyone will
acknowledge a certain resemblance between these two situations, as a
parent articulates an expectation of love which the child is supposed to
show, but at the same time we can all see the differences. *King Lear* begins
with an abdication and inheritance ritual, a highly artificial ceremony
added by Shakespeare to his sources (no other version of the Lear story
included this point),[28] designed to legitimise the King's *de facto* division of
his kingdom. The ceremony goes hideously wrong when Cordelia refuses
both the flattery and the reification of love that Lear expects. There is no
question of 'disciplining' her in the sense of improving her future conduct,
for whatever Cordelia has learned from her upbringing has not, thankfully,
stamped out her individual integrity, and it is too late to change that.
Greenblatt recognises as much (p. 83), and subsequently offers a sensible,

if conventional (none the worse for that!) analysis of the play in terms of its network of rights and obligations (pp. 95–6). In between these points, however, he builds up a structure of inference that the anecdote from Wayland seems too slight to support.

In effect, Greenblatt develops the 'continuity' option (rather than 'analogy'), seeking to link Shakespeare's England directly with 'Jacksonian America', notwithstanding the many different factors shaping each society. He argues that one 'crucial difference' between the two texts is that 'by the early nineteenth century the age of the child who is tested has been pushed back drastically'. The fact that Wayland expected his 15-month old son to understand him, we are told, 'reflects a transformation in cultural attitudes towards children, a transformation whose early signs may be glimpsed in Puritan child-rearing manuals', and which 'culminates in the educational philosophy of Rousseau and the poetry of Wordsworth'. (I doubt if either of those had much to say about bringing up one-year old children . . .) Cordelia, however, is tested at '*precisely* [*sic*] the age that demanded the greatest attention, instruction, and discipline' in Shakespeare's England, *the years between 15 and 26* (p. 83; my italics). For, according to Lawrence Stone, 'the floating mass of young unmarried males' constituted an unruly element in society, whose spirits had to be curbed by educational and social pressures, while girls, too, had to be taught to move 'from the authority of the father or guardian to the authority of the husband' (p. 83–4). Setting aside for the moment Stone's extremely dubious history of family life (see Chapter 6), I note here the whole series of assumptions that Greenblatt has quietly made, whether or not with full awareness: that a literary text is reliable evidence for Elizabethan society; that each of these two texts is representative of their period; and that the differences between them represent actual historical changes. Assumptions of such magnitude surely deserve some methodological discussion.

Greenblatt, unconcerned with method, claims that by the nineteenth century 'the temporal frame has shifted from adolescence to infancy', and, 'equally significant, the spatial frame has shifted as well, from the public to the private' — shifts, that is, which are representative of their period. 'Lear is of course a king', Greenblatt hurriedly adds, but asserts that Renaissance writers conceived the family as continuous with public life, so that 'Lear's interrogations of his daughters' feelings toward him' can be seen as registering 'a central ideological principle of middle- and upper-class families in the early modern period' (p. 84). This is to assume, without argument, that a play whose known sources include a folk-tale story as retold by a legendary Celtic history of Britain, medieval chronicles, a contemporary novel inspired by Greek romance, and a tract exposing Jesuit exorcisms, not to mention Shakespeare's creative re-shaping of all this material, nevertheless presents a typical image of contemporary family life. Equally tendentious, it seems to me, is the remark that 'By the time of Jacksonian America, the family has moved indoors, separated from civil society . . .' (p. 85). But surely the family of a Baptist minister was more or less on public display, meant to be seen as exemplary to society at large? To generalise on such slender evidence is a prime example of the faulty nature of arguments that do not recognise the necessity of confronting 'negative instances', as Bacon emphasised; the fact that an observation of 1,000 white swans concluding that all swans are white would be negated by the discovery of a single black one. All that is needed to destroy Greenblatt's thesis would be to discover a Renaissance text in which a father disciplined his child in the same way as Wayland, and/or a nineteenth-century one where a father disinherited a child for not giving him love on the terms he expected. But in any case the generalisations rest on the flimsiest base.

Greenblatt's desire to bring his two texts into more than accidental contiguity leads him to argue for the 'continuity' option in his linking of past and present, now claiming several 'significant continuities between Renaissance child-rearing techniques and those of nineteenth-century American evangelicals', the first being parental observation of children. Where Wayland scrutinises his son carefully, Lear and Gloucester 'seem purblind by comparison': Lear can't distinguish the elder daughters' hypocrisy from the youngest's truth, while Gloucester can't even recognise Edgar's handwriting (p. 85). But it is surely pointless to apply naturalistic criteria to the behaviour of characters in a play, and then argue outwards from this point to history. Lear's inability to evaluate Cordelia properly is the starting point of the play's action, an artificial situation in itself, of course (I mean, that an action should have such a clear-cut beginning), but it is perhaps the culmination of a lifetime's ethical blindness. As for Edgar's handwriting, a competent trickster like Edmund could easily forge that (just to accept for the moment these naturalistic expectations). But all this is irrelevant, in any case, for Greenblatt was meant to be showing 'significant continuities' between England in 1605 and America in 1831, and the fathers here are behaving quite differently. At least in *Lear*, he can add, the daughters 'scrutinize their fathers', the remarks of Goneril and Regan at the end of the first scene ('how full of changes his age is') thus being taken out of the play and generalised as a social practice. Widening his historical scope still further, Greenblatt tells us that 'there is virtually no evidence' of 'intense paternal observation of the young' in 'late medieval England' but 'quite impressive evidence' of it in the seventeenth century, as in Puritanism, witness the diary of Ralph Josselin (p. 86). Such reckless assertions, which claim to know social attitudes over a three-hundred year period, are familiar from the works of Foucault and Stone, but here read more like a parody of them.

Bringing together two such different texts is a difficult task, 'yet in the trial', as Nestor says of the combat between Hector and Achilles, 'much opinion dwells' — and some danger. The person juxtaposing the two may be tempted to snatch at slight resemblances. The fact that Josselin threatened to disinherit his unruly heir John, in 1674, Greenblatt claims, 'provides an immediate link to *King Lear*' (not surprisingly, since Greenblatt has chosen to quote only this one passage about disinheritance), but also, he finds, 'Josselin's threat to "make only a provision . . . to put bread in your hand" curiously anticipates the symbolic object of contention in the Wayland nursery . . .' (pp. 86–7). An equally flimsy parallel — recalling Fluellen's unwitting parody of Plutarch's 'Parallel Lives', the telling comparison between Macedon and Monmouth being that each town has a river 'and there is salmons in both' — is that Lear's pathetic 'dream of the prison as nursery' distinguishes him from Wayland, who 'used the nursery as a prison'. This is one of 'the crucial differences' between two cultures (p. 98): not everyone will agree. The last of these supposed historical categories that Greenblatt invokes is what he calls 'salutary anxiety', the deterrent effect of the fear of punishment, which in Renaissance England was at 'the symbolic center of society', in royal power, but had been 'lost by early nineteenth-century America' (p. 91–2). What concerns me is not the Americans' 'loss' (hardly surprising, given their rejection of a monarchy), but Greenblatt's attempt to diffuse the concept of anxiety first to Renaissance theories of tragedy and thence to Shakespeare. As a dramatist, Greenblatt suggests, Shakespeare creates authority figures, such as the Dukes in *Measure for Measure* and *The Tempest*, both of whom 'systematically awaken anxiety in others and become, for this reason, images of the dramatist himself' (pp. 91–2). This double claim, already made earlier,[29] must be dismissed as wholly anachronistic, proto-Freudian, lacking any grounding either in literary theory or dramatic practice. It seems a suspiciously easy way of associating Shakespeare with the state and its exercise of power.

*   *   *

From this first experience of New Historicist practical criticism we can deduce that the juxtaposition of two items, texts, cultural samples, or whatever, if it is to suggest similarities as well as differences, has to find a common point, a *tertium comparationis*. In the Wayland/Lear essay Greenblatt's similarities sometimes turned out to be differences, at other times just trivial. The element of risk involved is great, but the 'opinion' or reputation, the symbolic capital that can accrue if performed to the general satisfaction, is also great. In an essay called 'Fiction and Friction' Greenblatt links *Twelfth Night* with two cases of transvestism recorded in France in and after Shakespeare's lifetime. In one of them, reported by Montaigne, a girl posed as a man, married a woman and lived together with her for several months 'to the wife's satisfaction', before the girl was exposed, tried and executed (Greenblatt 1988, pp. 66–8). According to Greenblatt, in *Twelfth Night* 'Shakespeare almost, but not quite, retells' this story. Presumably he means that Viola in her disguise as Cesario might have actually gone through a ceremony with Olivia (despite Viola's own love for Orsino), and then . . . and then . . . — but the more we begin to think the suggestion through, the more absurdly impossible it seems. To Greenblatt it is 'one of those shadow stories that haunt the plays' (p. 67). Yet, to scrutinise that metaphor for a moment, how can the story be said to 'haunt' the plays when the chances are that neither Shakespeare nor the majority of his audience had ever heard of it? And in what sense is it a 'shadow'? As the *persona* in Donne's 'Nocturnal upon St. Lucy's Day' puts it, 'If I an ordinary nothing were, / As shadow, a light and body must be here'. Where is the light, and which is the body?

To anyone familiar with English Renaissance drama it is surprising that Greenblatt, looking for examples of female transvestism, should go so far afield. It is odd, to start with, that he should have taken his examples from France, when the English public theatre alone in Europe did not allow women on the stage. Better instances of actual female transvestism would have been Richard Brome's comedy, *A mad couple well match'd* (1639), or Ovid's fable of Iphis and Ianthe (*Metamorphoses*, 9.673–797).[30] But a more pressing objection must be against the use of actual transvestism as a parallel for romantic drama, in which — with the familiar paradoxes of reversal within English drama — a boy actor dresses as a woman who then disguises as a man. This is an artificiality peculiar to the theatre in those days, of course, but it remains a convention or contract that must simply be accepted before drama can at all take place. Such disguises within the play are short-term, achieve a specific aim — self-preservation, suspension of identity, the achievement of some romantic goal — and are abandoned once that goal is achieved. In this form ♂ *pretends* to be ♀, up to the denouement, whether voluntary or not. But there is an enormous jump from here to the two historical topics that Greenblatt brings in, transvestism (♀ *functioning* as ♂) and hermaphroditism (*being simultaneously* ♀ and ♂). And for someone pretending to recreate the Renaissance social context it is surprising that Greenblatt should not have observed the fierce disapproval, in those days, of what is now lightly termed 'cross-dressing'. This is a well-known point to anyone familiar with the connotations of 'effeminacy' then, or with the exemplum of Hercules reduced to spinning for Omphale, or the biblically-inspired diatribes of Elizabethan moralists, or Sidney's difficulties with the 'womanish man' produced by the disguised prince in *Arcadia*. This whole topic has been recently treated with great historical range and critical intelligence by Linda Woodbridge,[31] in a book unwisely ignored by Greenblatt, which shows that the Renaissance knew 'a tradition of fear and of contempt for physical androgyny and transvestism which went back to the Greeks' (and presumably explains why the legal sentences punishing it were so savage). Ovid's myth of Hermaphroditus became 'an emblem of bestial transformation' in Renaissance culture (Woodbridge 1984, p. 141). In Shakespeare's plays the dramatist reminds us each time that female transvestism, 'however necessitated by emergency

circumstances, is unnatural' and 'shameful'. When Shakespeare's heroines
don male weapons they are given 'the feigned masculinity of the braggadocio'
(*ibid.*, pp. 153–4) as a sign of the role being played. In the Renaissance
male transvestism was regarded as even more shameful, horrible, or comic
(p. 157).

   Greenblatt claims to be 'break[ing] away from the textual isolation that
is the primary principle of formalism' (Greenblatt 1988, pp. 72–3). The
dichotomy is attractive, but specious: the alternative to 'isolation' can
be irrelevant contextualisation. Greenblatt's ambition to 'historicize
Shakespearean sexual nature' (p. 72) will not be fulfilled by ignoring the
central issues of normal male-female sexual behaviour for such 'newer'
topics as Renaissance attitudes to hermaphroditism, or the belief — of
some theorists only[32] — that the male and female genitalia were structurally homologous (pp. 72–85), topics which are in any case completely
marginal to the plays. Greenblatt finally returns to the text (*Twelfth Night*,
we recall) from his background reading via a new *tertium quid*, namely the
concept of heat. In most physiology descending from Aristotle and Galen
heat is a crucial factor in distinguishing the sexes. The male's greater body
heat was thought to produce 'the most perfectly concocted semen from
which the male will be born', and to give the male child superior mental
characteristics: 'courage, liberality, moral strength, honesty'.[33] Heat is a
functional part in theories of sex (not gender!) differentiation, another
topic of marginal interest to Shakespearian drama. Greenblatt, however,
treats heat as he pleases, now in concrete terms in the medical writings,
then in abstract or metaphorical terms in literature, locating it as verbal
wit, in turn redefined as 'pleasurable chafing', or 'erotic chafing'. His
theory (a strikingly improbable one, depriving the dramatist of anything
approaching common sense) is that 'Shakespeare realized that . . . sexual
chafing could not be presented literally on stage' (what does this mean:
sexual foreplay? masturbation?), and so resorted to 'verbal wit' as a substitute (pp. 88–9). Having ascribed this remarkable piece of logic to
the dramatist he concludes that 'dallying with words is the principal
Shakespearean representation of erotic heat' (p. 90). By this concept he
does not mean, surprisingly enough, Shakespeare's use of bawdy, but the
kind of obstructive punning made by Feste against Viola, or — we might
add, finally ruining his gossamer theory of the 'eroticism' involved — by
the gravedigger to Hamlet. Few things have been less erotic to readers and
theatregoers in these last three hundred years than this kind of wit, and it
is a sad instance of the gap between critical ambition and performance
that, after this long haul through the medical background, we are given
such a brief and unoriginal discussion of *Twelfth Night*, with an unrelated
switch from *res* to *verba*. As one critic has said, in a different context, 'of
all activities, the consumption of words is the most remote from pure or
bodily sensation' (Tallis 1988, p. 118).

   It is always hard for the reader to know how much self-criticism lies behind the book he is reading, how many times the author has scrapped material that he found inadequate, rewritten passages that were clumsy or confused. While ready to credit Greenblatt any amount of *labor limae*, for such smooth eloquence as his does not come easily, an essay like 'Fiction or Friction' seems to me to show a disregard for, or unawareness of, normal scholarly criteria of argument and evidence. Some readers object that it only uses the medical material in a subsidiary way;[34] my objection is that it neither masters that material nor uses it to illuminate the drama. A more promising subject is offered by an essay called 'Shakespeare and the Exorcists', which brings together *King Lear* and Samuel Harsnett's *Declaration of Egregious Popish Impostures* (1603). Harsnett, who had previously exposed the Puritan exorcist, John Darrell, here unveiled the practices of the Jesuit Edmunds in persuading three chambermaids in the family of Edmund Peckham ' "to seeme as though they had been possessed, when as in truth they were not" '. The priest's motive was to reconcile the 'supposed demoniacs and others . . . to the old Church', and he was successful (Muir 1961, pp. 149–50). The main link between Harsnett and Shakespeare consists, as Lewis Theobald first showed in 1733,[35] in the fact that Edgar, in his assumed *persona* as Poor Tom, uses the names of the several devils who supposedly possessed the serving maids:

> Five fiends have been in poor Tom at once; as Obidicut, of lust;
> Hoberdidance, prince of dumbness; Mahu, of stealing; Modo, of murder;
> Flibbertigibett, of mopping and mowing. . . .   (4.1.58ff)

There are numerous smaller echoes, but that is the most concentrated. Shakespeare shows no interest in the supposed 'exorcism', nor in the Jesuits' doings, but uses the text for its authentic details of devils' names, and seems to have been attracted by its great range of unusual words, which crop up in *King Lear* and almost nowhere else in the canon.[36] Given the evidence of these verbal borrowings, what then?

Greenblatt is aware that this link has been 'known for centuries', but complains that 'the knowledge has remained almost entirely inert, locked in the conventional pieties of source study' (Greenblatt 1988, p. 94; in an earlier version source study was said to be 'the elephant's graveyard' of modern criticism). Ready to vitalise and release it, Greenblatt starts from the Foucault-like approach of locating the 'institutional strategies' in which both texts are 'embedded', and makes the following grandiose statement: 'These strategies, I suggest' — the reader soon learns to beware of such ingratiating and modest-seeming claims — 'are part of an intense and sustained struggle in late sixteenth and early seventeenth century England to redefine the central values of society', a process of 'transforming the prevailing standards of judgment and action, rethinking . . . conceptual categories' (p. 95). The subsequent discussion does nothing to justify this grandiose claim: what was the struggle? which — or whose — were the values? which categories were rethought? These are all questions that are never posed, let alone answered. This claim illustrates Alastair Fowler's judgment on New Historicism's 'fondness for exaggeration': 'Overstated epistemes are unsusceptible of demonstration; so the new historicists tend to rely on unargued assertion, or on selected instances' (Fowler 1988, pp. 967–8). Greenblatt's point of departure here is Harsnett's denunciation of exorcism (following Reginald Scot) as 'juggling and deluding the people by counterfeit miracles' (Greenblatt 1988, p. 100). Other opponents of exorcism described it as false or 'theatrical', drawing on the pejorative metaphors traditionally attached to the theatre. In fact, although Greenblatt sweepingly dismisses source studies, credit for first commenting on the theatrical imagery in Harsnett must be given to Kenneth Muir, a leading source scholar of modern times. 'One of the first things . . . to strike a reader of Harsnett's *Declaration*', Muir writes, 'is his detailed and unclerical knowledge of the theatre'. There are many references to Plautus and Terence, to medieval miracle-plays, and a memorable description of the Vice (Muir 1961, p. 148).

> But Harsnett's acquaintance with the stage can best be gauged from the way he continually returns to his comparison, made on the first page, of the tricks of the exorcists to a stage performance. There are scores of references to actors, comedians, players, tragedians, cue-fellows, playing, acting, performing, feigning, counterfeiting, acts (of a play), dialogue, prompter, cue, *plaudites*, puppets, scenes, hangings, &c. (*ibid.*, p. 149)

The fact that Harsnett uses 'some 230 words derived from the theatre' may reveal a private passion for the stage, but, 'as Chaplain to the Bishop of London he had the job of licensing books for the press . . . and he read plays as part of his job'. His publisher, James Roberts, was also connected with the theatre, having printed the Second Quarto of *Hamlet* and other plays (*ibid.*).

The originality of Greenblatt's link between exorcism and drama is much diminished once we read Muir's analysis. Greenblatt's treatment of the material, however, is original. His strategy is to emphasise the fact that although some echoes of Harsnett appear from other characters, the main list of devils is given to Edgar, who is 'counterfeiting' madness, or as he misleadingly puts it, displaying theatricality. From this point the argument develops as a (fallacious) syllogism: exorcism was denounced as 'counterfeit'; but drama was also counterfeit; *ergo*, drama is a form of exorcism, or exorcism a form of drama. But the fact that opponents of exorcism used derogatory metaphors from the theatre does not mean that these are convertible propositions. Then to say that Edgar's claim to have seen a 'fiend which parted from' Gloucester before his attempted suicide (4.6.69ff) — and not, notice, emerging from his mouth, as supposedly happened in exorcism — constitutes 'the play's brooding upon spurious exorcism' (p. 118), or shows that the play effects a 'convergence of exorcism and theater', to make such judgments is to build not upon sand but on air. The references to devils in *King Lear* have nothing to do with exorcism, and Shakespeare shows no interest either in the Jesuits or in what Greenblatt misleadingly describes (without ever defining) as 'charismatic exorcism' (pp. 10, 120). Greenblatt can be judged to have succumbed to the 'continuing temptation' in his method, as Garry Wills puts it, to 'use . . . historical data outside their full historical context'. In this essay, Wills judges,

> Greenblatt ignores the several meanings of 'exorcism' at the time, and entirely misses a polemic from the same years that *did*, explicitly, attack Jesuit exorcisms-by-relic — Thomas Dekker's play *The Whore of Babylon*, in which priests are dispatched from Rome to England to undermine the regime with exorcisms. Greenblatt thought there should be an anti-exorcism play, given the salience of the issue; but he got the wrong one. . . .[37]

Among the fragments of reading Greenblatt uses to bolster up his argument is the fact that *Lear* was once performed at the manor house of a recusant couple in Yorkshire, which to him suggests that the play itself was 'strangely sympathetic . . . to the situation of persecuted Catholics' (p. 122); and the remark that Cordelia 'redeems nature from the general curse', which to him suggests a link with medieval Resurrection plays which offered ocular proof that Christ has risen (p. 125), two comments that show some uncertainty about the nature of religion in the Renaissance.[38]

The *tertium comparationis* in this essay, exorcism, supposedly linking Harsnett with Shakespeare, again fails to fulfil the demands Greenblatt makes on it. He ascribes a wholly illusory idea to the dramatist by saying that 'In Shakespeare, the realization that demonic possession *is* a theatrical imposture leads not to a clarification . . . but to a deeper uncertainty in the face of evil' (p. 122; my italics). Greenblatt reports Harsnett as saying that 'the hidden reality' behind the imposture '*is* . . . the theater' (p. 126; my italics): but all that Harsnett says is that it is, like the theatre, a 'performance'. Greenblatt arrives at the conclusion that 'if false religion is theater' (p. 126) then — the suggestion is — theatre is false religion, as proved by 'Edgar's fraudulent, histrionic performance' (p. 127). Somehow all this is said to show that 'the official position is *emptied out*, even as it is loyally confirmed' by Shakespeare, 'dutifully' writing a play to show the identity of theatre and imposture (*ibid.*). (For a self-proclaimed New Historicist Greenblatt is all too often ready to commit the old heresy of biographical criticism, ascribing political motives to Shakespeare outside the plays themselves.) The further argument, that mad Lear's discovery of 'the thing itself' is actually 'a man playing a theatrical role' (p. 126), is fallacious: what Lear *has* discovered is a near-naked man, a poor forked animal. To start calling in question the theatricality of the theatre in these terms is to step into a spiral that descends rather quickly, into itself. The link that Greenblatt attempts to forge between exorcism and *King Lear* is self-deluding, illusory.

IV

The other axis in Greenblatt's linking up the present age with the Renaissance, I suggested, was the motive of indictment or incrimination, briefly glimpsed in those remarks on Edgar's 'fraudulent' performance. The form this usually takes is to attempt to upset the accepted distinction between dominant and subordinate, legitimate and illegitimate pretenders to power. A key text for Greenblatt, as for the English neo-Althusserian 'Cultural Materialists' is *The Tempest*, now unfortunately reduced to an allegory about colonialism, in which Prospero becomes an exploitative protocapitalist and Caliban an innocent savage, deprived of his legitimate heritage. In an essay called 'Learning to Curse: Aspects of Linguistic Colonialism in the Sixteenth Century' (Greenblatt 1990, pp. 16–39), the play is said to present 'the startling encounter between a lettered and an unlettered culture' (p. 23). Greenblatt refers to the scene where Caliban invites Stephano and Trinculo to ambush Prospero during his afternoon sleep:

> There thou mayst brain him,
> Having first seiz'd his books . . . Remember
> First to possess his books; for without them
> He's but a sot, as I am, nor hath not
> One spirit to command. They all do hate him
> As rootedly as I. Burn but his books.   (3.2.88ff)

Books

(Caliban lyingly attributes hatred to the other spirits: Ariel, although anxious to regain freedom, is still loyal to Prospero and is actually present throughout this scene, sowing discord among these plotters and foiling their murder plot). The crucial point is, what these books represent?

*   *   *

How to place Caliban is a delicate question for the critic. He is the traditional 'wild man' in European travellers' encounters with primitive communities; he is an embodiment of lawless appetite, who would kill Prospero and rape Miranda if he could. His rape attempt on Miranda was evidently the point at which Prospero abandoned his goal of educating Caliban. Until then, Caliban recalls,

> Thou strok'st me and made much of me, wouldst give me
> Water with berries in't, and teach me how

To name the bigger light, and how the less,
That burn by day and night; and then I lov'd thee
And show'd thee all the qualities o'th'isle . . .   (1.2.334ff)

Up till that point, Prospero interjects, he had used Caliban 'with humane care, and lodg'd thee / In mine own cell, till thou didst seek to violate / The honour of my child' (347ff). Caliban is unrepentant — 'Would't had been done! . . . I had peopled else / This isle with Calibans' — evidently not acknowledging the traditional moral emphasis on controlling the appetites of lust, greed, anger, and so forth. The best way to see Caliban, I suggest, is as an anomalous category within the Great Chain of Being. He is capable of language, and thus above the animals, but incapable of reason, that ability to control the appetites and live peaceably in the social group. Reason has been, since the time of Isocrates and Cicero, the other traditional attribute linking language with humanity. As Prospero says when he learns of Caliban's plotting with Stephano and Trinculo to murder him, he is innately resistant to reason and education ('nurture'),

> A devil, a born devil, on whose nature
> Nurture can never stick; on whom my pains,
> Humanely taken, all, all lost, quite lost!
> And as with age his body uglier grows,
> So his mind cankers.   (4.1.188ff)

Again at the end, when the comic villains in the subplot are exposed, Prospero can say 'this thing of darkness I / Acknowledge mine' (5.1.278ff), his failed experiment, the limit case of the civilising powers of language.

I would argue that Shakespeare is here challenging the humanists' automatic equation of *ratio* and *oratio*, their assumption that the gift of language necessarily endows speakers with reason. The tradition descends directly from the prooemium to Cicero's *De Inventione*, which records how at some time in the past 'men wandered . . . in the field like animals and lived on wild fare', lacking reason, religion, society and law, until one 'great and wise man transformed them from wild savages into a kind of gentle folk' by the use of 'reason and eloquence', *ratio et oratio* (cit. Vickers 1988, pp. 10–11). This tradition, communicated in texts that formed part of the basic curriculum for rhetoric and literature at both grammar school and university, was very familiar in the English Renaissance. As Sir Philip Sidney wrote in his *Apology for Poetry*,

> For if *oratio* next to *ratio*, speech next to reason, be the greatest gift bestowed upon mortality, that cannot be praiseless which doth most polish that blessing of speech. . . . (Sidney 1965, pp. 121–2)

And in a poem called 'Man', George Herbert rephrased the tradition:

> Man is ev'ry thing,
> And more: He is a tree, yet bears more fruit;

A Beast, yet is, or should be more;
Reason and speech we onely bring.

As part-man, part-beast, Caliban has acquired only half of these twinned faculties, having *oratio* but lacking the more important *ratio*, that faculty praised by Martin Luther as 'an excellent gift of God, . . . indispensable to human welfare; without it, men could not live together in society, but would devour one another like the irrational animals. Therefore . . . it is the function and honor of civil government to make men out of wild animals and to restrain them from degenerating into brutes' (*cit.* Frye 1963, p. 101). I have argued elsewhere that Shakespeare calls in question the humanist belief that eloquence is the defining mark of a good man by making so many of his most persuasive talkers evil.[39] Caliban, I suggest, is another challenge to the humanists' naïve belief that the gift of speech is inherently civilising. He is resistant to nurture, impervious to reason, a creature that can only be counted on to follow its own desires, however violent.

But as so many instances show, Shakespeare seldom created wholly evil characters with no redeeming features. He regularly allowed his anarchic or criminal people some basic vitality, some engaging characteristics, or just the ability to survive in society — as Parolles says, 'Simply the thing I am / Shall make me live'. Creating Caliban involved the coherent mixture of attractive and unpleasant features. He is the son of the 'damned witch Sycorax', who had imprisoned Ariel within a cloven pine until Prospero's superior magic had released him. Caliban was the child that Sycorax 'did litter here, / A freckled whelp hag-born — not honour'd with / A human shape' (1.2.283ff). This curious mixture, part-human, part-animal, lives off what it can catch with its bare hands. Terrified of Stephano and Trinculo, Caliban offers to pluck them berries, catch fish, pick crab-apples, dig up peanuts 'with my long nails', steal birds' eggs (2.2.158ff). His naïve wonder at the drunken butler and servant —

> These be fine things, an if they be not sprites.
> That's a brave god and bears celestial liquor.
> I will kneel to him.   (2.2.116ff)

parallels that of Miranda, on first seeing the assembled court of Milan, the usurping Duke and his followers:

> O wonder!
> How many goodly creatures are there here!
> How beauteous mankind is! O brave new world,
> That has such people in't!   (5.1.183ff)

And just as her naïveté is exposed by Prospero's laconic 'Tis new to thee', so is Caliban's, by Trinculo: 'A most ridiculous monster, to make a wonder of a poor drunkard!' (2.2.163ff). Yet, as the very medium in which Trinculo and Stephano express themselves shows, Shakespeare has confined them to prose, giving Caliban the higher register of verse,[40] and a responsiveness to the natural world that shows again his anomalous placing between the human and the animal: 'Pray you, tread softly, that the blind mole may not / Hear a foot fall' (4.1.194). No one else in Shakespeare could have said that.

The balancing of attractive and loathsome qualities, this placing of him in anomalous categories, may explain why Caliban can only take over part of the humane culture symbolised by the gift of language. So his desire to burn Prospero's books should be taken in the first instance as identifying the source of superior magical power, 'my so potent art', as Prospero calls it (5.1.50), an art even greater than Sycorax, who could 'control the moon' (5.1.212ff). It can also be taken, as Greenblatt does, to show a hostility to letters — 'without them / He's but a sot, as I am'. If so, Caliban, who has learned to talk but not to read and write, comes in the same class as Jack Cade, the rebel leader, who proclaims a totalitarian Utopia in which 'there *Cade* shall be no money', and everyone will 'agree like brothers and worship me their lord'. The first victim of the mob is a clerk, who 'can write and read and cast account' — 'O monstrous!', Cade says, and cross-examines him: 'Dost thou use to write thy name? Or hast thou a mark to thyself, like an honest plain-dealing man?' When the clerk admits, 'I thank God, I have been so well brought up that I can write my name', the mob shouts 'He hath confess'd. Away with him! He's a villain and a traitor'. So he is taken off to be hanged, 'with his pen and inkhorn about his neck' (*2 Henry VI*, 4.2.70ff). A later victim is Lord Say, whom Cade formally indicts:

> Thou hast most traitorously corrupted the youth of the realm in erecting a grammar school. . . . It will be prov'd to thy face that thou hast men about thee that usually talk of a noun and a verb, and such abominable words as no Christian ear can endure to hear.   (4.7.30ff)

That is an amusing charge, of course, but when the head of Lord Say *Say* appears on a pole a few minutes later the link between 'hostility to letters' and anarchy is not so comic any longer.

For Greenblatt (like the Cultural Materialists to be discussed in Chapter 7) Caliban is the hero of the piece, with Shakespeare a dubious accomplice in his oppression and exploitation. Quoting a critic who believes that every dramatist is a colonist, and that in creating Prospero 'Shakespeare's imagination was fired by the resemblance he perceived between himself and a colonist', Greenblatt announces that 'the problem for critics' — as if this rather dotty idea had had a wide uptake — 'has been to accommodate this perceived resemblance between dramatist and colonist with a revulsion that reaches from the political critiques of colonialism in our own century back to the moral outrage of Las Casas and Montaigne' (Greenblatt 1990, p. 24). That flimsy idea having been assimilated, without any methodological discussion, to the general outrage that all decent people today feel about colonialism, Greenblatt can capitalise on this indictment, declaring that

> many aspects of the play itself . . . make colonialism a problematical model for the theatrical imagination: if *The Tempest* holds up a mirror to empire, Shakespeare would appear deeply ambivalent about using the reflected image as a representation of his own practice. (*ibid.*)

In one stroke Greenblatt has taken the trivial analogy between dramatist and colonist to express a general historical law about drama, and then made some ungrounded biographical insinuations about Shakespeare's uneasy feelings at being involved in this enterprise. All this from a critic who professes fidelity to the text (Greenblatt 1988, p. 4).

But let us first deny your major: dramatists are not colonists. They create in language both a world and its inhabitants. That world did not belong previously to any other group of people, who have been driven out or exploited; it has been created specifically for this play. Apply any weight to such an argument and it collapses. Shakespeare is not a colonist, nor is Prospero. He was cast away by his usurping brother and landed on an island previously inhabited by Sycorax. But she, too, had only landed there having been cast away, this time legally, by the citizens of Argier, 'for mischiefs manifold and sorceries terrible', who only spared her life because she was pregnant. Whether Sycorax as an exiled aggressor has more right to the island than Prospero as an injured victim, is a moot point, but it is in any case not one raised by the play. After Sycorax's death Prospero landed there, freed Ariel, and attempted to educate Caliban (1.2.257ff). Prospero has made the island as inhabitable as he could, until the propitious time arrived when he could bring his enemies within his power and go home. Having not killed but forgiven them — which is after all the main and surprising event of the play — he will return to Naples to celebrate the marriage of Ferdinand and Miranda, thence 'retire' to his *vita contemplativa* in 'Milan, where / Every third thought shall be my grave' (5.1.310ff). He is happy to leave 'this bare island' (Epilogue 8), where Caliban can now live alone, if he wants to, whatever the legitimacy of his claim. (From his final words, 'I'll be wise hereafter / And seek for grace' (5.1.198f) it looks as if Caliban prefers to serve Prospero. Since Ariel will 'to the elements / Be free' (321f), the island may well be uninhabited again.) Prospero's stay on the island, then, is enforced, not voluntary, and while he can use its natural resources to stay alive, all the normal features of the hated colonist — murdering the natives, stealing their land, exporting their goods, produce, and wealth for profit back to one's home country — are conspicuously lacking. If modern critics want to denounce colonialism they should do so by all means, but this is the wrong play.

The terms with which Greenblatt has presented the issue make it inevitable that he will side with Caliban in the scene where Miranda (according to the Folio text; some modern editors re-assign the speech to Prospero) describes just how Caliban's nature was resistant to nurture:

> Abhorred slave,
> Which any point of goodness will not take,
> Being capable of all ill! I pitied thee,
> Took pains to make thee speak, taught thee each hour
> One thing or other: when thou didst not, savage,
> Know thine own meaning, but wouldst gabble like
> A thing most brutish, I endow'd thy purposes
> With words that made them known. But thy vile race,
> Though thou didst learn, had that in't which good natures
> Could not abide to be with. . . .   (1.2.353–62)

The traditional schoolbook definition of man was *animale rationis capax*:[41] Caliban, capable of *oratio* only and otherwise 'capable of all ill', retorts:

oratio not ratio

> You taught me language; and my profit on't
> Is, I know how to curse. The red plague rid you
> For learning me your language!   (365–7)

At one level, that again defines Caliban's anomalous position, his resistance to nurture, reason, sociableness ('conversation', in the old sense of that word). On another level, though, as several writers point out, it is only part of the truth. Caliban can do much more with language than curse. He speaks in verse, and Shakespeare has deliberately given him that great speech of assurance and consolation:

> Be not afeard. The isle is full of noises,
> Sounds and sweet airs, that give delight and hurt not.
> Sometimes a thousand twangling instruments
> Will hum about mine ears, and sometimes voices. . . .
>   (3.2.127ff)

(Within the series of plot-parallels created by Shakespeare that speech matches Prospero's reassurance: 'Be cheerful, sir. / Our revels now are ended . . .'). Our sense of Caliban being always out of place in whatever hierarchy we evoke is confirmed by the coarse reaction of Stephano to this description of the isle, full of sweet airs: 'This will prove a brave kingdom to me, where I shall have my music for nothing'. Caliban, we are glad to see, has a brain ultimately able to perceive how he wasted himself on this couple: 'What a thrice-double ass / Was I to take this drunkard for a god / And worship this dull fool!' (5.1.299ff).

I insist on the range and complexity of attributes that Shakespeare has given Caliban because Greenblatt ignores them, simplifying him as the oppressed underdog. Commenting on 'You taught me language', he says that it 'might' be taken as a self-indictment, that Caliban's nature is too debased to take on the full range of humanity.

But the lines refuse to mean this; what we experience instead is a sense of their devastating justness. Ugly, rude, savage, Caliban achieves for an instant an absolute if intolerably bitter moral victory. There is no reply. . . . (Greenblatt 1990, p. 25)

It is, he repeats, 'a momentary victory that is, quite simply, an assertion of inconsolable human pain and bitterness' (p. 26). Greenblatt's hatred of colonists and sympathy for the oppressed leads to a romanticisation or sentimentalisation of Caliban. I see, 'quite simply', no such 'inconsolable human pain', only anger and frustration, one register among many in Caliban's power over language. (The term 'human' is in any case too simple.) This sentimentalisation reaches its highest point in Greenblatt's comment on the speech where Caliban offers to show Trinculo and Stephano where to find apples, nuts, and other food: 'sometimes I'll get thee / Young scamels from the rock'. Greenblatt speaks admiringly of 'the rich, irreducible concreteness of the verse' as showing 'the independence and integrity of Caliban's construction of reality' (now he's a post-structuralist, too), and says that the proof of the opacity of Caliban's world 'is the fact that we do not to this day know the meaning of the word "scamel"' (p. 31). True, that word is baffling, whether it refers to sea-mels (seamews), shellfish, or perhaps, as has recently been suggested, derives 'from squamelle, furnished with little scales. (Contemporary French and Italian travel accounts report that the natives of Patagonia in South America ate small fish described as fort scameux and square)'.[42] Whether the indeterminacy of the word is due to Shakespeare's handwriting, the printers' misreading, or just an unfamiliar expression from a garbled traveller's manuscript, it seems the height of empathy with the oppressed to ascribe to Caliban this proof of the authenticity of his world, before the colonists overran it. And meanwhile the long discredited biographical approach has been revived to stigmatise the dramatist, claiming that 'Shakespeare even appeals to early seventeenth-century class fears by having Caliban form an alliance with the lower-class Stephano and Trinculo to overthrow the noble Prospero' (p. 38, note 46). The desire to find guilty men is often not too fussy about the kind of evidence it uses.

The discourse about colonialism in modern criticism is a one-sided affair, heroes and villains instantly recognisable, a narrative in which the seven deadly sins each get starring roles. The question for literary critics is not whether colonialism is detestable — that needs no discussion — but which works of literature, which authors, which characters can be judged, legitimately and fairly, having weighed the evidence and given everyone their say, to be guilty of endorsing colonialism and its evils. The Tempest has become the display ground for critics eager to vent their righteous indignation and to show that they, at least, are not guilty of that complicity with the repressive forces of history shown by those who have previously read, taught, and admired Shakespeare. One could expect Greenblatt, too, to take the play as an allegory of colonialism, and his reading had the expected results. It is more surprising to find him applying the same incriminatory methods to the *Henry IV* plays. After all, if anyone leaves England in those plays it is not to colonise anywhere but to attack our ancient enemies the French, and to dispute areas of land in a process that started in 1066 and continues to this day in the form of rugby-matches. There are — surely! — no colonists, and no colonised there, unless we refer to the 'four nations' scene in *Henry V*. How can Greenblatt possibly use these texts to indict colonialism?

The answer is, of course, by means of a parallel text, between which and Shakespeare a network of common points can be established to show 'the embeddedness of cultural objects in the contingencies of history' (Greenblatt 1990, p. 164), a phrase which may here seem euphemistic. Greenblatt's essay in incrimination, 'Invisible Bullets' (which on its original appearance in *Glyph*, 1981, had the subtitle: 'Renaissance Authority and Its Subversion'), has been much admired by followers of New Historicism. Robert N. Watson writes that 'Stephen Greenblatt's wonderfully fresh and insightful "Invisible Bullets" is of course a seminal document in the New Historicist Movement'.[43] Arthur F. Kinney, editor of *English Literary Renaissance*, has hailed it as 'perhaps the most important, and surely the most influential essay of the past decade in English Renaissance cultural history'.[44] Given such a glowing reception, this essay seems worth examining closely.

Arthur Kinney!

Greenblatt sets out to relate Thomas Harriot's *Briefe and True Report of the New Found Land of Virginia* (1588)[45] to Shakespeare's Hal/Henry V, the *tertium quid* being the familiar pair of 'orthodoxy' and 'subversion', both terms being echoed over and over in that primitive but for some readers evidently effective form of rhetorical repetition (see pp. 21ff, 30–35, and especially p. 39, where the word 'subversion' appears ten times on one page). To anyone familiar with the values and practices of New Historicism it will be immediately apparent that to cite a 'colonialist' text can only bode ill for the literary work ultimately involved in the comparison. But here even the text from socio-cultural history comes in for attack. Greenblatt accuses Harriot of exemplifying the 'Machiavellian' argument that Christianity 'originated in a series of clever tricks, fraudulent illusions perpetrated on Moses' by the Hebrews using Egyptian magic (pp. 24–5). The page-reference given is to chapter vi of *The Prince*, where Machiavelli merely mentions Moses in a list of founders of kingdoms and says nothing about fraud or magic. A few lines later Greenblatt candidly admits that this argument 'is not actually to be found in Machiavelli' (p. 25), thus destroying whatever historical status he claims for the reference, but he reports that it can be found in the 'notorious police report of 1593 on Christopher Marlowe' made by the government spy Richard Baines

(p. 24). Why Greenblatt should drag in Machiavelli is not clear, unless as a modern bogey-man or smear word (totally unhistorical, if so), but he repeatedly ascribes to Machiavelli the 'sense of religion as a set of beliefs manipulated by the subtlety of priests to help instill obedience and respect for authority' (p. 26). The passage in Machiavelli he refers to is his commentary on Livy,[46] *Discorsi*, I.xi, which describes how Numa Pompilius, newly elected king of Rome, 'finding a very savage people, and wishing to reduce them to civil obedience by the arts of peace, had resource to religion as the most necessary and assured support of any civil society' (p. 146). Greenblatt has failed to understand several issues here. The first thing he has not noticed is that Machiavelli is quoting Livy practically verbatim, and enlarging Livy's account with glowing approval of the social efficacy of religion, in a theory not unlike Emile Durkheim's.[47] Fear of the gods, Machiavelli emphasises, makes men keep their oaths and also unites the people, 'keeping them well conducted, and covering the wicked with shame' (p. 147). Machiavelli says nothing about faith, nor does he — any more than Livy — see this as constituting the *origin* of religion, which already existed and was simply applied by an enlightened ruler to a civic purpose. Machiavelli actually grants Numa 'the highest merit' for using religion as a means of establishing social concord, his 'wisdom and good-ness' bringing Rome peace and prosperity (p. 148).

Furthermore, Greenblatt has failed to realise that Machiavelli is holding up ancient Rome as an explicit rebuke to the modern papacy. As Machiavelli writes in the following chapter, 'Princes and republics who wish to maintain themselves free from corruption must above all things preserve the purity of all religious observances, and treat them with proper reverence; for there is no greater indication of the ruin of a country than to see religion contemned' (p. 199). If the Christian religion had been maintained 'according to the principles of its founder', the Christian states and republics might have remained happy and united. The greatest proof of its current 'decadence' is

> the fact that the nearer people are to the Church of Rome, which is the head of our religion, the less religious are they. . . . [The] evil example of the court of Rome has destroyed all piety and religion in Italy, which brings in its train infinite improprieties and disorders . . . . (p. 151)

The Church has kept Italy divided, Machiavelli alleges, by resting com-fortable in its temporal dominion and not trying to enlarge it to take control of the whole country, while blocking any other attempt to do so (p. 152). The court of Rome is such a source of dissension and weakness that if it were transposed en bloc to 'the Swiss, who of all people nowadays live most according to their ancient customs so far as religion and their military system are concerned', in no time at all 'the evil habits of that court would create more confusion in that country than anything else that could happen there' (p. 152–3). To reiterate his point, Machiavelli returns to Livy and Rome in the next chapter, describing 'How the Romans availed of religion to preserve order in their city, and to carry out their enterprises and suppress disturbances' (pp. 153–5).

Not everyone accepted Machiavelli's recommendation of a state power using religion in this way, and the Catholic church was predictably outraged. This 'famous indictment of the Church', as Mark Phillips records, provoked much discussion. Francesco Guicciardini, for instance, did not share Machiavelli's early humanist reverence for Roman history as exemplary. While he 'accepts and redoubles (the) invective against' the modern papacy, Guicciardini argues that 'the peculiar conditions' of ancient Rome's greatness invalidated 'any argument from Roman example'.[48] Whichever writer we side with, this is the proper historical context within which to discuss Machiavelli's invocation of Numa Pompilius and the social function of religion. Greenblatt, drawing on what he elsewhere despises as 'vulgar Machiavellianism', and on the reports of Elizabethan informers (thus aligning himself with the government that employed them), first travesties Machiavelli and then transfers the smear words — 'fraudulent imposition', 'coercive' — to Thomas Harriot's account of the Algonquian Indians. His sense of historical accuracy, presumably, makes him add that 'Harriot does not voice any speculations remotely resembling the hypotheses that a punitive religion was invented to keep men in awe and that belief originated in a fraudulent imposition by cunning 'jugglers' on the ignorant...' (p. 26). But that smear is allowed to stand as concerns Machiavelli, and Harriot is soon linked with it. No doubt aware that if a description is repeated often enough, the unwary reader will accept it as true ('lie boldly', as Coleridge wrote, 'some of it is bound to stick'), Greenblatt presents Harriot throughout as a cynical exponent of what he calls 'the Machiavellian anthropology that *posited the origin of religion* in an imposition of socially coercive doctrines by an educated and sophisticated lawgiver on a simple people' (p. 27; my italics: repeated on p. 28). Again invoking Machiavelli and the term 'coercive belief', as if to create a reflex or subliminal association, Greenblatt claims that Harriot uses 'the most radically subversive hypothesis in his culture about the *origin and function of religion* by imposing his religion... on others', and so subverting that religion (p. 30; my italics). (This is an extraordinarily disabling modern idea, incidentally, that to try to disseminate your faith is to 'subvert' it. It is another post-Derrida way of attacking the enemy, claiming that their acts achieve a goal exactly opposite to that intended. Where is the evidence?)

Anyone who takes the trouble to consult Harriot's text will find that Greenblatt gives a wholly false impression of it, by selective quotation and persistent distortion. Harriot was not a 'lawgiver', to start with, but an observer, 'specially imploied... in dealing with the naturall inhabitantes' (H., p. 321), as he put it, due to his mastery of their language (which he had probably learned from two Indians who had been brought to England in 1584, and whom he may have taught English). Harriot was engaged to draw up a report on the colony in the course of one visit; he had no official administrative post. He was an orthodox Christian, too, and there is no evidence at all for the claim that he shared the supposedly 'Machiavellian' belief that religion was a fictitious belief-system invented by cynical rulers in order to dupe their subjects. (There is no evidence that Machiavelli believed this either; I could surmise, with just as much authority, that this is actually Greenblatt's theory of religion.) Harriot, dutiful student of all aspects of this potential colony, having spent a year there collecting and analysing material, hoped that by publishing his account he would counteract the 'slaunderous and shamefull' reports put about by other Englishmen who had only visited it briefly (*H.*, p. 320), not explored the whole country, and who were frustrated at not having instantly struck rich: 'after gold and silver was not so soone found, as it was by them looked for, [they] had little or no care of any other thing but to pamper their bellies' (*H.*, p. 323). Harriot writes as an all-round scholar hired by a group wanting to attract investments in the 'enterprise for the inhabiting and planting in Virginia' (*H.*, p. 320). His brief was to ascertain whether the country was fruitful, would both support human life and allow the production of enough exports to make it commercially viable. Although the mere fact that he agreed to work for his patron Raleigh will be enough to make him suspect to haters of colonialism (for whom all are guilty), he was not a colonist himself but a poor scholar. Arguably the most outstanding English mathematician of his generation, Harriot never found a niche in the university system and, like so many scientists in early modern Europe (as we are beginning to realise), depended on patronage.[49]

Harriot divides his treatise into three parts, first considering those 'merchantable commodities' already found in Virginia, or which could be planted: grass silk, flax and hemp, alum, sassafras, cedar, wine, oil, furs, minerals, pearls, dies, and other things which could be exported (*H.*, pp. 325–37). In the second part (*H.*, pp. 337–62) he surveys the commodities that can yield 'victuall and sustenance of mans life', grain, pulses, fruit, herbs, including a remarkably precise observation of the indigenous people's ways of sowing grain, and one of the earliest descriptions of tobacco as used both medicinally and in religious rituals (*H.*, pp. 344–5). In the third part he discusses those resources that can be used for building houses (*H.*, pp. 362–68), and finally surveys 'the nature and maners of the people' (*H.*, pp. 368–82). The qualities of open-minded observation and natural curiosity evident throughout the treatise — listing 86 different kinds of fowl as distinguished 'in the country language', for instance, of which he also had a visual record in the drawings made by the artist John White, who accompanied the expedition — are strikingly evident in Harriot's account of the people.[50]

Future investors in a frankly commercial enterprise are not normally interested in ethnographical description for its own sake, being basically concerned whether the inhabitants are 'friendly' or not. (Once again I record, should anyone doubt it, my disgust at how colonists have treated indigenous peoples. Greenblatt has no monopoly on this feeling.) At pains to reassure potential 'Adventurers' (putting out their risk-capital) on this head, Harriot describes the natives as 'not to be feared, . . . having no edge tooles or weapons of yron or steele to offend us withall, neither knowe they how to make any'. Their only weapons are bows and arrows, their sole defence shields 'made of barks, and some armours made of stickes wickered together with thread' (H., pp. 368–9). If it should come to 'warres between us and them, . . . wee having advantages against them so many maner of waies, as by our discipline, our strange weapons and devises else, especially by ordinance great and small', the outcome can be 'easily imagined' (H., p. 37f). In other words, the settlers will be safe, the investors' capital will be safe, and a goodly return on investment can be expected from this fruitful land. *Safety*

Having thus completely satisfied the commercial readers' interest in this people (in much the same way as the *Wall Street Gazette* or *Financial Times* might evaluate investment risk) Harriot, unasked and unprompted, adds half-a-dozen pages describing the Algonquian Indians as a people, and especially their religious beliefs. This is another instance of Harriot's disinterested curiosity in the world about him, for no colonialist in the stereotype of rapacious exploiter cares two cents about the theology of the people he is about to rape. Yet, ironically, this is just the passage that Greenblatt seizes on to accuse Harriot of writing his description of the Indians purely 'to prove that the colony could impose its will on them. The key to this imposition, as we have seen, is the coercive power of religious belief, and the source of the power is the impression made by advanced technology upon a "backward" people. Hence Harriot's text is committed to record what I have called his confirmation of the Machiavellian hypothesis' (Greenblatt 1988, p. 31; I have not already quoted this passage). Whoever opens Harriot's text, however, will find something very different. Far from using 'advanced technology' to oppress or terrify them, Harriot juxtaposes European civilisation with the inhabitants' natural gifts, a comparison from which the Algonquians emerge rather well:

> In respect of us they are a people poore, and for want of skill and judgement in the knowledge and use of our things, doe esteeme our trifles before thinges of greater value: Notwithstanding, in their proper manner (considering the want of such meanes as we have), they seeme very ingenious. For although they have no such tooles, nor any such *wit* crafts, Sciences and Artes as wee, yet in those things they doe, they shewe excellencie of wit. (H., p. 371)

That combination of self-deprecation ('our trifles') and praise of the indigenous people's native intelligence is far removed from the Eurocentric superiority recorded by some early visitors to unexplored lands. True, Harriot does write that the more the Indians discover 'our manner of knowledges and craftes to exceede theirs in perfection and speed . . . by so much the more it is probable that they shoulde desire our friendship and love, and have the greater respect for pleasing and obeying us' (H., p. 372). This belief may well seem naïve, but it also expresses his continuing emphasis on the need to live together in peace — peaceful subjection, of course.

No modern reader, obviously, can accept at face value Harriot's further hope that if 'good government be used', the Indians may soon 'be brought to civilitie, and the imbracing of true Religion' (ibid.). We are all too conscious that our 'civilitie' is only one of many possible types, and that in destroying others to make them conform to ours we are calling the very notion of civilisation in question. As for 'true Religion', we may be prepared to accept the sincerity of each believer that his or her system of belief is the true one, but we do not think sincerity sufficient ground for imposing any belief system on another people. I do not wish to endorse Harriot's beliefs in any way; merely to record that Greenblatt has misrepresented them, and to that degree failed in the first duty of a historian. The major feature of the Algonquians' religion, which Greenblatt never mentions, is that it is polytheistic.

> They beleeve that there are many Gods, which they call Montoac, but of different sortes and degrees; one onely chiefe and great God, which hath bene from all eternitie. Who, as they affirme, when hee purposed to make the worlde, made first other goddes of a principall order, to bee as meanes and instruments to be used in the creation and government to follow; and after the Sunne, Moone, and Starres as pettie gods, and the instruments of the other order more principall. . . . For mankinde they say a woman was made first, which by the working of one the goddes, conceived and brought forth children: And in such sort they say they had their beginning. . . . They thinke that all the gods are of humane shape, and therefore they represent them by images in the formes of men. . . . (H., pp. 372–3)

The Algonquians 'beleeve also the immortalitie of the soule', Harriot records, and (perhaps already influenced by earlier Christian visitors: H., p. 373 note) they posit the existence of heaven and hell after death, the deterrent fear of hell making 'manie of the common and simple sort of people . . . have great respect to their Governours, and also great care what they do, to avoid torment after death, and to enjoy blisse'. In addition, the Algonquians have a code of punishment for various kinds of wrongdoing on earth, 'according to the greatnes of the factes' (H., pp. 374–5).

Although not entirely consistent with other sources, Harriot's remarks are respectful, neither antagonistic nor exploitative, and address the concerns of many of his non-capitalist readers by considering the inhabitants' possible conversion to Christianity: 'some religion they have alreadie, which although it be farre from the truth, yet being as it is, there is hope it may bee the easier and sooner reformed' (*H.*, p. 372). In order to emphasise their potential for conversion he notes that the Indians 'were not so sure grounded' in their religion, 'but through conversing with us they were brought into great doubts of their owne, and no small admiration of ours' (*H.*, p. 375). An instance of the Algonquians' tendency to 'esteeme our trifles before thinges of greater value' was their reaction to the explorers' 'Mathematical instruments' — a compass, a lodestone, perspective glass, fireworks, guns, clocks. The Indians were so impressed that they thought these instruments 'were rather the works of god than of men, or at the leastwise they had bin given and taught us of the gods', so making the English a people 'whom God . . . specially loved' (*H.*, pp. 375–6). These are familiar enough reactions by any primitive people confronted for the first time with European technology, and could be duplicated many times over. Greenblatt uses them, however, to make the very serious charge (fundamental to his thesis) that Harriot 'undermined the Indians' confidence in their native understanding of the universe' by the 'marvels' he showed them, so subverting their religion (p. 27).

Unfortunately for Greenblatt's thesis, though, there is no evidence that Harriot did, or even thought that he had done, such a thing. The fact that one Indian chief, when ill, 'sent for some of us to praie' to the Christian God, and that others made the same request when their corn 'began to wither by reason of a drought' (*H.*, p. 377), is unsurprising in a polytheistic system confronted with gods of apparently greater power. Some of the Algonquian priests and people, Harriot records, 'sometimes accompanied us, to pray and sing Psalmes; hoping thereby to bee partaker of the same effects which wee by that meanes also expected' (*ibid.*). Although willing to expound the Bible to them, Harriot refused to compromise his own religious beliefs, rejecting some of the Indians' appeal to call down divine wrath on their enemies because 'our God would not subject himself to any such prayers and requests of men' (*H.*, p. 379). Harriot, at least, was quite clear about the differences between polytheism and Christianity. Whether Greenblatt is or not, it is unfortunate that he should have failed to inform his innocent and trusting readers about the Algonquians' polytheism, the crucial fact which casts doubt on his claim that Harriot, or anyone else, could bring about the *collapse* of their belief system. Greenblatt is reading with Western eyes, creating a wholly imaginary religious crisis from the assumptions of a monotheistic religion. In polytheism, witness modern Japan, believers regularly turn from one religious system to another as circumstances arise, or pursue both simultaneously. The further, and quite unrelated fact that many Indians contracted fatal diseases from the Europeans (measles, smallpox, perhaps influenza), whom they suspected of killing with 'invisible bullets' (*H.*, pp. 378–80), is indeed tragic, and one of the most disturbing features of colonisation, but it is in any case an issue

of a wholly different kind. Harriot neither willed nor caused — could not
have caused — that. Nor, when Harriot made some missionary attempts, is
there any evidence of him practising 'fraud' or 'coercion'. He simply did
what every responsible Christian, Protestant or Catholic did in those days,
sincerely try to convert what they thought to be heathen souls. Of course,
Greenblatt adds, the 'subversiveness' of Harriot's 'confirmation of the
Machiavellian hypothesis' — an illusory confirmation of an illusory hypothesis! — may have been invisible to most readers, and even to Harriot
himself. Indeed, he suggests, 'it may be that Harriot was demonically
conscious of what he was doing' (p. 31) — a remark that opens an infinite
field of insinuation.

    For a less biassed account we could turn — as Greenblatt could have
turned, since the book was published in 1983 and his essay has appeared
in several revised versions since then — to the standard biography of
Harriot.[51] Here we learn of Harriot's scientific preparations for Raleigh's
expeditions of 1584–5, including the lessons he gave to the ships' captains
on navigation, a science in which Harriot achieved quite remarkable
accuracy (Shirley 1983, pp. 85–95). Harriot consulted sea masters arriving
in the London docks, studied critically the instruments available, devised
new instruments and even produced new charts, with an unusual mastery
of both theoretical and practical knowledge. His curiosity in the world
around him led to him compiling for his own use a glossary of sea terms
(ibid., pp. 96ff). The same spirit of enquiry made him master the Algonquian
language, becoming the main spokesman and translator for the expeditions,
'one of the most advanced linguists of his time and the first Englishman to
master this highly complicated language' (p. 107). In his published Report
he noted that 'the language of every [Algonquian] government' — or
settlement — 'is different from any other, and the further they are distant,
the greater is the difference' (H., p. 370), revealing a surprising sensivity
to dialects. His surviving papers include some in a strange script which was
formerly interpreted as 'cabalistic': in fact, we know now that this was
a surprisingly original phonetic transcription of Algonquian, for which
Harriot invented a new cursive script (Shirley 1983, pp. 108–12). One
would never guess from Greenblatt's reduction of him to the level
of a fraudulent colonist that Harriot was a veritable uomo universale:
but then, Greenblatt is disillusioned with celebrations of Renaissance
accomplishments.

    On his first expedition to Virginia Harriot was already noting Indian
names, customs, and beliefs (ibid., p. 133), showing his characteristic
'accuracy and completeness' (p. 146). In his dealings with the Indians, his
biographer judges, Harriot revealed 'his personal warmth and sympathy
for men of a totally alien culture, and his willingness to accept their
unorthodox beliefs with understanding' (p. 151). Although biographers
sometimes tend to overvalue their subjects, that seems to me a fair assessment of Harriot, and any reader of the Report can see how critical he was

of those members of the colony who had been cruel to the Indians (H., p. 381; Shirley 1983, p. 152). In attempting to bring Christianity to them 'he expressed none of the militant zeal' of the Catholic Spaniards, but rather a tolerance and receptiveness which was as much interested in learning their religious views as imparting his own (pp. 152–3). He was impressed by the seriousness with which the Algonquians held their religious beliefs, their '"solemne feastes"' and '"solemne prayers"', praising their integrity and peace of mind: '"This people therefore voyde of all covetousnesse, lyve cherfullye and att their harts ease"' (p. 153). Their moral superiority to Europeans was thus evident. It seems fair to conclude that, rather than an unscrupulous manipulator trying to bring down a whole belief-system, in his dealings with the Indians Harriot showed the same open-mindedness and willingness to entertain 'unusual premises' that made him the outstanding English scientist of his age (p. 154).

The motivating force behind Greenblatt's distortion of Harriot's *Briefe and True Report* is obviously the politicisation he admits to in his own criticism since the Vietnam War, the belief that 'neutrality was itself a political position, a decision to support the official policies in both the state and the academy' (Greenblatt 1990, p. 167). His way of connecting 'the present with the past', we recall, was either by representing 'a particular set of historical circumstances . . . in such a way as to bring out homologies with the present', or else to analyse 'those circumstances . . . as the generative forces that led to the modern condition' (*ibid.*). Either way, representation or analysis, Greenblatt has given a false and tendentious account of Harriot, intended to associate him with a whole series of New Historicist targets. The *ressentiment* behind the misrepresentation comes out most clearly in Greenblatt's bitter comment at the end of his account of the *Report*, on 'the pious humbug with which the English conceal from themselves the rapacity and aggression, or simply the horrible responsibility implicit *in their very presence*' (Greenblatt 1988, p. 38; my italics). Such a general indictment can raise uncomfortable questions, though. Granted that the original colonists are most to blame, what about later immigrants? Perhaps their decision to emigrate in search of work can be faulted as endorsing the colonialists' original 'seizing' of the land, in which case which of us would be free from blame?[52] The discourse on colonialism seems to find dangerously easy targets.

*   *   *

I have dealt with Harriot's treatise at some length because it is obviously unfamiliar to most readers, even to those academics who have praised this essay 'Invisible Bullets' so highly. (I can't imagine that they will continue to do so once they know what Harriot actually says.) With Greenblatt's account of *Henry IV* and *Henry V* I can be briefer, since the critical bias will be more visible to readers who know those plays. Greenblatt applies to

them the familiar New Historicist interest in 'the production and containment of subversion and disorder' (p. 40). The villains of the piece turn out
to be not the rebels, Hotspur, Northumberland and Co., nor the parasites
and rogues, Falstaff, Pistol and Bardolph, but the forces of ostensive law
and order, especially Prince Henry. Hal is seen from the outset in extraordinarily unsympathetic terms, as 'a "juggler", a conniving hypocrite'; the
'power he both serves and comes to embody is glorified usurpation and
theft' (p. 41). This interpretation deliberately ignores, or discounts, the
quite explicit passages in which Shakespeare presents a very different
judgment. At the end of his first scene in *1 Henry IV*, the dramatist gives
Hal a self-declaratory speech — 'I know you all' — to reassure those
members of the audience who did not know the chronicle history that the
Prince is simply enjoying himself until the time comes for him to take up
his responsibilities:

> So when this loose behaviour I throw off
> And pay the debt I never promisèd,
> By how much better than my word I am,
> By so much shall I falsify men's hopes; . . .   199
> I'll so offend to make offence a skill,
> Redeeming time when men think least I will.   (1.2.196ff)

Although the speech is an unambiguous declaration of Hal's intent to foil
the many backbiters who, as Holinshed records, were constantly spreading
evil stories about him, Greenblatt reads it 'against the text', as modern
theorists quaintly put it, to present it in his negative light. Ignoring the
obvious sense of 'hopes' in line 199 — that is, 'the expectations of my
enemies and critics that I will turn out a ne'er-do-well' — Greenblatt sees
it as implying barefaced deception and betrayal (p. 41). At one level this
'partial' interpretation of the sense is old-fashioned character criticism,
which isolates one character from the play, ignoring the context and
the playwright's design. Within character criticism it belongs to the
vituperative pole, what Richard Levin has called 'character assassination',[53]
namely the building up of 'a "case" against the targeted character by going
through, or at least claiming to go through, his entire career within the
play in such a way as to put him in the worst possible light' (Levin 1979,
pp. 85–6). In this mode of reading 'the critic treats only those facts which
reflect (or can be made to reflect) unfavorably upon the character, and
silently passes over all the others'. As Levin shows, this strategy also
involves selecting only 'those aspects that will submit to his negative
thesis'; emphasising 'relatively trivial facts at the expense of the important
ones' which establish a correctly balanced attitude to the character, so
distorting the play; and taking those facts 'out of the context established by
the playwright to guide our response to them' (*ibid.*). Greenblatt does all
of these.
  Since the New Historicists, in the wake of Barthes and Foucault,

generally dismiss the notion of the author having shaped his materials with a coherent moral and aesthetic design, they end up committing the same error as do thousands of unsophisticated readers who regard characters in literary works as if they were people you could meet on the street. Greenblatt has taken an instant dislike to Hal for what he thinks Hal represents, and proceeds to damn him like some wholly unprincipled prosecuting attorney. Earlier Greenblatt had professed his belief that 'sustained, scrupulous attention to formal and linguistic design will remain at the center of literary teaching and study' (Greenblatt 1988, p. 4): by these criteria his account of *1 Henry IV* is fragmented and unscrupulous. To present Hal as 'the prince and principle of falsification . . . a counterfeit companion . . . an anti-Midas: everything he touches turns to dross', resulting in a 'devaluation' that reduces him to 'counterfeit coin' (p. 42) — such a totally unsympathetic reading seeks no justification in the text (95% of which is never referred to) and is more concerned to legitimise itself as a politically correct opposition to 'the official policies in both the state and the academy'.

Greenblatt is echoing, whether he knows it or not, other hostile accounts of Hal, such as those by Richard Simpson, the Victorian, and D.A. Traversi, a 1940s *Scrutiny* critic. His account is just as one-sided as theirs, but serves a different goal. Embodying as he does the New Historicist fascination yet disillusionment with the sources of power and authority, Greenblatt must ignore not only the positive aspects of Hal as a character in the play, but also the historical record of him as embodying legitimate rule. Bolingbroke had seized the crown from Richard II, and his reign was 'unquiet', as a Tudor historian put it, a tissue of rebellion on the outside and guilt within, the nemesis of conscience sapping any enjoyment of his rule. But, by a sleight of hand in the Tudor historians, one sometimes feels, when Hal succeeded to the throne he cast off his father's guilt and became the legitimate ruler, Henry V, whose achievements in war and peace assured England prosperity throughout his reign, and great victories in France. His positive gains, in turn, were dissipated by the imprudence of Henry VI and the recurrence of civil conflict, leading to the disaster of the War of the Roses, from which Henry VII and the Tudor dynasty saved us. All this is familiar from the historians or Shakespeare's *Henry VI* cycle, as every schoolboy knows. References to the sources will show that Shakespeare's synthesis from Hall, Samuel Daniel, Holinshed, and half-a-dozen other versions gives a coherent and consistent picture of Hal embodying maturity, decency, chivalry, courage, wit, authority, and a sense of future responsibilities which he must and can assume with dignity and justice.[54] To realise this, it is only necessary to read the plays with an open mind.

One of the main changes that Shakespeare (following Daniel) made from the chronicles was to reduce the age of Hotspur, who was historically older than King Henry IV, in order to make him the rival of Hal. From the first, Geoffrey Bullough writes, Shakespeare's 'intention was to make the Hal-Hotspur antithesis culminate in the physical and moral triumph of the former at the battle of Shrewsbury. Yet to give this any weight the Prince must be shown in action as a madcap' first (Bullough 1962, p. 159), those legendary incidents involving his misbehaviour as the wild young man who reformed on succeeding to the crown. In another source, the 'rowdy and chauvinistic play' called *The Famous Victories of Henry the Fifth* (ca. 1587–88), as David Bevington points out, 'Hal is truly unregenerate. He not only robs and wenches, but endorses the idea of plundering the rich and encourages his companions to look forward to unrestricted license when he is King. The blow he delivers the Chief Justice is a blow for freedom. Hal seems consciously to desire his father's death. Yet he does reform', albeit in a 'crude and sudden' way (Bevington 1980, p. 1641). Shakespeare preferred to follow the chronicles in recording that none of Hal's exploits actually harmed anyone; indeed Shakespeare (like Stow) has him repay to the victims the purses Falstaff managed to steal on Gadshill. Hal performs a double restitution: of the money to the travellers, of the kingdom to its legitimate officers. Hal's intention to 'redeem time' — to buy it back, as if a debt, or make amends for time lost — is a motif which Shakespeare deliberately emphasises. In his first long confrontation with his father, whose praise of Hotspur is obviously designed to build him up as a worthy rival (3.2.97–128), Hal defends himself from the slanders of 'smiling pickthanks and base newsmongers' and twice vows: 'I shall hereafter . . . / Be more myself' (92–3), promising to 'redeem all this on Percy's head', who shall 'exchange / His glorious deeds for my indignities' (132ff). When he confronts the rebels before the battle of Shrewsbury Hal generously praises Hotspur and acknowledges his own falling-off until now:

> I do not think a braver gentleman,
> More active-valiant or more valiant-young,
> More daring or more bold, is now alive
> To grace this latter age with noble deeds.
> For my part I may speak it to my shame,
> I have a truant been to chivalry. . . .   (5.1.87ff)

Hal's generosity (another positive side of his character that Greenblatt either cannot or will not see) is praised by Vernon as he reports back to Hotspur how Hal

> gave you all the duties of a man,
> Trimmed up your praises with a princely tongue,
> Spoke your deservings like a chronicle. . . .

Not only generous in praising his rival, Vernon reports, Hal 'made a blushing cital of himself / And chid his truant youth with such a grace' as if he had acquired the ability 'Of teaching and of learning instantly'. In addition to giving an independent testimony of Hal's positive qualities,

Vernon's report repeats the dialectic of truancy and reform that was estab-lished at the play's outset. When Hal has fulfilled his promise, killing Hotspur, routing Douglas, and saving his father's life, the King duly acknowledges his reformation: 'Thou hast redeemed thy lost opinion' — that is, reputation (5.4.47).

In the sequel Shakespeare twice gives Hal a self-reproach for not yet having 'redeemed' his lost time, first in the jaded scene with Poins: 'Well, thus we play the fools with the time, and the spirits of the wise sit in the clouds and mock us' (2 Henry IV, 2.2.134); and secondly at the end of the Eastcheap scene with Falstaff: 'I feel me much to blame/So idly to profane the precious time' (2.4.364–5). Awaiting news of the confrontation with the rebels, the sick King also praises Hal's generosity: he has 'a tear for pity, and a hand / Open as day for melting charity' (4.4.30–32). In the great scene between them that follows — when Hal's 'trying' with the crown, 'as with an enemy', produces the last misunderstanding between them, the son's self-defence settling his father's anxieties once and for all — Hal affirms his integrity and the sense of duty he is now ready to accept:

> If I do feign
> O let me in my present wildness die,
> And never live to show th'incredulous world
> The noble change that I have purposed!   (4.5.151–4)

Finally, having acceded to the throne and endorsed the Lord Chief Justice, the new King declares that he has buried the 'affections' or passions of his prodigal years, and will now live — echoing the words of his first soliloquy —

> To mock the expectation of the world,
> To frustrate prophecies, and to raze out
> Rotten opinion, who hath writ me down
> After my seeming.   (5.2.123–30)

Hal's abandonment of 'vanity' shows his underlying virtue, making the prophecy of his conversion to the responsibilities of office a coherent ethical motif with which Shakespeare organised both plays. (To some modern critics, of course, any character who overtly takes up an ethical position must be suspected of hypocrisy. The clarity with which much literature of the past uttered ethical evaluations is a source of considerable difficulty to some critical schools today.)

This exemplary story of the emergence of a supremely successful and legitimate ruler can be of little interest to the avowedly politicised New Historicist, disillusioned after Vietnam, Watergate, the Gulf War, or any of a dozen episodes in contemporary history that reveal our governors in the worst possible light. The jaundiced idealist Greenblatt, preferring to side with 'rotten opinion' and 'base newsmongers', writes a sustained indictment of Hal. He ignores history and draws opportunistically on his 'background' source, Harriot, whose attempt to supply an Algonquian-English dictionary is now said to have been made to 'consolidate English power in Virginia' (Greenblatt 1988, p. 45) — the 'politicized' nature of that remark, ascribing the worst possible motives to Harriot the inquiring scholar, needs no comment. In the same way, Greenblatt continues, Hal studies the tavern slang of his cronies in order 'to understand and control the lower classes' (p. 49). In order to make this analogy, Greenblatt has had to ignore the dramatic context, from which it is clear that Hal is performing neither a Henry Mayhew exercise in social reporting nor a Basil Bernstein one in socio-linguistics, but is actually enjoying himself. At the 'olde Taverne in Eastcheape' in Part One of the play, he calls on Poins to 'lend my thy hand to laugh a little', having been 'with three or four logger-heads, amongst three or fourscore hogsheads' — that is, drinking in the cellars with the tapsters, with whom he is on Christian name terms. He is proud to have been accepted by them, for they 'tell me flatly I am no proud Jack like Falstaff' — note that comment on Falstaff's egoism —

> but a Corinthian, a lad of mettle, a good boy (by the Lord, so they call me!), and when I am King of England I shall command all the good lads in Eastcheap. They call drinking deep 'dyeing scarlet', and when you breathe in your watering they cry 'Hem!' and bid you 'Play it off!' To conclude, I am so good a proficient in one quarter of an hour that I can drink with any tinker in his own language during my life. (2.4.2–19)

This sense of Hal's enjoyment at having been accepted into the Eastcheap world, with its ludicrously serious rules for drinking and its special cant, the feeling of 'play' involved, is totally absent from Greenblatt's account. Equally ignored is the Prince's zest for play-acting with Falstaff, putting serious affairs in a comical light. At one point Hal imagines them personating the rebels: 'I prithee call in Falstaff. I'll play Percy, and that damn brawn shall play Dame Mortimer his wife . . . . call in ribs, call in tallow' (2.4.108ff). Falstaff shares, indulges this delight in improvisation and fantasy: 'What, shall we be merry, shall we have a play extempore?' (279–80), an invitation that he repeats when they imagine Hal being rebuked by his father when he returns to court:

FALSTAFF.   If thou love me, practise an answer.
PRINCE HENRY.   Do thou stand for my father and examine me upon the particulars of my life.
FALSTAFF.   Shall I? Content.

There follows what the Hostess rightly describes as 'excellent sport i'faith', that marvellous scene in which each in turn acts out accusation and defence, Hal being accused by his father, as agreed, but Falstaff then unexpectedly attacked by Hal, producing Falstaff's superb *apologia pro vita sua* (2.4.373–485). In addition to its structural importance for the father-son relationships in the play, and the related issues of truancy and corruption, few comic scenes have given greater pleasure on the English stage than this one. Here, if anywhere, would have been the place to invoke that otherwise popular ingredient in Current Literary Theory, Bakhtin's notion of carnival. But such sympathetic critical paradigms may only be used for openly subversive characters, ideologically approved.

Greenblatt bolsters his indictment of Hal by citing a passage in the sequel, the scene where Warwick tries to reassure the dying Henry IV that his son is no wastrel. But our New Historicist once again betrays history, failing to provide the background needed to understand it. Warwick states that

> The Prince but studies his companions
> Like a strange tongue, wherein, to gain the language,
> 'Tis needful that the most immodest word
> Be look'd upon and learnt; which once attain'd,
> Your Highness knows, comes to no further use
> But to be known and hated. So, like gross terms,
> The Prince will in the perfectness of time
> Cast off his followers,

Going about in disguise

memory of their wrongdoings aiding the future King's knowledge of crime and punishment (*2 Henry IV*, 4.4.68ff). It was a widely-understood principle in classical and Renaissance politics that a ruler should get to know his subjects — indeed, a whole school of texts describes how a wise ruler did so by going among them in disguise. As Sir Thomas Elyot wrote in *The Governor*, rulers will never discover the causes of sickness or health in society 'except they them selfes personally resorte and peruse all partes of the countrayes under their governance, and inserche diligently . . . what be the customes and maners of people good and bad', in order to 'here what is commonly or privately spoken'.[55] This is to give a serious, not to say a studious explanation, which might indeed be open to the charge of hypocrisy. But as we have seen, Shakespeare presents a Hal who is not pretending, but really enjoying this carefree time before taking on the pains of office. Greenblatt ignores the 'carnival' aspect of his behaviour, accepts Elyot's serious explanation, as it were, but only to put it to the worst possible application. He actually accuses Hal of seriously compiling that 'kind of glossary . . . specifically linked to the attempt to understand and control the lower classes', namely 'the sinister glossaries appended to sixteenth-century accounts of criminals and vagabonds' (p. 49: one detects in the New Historicists, and not for the first time, a touch of paranoia in their attitude to the 'ruling classes'). But first — to state the obvious! — criminals and vagabonds did not constitute the 'lower classes' in Elizabethan England, who were for the most part honest working men and women who regarded criminals with fear and disapproval. Secondly, the aim of the compilers of such glossaries was not to 'control' the criminals but to have their canting terms and crooked practices known, so that honest citizens would not be deceived by them, and the laws of the realm upheld. These are the explicit motives of such a typical text as Thomas Harman's *Caveat for Common Cursitors* (1566), and Harman would have agreed with Warwick's insistence on the need to learn such 'immodest terms' so that they 'be known and hated'. Thirdly, Hal is not compiling a glossary of any kind. That Greenblatt should put on the same level Harriot's list of Algonquian words, Hal's delight at such phrases as 'Hem!' and 'Play it off!', and Harman's account of thieves' slang is a trivial, and at first sight puzzling manoeuvre.

But there is a link, in Greenblatt's eyes: namely, he accuses Harman of having 'betrayed' his informants by printing information given to him in confidence (for the public good, we recall), and argues that similarly 'the "larger order" of the Lancastrian state in this play seems to batten on the breaking of oaths' (p. 52). It is a characteristic New Historicist procedure, as we know, to find the Renaissance guilty of having created unpleasant aspects of modern society. So here, Greenblatt writes, 'the founding of the modern state, like the self-fashioning of the modern prince, is . . . based upon acts of calculation, intimidation, and deceit'. But Hal betrays no one. The breaking of the assurance of safe conduct given to the rebels is assigned by Shakespeare, following his sources, to Prince John (*2 Henry IV*, 4.2.110ff). Changing the emphasis in his sources, Bevington writes, 'Shakespeare puts Northumberland in a more dishonorable position than in Holinshed, and emphasises the perfidious dastardy of Prince John. Seemingly, Shakespeare wanted to stress the coldness and cynicism of Machiavellian politicians on both sides of the rebellion, as a contrast with the more enlightened policy to which Prince Hal aspires' (Bevington 1980, p. 1641). Whatever we might feel about deceiving our enemies (if it spared a lot of lives, as the disinformation techniques used by allied espionage during the second world war did, there might be something to be said for it), in Elizabethan terms it could be justified, since rebels are guilty of treason: they have betrayed the oath of allegiance that every subject is deemed to have sworn, to obey the sovereign and the law of the land. Greenblatt does not make Hal guilty of this act, but he says in general that 'out of the squalid betrayals that preserve the state emerges the "formal majesty" into which Hal at the close, through a final, definitive betrayal — the rejection of Falstaff — merges himself' (p. 53). Greenblatt has not, unfortunately, examined the text here with the 'sustained, scrupulous attention to formal and linguistic design' that he claims to respect. Had he done so, he would have found that Hal does not 'betray' Falstaff since he never promised him anything, indeed explicitly predicted his ultimate banishment at the start ('I do, I will': *1 Henry IV*, 2.4.475).

More important, had Greenblatt approached the play with an open mind in the first place, he might have realised that Falstaff, despite all his engaging qualities, is the great predator, an unscrupulous parasite who

[handwritten margin note: And how else does one rule?]

never has a good word to say about anyone, never does a good deed, and, if he had the power, would corrupt the whole state.[56] Falstaff is not 'betrayed': he betrays himself, most seriously in the grotesque act, 'alone' on stage — 'Nothing confutes me but eyes, and nobody sees me' (5.4.128: 'O wie gut, dass niemand weiß, / Dass ich Rumpelstilzchen heiß '!') — of stabbing the corpse of Hotspur, whom Hal has killed, and claiming credit for his defeat (*1 Henry IV*, 5.4.120ff). Greenblatt comments neither on this episode nor on the amazing generosity which Shakespeare ascribes to Hal when, having protested at Falstaff's lie — 'Why, Percy I kill'd myself' — he nonetheless lets Falstaff take credit for the victory: 'if a lie may do thee grace, / I'll gild it with the happiest terms I have' (5.4.142–56). In terms of dramatic technique (needless to say, ignored by New Historicism), the 'counterfeit' and 'honour' soliloquies in Part One show Falstaff still as an engaging rogue but isolate him and involve the thinking spectator or reader in some moral problems. Shakespeare heightens both effects in Part Two, where the nature and frequency of the soliloquies confront the audience more and more with his unpleasant qualities.[57] Greenblatt finds 'the mood at the close' of the play, after Falstaff's rejection, 'unpleasant' (p. 55, reading 'against the text' once more), but it depends whose side you *Falstaff* are on. Had Falstaff been given power, we may be sure, the result would *as Jack* not have differed much from the anarchy incarnated in Jack Cade (*2 Henry* *Cade* VI, 4.2.61ff, 4.6, 4.7). It is Cade who says 'And when I am King, as King I will be, . . . there shall be no money'; all men shall wear the same 'livery, that they may . . . worship me their lord'; and: 'Away! burn all the records of the realm; my mouth shall be the parliament of England'; and: 'there shall not a maid be married, but she shall pay to me her maidenhead, ere they have it'. For law and order Cade wants to substitute a grotesque version of feudalism with himself as the ruler living off his people. (Twentieth-century history has given us more than enough examples of leaders of religious groups or political states indulging their own appetites for greed, sex, or riches.) Falstaff's Utopia is less explicit, but includes the request to Hal to banish the gallows when he succeeds to the throne: 'Do not thou when thou art king hang a thief' (*1 Henry IV*, 1.2.56ff). And when the news reaches him that Hal has become King he proclaims: 'Let us take any man's horses — the laws of England are at my commandment. Blessed are they that have been my friends, and woe to my Lord Chief Justice!' (*2 Henry IV*, 5.3.119ff).

Once again, for all his apparent contemporaneity, Greenblatt is here repeating traditional attitudes in Shakespeare criticism, for protests at Falstaff's rejection go back to A.C. Bradley in 1909, and beyond him to Maurice Morgann, much discussed — and ably refuted — in the 1770s.[58] Scratch a New Historicist and you find a disappointed romanticist. But whereas earlier sentimentalists protested out of affection for the fat rogue, Greenblatt displays no affection for him, taking Falstaff's side merely as a weapon in his own opposition to the powers of legitimacy and authority.

Turning to *Henry V*, then—in which he predictably finds 'every nuance of royal hypocrisy, ruthlessness, and bad faith' (p. 56) — and anxious at every stage to attack established authority, our critic is reduced to siding with Pistol and Bardolph against Fluellen and the King. According to Greenblatt, Pistol 'pleads that Fluellen intervene to save Bardolph, who has been sentenced to die for stealing a "pax of little price"' (p. 58). But this is to accept Pistol's view of the affair! Robbing churches, to the Elizabethans, was a serious crime, and the punishment exemplary. To Greenblatt 'this attempt to save his friend's life is the ground for Fluellen denouncing Pistol as a "rascally, scald, beggarly, lousy, pragging knave"': as if those two incidents were connected, and as if there were not ample, indeed unanimous evidence in the play to endorse Fluellen's judgment. Greenblatt conveniently overlooks the denunciation of the whole crew of parasites that Shakespeare gives to a choric character, the Boy:

> As young as I am, I have observed these three swashers: I am boy to all three, but all they three, though they would serve me, could not be man to me; for indeed three such antics [buffoons] do not amount to a man . . . They will steal anything, and call it purchase. . . . They would have me as familiar with men's pockets as their gloves or their handkerchers: which makes much against my manhood. . . . I must leave them, and seek some better service: their villany goes against my weak stomach, and therefore I must cast it up. (3.2.28ff)

Pistol's whole career of crime, rant, and ignoble cowardice — unforgettably conveyed when he grovels to Fluellen and eats the leek he has mocked (5.1.14ff) — is presented by Shakespeare throughout in the worst possible light. Pistol is explicitly condemned by the Boy here and later (4.4.66ff); by Gower, who describes him as 'an arrant counterfeit rascal, . . . a bawd, a cutpurse . . . , a rogue' who poses as a soldier, one of the 'slanders of the age' (3.6.61ff), 'a counterfeit cowardly knave' (5.2.69); and by Fluellen (notable for 'care and valour', as Shakespeare makes the King say at 4.1.84), outraged by this 'rascally, scald, beggarly, lousy, pragging knave' (5.1.5ff).

The consistency of Shakespeare's critical view, and an example of the early theatrical convention of self-presentation, can be seen from the number of times he makes Pistol describe himself as a parasite — on his way to the wars: 'Let us to France, like horse-leeches, my boys, / To suck, to suck, the very blood to suck!' (2.3.55–6); after his defeat of a French soldier, taken in by his bluster: 'As I suck blood, I will some mercy show' (4.4.64); and at his dismissal from the play, vowing to become a 'bawd' and 'cutpurse of quick hand. / To England will I steal, and there I'll steal' (5.2.85ff). Yet his desire to perform a character assassination of Hal means that Stephen Greenblatt voluntarily allies himself with Pistol — an uncomfortable bedfellow for a Berkeley professor. As for the presence of the 'four nations' (English, Welsh, Scottish and Irish) in Henry's army, where generations of readers have taken this as a symbol of the new spirit of national unity embodied in the King (a unity of mutual support, as anyone with an inkling of geography or history would know, since the destruction of any of these countries by a foreign power would spell the ruin of them all), Greenblatt sees them through New Historicist spectacles as signifying coloniser and colonised (p. 56). At least this is predictable.

In the scene on the eve of Agincourt, finally, Greenblatt claims that the soldier Williams challenges the king's authority effectively, Henry being forced back on 'a string of awkward "explanations" designed to show that "the king is not bound to answer the particular endings of his soldiers" — as if death in battle were a completely unforeseen accident' (p. 61). The critic's sarcasm cannot conceal the fact that the burden of this discussion is indeed to absolve the king of personal responsibility for the deaths or injuries of his soldiers. He is only the head of a state which goes to war collectively, and is collectively responsible. Greenblatt's further claim that Henry is 'almost single-handedly responsible' for the war ignores the evidence from this play — or from the *Henry VI* cycle, or from the Tudor historians — that the king had the backing of the whole nation; that he achieved a glorious victory; and that the prestige of England was never greater. After Vietnam, after the Falklands, it takes more effort of the historical imagination to think oneself back into a position where Henry V can be seen as a hero who unified his country, bringing peace and prosperity. It is all too easy to ignore history and see him in the jejune and jaundiced terms of disillusioned liberals.[59] But to do so while practising something claiming to be 'historicism' becomes an act of self-deception.

V

If Greenblatt's work represents the *acme* of New Historicism then the number of grave defects it contains must arouse doubts about the value or validity of this whole school of criticism — if that is not to grant it a spurious unity (time will tell). A disregard for the integrity of the literary text; a bending of evidence, background and foreground, to suit one-sided interpretations; the foisting of modern cultural and political attitudes on to Renaissance texts — these are serious deficiencies for a movement which claims to avoid the mistakes of the past and provide a model for the future. To many readers this will constitute sufficient reason to view their work with cautious scepticism.

To some critics, however, New Historicism does not go far enough. One writer frequently associated with the group, Jonathan Goldberg, published an essay on *Macbeth* specifically designed to advance a new cutting edge. Goldberg refers to Greenblatt's essay on *King Lear* and the exorcists but rejects its method, not on the historical or critical grounds that I have outlined but because it 'does not ultimately call into question the value system upon which it rests. Greenblatt's *King Lear* is, in many ways, perfectly recognizable' (Goldberg 1987, pp. 242–3), evidently a major defect in Goldberg's eyes. Greenblatt's argument, he complains, 'does not . . . go far enough in distinguishing itself from more conventional literary criticism. It seeks to preserve the very notion of literalness it calls into question' (p. 244). Summoning up a more powerful magic, Derrida's concepts of 'répétition', 'trace', and 'différance', Goldberg announces that he will now 'call into question the methods of literary critics, and the practices of textual, historical, and formalistic criticism' (p. 245) — with an appropriately de-centred view of history as 'heterogeneous dispersal' (p. 247).

Stimulated by this prospect of a total rejection of all extant systems, the reader of the discussion of *Macbeth* that follows is sadly disappointed to find that most of it is entirely traditional criticism, discussing Shakespeare's sources and his deviations from them, mirror-imagery, possible revisions of the text, Ben Jonson's masques, Jacobean absolutism, and panegyric. As for the comments on Shakespeare's plays, although they pay homage to the current concern with gender they read more like old-fashioned judgmental character criticism, only worse in that they ignore motive and context. Masculinity in *Macbeth*, Goldberg declares, 'is directed as an assaultive attempt to secure power, to maintain success and succession, at the expense of women. *As is typical of many of Shakespeare's tragedies, the play is largely womanless and family relationships are disturbed*' (p. 259; my italics). As it happens, there are three women in *Macbeth* (excluding the witches), as there are in several of Shakespeare's tragedies, a reasonable complement given the make-up of the average Elizabethan theatre-company, and two of them have important roles. But it would not suit Goldberg's argument to note this. True, family relationships are disturbed: that is indeed one of the characteristics of tragedy as a genre. For Goldberg, however, it is proof of the dramatist's misogyny. Pursuing his thesis that Shakespeare is 'anti-feminine', he states that when Macbeth is killed he

is replaced by two men who have secured power in the defeat of women. Indeed, Macduff has not only abandoned his wife and family, his very birth represents a triumph over his mother's womb, the manifest fantasy of being self-begotten that also deludes Macbeth in his final encounter. (p. 259)

Readers will not need me to remind them that Macduff's flight was an emergency to preserve his life on the outside chance that he might be able to defeat the tyrant; and that the loss of his family causes him more anguish and remorse than anyone else in the play is capable of, an ability to care about others against which we can gauge Macbeth's concern solely with himself. There is no evidence in the text or anywhere else that Macduff has 'secured power' by 'the defeat of women'. As for his birth by Caesarian section, that is such a singular donnée of plot, the special case that would fulfil the witches' prediction of Macbeth's invulnerability to man 'born of Woman', that it would be folly to base any normative argument on it. And to call this birth a 'triumph over his mother's womb' is an unpleasantness which may be a peculiarly modern form of misogyny on Goldberg's part, but is nowhere found in the play. As dramatic criticism Goldberg's is no better than Greenblatt's on Hal in disregarding the play's integrity, both critics displaying a self-willed quality that can only be described as ruthless. More striking, though, is the gap between the critic's ambitions for a wholly new discourse and what he actually produces.

Everyone will agree with the principle from which these critics apparently began, that the writing of history is a construct in which the historian evaluates evidence and organises a narrative that fulfils contemporary expectations of coherence and consistency — that, in these respects at least, all narrations of the past, far from being 'objective', bear the marks of the individual writer and of the age in which they were produced. Paradoxically (to adapt a phrase), the 'poverty of the New Historicism' lies in its being subject to the same constraints. Its own critical practice is just as much a product of its time, of an ideology that only allows it to deal with a part of Shakespeare, reshaped to suit its own purposes. It is not the proclaimed historicist approach that, in the end, mars this form of criticism, nor its flirtation with Current Literary Theory, but its relentless politicising. The general form this politicising takes is a monotonous preoccupation with the triad of power, containment, and subversion. Greenblatt, in addition, uses both literary texts and the cultural context to indict aspects of modern society of which he disapproves. It is the present that controls his work, not the past. Frank Lentricchia has described Greenblatt as endorsing a version of determinism that is 'the typically anxious expression of post-Watergate American humanist intellectuals' (Lentricchia 1988, p. 93; 1989, p. 235), and Louis Montrose has recorded his feeling that New Historicist concerns are 'partially impelled by a questioning of our very capacity for action — by a nagging sense of professional, institutional, and political powerlessness or irrelevance' (Montrose 1989, p. 26). Everyone must have days when they feel powerless or irrelevant, and citizens of a democracy that only get to vote every four or five years often feel that their participation in political life is nominal.

While sharing and understanding Montrose's feelings, though, a deeper and more important issue may be involved. Montrose does not suggest that their academic work is only 'a psychological compensation for social inactivity and political quiescence' (ibid.), but Lentricchia's critique of Greenblatt accuses New Historicism of encouraging — in the wake of Foucault — a cynically passive acceptance of a corrupt society over which we supposedly have no control. The Foucauldian belief in 'a power that coerces all practices' produces 'the desire to get outside politics' (Lentricchia 1988, p. 95; 1989, p. 237). The New Historicist, powerless to act, longs for 'a space of freedom' where he will not feel enabled by vast, impersonal systems. There, in that special place, we know we are because we feel ourselves to be discontented; in that reflective space we make the judgement that no system enables — that we are unhappy. And we locate our unhappiness precisely in those systems that have produced and enabled us as selves. (*ibid.*, pp. 100–101/241)

Hence the attraction of literary criticism written by disaffected subjects who, as Hooker put it, 'openly reprove supposed disorders of state' and thus appear 'principal friends to the common benefit of all'. Hence, too, the parallel indictment of the Renaissance, as Lentricchia also notes, for being 'peculiarly modern', but '"modern" not only in a sense not intended by Jacob Burckhardt but in one which would have horrified his liberal confidence: the Renaissance is *our* culture because it is the origin of our disciplinary society' (pp. 97/238).

Lentricchia's target is the 'political quandary' he diagnoses in New Historicism: 'hating a world that we never made, wanting to transform it' but believing that impossible, 'we settle for a holiday from reality, a safely sealed space reserved for the expression of aesthetic anarchy' as a substitute for political action (pp. 101/241–2). He is concerned that this cynical acceptance of power and passivity encourages quietism and an illusory picture of democracy as totalitarian. My concern, rather, is with the discrepancy between Greenblatt's claim that the value of New Historicism is its 'intensified willingness to read all of the textual traces of the past with the attention traditionally conferred only on literary texts' (Greenblatt 1990, p. 14), and the travesties that he performs on Harriot, Harsnett, and several other writers called up to provide contextual material. The fact (already noted by several critics)[60] that Greenblatt regularly misrepresents the cultural or literary text that he discusses, suggests to me that his desire for revenge or retribution has overcome his better judgment. Taking up but redirecting the remarks of Montrose and Lentricchia, I see this distorting process displaying what Max Scheler described in his classic analysis as *Ressentiment*, that stifling feeling of impotence, born of the mentality (originally defined by Nietzsche's attack on Christianity), in which the dominated helplessly seeks to subvert and overturn the values of the master.[61]

The feeling of powerlessness, Scheler showed, gives rise to such 'emotions and affects' as 'revenge, hatred, . . . the impulse to detract' (p. 46). The desire to detract seeks 'those objects . . . from which it can draw gratification. It likes to disparage and to smash pedestals, to dwell on the negative aspects of excellent men and things, exulting in the fact that such faults are more perceptible through their contrast with the strongly positive qualities' (*ibid.*, p. 47). Or, as in the case of Harriot or Hal, denying them any 'positive qualities' at all. The crucial element for Scheler is the simultaneous presence of bitter feelings and the inability to turn them into action.

Ressentiment can only arise if these emotions are particularly powerful and yet must be suppressed because they are coupled with the feeling that one is unable to act them out — either because of weakness, physical or mental, or because of fear. Through its very origin, *ressentiment* is therefore chiefly confined to those who *serve* and are *dominated* at the moment, who fruitlessly resent the sting of authority. (p. 48)

To Scheler's suggested motives for the non-expression of feelings we can now add the Foucault-derived belief that there is no point in uttering them, because subversion will in any case be contained and rendered meaningless. Uncannily like Foucault is Scheler's account of how 'the delights of oppositionism' depend on a negative view of the situation: 'It is peculiar to *"ressentiment"* criticism that it does not seriously desire that its demands be fulfilled. It does not want to cure the evil . . .' (p. 51). Society must go on being conceived as composed of anonymous power-structures that determine us and deny our selfhood. The Renaissance can go on being re-defined as the origin of our discontents, while Shakespeare can go on being shown — with a mixture of regret and satisfaction — to be guilty too.

CHAPTER FIVE

Psychocriticism: Finding the Fault

In the cultural desert created by the prejudices of the liberal intelligentsia of New York or of the Californian cities, the questioning of the scientific pretensions of psychoanalysis is restricted almost entirely to those concerned with the philosophy of science. The therapeutic needs of such aids perhaps makes intelligible the extraordinary situation whereby a theory that is certainly no better confirmed — and perhaps not as well confirmed — as witchcraft or astrology should have gained the credence it has.
                                                                      Alasdair MacIntyre[1]

I suspect that much of the resistance to Freudian interpretations is based on dissatisfaction with Freudian theory itself.   Kendall Walton[2]

Psychoanalytic theory has become widely dispersed in the last fifty years, the influence of Freud, in particular, having reached the point where many of his concepts seem part of the furniture of the twentieth-century mind, as if they have always existed, and need no further justification. In America the cultural conquest of psychoanalysis is complete: a revised Webster's Dictionary in the 1970s listed 140 words beginning in *psycho*, 'exactly twice as many as in the previous edition twenty-five years earlier' (Barzun 1974, p. 13). America currently recognises no less than eight different schools of psychoanalysis, of which the Freudian is dominant (*ibid.*, p. 31). But of course psychoanalysis — which involves patients either free-associating or recalling their dreams so that the analyst can diagnose whatever past event or unconscious activity created the psychic disturbance for which they are being treated — is only one of many forms of psychotherapy. A little known fact in literary critical circles is that Freudian analysis has been compared with up to two hundred other therapeutic systems, and has been shown to have no better success-rate than its many rivals, and to suffer from two serious disadvantages, the length of time it takes and the consequent expense in analysts' fees.[3] Few of these other therapies have so far been used as models by literary critics, for whom Freudianism has long been the single system.

The temptation to seek psychological causes or explanations for the behaviour of characters in literature is not new. Already in the 1830s Hamlet or Ophelia were being classified according to one or more theories of hysteria.[4] The Freudian appropriation of literary criticism began in 1910 with Ernest Jones's essay, 'The Oedipus-complex as an explanation of Hamlet's mystery', a topic finally given full-length treatment some forty years later.[5] While other writers underwent similar treatment — Ben Jonson was classified by Edmund Wilson as an anal erotic[6] — it has always been Shakespeare who has attracted the most attention. The bibliography of psychoanalytical criticism of Shakespeare is already extensive, and grows exponentially every year.[7] In 1987, for instance, at least four full-length books appeared analysing Shakespeare's characters — there seems to be a temporary lull in pursuing the dramatist himself — in Freudian and/or Lacanian terms, and most of this chapter will be given to an examination of these works.[8] For some readers and historians it might seem sufficient to analyse the criticism without bothering about the system of ideas behind it. To me it seems more honest to recognise, as Kendall Walton puts it in the second epigraph above, that my problems with the criticism derive in the first place from my objections to Freud. Furthermore, since Freudians have simply ignored the many critiques that have been appearing with increasing frequency over the last twenty years, it seems important to point out that the whole Freudian edifice has been drastically undermined, with severe consequences for any literary criticism based on it.

I

Alasdair MacIntyre's comment, in my first epigraph, that 'the questioning of the scientific pretensions of psychoanalysis' was virtually restricted to philosophers of science, was certainly true for the late 60s. An essay he wrote in 1968, 'Psychoanalysis: the future of an illusion?' (MacIntyre 1971, pp. 27–37) described the 'intellectual boredom' he felt at the constant respectful recycling of Freud's ideas, and outlined some telling theoretical objections to them. MacIntyre was one of the first critics to object that in Freudianism 'the explanatory theory helps to provide a vocabulary for the description of the very facts which the theory is designed to explain' (ibid., p. 28). If we describe adult behaviour as Oedipal, for instance, a resemblance with childhood behaviour is brought out by using a term 'which already half-commits us to a particular explanation of this resemblance' (ibid.). Writing in 1968, MacIntyre could think of

> no discipline to compare with psychoanalysis for the way in which the
> very use of the vocabulary commits the novice — quite unconsciously —
> to acceptance of a complex theoretical framework. (p. 29)

(Students of the cultural scene in the intervening period know of at least one critical school that rivals Freudianism in this respect, Derridian deconstruction.) MacIntyre also showed that Freud never offered adequate criteria by which his concept of repression could be tested (p. 30), and that other Freudian hypotheses are unfalsifiable because they contain too many variables. In his 1908 essay on 'Character and Anal Erotism' Freud hypothesised that instinctual drives might manifest themselves in one way, or — by 'the processes of reaction formation' — in precisely the opposite way. 'The same type of background may result in sadistic, aggressive behavior or in gentle, nonviolent behavior. The hypothesis has become a bet that cannot lose', but also cannot win. Either way, 'its unfalsifiability is fatal to its status as a hypothesis' (ibid., p. 31). Judged by our criteria for logic or scientific argument, MacIntyre's assessment of Freudianism as having less demonstrable validity than witchcraft or astrology had in the Middle Ages seems sober rather than provocative. All three were closed systems that defied verification or falsification.

The stagnation that MacIntyre complained of in Freudian studies was soon to change. At this time Henri F. Ellenberger was preparing his substantial book, The Discovery of the Unconscious: The History and Evolution of Dynamic Psychiatry (New York, 1970), which devoted a long chapter to Freud (pp. 418–570), a chronological survey of life and work which dispassionately placed Freud in his historical context. Ellenberger revealed Freud's many unacknowledged debts to his predecessors, and showed how from an early stage Freud gave misleading accounts of the cures he had effected, creating a series of myths about himself and his work. (I shall be returning to Ellenberger for my brief summary of the Freudian system below.) Also in 1970, Frank Cioffi published a shrewd and concise analysis which judged Freudianism to be no more than a pseudo-science.[9] The actual scientific status of Freud's work was called in question over the next decade in a number of studies by experimental psychologists, including Hans Eysenck and Glenn D. Wilson (eds.), The Experimental Study of Freudian Theories (London, 1973); Seymour Fisher and Roger P. Greenberg, The Scientific Credibility of Freud's Theories and Therapy (New York, 1977); and B.A. Farrell, The Standing of Psychoanalysis (Oxford, 1981). Although some of these writers continued to respect Freud's scientific work, the cumulative effect of their sober enquiries enforces a quite contrary assessment (Gellner 1985, pp. 158–63, 197–9, 204; Crews 1986, pp. 20–4, 37–41).

The most comprehensive study of Freud in English, which placed him in the Lamarckian tradition of biological determinism and revealed many unscientific aspects in his work (although still expressing admiration for him as a scientist), was Frank J. Sulloway, Freud, Biologist of the Mind. Beyond the Psychoanalytic Legend (London, 1979; rev. ed. 1983). As Sulloway decisively shows, a biographical approach is vital to understanding the genesis of Freud's theories, which stand in no coherent relationship to his so-called clinical work, and to appreciate the quite extraordinary amount of myth-making that Freud indulged in, and which made his system so successful. Sulloway's chapter on 'The Myth of the Hero' (Sulloway 1983, pp. 445–89) is summed up in his 'Catalogue of

Major Freud Myths', presented in tabular form (pp. 489–95), which sets out twenty-six myths put about by or attached to Freud. In each case Sulloway briefly describes the myth, its function (legitimation of one or more facets of Freud's heroic self-image as an isolated man of science, or nihilation of evidence giving credit to others working in the field); the myth's sources (mostly the writings of Freud and his early associates); and its rebuttal (Sulloway's own book, citing the work of some twenty or thirty other writers). These myths include such key ideas as that psychoanalysis is essentially the product of Freud's self-analysis, a 'herculean' and totally 'unprecedented' feat, that this self-analysis led to Freud's abandonment of the seduction theory and his discovery of infantile sexuality and of the unconscious. In fact, Freud drew most of his formative ideas from the contemporary sexology movement, especially the work of Wilhelm Fliess, whom he subsequently tried to both discredit and ignore (Sulloway 1983, pp. 135–237). Freud's claims to originality were illusory, and his professed indifference to questions of priority was mere evasion.

Far from Freud's theories having derived from his self-analysis in 1897 (a dubious episode in any case: *ibid.*, pp. 18–19, 207–10, 447), or from his purely clinico-psychological observation, 'it was Fliessian sexual biology, evolutionary theory, and the biogenetic law' that really animated Freud's work (p. 237). In his conclusion Sulloway writes with some authority that 'Freud's theories reflect the faulty logic of outmoded nineteenth century biological assumptions, particularly those of a psychophysicalist, Lamarckian, and biogenetic nature' (pp. 497–8). The psychophysicalist inheritance was Freud's notion of 'psychical *affect*' as a 'quantitative measure of . . . excitation or "emotion"', a finite amount that could be 'discharged' (pp. 91, 109 note), while the related conception of neurosis, as he put it in 1894, applied ' "in the same sense as physicists apply the hypothesis of a flow of electric fluid" ', with hysteria becoming 'equated with a "short circuit"' (pp. 61–2). The 'biogenetic law', propounded by Ernst Haeckel in the 1860s, was that 'ontogeny recapitulates phylogeny', the development of humans from foetus to adulthood (ontogeny) re-enacting the entire history of the race (phylogeny). Freud's 'endorsement of this law', Sulloway judges, was the biggest 'a priori biological influence in all of psychoanalytic theory', for he claimed that the developing child in its progress through erotogenic zones necessarily 'recapitulates the *sexual* history of the race' (p. 259). This assumption made Freud equate the pleasure that a baby receives suckling at its mother's breast with the pleasure that animals received from sex, a theory widely disputed by his early associates, notably Jung, and opposed by many psychologists since (pp. 258–61). Sulloway points out that the child may recapitulate the history of the race in some aspects, 'but it recapitulates the embryonic, not the adult stages', as Freud mistakenly thought. His biogenetic assumptions were plausible in his day, but they were 'nevertheless wrong; and much that is wrong with orthodox psychoanalysis' derives from them (p. 498).

As for his work with patients, Sulloway respectfully suggests that 'Freud was not always aware of how much faith he placed in' his biodeterminist assumptions, or of 'how much his clinical observations absorbed from them "empirical" meaning'. In other words, Freud constantly 'saw in his patients what psychoanalytic theory led him to look for and then to interpret the way he did; and when the theory changed, so did the clinical findings'. Sulloway cushions the blow, but it is a stunning one, and much of his book bears it out: Freud only saw in people what his theories at any one point would allow him to see. His biogenetic assumptions affected all his work, from his 'discovery of spontaneous infantile sexuality (1896/97) to the very end of his ·life'; they led him to make controversial claims for their universality, and — worst of all — they 'prevented Freud from accepting negative evidence and alternative explanations for his views' (ibid.). These objections constitute, in somma, a severe charge, and several reviewers, while praising Sulloway's scholarship and historical breadth, criticised him for not having fully faced the devastating implications of his own work for Freud's standing as a scientist, in particular his mendacity and deliberate manipulation of evidence in his case histories.[10] Acknowledging the justice of these criticisms, Sulloway recently returned to the issue, and in an essay called 'Reassessing Freud's Case Histories. The Social Construction of Psychoanalysis', admitted that 'the erroneous and now outmoded assumptions from nineteenth-century biology' on which Freud based his 'essential psychoanalytical concepts' and 'assembled his "empirical" obser-vations' were 'more lethal to his enterprise than I had previously concluded' (Sulloway 1991, pp. 245–6).[11] By way of making good, Sulloway syn-thesises and extends previous studies to show how Freud broke many fundamental principles of scientific research. He manipulated the events described by his patients and changed them to suit his bias (p. 254); his published case histories exhibit 'glaring' omissions of information (typically, over-emphasising the father's role and excluding the mother's), often amounting to deliberate distortion (p. 256); he made 'fictionalized recon-structions' of his patient's histories, vastly exaggerated the therapeutic success of his treatment (p. 257), and constructed 'pervasive but spurious links' to claim that his theories were proved by the patient's symptoms (p. 273). Sulloway's considered judgment is that 'Freud erected his psycho-analytic evidence on a kind of intellectual quicksand, a circumstance that consequently doomed many of his most important theoretical conclusions from the outset' (p. 245). Many other studies of Freud's case histories have exposed his unscientific procedures and mendacity: in addition to those cited by Sulloway, I think of Ellenberger on Anna O.,[12] Anthony Wilden and Roy Porter on Schreber,[13] and a number of feminist critics on Dora.[14]

Dissatisfaction with the scientific status of Freud's theories was one of the motivating forces behind a series of essays published from the mid-70s by the literary critic Frederick Crews, first in a collection called Out of my System: Psychoanalysis, Ideology, and Critical Method (New York, 1975), and then more powerfully in a second volume, *Skeptical Engagements* (New York, 1986).[15] A single essay by Crews, 'The Freudian Way of Knowledge' (Crews 1986, pp. 43–74), should be enough to give any unaligned reader serious doubts about the scientific or ethical status of Freudian psychoanalysis. Drawing on a dozen or more independent evaluations of Freud's system, Crews finds him guilty of 'enumerative inductivism', the naïve belief that 'a certain number of confirmatory instances will establish a hypothesis without further enquiry' (Crews 1986, p. 80). Instead of a balanced suspension of judgment until adequate testing had been carried out, Freud displayed a 'monomaniacal quality . . . a tendency to generalize too hastily while slighting any factors, especially organic ones, that might lead to a diagnosis other than his own' (*ibid.*, p. 50). Freud regularly ignored any criticism that might reduce the universality of his claims (p. 51). The key notion of repression, the supposedly 'unconsciously compelled and traumatic forgetting that alters one's mental economy in certain drastic ways', was never confirmed by observation and experiment. Rather, Freud extrapolated other major tenets in his system from his unproven 'premise that repression is the mainspring of neurosis' (*ibid.*, p. 77). As for his case-studies, even pro-Freudian researchers have 'regretfully concluded that nearly all of Freud's substantially described cases were manifest failures' (p. 59). It is doubtful whether Freud actually 'cured' anyone. As Crews puts it, 'the consulting room was never a laboratory for Freud; it was only the area in which he applied his prior deductions to specific cases, reassuring himself that his patients had repressed the kind of material he demanded of them' (p. 69). His interpretive method 'allowed him, if other signs were supportive, to consider irrelevancies as "displacements", and even, if he wished, to claim as "conclusive proof" of reconstructed memories the fact that patients "have no feeling of remembering the scenes"'. It is hard not to agree with Fliess's cutting allegation (in 1901) 'that Freud . . . "perceives nothing in others but merely projects his own thoughts into them"' (p. 58).

The truth about Freud, as it has gradually emerged over the last twenty years, is profoundly disillusioning. Virtually every part of his system has been challenged, if not utterly destroyed. As Crews says, instead of asking himself whether 'his dubious hypotheses . . . might be wrong', Freud 'habitually buttressed [them] with ex post facto provisos', such as 'new theoretical entities and catch-all excuses', invoking for instance 'the hereditary factor', or what Freud called ' "the primaeval times of the human family" ' (p. 67), to which he claimed privileged access. Or else he 'coped with potential disconfirmation by brashly redefining his terms and stretching the scope of his concepts', or by simply inventing 'a new mental law to cover the case at hand', even though it contradicted a previous law (p. 104). Crews cites Cioffi's searching study of inconsistencies in Freud, which shows that he maintained at one time or another completely contradictory positions:

childhood trauma both is and is not a necessary condition for neurosogenesis . . . ; recall of sexual material from infancy is both necessary and unnecessary to the undoing of a neurosis; a strict superego is produced by the misfortune of having either a hard, cruel father or . . . an indulgent one; explicit castration threats are both required and not required for the generation of castration anxiety . . .

and so on (pp. 104–5). Freudian theory seems increasingly a series of *ad hoc* constructs, lacking all internal coherence, 'bewilderingly unsystematic' (p. 24). The conclusion that Crews reaches, to which literary critics should seriously attend, is that 'psychoanalysis was founded not on observation but on deductions from erroneous dogma, and as a result the entire system can make no claim on our credence' (p. 97).

All the pillars supporting the Freudian system have been examined and condemned as unsuitable for load-bearing. Another critic with a literary background, the Italian classicist Sebastiano Timpanaro, applied the techniques of textual criticism to Freud's theory of the verbal 'slip', showing how many more simple and more likely explanations there were than Freud's notion of parapraxis.[16] As for the famous *Interpretation of Dreams*, Clark Glymour has revealed Freud tendentiously selecting material to preserve his own hypothesis, violating all scientific procedures, making in the process 'half a rotation from scientist towards mountebank'.[17] Timpanaro pronounces the book 'capricious and scientifically dishonest' (Timpanaro 1976, p. 236). The last two evaluations I shall cite come from philosophical quarters, each in its own way devastating. Adolf Grünbaum, in *The Foundations of Psychoanalysis. A Philosophical Critique* (Berkeley and Los Angeles, 1984), evaluated Freudianism from the standpoint of a philosopher of science.[18] This is a demanding book, not easy to summarise without simplification, but repaying study. It includes a patient and thorough demolition of Freud's repression theory, showing it to be a tissue of assumptions, gratuitous extrapolations, begged questions, contrived selections, and manipulated data (Grünbaum 1984, pp. 174–89, 194, 210, 216–66). Another impressive sequence concerns the innately unscientific nature of the Freudian psychoanalytic situation, an especially important issue for Freudian Shakespeare criticism, where the critic plays the role of analyst. Briefly, Grünbaum shows that the basic analysis situation is contaminated by the selection the analyst must make from the vast amount of recorded material; by his explicit suggestions to his patients, often prompting them to continue free association 'until they yield *theoretically* appropriate results' — a technique of planting what Freud called ' "the conscious anticipatory idea" ' in the patient's mind so that he ' "then finds the repressed unconscious idea of himself on the basis of its similarity to the anticipatory one" ' (*ibid.*, pp. 127–8, 209–15, 242–3). At every stage we find circular arguments, only self-confirmatory evidence, supposedly reliable 'clinical' data that has been tampered with throughout. One point particularly relevant to literary criticism concerns the absence of external constraints, the result being that data can be selected or constructed to make whatever pattern is needed to confirm the theory. I refer to the often noted phenomenon that, as a practising psychoanalyst put it, 'the "free" associations of the patient are strongly influenced by the values and expectations of the therapist', so that

> the patients of each school seem to bring up precisely the kinds of phenomenological data which confirm the theories and interpretations of their analysts! . . . Freudians elicit material about the Oedipus complex . . . Jungians about archetypes, Rankians about separation anxiety, . . . Sullivanians about disturbed . . . relationships, etc. (Grünbaum 1984, p. 211; Gellner 1985, p. 92)

In this way, each theory can be self-validating.

The last critic of Freudianism whom I shall cite is Ernest Gellner, sociologist, anthropologist and philosopher, in a refreshingly trenchant and untechnical book, *The Psychoanalytic Movement. Or, The Coming of Unreason* (London, 1985). Gellner also shows how the hierarchical situation in Freudian analysis puts the analysand at a complete disadvantage, having lost his conceptual foundations by the very terms of reference used in the therapy he has agreed to undergo (Gellner 1985, pp. 47–8), all power being vested in an authority figure, member of a self-perpetuating guild which recognises no other form of authority than that descending, like some apostolic succession, from Freud himself.[19] The basic hypothesis, the existence of the unconscious as the location of all that is decisive in the patient's life and psyche, is 'not so much a hypothesis', Gellner writes, as 'a suspension of all other hypotheses', producing in turn 'the suspension of intuitive logical certainties (of what would normally be called reason) . . .'. It carries the related hypothesis, that the analyst alone has access to the patient's unconscious (pp. 47–8). The patient has to 'cooperate' with the therapy, as an analyst might say, which means that he has no 'stance from which he could attempt a critical evaluation of it' (p. 49). Should he venture one, he can be judged guilty of resistance, the notorious Freudian belief that 'the repudiation of an interpretation or of a theory is evidence of its validity, because it shows the desire of the Unconscious of a given person not to be unmasked . . .' (p. 153). For Gellner resistance is one of several 'falsification-evading devices' (pp. 153–4) that allows psychoanalysis to evade the normal post-Popperian criteria for the demarcation of science, notably the demand that theories can be falsified — that is, being sufficiently coherent and independently formulated to be testable. Freudian ideas cannot be tested since they cannot be formulated in an independent language that does not prejudge the issue (pp. 4–5). They are conceptually vague (pp. 53–4), and rather than constituting 'one optional possibility within a wider world', they 'define, constitute, fill out their own world' (p. 157). In this domain external criteria are rejected as irrelevant, and observed behaviour is no longer an independent corrective to theory. In a typically circular process, Freudian concepts classify human behaviour 'in terms of the theory which is built into the concepts themselves, and which they then illustrate at will from any data' (p. 156).

The concepts are not difficult to understand, indeed, the basics of Freudianism can be mastered in half a day's reading. But to Gellner this is one more proof of the non-scientific nature of psychoanalysis, its acceptance of a 'naïve realism' which assumes perception to be 'the innocent encounter of a pure mind with a naked object', and thinks that the analyst has only to remove the veil of repression or neurosis to disclose the truth (pp. 90–91, 104–105, 82–3). Psychoanalysis, ignoring the whole development of scepticism and the conjecturalisation of knowledge since Descartes, in effect reverts to the world-view of pre-scientific societies, where reality is comfortably solid (pp. 120, 125–8). Gellner, like other critics of Freud, recognises the existence of an unconscious (pp. 75, 96, 107, 199–200), but rejects as unproven the two major assumptions of analysis, that patients' verbal recollection of their past will necessarily cure them, and that the 'material retrieved' constitutes a liberation of memories originally repressed because of their sexual significance (pp. 149, 182–3, 208–209, 224–5). Psychoanalysis certainly fulfils a need for lonely or disturbed people to find a sympathetic listener, but the analyst is not so much a scientist as a secular priest within a belief-system.[20] As for the much-touted phenomenon of transference, Gellner agrees that talking to someone else about your problems can be therapeutic, yet offers nine different, non-Freudian explanations of why this should be (pp. 56–66). For anyone sceptical of the Freudians' claim to be able to decipher the workings of the unconscious it is refreshing to read Gellner's comment that 'Consciousness is in a way much more mysterious than the unconscious' (p. 95). In the Freudian unconscious, I add, there is nothing mysterious: we find the same half-a-dozen main ideas over and over, in one permutation or another.

The appropriate conclusion to this brief survey of some of the critical literature on Freud over the last two decades would be the remark by P.B. Medawar, Nobel prize-winner for medicine, that 'the opinion is gaining ground that doctrinaire psychoanalytic theory is the most stupendous intellectual confidence trick of the twentieth century: and a terminal product as well — something akin to a dinosaur or a zeppelin in the history of ideas, a vast structure of radically unsound design and with no posterity'.[21]

*   *   *

I have tried to condense as briefly as possible some results of the great amount of scholarship produced over the last twenty years which has challenged Freudianism. The system that continues to claim scientific status for itself can now *only* be seen as a structure of interlocking theories, none of which has ever been proved, each of which assumes the validity of the others as the basis for its own existence, a self-generating, self-protective construct full of ruses to avoid being called to account. In due time, perhaps, recognition of the devastation that Freudianism has suffered may filter through and cause its general discrediting. But as we well know, published refutations do not necessarily change believers' opinions, and anyone who thinks they do is in the uncomfortable position of Swift's Gulliver, manically convinced that the world consists only of Houyhnhnms (horse-like creatures having reason) and Yahoos (man-like creatures of unreason), and protesting that the publication of his book has not managed to cure human vices:

> instead of seeing a full stop put to all Abuses and Corruptions, at least in this little Island, as I had Reason to expect: Behold, after above six months Warning, I cannot learn that my Book hath produced one single Effect according to mine Intentions: . . . And, it must be owned that seven months were a sufficient Time to correct every vice and Folly to which *Yahoos* are subject; if their Natures had been capable of the least Disposition to Virtue or Wisdom.[22]

The laugh is on Gulliver there, impatient and simple-minded moralist, but the residual irony affects us all. As for Freudianism, the verdict of two experimental psychologists still stands, that ' "A theory which fails consistently to predict . . . may nevertheless survive, due to the vagaries of the *Zeitgeist*" ' (Eysenck and Wilson, *cit.* Gellner 1985, p. 204).

In literary criticism the *Zeitgeist* continues to flourish. The anomaly may eventually become visible, however, that literary critics are still unquestioningly adopting a system that owes its whole prestige to its supposed ability to describe or explain human behaviour in real life. But if the system is bogus, the explanations erroneous, the very concepts and terminology question-begging, what status shall we assign to literary criticism based on it? One issue that literary critics can no longer ignore is the dubious status of Freudian argument, with its ability to control what counts as evidence, self-protectively excluding other criteria. Not many people now believe that a training in English literature makes us better men and women: but at least it should help us to spot what Frederick Crews has described as 'the ambiguous and opportunistic character of the whole Freudian system' (Crews 1986, p. xvi), its 'fatal readiness to corroborate any number of incompatible hunches about a given phenomenon, which can, according to the analyst's whim, be taken to mean either what it seems to mean, or exactly the opposite, or some other idea which it has supposedly "displaced" ' (p. 9). Adopted for literature, such opportunism can be convenient. Freudian Shakespeare critics, as we shall see, allow themselves the same liberty, the same 'elasticity of . . . rules', the same 'absence of constraints' on the production of evidence (p. 26). For some post-modernists, who have abandoned the whole notion of evidence, that may not matter. For others the complete liberty of interpretation that it claims is good reason for regarding psychoanalytic criticism with suspicion, at its worst legitimising self-pleasing speculation.

The demonstration of Freudianism's inability to explain real-life behaviour other than with its own question-begging categories might make its exponents defensive, claiming that the system nevertheless provides a usable model for analysing literature. If so, we would have to ask what use a system is that has such a limited range of interpretive possibilities, reproducing the same basic patterns time and again? Any sustained analysis of Freudian-inspired criticism eventually becomes monotonous, a condition that (I fear) the following discussion will not manage to escape. In order to refresh some memories, and to have a common reference-point for the analyses that follow, I now give a brief (but not uncritical) résumé of Freudian theory. This is the basic dogma that we can expect to find reproduced in psychoanalytical Shakespeare criticism.

The fundamental principle is that neurosis is a form of pathological behaviour which always has a sexual cause. Freud defined neurosis as 'a pathologically repressed, or "*negative*", state of sexual perversion' (Sulloway 1983, p. 277). Every neurosis has a determinant cause, Freud believed, in the repression of sexuality during childhood (*ibid.*, pp. 359, 364). From his first classification of neuroses (1896) to the posthumously published *Outline of Psychoanalysis* (1940), Freud never altered his opinion that repression-producing neuroses '"arise from the component instincts of sexual life . . . without exception"' (*cit. ibid.*, pp. 375–6). Systematising the theories of many psychologists in the late nineteenth century, Freud divided the development of infantile sexuality into a movement through three erogenous zones, oral to anal to genital (*ibid.*, pp. 203, 259–61, 377–81, 383–4). On the truth of this theory '"of the sexual component instincts"' in childhood, he declared in 1913, '"psychoanalysis stands or falls . . ."' (*cit. ibid.*, p. 259).

Sexual causes animate dreams, as well as neuroses. Every dream, Freud taught, is '"a (disguised) fulfilment of a suppressed or repressed wish"', in which '"the sexual material [plays] a decisive role"', for '"the dream represents the fulfilment of disguised *sexual* wishes"', sometimes discernible in what he claimed to be '"the fixed symbolism of dreams"' (*cit. ibid.*, pp. 320, 329–30, 350). Even anxiety dreams, Freud claimed, could be explained as wish-fulfilment. Freud drew most of his ideas on symbolism from current popularising books such as Karl Scherner's *Das Leben des Traums* (1861), but was more single-minded than other theorists, referring most of the 257 dream symbols mentioned in his writing to 'the human body (and its separate organs, particularly the genitals)' and to 'numerous other aspects of sexual life' (*ibid.*, pp. 325–7, 337–8). Thus boxes or cases meant the womb; walking up or down steps meant coitus; baldness, decapitation, or hair-cutting meant castration. Freud enlarged interpretive possibilities, as one might put it, with the suggestion that some symbols need to be interpreted in inverted terms, as one of his students recorded, '"since dreams often showed the opposite of what they mean"' (ibid., pp. 350–1). Among the material surfacing in dreams, or in free association, would be the repressed sexual desires of childhood — especially the famous Oedipus complex, in which, as one commentator reminds us, 'the little boy wants to possess his mother, wishes to get rid of his father, but is frightened of this threatening rival and of castration as a punishment for his incestuous feelings towards his mother' (Ellenberger 1970, p. 492). This theory was initially conceived in terms of the male sex, and Freud 'subsequently admitted that matters were far more complicated in the female sex owing to the little girl's preoedipal attachment to her mother, her lack of castration fears, and the paramount role of penis envy in her Oedipus complex' (Sulloway 1983, p. 374). Castration-anxiety was also taken to be a cause of neurosis, essentially a defence against passive homosexual fantasies (ibid., p. 383). Like so many Freudian concepts, castration was subsequently given a putative historical status, surviving in modern man as 'phylogenetic residues of actual deeds' in the prehistory of the species (ibid., pp. 386, 392). Totem and taboo (1912–13) is a kind of mythical fantasy on Darwinian themes, involving the powerful and castrating father, the struggle between males for dominance, and so on (ibid., pp. 372–3, 381).

As these examples show, much of Freud's thinking was based on male experience. In his eyes woman is born incomplete, never achieves the wholeness of man, and is subordinate in other ways. As he said in 1910, '"Neurosis always has a 'feminine' character. . . . Whatever is of the libido has a masculine character, and whatever is repression is of a feminine character"' (cit. ibid., p. 202 note). In Civilization and Its Discontents (1930) Freud gave as an example of the renunciation of instinctual gratification necessary to civilisation, man's taming of fire: 'Whenever primitive man came upon fire, he would extinguish it by urination. Owing to the phallic shape of the flames, he experienced an erotic feeling of a homosexual contest. [Did Freud really think that homosexuals went in for phallic competitions?] The first man to renounce this erotic pleasure was able to put fire to practical use'. Woman, meanwhile, 'was constituted keeper of the hearth because she was anatomically incapable of extinguishing fire as a man does. In another place Freud suggested that woman was the inventor of clothing because she wanted to hide her shameful lack of a penis; pubic hair inspired the invention of weaving' (Ellenberger 1970, p. 529). Criticism never made Freud re-think his theory, indeed in 1931 he said that 'women who rejected his own view of penis envy were using psychoanalysis illegitimately, as "a weapon of controversy"' (Grosskurth 1991, p. 26). His disciples loyally supported him, using the crudest forms of exclusion to silence anyone who challenged him from within the fold, as the sad case of Karen Horney shows.[23] To an increasing number of readers such theorising can only seem ridiculous and offensive, the result of applying male-based nineteenth-century theories of gender. Freud's deliberate ignoring of the breast, together with women's reproductive capabilities, have aroused justifiable anger among feminists.[24] Yet a large number of feminist literary critics still use castration fears and penis envy as indispensable tools for the evaluation of male and female behaviour, unable to reject these convenient but demeaning reductivist concepts.

Freudian literary critics, feminists and others, continue to use his master theory of how the personality deals with instinctual desires for either gratification or repression, his division of the psyche into three parts. The id is 'the unconscious, the seat of both the repressed material and the drives' or passions, including unconscious fantasies and feelings, 'notably guilt feelings' (Ellenberger 1970, p. 516). The ego, Freud wrote, is '"that part of the id which has been modified by the direct influence of the external world"' (Sulloway 1983, p. 374). The superego, finally, is 'the watchful, judging, punishing agency in the individual, the source of social and religious feelings in mankind'. But since 'the superego receives its energy from the id', it frequently has a 'cruel, sadistic quality', producing 'neurotic guilt feelings' (Ellenberger 1970, p. 516). The superego arises in childhood, Freud taught, as '"the heir to the Oedipus complex"' — that is, being identified with the authority of the opposite-sex parent and the prohibition of the child's incestuous impulses (Sulloway 1983, p. 374). In this, as in virtually every part of his system, Freud was a psychological determinist, with a lifelong belief that 'all vital phenomena, including psychical ones, are rigidly and lawfully determined by the principle of cause and effect'. As Frank Sulloway shows, Freud 'did not believe that anything at all was truly "free" in the life of the mind' (Sulloway 1983, pp. 94–5; also pp. 138, 170; Ellenberger 1970, pp. 488–9, 494, 498). The diagrams that Freud's expositors provide of his theories of neurosis or dreaming show graphically his belief that everything is 'tied' or 'linked' in 'a chain of unconscious fixed ideas' back to childhood sexuality and its varying forms of repression (Sulloway 1983, p. 342; Ellenberger 1970, pp. 489, 491). Reductivism and determinism are among the more depressing features of Freud's legacy.

Literary critics apply this system to novels and drama, reproducing all its faults. They ignore the richness of the societies depicted, the forces of history, the role of institutions and office, conflicts of love and duty, or anything else except the psycho-sexual nature of the main characters. Freudian literary critics, like Freud himself, are not interested in love, normal sexuality, health, happiness, family-relations that are caring and supportive; friendships; work; the experience of art, music, literature. . . . Disregarding normal behaviour, they concern themselves with what *they* perceive to be the personality-problems of some few characters (those presented in enough detail to justify analysis). Psychocritics are essentially concerned with individuals, often 'analysing' them in separate character-studies, that most primitive of critical modes. Psychocritics in effect assume that Hamlet or Othello are patients whose 'data' can be collected in isolation from the literary work in which alone they have a meaning and function. Strangest point of all, to my mind, they also assume that the characters to be analysed will manifest a psychopathology, reveal that they are suffering from some pathogenic or traumatic experience either within the play or in their putative earlier existence. That is, the strategies of a disturbed consciousness, unable to deal satisfactorily with reality, having consulted or been referred to a psychoanalyst for treatment, are now taken as the models for a normative literary criticism. The resulting critical focus on a few disordered psyches is not interested in, could not in any case deal with literary history, the demonstrable evidence that each play was written at a certain period in a chosen form, and that each is completely individual. The psychoanalytic critic lays Congreve and Strindberg, Büchner and Feydeau, all on the same couch, applies the same categories to them all, gets the same results. Psychocriticism, not having any aesthetic categories or knowledge of literature, must also ignore questions of genre, authorship, and style, jettison or misread motivation suggested by the writer if it should not fit its system. As loyal as the analysts on whom they model themselves, for psychocritics the Freudian model is to be illustrated, never questioned.

II

Literary criticism that takes over Freudian ideas can hardly hope to escape their monocausal reductivism. In her book on *Shakespeare's Other Language*, Ruth Nevo affirms that Freud produced the three 'most seminally important books for the study of language and literature . . . in this century' (Nevo 1987, p. 9). As a model specimen of Freudian interpretation she cites an account of 'Three Blind Mice', by Robert Rogers, which she judges 'an exemplary instance of the primary and secondary processes in poetry'.[25] In this nursery rhyme — '. . . see how they run. / They all run after the farmer's wife,/ Who cut off their tails with a carving-knife' — Rogers 'discovers a precipitate of a fantasy rooted in deep-seated castration anxiety which the song "succeeds . . . in generating, controlling, and dispelling"'. What Rogers finds, Nevo writes approvingly, is a 'theme of vision and blindness as symbolic lust and castration'. That is, I imagine, the mice were not — as everyone has always assumed — born blind, but have been blinded as punishment for their scopophilia, their gazing lustfully at the farmer's wife. (What these little creatures thought they could get up to with her is difficult to imagine; just as one wonders how a rodent, lacking reason, can be guilty of lust; and how we, the readers or listeners, being

ordered or invited to 'see', can avoid committing the same sin.) *Ergo*, the
cut-off tails must 'figure' as penises. Nevo announces that in this 'rhyme,
exceptionally, crime follows punishment', which allows her to claim that
'blind' and 'tails' are related. This completely arbitrary handling of narrative
sequence is a liberty that psychocritics frequently allow themselves. Nevo
endorses Rogers's conclusion that ' "the stress on seeing . . . reassur[es] the
detached listener that since he can see . . . he is himself whole and hale" ',
— then the listener must be a man! — thus validating 'Freud's observation
that fear of the loss of the phallus is often represented by a multiplication
of the object which represents it' (*ibid.*, pp. 14–15). This 'exemplary'
account of poetry (some might have thought it a spoof) already reveals the
major (and unsolved, because unconsidered) problem for Freudian critics,
that of evaluating evidence, the absence of criteria which could tell them
when references to cutting are *not* castration-fears, when blindness is *not*
the result of scopophilia. But their ignoring of negative instances could be
seen as a loyal tribute to Freud.

Nevo's own approach, inevitably so for a Freudian, is resolutely ahistorical, sweeping aside the charges of 'anthropomorphism and anachronism'
often applied to psychoanalytic readings of Shakespeare in these terms:

> If we do not wish older works to become fossilized, simply archaeological,
> we *must* employ our contemporary conceptions in interpreting them.
> Both present and past are thus more fully understood. (p. 30)

The 'present', may be — or rather, some current trends within psychoanalysis and linguistics — but the past is not simply 'understood' in this
way, for in an ahistorical reading the present simply reproduces itself, using
the past as a vehicle. To overcome this dilemma the reader, and especially
someone who sets up as a critic, needs to develop the historical imagination
in order to reconstruct those attitudes to life and literature — social,
moral, and aesthetic (involving critical theories, notions of genre, the arts
of language) — which influenced the writing and reading of literature
at some past time.

Nevo, who has written some valuable historical criticism,[26] knows all
this, of course. She equally knowingly adopts as her critical model

> present-day post-psychoanalytic semiotics, which finds in *rifts* at the
> realist-rationalist level of plot, character and diction evidence of *uncon-
> scious signification*, of the language of dream and fantasy. It is the inter-
> play of *that other language* with the manifest events and dialogue which
> may yield the new insights we seek. (p. 8; my italics)

She invokes as exemplar Lacan's theory of 'the importance of "the unsaid
. . . that lies in the *holes* of the discourse" ', and his related belief that 'the
unconscious speaks as *something other* from within the speech of consciousness, which it undercuts or subverts', existing at a 'chaotic, preverbal' stage
beneath the externally 'regularized, rational order' (pp. 10, 24; my italics).

In psychoanalysis, apparently, what the patient doesn't tell you is the real give-away. As a follower of Lacan puts it, the psychoanalyst is only interested in the text's 'brutal silences, . . . blemishes, incongruities and neglected details' (p. 26).

Ignoring historical criticism, theatrical convention, genre, rhetoric, and Renaissance theories of literature, the Neo-Freudian critic approaches a non-realist literary form with expectations derived from realism and finds — incoherences. This is supposedly just like the psychoanalyst, who deduces what is really bothering the patient from omissions in the narrative of his or her inner life. (In any case the injunction to create an interpretation out of the silences – *ex lacunis, ex Lacanis* — gives the analyst a freedom of invention that raises major questions of relevance to the patient's case-history. That thought might well trouble doctors; to literary critics it merely offers more freedom.) It seems very dubious to apply this analogy to Elizabethan drama. The analyst's notes of extended conversations with the patient (or of the patient's monologues, rather), are not at all like the plays of Shakespeare, constructed in relative leisure over a long period (a total of 37 plays in a writing career of about 20 years), and with considerable planning. As I briefly showed in Chapter 2, Shakespeare's inventive treatment of his sources reveals a concern to create dramatic structures that will fulfil the criteria of genre and meet self-imposed demands of coherence (subject to theatrical conventions) in plot and motivation. Those are the dramatist's primary goals; secondary, though not easily separable, is his need to involve the spectators in the events represented, tragic or comic, arousing a complex range of feelings in response to character and issue. Nevo brusquely dismisses the notion of genre early on, listing the remarkable ingredients of the Romances in order to prove 'their defiance of common sense' (p. 3), their 'ungrammatical' nature compared to tragedy, with its 'masculine irresolvable either/or bind', and comedy, with its 'harmonizing feminine both/and' (p. 6). But it is very obvious that the remarkable ingredients listed by Nevo — shipwreck, separation, disguise, questing, reunion — are the basic narrative motifs of Greek romance, a genre that survived in unlikely places (such as medieval saints' lives and chivalric literature), and was rediscovered in the Renaissance. The influence of this genre on Elizabethan fiction has been long demonstrated, as has Shakespeare's frequent use of these structural motifs, from *Comedy of Errors* to *Twelfth Night* to *The Winter's Tale*.[27] Nevo praises 'the firm architectonic of most of the plays', saying that Shakespeare evolved forms 'based upon classical precept and example' (p. 4), which is perfectly true. But she conveniently fails to see that the Romances are equally 'classical', only deriving from a later period of antiquity, the Hellenistic adoption of patterns from the New Comedy for prose fiction.

It is regrettable that this historical dimension is ignored, but my argument against the kind of criticism that Nevo writes here is in any case not that it is non-historical, but nonsensical — taking the sense of the play to be the declared motives of action and reaction that Shakespeare gives his characters, and which are clearly accessible to the ordinary reader and theatregoer. Set against the manifest coherence of action and plot — all presented through largely recoverable theatrical conventions — the intention to discover 'rifts' seems like a game played without rules. The psychocritic, a specially enlightened Freudian or Lacanian, diagnoses a whole series of psychic disturbances in the play's characters as if revealed in 'dream and fantasy'. In order to deduce significance *ex silentiis* the critic must ignore the dramatist's explicit design and carefully-constructed settings of social and political conflict so as to focus, as Nevo puts it, on 'the overlooked detail, the marginal, the trifling or the trivial' (p. 22). The margin becomes the centre, and the centre is dispensed with, leaving a blank sheet on which the critic can invent a new play, with strikingly different emphases. Having put together the holes, the unspoken — which has to be seen as somehow 'subverting' the spoken, for the order of the day is not complementarity but radical opposition between the two levels (the usual simple binary model) — the critic must then interpret these discrepancies according to the Freudian-Lacanian paradigms. Ignoring the question of genre, Nevo treats Shakespeare's final Romances as four separate plays — indeed, any four plays would have served her turn equally well. Her goal is to find the 'informing or generating fantasy, or ensemble of fantasies, in each play' (p. 29).

It is worth noting at the outset that the essential stuff of Freudian literary critics is fantasy — presumably because patients referred to analysts have difficulty in dealing with reality — but that, in consequence, these critics regularly confuse the reality of the plays with the codified Freudian 'fantasy' plots. In *Pericles* (only partly by Shakespeare, of course, a point Nevo dismisses: p. 34), the terms of the competition to win Antiochus' daughter bind the suitors to solve a riddle correctly, or else be decapitated. Nevo is confident that 'Freudian symbologists will immediately identify a castration fantasy' in this plot (p. 37): but the rest of us see that unsuccessful suitors will have their *heads* chopped off, not their testes. The Freudian reading of texts in the terms of its own categories regularly substitutes fantasy for reality, lesser for greater. The recovery of Thaisa, wife to Pericles and mother to Marina, is said to be 'a compensatory birth or rebirth fantasy: out of the chest / coffin emerges a sweet-smelling "corse"' (p. 55). But as every reader or spectator of *Pericles* knows, the corpse moves, and speaks: it is alive! In the play's brothel scenes, Nevo writes, 'the metaphors are fantasies of injury, force, mutilation' (p. 57): but alas for poor Marina, they are neither metaphors nor fantasies but all too real, and imminent. *Cymbeline* is 'inundated by fantasies of dispersed and reassembled families' (p. 92): but no, these events actually happen to those families. Polixenes' remark about his nine-month visit at the outset of *The Winter's Tale* involves the number '9', which according to Freud *always* indicates '"the phantasy of pregnancy"' (p. 103): but no, Hermione is truly pregnant.

Prospero, similarly, is said to suffer from a 'fantasy of omnipotence' or domination (pp. 138, 150): but unless one is to reject the plot donnée of magic on which the whole play is built, he really *can* dominate man and nature with his art. As for Prospero disarming Ferdinand of his sword and setting him to chop logs, to the Freudian these are 'metaphorical castrations' expressing 'a possessive father's hostility to his usurper rival' (p. 135), for by the familiar Freudian licence in interpretation (that 'elasticity of interpretive rules', as Crews put it) 'in dreams, as we know, opposites obtain: Going is coming . . . log-chopping displaces a threat of castration' (p. 136). Since Prospero imposes 'log-bearing slavery' on Caliban, too, we may conclude that Prospero makes people chop firewood to allay his fears that they wish to castrate him — rather clever of him, since he can thereby kill two birds with (or, instead of) two stones, dispelling anxieties and warming his cave at the same time! As for the 'sunburn'd sicklemen' in the masque, they give 'intimations of mortality, and of castration' (p. 148) — to men only, one assumes, noting again the phallocentrism in so many of Freud's theories.

Each of the four Romances is distorted to fit Nevo's neo-Freudian template. The fact that Pericles twice refers to himself as 'son' to Antiochus reveals to Nevo that he is 'in the grip of the oedipal guilt which Freud . . . characterizes as "the pure culture of the death instinct"' (p. 42). (Freud's pessimistic-determinist belief in a human 'death instinct' is of course the most dubious of his later theories: Sulloway 1983, pp. 393, 404–14.) *Pericles*, like so many Romances, involves journeys by sea, storms, shipwrecks, separations, reunions, so it is no surprise that the hero should address the storm which has just cast him ashore:

> Yet cease your ire, you angry stars of heaven!
> Wind, rain, and thunder. . . .
> Alas, the seas hath cast me on the rocks. . . .
>
> (2.1.1ff)

Nevo ingeniously Freudianises the speech as an allegory of family conflicts. The 'wrathfully punitive sky elements' are paternal, the ocean maternal, and Pericles is 'a son whose rebellious urge against a parental couple — sky-father and sea-mother — has turned inward against himself' (pp. 45–6). It is Nevo, of course, who imports the parental symbols and adds the further idea of self-hatred, a projection or imposition onto the text which the psychocritic regularly performs. The fact that in a twelve-line speech by Pericles we find 'sun' in one line and 'son' three lines later prompts her to this critical flight: 'If we reverse the son/sun homonym, moreover, the tempting/frightening possibility of usurping the father figure comes again into view' (p. 51). But what possible warrant do we have for doing such a thing? Either texts have an integrity constructed by a writer with definite aims in mind, or they are truly random collections of signifiers which critics are free to arrange in any pattern that serves their own obsession. According to Lacan, Freud discovered '"that the displacement of the signifier determines the subjects in their acts"' (p. 52) — but who displaces the signifier here? And why? These 'phonemic ambiguities (son/sun)', Nevo goes on, 'may serve as cover for a considerable urge to self-assertion' (p. 52), that is, a 'cover' or 'screen' for what Pericles is incapable of stating directly. He would really like to be able to usurp his father: so the challenge to the diagnostician is to discover why the main protagonist should be *concealing* such urges. (Incidentally, Pericles' father never appears: either he is dead, or his son has usurped him — which, to the Freudian, may be the same: at all events, he now needs no 'screen'.)

Nevo's intense, if fruitless scrutiny of Pericles is typical of the psycho-critic's interest in one character at a time, for 'just as dreams are always about the dreamer, so there is always a central ego for a play to be about' (p. 67). But if a play is the dream of one of its characters, how are we to account for the presence of other people, each apparently acting with freedom of will and autonomy? Psychoanalytic criticism cannot deal with all the characters in a play (not all of them fit its templates); but it can relate a surprising number of them to the main figure (surprising since nobody else so far has related them), by a process known as 'splitting'. In the words of André Green, a follower of Lacan, '"in the dream, when the dreamer's representation becomes overloaded, the dreamer splits it into two and sets up another character to represent, separately, one or more of his characteristics or affects"' (*cit.* Nevo, p. 56). The analyst must then discover what caused the representation to become 'overloaded' (a metaphor from electricity? If so, echoing Freud's notion of hysteria as a 'short circuit'). This seems to me (no believer in psychoanalysis) a bizarre theory, but I can see that it gives the psychocritic still more freedom of manoeuvre. In Pericles' case, Nevo confidently states,

> the classic recourse, in psychoanalytic theory, of the maternally fixated libido is a debased sexual object — prostitute or courtesan. The trans-formation of Marina into such a figure liberates sexual fantasy, the brothel scenes providing a screen through which the deeply repressed sensuality of Pericles can find release. (p. 57)

But the desire to fulfil a Freudian paradigm makes the critic take her eye off the play. Marina is precisely *not* transformed into 'a debased sexual object': she is sold to a brothel-keeper, yet her remarkable combination of virtue and eloquence preserves her chastity (4.2, 4.6). And, of course, Pericles goes nowhere near the brothel, has no idea that his daughter is there. The psychocritic's 'description' is pure invention, an eagerness to apply the Freudian template blinding her to the play itself.

Nevo does pay occasional attention to the plot, saying that 'Pericles, himself absent from the stage, . . . is replaced by these fantasized figures . . .' (p. 57). But what sense does 'replaced' have in that sentence? Replaced not by Shakespeare but by the critic, in order to make up the neo-Freudian formula. Nevo believes it essential 'for both Marina's parents to be sexually in abeyance . . . while the screen fantasies of the brothel scenes are taking place. The psychic burden is shifted, so to speak, to the shoulders of the surrogate figure' (p. 58). But if Marina is a 'depersonalized sex object' on which Pericles' 'deeply repressed and traumatized libido' can release itself, why is it that *the man who visits the brothel is actually Lysimachus, governor of Mytilene*? Nevo tendentiously describes Lysimachus as 'a split character, indeterminately ravisher and protector' (p. 59), but the indeterminacy is hers. The play is quite clear: Lysimachus is a customer of the brothel who is converted to virtue by Marina, whom he subsequently marries. But having diagnosed a 'split', Nevo exploits it:

> this split, or anomaly, is our clue. For if the dream burden has been displaced to other figures in the way Green describes [*assuming that Green's approach is at all suitable to drama*], and we can read Lysimachus as a representation, or extension of Pericles, then the split in Lysimachus is the unconscious split in Pericles. (*ibid.*)

But what would this hypothesis achieve? It would be reductive, and tautologous, for Lysimachus would then be suffering from the same 'deeply repressed and traumatic libido' as Pericles, the only difference being that Pericles retreats, monk-like, into 'his mourning and his melancholy' (p. 57), while Lysimachus goes out to get a whore. His reality is to find a princess and a wife; Pericles' reality is to be reunited with both wife and daughter: what fantasies might be represented by these events in the play?

If the 'splitting' manoeuvre seems oddly redundant in *Pericles*, Nevo makes more of it in the other Romances. In *Cymbeline* she follows Murray Schwarz in diagnosing a '"tense and precarious balance"' in the psyche of Posthumus between 'alternative sexual modes'. So, 'by following Posthumus carefully through the play' — a rationale for old-fashioned one-at-a-time character criticism — we will find in him '"the tyranny of the superego which would split the psyche into diametric opposites, one part that worships and another that defiles"' (p. 74). If we do follow him through the play, though, we find that Posthumus appears in only 8 of the 26 scenes into which *Cymbeline* is conventionally divided, and — a remarkable plot-feature that shows all too clearly the influence of Greek romance — is separated from his newly-married wife, Imogen, between the first scene and the last. But the psychocritic can easily overcome this deficiency by diagnosing 'an inhibition of desire on Posthumus' part' which *splits itself*, note well, into 'two proxy suitors, the fastidious Iachimo and the unspeakable Cloten', who are both '"aspects or projections of Posthumus' psyche"', as Schwarz put it, 'for whom they substitute' (pp. 74–5). But, as with 'replaced' in *Pericles*, they only 'substitute' within the formulae of neo-Freudian criticism, always striving to reproduce and so validate its own limited plots. Cloten is said to represent 'pure sexual drive' (surely he is never as admirable as that?), while Iachimo stands for 'aim-

inhibited fantasy', a 'lust of the eyes' (pp. 75, 77). However, reference to
the scene (2.2) where Iachimo creeps out of the trunk in which he has
hidden in order to observe some intimate details of Imogen which will
enable him to win his wager with Posthumus, shows little, if any lust (he is
more concerned to record every detail of the room, to make his story
of having slept with her more plausible), and the critic who describes
Posthumus as being 'sexually aroused' by Iachimo's story in 2.4 (p. 78) is
similarly adding a sexuality that is not in the text. Posthumus is indignant,
hurt, but not lubricious. Later Cloten is said to represent 'the repressed
libido' in Posthumus, Iachimo his 'repressive superego' (p. 87), a typically
Freudian fragmentation of character into abstractions and allegories. But
although she emulates Freud by always pursuing the sexual element, Nevo
has forgotten Freud's theory that the role of the super-ego is to check and
control the ego. Here she attributes to the super-ego a voyeuristic desire,
trying not to quell but to arouse the sexuality of the ego: 'Posthumus . . .
is precipitated into his Cloten self, his unreconstructed . . . demeaning
sensuality' by Iachimo (p. 78). If I were Posthumus I would go and see an
analyst, happy in the knowledge that I would thereby be helping, as André
Green puts it, not the text's author ' "but the analyst-interpreter, who helps
himself through seeking to comprehend the emotions the text awakens
in him. Thus the patient, the potential analysand, is . . . the analyst
himself" ' (cit. Nevo, p. 26). Thus psychoanalytical criticism becomes a
mode of self-therapy. (The critic, Nevo adds, as if unhappy about the
implications of this role-reversal, is 'analyst too, and the text analysand'.)

Never mind who is analysing whom, wherever the Freudian looks in
Cymbeline, characters have sexual problems. Imogen is struggling 'to resolve
the ambivalence of untried sexuality' (p. 82). Since we know that, 'in the
symbology of dreams, crowns and wreaths, metamorphoses of that most
fertile of all figures, the circle, are genital displacements upwards' (p. 50)
— as it were, translating the groin to the head — then Imogen's declared
preference for even Posthumus' 'meanest garment' over Cloten and 'all
the hairs' on his head (2.3.129ff) now 'becomes explicable' (after four
centuries, for the first time) as a 'displacement upwards of the body-image'
(here, his underpants), which is 'a protection from the recognition, which
it also divulges, of a lively desire' (p. 81). But why should Imogen wish to
protect herself from this recognition? Everything she says about Posthumus
manifests her constant desire for him:

> I would have broke mine eye-strings, cracked them, but
> To look upon him. . . .
>   Ere I could tell him
> How I would think on him at certain hours
> Such thoughts and such . . .   (1.3.17ff)

— they were parted. Imogen has no need to hide, nor we to seek, anything
other than her freely-expressed sexuality.

Nevo at one point mocks an older style of Freudian criticism, 'the well-known parlour game of Hunting the Phallic symbol' (p. 18): but she plays it herself.[28] Not only are all circles 'upward displacements' of a genital instinct, but as Iachimo creeps out of his trunk in Imogen's bedroom 'the phallic flame of the taper is itself a voyeur as it "Bows toward her, and would under-peep her lids"' (p. 77). (Have you ever seen a phallus behave like that?) As for Cloten, he is beheaded, 'his "clotpole" sent down the stream "in embassy to his mother" (4.2.185), in a strange parody', Nevo informs us, 'of pagan fertility rituals. As a consequence, the Queen [his mother], bereft, so to speak, of her male organ, declines and dies' (p. 86). Readers who missed the incest motif must be kicking themselves! It is all too obvious to Professor Nevo, who now promotes 'Posthumus as a proxy [psychocritics may 'substitute' or 'replace' any character, ad libitum] for Cymbeline' — the father of Imogen — 'in the latter's absence', thus making this a play about 'a father's deeply repressed desire for his daughter' (p. 94). Since Posthumus is Imogen's husband, and they were involuntarily separated, the reference to incest is wholly fictitious. It would be hard to find a better example of the critic dragging a Freudian concept, willynilly, into a literary work. Pursuing her interpretation, Nevo rebukes Murray Schwarz for declaring the play a failure because Shakespeare lacks '"the psychic courage to admit that the fears and aggressions he invokes in Cymbeline reside in a father, and that their object is an unconsciously harbored mother imago"'. This, she comments, 'is absurd since either it postulates a Shakespeare who could only know what he knew by having undergone a course in the psychoanalytic theory of the Oedipus complex', or else it forgets that Shakespeare had written Hamlet ten years earlier (p. 92). One welcomes these lines as proof that Nevo has broken with the tradition of psychoanalysing the author; but on the next page we find her speculating on the fact that 'Shakespeare's mother died the year before Cymbeline' was written, that a grand-daughter was born to him at this time, and that he returned to Stratford after a 'twenty-year absence in London' (p. 93: a misleading description of his links with Stratford, to which he regularly returned.) So, behind the play, she detects 'a troubled author whose preoccupations the foreground stories screen, and while screening reveal . . .' (p. 94). Not revealing enough for Nevo to say what they were, but incestuous preoccupations, it seems, somehow involving his mother / daughter / grand-daughter in some unspecified way. Lucky the critic who has access to the author's psyche, and one who lived four hundred years ago, too.

The Winter's Tale needs no such critical exertions: Leontes is evidently suffering from 'infantile fears of isolation . . . for which the accusation of adultery is a cover', motivated by 'the archaic rage of a sibling rivalry for an undivided mother' (p. 105). In other words (theory A), Leontes casts his wife Hermione in the role of mother, with himself as the rival to his son Mamillius. 'There is', Nevo writes, 'in every delusion a grain of truth' (which grain? we wonder, and who can find it?). So, she goes on, Hermione does indeed 'betray Leontes, with her children' (p. 106) — that is, by loving them more than she loves her husband. But two pages later we are told (theory B) that Leontes loves Mamillius and identifies with him, since 'they are both ousted rivals for the mother's love' (p. 108). But either Leontes hates his son or he loves him; and either Hermione loves her children or she hates them. Which is it? To the Freudians, plot is some kind of flexible material which can be bent in any direction they please, with readers supposedly unable to remember what they have just been told.

Prospero, too, has infantile fantasies, only in his case (deluded fellow!) he believes that his magic gives him power over the people on the island, and over nature. 'Such grandiose omnipotence, psychoanalytic theory tells us, is a defense against its obverse, the infantile terror of total dependency, therefore it requires the fantasied destruction of maternal power' (p. 138). But there is, unfortunately for this theory, 'a notable absence, or repression of mothers in The Tempest' (p. 139 — a good example of finding meaning in the 'gaps' of a text), so the critic has to invent some. Nevo actually suggests that we see 'both Ariel and Miranda as fantasied beneficent surrogate feminine presences' (pp. 138–9): that is, Prospero, like Lear, makes his daughter(s) his mother(s). Whatever personae the dramatist has carelessly failed to supply for the Freudian plot, the critic can provide by substitution, inversion, or splitting. But any one identification may be limiting, so Nevo promptly adds that Ariel also represents 'the urge towards sublimation, and Caliban the drift towards regression — a Shakespearean Eros and Thanatos respectively — and it is the struggle between these two cardinal impulses that structures' the play (p. 139). Besides the deadening reification and abstraction involved here, which would reduce the play to allegory, we must protest that there is nothing of Eros in Ariel, and little of Thanatos (elsewhere associated with Oedipal conflicts) in Caliban — whom Nevo subsequently sees as the libido (pp. 140–1). Jacques Barzun has said that 'nothing is more impalpable than the Id', and Frederick Crews has described it as 'that amorphous and ambiguous concept'[29] — in any case, to Freud the id was before language. Caliban is such a superb creation, a natural savage, marvellously malevolent, marvellously eloquent, stupidly impressed by the drunken butler and his mate — who that cares about drama would wish to reduce him to the id? But Nevo goes on to see Antonio as 'Prospero's alter ego' (they are brothers, of course), who, 'like other sibling rivals in Shakespeare, . . . are split, antithetical, decomposed parts of a psychic whole' (p. 144). But in what sense is Prospero lacking in qualities that Antonio could give him? And what kind of creature would the composite Prospero-Antonio be? Nevo's confident pronouncements do not screen the fact that her imposition of Freudianism on the plays fatally distorts their structure and meaning.

III

The liberty of interpretation that Freudian critics appropriate to themselves can only result in a deformation of Shakespeare. Relationships between characters, political conflict, social discord, the clash between ambition and legitimacy — all these are swept by the board to make way for the stereotypes of psychoanalytic theory. In a book with the ominous title *Dream Works. Lovers and Families in Shakespeare's Plays*, Kay Stockholder sets out a thorough-going application of the method used several times by Ruth Nevo, a theory 'that permits one to assume that the protagonist of a literary work is analogous to the figure that we identify as ourselves' — let us hope with good reason! — 'when we awaken from dreaming' (p. ix). D.G. James, in *The Dream of Learning* (1937), thought that *The Tempest* was dreamt by Prospero, an idiosyncratic theory in an otherwise illuminating book. Without any justification, theoretical or textual, Stockholder systematically sees all the plays as having been *dreamt by the protagonists*. The play, then, is a dream that tells us what the protagonist is suffering from — by any criteria, an amazing idea. In general, she writes, '*any* figure may be regarded as the protagonist' (p. 19). If we make Claudius the protagonist of *Hamlet*, 'Hamlet then becomes a distanced representation of Claudius' incomplete filial drama, through whom he expresses his fearful desire to be punished' for his evil ambition (pp. 19–20). This manoeuvre illustrates Freud's principle that dreams are 'the imaginary gratification of unconscious wishes' (p. 6), and it is loyally Freudian in ascribing an inverted Oedipal complex to Claudius. But unfortunately it makes complete nonsense of the play, since Hamlet is not a figment of Claudius' dream, but a real character. If a critic's 'organising principle' consists of abandoning the whole design of action and motive, then it is a principle that destroys what it — presumably — set out to illuminate.

Stockholder believes that any situation, or any character, can have been 'dreamt' by the designated 'protagonist', however tenuous their role in the play. In *The Comedy of Errors*, 'though absent from most of the action' — he appears in the first and last scenes — *non obstante*, 'Aegeon is the figure around whom the action turns and for whom it has most consequence' (p. 27). What of the brothers Antipholus, their servants Dromio, assorted wives, mistresses, money-lenders, constables, and all the confusions of mistaken identity? They are surely central — if the word is to have any meaning — and Aegeon is truly marginal, the long-lost father whose reappearance in the final scene (the Greek romance, again) permits the multiple recognitions that resolve all the plot's crises. For *The Merchant of Venice* Stockholder elevates to the central position a character who does not appear in the play at all. The 'underlying connections' — that is, within the psychoanalytical template — 'are best revealed by taking Portia's father as dreamer, since his power initiates the plot configuration' of the three caskets. The fact that he is dead might deter another critic, but not one in possession of this 'organising principle': 'By dreaming himself dead [her father] has removed himself from the immediate experience of conflicting desires and fears, and has idealised his own image' (p. 33). But, we want to know, 'how can anyone *dream* himself dead? Does that mean he actually committed suicide? Or is he just dreaming and will wake up at the end of the play?' Both questions would be fatuous, but Stockholder actually answers the first of them, ascribing to Portia's father repressed incestuous desires, from which he 'withdrew into death', so escaping the conflict, but trying to control his daughter's sexuality from beyond the grave. The ordinary reader might protest that the caskets are designed to make sure that the man who wins Portia won't be motivated by desire for her money; and that in any case Portia is perfectly able to manipulate this condition to her own advantage — indeed, few characters seem less likely to be under anyone's control than Portia.

It is as if psychocritics have been issued with an instruction sheet alerting them to some standard issues:

> Indicate the main neuroses represented in this play; identify repressed traumas, displacement mechanisms, Oedipal complexes and their inversion, references to the primal scene, anal-oral-phallic fixations, and the patients' fear of their own sexuality. Remember that the unspoken is usually more significant than the spoken, for, as one of our colleagues has observed, out of the succession of linked signifiers which constitute the literary text, 'the unconscious signified rises . . . from the gulf or absence in which it resides . . . in order to indicate, by veiling it, what needs to be hidden.'[30]

Stockholder diligently obeys these injunctions to the letter, finding the same patterns recurring over and over (so the theory must be correct). When a dream becomes overloaded, as we know, 'the dreamer splits into two and sets up another character to represent, separately, one or more of his characteristics or affects.'[31] So Stockholder finds that Edgar divides from his 'sadistically moral' self the 'devil-ridden Poor Tom' (p. 18), presumably since the pressure of being 'a sanctimonious, self-righteous person' (p. 125) is too great. Later, though, 'Lear in Kent's disguise' becomes 'a semi-split dream figure' — we cannot admit this term: a figure is either split or not! — embodying moral authority and wilfulness, while Lear 'also partially splits the moral Edgar. In his own person Edgar betrays an underlying association of moral authority with a cruelty that participates in Goneril's and Regan's sexual sadism, while in the disguise as Poor Tom Lear associates moral authority with a sexualized masochism' (*ibid.*). That is, Edgar represents the sadism of the id which, according to Freud's ad hoc and flexible argumentation, sometimes surfaces in the super-ego (Ellenberger 1970, p. 516). The pattern is neat, we must admit, in its balancing of sado-masochist tendencies, but how can Lear 'dream' himself into the roles of Kent and Edgar, when they are simultaneously on stage with him? This begins to sound like a play in which one man plays many parts. (Perhaps Peter Greenaway got the idea for *Prospero's Books* here?) Anyone with ordinary access to the text will have difficulty in finding either sexual sadism in Edgar or sexualised masochism (a tautology?) in Poor Tom — or is it Lear who is dreaming the disguise of Poor Tom?

All the 'dreamer-protagonists', we discover, are sexually disturbed, and devise elaborate strategies for evading the consequences of their psychopathology. Take the incestuous (would-be, would-be-not) fathers, for instance: what extraordinary lengths they go to! Portia's father has not only dreamed himself dead to avoid his incestuous feelings for Portia, but he 'reveals in the two figures into which he splits himself, each of whom becomes the other's *alter ego*, his reason for obliterating his own figure'. So great is his 'negative sense of himself' — he must have a truly vicious super-ego — that he divides himself on the one hand into Shylock, to embody 'his desire for power and wealth with murderous hatred, greed, and . . . the reification of values', and on the other into Antonio, thus substituting 'a homo-erotic love choice for an incestuous one, a strategy to avoid the frightening feelings associated with heterosexual love' (pp. 33–4). Yet this attempted concealment was unavailing before the psychoanalyst's penetrating gaze.

If fathers have problems with their daughters, sons have even greater difficulties with their begetters. The first questions to ask of a dreamer-protagonist are 'who's his father?' and 'what has he done to his father?' — or, 'what has his father done to him?' This is not always easy to answer, since Shakespeare neglected to fit everyone out with parents, yet, with a bit of ingenuity, substitutes can be found. Othello has provided himself with one 'by means of splitting and distancing the paternal image into the abstract authority of the Venetian State' (p. 84). *King Lear* seems, to begin with, the kind of play that some feminists complain about, being rather short on mothers. (The three boy-actors playing the daughters might well have exhausted the stock of female performers in Shakespeare's company, one objects, before realising that to reason thus is to fall into the error of assuming that all plays *ought* to include mothers!) This play, we are told, disguises its contents 'by eliminating an actual mother', and shows Lear struggling with 'the world of infantile strife itself' (p. 146) — having made, as the Fool puts it, his daughters his mothers. But at the same time — a vertiginous effect, opening up glimpses into an unexplored realm of personality-transformation — Lear, 'by casting himself as father to all women figures . . . renders all sexuality incestuous' (p. 118). To be at the same time father *and* son. . . . 'To take't again, perforce'.

If this seems a rare and difficult transformation, other characters reveal a straightforward Oedipal fixation, despite occasional complications. By the end of his play Hamlet 'finally succeeds in eliminating paternal figures that bar his way to both his mother and Ophelia' (p. 40). To make a boringly obvious comment, Polonius is not a father-figure but a father (of someone else); Hamlet kills him by accident (hoping it's the King), and not to gain access to Ophelia (whom he has already rejected), and who of course, by the end of the play, is already 'eliminated'. The corollary of this whole extraordinary shuffling-around of character and motive is that it is 'Hamlet's fear of assuming his maturity' that 'has placed Claudius on the throne' (p. 40).[32] So there would have been no need to murder Old Hamlet at all! Macbeth wears his Oedipal kit with a difference:

> Having defined his desires for becoming father and King as illegitimate, Macbeth has reversed the classical Oedipal paradigm in which the son in order to marry the mother wishes to kill the father. Rather, he has married the mother, and included the implied sexuality in the project of killing his father. (p. 103)

This would make Lady Macbeth his mother, Duncan his father, an odd couple indeed. Truly, nothing is what it seems. But one mother is not enough for Stockholder, who also evokes the witches, and Hecate (if these scenes are indeed Shakespeare's) as 'a diabolically defined version of an offended mother' (p. 104). Now we know what makes Macbeth so murderous!

And so the book continues, to its own satisfaction, interpreting everything in terms of the same limited series of motives and goals. 'Ridicule is the test of truth', Shaftesbury wrote, and I have occasionally used ridicule as a way of exposing the absurd assumptions of this critical method, and its grotesque results. In its dedication to the Freudian location of sexuality as the motive force of human action Stockholder's book sees everything in Shakespeare as one form or another of malfunctioning — guilt, repression, fear, self-loathing. In this obsessive pathological probing, simple truths about plot and character become distorted, the language of the plays misinterpreted, often perversely. In one chapter, called ' "Blanket of the Dark": Stealthy Lovers in *Macbeth*', Stockholder somehow associates that couple with guilty or furtive love-making, ruining one of Shakespeare's most original metaphors in the process: 'neither our eyes nor Macbeth's peep through the blanketed dark to the invisible bedroom in which Macbeth and Lady Macbeth consummate their love' (p. 111). But why should we, and why should it be 'stealthy' if they are legally married? We can only conclude that Stockholder has misunderstood Shakespeare's bold metaphor for Lady Macbeth's invocation of night to conceal her murderous act, seeing it in terms of another form of concealment much more interesting to Freudians. So she writes of Antony that he, 'in contrast to Hamlet or Macbeth, . . . is not in pursuit of furtive pleasures while dodging parental spying eyes or hiding beneath a blanket of the dark' (pp. 148–9). (Since when was Hamlet chasing 'furtive pleasures'?) Evidently Freudians can take metaphors literally, if it suits them, at whatever cost to the imagination.

As for symbolism, phallicism is everywhere. A reference to a child's 'muzzled dagger' in *The Winter's Tale* suggests to Stockholder 'the erotically violent passions' hidden in childhood (p. 189). Seeing himself as Tarquin, Macbeth 'interprets his dagger as a bloody phallus, with which he violently penetrates the equivocating and seductive woman' (p. 111). (Who is he killing, Duncan or Lucrece?) Lear's ' "bare, forked animal" . . . calls oblique attention to his phallus' (p. 126) — Poor Tom's, presumably (yet the Fool says he has 'reserved a blanket, else we had been all shamed'); while Hamlet's reference to the ' "act' can only be to Gertrude's sexual act. . . . That act is associated with the day of judgment, on which, like a phallus, "foul deeds will rise" ' (p. 55). To the Freudians, anything that rises, stands, falls, or is kept confined, must be a phallic symbol. As in *The Tempest*, for instance:

> The image of Prospero's 'princely trunk' depleted by Antonio's ivy and of Ariel's imprisonment in Sycorax's cloven pine both carry phallic suggestions. The first one associates a homosexual encounter with evil, depletion, and impotence. . . . In the second image Ariel becomes as Prospero's phallus, or more precisely his phallic potency, refusing to yield to woman's pleasure and refusing to release the seed that will propagate more Calibans. She 'in her most unmitigable rage' imprisons the phallus, which will neither yield to orgasm nor lose its erection. . . . (p. 205)

— a remarkably uncomfortable state. But it explains why Ariel, having embodied Prospero's 'phallic potency', is invisible to everyone but Prospero. Yet Prospero's 'separated' organ sometimes wants 'premature release', thus threatening his self-control (p. 206) — with *ejaculatio praecox*, evidently.

Such distortions of the text to their own preoccupations are common-place in Freudian Shakespearians. What continues to surprise, though, is their unawareness of the repetitiveness of their project, how it reduces so many diverse characters to the same lowest common denominator, sexuality and its disorders. In the process it ignores essential elements of plot, characterisation, and theatrical convention. Portia must be a sadist, for 'from the very beginning she could have saved Antonio with the legal argument she later uses, but instead manipulates Shylock into showing his worst side'. Being one of those 'avenging and punitive women who enjoy humiliating men' she next turns 'the sadistic edge of her displeasure towards Bassanio', and enjoys watching him 'suffer in the impossible moral dilemma she has created through the strategy of the exchanged rings' (p. 32). Of course, the issues of contracts and reciprocity have a much more serious function in the play than Stockholder imagines. *As You Like It*, she complains, 'provides no explanation' for Rosalind's 'continued disguise. There is no apparent reason for her to conceal her identity from Orlando, except for her pleasure' in her own superiority (p. 37). This is to write as if one could judge any character, at any point in the action, simply in terms of modern interpersonal relationships, as if to say, 'I wouldn't behave like that!' The most banal twentieth-century motivations are ascribed to

characters in Elizabethan drama, ignoring the author's design, conventions
of genre or staging, and a whole range of relevant social attitudes. Instead
of seeing Hamlet's outrage at his mother's speedy marriage to his uncle
as sign of the normal contemporary definition of such relationships as
incestuous, Stockholder ascribes to Hamlet the view that 'sexuality in
itself' is 'the source of pollution' in the play (pp. 40, 55). Troilus manages
better, 'concealing his sexual disgust beneath his anticipation of sensual
delight' (p. 71). Only the Freudian can spot the disgust.

And so they line up, these poor people, to have their deficiencies
exposed and diagnosed. Angelo's 'hatred and fear of sexuality' has made
him avoid Mariana (p. 77). Isabella, too, 'has denied her sexuality'
(p. 79). Othello, also, 'struggles with the fears and anxieties around
heterosexuality' (p. 85), but in vain. Out of his 'eroticized self-hatred'
Othello 'generates the "ocular proof" of Cassio and Desdemona copulating
which in turn leads him to release his violent patterns' (p. 89). He is not
the only guilty party, for 'Desdemona's unconscious desire for Othello's
potential violence generates his suspicion' (p. 92: as if he should think,
'Ha! She wants me to be violent to her! What might that mean?').[33] In the
event Othello attaches 'homosexual eroticism' to Iago, economically fusing
his 'homosexual drives into the heterosexual love-death drama' by casting
Iago as the destructive power (p. 94), representing as he does 'Othello's
fulfilment of the homosexual desires that he morally condemns' (p. 97).
Not surprisingly, perhaps, Iago, too, suffers from self-hatred (p. 95), while
Edgar, split as he is into sadistic and masochistic halves, indulges in 'self-
laceration' (p. 126) — both characters have hyperactive super-egos, it
would seem. Cleopatra, too, being generated by Antony as a 'deadly
serpentine power' (p. 157), and representing 'the slime of sexuality' which
Antony, by his suicide, prefers to 'the paternal ghost' of Caesar (p. 162) —
so avoiding an Oedipal conflict — has her own problems with sex. She
loves Antony, but in order to draw him closer 'she betrays him, and finally
evades her fear of her own deadly sexuality by having him *die into her
language*' (p. 163; my italics) — whatever that might mean. Leontes has
'incestuous feelings for mothers and daughters' (p. 194 — presumably she
means '*his* mothers and daughters'), while Prospero manages 'to repress his
own passions for Miranda' by a 'definition of himself as magus' (p. 202).

IV

If a critical method produces, in an oeuvre as rich and varied as
Shakespeare's, so many repetitive, reductive readings, then it declares its
own deficiencies. This is not a matter of the intelligence of the critic who
uses it, since the method levels out not only the plays but the critics.
Stockholder is thorough, not deviating from the given paradigms into any

more unusual fields. In *Shakespeare's Ghost-Writers* Marjorie Garber is much sharper, more widely-read, but the total effect of her knowledge, when applied along Freudian templates, is just as reductive as Stockholder's. The psychocritical parts of this book are devoted to *Macbeth* and *Hamlet*. For the first, her starting-point is Macduff's remark on having discovered Duncan's corpse:

> Approach the chamber, and destroy your sight
> With a new Gorgon.   (2.3.71f)

The Variorum edition notes that Shakespeare probably got his knowledge of the Gorgon from Ovid's *Metamorphoses*, 5.189–210. Professor Garber gets hers from Freud's 1922 essay on 'Medusa's Head', where he states that 'The proliferation of swarming snakes compensates for and covers over the fear of castration', namely by 'a doubling or multiplication of the genital symbol' (Garber 1987, p. 15). (The same argument was used for 'Three Blind Mice'.)

Ordinary readers might be forgiven for thinking that Macduff's words mean 'the horror of this sight will turn you to stone', and others might be surprised to think that these one-and-a-half lines carry any substantial import for the play. But Garber unites feminism and psychoanalysis to assert that 'gender undecidability and anxiety about gender identification and gender roles are at the center of *Macbeth* — and of Macbeth' (*ibid.*, p. 97). The passages she has in mind — apart from the fact that the three witches have beards (1.3.45ff) — occur in the scene where Lady Macbeth tries to shame her husband into murdering Duncan by accusing him of cowardice (1.7.39ff). His reply is to assert

> I dare do all that may become a man;
> Who dares do more is none.   (46f)

— which means, 'beyond a certain point acts of daring may become inhuman'. This is the sense in which Lady Macbeth takes it in her scornful reply:

> What beast was't then
> That made you break this enterprise to me?
> When you durst do it, then you were a man;
> And to be more than what you were, you would
> Be so much more the man.   (47ff)

Her riddling and specious reply also takes 'man' in the sense of 'virile, courageous', and neither he nor she uses the word as a comment on gender as such. The issue is not one of biology, nor of socio-cultural conditioning, but of ethics. In the Renaissance 'courage', in the sense of being able to perform violent acts, was thought to be a male prerogative. So again, at the banquet when Macbeth alone can see Banquo's ghost, his wife rebukes him for his apparent cowardice with the taunt: 'Are you a man?', and he answers: 'Ay, and a bold one, that dare look on that / Which might appall the devil' (3.4.57–9). But to her his 'flaws and starts' are more suitable for 'A woman's story at a winter's fire, / Authoriz'd by her grandam' (62ff) 'What? quite unmann'd in folly?' (72) she sneers. To Macbeth the opposition man/no-man distinguishes between humanity and inhumanity; to Lady Macbeth it opposes courage and cowardice: Garber's references to 'gender undecidability' and 'anxiety' are wholly beside the point.

Interestingly enough, several feminist critics emphasise this fact. Joan Klein writes that Lady Macbeth epitomises 'the sixteenth-century belief that women are passive, men active: "nature made man more strong and couragiouse, the woman more weake fearefull and scrupulouse" . . .' (Klein 1980, p. 244). Sir Thomas Elyot's words, in *The Defence of Good Women* (1540), show the common idea that acts of violence can only be performed by men. Yet, as Klein puts it, despite her wishes, 'Lady Macbeth is never unsexed in the only way she wanted to be unsexed — able to act with the cruelty she ignorantly and perversely identified with male strength' (*ibid.*, p. 250). Linda Woodbridge also takes Macbeth's 'Who dares do more is none' to show that he sees 'pity and compassion as human rather than feminine attributes; pitilessness is not masculine but subhuman' (Woodbridge 1984, p. 170). As she perceptively notes,

> When Shakespeare's female characters express a wish to be men, it is almost always to shame some man into taking action; and they usually pervert the meaning of manhood to exclude pity and compassion, on the illogical principle that if women are compassionate, men cannot be.

As Woodbridge shows, the desire to suppress women's natural pity usually figures in the argument that if a tenderhearted woman can abandon pity, then a man, having a 'less developed' sense, ought to find it easier to suspend compassion.

> This is Lady Macbeth's line; its context in *Macbeth* establishes it as a villain's argument. Shakespeare usually sees something monstrous about a woman who wishes she were a man. (p. 200)

Those of his women who permanently abandon the feminine model of 'weak, tender, pitying vulnerability' are seen as 'dehumanized, warped, monstrous, "fiend-like"' (*ibid.*, p. 216).

These comments valuably remind us that the issue here is ethical, not psychosexual. Yet Marjorie Garber, ruthlessly Freudian — ruthless in ignoring the sense of the text — insists that what Macbeth's lines really express is his 'fear of castration' (Garber 1987, p. 108). She bases her argument on Freud's 'reading of the Medusa head', now said to refer to 'a fearful sighting of the female genitals' (p. 97). This contradicts her earlier linking of it with 'fears of castration', but in Freudian interpretation penises may be multiplied to compensate either for the presence of one, or the absence of any in the dreamer. (I still find it hard to imagine how a woman might experience castration fears.) For Freud, notoriously enough, women are seriously disadvantaged by lacking a penis, indeed he even speculated that nature's oversight as regards women could have disastrous effects on men, too. So he 'connected', as Garber puts it, Leonardo da Vinci's supposed 'homosexuality to his desire to see his mother's penis, and his "disgust" at the appalling discovery that she lacks one' (p. 121).[34] This is all fictive, needless to say, another instance of a Freudian obsession cloning itself on to otherwise intelligent followers. But in any case, we might ask, what has all this to do with *Macbeth*? Well, another Freud theory was that dislocated body parts in dreams, such as severed heads, also show 'the castration complex', and this play, Garber notes, includes the severed heads of Macdonwald and Macbeth (p. 105). But now she falls into the trap that always faces Freudians, of reducing everything to fantasy. What the ordinary theatregoer can tell her is that these are real heads, not imaginary ones, and for most people decapitation is more horrible — or at least, more terminal — than castration. According to Garber, and Freud, the representation of Medusa's hair by snakes in fact serves 'as a mitigation of the horror, for they replace the penis, the absence of which is the cause of the horror' (*ibid.*). Some people might find this more horrible, but to Freud, aspiring towards producing a scientific discipline, it was what he portentously affirmed to be a 'technical rule' that 'a multiplication of penis symbols signifies castration'. Who can argue with that?

The question of whether Freud was writing about men, or women, or both, seems to be settled by the following quotations that Garber makes from his 1922 essay: '"The sight of Medusa's head makes the spectator stiff with terror, turns him into stone"', which to Freud constituted a striking '"transformation of affect! For becoming stiff means an erection. Thus in the original situation it offers consolation to the spectator: he is still in possession of the penis and the stiffening reassures him of the fact"' (p. 106). By this token Macduff, if he has truly seen a Gorgon or a Medusa's head, should have an erection, which an enterprising neo-Freudian director could easily represent (or simulate). Now at least it is clear that Freud is writing about men, with his typical phallocentrism, and pursuing a puerile association of ideas. (Although it is not clear who 'the spectator' is at this point: not of the drama, presumably; and not of a dream, since dreams can't be witnessed from the outside — unless of course one can deduce from the subject's erection that he is dreaming about Medusa; or unless the dreamer is simultaneously a spectator of his own dream. . . .) But to Garber the question remains resolutely open, un-decided, indeed — best of all — undecidable:

> With its gaping mouth, its snaky locks and its association with femi-ninity, *castration, and erection* [my italics: a truly polyvalent symbol!] Medusa's head ends up being the displacement upward neither of the female nor of the male genitals but of gender undecidability as such. (p. 110)

At this point the reader is entitled to ask, 'but whose problem is this, anyway?' The discourse of Macbeth and Lady Macbeth is about virility in the sense of courage, gender as the conventional distinction (in those days) between woman as the weaker sex unsuited to acts of violence, and men as the performers of such deeds — but never about undecidability. Lady Macbeth's invocation 'unsex me here' lies in the realm of ethics, not gender, expressing her wish to overcome what she calls the 'compunctious visitings of nature', so that 'direst cruelty' and a 'fell purpose' can sweep aside 'remorse' (1.5.40ff); her sleep-walking shows that she failed to destroy nature. One cannot seriously take these, or any other lines in the play, as referring to 'gender undecidability'.

It must be obvious by now that Professor Garber has long ago lost contact with Shakespeare's text, and is performing a kind of fantasy on Freudian-Lacanian themes. Perhaps all this talk about real penises has been mistaken, a reification of what is actually meant allegorically, or metaphorically. At this point she invokes Lacanian theory, with its mangling of Saussurian linguistics, and the resulting orthodoxy in some current theoretical circles that language refers only to itself, and that signifiers now 'float', cut free from their erstwhile position as an integral part of the linguistic sign. Garber, having first accused Freud of enacting 'the *repression* of gender undecidability' by locating Medusa's head in the male world; and having then rejected 'the present-day tendency' to see *Macbeth* in terms of 'male homosocial bonding or anxiety about female power', finally comes down on both sides of the fence:

> Power in *Macbeth* is a function of neither the male nor the female but of the suspicion of the undecidable. The phallus as floating signifier is more powerful than when definitely assigned to either gender. (p. 110)

This incongruous, almost comic mingling of metaphors ('the phallus as floating signifier') may be 'more powerful' for her argument, but it will leave many readers uneasy as to how to take it — is 'floating' to be visualised, like those floating figures in Chagall? If the phallus is a 'signifier', is it a word or a thing? How can it be 'assigned' to both sexes? Is this a belated reparation of the Freudian-Lacanian 'lack'?

Garber's discovery of a 'floating signifier' in *Macbeth* comes from a short passage in the second witches' scene (1.3.4–29). The witches, she says, 'are in a sense pluralized, replicative dream-figures for Lady Macbeth', and therefore speak 'Medusa language, the language of gender undecidability and castration fear' (p. 110). She has three pieces of evidence: in order to plague a shipman, the first witch plans to take on the shape of 'a rat without a tail' and slip aboard his ship. This alludes to the ancient belief that although a female witch could assume the form of a (two- or four-legged) animal there was no part of her anatomy which could double up as the tail. What this obviously means is, 'since women do not possess a penis'. But in Garber's discourse, I presume (since she is not explicit), the female-witch once *had* a tail/penis but it was cut off (as in 'Three Blind Mice'). Once again, a psychocritical theory involves reading a great deal of its own 'affect' into Shakespeare's text. Garber's second piece of evidence is the witch's threat to punish the shipman and 'drain him dry as hay', deprive him of sleep so that he will 'dwindle, peak, and pine' (1.3.21–3). Many readers have taken 'drain' here to refer either to the witch's sucking blood or to her 'sleep torture'. Dr. Johnson noted on this passage that 'the common Afflictions which the Malice of Witches produced was Melancholy, Fits, and Loss of Flesh, which are threatned' here. Reginald Scot, in *The Discoverie of Witchcraft*, recorded among the 'lies' of Bodin and other demonologists the tradition that witches daily offered the devil 'bloude of their owne' to drink; but he sturdily rejected the idea that melancholy persons, suffering the delusion of being witches, 'can hurt and infeeble other mens bodies' as false. Yet, as Peter Burke has recorded, sixteenth-century theologians believed that witches drank blood, especially that of children, and Shakespeare seems to make Hamlet allude to the myth in his 'Now could I drink hot blood'.[35] To Garber, however, it can only refer to 'a man exhausted . . . by sexual demands made upon him . . . the drained husband will not, unlike the weird sisters, be capable of "doing"' (p. 111). To the Freudian all things are sexual: yet the witch's triple 'I'll do' (which is usually taken to mean 'I'll create havoc') can hardly be taken as a description of copulation since — although Garber describes her as 'androgynous' — she now explicitly has the form of 'a rat *without* a tail'. Thirdly, the witch says 'Look what I have . . . . a pilot's thumb', and for Garber, inevitably enough, this reference to a 'dismembered' bodily part 'culminates the implicit narrative of sexual disabling and castration', since 'the morphological similarity between thumb and phallus needs no elaboration, and the possession by the witches of a thumb/phallus as a fetishistic object would emphasize their ambiguous, androgynous character . . .' (p. 111).

But no, 'morphological' implies the study of the relation between form and function, and in the human body the thumb and phallus have anything but the same function. In the morphology of Freudian narrative they may have, but that merely shows again the self-confirming nature of Freudian criticism. 'These are our concepts; look, I locate them in the text; *ergo*, the author/text must be read in this way in order to make sense' — Freudian sense, though. So Garber returns to Medusa again to gloss the witch's 'look what I have' in terms of a 'childlike announcement of sexual display', that is, 'look at my genitals'. Now she adds a new explanation for Medusa: 'Just as the Medusa head incorporates the elements of sexual gazing (scopophilia) and its concomitant punishment, castration, so the First Witch's exhibition of a prize . . . invites a similar transgressive sight' (p. 111). But this is the first we have heard of scopophilia in this context, and it is also news that the castration fear is not just an — ungrounded — anxiety but punishment for actual misbehaviour. Freud's text, we see, is also flexible. Yet the connection between the witch and the shipwrecked pilot is, for the moment at least, obscure. Who is transgressing? Did *he* say 'look what I have'? Or was the First Witch guilty of scopophilia? And, if she is saying it, is she saying 'look at my thumb, i.e., penis'? And will she be punished for that? Or will the others be if they look at her? But if she/he is already androgynous why should she/he need another thumb/ penis? Ah, of course, since we know that doubling of the genital symbol represents a fear of castration, it is the witch's problem, then, not Macbeth's; nor the shipman's; nor mine now.

Freudian criticism opens up a vast indeterminate space for its activity. The witches are androgynous, gender is undecidable, the penises that might be lost might be either male or female, the discourse is either concrete or abstract, either literal or metaphorical, or both (or neither?). As we move from Freud to Lacan the possibilities for abstraction multiply exponentially. Lacan's essay, 'Desire and the Interpretation of Desire in *Hamlet*', has moved psychoanalytical semiotics on to an altogether more rarified plane, starting from yet another invocation of 'the castration complex', this time to associate the ghost in *Hamlet* with what Lacan calls the 'veiled phallus'.[36] Garber quotes Lacan's explanation of the ghost:

> 'The hole in the real that results from loss, sets the signifier in motion. This hole provides the place for the projection of the missing signifier, which is essential to the structure of the Other. This is the signifier whose absence leaves the Other incapable of responding to your question, the signifier that can be purchased only with your own flesh and blood, the signifier that is essentially the veiled phallus. . . .' (p. 135)

The problem, again, is that Lacan sometimes seems to be using words literally, sometimes metaphorically: 'hole', 'place', 'structure', 'flesh and blood', all imply some dimension of physical reality. Yet reality is at once undercut: '"the very source of what makes Hamlet's arm waver at every moment"' — we see that Lacan is still following the Romantic conception of Hamlet's delay, although he unfortunately translates to the whole of the action ('every moment') the single time when Hamlet raises his sword over the praying Claudius — the source of his delay is what Freud described as a 'narcissistic connection': '"one cannot strike the phallus, because the phallus, even the real phallus, is a *ghost*"'. That is, as Garber explains, 'not only is the ghost the veiled phallus, but the phallus is also a ghost' (p. 130). No wonder you can't strike it, then.

So many levels of discourse — symbolic, metaphoric, literal, Freudian, Shakespearian — have become fused together here that it seems impossible to separate out a clear statement on any level. Since my aim is to write, and to find criticism which illuminates Shakespeare's plays with some fidelity to text and context, I would have to say here that Hamlet's arm was once raised to strike not a ghost, nor therefore a veiled phallus, not even a real phallus, but his usurping incestuous uncle. That statement reads baldly, I know, and gets no marks for originality, modishness, or wit. But I make it in order to underline the degree to which neo-Freudian discourse on Shakespeare has become a discourse about itself, to itself, with the play text providing occasional 'confirmatory' instances.

As one follows Garber's dense involvement with Lacan on Freud on the Oedipus complex, occasionally a remark seems to refer directly to Shakespeare's play, but often in a way which gives us pause. Garber subsequently invokes Lacan's argument that 'the Name-of-the-Father is the dead father' in these terms: 'This father — the Ghost — isn't dead enough. The injunction to "Remember me" suggests that he is not quite dead' (p. 131).[37] But ancient tradition held that ghosts may rise from the dead, for certain times, with their vocal chords intact. In what way is the Ghost of old Hamlet not dead enough? Garber glosses another of Lacan's arcane pronouncements on doubt, 'the gap in certainty that instates paternal undecidability', with the explanation that 'psychoanalytic readers all comment on the splitting of the father into Claudius, Polonius, even old Fortinbras and old Norway'. In which case, we must add, the 'splitting' has been 'instated' by the Freudians, for to Hamlet there is only one father, and he is dead. But Garber, unable to stop elaborating her points, states that 'Hamlet finds both too many fathers and too few' — having it both ways, again — and concludes that, just 'as in the case of the Medusa, where a multiplicity of penises is imagined to cover the unimaginable horror of no penis, . . . so here the multiplicity of fathers covers the fact of lack' (p. 134) — that is, it is a state of mind in Hamlet, not an event in the play. Once again, Freudian discourse is seen to be self-confirming, as loyal epigoni strive to validate the theories which a few founding fathers have enunciated, re-casting the text in their own image.

Lacan has a still more extraordinary argument, that the anamorphic shape of a skull in Holbein's 'The Ambassadors' is a phallic symbol representing 'the subject as annihilated . . . the imagined embodiment . . . of castration'. He goes on to connect this truly original idea ('How is it that nobody has ever thought of connecting this?', he asks, not staying for the obvious answer) with 'the effect of an erection'. Not just any erection, however, but one in which 'a tattoo [has been] traced on the sexual organ *ad hoc* in the state of repose and assuming its . . . developed form in another state', thus symbolising 'the function of the lack, . . . the appearance of the phallic ghost' (pp. 134–6). Any doubts that have been expressed over Lacanians' slippery shifting between symbolic (phallus) and real (penis) seem all too justified.[38] Placing herself in the role of dutiful hermeneut, ignoring the element of clowning so frequent in Lacan, Garber attempts to explicate this Lacanian fantasy, citing passages from Shakespeare at every turn in his argument. So here she makes an awful pun on Hamlet's recognition of 'My father's spirit — in arms!', writing 'The anamorphic ghost of old Hamlet, *erected* to full form by the gaze, contrasts sharply with the same figure in the "state of repose", *recumbent*,

passive, "sleeping within my orchard"' (my italics). That is, to explicate
the explicator (and to play a little), *just as* the skull in Holbein's painting
seems from one viewing position to be a white oblique pencil-like shape,
but seen from the correct point grows into the full circle of a skull; *so* a
penis tattooed in its recumbent shape (although of course this would be an
extremely difficult operation, not to mention painful, since it would offer
an awkwardly small surface for the tattooist's needles to work on: the erect
state would be much easier — always assuming the erection could be
maintained for several hours) would look different when erect; *just so* does
the ghost of Hamlet's father look different when seen walking in full
armour — that is, *'erected to full form by his son's gaze'* (might he not be
guilty of scopophilia? But if the phallus is veiled then all may be well . . .).
Is this not, at every stage, a fantastic argument, especially as purporting
to be Shakespeare criticism? Psychocritics habitually construct a self-
contained, self-confirming discourse, in which, once again, a reference to
an actual, real death — the Ghost's account of how he was 'sleeping, by a
brother's hand / Of life, of crown, of queen, at once dispatch'd, / Cut
off' — is confidently interpreted as a 'fantasy-nightmare of his own
castration' (p. 136). That rather seems to miss the point.

Marjorie Garber, widely-read and intelligent though she is, seems to
have been Lacanned / trepanned (no apologies for punning: everyone's
doing it) into reading the same limited series of significances into very
varied and powerful texts by Shakespeare. *Macbeth* and *Hamlet* are reduced
in the process, for whether the discourse is about Medusa's head,
anamorphic ghosts, or tattooed penises, the critic always comes back to the
same *points de repère*, fear of castration in particular. There is a strange
disproportion between the erudition and energy with which the critical
model is erected and the actual insight that it yields. The journey is long
and arduous, the fruits sparse, and always the same. When Freud aired his
Oedipal theories once again, in connection with Schreber, he offered
'a characteristic explanation: "I must disclaim all responsibility for the
monotony of the solutions provided by psychoanalysis"' (Porter 1987,
p. 156). But he was responsible, and the literary criticism produced in his
image reproduces the repetitiveness of his theories.

V

Despite great differences in tone, style, and intellectual preoccupations,
the monotony experienced in reading Garber is also felt — although in a
more tortuous form — with the Shakespeare criticism of Stanley Cavell, a
philosopher who came to psychoanalysis in mid-career. His collection of
essays, *Disowning Knowledge In Six Plays of Shakespeare*, has a philosophical
orientation at the outset, at least, namely the concept of scepticism.

Cavell is convinced that Shakespeare engaged 'the depth of the philo-sophical preoccupations of his culture' (p. 2), a flattering but misguided eulogy which confuses the work of an alert and reasonably well-educated writer for the public theatre with the activities of professional philosophers during the Renaissance.[39] Cavell suggests that 'the advent of skepticism as manifested in Descartes's *Meditations* is already in full existence in Shakespeare from the time of the great tragedies', specifically the Cartesian 'way of raising the question of God's existence and of the immortality of the soul' (p. 3). One may reasonably doubt whether Shakespeare ever concerned himself with either issue (at any rate in the plays), and the invocation of Descartes is anachronistic for the obvious reason that he gave scepticism a quite different orientation than it had in the Renaissance, as Cavell could have discovered from the excellent studies by Richard Popkin and the late Charles Schmitt.[40] Luckily Cavell, no historian, prefers to leave the issue in the conditional (or counter-factual) form: 'If Shakespeare's plays . . . reinterpret the skeptical problematic — the ques-tion whether I know with certainty of the existence of the eternal world and of myself and others in it', then it follows that 'the plays find no stable solution to skepticism' (p. 3). But where is the evidence that Shakespeare ever thought in those terms, or addressed such a problematic? In the event Cavell takes scepticism in a much more personal sense, linking it to a bewildering range of factors, including the rise of science, the displace-ment of God, the romantic concept of marriage, narcissism, cannibalism, fanaticism, and nihilism.[41] The abstractionism implicit in such a discourse seems to move away from drama to allegory (Othello 'allegorizes' his sceptical doubt 'as some form of jealousy': p. 7 — the word 'allegory' is repeated several times), and to its own version of reductivism: Leontes is 'a portrait of the skeptic as fanatic' (p. 17), or 'as nihilist' (p. 208).

When we look at the evidence cited from the plays to justify these propositions we find a curious distortion of the evident sense of the text towards the philosophical abstractions. On Leontes' remarkable speech itemising to Camillo all the evidence he claims to have seen that his wife has betrayed him with Polixenes: 'Is whispering nothing? / Is leaning cheek to cheek? Is meeting noses? / Kissing with inside lip?' (1.2.286ff), Cavell writes that, as a 'punishment' of Leontes for disowning his child — but Leontes never disowns Mamillius, still acknowledging that 'he does bear some signs of me' (2.1.58), in any case a reaction that happens *after* this scene (another Freudian inversion of sequence?) — Leontes 'loses the ability to . . . account for the order and size and pace of his experiences. . . . I take the surface of the speech as asking whether anything counts: Does whispering count, does it matter, is it a criterion for what the world is, is anything?' (p. 206). But this is to misread as a metaphysical issue what is merely a deluded claim to have ocular proof of adultery, a mistake further compounded when Cavell says that 'Leontes' wish for there to be nothing' shows 'the skeptic as nihilist' (p. 208). However, Leontes is using the word 'nothing' not in this sense but as an ellipsis for 'evidence of adultery'. Nor does he 'wish' there to be nothing — in his delusion, indeed, he wishes there to be something, since it would justify his suspicions. Leontes' folly is to take a series of rhetorical questions as if they were evidence admissible in court; Cavell's folly is to treat them as metaphysics.

Competence, even distinction in philosophy is obviously no guarantee of sensitivity, tact, or inwardness with literary texts. If not controlled by a sense of the integrity of the play and its mode of existence as drama, not as disjointed verbal material open to any selective interpretation, the philosophical model can simply blot out the literary work it is intended to illuminate. This obliteration of the text is particularly noticeable when Cavell moves on from philosophy to psychoanalysis. In *The Winter's Tale*, he writes, Leontes interrupts Mamillius' tale 'Of sprites and goblins', revealing, Cavell claims, a competition between father and son; on which he remarks confidently (placing the point in a parenthesis, as if there were no need to argue it): 'while evidently I expect considerable agreement that in Leontes' intrusion we have an Oedipal conflict put before us . . .' (p. 199). But reference to the text at this point (2.1.32ff) will show that Leontes has come in great anger to his wife after receiving the news that Polixenes and Camillo have left in haste. He cannot know that Mamillius is telling his mother a tale, appears not even to have noticed it, since he enters impatiently questioning one of his attendants about Polixenes' hasty departure — 'Was he met here? His train? Camillo with him?' (2.1.33). Leontes in fact takes no notice of the child for 24 lines, until he orders him to be carried off lest Hermione corrupt him further. Leontes' jealousy may be manic, but he is in no sense a rival to his son for Hermione's love, so the 'conflict' here cannot be Oedipal.

The Freudian drive to give every form of human behaviour a psycho-sexual explanation comes out even in Cavell's brief account of *Hamlet*, where he interprets the dumb-show that the players mount as representing the 'primal scene — enciphering young Hamlet's delayed sense of Gertrude's power to annihilate all Hamlets' (p. 187). But in Freudian terms the 'primal scene' refers to the child unwittingly seeing its parents making love, whereas in the players' dumb show the Queen mimes a protestation of love to the King and then poisons him: 'annihilate' is here literally true, not in Cavell's metaphorical sense (I imagine) of 'overcome sexually, cause to "die"'. The imposition of a sexual interpretation is seen again in Cavell's account of the catastrophe in *Hamlet*, where Hamlet kills the King with his own poison: 'I can imagine that some will wish to speculate about the fact that Hamlet inseminates Claudius; and with Leartes' [*sic*] foil. And further, I guess, that he does so only after he has himself been inseminated by it' (p. 190). Where does Cavell, with his 'inseminate', get the idea of semen from? Ordinary people would say 'poisons', but to the Freudian evidently all activity must be sexual.

The problem over literal and metaphorical readings, as with 'annihilate', is one that besets Cavell several times. Writing of Cleopatra's death-speech, with its marvellous affirmation of mutuality, finally dedicating herself to Antony — 'Husband, I come' (5.2.286), Cavell refers to it as 'Cleopatra's presentation of orgasm' (p. 31; 'declaring of orgasm', p. 32). Of course, sex can be represented as death, but the reverse does not always hold, and certainly not here. To spell out the embarrassingly obvious, Cleopatra means: 'I am coming to join you in death', not 'I am having an orgasm'. Cavell falls into the same trap with *Othello*, declaring that 'the whole scene of the murder is built on the concept of sexual intercourse or orgasm as a dying. There is a dangerously explicit quibble to this effect in the exchange

OTH. Thou art on thy death bed.
DESD.   Ay, but not yet to die.   (5.2.74f)

— 'The possible quibble', he goes on, as if to modify his assertion, but the bawdy sense is irrelevant here. In the terms of Cavell's sexual discourse about marriage, and the question whether a man can be sure that he has given satisfaction to the woman, Desdemona's words would have to mean (however absurdly in a play performed in public) 'I am not ready for my orgasm yet'. What she actually means is, 'this may indeed be the bed in which I shall die' — a comforting image of an assured relationship extending over time (some people do indeed die in their marriage beds) — 'but surely not yet!' This much is clear from their earlier exchange, which Cavell does not quote:

OTH. I would not kill thy unpreparèd spirit;
   No — heaven forfend! — I would not kill thy soul.
DESD. Talk you of killing?
OTH. Ay, I do.
DESD. Then heaven have mercy on me!
OTH. Amen, with all my heart!
DESD. If you say so, I hope you will not kill me.   (5.2.32ff)

And it is in allusion to this established meaning that Othello says — in another part of the scene omitted by Cavell — 'Sweet soul, take heed, / Take heed of perjury: thou art on thy death-bed.' (Truly, from the passages left out by psychocritics one can really discover the burden of the text!)

Critics, like all readers, must know where to screen out irrelevant associations, else they cannot understand metaphor, which by a process of mental translation makes a temporary alliance between two concepts that resemble each other in some ways but not in others. ('My love is like a red, red rose' demands that we see some but also delimit other ways in which the woman resembles the flower.) When Othello approaches the sleeping Desdemona he reflects that he can extinguish a candle and re-light it, but no 'Promethean heat' could 'relume' her light.

> When I have plucked thy rose,
> I cannot give it vital growth again,
> It needs must wither. I'll smell it on the tree.   [*Kisses her.*

Plucking the rose here, obviously enough, is a metaphor for the irreversible process of extinguishing life. Yet to Cavell, Othello's 'private dream' of killing Desdemona 'is of contamination. The fact the dream works upon is the act of deflowering' (p. 134) — that is, the other metaphor of 'plucking the rose' as taking a woman's maidenhead (are we to take 'I'll smell it' literally, too?). After that literalist reading Cavell's comments on Othello's admiration for her beauty — 'Be thus, when thou art dead, and I will kill thee, / And love thee after' — come with an awful predictability:

> Necrophilia is an apt fate for a mind whose reason is suffocating in its sumptuous capacity for figuration, and which takes the dying into love literally to entail killing . . . or that turns its object to live stone. . . . (p. 135)

But it's the philosopher, rather, who takes things literally. To imagine an Othello actually contemplating necrophilia might be, in a previous generation, the effect of having dabbled too much in 'psychopathia sexualis'. The figure behind Cavell here, however, is not Krafft-Ebing but Lacan (or perhaps de Man), with the anachronistic notion of 'figuration'.

His puzzling account of Othello's reason 'suffocating in its sumptuous capacity for figuration' — that is, I presume, ability to make rhetorical figures and tropes — is clarified by his later remark that

> It is an unstable frame of mind that compounds figurative with literal dying in love; and Othello unstably projects upon her, as he blames her:
>   O perjur'd woman, thou dost stone thy [Q1; F1 reads 'my'] heart.
> As he is the one who gives out lies about her, so he is the one who will give her a stone heart for her stone body [that is,] his words of stone . . . confound the figurative and the literal. (pp. 136–7)

True, an ability to distinguish literal from metaphorical is occasionally invoked as a test of sanity, but Othello at least would pass it, since his words are entirely figurative, have no literal dimension. Othello means that Desdemona's denial of ever having given Cassio a token is an act of perjury that hardens his heart (it can hardly be hers), an ancient metaphor for the absence of pity, and that he will be unrelenting in punishing her. Where is the literal sense involving 'stone' here? — and, above all, where is the confusion between literal and figurative?

Cavell's essays in linguistic criticism are not disinterested, of course, but serve to buttress his psychoanalytical interpretation of the play. Unsurprisingly by now, this Freudian, too, sees the crucial issues as concerning the characters' sex lives. So Cavell urges that we must 'think in this play not merely generally of marriage but specifically of the wedding night', for 'the whole beginning scene takes place while Othello and

Desdemona are in their bridal bed' (p. 131). Since Cavell's whole interpretation is based on the parallel he sees between their wedding night and
the night in which Othello kills her — since, as he will claim, the murder
scene is a 'fatal reenactment of their wedding night' — we must see what
evidence the play offers. Cavell has obviously taken at face value (a
fatal error with this character) Iago's slanderous words, designed to upset
Brabantio: 'Even now, very now, an old black ram / Is tupping your white
ewe' (1.1.89f). What Roderigo tells Brabantio is that Desdemona, 'At this
odd-even and dull watch o'th'night' — that is, between midnight and one
o'clock — has been transported by 'a gondolier/ To the gross clasps of a
lascivious Moor' (1.1.123ff). Brabantio searches the house, finds that she
has gone, and asks 'Are they married, think you?', to which Roderigo
replies 'Truly, I think they are' (160f). Brabantio gets armed men together,
and Roderigo leads them to the Sagittary — as Iago has previously arranged
('there will I be with him': 158ff). The second scene (only 23 lines later)
finds Othello, who is normally dressed, having been joined by Iago,
recounting some imaginary slanders on Othello (by Roderigo?), and asking
'Are you fast married?' (1.2.11). There has been no time to consummate
anything, even granted the flexible conventions of the Elizabethan stage.
Iago then warns Othello that Brabantio's power in Venice is such that 'He
will divorce you' (14), and a few minutes later — that same night —
Brabantio appears before the Venetian Council to accuse Othello of having
'charmed' her (1.3.59ff, 102ff). Othello affirms his innocence, describes
how he and Desdemona came to fall in love, and she confirms in public
that her choice was freely made, 'preferring [him] before her father' as her
mother had preferred her husband (1.3.180ff, 248ff). Their marriage is
legitimate, a *matrimonium initiatum*, in Gratian's distinction, but not yet
ratum, consummated.[42]

The pressure of state business will send Othello off to Cyprus at once —
in effect, on their wedding night — for which the Duke seems to apologise:
'you must therefore be content to slubber the gloss of your new fortunes
with this more stubborn and boisterous expedition' (226ff). Othello
counters by asking that Desdemona be allowed to accompany him, and she
protests that 'if I be left behind, . . . and he go to the war, / The rights for
which I love him are bereft me' (255ff), 'rights' meaning the privilege of
sharing his life and dangers, but also the rites of marriage. When they are
finally reunited on Cyprus, the storm having destroyed the Turkish fleet,
Othello issues a proclamation of a general 'triumph', with feasting and
dancing, with the added justification: 'for, besides these beneficial news, it
is the celebration of his nuptial' (2.2.6f). Immediately afterwards we see
Othello setting the guard, and retiring for the night:

> Come, my dear love,
> The purchase made, the fruits are to ensue;
> That profit's yet to come 'tween me and you.   (2.3.8ff)

Readers of Shakespeare have long noted the parallel with Juliet, similarly
poised between a *matrimonium initiatum* and *ratum*:

> O, I have bought the mansion of a love,
> But not possess'd it; and though I am sold,
> Not yet enjoy'd.   (3.2.26ff)

As we follow through this carefully constructed sequence, every detail of
which was invented by Shakespeare, we are left in no doubt that Othello
and Desdemona consummate their marriage on Cyprus. Iago's plot against
Cassio succeeds in rousing them both from their marriage bed, to which
they return — 'Come away to bed . . . Come Desdemona. 'Tis the soldiers'
life / To have their balmy slumbers wak'd with strife' (2.3.159ff, 246ff).
  Since it is the vocation of psychoanalytic critics to identify a neurosis
and its sexual cause ('My vocation, Hal! 'Tis no sin for a man to labour in
his vocation'), Cavell needs to be able to attach some trauma to Othello's
sexual relations with Desdemona in order to motivate his killing of her. To
argue such a case, of course, means ignoring Iago's evil slanders and
Shakespeare's elaborately constructed account of the triple relationship
Desdemona-Othello-Iago, with all its overtones, personal (the slighted
subordinate wishing revenge) and social (the noble Moor needed by Venice
but still treated as a foreigner). Willing to abandon the play's whole 'overt'
motivation, Cavell wishes to attach to Othello a trauma that derives from
his own (Cavell's own) idiosyncratic concept of scepticism. His essay is
called 'Othello and the Stake of the Other', and perfunctorily explains
Othello's jealousy as a form of scepticism by a passing reference to
the *Meditations* of Descartes, and the problem of how one can know
the existence of another (pp. 125ff). But Cavell's metamorphosis from
Cartesian to Freudian causes him at once to collapse that abstract question
into one considerably more specific, and intimate, namely how do you
know if your wife was a virgin when you married her? He begins, unfortunately accepting as literal truth Iago's words designed to horrify Brabantio
('tupping') by stating 'We know — do we not? — that Desdemona has lost
her virginity . . . by the time she appears to us. And surely [*surely?*] Othello
knows this!' (p. 130). But he then begins to raise doubts, suggesting
that the 'conjunction of the bridal chamber with a scene of emergency'
in Cyprus is but a repetition of what happened on their first night in
Venice. Perhaps, he goes on, the 'conjunction' between love-making and
emergency that he has detected is meant to imply that 'their "hour of love"
(1.3.298–9), or their two hours, have each been interrupted' (p. 131).[43]
However, Cavell's quotation is only a partial one, as will be seen by
restoring Othello's whole sentence:

> Come, Desdemona, I have but an hour
> Of love, of worldly matter and direction,
> To spend with thee: we must obey the time.   (1.3.298ff)

Does Cavell seriously imply that, with so much else to do, Othello and Desdemona go off and make love at this point? That is what his insinuation amounts to. Yet such a degree of certainty would not fit his 'skepticism' hypothesis, so he withdraws it, although at the cost of making Othello seem an idiot: 'There is reason to believe that the marriage has not been consummated, anyway reason to believe that Othello does not know whether it has' (p. 131). But what sort of a 'lunkhead', as he subsequently calls Othello, would not know whether he has consummated the marriage or not, especially since Cavell has declared that we know that Desdemona is no longer a virgin?

But Cavell is contradicting one phase of his argument here in order to enable another phase, namely the suggestion that Desdemona may *not* have been a virgin when Othello 'tupped' her in Venice, on their 'one shortened night [*sic*!] together' (p. 132). Referring to Othello's speech just before they actually consummate their marriage on Cyprus, Cavell picks out the 'purchase . . . fruit' metaphor and asks

Is the purchase their (public) marriage? Then the fruits and profit are their conjugal love. Then he is saying that this is yet to come.

— which most people would see as the correct interpretation of the lines. But, unsatisfied, Cavell goes on:

It seems to me possible that the purchase, or price, was her virginity, and the fruits or profit their pleasure.

Cavell seems to be reducing loving mutuality to the 'price' of a maidenhead, an attitude which might be appropriate to the brothel scenes in *Pericles*, but which seems horribly out of place here. I must honestly say that I am not sure what Cavell is arguing at this point, whether premarital sex is wrong, or whether Desdemona cheated Othello about her virginity. . . . What he is certainly aiming at, though, is to arouse doubt. He initially takes Othello's metaphor for Desdemona's sleeping beauty —

> Yet I'll not shed her blood,
> Nor scar that whiter skin of hers than snow
> And smooth as monumental alabaster —   (5.2.3ff)

as implying 'a piece of cold and carved marble' (pp. 125f; overlooking the purity and smoothness in order to insinuate the cold), but he subsequently reifies the metaphor, now seeing it as somehow describing 'Othello's turning of Desdemona to stone' (perhaps Othello is the Gorgon now!). Further, Cavell then manages to link it to the issue of virginity: 'His image denies that he has *scarred* her and shed her blood. It is a denial at once that he has taken her virginity and that she has died of him' (p. 134; my italics for the insinuation of a point to be developed later). Desdemona is still alive at this point, so 'died' must be meant metaphorically. But why should Othello want to deny that he has taken her virginity? That is surely the normal and natural consequence of marital consummation. As we have seen, Cavell — thanks to taking the metaphor of 'plucking the rose' literally — believes that Othello's plan to kill Desdemona is a dream of 'contamination' based on 'the act of deflowering' (p. 134). So perhaps he hasn't consummated it after all? And who contaminated whom?

Here the wedding sheets may be called in as evidence (*Exhibit two*). After Othello in his dementia has accused her in public of being a whore Desdemona, stunned and broken, asks Emilia: 'Prithee, tonight / Lay on my bed my wedding sheets' (4.2.105ff). This refers, most readers and theatregoers have thought, to a more richly embroidered set of linen that, she hopes, will remind Othello of the love that brought them together. To Cavell, however, this can mean 'only' one thing: 'The exhibition of wedding sheets in this romantic, superstitious, conventional environment can only refer to the practice of proving purity by staining' (p. 135). To which we might want to ask, was this practice common in Shakespeare's England, or Renaissance Venice — were it not for a far more important question, namely, why would Desdemona want to put on her bed a pair of sheets already dirty with hymenal blood? (It is just as well that Thomas Rymer did not know of Cavell's interpretation, which would have given greater force to the notorious moral he deduced from the play: 'this may be a warning to all good Wives that they look well to their Linnen'.)[44] Furthermore, to follow out the logic of Cavell's suggestion, it would have to have been a copious discharge indeed to be visible as Desdemona lies asleep, her sheets, presumably, tucked under her chin. These are unpleasant speculations, I know, but the questions Cavell asks are not concerned with tact or sensibility. He is after proof, sounding like an attorney in court:

> Well, were the sheets stained or not? Was she a virgin or not? The answers seem as ambiguous as to our [*that is, Iago's*] earlier question whether they are fast married. Is the final, fatal reenactment of their wedding night [*sc. Othello's suffocating Desdemona*] a clear denial of what really happened, so that we can just read off, by negation [*a psycho-analytical practice*], what really happened? Or is it a straight reenactment, without negation, and the flower was still on the tree, as far as he knew? In that case, who was reluctant to see it plucked, he or she? On such issues, farce and tragedy are separated by the thickness of a membrane. (p. 135)

Before attending to those questions, a word on Cavell's use of the word 'farce'. He has just claimed that his theory of blood-stained wedding sheets 'provides a satisfactory weight for the importance Othello attaches to his charmed (or farcical) handkerchief, the fact that it is spotted, spotted with strawberries' (p. 135). Why should the fact that Othello believes it to be charmed make it 'farcical'? Such a plot-donnée had better be accepted, if we are to be able to read literature at all. Earlier Cavell wrote that 'It has been felt from Thomas Rymer to G.B. Shaw that the play obeys the rhythm of farce, not of tragedy' (p. 132). But Rymer had no aesthetic interest in 'rhythm', merely wanting to dismiss the play as brutally as possible: 'There is in this Play some burlesk, some humour, and ramble of Comical Wit; . . . but the tragical part is, plainly, none other than a Bloody Farce, without salt or savour'.[45] As for the handkerchief with its embroidered strawberries, are we seriously to believe that Othello values it for being in some way proleptic of his (according to Cavell, blood-stained) wedding sheets? And can anyone seriously accept the grand Freudian assumption behind all this insistent prying, namely that the murder scene is 'the final, fatal reenactment of their wedding night', and that whatever went wrong then causes all the destruction now?

Cavell's questions, to return to them, imply, first of all, that the issue whether Desdemona was a virgin on her wedding night in Cyprus is still open. Earlier, of course, he proclaimed that she was no longer a virgin on her first appearance in the play. Clearly, his scepticism cannot abide certainty. Secondly, he asks which of the two, Othello or Desdemona, 'was reluctant to see it [sc. Desdemona's 'flower'] plucked, he or she?' I note in passing that the verb 'see' is inappropriate to the activity that Othello and Desdemona were involved in (though it does of course fit the critic poring over the play) but this question insinuates the further possibility, that Othello might have been reluctant — whatever that might mean — for Desdemona to lose her virginity. Well, the reader of this page might now irascibly enquire, did they or didn't they? Cavell cannot, or will not, tell us:

> We of course have no answer to such questions. But what matters is that Othello has no answer [where is the evidence that he ever asked them?]; or rather he can give none, for any answer to the questions, granted that I am right in taking the questions to be his, is intolerable. The torture of the logic in his mind we might represent as follows: Either I shed her blood and scarred her or I did not. If I did not then she was not a virgin and this is a stain upon me. If I did then she is no longer a virgin and this is a stain upon me. Either way I am contaminated. (I do not say that the sides of this dilemma are of equal significance for Othello.)
>
> But this much logic anyone but a lunkhead might have mastered apart from actually getting married. (pp. 135–6)

But the 'torture of the logic' here is in the mind of the critic, not the character, for Cavell's dilemma is based on a grotesque misreading of Othello's lines 'I'll not shed her blood, / Nor scar that whiter skin of hers than snow'. Here Othello obediently mouths the idea that Iago put in his head, revising his own plan to poison her: 'Do it not with poison: strangle her in her bed, even the bed she hath contaminated' (4.1.203ff). But Cavell, brooding on this issue, has conflated Othello's words over the sleeping Desdemona, which we can all see and hear, with what may have

taken place on their wedding night (which even this critic fails to reconstruct, despite his efforts), or what may be going on in Othello's mind.
True, Othello may have 'shed her blood' in making love for the first time,
but he has certainly not 'scarred' her, since — as I imagine Cavell knows,
and I apologise to the reader who might be offended by this observation,
but it is he, after all, who has pitched the discussion at this level — the
perforation of the hymen does not leave a scar but opens a natural orifice.
The 'dilemma', like the scar, is of the critic's making, then, and can be
discarded. It is cleverly constructed, to leave no exit — 'if I did not shed
her blood', Othello thinks, 'this is a stain on me' — where Cavell means
'stain' in the metaphorical sense of 'reproach', or dishonour (if Desdemona
wasn't a virgin); but 'if I did shed her blood' then this, too, is 'a stain on
me' — where Cavell presumably invokes the literal sense of 'pollution that
can be washed off' (if people did wash in those days). Spelling it out like
this allows us to see that Cavell's 'dilemma' is a spurious verbal construct,
collapsing the difference between literal and metaphorical senses, and
revealing (to me, at least) a truly contorted form of reasoning in the critic's
mind. Cavell patronisingly excuses Othello for not seeing both sides of
the dilemma as 'of equal significance': but the problem is Cavell's, not
Othello's.

Readers need stamina: Cavell has not yet finished reconstructing the
sexual relationship between Othello and his wife. He states that Othello
'fails twice at the end to kill Iago, knowing he cannot kill him' (p. 136).
Reference to the text reveals one moment when Othello *runs at Iago, but
Montano disarms him*' (stage-direction in the New Cambridge edition, at
5.2.238), and another when Othello *wounds Iago* with his sword, saying 'If
that thou be'st a devil, I cannot kill thee' (5.2.287f). It is, I imagine most
people would agree, deliberate design on Shakespeare's part that keeps Iago
alive throughout this final scene, and a remarkable dramatic stroke to show
him, the man who has poisoned human society with his lies, now, found
out, refusing language: 'Demand me nothing; what you know, you know; /
From this time forth I never will speak word' (305f).[46] To Cavell the half-
hearted Cartesian this should make Iago the sceptic, not Othello; but to
Cavell the fully-convinced Freudian Othello's failing to kill 'this nobody' is
'the point of his impotence, and the meaning of it'. Here is a new
argument, adumbrated by the earlier hint of Othello being 'reluctant' to
pluck Desdemona's 'flower', namely that Othello may be impotent. But let
Cavell present his own case, in his best Jamesian style:

> In speaking of the point and meaning of Othello's impotence, I do not
> think of Othello as having been in an everyday sense impotent with
> Desdemona. I think of him, rather, as having been surprised by her, at
> what he has elicited from her; at, so to speak, a success rather than a
> failure. . . . Surprised, let me say, to find that she is flesh and blood. . . .
> It is the dimension of her that shows itself in that difficult and dirty
> banter between her and Iago as they await Othello on Cyprus. (p. 136)

(I have altered the order of the last two sentences quoted, to bring out more clearly what Cavell means by 'surprised': that is, Othello is surprised at Desdemona's sexuality; and I leave out a repetitive and circling, indeed tortured continuation of this argument over the next page.) Two points need to be made here: first, despite Cavell's disclaimer that he does not think of Othello as having been 'in an everyday sense impotent with Desdemona' that is certainly what he implies later on (and one wonders what other sense the word might have — 'well,' as Cavell might put it, 'could he get it up or couldn't he?'). Secondly, he imputes to Desdemona a female sexuality as revealed in the 'dirty banter' she has with Iago while awaiting Othello's arrival. Reference to that scene, however (2.1.109–162), which moves from Iago's attack on women ('you are pictures out of doors . . . hussies in your beds') to his insinuation that women would never 'change the cod's head for the salmon's tail', will show that all the bawdy in it (and there is not much) comes from Iago, not Desdemona, who remains as chaste as ever, amused but shocked at his insinuations. 'Dirty banter' has such a Puritanical disapproval about it[47] that we turn to Rymer wondering if Cavell took it from there, but Rymer only dismisses the dialogue as 'a long rabble of Jack-pudden farce . . . that runs on with all the little plays, jingle, and trash'.[48] Cavell seems in two minds about Desdemona's 'flesh and blood'; welcoming but disapproving, too.

Returning to that wedding-night, wherever it took place, and whatever happened — not to mention whatever relevance such a non-represented, non-reported event could possibly have for the interpretation of a play — Cavell now decides that Desdemona *was* a virgin, but that Othello somehow could not 'accept' her chastity (a further level of confusion, for to judge by his account they certainly made love). He writes of Desdemona:

> Her virginity, her intactness, her perfection, had been gladly forgone by her for him, for the sake of their union, for the seaming of it. It is the sacrifice he could not accept, for then he was not himself perfect. It must be displaced. The scar [sic] is the mark of finitude. . . . (p. 137)

(Cavell's discourse, I should add, takes place on several levels simultaneously, from speculation about the wedding-night to the higher, more abstract thesis that Othello 'cannot forgive Desdemona for existing, for being separate from him'.) Here, as with other sore points in Cavell's argument, the question of chastity is simultaneously resolved and left open. Desdemona sacrificed her 'intactness' to Othello, but he could not accept it, although there still seems to have been a 'scar' on one of them, however produced. Cavell's argument, which is developed in the shadows of his other speculations, is — to put it very baldly, with a directness that Cavell fastidiously shuns — that Othello's impotence is the clue to it all. His inability to accept Desdemona's gift of her virginity ('It must be displaced') results in an obsession with 'defloration' that causes him to murder Desdemona, since he is powerless to deal with a sexuality that he has himself released. He should never have made love to her in the first place, for he let loose forces that he was powerless to control. And there are warnings in this for the rest of us:

> If such a man as Othello is rendered impotent and murderous by aroused, or by having aroused, female sexuality — or let us say, if this man is horrified by human sexuality, in himself and in others — then no human being is free of this possibility. (p. 137)

It seems to me that every suggestion or conclusion in that sentence is fictitious. Cavell's remarkable torturing of logic pulls the play into a private nexus of interests, from philosophy to psychoanalysis, and finally to a spurious form of etymology, for in conclusion he calls 'attention — I cannot think I am the first to say it out loud — to the hell and the demon staring out of the names of Othello and Desdemona' (p. 140) — staring, that is, for English readers not Italian (in his linguocentrism, Cavell resembles Freud, who thought that the Egyptian hieroglyph *Mut* indubitably suggested *Mutter*). This remark recalls the comic denouement in *Cymbeline*, that parody of Renaissance etymology, where Philharmonus, a soothsayer, interprets the oracle's reference to 'tender air' as being the same as 'mollis aer; and mollis aer / We term it mulier' (5.5.448f). That Cavell should reduce Shakespearian characters to word-games, to accidental (non-phonemic) similarities which suggest to him deep symbolic significance (a game that has been called 'the impotent remarking of particulars'),[49] is the last of many proofs that Freudians lack any sense of self-criticism, have no criteria by which to question either the model or their application of it. Here, too, a form of determinism seems to have taken over.

VI

I have attempted to give sustained critical analyses of four recent psycho-analytic studies, readings of their misreadings, as it seems to me (to them, no doubt, the opposite). This may have placed a strain on the reader's patience, but it seemed to me an exercise worth performing once with the kind of close scrutiny that those critics, presumably, gave to the plays. Monotonous it certainly was, but that merely reflects the monotony of their interpretive model. At any rate, I think we can now fairly conclude that the damage that Freudian Shakespeare criticism does to the plays consists of both omission and distortion. Those elements are omitted that do not fit — not even with the super-flexible method of 'splitting' characters into constituent mini-selves to be identified with whatever other character one pleases. Despite this useful device, major parts of the play, involving plot and motivation, still have to be ignored, social and political aspects passed over (the pressures of class and party politics in *Coriolanus*, for instance, disappear altogether in Freudian readings),[50] many scenes and characters discarded altogether. The playwright's carefully organised dramatic structure, unifying several plots, focussing the issues that unite and divide the people in the play, is either ignored or rearranged to privilege Freudian narrative models, the primal scene, Oedipal hatred, the workings-out of repressed homosexuality, anxiety, or whatever. Analytical interest is focussed on the personality of one or two main characters, in the usual search to identify pathological neuroses, the assumption always being that the causes of unhappiness (no psychocritic is interested in happiness) are internal. As Ernest Gellner has said of Freudian theory in general,

> The real obstacles and impediments in life are generally *inside*. . . . The whole system is pervaded by the assumption that tragic predicaments are indeed self-imposed. Presumably by definition, neurotic unhappiness can originate only inside the psyche. (Gellner 1985, p. 71)

Uncritically accepting that principle, in all its circularity, Freudians look 'inside' Othello to find the 'neurotic unhappiness' they have been trained to identify. In the process they leave out Iago as engine and motive, oddly enough, perhaps because his deeds seem less spectacular, or perhaps because he always acts with such apparent rationality. Under further scrutiny, of course, Iago can also be shown to be an anal erotic (with-holding language), a frustrated homosexual, and much else. But so far, at least, Freudians have simply ignored the 'overt' motivation (my inverted commas mock their assumptions) of Iago, which for other readers massively dominates the drama.

What remains after the omissions is then distorted by the very process of Freudian reading. In the work of Cavell, Garber, Nevo, and many, many more, the critical enterprise consists of applying an interpretative model (A) to the literary text (B). But instead of a genuine illumination by the A/B comparison the literary work is made to conform to the model, and in effect reproduces it: A-A$_1$-A$_2$ (Freud to Lacan to whoever's next). The pre-selected parts of the play are subjected to what is currently known as a 'strong' or 'powerful' reading, which distorts them so much that they are no longer recognisable as the *Macbeth* or *Othello* we have always lived with. This process of fragmentation and distortion reduces the literary work to a loose conglomerate of signifiers on to which the psychocritic can impose his or her interpretive model. The psychoanalytic paradigms, in other words, are too strong, too individual to serve as critical tools without just rewriting literary works in their own image.

This conclusion, unwelcome though it will be in those places where psychoanalysis has become not so much a technique for therapy as a way of life, seems unavoidable. Literary critics may have something to learn here from historians, in their sceptical response to a subsection of Freudianism called 'psychohistory', a genre which finds that world-historical events, too, exemplify what Freud might describe as certain 'technical rules'.[51] Gertrude Himmelfarb has noted how in this approach, as in Freudian literary criticism, the centre of gravity shifts. Psychohistory 'derives its "facts" not from history but from psychoanalysis, and deduces its theories not from this or that instance but from a view of human nature that transcends history' (Himmelfarb 1987, p. 35). One of its leading American practitioners claims that psychoanalysis is actually superior to history in that it possesses ' "a scientific system of concepts, based on clinical data" ' (*cit: ibid.*, p. 114), which is true for all ages, inherent in human nature itself. The resulting application of this system, however, can only be ahistorical, as Erik Erikson candidly admitted in his *Young Man Luther* (1958), willingly accepting ' "half-legend as half-history" ', and invoking his ' "clinician's training" ' as the authority permitting ' "him to recognize major trends even where the facts are not all available" ' (*cit. ibid.*, pp. 38–9). In this way the psychohistorian gives himself *carte blanche* to rewrite biography or even political history in Freudian terms.

Undeterred by the unavailability of the subjects for analysis, hailing Freud for positing the Oedipus complex as 'a "constant" of human nature (a "biological given")', the psychohistorian assumes that President Nixon, too, must have gone through the Oedipal phase, and proceeds retrospectively to explain his adult behaviour from this phase, so crucial for the 'identification with a model of a mature man' (*ibid.*, pp. 114, 117). (Does this also explain Nixon's many faults as a president?) As with the patient on the couch, psychohistory ignores 'the conscious, manifest level of behaviour' (p. 46), and takes any 'utterance or action . . . as an involuntary symptom which, when properly interpreted, discloses a meaning hidden from the agent and from common observers' (p. 35). In Shakespeare criticism, as we have abundantly seen, manifest and declared motives are dispensed with; actual dreams (those by Bottom, Clarence, Duke Humphrey and Eleanor) are ignored, presumably because Shakespeare has made their meaning crystal-clear. Psychohistory, deterministic and mechanistic, 'reduces history to the status of "epiphenomena", the superficial expression or manifestation of reality' (p. 43). When confronted with the deeper level excavated by the psychohistorian, however, we may be appalled by the vast disparity between the complexity of the character or issue under discussion and the triviality of the explanation. Hitler's hatred of the Jews and advocacy of gas-chambers to destroy them have been said by psychohistorians to derive from an unsuccessful cancer operation on his mother by a Jewish doctor, and his own gas poisoning in 1918 (the *tertium quid* being an iodine compound called iodoform). His desire for more *Lebensraum* reflects his mother's maternal trauma (three infants died before he was born), which resulted in 'her compensatory overfeeding of him', producing an 'oral-aggressive fixation' as he relived his mother's trauma: *ergo*, 'Germany could not feed her children adequately' (pp. 37–8).

I take it that the trivialisation effected there is far more damaging than anything that Freudian critics do to Shakespeare. Yet the difference is one of degree only. The accounts that Nevo or Garber give of Prospero or

Macbeth are similarly said to 'correspond' to a Freudian or Lacanian model, are subsumed under favourite explanatory schemes. In the process, as in psychohistory, another historian has objected, 'events and agents lose their individuality and become illustrations of certain automatisms' (Barzun 1974, p. 23). Both schools seek to 'diagnose' specific instances by reference back to a limited set of explanatory models, whereas, Barzun insists, true 'understanding in human affairs means imagining, visualizing, reliving, and above all *individualizing*, not reducing to type and kind, as diagnosis is meant to do' (p. 64). The mechanistic approach of psychohistory is a legacy still of Freud's ambition to found a science, his hope to discover universal laws governing human behaviour. Freud believed that 'man's evolutionary past . . . had originally decreed the psychoanalytic laws of human behaviour', endowing 'these laws with a universal, transcultural validity' (Sulloway 1983, p. 367). Had he succeeded, psychoanalysis might have achieved the status of the empirical sciences, with the law-giving power which nineteenth-century historians of ideas defined as *nomothetic* (as opposed to the procedures of the humanities, which they saw as *idiographic*, concerned with individual writers and artists, individual works of art). Psychoanalysis, we now know, achieved no more than the status of a pseudo-science, but in making an alliance with it both history and literary criticism are being false to their true natures. As Michael Baxandall has recently commented, the idiographic model 'demands that we attend formally to the actor's purposes: we identify the ends of actions and reconstruct purpose on the basis of particular rather than general facts'. As 'historians and critics' of the arts, Baxandall writes, our interest is 'more often idiographic, towards locating and understanding the peculiarities of particulars. We seek differentiating tools . . .'[52] — whereas, I add, the psychoanalyst seeks 'general laws' about human action under which he can subsume, and so treat, individual cases. For a literary critic, then, to handle in a nomothetic way material demanding an idiographic approach is to commit a grave category error, which can only distort the work of art in question. The schematism and repetitiveness that results can best be described in the terms of Coleridge's familiar distinction — borrowed from Schelling — between mechanical regularity and organic form. As he wrote in 1808, much damage can be caused by confusing

> mechanical regularity with organic form. The form is mechanic when on any given material we impress a pre-determined form, not necessarily rising out of the properties of the material. . . . The organic form, on the other hand, is innate; it shapes as it develops itself from within, and the fullness of its development is one and the same with the perfection of its outward form. . . .

Nature is inexhaustible, Coleridge writes, in powers as in forms, each exterior being 'the physiognomy of the being within'. And so, to return to drama, even such is the appropriate excellence of her chosen poet, of our own Shakespeare, himself a nature humanized, a genial understanding directing self-consciously a power and an implicit wisdom deeper than consciousness.[53]

Setting aside (if one can) the bardolatry there, I would underline two of Coleridge's remarks, although apparently contradictory: the sense that a play 'shapes as it develops from within', with at the same time Shakespeare's 'understanding directing self-consciously'. The 'pre-determined forms' of psychoanalysis offer no help in understanding either process.

CHAPTER SIX

Feminist Stereotypes:
Misogyny, Patriarchy, Bombast

We know well that habits and institutions which are now reasonably criticized as grossly unfair and unjust — for example, in the relations between rich and poor — were not criticized by our ancestors in this way, partly because, embedded in a different way of life, our ancestors had different targets for criticism from the standpoint of justice, and needed to imagine, or to anticipate, a different way of life, if they were to see the then prevailing relations between rich and poor as grossly unjust. Stuart Hampshire[1]

Feminist Shakespeare criticism is a relatively recent genre. The first courses in Women's Studies were set up in America in 1966, leading to the foundation of the National Women's Studies Association in 1977; the first feminist book explicitly devoted to Shakespeare, Juliet Dusinberre's *Shakespeare and the Nature of Women*, appeared in 1975; while 1976 saw the formation of the Modern Language Association sections on 'Feminist Criticism of Shakespeare', and on 'Marriage and the Family' in Shakespeare (Greer 1988, pp. 616, 629). Thereafter national and regional meetings spread across America at such a rate that by 1988 an editor of a journal's special issue concerned with 'Women in the Renaissance' could write that it is now 'difficult to imagine a Renaissance conference that would not include a wide range of papers devoted to women writing and / or representations of women in works by male authors'.[2] The success in the universities has been astonishing, with '250,000 students at present reading Women's Studies of one sort or another' in America alone (Greer 1988, p. 616). A veritable explosion of publications — book-length studies, collections of writing by Renaissance women, anthologies of modern criticism — have transformed the subject in a remarkably short time.[3]

At this point I feel the need to distinguish between feminism as a political movement intended to correct unjust discriminations that go back, in Western society, to Aristotle and beyond (I need hardly mention Islam), and feminist literary criticism. On the political issue, it is surely right that here, as with other marginalised groups — the elderly, the handicapped, blacks, people of minority religions or lower castes, ethnic groups, political prisoners — our feelings of concern and compassion ought to issue into whatever forms of action are available to us as agents in a free society. But does that include the activity of literary criticism? Must we demonstrate our virtue, our ideological or religious correctness, by the way in which we write about literature? Ought we to seek out novels or plays which we can excoriate for endorsing colonialism, anti-Semitism, misogyny, class-hatred? Yes of course, one answer would be, provided that you find the right books, those that really do encourage such repulsive attitudes. The danger is, though, that the resulting criticism, although displaying the right social virtues, may be completely uninteresting as literary criticism, or even totally misguided. Politically motivated, perhaps ethically justifiable, it will not necessarily tell us anything about the way in which a novel or play works, how it is structured in terms of plot and language, what qualities of creativity or imagination it may display, what ethical position it takes up on other issues. Politically guided criticism might even value, on ideological grounds, work that other critics would dismiss as propaganda, not art.

Throughout this book I have been arguing for a literary criticism that respects the integrity of a play or novel, addresses itself to the individuality of each work in its historical context, without reducing the enormous range and variety of imaginative writing to some lowest common denominator. The problem with explicitly political criticism is that it tends to politicise virtually every element of a work, and to ignore non-political issues. Some writers even claim that all writing is political, and that to deny literature an inherent politics would be 'quietistic'. But, as the Marxist critic Catherine Gallagher replies, the argument is tautological: 'Such reasoning begins with the assumption that everything has *a* politics; a denial of this assumption must also have *a* politics, no doubt reactionary. Such reasoning is impervious to evidence...' (Gallagher 1989, p. 44). Anyone willing to consider the evidence, I maintain, will concede that while some works do indeed raise political issues, others do not, or only faintly; and that to impose the expectation of a political dimension on everything we read is as unreasonable as to impose a religious dimension on it. Both expectations will distort the text, expecially since the 'politics' or 'religion' imposed will be our politics, our religion. For instance, 'the politics of the family' is a recognisable post-1960s concept which, when applied to literature of the past, may perhaps produce data which speak to our preoccupations, but will not attend to those in the texts of that age, or may actively falsify them. For, as my epigraph from Stuart Hampshire puts it, our ancestors were 'embedded in a different way of life', had different concerns, took for granted situations which seem to us unjust, and devoted much energy and concern to issues — such as the salvation of their souls in the after-life, or the maintaining of their virtue in this world — which seem to many people today of little importance. A properly historical approach would recognise this.

If 'first-wave' feminism refers to the generation of Virginia Woolf, its 'second wave' arriving in the late 1960s, the general issue is whether such a new school of criticism can adapt itself to the literature of the past, especially something as remote as the Renaissance. In particular, we must ask, has this second wave produced independent criticism, or does a group having shared assumptions, common methods, produce identical readings? As recently as 1980 the editors of an influential symposium could declare that 'feminist criticism of Shakespeare is still too new to have established any orthodoxies' (Lenz et al. 1980, p. 12). But already then, I think, and certainly in the decade since, a number of orthodox positions can be clearly defined and evaluated, some of which, I shall argue, damage our chances of understanding Shakespeare. What follows is a critique of those aspects which, as with other critical schools evaluated here, result in a partial Shakespeare — seen in part; used for a partisan goal. I repeat, my remarks do not presuppose any hostility to the cause of women's studies; nor, even less, to the movement seeking to redress the injustices done to women since the beginning of Western civilisation. What concerns me here is the injustice done to Shakespeare.

I

Carol Neely, writing in 1981, defined three modes of feminist criticism, which she called 'compensatory, justificatory, transformational'. The first type, compensatory, 'declares women characters (or authors) worthy of and in need of a new kind of attention'. It has focussed on the 'powerful, prominent women' in Shakespeare, restoring to them 'their virtues, their complexity, and their power, compensating for traditional criticism which has minimized or stereotyped them' — Kate in The Taming of the Shrew, Cleopatra, and Desdemona are all up-valued in the process (Neely 1981, p. 6). Neely recognised that this search for 'positive role models' has certain dangers: 'the heroines tend to be viewed in a partial vacuum, unnaturally isolated from the rest of the play, the Shakespearean canon, and the culture in which that canon is rooted' (ibid., pp. 6–7). Further, the process of singling out these women and 'the framework within which they are valued', she observed, can become biassed, 'subject to contamination by the sex-role stereotypes of the culture in which the criticism exists and which it is reacting against' (p. 7). That is, feminist critics, 'influenced by their own battles for equality, . . . may overcompensate and attribute inappropriately or too enthusiastically to women characters qualities tra-ditionally admired in men — power, aggressiveness, wit, sexual boldness'. This is a case of 'reversing but not discarding the conventional stereotypes', and it cannot easily cope either with the women who are not heroines, or — a more damaging concession, one may feel — 'with the men who are important to all of Shakespeare's women' (p. 7).

Neely's second mode was 'justificatory criticism, which acknowledges the existence in Shakespeare's plays and in his culture of the traditional dichotomy, of the stereotyping of women, of the constraints of patriarchy', and then applies this knowledge to justify 'the limitations of some women characters and the limiting conceptions of women held by male characters' (p. 7). These 'limitations' are then said to be culturally induced. Critics using this approach explore the roles of 'women — heroines, and especially, victims — in the male-defined and male-dominated world of the plays, showing how their roles are circumscribed by political, economic, familial, and psychological structures' (p. 8). Such critics find support, as Neely put it, in 'varied analyses of patriarchal society by historians like Lawrence Stone or anthropologists like Claude Lévi-Strauss', who have traced the 'dominance-subordination relations' between men and women. This mode, too, has its dangers. Just as the first approach finds it hard to define the heroines' characteristics 'without reverting to some version of sex-role stereotypes, the second mode has difficulty assessing patriarchy's varied quality and weight from play to play without falsely rigidifying it. Justificatory critics differ over whether Shakespeare defends patriarchal structures, attacks them, or merely represents them'. Whatever their conclusion, Neely believed, the approach itself 'may be led to make the structures more monolithic or oppressive than they are, to minimise both the freedom of action of individual women within them' and the influence these women have on the patriarchal structures themselves: 'the result may be depressing — and also unbalanced' (p. 9).

Faced with these opposed goals, 'powerful women' as against 'oppressive patriarchy', a third mode examines the interaction between the two, asking 'not simply what women do or what is done to them, but what meaning these actions have and how this meaning is related to gender'. Neely called this mode 'transformational because of its subject — the mutually transforming roles and attitudes of men and women . . . and because of its goal — which is not only to compensate for or justify traditional criticism but to transform it' (p. 9). Although she did not recognise it, Neely's account of this third mode shows that the background discipline that underpins the literary criticism has also shifted. If in the first mode it was basic feminism (putting more emphasis on neglected women), and in the second social history of a particular kind (patriarchal society), in this third mode the relevant background authority is psychoanalysis. Critics in the transformational mode, as she put it, 'interrogate the relations between male idealization of and degradation of women', some showing how the 'idealization of women in the comedies serves to alleviate the heroes' anxieties about sex — as does the disguise of the heroines and their ultimate submission to men in marriage' (revealing, I presume, the women's matching 'anxieties about sex'). Other critics 'show how male misogyny in the tragedies is a defense against male fears of feminization and powerlessness, and, ironically, brings about the very loss of potency which men fear'. In these concepts of anxiety, fear, compensation we recognise, as

Neely did not, the mental world of Freudianism, and it is perhaps because of her closeness to that world that Neely confessed that her perspective on transformational criticism was 'not detached enough for its limitations to be fully apparent' (p. 10).

Carol Neely's account of these three modes was clearly conceived and balanced in judgment. Other feminists confirm, but also qualify her emphases. There are, it seems to me, two main issues, one contemporary, the other historical. The contemporary issue is the ultimate goal of feminist Shakespeare criticism. According to the editors of one of the earlier anthologies, such criticism 'is not only and not always feminocentric, for it examines both men and women and the social structures that shape them'; but it is nonetheless 'avowedly partisan; it takes the woman's part' (Lenz et al. 1980, pp. 3, 12). According to Gayle Greene, such criticism 'presupposes a feminist perspective', one that 'both originates from and participates in the larger effort of feminism — the liberation of women from oppressive social structures and stereotypes' (Greene 1981, p. 30). It has a commitment to 'social change' that makes it ' "criticism with a cause, engaged criticism . . . revolutionary" ' (ibid., pp. 33–4). Or, as an Australian feminist puts it, its goal is ' "to search for the origins of women's oppression and therefore to develop strategies for changing that oppression" ' (cit. Greer 1988, p. 616).

The fullest recent statement of this conception of feminist literary-critical goals comes from Lynda E. Boose. Responding to criticisms that 'the past decade of feminist analysis of family, sex, and marriage' had not been historically grounded, but was 'psychoanalytically based and textually rooted' — that is, supposedly, directly derived from the reading of texts — Boose acknowledges their truth. Indeed, she finds it

> thoroughly consistent with the feminist goal of liberating women from their history that the mainstream feminist interpretations of Shakespeare did indeed marginalize the historical and concentrate instead on the literary text. The text, at least, contained representations of women and could thus be used as a mirror in which modern women and men could recognize — and begin to change — the reflected image of a history of oppressive sexual and familial relations. (Boose 1987, p. 735)

However, the 'psychoanalytical approach adopted within the academy' — reproducing what she calls 'the essentialized notion of gender embedded in Freudian determinism' — had its disadvantages, too, chiefly in keeping 'feminist investigations focussed on given relationships within patriarchal family structure rather than on stepping outside and demanding an over-turning of the structure itself' (ibid., pp. 736–7).

The obvious contemporary issue, then, is whether it is right to 'use' a Shakespeare play as a text for what Boose describes as 'applied politics', an attempt to change not just the academy (as Neely wants), but society itself. What happens to works of literature when put to these uses? The further question is whether Shakespeare's plays actually do contain 'representations' of women, or of contemporary social attitudes and structures, in sufficient detail, or as a conscious programme, for us to be able to use them as reliable raw material for a sociohistorical analysis. That seems to me an enormous assumption, made unconsciously or at any rate unquestioningly by all feminist critics. Do the plays 'represent' their society accurately? Was that their main aim; and is it an inevitable component of every literary work? Does Shakespeare, dramatizing Greco-Roman history, Italian romance, medieval-Tudor chronicles, invariably — irrespective of the genre and dramatic conventions within which he worked — reveal the attitudes of his society, or indeed his own attitudes? Such awkward questions are not often asked.

The second issue, involving historical attitudes to women, has had some discussion, along a pleasantly wide spectrum. At one extreme is Juliet Dusinberre, enthusiastically stating that feminism, 'the struggle for women's rights', existed in Shakespeare's day, with all the attendant properties of the modern women's movement: 'the ideology, the literature, the social reform, the activism, and the increased awareness necessary to all of them dominated the society for which Shakespeare and his contemporaries wrote their plays' (Dusinberre 1975, p. 1). This claim, although still echoed by uncritical writers (Dreher 1986, p. 115), has not found much endorsement from feminist critics with a historical training.[4] Lisa Jardine distanced herself from these 'extravagant claims', expressing puzzlement that some feminist historians should be 'so eager to see emerging emancipation in the seventeenth century, and especially to read liberation into concessions which they would readily recognise as trivial in their own day' (Jardine 1983, p. 63). Linda Bamber also rejected the assimilation of Shakespeare 'into the system of feminist ideas', insisting on his 'indifference to, independence of, and distance from this system'. As she put it, 'only some plays, or some portions of some plays, can satisfy our desire as feminists to share common ground with this great writer' (Bamber 1982, p. 2). Marianne Novy agreed: 'we can learn a lot from Shakespeare about how far a brilliant man can go in trying to understand women. . . . We cannot learn from him the new possibilities for being a woman in the nonsexist society that feminists hope to create, nor should we expect to' (Novy 1981, p. 26).[5]

Linda Woodbridge, in the most impressive book yet written on women in the English Renaissance, found, indeed, an inherent contradiction in the claims that Shakespeare 'anticipated the women's movement by four hundred years'. Modern feminism, she wrote, believes in 'the essential intellectual, emotional, and moral equality of the sexes', independent of the valuations of gender made by the culture around them, while 'Renaissance *defenses* of women' — I italicise the word to make it clear that such works are produced by the supporters of women, not their enemies — 'constantly emphasize the differences between men and women' as if these belonged to nature, not culture (Woodbridge 1984, p. 3). These culturally produced attitudes — admirably analysed by Ian Maclean (Maclean 1980) — were almost universal in this period, and Shakespeare was no exception, however much we try to remake him in our image. As Woodbridge put it:

> We are tempted to assume that not only did Shakespeare know and love women, as he truly did, and not only does he occasionally allow them to speak movingly in their own defense (a privilege he grants even to villains, so why not to women?), but he was also conversant with all the modern notions about sex-stereotyping, socialization, the economics of sexism, and so on.

But the fact is that 'feminism as we know it did not exist in Shakespeare's time', and there is 'little evidence that he was ahead of his time in his attitudes toward women' (ibid., p. 222). Where Shakespeare differs from other writers, we might want to say, is in the breadth of his depiction of life, and the depth of his sympathy for almost all facets of human behaviour — setting aside hypocrisy, evil, and other forms of destructiveness. Given an oeuvre of such richness it is inevitable that he will dramatise issues which speak to us, the relationships between men and women forming, obviously enough, an important element in the construction of a good society in the comedies, and its destruction in the tragedies. But to concentrate on this element alone, or this at the expense of others, can distort the plays, sometimes subtly, sometimes blatantly.

II

Where Lynda Boose saw feminists 'using' Shakespeare's texts 'as a mirror' showing 'the reflected image of a history of oppressive sexual and familial relations', it seems to me that what some feminist critics put between the reader and the play is not a plane but a distorting mirror, in particular one that produces an anamorphic image. In anamorphic or 'perspective' art, as the Renaissance called it, the artist creates either specific objects (such as the skull in Holbein's painting 'The Ambassadors') or whole compositions which appear distorted unless they are seen from a coded viewing-point. Once the spectator takes up the right position the forms are restored to their normal shape and size:

> Like perspectives, which rightly gazed upon
> Show nothing but confusion; eyed awry
> Distinguish form.   (Richard II, 2.2.18ff)

If Shakespeare's plays are viewed exclusively in terms of women, men, sexual relationships, social attitudes, or used by a pressure-group for explicit political purposes, the distortion becomes general and permanent, 'nothing but confusion'. There is no longer any viewing-point which will resolve the plays back into their original proportion, or 'distinguish form'.

The simplest type of distortion is to see these plays as documents in the wars between the sexes. Carol Neely has noted that feminist criticism 'may tend to employ what might be called reverse sexism, attacking and stereotyping male characters and male critics'. This becomes a way of reversing 'the conventional stereotypes, representing female characters as active, powerful, rational, and male characters as passive, weak, unhinged'. She finds this approach 'understandable', but judges it 'neither a necessary nor a sufficient determinant of feminist critical style' (Neely 1981, pp. 4–5). The problem with this approach is that it tends to indict 'men' as such. Paula S. Berggren writes disapprovingly of 'the men' at the end of Shakespeare's tragedies having 'a glory of self-delivery (Hamlet leaping in Ophelia's grave, Othello pulling out his weapon, Lear with his looking glass)' (Berggren 1980, p. 25): the women have no such heroic moment. In the late plays, she feels, 'the tragic predicament afflicts male and female protagonists equally, but the men remain more comfortably self-indulgent in their pain' (*ibid.*, p. 28). As for the 'misogyny' she finds there, it is obvious who's really to blame: 'when men revile women, they cry out against their own failures' (p. 26). The editors of this volume take the same line about the misogyny in *Cymbeline* (2.5.19–33): it 'degrades women, but it degrades Posthumus more. The vices he attributes to women are, of course, his own' (Lenz *et al.* 1980, p. 14). In rather similar vein Janice Hays discusses 'the Distrust of Women' in Shakespeare, and finds that in Shakespeare, as throughout human history, women are 'always the agents of giving and sacrifice, men the receivers of their sacrificial gift' (Hays 1980, p. 92). This is perhaps what Neely means by 'reverse sexism': if so, it is hard to see why we should take it any more seriously than sexism itself. If the human race has been blind in one eye for so long, does it help to put out the other?

If 'men' are not the target, then 'patriarchy' is. Here feminists have drawn on social history, particularly the kind of social history written by Lawrence Stone, who is immensely popular with some feminists because he tells them what they want to hear. Often quoted, for instance, is his description of the 'sixteenth-century aristocratic family' as being patrilinear, primogenital, and 'patriarchal, in that the husband and father lorded it over his wife and children with the quasi-absolute authority of a despot'.[6] This account of the aristocratic family is then taken as describing all other families, at whatever place in society or point in time, and generalised as an invariant feature of Renaissance life. Many readers of Stone's later book, *The Family, Sex, and Marriage in England, 1500–1800* (London, 1977) have been so impressed by the amount of data it contains that they have not realised the degree to which Stone slanted his interpretation towards very personal emphases, and how bitterly many of his points have been contested by other historians.[7] The now-canonical view of the rigidly authoritarian family in the seventeenth century, dominated by the father, has been vigorously challenged by several recent researchers, and the case against Stone seems unanswerable.[8]

Stone attempted to overturn our whole perception of human relationships in early modern England, describing it as a period starved of warmth, riddled with neurotic distrust and hostility. According to his idiosyncratic mixture of neo-Freudianism and Whig history, in the period from 1500 to 1700 children were treated in ways which permanently distorted their psyches and made them warped adults. The practices of swaddling babies for the first few months, of giving them to wet-nurses (in fact, less than 5% of the population could afford to do this), of systematically breaking their wills by prolonged physical and psychological punishment (Stone's sensationalist account of flogging in schools may have some basis in fact, but there are no grounds for thinking that parents practiced such violence) — all these evil habits, together with the fact that many parents died prematurely, meant that children suffered forms of deprivation that scarred them for ever. Their parents were not over-concerned at their children's deaths, for they knew that child mortality rates were high, and so did not bother to invest any love or feeling in their offspring. As for marriages, they were loveless, on the whole, the father and husband forcing his family to obey his repressive wishes (such as attending household prayers!), denying the wife any independence or status. Children were just disposed of in marriage by the father, whose only considerations were money and land. This whole repressive structure began to collapse in the eighteenth century, age of enlightenment, when people suddenly learned to trust each other, discovered parental love and companionate marriage for the first time, and slaughtered the patriarch. At this point, too, thanks to the influence of the novel, men and women allowed the idea of romantic love to enter their lives, for all the output of poets and dramatists over the previous three hundred years concerned with love as the basis for marriage and indeed all other relationships had been regarded as a dangerous fantasy, indulged in only by a handful of idle young courtiers. The poetry of Wyatt and Surrey, Spenser, Sidney, Donne, the Cavaliers, Rochester, or the plays of Shakespeare, Dekker, Fletcher, and all the rest, were mere escapist fodder, neither reflecting real-life attitudes nor influencing behaviour.

Every detail in Stone's thesis has been questioned by competent historians, and I need neither summarise nor extend their refutation.[9] But a few points should be made here, in the interest of balance. One source of evidence mistreated by Stone is the literature on marriage, first analysed by Chilton Powell in a pioneering study published in 1917, and recently given an important corrective by Kathleen Davies.[10] Powell argued that whereas Catholicism, and conservative elements of the Church of England, continued to regard marriage as 'a kind of necessary evil' intended for the procreation of children and the avoidance of sin, the Puritans (or Reformers), influenced by Luther and his followers, had a much more positive concept of matrimony'. They saw it as an 'honourable and natural society of man and woman', having been 'instituted for the mutual blessing and benefit of husband and wife', and their teaching emphasised 'mental and spiritual satisfaction in marriage rather than mere physical' (Powell, pp. 94, 121). Davies showed that while Powell was correct in emphasising the importance of mutuality in Puritan attitudes to marriage, this was neither new nor specifically Puritan, since similar pronouncements can be found in pre-Reformation texts, and even in some medieval sources. In these treatises, often reprinted, marriage is seen as a partnership in which each party has duties towards the other: to love and worship with the body, as the English marriage service had stated since the Middle Ages, to comfort each other in sickness, to share the responsibilities of providing for the family (which in many cases made women working partners), to bring up children in godly ways, to care for their health, education and welfare throughout the parents' lives and after their deaths, by the careful maintenance of land and property. And these injunctions were no idealising theory: as many studies have shown, marriage granted women far more power and status than some feminists care to acknowledge, and wives, mothers and daughters were just as much the object of love and nurturing as were husbands, fathers, and sons. Of course, many inequalities persisted, both in law and in social practice, but the overall picture was far less bleak than some historians would have it.

It is heartening to see that this much-needed corrective research is coming from women historians, too. Not only do we have the excellent studies by Linda Woodbridge, Kathleen Davies and Vivien Elliott, but a recent book by Margaret Ezell has undermined still more of Stone's thesis and demonstrated the proper historical approach.[11] Ezell proves Stone wrong in his contention that children were usually given in marriage by their father. For one thing, the high mortality rate meant that many children were left fatherless, so that wedding negotiations (where they took place, in the higher realms of English society) were carried out by the mothers, especially, sometimes aided by aunts or grandmothers (Ezell 1987, pp. 18–32). Even when the father was alive, women still played the major role in these matters, and many instances show that the children's wishes, too, were taken into account. In the children's education and careers it was not the case that the patriarch laid down the law with unbending rigidity: mothers also had their say, indeed Ezell emphasises that the responsibility in these matters was not so much patriarchal as parental (*ibid.*, pp. 13, 34–5, 161). From her survey of women's education we can also reject Stone's picture of women receiving a formal classical education only for a brief period in the sixteenth century, under the influence of humanism, from which, he claims, in the not yet enlightened seventeenth century they slipped back into 'feminine acquirements'. The fact is that many more women received education in the seventeenth century than ever before, in a wider range of schools (pp. 11–15). Ezell also does much to dispel the false notion that the patriarchal oppression of women reduced them to silence both in the home and outside it, as seen by the scarcity of women authors. There was in fact a large literature by women (the better we research the subject the more we find),[12] much of it still extant in manuscript, as Ezell shows for the first time (pp. 62–100). Women's reluctance to venture into print can now be seen as deriving not from 'sexual intimidation' but from a clear decision to avoid the risk of being misunderstood and to select readers of their own choice (pp. 65–71, 85). This valuable study reinforces the case against Stone so tellingly made by Macfarlane, Wrightson and other critics, giving us a much more balanced picture of relationships between men and women. We can now accept the fact that women's competence was recognised in many areas of life, and that the success of marriage and parenthood was seen as depending not on some arbitrary male authority but on the mutual exchange of love, care, and nurturing. A leading feminist historian recently rebuked feminist critics for focussing on power but tending 'to homogenize its dynamics under the mindlessly simplistic category of "patriarchy"' (Fox-Genovese 1989, p. 237). That may be the signal for a welcome change of emphasis in women's studies.

For the great majority of feminist Shakespeare critics, however, blissfully unaware of the weakness of Stone's thesis, patriarchy continues to serve as a monolithic, reified bogey-man. In Charles Frey's reading of the great tragedies, 'Lear, Othello, and Macbeth, plays shot through with sexual and familial confusion, we see the inability of an authoritarian, aggressive male to enter reciprocal, fruitful relations with women or to foster life or line'. In the face of 'such often disastrous results generated by the system of near-absolute male authority', Frey can only conclude that 'Shakespeare's women are to some degree victims of patriarchy' (Frey 1980, p. 296). What we really see, however, is the distorting effect of this topic-determined approach, with its normative viewpoint or expectation that literary works — indeed, whole genres — can be reduced to the level of gender and still yield a meaningful statement. I dare say that no tragedy, by any writer, shows men entering into 'reciprocal, fruitful relations with women', or fostering life and line. But that is a necessary consequence of tragedy's concern with breakdown, and its presentation of the human evil that destroys almost everything and everyone we value in these plays. The genre is by definition committed to dramatising destruction, loss, waste. Ignoring this point, feminists make the further error of generalising the faults of specific characters, which involve a wide range of motivation — the mistaken love in Lear and Gloucester which displaces Cordelia and Edgar, empowering Goneril, Regan, and Edmund; Iago's hatred and brilliant manipulation of Othello, Desdemona, and almost everyone else in that play; Lady Macbeth's readiness to abandon human nature and social order to further her ambition, and her husband's inability to escape being manipulated by her — feminists generalise these diverse and individual motives into some supposed characteristic of Shakespeare's society and of the attitudes he derived from it, or see them as the mark of 'men' or 'women', *tout court*.

The disappointing aspect of much feminist Shakespeare criticism so far is that it seldom analyses drama in a spirit of open enquiry. It uses highly selective reference to the plays to make a slanted interpretation of them, with the aim of attacking specific political targets: male behaviour, patriarchy, injustice to women — then as now. The editors of that anthology, *The Woman's Part*, predictably emphasise the presence of patriarchy in Shakespeare and describe it as 'oppressive':

> Its lethal flaws are made manifest in the presentation of rape and attempted rape, in the . . . spurious manliness and empty honor that generate the tragedy of *Othello*. . . . Many other plays as well reveal the high cost of patriarchal values; the men who uphold them atrophy, and the women, whether resistant or acquiescent, die. . . . Cordelia . . . dies a victim of a chain of brutal assertions of manhood — Lear's, Edmund's, the Captain's. (Lenz *et al.* 1980, pp. 5–6)

Again the indictment of a generalised target distracts the attention from the specific actions within the play. Iago's hatred is the single generative factor in *Othello*, not manliness, nor honour; and Cordelia's death is due to a whole complex of desires — not excluding Goneril and Regan's cruelty and lust (their rivalry for Edmund consolidates his power at a crucial phase). As for rape, I trust that feminists will recognise the disgust with which Shakespeare presents that act, whether in *The Rape of Lucrece*, *Titus Andronicus*, or *Cymbeline*.[13]

One of the editors of this anthology, co-editor of a later one, writing in her own person, similarly affirmed that feminist critics 'find frequently an implied critique [that is, she suggests, *in Shakespeare, by Shakespeare*] of the values of patriarchy: of the aggressive individualism of an Edmund or Iago', or of the 'destructive effects' that 'patriarchal hierarchy' has on Desdemona, Othello, Coriolanus. Indeed, the whole genre of tragedy, it seems, is marked by this social system: 'lives are brought to tragic conclusions in these plays by the weight of a destructive patriarchy' (Greene 1981, pp. 30–31). We have been assured that feminism has no orthodoxy yet — but surely this is it! However, the reader concerned with the whole of Shakespeare must object that in his plays men and women are good or evil in themselves, not because of the social structure in which (supposedly) they find themselves. As an explanation of human behaviour this is rather like the reductivism and attempt to avoid responsibility which Shakespeare mocked, through the persona of Edmund, in judicial astrology: 'as if we were villains on necessity, fools by heavenly compulsion, knaves, thieves, and treachers by spherical predominance, drunkards, liars, and adulterers by an enforc'd obedience of planetary influence' — and rapists, duellists and murderers by the overwhelming weight of patriarchy. The amount of blurring and distortion created by this type of explanation is seen in Greene's identification of patriarchy with the 'aggressive individualism' of Edmund or Iago. In fact, the ruthless egoism of those two villains is actually hostile to, and subversive of, all forms of social order.

Another automatic, unthinking orthodoxy in current feminist circles is to equate patriarchy with misogyny. (I am aware that 'misogyny' is sometimes used loosely, to describe any system that under-privileges women, but from the contexts in which these critics use the term it seems to be meant literally.) Paula Berggren thinks that 'the central element in Shakespeare's treatment of women is always their sex, . . . primarily as a mythic source of power, an archetypal symbol that arouses both love and loathing in the male' (Berggren 1980, p. 18). Where does this loathing come from? Janice Hays diagnoses a generalised 'sexual distrust of women' frequently expressed in Shakespeare (Hays 1980, pp. 79ff). Madelon Gohlke believes that 'violence against women as an aspect of the structure of male dominance in Shakespeare's plays' indicates a deeper conflict in which women in general, as lovers and mothers, are 'perceived as radically untrustworthy' (Gohlke 1980, p. 161). Linda Bamber finds misogyny frequent in Shakespeare, but conveniently explains it with the psychoanalytic theory of projection. The misogyny of Hamlet, Lear, Antony, and Othello, she writes, is a

> projection onto women . . . of incoherence within the male. It is only when his sense of his own identity is threatened that the hero projects onto women what he refuses to acknowledge in himself. Only when he finds himself cowardly, appetitive, shifty, and disloyal does the sexuality of women disgust him. (Bamber 1986, p. 14)

In other words, 'misogyny and sex nausea' are born of what men find 'unacceptable in the male self — vicious, single-minded aggression' (pp. 15, 19). This is called, 'turning the tables'.

To some readers such arguments might be reassuring, perhaps even offering consolation that men are just as bad. But to me, critics who make such generalisations have simply ignored whole sections of the action, sequences of perfectly coherent causation which explain precisely why some men, sometimes, express resentment against women. In general, the diatribes against women are not, as elsewhere in drama and literature of the 'anti-feminist' tradition, the utterances of characters who can be identified as permanent misogynists, whether comic or vicious. In Shakespeare's men misogyny is (with two exceptions) a passing state, for which we see clear and adequate causes. The exceptions are, first, Timon of Athens, whose disappointment at the ingratitude of those he took to be friends, not parasites, becomes so obsessive that it deranges his feelings towards the whole of humanity. Timon becomes misogynistic *and* misanthropic. The same might be said of Iago, whose resentment of women (an irrational suspicion of Emilia constantly betraying him, which makes him well qualified to arouse similar fears in Othello) is equalled by his dislike of men, apart from himself. All the other misogynistic phases that men go through in Shakespeare occur in response to real or imagined betrayals of love. Hamlet is disgusted by his mother's speedy and incestuous marriage, which shows how little she loved his father; and he also has reason to believe that Ophelia is being used as a decoy. True, his diatribe against women is unbalanced, his generalisations extreme, and he lapses into the stock postures of misogynist satire.[14] It is not always easy to be sure what Shakespeare intended in this play, given the many and perhaps irreconcileable aspects of Hamlet's character as he created it, and one may well feel, with T.S. Eliot, that Hamlet's emotion 'is in excess of the facts'. I for one would regard the disproportionate intensity of feeling as yet another sign of the play's failure to integrate character, motive, and action. But Hamlet does have a reason for the disappointment he expresses, it is not because he himself is 'appetitive' or 'disloyal'.

Troilus, too, has ample reason to feel bitter at Cressida betraying him with Diomedes. But his outburst, which also generalises about the whole of the female sex on the basis of this one disappointment — 'Let it not be believed for womanhood. / Think, we had mothers' — is instantly mocked. As we have seen in Chapter 3, Shakespeare has Ulysses standing by in order to expose this superficiality — 'What hath she done, prince, that can soil our mothers?' (5.2.129ff). Troilus' attempt 'to square the general sex / By Cressida's rule' is so patently ridiculous that it deserves to be put in the same category as those inherently meaningless generalisations that begin 'Men . . .' or 'Women . . .'; or 'Englishmen . . .' or 'Germans . . .'. One character in Shakespeare who launches an attack on women's infidelity will be seen later to have spoken the truth without knowing it, since it has yet to happen. King Lear's intuition about his hypocritical daughters' appetite — 'Down from the waist they are centaurs' — actually precedes the outbreak of lust and rivalry between his two elder daughters, but many people would agree that 'the promiscuity of Goneril and Regan is predictable from their self-selling in the opening scene of the play' (Dusinberre 1975, p. 63). Lear's disgust is proleptic, then, and what he describes does actually happen in the play.

All the other men who attack women do so in the mistaken belief that their love has been betrayed. Antony's anger with Cleopatra comes when he finds her apparently making a deal with Caesar's messenger, and being over-generous with her person. In *Much Ado* Claudio is gulled by Don John's plot into thinking that Hero has deceived him. Othello has been convinced by Iago of Desdemona's infidelity, he has his 'cause', deluded though it is. Similarly with Posthumus, gulled by Iachimo into believing that Imogen has been unfaithful. As for Leontes' jealousy, it is not fully motivated, deliberately so, in order to show it as a sudden and irrational collapse. With the exception of Othello, none of these mistaken beliefs of betrayal has any tragic outcome: they belong to the plot-world of comedy, a temporary mistaking that is cleared up once greater knowledge of the real situation unfolds. In several cases the men's behaviour takes on some of the ridiculous forms that Woodbridge shows to be characteristic of the stage misogynist, who is typically a figure of ridicule or contempt (Woodbridge 1984, pp. 275–99). Leontes has something of the character of the stage-tyrant, whose outbursts do not really frighten. Indeed, when Paulina stands up to him he becomes a comic figure, a version of the hen-pecked husband ('Away with that audacious lady. . . . / I charged thee that she should not come about me, / I knew she would': 2.3.42–131). The only character whose misogyny is caused by a jealousy wholly self-produced is Ford in *The Merry Wives of Windsor*, and Shakespeare gives him, appropriately, a number of ludicrous soliloquies: 'Heaven be praised for my jealousy!' (2.2.309); 'This 'tis to be married! This 'tis to have linen and buck-baskets!' (3.5.42ff); reaching the absurd degree of holding himself up as a type of foolishness — 'Let them say of me, as jealous as Ford, that searched a hollow walnut for his wife's leman' (4.2.161ff).

Ford is a character who fully bears out the conclusions of Linda Woodbridge, that 'many stage misogynists are basically comic figures' (Woodbridge 1984, p. 285), and Margaret Ezell, that they became figures of fun. Joseph Swetnam, whose *Arraignment of Lewd, Idle, Froward and Inconstant Women* (1615) is naïvely seen by Stone as typifying 'the "sharpening acrimony against women in general"', ended, as Ezell points out, as 'a buffoon villain in a play' called *Swetnam the Woman-hater* (1620), a treatment meted out to other embodiments of 'mean-spirited misogyny' (Ezell 1987, pp. 46–51). Equally ridiculous is Posthumus, whose mis-ogynistic soliloquy oscillates between violence and impotence. He starts with the blanket indiscrimination of a Troilus or Timon — 'Is there no way for men to be, but women / Must be half-workers? We are all bastards', a deduction of such illogic as to be patently ridiculous. He is satirised throughout, and appropriately concludes by reducing himself to the level of an ineffective satirist denouncing women: 'I'll write against them, / Detest them, curse them' (*Cymbeline*, 2.5.1–35). 'Get on with it' is all that we can say, dismissively. In these men jealousy, like misogyny, is a temporary sickness — 'thou hast some crotchets in thy head now', Mistress Ford says to her husband (2.1.154f); or, as Mistress Page tells her,

> Why, woman, your husband is in his old lunes again. He . . . so rails against all married mankind; so curses all Eve's daughters, of what complexion soever; and so buffets himself on the forehead, crying 'peer out, peer out', that any madness I ever yet beheld, seemed but tameness . . . to this his distemper he is in now. (4.2.21f)

All these men resemble Leontes, of whom Paulina — a central spokes-woman and moral authority if ever there was one — says: 'These dangerous, unsafe lunes i'the King, beshrew them!' (2.2.30). Once they recover from their 'lunes' or periods of temporary madness (male menstruation?), they beg the woman's pardon for the wrongs their mistaking has created. Let

Ford speak for them all, translated as he is to the dignity of verse to match
the seriousness of his utterance:

> Pardon me, wife, henceforth do what thou wilt.
> I rather will suspect the sun with cold,
> Than thee with wantonness.   (4.4.6ff)

The distemper has been cured.

Of course, the language used against women by a Lear or a Posthumus is
degrading, deeply offensive: but we know that it is the language of a man
in a state of violent passion, justified or not, and that it in no way presents
a norm either for them or for Shakespeare's men in general. Many misogynists in Elizabethan drama, as Woodbridge has shown, turn woman-
haters out of one unhappy experience. But, as she points out, 'the
misogynist's credibility is continually undercut by his subjectivity and his
habit of jumping to conclusions'. The dramatists unanimously establish
'the character type as discreditable by nature — no less suspect as a
commentator than the braggadocio' (Woodbridge 1984, pp. 282–3), being
linked to 'a related type, the slanderer' (p. 288). In Shakespeare the
misogynist is more often the victim of a slanderer than a slanderer himself
(a significant point), but his plays conform to the general pattern in which
misogynists are discredited. In Shakespeare, as in other dramatists, the
misogynist performs what Woodbridge calls 'an antimasque function',
objectifying 'doubts, fears, and antagonisms' which can be thought to be
banished when the misogynist is 'converted, discredited, or simply drops
out of the play'. In effect the plays become 'almost ritual vindications of
Woman' (p. 290), and so, she concludes, paradoxical though it may seem,
that 'the stage misogynist is a figure belonging to the defense of women' (p.
297). This is certainly true when we think of the attacks of Leontes on
Hermione, Enobarbus on Cleopatra, Claudio on Hero, Ford on his wife,
Posthumus on Imogen, and — belatedly, as Othello himself realises, of
Desdemona too. All these women are comprehensively vindicated from the
misogynist attack. The example of Othello, suddenly and painfully realising whom he has destroyed —

> My wife! My wife! What wife? I have no wife.
> O insupportable! O heavy hour!
> Methinks it should now be a huge eclipse
> Of sun and moon. . . .   (5.2.61ff)

— is the most painful proof of the rule that misogyny in Shakespeare is the
result of mental imbalance, not a permanent state of the psyche which
can only be eased by the phenomenon of 'projection'. The state is only
temporary, for with the exception of Timon (permanently estranged from
the whole of humankind) and Iago (liking nobody), it is noticeable that
Hamlet shows no lasting resentment to either Ophelia or Gertrude, and

FEMINIST STEREOTYPES

341

that all the others recover their love again, retaining it, in romance, losing it for ever in tragedy.

There is, we may conclude, not much misogyny in Shakespeare, and what there is derives from causal plot structures, not from diseased psyches. There is not much misogyny in the supposedly patriarchal Renaissance either, as Linda Woodbridge has conclusively shown. Her outstanding study of the controversy over women in England between 1540 and 1620 establishes that there were many more defences of women published than attacks on them; that the defences came first, as part of a formal, debate-like structure (she makes good use of contemporary practices in rhetoric); that the debate was more of a literary convention than a reflection of real life; and that it was possibly damaging to the actual cause of women, since it deflected attention away from real issues (financial and legal bondage) to literary topoi (pp. 134–5). Yet, as she observes, 'Renaissance attacks on women are more congenial to modern feminists than are Renaissance defenses of women' (p. 8). There is perhaps something of a rallying-point about the image of a hostile, oppressive enemy: it unites those threatened into a group, justifying their aggression as legitimate defence. As Woodbridge writes of the morality plays, 'the presence of the formal detractor, in the person of the Vice, is a structural and genetic necessity: the defense of women had always adopted a position of rebuttal; if a contemporary detractor did not exist, the formal defense had always found it necessary to invent one' (p. 278). The current enemy is the patriarchal society. But that, too, is an unhistorical modern illusion, a cultural construct.

Whoever approaches English social history in the sixteenth and seventeenth centuries with an open mind will find ample evidence that women were not uniformly oppressed, but treated with respect, given status and power — albeit within boundaries — and were associated with such qualities as love, sharing, and nurturing. Those feminists who are aware of this historical fact but suppress it, preferring to see hatred, oppression, and violence, are distorting the real situation, whether or not for self-serving ends, and what they gain in the short term (a sense of unity in the face of oppression) they will lose as the true picture comes to be more widely known. Lynda E. Boose, for instance, who believes that 'misogyny . . . indelibly marks both the literary and non-literary texts of the English Renaissance' (Boose 1987, p. 712), defends feminists' use of psychoanalytic approaches, even though they accept 'Freud's essentialist presumption' of 'the transhistorical nature of the family unit' (pp. 715, 720) — that is, as retaining the same identity and behaviour-patterns at whatever point in history. Boose then faces the charge that such criticism is 'ahistorical' in 'its failure to recognize the historical specificity of psychic and social structures that produce gender and family' (p. 733). As we saw above, in reply she effectively dismissed history. Feminists rightly 'privilege' the literary work over its historical context, she claimed, because the work's 'ability to survive massive social changes and still fascinate a modern reader' (whether or not they have understood it!) means that to them

> a historical text is seen as fully approachable through contemporary ideas — nor are those ideas assumed to be projections backward from the present. Even though a social idea may not have been articulated during the historical moment in which the text was produced, such ideas are imagined as being potentially fully present, latent within earlier times, but, like the late discovered planets, awaiting the invention of a telescope, a discourse, that could articulate them. (p. 734)

But the analogy is false: those planets have been there since the world began, while the 'psychic and social structures' of 1580, say, are the result of a whole complex of historical factors specific to that time (and indeed to each place), and totally different to those of 1780, or 1880. Lacking an open-minded approach to the past, such reading into the literary text of social ideas that may post-date it is indeed nothing other than a projection of our concerns 'backward from the present', a re-writing of the text in our terms which freezes it at this moment in time, detached from both past and future. In twenty years' time such criticism may seem archaic. For Boose, however, 'the feminist investment in history' is and should be 'not only minimal' but actively sceptical of the whole possibility of historical understanding, since 'Western history is essentially a transmitted record of upper class white males' (p. 735), a 'monological narrative of male-male conflict' (p. 737). After this absolute dismissal of the historical approach we are left with 'feminist analyses [grounded] inside the text' (p. 714). To some readers this will seem like a poor exchange.

III

If we leave the historical issue and turn back to Shakespeare's plays, examining those forms of 'pure' criticism which disavow reconstructing a Renaissance or any other context, we find that several feminists pride themselves on their close scrutiny of the text. The editors of the first anthology of their work say that feminist critics reading Shakespeare 'trust their responses . . . even when they raise questions' that challenge prevailing assumptions, and that 'conclusions derived from these questions are then tested rigorously against the text'. All their contributors are said to 'owe a substantial debt to New Criticism. All use techniques of close textual analysis . . .' (Lenz et al. 1980, pp. 3, 10). But the dichotomy is misleading, for textual analysis is only convincing when it can claim to have understood the meaning of a text, and meaning is, to begin with, lexical, depending on the history of the language at that point in time, acquiring more specific contextual detail from the genre in which it occurs, and the conventions of the work's literary form. In pastoral love-poetry or madrigals 'to die' is a euphemism for orgasm, but to find in Othello's last words as he kills himself ('No way but this, / Killing myself, to die upon a kiss') an 'appalling pun', as Madelon Gohlke does (Gohlke 1981, p. 164), is to lose the literal in the metaphorical. In modern (especially American) slang 'grope' as a transitive verb without a preposition means something like making physical contact, sexually. To Linda Bamber Hamlet's description of how he searched the sleeping Rosencrantz and Guildenstern for evidence of the death-sentence Claudius has given them — 'in the dark / Groped I to find out them, had my desire, / Fingered their packet' (5.12.13–15) — 'the language implies a heavy investment of libido in the action' (Bamber 1982, p. 90). But no, 'groped' here simply means 'fumbled around', looking for something, while 'fingered' means 'stole, extracted', as in that description of the kidnapping of Henry VI with a metaphor from card-games: 'The king was slily finger'd from the deck' (3 Henry VI, 5.1.44). There are no sexual undertones here.

Other feminist critics reveal anachronistic aesthetic attitudes, derived from nineteenth-century naturalism, which make them insensitive to the theatrical context of Elizabethan drama, with its many conventions governing language, symbolism, and plot-forms. Commenting on the scene in Richard III (2.2) where the surviving relatives of the murdered Clarence and the dead King Edward express their griefs, Madonne M. Miner complains that the characters 'engage in a chorus of moans, each claiming the greater loss. An appalling absence of empathy characterizes this meeting . . . . a selfish indulgence' (Miner 1980, p. 46). This is to judge from a disablingly modern viewpoint, unaware of both dramatic purpose and the lament-form, which serves both to express the characters' grief and to arouse feeling in the audience. Janice Hays, discussing Much Ado about Nothing, finds it 'reasonable and even probable' that Claudio should ask Don Pedro to make a courtship approach on his behalf to Leonato, but observes disapprovingly that 'it does not at all follow that Don Pedro should disguise himself as Claudio, approach Hero, and woo her' (Hays 1980, pp. 83–4). She invokes Lawrence Stone and Freudian theories of 'latent content' shaping 'manifest presentation' to explain this: but she might simply have reflected that such behaviour is perfectly normal in an Elizabethan play. This lack of any sense of the dynamics of plot or dramatic structure also characterises David Sundelson's disapproval of the Duke in Measure for Measure, whose concealment of his plot to save Claudio is described as a 'protracted torment' of Isabella. He lets her 'believe that her brother has been executed, and, as if that were not enough, accuses her of madness and drives her uncomfortably close to it by pretending not to believe her denunciation of the deputy' (Sundelson 1981, p. 87). Such comments ignore the logic of plot and treat characters in Elizabethan drama by the standards of contemporary psychological naturalism, as if to say, 'I'd never behave like that! What a nasty man! How inconsiderate!'

If plot and dramatic structure go by the board, so do theatre conventions. It was a convention in the Elizabethan theatre for women's roles to be taken by boys (apart from some older comic female parts, played by men). The disguise involved was sometimes reversed, so to speak, in that the female characters subsequently adopted male disguise in order to fulfil their plots within the play, usually romantic, and usually involving a happy ending. This curious A/B/A structure has been commented on in English literary criticism for centuries, but feminism, sometimes aided by psychoanalysis, wishes to give it a quite new significance. As we briefly saw with Greenblatt's ('Fiction and Friction') unsuccessful search for 'heat' in the comedies, theatrical disguise is being increasingly discussed in terms of transvestism ('cross-dressing') or even androgyny. Both concepts seems to me glaringly anachronistic and inappropriate to what was a theatrical necessity, given the English ban on actresses. Outside the theatre transvestism is the action of sexually mature adults who feel unhappy with their biological destiny, sometimes wishing to attract attention from their own sex by posing as the other. The motivation behind it is complex, but it is a freely-chosen act, often with sexual consequences; for a boy-actor, apprenticed to the company and likely to stay with it once his voice had broken, it did not have these connotations.

Although unsuitable as descriptions of boy-actors, both notions obviously appeal to the current fascination with gender. Transvestism is an instance of 'gender-swapping' that can be taken to show either male anxieties with their biological sex, or women's wishes to overturn the cultural category of gender; androgyny is a crossing of categories for the boy-actor, who — for the duration of the play, at least — is supposedly both male and female. The direction this second concern can take is shown by recent studies which see the characters of Portia, Rosalind and Viola, played by male actors, as representing to Shakespeare's audience 'celebrations of an idealized androgyny unavailable in real life'. However few spectators then, or now, aspire towards the androgynous condition, the vogue for essays, and soon books, on cross-dressing since the 1970s has been astonishing, making it the 'fastest-growth area' in Renaissance drama studies. Some of this work is historically well-founded (that by Linda Woodbridge exceptionally so), some not; some of it preserves a sense of the plays as drama, 'doings' which have distinct and differing structures; some of it ignores all aesthetic considerations and picks out only those elements fitting current feminist preoccupations. I shall cite one critic who preserves the notion of structure, another who destroys it, beginning with the second.

Jean Howard's essay on 'Crossdressing . . . and Gender Struggle' draws eclectically on several current routines: first, New Historicism (her readings 'are motivated by present concerns', she states, citing Montrose in support: Howard 1988, p. 418 note), with its Foucauldian concern for 'sites of resistance to the period's patriarchal sex-gender system' (pp. 419, 439);

secondly on 'Materialist or socialist feminism' (p. 419 note); and thirdly —
and inescapably — on psychoanalytic criticism (in *Twelfth Night* Orsino's
'narcissism and potential effeminacy are displaced, respectively, onto
Malvolio and Andrew Aguecheek': p. 432). I pick out, for brevity's sake,
her account of *Twelfth Night*, a play in which some feminists take Viola
as representing what they call androgyny, 'the erasure of sexual determinacy' (pp. 430–33). Howard in fact disagrees with feminists who see
such 'blurring of sexual difference' as offering 'the liberating possibility of
undoing all the structures of domination and exploitation' involved in a
binary sexual system. She believes that Viola's gender identity is never
'made indeterminate and thereby . . . threatening *to the theatre audience*' (a
diametrically opposed reading to those who see androgyny as a blessed
transformation!), since the audience never doubts her heterosexual
orientation, what Howard tendentiously labels 'her properly "feminine"
subjectivity'. Viola, that is, does not attempt 'a dismantling of a hierarchical gender system', and her 'self-abnegation' thus makes her acceptable
to men. While making sense within one current feminist paradigm,
Howard's categorisation reduces Viola to a bleached, rather passive role,
far removed from what we perceive as an active presence in the play, a
woman who can turn many situations to her own advantage, that side of
her caught so well in Johnson's laconic note: 'Viola is an excellent schemer,
never at a loss'.[15] To Howard the play as a whole 'seems to . . . embody a
fairly oppressive fable of the containment of gender and class insurgency
and the valorization of the "good woman" as the one who has interiorized'
her 'subordinate relations to the male'. That is a dispiriting example of how
gender criticism can drain life and movement from a play.

   Howard's paradigm has a much stranger effect on Olivia, whom she
regards as 'the real threat to the hierarchical gender system in this text'.
Joining hands with Stephen ('Fiction and Friction') Greenblatt, Howard
agrees that 'Olivia is a woman of property, headstrong and initially
intractable', who 'lacks any discernible male relatives, except the dis-
reputable Toby, to control her and her fortune'. This is apparently a
suspicious degree of independence, and another fact to be held against her
is that 'at the beginning of the play she has decided to do without the
world of men, and especially to do without Orsino. These are classic marks
of unruliness', Howard deduces, and thus Olivia 'is punished, comically
but unmistakably, by being made to fall in love with the crossdressed
Viola'. The 'humiliation' of Olivia — by 'the play', Howard says, not
by Shakespeare — is appropriate for a woman who has 'jumped gender
boundaries to assume control of her house and person and refused her
"natural" role in the patriarchal marriage market'. Viola is the agent of this
humiliation, and is thus 'used to enforce a gender system', while at the
same time 'the oft-repeated fear that boy actors dressed as women leads to
sodomy is displaced here upon a woman dressed as a man'. (I confess not to
understand this point: what is 'displaced' on to Viola, and how can there

be any 'fear of sodomy' if a woman falls in love with her? In any case, the fact that some hysterical moralist like Stubbes invoked sodomy to attack theatrical disguise proves nothing about general attitudes.)[16]

Imposing a modern gender-paradigm on *Twelfth Night* simply applies normative expectations to it from a distance of four centuries, distorting the play until it fits the present-day paradigm. Howard never mentions that, at the beginning of the play, Olivia has vowed to mourn seven years to 'keep fresh . . . / A brother's dead love' (1.1.29f), the brother who had presumably been in charge of their household. Olivia has not 'jumped gender boundaries to assume control of her house': she has inherited it, and is no doubt capable of managing it, as many Elizabethan women (usually widows) did, given reliable help from their steward and others. As Sebastian records, baffled by the sudden 'flood of fortune' that overwhelms him with Olivia's proposal to marry him virtually at first sight (as far as he is concerned, at least), she cannot be mad, for if she were

> She could not sway her house, command her followers,
> Take and give back affairs and their dispatch
> With such a smooth, discreet, and stable bearing
> As I perceive she does.   (4.3.11ff)

In her mourning Olivia has rejected not 'the world of men', as Howard claims, but the world in general; or if not that, Orsino, whom she does not like (but then, apart from Viola, not many people do). Howard's description of Olivia as 'headstrong . . . intractable', having 'refused her "natural" role in the patriarchal marriage market', is presumably intended to spell out (and parody) male chauvinist attitudes. In our theatrical experience, reading or seeing the play, Olivia becomes a comic figure when she falls in love with Cesario-Viola — so does Viola — but any notion that 'the play' (once again detached from Shakespeare's authorship) intends this to be seen as a *punishment* for challenging the patriarchal order is a figment of this critic's imagination ('classic marks of unruliness' is a fine invention). The Elizabethan property-owning woman was self-reliant to a degree that modern feminists of the incriminatory school evidently find it uncomfortable to admit. Following her ideological bias, Howard concludes that the play 'disciplines independent women like Olivia', not noticing that it (or rather Shakespeare) actually rewards her with Sebastian — 'Would thou'dst be ruled by me!', she says to him (4.1.63), and he gladly agrees. It is symptomatic of Howard's involvement with the 'gender struggle' that she never even mentions Sebastian, nor the comic resolution of the play in marriage, precisely those points that would have undermined her thesis. The play's ingenious structure, its beautifully articulated development of disguise and deception leading to cross purposes and comic misunderstanding as a means of exposing character and false values — think of Malvolio, and the reversals in the duel-scene involving Toby, Aguecheek and Sebastian — all this disappears from view.

Feminist criticism need not be so reductive and blind to drama as a highly-organised structure and a complex unfolding experience. This can be seen from an essay by Nancy K. Hayles on sexual disguise in the comedies, from which I select the discussion of *As You Like It* (Hayles 1979, pp. 63–8). Criticising the tendency to regard 'this complex dramatic device . . . solely in terms of social and sexual roles', Hayles urges that while some aspects of disguise are 'common to all the plays in which it appears, its dramatic function is shaped by the particular design of each play'. In *As You Like It*, she suggests, disguise proceeds in two separate movements: first, 'layers of disguise are added as Rosalind becomes Ganymede, and then as Ganymede pretends to be Orlando's Rosalind' — the unique extra level of pretence in this play; secondly, 'the layers are removed as Ganymede abandons the play-acting of Rosalind, and then as Rosalind herself abandons the disguise of Ganymede'. In the 'most complex layering, Rosalind-as-Ganymede-as-Orlando's Rosalind', Hayles points out, the heroine persuades her beloved to accept a more realistic version of herself than the Petrarchised idol of his love-verses. 'When Rosalind-as-Ganymede insists that Orlando's Rosalind will have her own wit, her own will and her own way', Rosalind is in effect insisting that Orlando confront the discrepancy between his idealised expectations and her needs, so 'claiming the right to be herself'. As Hayles finely puts it,

> In playing herself (which she can apparently do only if she first plays someone else) Rosalind is able to state her own needs in a way she could not if she were simply herself. It is because she is disguised as Ganymede that she can be so free in portraying a Rosalind who is a flesh and blood woman instead of a Petrarchan abstraction.

That sensitive observation, made by attending to the language of the play as it reveals feelings and motives, is at a far remove from the imposition of gender paradigms.

Hayles is also responsive to the dramatic structure, as two plot-levels become intertwined when Rosalind's male disguise makes Phebe fall in love with Ganymede.

> Rosalind's on-layering, which inadvertently makes her Silvius's rival, causes Phebe's desire to be even more at variance with Silvius's hopes than before. It takes Ganymede's transformation into Rosalind to trick Phebe into accepting her swain, as the off-layering of Rosalind's disguise reconciles these two Petrarchan lovers.

Hayles links the two stages of disguise to the general movement of this comedy, from conflict and competition (the exile by Duke Frederick of his brother, the rightful Duke; the mistreatment of Orlando by his brother Oliver) to reconciliation and co-operation. The Silvius-Phebe plot 'shows in simplified form the correlation between on-layering and rivalry, and off-layering and co-operation'. It also allows us to see a resemblance between the two pairs of lovers as 'reflections of stereotypical male and female postures, familiar through the long tradition of courtly love'. Hayles suggests that Rosalind's disguise, inasmuch as it allows her 'to hear Orlando's love-confession without having to take any comparable risks herself', gives her a superiority over him which is another instance of 'female manipulation', also caricatured in Phebe. If so, the superiority is shortlived, for — I suggest — just as in *Twelfth Night*, when Shakespeare engineered the comic duel with Aguecheek to deflate some of the advantages that Viola has gained through disguise, so here, when Rosalind hears from Oliver of Orlando's fight with the lioness, she faints. Within the play's conventions, Hayles argues, this is 'an involuntary revelation of female gender because fainting is a "feminine" response', but it also represents 'the loss of her manipulative control over Orlando'.

Rosalind regains self-control, and with it her disguise, but when she next meets Orlando she realises that the pretence is no longer needed. 'From this point on, the removal of the disguise signals the consummation of all the relationships as all four couples are married'. Hayles sees much of the play, including the disguising, in terms of 'control', however, which seems to me to miss the point. I see disguise as a way of gaining an (often unfair) advantage over other people, so that Rosalind's abandonment of disguise puts her back on the same level as Orlando, acknowledging his rights and needs as well as her own. But I agree with Hayles that the removal of disguise is 'an act of renunciation', and that (as with Portia's gift of herself to Bassanio)

> what appears to be a generous surrendering of self-interest can in fact bring consummation both to man and woman, so that rivalry can be transcended as co-operation brings fulfillment. In *As You Like It*, fulfillment of desire, contentment and peace of mind come when the insistence on self-satisfaction ceases.

As Hayles shows, the several events in the closing stages of the play bringing about reconciliation 'all express the same paradox of consummation through renunciation that is realized in specifically sexual terms by the disguise'. (What a refreshingly sane and coherent account of the play's resolution this is compared to Malcolm Evans's Derridian fissurising, discussed in Chapter 3.)

Yet there is one more level of disguise to be removed in *As You Like It*. In the Epilogue Rosalind addresses the audience, first charging the women 'for the love you bear to men, to like as much of this play as please you', and then charging the men 'for the love you bear to women' with the same task. 'If I were a woman', the actor adds, 'I would kiss as many of' the men as she liked, and hopes that they all 'will for my kind offer, when I make curtsy, bid me farewell'. At this moment, Hayles writes, the boy actor 'relinquishes the last level of the sexual disguise', the 'unlayering' being once more 'linked with a reconciliation between the sexes' as he appeals to each in turn. Through the figure of Rosalind, who has been mistress of ceremonies in the closing scenes, a 'surrogate playmaker', Shakespeare 'uses his relinquishing of control over the play to signal a final reconciliation between the men and women in the audience'. There Nancy Hayles neatly indicates the multiple connections between playwright and actors, playwright and audience, actors and audience, and the whole structure of make-believe in which we have been participating, a dramatic experience unfolding simultaneously on several interconnected levels and involving us in the hopes and fears of many characters and their resolution, successful or otherwise.

Such sensitivity to the relation of characters' intentionalities to the play as a whole is rare in feminist criticism (and not only there, I should add in all fairness). Far too many feminist analyses of Shakespeare consist of character studies, often one at a time, with moralising judgements from a superior modern viewpoint. So Diane Elizabeth Dreher passes her verdict on Shylock's daughter: 'Bored, restless, and superficial, eager for the acceptance of her peers and resentful of her father, Jessica is a typical adolescent. She embodies the worst qualities of youth without its fervent idealism' (Dreher 1986, p. 102). Such a comment is not merely modern and anachronistic, it shows the danger of ignoring the specific identity of this character in this situation (there is only one Shylock), in order to generalise about supposedly typical behaviour-patterns. Feminism has a tendency to see everything in terms of family-structures, inevitably distorting or falsifying the play as a result. Dreher makes many such generalisations:

> Research has correlated schizophrenic young women with rigid, authoritarian fathers who refuse to acknowledge their daughters' autonomy. Such is the relationship of Polonius with Ophelia, who, understandably, goes mad. (p. 12)

This glib comment overlooks, first, Ophelia's rejection by Hamlet; and secondly, the fact that it is not life with her father that drives Ophelia mad but the shock of his death, also caused by Hamlet. Dreher leaves out the unhappy love affair, because her Freudian-feminist alignment leads everything back to parent-child relationships. So, she adds, 'Shakespeare's fatherless daughters' — but one should not cite such remarks without noting the tendentious assumptions of this critical school that such 'omissions', like that of Shakespeare having 'failed to provide a wife' for Lear or Prospero, or sufficient mothers elsewhere, are somehow significant: if every character had to be fitted out with the standard allocation of spouses, parents, and/or children, the casts of these plays would be immense — such fatherless daughters as Olivia in *Twelfth Night* are, *therefore*, 'defensive and hesitant to commit themselves to men. Olivia hides behind her veil . . .' (p. 13). But only because she doesn't give a fig for Orsino! When Cesario comes along she is anything but hesitant, indeed marries

Sebastian with what seems to many theatregoers and readers like comical haste.

Such elementary misreadings of the play are not due to the lack of a historical perspective: but they are endemic to the whole feminist enterprise of locating 'the woman's part' and judging from there. A non-historical critical reading of Elizabethan drama is valid at any time provided that it respects what I take to be the fundamental, if often unstated principle of literary criticism dealing with a mimetic work of literature, that one should accurately and faithfully describe what happens in it, and why. (We require other things of the critic too, of course, but this one is essential.) Paula Berggren criticises Posthumus for 'his show-stopping theatrics' when he strikes 'the disguised Imogen' who is 'so bold as to answer his cry by identifying herself' (Berggren 1980, p. 28). But since he has every reason to believe that Imogen is dead, there is no way that Posthumus can identify her with this person in a page's clothing. Berggren's real target is 'self-indulgent' men, and she mocks the 'egotistical humility' of Posthumus, his 'colossal self-absorption'; to be fair, she might have commented on his anguish and self-accusation, too. Berggren states that disguise 'remains incidental, though useful, for Shakespeare's women; for his men, it is the very core of experience' (p. 20). But this superficial and hostile generalisation leaves out the fact that most of the men who use disguise and dissimulation do so for evil and destructive purposes, such as Richard III, whom she cites. In Shakespeare women disguise to achieve their (usually romantic) goals, because the plot-situation, or society, offer them no alternative. Hamlet's feigned madness is just such a protective disguise, but with male characters otherwise there is an alternative to disguise, namely open and honest behaviour. Berggren uses *King Lear* to show what she describes as 'the Manichean view of female sensuality in Shakespeare's high tragic world': that is, in 1.1 Lear offers his daughters 'plenteous rivers and wide-skirted meads', while in 1.4 he 'reverses his promise to Goneril and Regan, bidding Nature instead "dry up [their] organs of increase". They consequently manifest [a] depraved and nonprocreative lasciviousness' (p. 24). Something, indeed, happens between those two points, but readers will not need me to summarise the plot there. I just express disappointment at this kind of superficial man-nailing, a *ressentiment* that does not fulfil even the minimal requirements for literary criticism.

Feminist critics, like everyone else, tend to overlook or reject the things that displease them. Lisa Jardine cannot accept the absolute gift of the self that Portia makes to Bassanio:

Myself and what is mine to you and yours
Is now converted. But now I was the lord
Of this fair mansion, master of my servants,
Queen o'er myself; and even now, but now,

This house, these servants, and this same myself
Are yours, my lord's. I give them with this ring. . . .

                                                        (3.2.149–72)

For Jardine it is 'a financial balance sheet' that 'simply will not balance',
for Portia has 'rhetorically contrived' her 'capitulation' (Jardine 1983, p.
61). To me it reads like a spontaneous and convincing gesture, all of a
piece with her feelings and values as we have known them since the
beginning of the play. Must I qualify these words by adding 'but then, I
write as a man', as if my sex were congenitally used to women offering
themselves to us, since we are incapable of giving ourselves to them? That
would be a submission gesture, admitting defeat or appeasing a victorious
enemy (in the animal kingdom, at least). But this is precisely what
feminists, in another new orthodoxy, accuse the heroines of Shakespeare's
comedies of doing: 'even the strongest, most resourceful of the heroines
end their comedies with ritual gestures of submission' (Novy 1981, p. 20;
Park 1980, pp. 106ff). The words of Rosalind, Beatrice, and Portia are
cited: but not those of Orlando, Benedick, and Bassanio. Yet this is to put
the whole issue in a negative light. Each of those heroines wants her man,
gives herself and receives him in turn. To leave out the women's desires,
on the description and fulfilment of which Shakespeare lavishes a great
part of his energies in comedy, is to lessen the plays, and falsify them.

IV

The most damaging effect of these partial, distorted readings concerns
ethical issues, where the feminist displacement of interest towards the
family leads to them omitting or ignoring crucial acts of evil and destructive
behaviour, from both men and women. One feminist has fairly criticised
Linda Bamber and Marilyn French for making an 'essentialist' definition of
male (evil) and female (good) principles — 'the ability to kill' being set
against 'the power to nurture and give birth' — independent both of
historical particularity and the effects of genre and literary tradition.[17] This
is a valuable comment on the tendency to reduce complex issues to their
simplest binary opposition (as if we were to evaluate the food we eat in
terms of the proportion of hydrogen and carbon molecules it contains).
Unfortunately, however, this critic herself goes on to describe *King Lear* as
linking 'sexual subordination and anarchy' but with 'an explicitly misogynist emphasis', namely the idea that 'fathers are owed particular duties
by their daughters' (McLuskie 1985, p. 98). But parents also had their
duties, according to Renaissance social theory, and the expectation of 'filial
gratitude', as she calls it (p. 104), applied just as much to sons — even to

bastard sons, when legally recognised — as to daughters. It is significant of her one-sided approach that she never mentions Edmund, who not only betrays his natural father but whose destructive involvement in a sexual triangle with Goneril and Regan shows that 'atavistic selfishness and the monstrous assertion of individual wills' — which she fears would become the image of 'feminist ideology' if those two daughters' rights were to be asserted (p. 102) — is just as much a mark of the male sex, when external legal or moral constraints are abandoned.

The focus on gender issues regularly distorts issues of ethics and motivation. Janice Hays, discussing 'Much Ado and the Distrust of Women', believes that 'Shakespeare's purpose in the Hero-Claudio plot is . . . to confront the psychological difficulties of joining the traditional arranged marriage, which takes into account social and economic reality, with romantic and erotic love' (Hays 1980, p. 81). But Claudio has no qualms about the choice of Hero or the arrangements for the marriage. It is only when the malice of Don John produces the false disguise plot, where Claudio is led to believe that his intended has been having nocturnal assignations with another man, that the marriage arrangements break down. Hays explains Claudio's behaviour with a mixture of Lawrence Stone and Freud, to which I shall return. As for Don John's evil, Hays describes him as planting 'the seeds of distrust in Claudio's mind' (in fact he gives him 'ocular proof'), but doing so merely 'by externalizing unconscious aspects of Claudio's psyche' (p. 84). The real cause of the discord, then, is the psycho-social structure. A similar formulation by Diane Dreher links the heroines of comedy and tragedy: 'Ophelia, Hero, and Desdemona are victimized by the traditional power structure that identifies women exclusively as child-bearers, insisting on a rigid model of chastity to ensure the continuity of pure patrilineal succession' (Dreher 1986, p. 76). Readers who stop to wonder what child-bearing and chastity have to do with those three women soon realise that the critic's target is not the play but the 'power structure' supposedly behind it. Shakespeare becomes a tool in the indictment of the family, source of our present discontents.

The displacement of attention away from ethical issues sometimes takes the form of reinstating female characters and indicting males. Madelon Gohlke's description of Hamlet would shift the whole focus of the play: 'obsessed as he is with sexual betrayal, the problem of revenge for him is less a matter of killing Claudius than one of not killing his mother' (Gohlke 1980, p. 153) — so critics have been wrong for centuries concerning Hamlet's real motives. But rather than simply ascribing a generalised 'anger against women' to him, we ought to remind ourselves that his mother has betrayed her dead husband with what she herself describes as an 'o'er-hasty' (not to mention incestuous) marriage. To Rebecca Smith, though, Gertrude is a character to be exculpated from the traditional charges of vanity and lust, being only 'a soft, obedient, dependent, unimaginative woman' (Smith 1980, p. 194), 'merely a quiet, biddable, careful mother and wife' (p. 201). Smith finally approaches the issue of Gertrude's 'hasty, *apparently casual* betrayal of the memory of her first husband' (p. 202; my italics), and comments:

> Although Gertrude is not an adulterer, she has been 'adulterated' by her contact, even innocently in marriage, with Claudius. Similarly, his crimes and deceit have, in fact, made Gertrude guilty of incest. In order to marry, Claudius and Gertrude would have been required to obtain a dispensation to counteract their canonical consanguinity or affinity. Obviously, if his crime of fratricide were publicly known . . .

permission would not have been granted. The Ghost and Hamlet know of the fratricide, and 'persist in terming the relationship incestuous [as well they might!]; but Gertrude has married in innocence and good faith, not as a party to the deception' (p. 203). But the issue of fratricide is irrelevant here: by the standards of Elizabethan society Gertrude has committed incest, and in haste, and that is enough to explain Hamlet's anger. The desire to exculpate Gertrude can result in her being described as 'morally neutral' (Bamber 1982, p. 77), but her acceptance of Claudius results in her becoming the instrument of his evil, and ultimately its victim. To describe her, as Smith does, as 'a compliant . . . woman whose only concern is pleasing others' (Smith 1980, p. 207) locates precisely the weakness that the critic is attempting to excuse.

I feel sympathy for Gertrude, just as I feel pity (at the end) for Lady Macbeth, but to attempt to screen them out of the play's moral system is to confuse sympathy and understanding. It is, of course, much more damaging to whitewash Lady Macbeth, but some feminists do so. Paula Berggren says that when we see her in the sleep-walking scene 'she is caught in the web that cripples women in a paternalistic society'; and, furthermore, 'is doomed to frustration in any case, for the husband who is neither father nor lover is beyond helping her' (Berggren 1980, p. 27). The significance of Macbeth not being her father and not helping her is unclear to me, if the 'paternalistic society' is to blame. For Madelon Gohlke once again, the husband is to blame:

> The world constructed by Macbeth attempts to deny not only the values of trust and hospitality, perceived as essentially feminine, but to eradicate femininity itself. Macbeth reads power in terms of a masculine mystique that has no room for maternal values. . . . To be born of woman, as he reads the witches' prophecy, is to be mortal. (Gohlke 1980, p. 158)

Almost everything there is wrong. The values of 'trust and hospitality' are in fact urged, painfully and from deep within his social and moral being, by Macbeth himself, and ruthlessly thrust aside by his wife. She it is who wishes to 'eradicate femininity'; she it is who despises 'maternal values'. And to be born of woman is indeed to be mortal — an absurd comment, made by taking the highly specific feature of Macduff's birth by Caesarian section and generalising it to a statement about men and women.

Joan Larsen Klein approves Lady Macbeth in her madness for being unable to deny her links with womankind — 'unlike her husband' (Klein 1980,[18] p. 241): but has this critic never read the final scenes of the play, with Macbeth's devastated sense of futility and non-existence? For Klein, too, an element in the tragedy is the couple's 'badly founded marriage' (p. 243). After such apologies it is good to read Linda Bamber's comment on Lady Macbeth's 'gratuitous fantasy of infanticide' in the speech 'I have given suck . . .' (1.7.54ff):

> Lady Macbeth's murderous ambition is more horrible than her husband's because a woman, as this speech reminds us, should represent nurture and human connectedness. Lady Macbeth is not entirely a monster; she does refrain from stabbing Duncan herself, and her moral feelings ultimately do assert themselves in her madness. But to argue for a redistribution of sympathy in *Macbeth*, as some feminists have done,[19] is a pretty desperate measure. (Bamber 1982, pp. 2–3)

And to indict the paternalistic or masculine world is equally desperate. Shakespeare's real interest in the tragedies is in these human beings in these situations, and the desires or principles that move them towards, or away from, the destructive elements in our behaviour: '"ruthlessness, callousness, power, lust, domineering self-assertion"'.[20]

*   *   *

Of all the distortions of an ethical structure made by feminist Shakespeare critics, the most damaging (to my mind at least) concerns *Othello*, and the role in it of Iago, who is not so much exculpated (he is a man, after all), as ignored. Having seen (in Chapter 1) how Iago's intentionality perverts all forms of human intercourse in order to fulfil his destructive wishes, and having followed (in Chapter 2) some of the ways in which Shakespeare adapted his source-material in order to make the play's action turn, time and again, around Iago's plots and fantasies, it is rather unnerving to find him virtually screened out of the play. '*Hamlet* without the prince' is an expression describing the absurd situation of a structure lacking a vital element that has passed into the language (although it did once happen):[21] '*Othello* without Iago' would be equally absurd. To ignore this agent of chaos is to falsify the play beyond recovery; yet some feminists do so. According to Berggren, Desdemona's tragedy illustrates the way in which tragic heroines 'must be desexualized' (Berggren 1980, p. 24): her summary of the play omits any mention of Iago. Marianne Novy, also generalising about tragic heroines, finds in Desdemona a typically Shakespearian mixture of assertiveness and submissiveness which is apparently sufficient in itself to bring about her catastrophe: 'she has put herself in the vulnerable position in which Othello can kill her' (Novy 1981, p. 21). Truly, to pick out 'the woman's part' can be a curiously myopic process, what J.H. Hexter has described as 'tunnel history', pursuing one track, blind to all the rest.[22] Marilyn L. Williamson also sees Othello in terms of Desdemona's pattern of assertiveness and submission, contrasted with Emilia (Williamson 1981, pp. 112–15), and also finds it unnecessary to mention Iago's plotting. Diane Elizabeth Dreher meditates at some length on this play (Dreher 1986, pp. 88–95), in a mixture of feminist and psychoanalytical criticism which succeeds in leaving Iago out of the reckoning and locates the cause of the tragedy within Othello and Desdemona, both in their psyches and in their social roles (since the latter determine the former):

> Both Othello and Desdemona err in conforming to traditional male and female stereotypes, adopting personal behavior which prevents real intimacy and trust. Desdemona's chastity becomes more important to both of them than Desdemona herself. Othello kills her and she sacrifices herself to affirm the traditional ideal. . . . In the world of traditional male-female roles, males act and females react. (Dreher 1986, pp. 93–4)

Had Shakespeare's society been different, ergo, there would have been no need to write Othello.

Madelon Gohlke does notice the presence of Iago, but characteristically deflects interest away from him as a source of evil to a favourite feminist concern, namely 'Shakespeare's exploration . . . of male sexual anxiety' (Gohlke 1981, p. 158). Her exploration of the play begins so late as to disqualify itself as a coherent study, namely at Iago's statement to Othello, when he has wholly manipulated and dominated him: 'I am your own forever' (3.3.476). This sentence, she suggests, can mean Iago's acceptance of 'Othello's naming him his lieutenant'; but it can also mean that Iago 'devotes himself entirely to his master', and thus 'uses the language not only of fealty, but of love. His desire, it seems, is to be possessed by' Othello (p. 158). Having made this stunningly literal reading, she finds it 'consonant with a psychoanalytical view of' Iago — a compound, we are told, of 'sadism and homosexuality' (p. 173, n. 3) — although it disagrees with the first meaning, so she offers to reconcile the two. But a third possibility has been crushingly obvious to anyone attending to the first 60 lines of the play, namely that Iago explicitly declares that he always serves himself, that his 'following' Othello is but 'seeming', that his 'outward action' never demonstrates the 'native act and figure of my heart': 'I am not what I am' (1.1.56–62). In other words, any statement of love that he makes must be read as hatred, and a desire to destroy, for as he tells us several times, 'I hate the Moor' (1.3.386). Gohlke actually quotes the first of these statements (p. 159), but interprets it in bizarre psychological terms: 'To be revealed is to be victimized. For Iago, direct statements of feeling or intent leave him open to injury or attack', so he 'adopts the strategy of the liar' (p. 159) — as if he had some unusually tender psyche.

Gohlke's motive for ignoring the issues of evil, malice, destructiveness and
dissimulation is that she wishes to explain Iago's self-concealment as a
mark of what she calls 'femininity', which characterises — paradoxically!
— not only Desdemona (pp. 164–8) but all the *heroes* in Shakespeare's
tragedies, who all, apparently, experience 'male sexual anxiety', 'fears' of
heterosexual relationships, 'profound ambivalence in the sexual sphere',
manifested as a 'resistance . . . to heterosexual bonding'. The tragic hero,
'*like Iago* . . . assumes that to be vulnerable is to be weak, exposed, even
feminine, and it is the feminine posture, above all, which he fears' (pp.
169–71; my italics). Yet the tragic hero, in the end, loses his 'facade of
masculinity', and 'finds himself in the typically feminine posture of telling
the truth through lies' (p. 172). Other readers must make what they can of
this essay, which seems to me irredeemably confused, but it certainly shifts
the emphasis away from the ethics of the tragedy to the issue of gender,
however vaguely defined.

Carol Thomas Neely is more straightforward, though equally biassed
against men. She distinguishes three schools of criticism concerning *Othello*.
There are 'Othello critics', who sympathise with the hero 'and, like him,
are overwhelmed by Iago's diabolism'; also like Othello, 'they do not
always argue rationally or rigorously' (which, lacking any specific citation,
would be described in boxing circles as a low blow). Then there are 'Iago
critics', who admire the villain's realism and dislike Othello, devaluing his
love (Neely 1980, pp. 211–12). Both schools 'badly misunderstand and
misrepresent the women in the play', the first group idealising Desdemona
but turning her into 'an object', the second group demeaning her. Both
schools neglect Emilia and Bianca, too. Neely offers to 'show that the
play's central theme is love — especially marital love; its central conflict is
between *the men* and *the women*' (p. 212; my italics). The character who
'most explicitly speaks of this theme' is Emilia, who is 'dramatically and
symbolically the play's fulcrum',[23] and so Neely constitutes a third school,
declaring herself 'an Emilia critic' (p. 213). No objection, the reader
thinks, until we see that this shift of focus again minimises Iago, virtually
writes him out of the play. Neely briefly judges Act II 'a repetition of
Act I', without having discussed either. In her summary 'Iago plots the
remainder of the play, but his scheme is slight, repetitive, and flawed'
(p. 124). But no, it is tremendous, hypnotic, and totally successful! Neely's
fastidious aesthetic judgements seem to prevent her from actually noticing
what happens in the play. Admitting the play's 'increasing intensity', she
still finds 'little actual plot development', ignoring Iago's gradual but total
undermining of Othello's trust in Desdemona and even in his own perception, comparing Iago rather disparagingly with Rosalind: 'Iago works to
induce fantasy, and Rosalind to dispel it. Neither entirely succeeds. [*Come
again?*] Iago's plot, like those of the comedies, rests on coincidence and
absurdity. The handkerchief is . . . trivial and ridiculous but symbolically
all-important' (p. 214). But no, again, the handkerchief is an agent of

plot, where it fulfils the functions expected of it, as I have shown, both to inculpate Desdemona in Othello's demented eyes, and subsequently to prove Iago's guilt, when Emilia reveals how they have all been deceived.

Iago and his 'absurd' plot out of the way, Neely can now focus on the play's real theme, 'the opposition of attitudes, viewpoints, and sexes'. She does so by an extraordinary reiteration of the opposition (to which my italics have called attention) between 'the men' and 'the women', or 'masculinity and femininity' in Shakespeare's comedies and tragedies (these terms recur, for instance, 19 times on p. 215 alone). 'The men' in *Othello* 'are, in Emilia's words, "murderous coxcombs". Three out of the five attempt murder' (p. 216) — as if this were somehow the consequence of them being men (no mention of Iago's destructive manipulations). The whole sex has a moral failing: 'vanity is the central characteristics of coxcombs and is at the root of the men's murderousness in *Othello*' (p. 221). The other sex, needless to say, sets a much better example: 'The women in *Othello* are not murderous, and they are not foolishly idealistic or foolishly cynical as the men are' (p. 218). Bianca's 'active, open-eyed, enduring affection' is superior to Cassio's 'indifference, to Roderigo's passivity, and to Othello's naïveté' (pp. 218–19). Emilia, as we might expect by now, 'articulates the balanced view': 'her views are midway between Desdemona's and Bianca's and between those of the women and those of the men' (p. 219). And so the critic goes on, elevating one sex and damning the other: 'the men's vanity, their preoccupation with rank and reputation, and their cowardice render them as incapable of friendship as they are of love. The women, in contrast . . .' (p. 224).

Iago's supreme plotting, his total control over Othello's view of past and present (Iago is the 'catalyst', Neely writes, of 'Othello's shifts from the idealization of women to their degradation . . . but Othello makes the task easy': p. 216), Othello's vulnerability as an outsider, Cassio's shame at his humiliation, Desdemona's well-meaning attempt to play the scold and pressurise her husband into relenting — this whole interlocking structure of dislocated virtue, where every attempt by Othello to free himself from his trap is outwitted by Iago, where all the goodness of Desdemona's pleading on behalf of another merely serves to incriminate her further in the eyes of Othello, who has been made to see the opposite of the truth[24] — this whole superbly articulated, claustrophilic, deeply painful plot-structure is ignored by the feminist critic, reduced to its simplest components — 'the men and the women' — and rearranged into two piles. Neely puts the men's faults on one side, the women's virtues on the other, and thinks that this amounts to literary criticism. All she does is to dismantle the play and use it as a vehicle for somehow getting even with men. Towards the end of her essay, admittedly, she concedes that the women are also partly to blame: 'the men . . . persistently misconceive the women; the women fatally overestimate the men. Each sex, trapped in its own values and attitudes, misjudges the other' (p. 228), but this still represents a reduction of the play to its lowest common denominator — if, indeed, it denominates anything at all. It is *this* man, and *this* woman, in *this* situation, that we should be attending to, a unique and carefully contrived plot-structure that, if decomposed into the genders of the protagonists, loses its wholly specific nature and results in predictable and repetitive generalisations.

To say that 'in the last scene the gulf between men and women widens' (p. 232) is to blind oneself to the painful sight of the deluded Othello killing the woman he loves; to Desdemona loyally trying to exculpate him with her dying words; to Emilia's disgust with Iago, and Othello's disgust with himself once he learns the truth — a complexity of alignment, the false against the true, the true against the false, of deception and discovery, a murder which affirms evil and a suicide which rejects evil and reinstates good (for the record, as it were, not for any usable future) — a complex and shifting alignment that makes any simple reduction of it to 'the men' and 'the women' futile, were it not so obviously serving an ulterior motive. Neely's own *ressentiment* against 'the men' in the play appears openly, at the end:

> Although male bombast is virtually silenced at the end of this play . . .
> — Iago 'never will speak word' (305) and the terseness and precision of
> Roderigo's dying epithet for Iago ('O inhuman dog') are equalled in
> Cassio's epitaph for the dead Othello ('For he was great of heart') —
> Othello's rhetoric continues unchecked. His last speech is his own brand
> of Iago's 'motive-hunting'. (Neely 1980, p. 233)

Anyone who can equate the speeches by those four men (poor Roderigo manages to gasp out his last breath: was he ever bombastic?), or can accuse Othello in his final speech of merely 'seeing himself . . . as ill-fated, unlucky . . . extolling his services to the state, confessing, asking for justice and judgement, telling stories about the past' — and not register his profound disgust with himself, a 'cursed dog' who deserves to be slain — anyone who can reduce all this to 'male bombast' is allowing her own partisanship for one sex over the other to prevent her actually experiencing the play as a human being. If this is feminism's answer to male chauvinism, then it is like someone whose legs have been cut off cutting off their arms, too.

V

Carol Neely's may be an extreme case, but the temptation to reduce the complexities of Shakespeare's drama to the simplifying generalisations of 'patriarchy', 'patrilineal society', or 'male vanity' is one that many feminists have fallen for. The last mode of distorting generalisation that I wish to

look at is that caused by feminism's enthusiastic alliance with psychoanalysis. I don't pretend to understand the reasons for this alliance (other
than the great prestige of psychoanalysis in American academe, already
noticed), but I am disturbed by its effects. Chiefly, it allows endless
possibilities of resolving complex plot-structures into simple instances of
male this, or female that, merely reinforcing the critic in his or her state of
omniscience. It is — who would have guessed? — the men who are
primarily exposed by this process, diagnosed, fitted into slots that make
their failings more obvious, easily understood, but hardly forgiven. The
editors of *The Woman's Part* note that 'as they explore the psychosexual
dynamics that underlie the aesthetic, historical, and genre contexts,
feminist critics find themselves in an increasingly close alliance with
psychoanalytic critics'. Although not altogether happy with Freud,

> they make extensive use of psychoanalytic insights into male ambivalence
> toward female sexuality. Throughout the canon these critics trace a
> persistent theme — men's inability to reconcile tender affection with
> sexual desire and their consequent vacillation between idealization and
> degradation of women. They suggest how structures of male dominance
> grow out of and mask fears of female power and of male feminization and
> powerlessness. (Lenz *et al.* 1980, p. 9)

Here is indeed the most popular psychoanalytic paradigm in the whole of
feminist criticism: men dominate women because they are afraid of them.
The 'profound fears of female sexuality and the desperate attempts to
control it in the plays [are] reflections of male ambivalence . . .'.

This seems to me a myth. The 'degradation' of women that is referred to
is the 'misogyny' so often alleged on so slender a basis. As I have shown,
misogynistic utterances are the consequence of men thinking that they
have been deceived or betrayed by women they love. There is no unmotivated misogyny in Shakespeare, and it is difficult to recall any men
who 'fear women's sexuality', or who 'have doubts about their own
masculinity' (wholly anachronistic concepts as these are). Yet the frequency with which feminists allege these psychic states shows how essential
this mode of explanation has become. Madelon Gohlke states that
'Antony's relation both to Cleopatra and to Caesar may be read in terms
of his anxieties about dominance, his fear of self-loss in any intimate
encounter' (Lenz *et al.* 1980, p. 159: intimate encounter with Caesar?
That's a new angle!). Peter B. Erickson finds that *Love's Labour's Lost*, 'for
all its comic charm, . . . presents an extraordinary exhibition of masculine
insecurity and helplessness. While the veneer of male authority is brittle
and precarious from the outset, female power is virtually absolute', the first
scene quickly exposing 'the pretensions of masculine idealism and the fear
of women which underlies it' (Erickson 1981, p. 65). From this surprising
statement Erickson rapidly runs through the play, seeing the women as
'torturing' the men, finding the four courtiers who 'catch one another with

love poems' in 4.3 guilty of 'fraternal voyeurism' (p. 76), and so on. But he never mentions Berowne's superb speech, 'Have at you then, affection's men-at-arms' (4.3.290–365), with its great defence of heterosexual love as a healthy, necessary human activity, not to be denied by a jejune dedication to study or the contemplative life. Feminists have developed a truly remarkable capacity to ignore whatever doesn't fit their interpretations. In the same collection David Sundelson finds at the 'heart' of *Measure for Measure* 'grave fears about the precariousness of male identity and . . . fears of the destructive power of women' (Sundelson 1981, p. 83). No doubt the same judgement will come to be made of every other Shakespeare play, many times over. With such a limited range of templates, psychoanalytic criticism must soon repeat itself.

Another way of classifying male mistreatment of women is to diagnose incestuous desires. For Paula S. Berggren, indeed, 'incest . . . is the obverse of misogyny: it reveals the narcissism underlying the vilification of the female that Shakespeare's tragic heroes so arbitrarily indulge in' (Berggren 1980, p. 26). But not only is there no arbitrary misogyny in the tragedies, incest exists on a very different plane from misogyny: the one is an indiscriminate hatred of all women, the other a sexual desire for women who belong to a close-kin category, variously defined in different cultures. Such fine distinctions are lost on some feminists, who invoke not only incest but even 'pseudo-incest': surely this is too grave an accusation to be blurred in this form. So Diane Elizabeth Dreher appeals to statistics: 'statistical profiles made during the 1970s of incestuous fathers and daughters correspond to many of Shakespeare's characters. He depicted only one case of incest, that of Antiochus in *Pericles*, but the proclivities are obviously there' (Dreher 1986, p. 10). Aren't they just, everywhere! For instance, the Duke in *Two Gentlemen* locks his daughter in 'a high tower to which he himself keeps the key. . . . The tower image, obviously phallic, also suggests hidden incestuous urgings' (p. 49) — not hidden to this critic, at all events. Dreher defines 'pseudo-incest' as the state where 'women remain children emotionally', such as Cordelia and Ophelia, grown women who tend for their father (this is known to others as nurturing), or allow him to meddle in their personal affairs, or like Desdemona, who transfers her obedience to father surrogates (p. 11). This seems to widen the category sufficiently to embrace any father, and any daughter. Dreher hesitantly describes Lear's love for Cordelia as 'pseudo-incest' (p. 69), but Madelon Gohlke is, as ever, more assertive: 'Lear incestuously marries his daughter in the manner of his death' (Gohlke 1981, p. 170). — I like 'marries'.

Some feminists use the widespread psychoanalytic concepts of Self and Other to describe 'the barrier of sexual differentiation' that separates masculine and feminine (Bamber 1982, pp. 4ff) — yet, by the same token, makes their physical and psychic union possible. (But as soon as we think that, we realise that in this school there is no accepted terminology for a couple, say: we are doomed to monism and separation.) Others invoke Lacan's concept of the phallus (Bamber 1982, p. 156), or Jung's categories animus/anima (Dreher 1986, p. 7), and some contest Freud's phallocentrism.[25] One example of an eclectic — and confused — use of several schools is Janice Hays, commenting on *Much Ado* (Hays 1980: pp. 95–9 list her many 'authorities'). The target of her analysis is, of course, a man — Claudio, who no sooner feels a 'surge of sexuality' for Hero than he tries to 'defend himself against' it (p. 82): readers may search the text in vain for that reaction. For to love a woman sexually, it seems, mobilises fears about the '"bad mother" who, in the male child's eyes, betrayed and abandoned him'. Hays draws on the psycho-social history of Lawrence Stone and his belief that 'most upper-class Renaissance adults' experienced 'severe separation anxiety' when weaned from their wet nurse, a deprivation which, Stone claims, regularly resulted in '"psychotic-like attacks of rage"', paranoia, and an '"inability to maintain human relations"', all the results of this childhood trauma' (p. 83). Whether this experience was at all known then, despite Stone's categorical pronouncements (another master of the rhetoric of assertiveness — 'overwhelmingly obvious in all the documentation of the period'), and what, in any case, its relevance to Claudio might be, — these are points simply taken as granted.

'Further', Hays goes on, 'for the young adult male to relate to a tenderly regarded woman sexually might seem perilously akin to incest, since the idealized woman would recall the nurturing women who were the objects of the boy's earliest tender feelings' — wet nurse, natural mother, or sister, 'all these women, in Renaissance patriarchal society, clearly the property of the father or father-figure'. (Hays usefully recapitulates most of the older feminist orthodoxies.) 'Poor Claudio!' we may well feel at this point, as our psychocritic has virtually closed off all the avenues to a normal, happy sexual relationship. Who would dare love a woman with such perils all around? If we turn to Claudio's relationship with men, notably his appeal to Don Pedro to help him in his suit for Hero, we find further dangers. The older man's encouragement to 'proceed without delay', although meant kindly, is now presented as a further crisis:

> Such permission from a parental authority-figure to follow the prompt-ings of desire, which in any adolescent male might well contain remnants of his feelings toward the original woman or women in his life, could let loose a flood indeed of incestuous fantasies and consequent fears of retaliation from the 'father'. (p. 84)

What is really 'let loose' here, I fear, is the psychocritic's desire to re-write the play according to neo-Freudian narrative models. She no sooner imagines Claudio's reaction to a father-figure giving him licence to woo than she makes the young man recoil on himself, his 'punitive conscience' expecting 'retaliation as a consequence of wishing to compete against the father-figure repesented [sic] by Don Pedro' (p. 85). But if Don Pedro has just given him the go-ahead, how can Claudio be competing with him? The author prefers to cite Lawrence Stone, again, on the apparently never-ending 'struggle', in the Renaissance, 'between fathers and sons, with consequent guilt and vindictiveness on both sides'. Life must have been awful then.

In the masked-ball scene Don Pedro disguises as Claudio, and exchanges some badinage with Hero, which the audience can hear but Claudio not (2.1.86ff). Penetrating Claudio's disguise, the villain Don John maliciously tells him that Don Pedro is actually 'enamoured on Hero', and — it being a convention in Elizabethan drama that slander is believed — Claudio concludes that 'the Prince woos for himself. . . . Farewell therefore Hero!' (161–182). But this false impression is soon cleared up, and Don Pedro tells him that he has gained the consent of both Hero and her father to the marriage. As Janice Hays reads the scene,

> Claudio stands to one side, watching but not participating, shut out from the interaction between Don Pedro and Hero, his posture suggesting what psychoanalysis terms a 'primal scene', in which the child sees (or fantasizes seeing) sexual relations between the parents and feels excluded and thus defeated in the hopes of securing idealized parental love. (p. 85)

But Claudio is not at all concerned with Don Pedro (who is not his father, in any case), but with Hero; and anything less like the primal scene than this courtly dance could hardly be imagined. Wheeling up yet another psychoanalytic concept, in a kind of fantasia on feminist themes, Hays suggests that the speed with which Claudio rejects Hero shows that he is afraid to 'compete with Don Pedro', which suggests in turn that he clings to 'male bonding . . . as a defense against the anxieties occasioned by heterosexuality'. If so, he is soon plunged into them by the announcement of parental consent: he makes a brief speech, kisses Hero, who — as Beatrice perceptively sees — 'tells him in his ear that he is in her heart' (2.1.315).

Happy end to the wooing stage, we might feel. But not for Hays: this paternal restraint 'out of the way, Claudio is now forced to confront the incestuous fantasies that have hitherto been held in check'. What fantasies? Whose incest? How do you know? Well, the critic goes on, 'Shakespeare uses the mock-assignation scene' — she means Don John's disguise plot, aided by Borachio, to make Claudio think Hero promiscuous — in order 'to externalize . . . Claudio's sexual fantasies about Hero' (p. 86). What she has in mind is the fact that when Borachio outlines the plot, he says that Claudio will 'see me at her chamber window, hear me call Margaret Hero, hear Margaret term me *Claudio*' (2.2.33ff). This is apparently a slip of Shakespeare's pen, and some editors follow Theobald in emending to Borachio. To Hays, though, it can only be a Freudian 'parapraxis', and 'it is axiomatic in psychoanalytic theory that when the ego dozes, id material works its way to the surface . . .': the question is, though, whose id? To Hays

> What the mock-assignation suggests is a disguised version of Hero being made love to by a Borachio who bears enough resemblance to Claudio [an illicit deduction!] so that Shakespeare could inadvertently confuse their names. Its outlines resemble what Freud reported as being certain masturbation fantasies, common during male adolescence, in which the young man imagines the mother and sister . . .

— but you can guess the rest. Don John's staging of this scene, then, 'is a dramatic enactment of Claudio's internal conflict', and reveals 'the incestuous root of Claudio's anxiety' (p. 86).

So, just to recapitulate the plot so far: Claudio is a young man unsure of his own sexuality who fears to express affection for any woman lest this revive the incestuous feelings which he had, as a child, for whatever woman with whom he had had close contact — wet nurse, mother, sister. So that, when he sees Borachio wooing Hero, it is not the spectacle of his fiancée apparently betraying him with another man that disturbs him, but the anxiety he feels at the thought that he might — or soon will — have to fill the part that Borachio is playing now, with all its overtones of incest. Can one imagine a more wilfully distorted reading of a crystal-clear plot-sequence? To Hays, though, the fact that Claudio affirms that he never 'tempted' Hero with immoral suggestions, but behaved 'as a brother to his sister', with 'bashful sincerity and comely love' — this is the real give-away, declaring his 'unconscious incestuous fantasies' (p. 87), further glossed by an elaborate citation from Freud (p. 98, n. 21). Also to blame, of course, is 'a patriarchal value system' that treats 'woman and her sexuality as a man's exclusive possession', and 'makes a woman's virginity an extension of male pride — particularly when no one has ever thought to ask about Claudio's sexual purity or lack of it' (pp. 87–8) — truly an oversight.

One might have thought that this play had now been totally explicated, every fantasy put in its appropriate slot. But as if not wholly satisfied with the psycho-feminist approach, Hays now switches registers rather opportunistically, drawing on religious and philosophical sources, and reading the apparent death of Hero as 'an aspect of the Christian concept of grace'; also as an instance of the '"Demeter-Persephone life style"' which women have developed to cope with human 'vulnerability and weakness' — that is, 'a "going down in order to come up"' (the collocation of these mythical figures and modern colloquialism is incongruous, to say the least); and finally in terms of Renaissance Neoplatonism, with its model of separation and return (pp. 88–92). Despite this upbeat argument, which now sees Claudio (almost forgivingly) as having gone through 'a ritual of atonement' to acquire 'God's extension of Grace' (p. 93), Hays ends by finding the Hero-Claudio plot 'not fully credible and convincing'

(p. 95). But this is to call in question the success of her own various
interpretive strategies, an unusual admission from a school which usually
evinces total self-belief.

No such doubts afflict Karen Newman, making a heady mixture of Freud
and Lacan in order to link 'Femininity and the Monstrous in *Othello*'. One
of the key pieces of evidence for this linkage is Othello's handkerchief,
which Newman describes in 'post-Saussurian' terms as 'snowballing signifier,'
— an unfortunate metaphor for a piece of linen — 'for as it passes from
hand to hand, both literal and critical, it accumulates myriad [which
means 'ten thousand', or 'countless'] associations and meanings.' In psychoanalytic terms, Newman writes,

> the handkerchief which Othello inherits from his mother and then gives
> to Desdemona has been read symptomatically as the fetishist's substitu-
> tion for the mother's missing phallus. Like the shoe Freud's young boy
> substitutes 'for the woman's (mother's) phallus which the little boy
> believed in and does not wish to forego', the handkerchief is the fetish
> which endows [women with a penis and so makes them] 'acceptable as
> sex objects' — that is, makes them like men. (Newman 1987, p. 156)

Those naïve people who believed that women were 'acceptable' — but
much more than as 'sex objects' — precisely because they were not like
men, had better think again, especially if they meet a woman carrying a
handkerchief, which may be a phallus-endowing fetish. To even understand this argument it is first necessary to accept Freud's theory of fetishism
and the (felt) anomaly of the woman's 'missing' penis. Commenting on
Barbara Johnson's discussion of Derrida's surmisal that in Lacan's interpretation of Poe's 'The purloined letter', 'the letter is [for Lacan] a symbol
of the *mother's* (missing) phallus', A.D. Nuttall observes that in this
sophisticated discussion 'the sheer improbability of the central notion is
not noticed' (Nuttall 1983, p. 29). This is now unquestioned dogma.

Having accepted, like so many psycho-feminists, the Freudian repertoire
of phallic symbolism, Newman suddenly changes course, objecting that 'the
psychoanalytic scenario is problematic because it privileges a male scopic
drama, casting the woman' — as so often in Freud — 'as a failed man'
(Newman 1987, p. 156). Further, she argues, the handkerchief figures
not only a lack, 'the missing penis', but a much more serious one, namely

> a desiring femininity which is described in the play as aberrant and
> 'monstrous' or a 'monster'. The handkerchief, with its associations with
> the mother, witchcraft, and the marvelous, represents the link between
> femininity and the monstrous which Othello and Desdemona's union
> figures in the play. It figures a female sexual topography that is more
> than a sign of male possession, violated virginity, even deceit, and more
> than the fetishist's beloved object. It figures not only Desdemona's
> lack . . . but also her own sexual parts —

since it has strawberries embroidered on it, which could represent her nipples, 'lips, and even perhaps the clitoris'. The handkerchief has (if not 'myriad' still quite a few) other significances in this critic's eyes: 'psychologically, because it signifies male fears of duplicity, consummation, and castration', and also 'politically . . . because it has become a *feminine trifle*', so that the whole play's 'tragic action is structured . . . around a trifle, a feminine toy' (*ibid.*). Despite the immense growth in critical sophistication since 1693, that argument matches Rymer in once again reducing the multiple motivation of a complex drama to a single item of linen.

The striking feature of the modern sequence is the speed and confidence with which it delivers its interpretation: evidently Newman derives from, and writes for, a context in which such interpretations are common sustenance. Yet the goal of her essay — equating femininity with the monstrous and with miscegenation — is not only depressing (is Desdemona, or woman in general, really to be understood as the product of inter-racial breeding?), but misguided. Her evidence for saying that femininity is described in the play as 'aberrant' — which, if true, would put *Othello* on the same level as Aristotle's statement that the male sex is the norm, the female 'as it were a deformity', though required by nature[26] — consists of three moments: first, Iago's declaration, at the end of his first soliloquy —

> I have't. It is engendered. Hell and night
> Must bring this monstrous birth to the world's light.
>
> (1.3.395ff)

Second, Othello's anguished response to Iago —

> 'Think, my lord?' By heaven, thou echo'st me
> As if there were some monster in thy thought
> Too hideous to be shown! (3.3.110ff)

Third, Othello's reaction to Iago's false story of Cassio's erotic dream — 'O monstrous, monstrous!' (3.3.431). The first use of the word gives us Iago's estimate of his plan to destroy Othello; the second use describes the ominous hints (as yet quite undefined) that Iago is signalling to Othello; the third use is for Othello's horrified reaction to the invented story about Cassio kissing Iago in his dream, thinking him Desdemona. All three uses, as anyone can see, refer to men, not women. There are, as it happens, three other uses of the word 'monster' in *Othello* (most familiarly, Iago's description of jealousy as 'the green-ey'd monster') and four of 'monstrous', but at no time do they refer to female sexuality. Newman has violated one of the fundamental principles of literary criticism, or indeed of any argument that purports to support itself by reference to a text, namely that the critic using such quotations must pay attention (in drama) to who speaks the words in question, in what situation, and to what purpose. If this principle is not observed then texts become merely random collections of lexical items, any of which may be cited by any reader to prove any argument.

One might have imagined, without referring to the play, that in the super-heated world of delusions that Iago creates in Othello's mind, female sexuality could seem 'monstrous' to either the guller or his dupe. But — perhaps surprisingly — it doesn't, and there is simply no basis for Newman's claim that 'the play' describes femininity as aberrant. Whatever the cause of this error — hasty misreading, determination to find evidence to support one's thesis — Newman's equation of the feminine with the monstrous, on which the rest of her essay is based, is self-generated, illusory, and monstrous. (Do editors no longer read, or check what their contributors say?)

The other notable features of Newman's account are its unrelenting search for sexual significances, and the plasticity of its so-called sexual symbolism. As one critic observes, 'the reintroduction of Freudian notions in a poststructuralist critical environment can afford little more than a set of mental toys' (Nuttall 1983, p. 29). The game is easy to play because the counters involved are so insubstantial, so weightless that one can be easily substituted for another. The handkerchief not only symbolises Othello's mother's missing penis, *and* Desdemona's missing penis, *and* Desdemona's female genitals, *and* inter-racial copulation, it also (multi-potent symbol!) signifies male fears both of 'consummation, and castration' — as if Desdemona represented a version of the *vagina dentata* myth. This reduction of all human activity to the sexual plane — 'Is man no more than this?' — is all too typical of Freudian literary criticism. What is particularly disturbing, in this free-for-all discovery of whatever meanings the critic wishes to attach to a symbol, is the absence of any constraints. As the previous chapter demonstrated so often, Freudian literary criticism is wholly lacking in any principles that could lead it to disqualify some interpretations as unfounded. Free association, it seems, is the law for both analysands and analysts. Occasionally one does not know in which category to put the critic.

VI

Psychoanalysis may come to seem, in time, a discipline from which feminist criticism will wish to distance itself. I hope so, for it can only support those dangerous temptations to reduce the complexity of the plays to the self-pleasing, simplistic, and repetitive categories of gender, or patriarchy, or the weaknesses of the male species. As Richard Levin has shown in a penetrating analysis,[27] feminist commentators on Shakespeare's tragedies have in effect agreed that the plays are 'not really about the particular characters who appear there but about some general idea', the woman's world on the one hand, and 'patriarchal society' or 'masculine consciousness' on the other (Levin 1988, pp. 127–8). Predictably enough, these critics find 'the concept of masculinity . . . to blame for the tragedy'

(p. 132). Yet, as Levin points out, 'gender relations are only one of the components' of the world of each play, and are not so much causes as 'necessary *conditions* of the action' — Lear as father and King, Cordelia as daughter. In themselves gender relations are incapable of generating a tragic action. Lear's rejection of Cordelia in the opening scene is said by one feminist to illustrate the tyranny of patriarchy, but, Levin notes, 'the witnesses to this rejection — Kent, Gloucester, Burgundy, France, even Goneril and Regan — all of whom presumably share these patriarchal assumptions, regard his behaviour as a shocking abnormality' (p. 127). What is at stake, I would add, is not patriarchy but Lear's inability to distinguish integrity from ingratitude, and his readiness to break a natural bond to assuage his injured vanity. The play does not divide here into men and women but into flatterers and truth-tellers, those who respect natural bonds and those who can deny them. At this point in the play Lear shares the values of Goneril, Regan, and Edmund, and he (like others) pays most bitterly for it. In *Othello*, another feminist claims, Othello's killing of Desdemona is 'the consequence of the gender roles imposed on the pair by their patriarchal society'. Yet, Levin rightly rejoins, 'the characters who comment on it (including Othello himself after he learns the truth) do not view it as one of your everyday patriarchal events' but rather as a 'horrifying violation of the norms of their world' (*ibid.*).

In feminism, Levin concludes, the relationship between 'the facts' of the play and 'the theme' explored by the critic undergoes a strange reversal. Feminist critics 'can always make their thematic concepts of gender fit the facts of the play, because the facts are defined by the theme, rather than the reverse'. So when a feminist asserts that the jealousy of Leontes is 'intrinsic to the male psyche' — ignoring the fact that 'all the men who comment on Leontes's accusation of Hermione take *her* side' — the critic is not deriving his concept of the male psyche from *The Winter's Tale* but is 'imposing it on the play' (p. 130). As with other thematic criticism, in order to make the untidy complexities of a play fit the paradigm writers either omit material not relevant to the 'formulation of the theme' (p. 128: the cashiering of Cassio, say), or else ignore passages in the text which would contradict it. Harry Berger, eager to find an all-pervasive *machismo* in *Macbeth*, cites the episode where Macduff learns that his family has been killed, quoting Malcolm's line urging Macduff to 'Dispute it like a man', an obviously suspect sexist remark. But he leaves out Macduff's answer, 'I shall do so; / But I must also feel it like a man' (4.3.220ff), which, as Levin says, 'asserts a very different sense of manhood' (p. 129). Carol Neely, seeing all the evil in *Othello* as proceeding from the men in the play, accuses them of persistently blaming others for their actions, citing Desdemona's last words, exonerating Othello from responsibility. But she fails to mention Othello's response: 'She's like a liar gone to burning hell: / 'Twas I that kill'd her'. Levin summarises the direction of Neely's reading of *Othello* (in terms that we could apply to much feminist criticism) as being to homogenise male behaviour in the plays and level it down 'to the lowest common denominator': the men are 'all supposed to be competitive, cowardly, foolish, jealous, passive, vain, swaggering, and murderous', evading responsibility and incapable of friendship (p. 129). In this reductive and repetitive process the heroes of the plays 'emerge as a sorry lot indeed, having lost virtually all their admirable qualities and even their individuality' (p. 131). Ironically, having freed Shakespeare's women of 'negative [sexist] stereotypes' feminists are now 'imposing such stereotypes on his men'. Yet, Levin observes, in Shakespearian tragedy — and, I would hope, in life — 'our appreciation of one sex never depends on the depreciation of the other' (p. 131).

*   *   *

This 'sexist stereotyping' of the male protagonist shows, finally, that feminist Shakespeare criticism has got stuck in the attitudes of the so-called second wave, that antagonistic phase of the 1960s which defined woman as 'person oppressed by a male power system' (Vendler 1990, p. 21). In the last ten years or so attempts have been made to refine simplistic feminist concepts, attempts which must be welcomed, as Helen Vendler puts it, as a sign that feminists are recognising the 'sheer diversity among women, and the insufficiency of any one definition of them (whether psychoanalytic, sociological, or political)' (ibid.). Such 'essentialist' theories as (Nancy Chodorow's) that 'universal models of "the reproduction of mothering"' exist, or (Carol Gilligan's) that 'women in general "have a different voice"', Vendler writes, 'have been plausibly accused of drawing wide conclusions about "women" from samples drawn from a single culture or social class or historical moment' (ibid., p. 22). Whereas the real issue, as one feminist recently declared, is that

'For some writers, gender is no more and perhaps not even as basic as poverty, class, ethnicity, race, sexual identity, and age, in the lives of women who feel less divided from men as a group than, for example, from white or bourgeois or Anglo or heterosexual men and women.' (cit. ibid.)

Vendler herself sees the 'unacknowledged problem' of feminism from the outset as having been its 'ascription of special virtue to women', either in the sentimental version, that 'men, as a class, are base and women are moral', or in the angry version, 'that men are oppressors and women are oppressed'. To 'cooler feminist minds', however, 'the possession of power, rather than whether one is a woman or a man, is what determines the act of oppression' (ibid.). Citing evidence of '"egregious selfishness"' in women, not physical violence but rather 'the character-destroying behavior — harshness, hatred, silence, and neglect — of some mothers' (pp. 21–2), Vendler describes 'the truth concealed by feminism' as being 'the abuse of power by both sexes, and the deficient moral behaviour of both men and women to each other and to children' (p. 22). She argues that feminism must achieve a 'de-idealizing of women', recognising that they can be 'victimizers as well as victims', and can be 'bigoted against men just as men are bigoted against them'. This change of attitude, obviously enough, 'in no way precludes protest of ill-treatment of women', but it will stop the falsifications produced by idealising women and degrading men.

In *Feminism without illusions: a critique of individualism* (1991), the feminist historian Elizabeth Fox-Genovese has drawn on a wide range of contemporary work that also criticises the simplistic paradigms of the 60s. One chapter is called 'Beyond sisterhood', showing how that metaphor encouraged solidarity but produced a false image of womanhood as 'a universal condition', ignoring vast differences in 'cultural, social and economic realities' (Fox-Genovese 1991, p. 17). That 'white middle-class women' should have assumed the right to speak for all women merely 'alienated many lower-class and black women, who see their primary oppression as deriving from their class or race', and it also blinded main-stream feminism to its responsibility to 'defend social and economic changes that can ensure decent lives for all people' (pp. 18–19). The model of sisterhood, further, placed woman within the family and encouraged 'the myth of separate spheres, which has cast women as the softening antidote' to male competitiveness, 'innately nurturing and dependent', thus locating women in the domestic not the public world (pp. 20–21), and promoting '"a biologistic and fatalistic interpretation of the inevitability of men's power"' (p. 20). The 'myth of separate spheres is bankrupt' now, Fox-Genovese writes, along with 'the vision of distinct women's values', for 'in representing "women as essentially virtuous and men as essentially vicious"', as one feminist put it, 'it "serves the forces of reaction as surely as it serves the forces of progress"' (p. 32).

Other concepts of 1960s feminism also need revision. The popular tactic of blaming all forms of oppression on misogyny continues to 'personalize gender relations' and to ignore 'the ways in which societies construct men's and women's roles and identities'. Also deficient as a theoretical explana-tion is what some feminists now see as the 'ahistorical' and 'conspiratorial' concept of patriarchy:

> To group all forms of male dominance under the single rubric of patriarchy is to fall into the similar trap of homogenizing all forms of male domination and thereby obscuring their specific characteristics. (p. 143)

It also risks 'homogenizing the experience of women themselves', for the 'familial metaphor' of patriarchy 'implicitly holds that men justify their rule over women on grounds of innate physical superiority', and so 'reduces women to their physical attributes', reinforcing 'precisely that view of women as innately "other", against which many feminists protest'. Worse still, in some feminists' eyes, the essentialist theory of patriarchy 'reduces the significance of differences among women and thus minimizes the social dimension of women's experience and identities' (p. 145). The economic (and partly Marxist) emphasis of some current feminist thought would identify a much more serious threat to women's existence in capitalism, likely to produce 'yet more humiliation for most, if not all, women' (p. 29), for the 'corrosive' effect of 'the market' as the sole criterion of socio-economic existence erodes the notion of community and encourages individualism (p. 44), makes households increasingly dependent on two salaries (pp. 63–4), and has 'destructive effects on the lives of women throughout the world' (p. 185).

Fox-Genovese summarises and extends much feminist writing of the 1980s in seeing the need to formulate 'a new conception of the economy and polity than can take account of sexual asymmetry without subjugating women to men' (p. 86). Rejecting the 'postmodernist dismissal of difference' as a mere product of language (pp. 238, 145–8), she urges feminists to see difference as a reality in human experience, not an 'unchanging polarity' but something that is 'historically as well as biologically grounded and interpreted', and is thus 'subject to constant reinterpretation' (p. 238). Women's needs must be fought for not 'in the name of atomistic individualistic principles', but 'in the name of social justice for all . . . viewed as responsible and interdependent members of society' (p. 86). The need to avoid one-sidedness is particularly pressing in the writing of history. Although it rightly judges the past to have been unjust, feminism 'cannot afford uncritically to glorify women's discrete part of it', nor assume 'that the male-dominated historical context contributed nothing to it'. Many readers, I hope, will agree with the corollary she draws:

> If feminism indeed contains redemptive promise for our society and culture, it can only realize that promise by cultivating both a critical attitude toward the past and a commitment to our history — whatever its injustices — as the history of women as well as of men. (p. 235)

*   *   *

So far, at any rate, the achievements of feminist history seem greater than those of feminist literary criticism. This may be because the record of the past offers much significant material that has never been properly used. For centuries social history was not deemed worthy of serious attention, or only treated in an ephemeral fashion, so that the historiographical innovations of the last forty years or so have been able to use fresh material and to reinterpret familiar material according to fresh interpretive models. Literary texts have never been neglected to this extent; indeed the intensive study of sixteenth- and seventeenth-century literature that has been going on since the eighteenth century has made a great amount of writing, with all its strengths and weaknesses, common property. There is no comparable body of unused material. Feminist literary criticism of a historical kind has unearthed some unknown or lesser known literature, much of it historically illuminating about the role of the woman writers of the Renaissance, who (with the solitary exception of Aphra Behn) were amateur, non professional. Their work has the same limitations as that of amateur men writers, cut off from the public arena which discourages so many of the untalented, and exposes those who do find a footing to the necessity of satisfying a reading or theatre-going public. That challenge, together with occasional feedback from readers or critics, is the greatest stimulus to the self-criticism by which a writer develops. Denied that arena and that stimulus, the writings of most amateur writers, male or female, hardly repay prolonged study (e.g., Vendler 1990, p. 22).

As for reinterpreting well-known literature, my complaint would be that feminist criticism has not developed any fresh interpretive models. Its massive assumption, that the literature of the past can be scrutinised in the light of our politically-based categories of gender, patriarchy and oppression, and can still yield criticism that illuminates it as literature, rather than as proto-political documents, is seldom questioned, with the predictable result that much recent work is anachronistic, alien to the mental and social world of the literature studied. The great majority of the Shakespeare criticism I have read has not progressed beyond the stereotyping, incrimina-tory mode, or has allied itself with the easy routines of psychoanalysis, Freudian and after, which provide convenient templates for the old family-guilt narratives, but are incapable of innovation. The challenge for a feminist Shakespeare criticism in the next generation will be to absorb the self-critical developments in feminist theory while acquiring a far greater knowledge of social conditions in the Renaissance, more familiarity with Renaissance literary theory (genre, convention, structure, rhetoric), and a far deeper understanding of the ways in which literature functions. Those feminists actively concerned with furthering the place of women in the academy should also not forget the enormously valuable work done in precisely these areas by a distinguished roll of women scholars, whose publications have been neglected of late as not fitting the current political paradigms. Like many other students of this period, I owe a great deal to the writings of such scholars as Rosemond Tuve, Sister Miriam Joseph, Muriel Bradbrook, Madeleine Doran, Alice Walker and Gladys Willcock, Molly Mahood, Jean Robertson, Anne Barton, the late Margot Heinemann, and others. That tradition, which had no immediately political goal in view, still offers many renewing sources of energy and insight.

At all events, whatever agenda we propose for feminist criticism, the settling of immediate political scores is no longer sufficient.

CHAPTER SEVEN

Christians and Marxists: Allegory, Ideology

It is among the miseries of the present age that it recognizes no medium between *literal* and *metaphorical*. Faith is either to be buried in the dead letter, or its name and honours usurped by a counterfeit product of the mechanical understanding, which in the blindness of self-complacency confounds symbols with allegories. Now an allegory is but an abstraction of abstract notions into a picture-language which is itself nothing but an abstraction from objects of the senses; the principal being more worthless even than its phantom proxy, both alike unsubstantial, and the former shapeless to boot. Coleridge[1]

With the exception of deconstruction — ceaselessly fissuring Shakespeare's text to prove its theory of the indeterminacy of language and meaning, in the process reducing characters to mere 'traces', purely verbal effects — all the critical schools so far discussed accept the substantiality of the characters within the play, but then force them into preconceived patterns. For the feminists it is essential that characters be seen as gendered, culturally superior or inferior, oppressor or oppressed. For the New Historicists the people in a play can be criticised for being in a dominant, exploitative relationship, or sympathised with as the victims of power, colonialism, or whatever. To the Freudians, they are individual case-studies, each manifesting one version or other of a limited, but endlessly recombinable repertoire of fantasies and neuroses. All these forms of criticism can be described as only partly literary, for they all ignore the primary experience of drama as a sequence of action which unfolds over time. Literary criticism which is not serving some political ideology or reductive theory of human behaviour holds that characters in a work of literature are figures in an organised whole which is structured on various levels, its outcome achieving a decisive re-disposition of the characters' relations to each other. Whether experienced in the theatre or in private reading, drama is a representation of human interaction which demands an intellectual, emotional, ethical response and is pleasing in itself. — That is a brief and all too sketchy description, but it suffices to show that none of these schools of criticism has an aesthetic or literary theory derived from, or applicable to the plays as theatrical or reading experiences. Each of them uses the plays to validate its own theories, overlooking, rejecting, or falsifying whatever does not match the template which they superimpose on literature. The play is subordinated to the paradigm.

The last two critical approaches I discuss, Christian and Marxist, go a stage farther than any of the others. They, too, ignore the theatrical experience, dramatic structure, aesthetic properties of the plays. They, too, use them to demonstrate the truth or applicability of their own paradigms, ignoring whatever does not fit. Here, too, the characters are not regarded as parts functioning in a complex whole having its own rationale. But these two schools take the abstracting process to its extreme, regarding characters not in gender-roles, nor even as clinical types, but as mere *representatives*. They 'stand for' something else in an external allegory, to be read outside, and independent of the play, having its own narrative-pattern, and a quite different conclusion. For Christian interpreters Shakespeare's characters represent Biblical personages (Christ, the Virgin Mary, Judas, and so forth), or religious figures from a later period (medieval Saints, say), or such Christian virtues as Mercy, Pity, Love. For Marxist interpreters they represent levels in society, viewed either synchronically (ruling class, bourgeoisie, proletariat), or according to a Marxist view of history (decaying feudalism, emerging bourgeoisie). This shared practice of allegorising, each in its own way abstracting characters from being, in Coleridge's words, 'objects of the senses' to figures in an alien scheme, is the main focus of this chapter.

That Christian and Marxist approaches share this type of abstraction when interpreting literature may seem accidental. On a wider view, how-ever, it may derive from their common status as belief-systems, or ideologies. As Christopher Butler observes in a shrewd analysis of the ideological element in literary criticism, ideology can provide an individual belonging to a group with 'an overall "framework of belief" or "world picture" giving rise to moral norms which typically guide his actions' (Butler 1984, p. 95). It is important that such beliefs cohere, forming an inter-related whole, but an ideology goes beyond 'a framework of belief, in that it is wedded to a programme for action in the light of a *model* of the nature of human society'. For Lenin the ideology of the labour movement was '"the set of those attitudes and beliefs which would best enable the workers to reconstruct society in their own interest"' (*ibid.*). Ideologies are developed by separate interest groups, each claiming a universal appeal, and are thus always in competition. Roman Catholic and Marxist ideologies, in Butler's example, each

have a peculiar certainty about the truth revealed to them, and indeed about the direction of history, towards revolution or salvation. They are thus also teleological, setting before us a goal, an ideal state of earthly or heavenly society. . . . The end-states they aim at, including that of a liberal democracy, are often justified by the freedom which we are expected to enjoy within the society they project. Paradoxically enough, the process of obtaining this freedom within history may involve a high degree of obedience to authority and extinction of self-will. (p. 96)

Theological dogma, the party-line, both regard those who question the authority vested in an institution as heretical, displaying a form of deviance which cannot be tolerated beyond a certain point, either in time or in degree. The subordination of the individual to the system is echoed in literary criticism, I suggest, by the way in which characters in literary works are subordinated to an overall scheme, which they are seen as illustrating or validating, reduced to 'figures' or 'types'.

Ideological interpretations of literature, as we shall see shortly, also move outside the individual work of art, involving readers, texts, and other readers in various forms of collision. Since ideologists have definite ideas 'about human nature or human values', Butler observes, they 'invade the sphere of moral values' and project their ideas as 'certainties' — man is born to serve God; his value for society consists in his labour. This sense of certainty may produce 'a direct confrontation between the beliefs of the interpreter and those supposedly asserted by the text' (p. 97), when the potentially literary response becomes a political one, posing the question: 'does the text confirm or contradict the beliefs independently held by the interpreter?' (p. 100). In terms of Christian interpretation, this juxta- position of incompatible belief-systems led to an initial rejection of the literature of the Greeks and Romans as heathen, a reaction which put the Church Fathers in a difficult position, since classical literature was also the single available body of knowledge, which — from the fundamental educational triad of grammar, rhetoric and logic up to the moral philosophy of Plato and Cicero — had formed men like Jerome and Augustine, and to which they themselves made notable contributions. The Church's response to this dilemma, familiarly enough, was to develop allegorical interpreta- tion as a way of saving heathen texts by attributing moralising meanings to them. In recent Marxist criticism, as we shall see, a comparable move towards allegory has taken place, for not dissimilar reasons. Linking these two ideologies, then, is not an arbitrary procedure.

I

To begin with the Christian readings, and acknowledging the fact that, as Richmond Noble definitively showed in 1935,[2] Shakespeare was himself well acquainted with Christianity and quoted from or alluded to the Bible and prayerbook hundreds of times, the basic question remains: by what criteria can an interpreter argue that a character in the plays 'represents' a person from holy writ or Christian legend? The prior condition to be fulfilled, one answer holds, would be to show that allegorical interpretations of secular texts were common in the Renaissance. R.M. Frye, in his sober and reliable study of *Shakespeare and Christian Doctrine*, showed that this was not common. Even professional theologians, who read classical literature in traditional ethical and rhetorical terms, did not try to find theological meanings in it (Frye 1963, pp. 65–90). A supporting argument would concern the nature of allegory as commonly understood in the Renaissance. Medieval exegetes used a four-fold scheme, conventionally illustrated by reference to Jerusalem: on the literal level, it is the holy city; on the allegorical (or 'figurative') level, the Church militant; on the tropological (or moral) level, the just soul; and on the anagogical (or analogical) level, the Church triumphant.[3] But Renaissance writers, as William Nelson showed, did not adopt this elaborate structure, and commonly took 'allegorical' to mean 'moral'.[4] An allegorical reading in the Renaissance sense would bring out the ethical implications of the represented action, without necessarily reducing the characters to types or personifications. One well-known characteristic in Renaissance hermeneutics, exemplified by Erasmus, was indeed the rejection of four-fold exegesis as scholastic, typifying medieval pedantry.[5]

Consideration of historical issues is in any case irrelevant to most modern Christian allegorical readings of Shakespeare, which ignore history and simply assume that the Bible has meant the same thing in all ages, and that the parallels they detect in Shakespeare's text are really there, whether or not consciously meant. The result is a general free-for-all, a game which anyone can play, since the rules are so easy to learn. The simplest move is to connect one Shakespeare character with one Christian. To Paul N. Siegel Lear's death has 'a deeper meaning', the 'miracle' being Lear's redemption 'for heaven, a redemption analogous to the redemption of mankind, for which the Son of God had come down to earth. The analogy between Cordelia and Christ . . . is made unmistakable' by the choric commentator who says that she 'redeems nature from the general curse / Which twain have brought her to' (*King Lear*, 4.6.210–11). Wrongly taking 'twain' to refer not to Goneril and Regan but to Adam and Eve, Siegel suggests that 'the Elizabethans . . . would have more readily apprehended than we do that Cordelia's ignominious death completes the analogy between her and Christ' (Siegel 1957, p. 186). Desdemona, too, dies an ignominious death, but takes on a redemptive function far wider than Cordelia (who only saved her father, after all):

> Desdemona raises and redeems such earthly souls as Emilia. Belief in her, the symbolic equivalent in the play of belief in Christ, is a means of salvation for Cassio as well as for Emilia. (*ibid.*, p. 134)

Othello, however, is not saved. 'Crushed by the sight' of Desdemona on her death bed, 'he calls to be transported to hell at once', in words which remind Siegel, at least, of what an Elizabethan homily calls 'Judas' repentance', a parallel which is instantly endorsed: 'In committing self-murder at the conclusion he is continuing to follow Judas' example. His behavior in his last moments, therefore, would have confirmed Elizabethans in the impression that his soul is lost' (p. 131).

Siegel frequently invokes Elizabethan attitudes as confirming his allegorising readings, but never proves that this habit of mind existed then. The truth seems to lie with R.M. Frye's counter-assertion: 'there is no evidence from any source contemporary with Shakespeare to support the notion that Elizabethan audiences customarily allegorized the plays they saw or that Elizabethan dramatists (save, possibly, in rare instances of clearly topical interest) allegorized the plays they wrote' (Frye 1963, p. 33). Such observations, although true, have no effect on critics who wish to draw large and precise parallels between Shakespeare and Christian story. Thus on one page discussing Othello, Roy W. Battenhouse finds in Othello's 'Keep up your bright swords, for the dew will rust them' an irresistible echo of Christ's words to Peter at Gethsemane: 'Put up your sword into the sheath; the cup which the Father hath given me, shall I not drink it?' (John 18:11). To Battenhouse 'the two scenes have a strange affinity, as if Othello were revealing to us a grotesque version of the biblical Christ' (Battenhouse 1957, p. 209). What purpose this 'affinity' could have in the structure of the play, and in what sense Othello could be even a 'grotesque' version of Christ, are questions not discussed. Instead, Battenhouse rushes on to identify more 'analogues':

> Another analogue is suggested by Act III, scene iii, when Desdemona, like Veronica of Christian legend, would soothe her lord's anguished face with a handkerchief. Othello brushes her off and the handkerchief is dropped and lost. Thus the analogue is both like and unlike the Christian legend, a kind of antitype to it.

That selective attention, however improbable, typifies the method of Christian allegorising: pick out the one detail that makes a parallel, ignore the rest. As Richard Levin has said, such 'parallels' are merely 'pieces of special pleading, in that they have always been subjected to a double screening in advance' by the allegoriser: 'out of all the facts in the play he selects only those suiting his purpose, and since each of these chosen facts has many aspects, he selects again those of its aspects that he will consider relevant and ignores all the others. The result is therefore never in doubt . . .' (Levin 1979, p. 221).

To return to Battenhouse, still on the same page, is to see him finding 'still another analogue, this time to Job', when Othello exclaims that he 'could have had patience, had it pleased Heaven "To try me with affliction" and "all kinds of sores" . . .'. This parallel, if reflected on, would suggest certain difficulties (notably that God must be punishing Othello). Battenhouse meets these by saying that 'Othello is suffering no sores other than of his own making', that he trusts in 'a Satan-like Iago', and that Othello also trusts 'in his own righteousness substituting as god' (with a small G!). So the Job analogue makes this 'an upside-down parallel of Christian story'. (Who is on top?) Battenhouse feels much happier with his final analogue, as Othello, having in one page been identified with Christ and Job, is now equated with Judas. His dying words to Desdemona, 'I kissed thee ere I killed thee', Battenhouse writes, 'bring to mind Judas', as does his (earlier) 'remorseful cry that "like the base Judean" he has thrown "a pearl away/Richer than all his tribe"'. Although he doesn't tell his readers, Battenhouse is quoting the Folio reading *Iudean* or *Judean*: the Quarto text gives *Indian*, and the majority of editors have opted for this reading.[6] Undeterred by textual considerations, Battenhouse comments:

> Here we have a true parallel. Judas was the Judean who threw away the pearl-of-great-price (charity, or Christ), and then committed suicide.

Battenhouse, who never faces the fact that the jewel Othello laments having thrown away is not Christ but Desdemona, goes on to discover other parallels between Othello, Judas, and the Pharisees. Finally, by saying 'Put out the light . . .' Othello is said to be 'enacting unwittingly a kind of *tenebrae* service' (Battenhouse 1957, p. 210) — that is, we recall, the Roman Catholic service on Good Friday. That Othello enacts it 'unwittingly' makes it perhaps not quite so inappropriate that Judas officiates at this ceremony.

*   *   *

We can already see the criteria by which a Christian allegoriser finds a significant parallel: any resemblance to anything in Biblical or legendary material will do, any handkerchief can be Veronica's, any sword Peter's. As for the negative instances, that recognition of contrary evidence which makes us qualify an interpretation, or abandon it altogether, they are thin on the ground. The result is a veritable *fay ce que vouldras*, to re-apply Rabelais. Staying with *Othello*, and drawing on a recent analytical bibliography,[7] we find that Desdemona was seen in 1939 as Christ (#30) and in 1950 as 'both the soul and the Redeemer', with her handkerchief 'a "sacred talisman", a necessary possession for anyone seeking "the harmony of the Divine Union"' (#140) — unfortunate to lose it, then. To Peter Milward in 1967, drawing on medieval moralities, Desdemona was the Virgin Mary (#633), but in 1985 he identified her with Christ (#1379). For Arthur Kirsch in 1978 Desdemona 'embodies the Christian value of pity', but is also 'an "incarnate ideal of marital love and of the charity which subsumes it"' (#1068). In 1981 Kirsch saw her as exemplifying 'the religious and psychological commitments of marriage as articulated by St. Paul and Freud' (#1204: does Freud ever write about commitments in a healthy relationship?). As for Iago, most allegorisers have seen him as a Satan figure, Battenhouse repeatedly, in 1969, 1964, and 1957 (#696, 488, 278). Going back to 1952, however, Battenhouse saw Othello as 'the "liberal humanitarian" of today', setting himself up outside Christianity, while 'his entrapment by the Satanic Iago offers a message to us today, who are "so easily victimized by the Communist conspirator"', with his 'materialistic deceit' (#173). So the Cold War claimed another victim.

*   *   *

The liberty of interpreting that the Christian allegorisers grant themselves is total. J.A. Bryant, Jr., in one of the most bizarre examples of this art, equates Othello with God, Cassio with Adam, Iago with Lucifer (also 'passed over for promotion'), Desdemona with Christ.[8] As R.M. Frye drily comments, 'we may perhaps be pardoned for feeling some slight anxiety along the way as to the approaching suicide of God the Father' (Frye 1963, p. 31). That suicide, indeed, for the majority of allegorisers, places Othello in hell, on the simple process of what Frye calls 'proof by assertion' (ibid., p. 22). For Paul Siegel it is self-evident that Gertrude is damned, Cassio saved, Roderigo damned. Desdemona, meanwhile, gains heaven by her 'martyrdom', with Emilia to attend her, while Othello and Iago are damned beyond redemption (Siegel 1957, pp. 114–15, 134–9). Sitting in judgment over characters in tragedy may give one a comforting sense of power, but it wholly mistakes the nature of that genre, and is in any case irrelevant. As Sylvan Barnet observed in a penetrating essay, the ethics in Shakespeare's plays

> partake of Christian ethics, but they are not based, as Christian ethics in fact are, upon the eschatology of the Christian system. Shakespeare . . . does not concern himself with the fortunes of his lovers and haters in the next world, nor does he insist that the meek shall inherit the earth.[9]

The plays 'partake of Christian ethics', we might add, in the sense that the Church shared a broad band of ethical teaching with classical moral philosophy. Luther (like many Christians) could praise both Cicero and Aristotle for their writings on ethics, but still believe that, '"however excellent they are . . . they cannot show the way to God into the kingdom of heaven"' (cit. Frye 1963, p. 79). Similarly, although characters in the plays may refer to the 'four last things' comprised in Christian eschatology (death, judgment, heaven, hell), Shakespeare never uses this scheme to suggest what happens to his characters 'after the play is over'. He, at any rate, could tell the difference between life and art.

Refutations of Christian allegorical interpretation have long ago pointed out its deficiencies,[10] but are unlikely to extinguish it as a critical option. For one thing, its very flexibility, the absence of limiting criteria, makes it combinable with other approaches, directed by the intentionality of the critic. Arthur Kirsch, as we briefly saw, could combine St. Paul and Freud in describing Desdemona. Stanley Cavell, writing about Coriolanus, starts with a psychoanalytic reading and ends up with a Christian one. This essay has been so much admired, especially in psychoanalytical-feminist circles, and Cavell's standing as a philosopher is so high, as to make it worth more detailed discussion. Although the essay is called 'Coriolanus and Interpretations of Politics', Cavell wholly ignores the political dimension of the play, that re-working of Plutarch in which Shakespeare made the family conflict between Coriolanus and his mother an integral part of the political situation, so that tensions in each exacerbate the other, with Coriolanus being caught in a series of dilemmas that destroy him.[11] His real interests psychoanalytical, Cavell baldly classifies Coriolanus as a Narcissus figure in whom, moreover, 'narcissism' is 'another face of incestuousness' (Cavell 1987, p. 144), a juggling of categories which it must take a Freudian to understand. Cavell's psychoanalytical model (Adelman 1978) encourages him to lump Volumnia and Coriolanus together in a complicated sequence of 'feeding, dependency, and aggression', based on just two passages in the play. First, Volumnia's reply to Menenius' invitation to dinner, immediately after Coriolanus' banishment:

> Anger's my meat; I sup upon myself
> And so shall starve with feeding.   (4.2.50–1)

In its context this means 'I shall go on being angry: I can sustain my anger indefinitely, simultaneously consuming and renewing itself' — a paradox, perhaps, but not too unfamiliar from angry people in life. Second, Coriolanus' bitter soliloquy, earlier on, as he goes through the to him degrading ceremony of begging from every 'Hob and Dick' the recognition by Rome which his bravery in war has already earned him:

> Better it is to die, better to starve,
> Than crave the hire which first we do deserve.   (2.3.118f)

Ignoring the dramatic situation and the conflicts arising out of the notions of class and service, the curiously anachronistic and pseudo-democratic voting customs in early Rome, that tension between enforced and voluntary recognition of the ruling patrician class which Shakespeare exploited to form a tragedy, Cavell takes these two remarks, a total of four lines made by two characters many scenes apart, for very different ends, as proving that mother and son are 'starvers, hungerers', expressing 'a condition of insatiability' (p. 148).

In ascribing to both mother and son the 'presiding passion' of 'human insatiability' (pp. 148–9), Cavell reduces to one level two very different people. Volumnia is indeed greedy, but on behalf of her son, that he fulfil her supreme ambitions by becoming consul (e.g., 2.1.146–9, 196–200). She has bred him to military and political success since he was a boy, perverting maternal love in the process (e.g., 1.3.1–25). For his part, although happy to fight for the ideal of Rome (2.2.131f; 3.1.76f), Coriolanus wants no part in politics, and loathes the sycophancy expected of him (e.g., 2.1.200ff; 2.2.135ff; 2.3.48ff; 3.1; 3.2; 3.3). The voting scenes, with the demagogic activities of the tribunes being juxtaposed with the ineffective efforts of the patricians to make Coriolanus a tactful vote-catcher, enact a collision that fills up the centre of the play. Coriolanus' resentment of political vote-begging produces conflict within the family, for Volumnia puts her role as Roman before that as mother. In rebelling against the one, Coriolanus inevitably rejects the other, making protests which Volumnia crushes by tactical withdrawals of love, culminating in his disastrous capitulation after he has defeated Rome for the Volsces (3.2.7–147; 5.3.19–209).[12] Ignoring the interweaving of politics and family which sets Volumnia and Coriolanus on opposed paths, using his Freudian idea of 'insatiability' to level out the opposition between them (as if you were to put Claudius and Hamlet on the same side), Cavell lumps mother and son together not only in their 'way of starving . . . their hunger', but in a further and more dramatic stage, 'their sense of being cannibalized'. If this word describes a human being eaten by another human, readers will look in vain to find either Volumnia or Coriolanus complaining of it happening to them. To Cavell, however, they do feel this, and are not alone, for he finds that 'the idea of cannibalization runs throughout the play' (p. 150).

But as any reader with a literary training can see, it is not so much an 'idea' as a metaphor for human relationships — especially ingratitude — which is never meant to be taken literally. Furthermore, like so much of the language in this play, it has been politicised. Each political group using this metaphor does so for its own polemical purposes. One of the tribunes says of Coriolanus, 'May the present wars devour him!' (1.1.257); Menenius says that the plebeians would like to 'devour' Martius (2.1.9); Coriolanus says that were it not for the Senate the plebs 'Would feed on one another' (1.1.192); the plebeians argue that the patricians are trying to 'eat us . . . up' (1.1.87); Coriolanus attacks the Tribunes: 'You being their mouths, why rule you not their teeth?' (3.1.36f); Menenius hopes that ungrateful Rome will not 'like an unnatural dam . . . eat up her own' by expelling Martius (3.1.288ff); and when Coriolanus goes over to the Volsces he complains that he has only his name left, the people's 'cruelty and envy . . . hath devoured the rest' (4.5.82). In all these instances the reader must decode 'eat', 'feed', 'devour' (none of which, incidentally, is used with unusual frequency in this play), as meaning 'destroy' or 'deprive', not taking the metaphor literally, and seeing it as embodying political rivalry, expressed throughout this play as intense hatred.

Such considerations would be lost on Cavell, who regularly conflates literal and figurative meanings. According to him Cominius comes 'to battle as to a feast', suggesting that Coriolanus sees it in those terms: but the metaphor is Cominius' own: 'Yet cam'st thou to a morsel of this feast' (1.9.10), in any case a metaphor for 'part of'. When Menenius prays that Rome will not behave 'like an unnatural dam', Cavell hopes that 'all readers . . . will recognize in this description of Rome as potentially a cannibalistic mother an allusion to Volumnia', suggesting to him not merely an 'identification of Volumnia and Rome' but 'an identity . . . between a mother eating her child and a mother eating herself' (p. 151). Pursuing a metaphor in this literal-minded way leads Cavell to the absurdity of imagining Volumnia first eating her child (Coriolanus is a grown man by now), then eating herself, a grotesque idea which is peculiarly hard to visualise. The resulting 'identity', or 'identification', as Cavell puts it, cannot distinguish cannibalism from metaphor, as if this play presented another banquet of Thyestes. The culminating point in this muddle is Cavell's reading (following Adelman 1978) of the lines where Volumnia rebukes Virgilia for expressing anguish at her mother-in-law's auto-induced militaristic vision of Coriolanus victorious in battle, covered in blood. 'The breasts of Hecuba', Volumnia contemptuously replies, 'When she did suckle Hector, look'd not lovelier / Than Hector's forehead when it spit forth blood / At Grecian sword, contemning' (1.3.39ff). This (horribly militarist) contrast between Hector as baby and Hector as grown man was fated to be destroyed by these Freudian critics, Adelman and Cavell agreeing that it transforms Hector from 'infantile mouth to bleeding wound', and Cavell adding his further insight that 'the suckling mother is presented as being slashed by the son-hero, eaten by the one she feeds', a typical Volumnia fantasy, he suggests (p. 154). But no, a typical Freudian fantasy, rather, as the learned philosopher shows that he is unable to read the lines that Shakespeare has written, collapsing a time-scale of twenty years, at least, between baby and warrior, into one garbled and violent phrase ('slashed . . . eaten'), again confusing literal and metaphorical.

The turning-point in Cavell's essay, from psychoanalysis to Christian allegorising (it could be subtitled 'Cannibals and Christians'), comes with his further misreading of Volumnia's lines. Where she made a nauseating comparison of the *beauty* of Hecuba's suckling breasts with the *beauty* of Hector's battle-wounds, for Cavell 'the lines set up an equation between a mother's milk and a man's blood'. Pushing ahead with the consequence of what it would *literally* imply if blood were the same as milk, he suggests that 'the man's spitting blood in battle' is a way of 'providing food, in a male fashion', so that Coriolanus' 'spitting blood in battle is his way of deserving being fed, that is to say, being devoured, being loved unconditionally' (p. 154). Thus 'effective bleeding', then — as if Coriolanus should say, 'here, drink my blood while it is still warm' — 'depends (according to the equation of blood and milk) upon its being a form of feeding, of giving food, providing blood identifies him with his mother' (p. 155). But it is only Professor Cavell who wishes to equate blood and milk, to identify Coriolanus and Volumnia, to suggest that battle-wounds provide food 'in a male fashion'. His perverse reading of these lines, the product of a long, intense, and tortuous meditation on the issues of feeding, cannibalising, and killing, reaches its improbable climax as he begins to plot a relation between Coriolanus and 'the other sacrificial lamb I have mentioned, the lamb of God, Christ', — not to 'identify them', he hastens to add: 'I see Coriolanus not so much as imitating Christ as competing with him. These are necessarily shadowy matters . . .' (p. 157).

But what would it mean to see Coriolanus, who lived some centuries before Christ, as 'competing with him'? Competing for Shakespeare, as if the dramatist were somehow associating the two? Or competing for Cavell, as if they were simultaneously present in his consciousness, role models perhaps? Whichever it is, Cavell now inserts Christ into his own interpretation of 'food' in *Coriolanus*. 'Christ is the right god' — I presume he means 'right' for *his* interpretation — 'because of the way he understands his mission as providing nonliteral food, food for the spirit, for immortality; and because it is in him that blood must be understood as food' (p. 157). We are grateful for the word 'nonliteral' there, but must say all the same that the difference between Coriolanus' imputed equation of blood and milk — based on Cavell's perverse interpretation of Volumnia's reference to Hector — and Christ's 'this is my blood of the new testament, which is shed for many for the remission of sins' (Matt. 26:28) is so great that it may seem an act of astonishing insensitivity, or critical hybris, to compare the two. But Cavell finds 'surprising *confirmation* for it' in two of Coriolanus' actions.

> First is his pivotal refusal to show his wounds. I associate this generally with the issue of Christ's showing his wounds to his disciples, in order to show them the Lord — that is, to prove the Resurrection . . .

and in particular his rebuke of doubting Thomas. 'Thomas would not believe until he could, as he puts it and as Jesus will invite him to, "put mine hands into his side"; Aufidius declares the wish to "wash my fierce hand in's heart" (1.10.27)' (p. 158; my italics). Every reader must judge whether they find this parallel convincing. To me it seems a desperate, superficial, fortuitous link between two utterly different incidents. Aufidius does not want to see, and know, the risen God: he wishes to cut his enemy's heart out and wipe his hands in its blood.

Cavell's second 'confirmation' of his thesis is even more fantastic, describing the scene where 'Volumnia, holding her son's son by the hand, together with Virgilia and Valeria', intercedes on behalf of Rome. Now what does this remind you of?

> I take this to invoke the appearance, while Christ is on the cross, of three women whose names begin with the same letter of the alphabet (I mean begin with M's, not with V's), accompanied by a male he loves, whom he views as his mother's son (John, 19:25–7). (Giving his mother a son presages a mystic marriage.) (p. 158)

So that young Coriolanus is to be archetypically equated with John the Evangelist, then . . . — but there would be no point in pursuing the issue. One can only wonder to what depths of introversion a scholar's mind can have descended for him to regard this as a proof of anything. The propensity to make your own meaning out of isolated letters of the alphabet suggests the gulled Malvolio ('what should that alphabetical position portend? If I could make that resemble something in me. Softly. M, O, A, I . . .': 2.5.130ff), or poor mad Kit Smart.[13] But Cavell has a 'second source of confirmation for Coriolanus' connection with the figure of Christ', namely 'some parallels that come out of Revelation'. He summarises that book as briefly as possible — a rhetorical effect — as containing a lamb, a dragon, 'and a figure who sits on a special horse and on a golden throne, whose name is known only to himself, whose "eyes were as a flame of fire", and who burns a city that is identified as a woman; it is, in particular, the city (Babylon) which in Christian tradition is identified with Rome' (p. 159). But where, in Shakespeare, are the seven beasts, and the four and twenty elders, and the book with seven seals?

'And I associate', Cavell continues, sure in the knowledge that he cannot be refuted (that is, he truly does associate) Coriolanus' first diatribe against the citizens with Christ's warning 'I shall spew thee out', the common factor being a passage in North's Plutarch. But in fact Plutarch writes that Coriolanus *lacked* (Cavell hasn't noticed this) the 'base and faint corage, which spitteth out anger from the most weak and passioned parte of the harte' (p. 158). Fortified by such hasty misreadings Cavell moves on into a realm of purely private associations. To him Coriolanus and Christ 'are identified as banished providers of spiritual food' (p. 160): what could possibly be 'spiritual' about Coriolanus? Yet another 'equation' that he finds in the play, again collapsing difference into identity, that between 'words and food', links Coriolanus further with Christ, 'invoking the central figure of the Eucharist' (pp. 163, 167). But Christ's 'food' is for others, and Cavell's point has been that people in this play eat each other, so he has to add that to Coriolanus 'the circulation of language is an expression of cannibalism' (p. 165). I can only hope that Cavell will one day eat his words.

Cavell pursues his parallel to the extent of seeing Coriolanus as a kind of failed Christ figure — for which, of course, his mother is to blame:

> She has deprived him of heaven, of, in his fantasy, sitting beside his father, and deprived him by withholding her faith in him, for if she does not believe that he is a god then probably he is not a god, and certainly nothing like the Christian scenario can be fulfilled, in which a mother's belief is essential. If it were his father who sacrificed him for the city of man then he could be a god. But if it is his mother who sacrifices him he is not a god. The logic of his situation, as well as the psychology, is that he cannot sacrifice himself. (p. 161)

I can find no comment adequate to such a serious pursuit of the parallel between Coriolanus and Volumnia on the one hand, Christ and the Virgin Mary on the other, with a missing father-figure as the excluded middle.

(Cavell has a few suggestions, by the way, as to who Coriolanus might conceivably have lined up as a father-figure.)

Cavell's final point about *Coriolanus*, his Parthian dart, the butt-end of his discourse (as in *Othello*), concerns the significance of a name. When I reviewed Janet Adelman's essay on its first appearance, I made the jocular suggestion that 'If Volumnia is castrating Coriolanus, . . . and if Corioli represents defloration', as Adelman suggested, 'then what dark deed is commemorated in our hero's honorific soubriquet, Coriol-anus? You may laugh, dear reader, but thin partitions do the bounds divide.'[14] I should have been more careful: whatever fantastic Shakespeare interpretation one can think of, it either has been or one day will be made. So for Cavell — to whom, as we recall, 'farce and tragedy are separated by the thickness of a membrane' — the 'anality in the play is less explicit than the orality', but he finds, all the same, that 'the issue [is] given full explicitness in the play's, and its hero's name'. Kenneth Burke once pronounced that 'in the light of the Freudian theories concerning the fecal nature of invective, the last two syllables [-*anus*] are so "right" . . .', so right that Cavell can find 'a kind of poetic justice' in the language having given 'the same sound equally to a suffix that encodes a name's military honor and to the name of the shape of a sphincter . . .' (p. 174). While feeling sorry for German readers who can't share the joke in Coriolan, just like the Italians who can't see 'hell' in Otello, and while wondering how many dozens of Latin names end in the suffix -*anus*, the real question that this comment raises is what, for the psychoanalytic critic, as for the Christian allegoriser, would constitute inadmissible evidence? Where could they draw a line between the relevant and the fortuitous, between the statistically improbable and the simply silly? Cavell's account of *Coriolanus* will long remain one of the most bizarre episodes in modern Shakespeare criticism.

II

While drawing certain parallels between Christian and Marxist approaches, I must say at once that the latter are more restrained, less fantastic. Whatever we may think about Marx's theory of society and history, or the many divergent theories of those who call themselves Marxists, no critic I know is quite as eccentric as J.A. Bryant or Stanley Cavell. The most common objection to Marxist literary criticism is, indeed, its lack of imagination, its mechanical discovery of Marxist concepts in literary texts on a 'one here, one there' basis (e.g., Barthes 1972, p. 255). Some thirty years after his Christian allegorising of the tragedies, Paul N. Siegel produced what he claimed to be 'a Marxist approach' to Shakespeare's history plays, English and Roman (Siegel 1986), with much the same simple stereotyping.[15] Quoting Marx and Engels on Shylock as a 'representative of the capitalist ethic' (p. 25), and E.C. Pettet's comment on Timon in his philanthropic phase as '"the representative of specific medieval values, a dispenser of feudal bounty"' (p. 26), and T.A. Jackson's view of Falstaff and his crew as representing the '"decomposition of an absolute class... dependants upon the feudal order"' (p. 21), Siegel continues in the same vein of simply labelling characters as 'representative'. Falstaff and Hotspur are 'representatives of social classes', Falstaff 'a member of the decadent feudalistic aristocracy, Hotspur a member of the same class at its best' (p. 34). Richard III is a 'representative of the spirit of capitalism', a claim that Siegel supports with a relentless list of every 'monetary' or 'commercial' term used by Richard, interspersed with disapproving reference to 'the bourgeoisie' (pp. 80–85). This approach depersonalises Richard, turning a uniquely daemonic figure into the mere representative of a class, and in the process destroys the play's ethical structure, responsibility for Richard's evil deeds now being transferred to the 'rampant individualism' of capitalism. In addition to damaging both character and play, this approach notably fails to explain why Richard was defeated, especially as capitalism subsequently 'gained world domination' (p. 85). Was Shakespeare a closet feudalist?

Eroding individuality, creating deterministic models of human behaviour, naïve Marxism resembles naïve Freudianism. The privileged categories are supposedly higher-level generalisations, but they produce just that 'abstraction from objects of the senses' which Coleridge complained of, losing the reality and vitality of the individual in bland and repetitive abstractions. More complex theoretical models now exist, as we shall soon see, but the paradigmatic structures used by naïve Marxism are incapable of being further energised, and the syntagmatic structures — the overthrow of capitalism, the withering away of the state — propose a narrative line which cannot be echoed in Shakespeare or any work not deliberately constructed on millenarian lines. The parallel with Christian narratives is again close, as Raymond Aron observed:

> In Marxist eschatology, the proletariat is cast in the role of collective saviour. The expressions used by the young Marx leave one in no doubt as to the Judaeo-Christian origins of the myth of the class elected through suffering for the redemption of humanity. The mission of the proletariat, the end of pre-history thanks to the Revolution, the reign of liberty — it is easy to recognise the source of these ideas: the Messiah, the break with the past, the Kingdom of God. (Aron 1957, p. 66)

The political reality, however, Aron could observe in the mid-50s, was that in communist countries 'it is the Party rather than the proletariat which is the object of a cult', and that whenever socialism has succeeded in democracies, 'the factory workers, having become petty bourgeois, no longer interest the intellectuals and are themselves no longer interested in ideologies' (ibid.).

Yet the proletariat remains the hero in much Marxist criticism, the role of enemy being played by the bourgeoisie and capitalists, with the intellectuals occupying an uneasy middle ground. A striking example of this idealisation of the people is Robert Weimann's book on Shakespeare and the popular tradition in the theatre, whose very favourable reception among Cultural Materialists again makes it worth examining in more detail.[16] His broad argument is that drama originated in folk-rituals, whether in ancient Greece or medieval England; that the 'popular' element is always fresh, 'realistic'; that intervention by 'humanists' or other intellectuals damages the true nature of drama; and that Shakespeare's best work derives from the popular tradition. None of these ideas is new, indeed the superiority of *das Volk* is a fixed principle having a venerable tradition in Marxist criticism. Weimann supports his argument with the citation of a great deal of secondary literature, some of it relatively modern and reliable (restating the views of C.L. Barber, Bernard Spivack, Alfred Harbage), but much of it obscure and obsolete, dating from the end of the nineteenth century.[17] The fact that Weimann can seriously cite Franz Mehring's view that Shakespeare's stage 'still had one foot in the Germanic Middle Ages' shows how much he relied on German sources which have been totally superseded, and is a sad testimony to the difficulty writers in the former DDR had in obtaining access to modern, non-communist scholarship. Perhaps as a result of his cultural isolation — or perhaps because it fitted his Marxist simplification of Elizabethan drama — Weimann based a large part of his argument on amazingly outdated works of anthropology and social history. His views on the ritual origins of drama derive from Frazer's *The Golden Bough* (p. 218), that 'monumental exercise in futility', as a modern anthropologist described it,[18] backed up with Gilbert Murray on 'Hamlet and Orestes', and those predictable Marxist studies of Greek tragedy by Thomson and Lindsay. The most glaring example of his reliance on outmoded sources is his citation of Margaret Murray's totally discredited book, *The Witch-Cult in Western Europe*.[19] These are not just 'old' books: they simply offer an unscholarly mess of speculation without evidence, or with evidence cooked to fit a thesis. Weimann knows that some of them have been discredited, but shows a rather slippery readiness to use them when it suits his argument.[20] It is remarkable that such work could be published in 1978 by an American university press which prides itself on being out front in critical theory.

The result of Weimann's reliance on such bad secondary material is that he accumulates a morass of unproven and unprovable theories about the origin of drama, linking 'miming' (whatever that was) with magic, with the 'cultic sphere', with the 'orgiastic cult' (p. 3), and with 'ecstatic or magic ritual', 'the shaman, the poet-priest', and the 'initiation ceremony' (p. 5). There is no evidence, of course, for any of these links, nor for a connection between 'magical rite and mimic representation (which survived in phallic fertility symbolism)' (*ibid.*). These are the detritus of nineteenth-century whimsical speculations about the pre-history of the race. Weimann gives wholly imaginary accounts of the Ur-form of drama, describing the fool as a 'descendant of a ritual', an 'atavistic agent of the cult' (p. 11); he blurs Dionysus, 'Orphic and shamanist traditions' (p. 14); dabbles indiscriminately with satyr cults and tribal culture (p. 19), saturnalia, seasonal rites, and vegetation magic (p. 23); and discourses on 'the relationship between the fool's motley and the pagan traditions of vegetation magic' (p. 31). This is all wild invention.

The fictitious nature of such speculations may be only fully evident to those who have worked in these fields, but every reader can see the methodological faults in Weimann's treatment of the Mummers' Play. He knows that our sole evidence for this 'tradition' consists of 'nineteenth-century versions [sic] of the texts' (p. 18), but he still credulously takes something set down at Weston-sub-Edge in 1864 as showing how the fool traditionally (on his vague time-scale, anything from one to three thousand years ago) had a 'ritual' connection with inversion, a topic which, he assures us, 'can best be studied in plays where this ambivalence is *reflected* in modern verbal structures' (pp. 33, 36; my italics).[21] Such a self-confirming attitude to evidence or proof, not even bothering to consider that this text might derive from more immediate dramatic traditions, written and printed drama performed in urban theatres, has no claim to be taken seriously as scholarship, Marxist or otherwise.

Throughout Weimann's book, from his discussions of medieval plays to his survey of late Elizabethan drama, it is simply assumed that drama retains in one way or another its 'cultic' or 'postritual' origins. All such references beg the question and pile myth on myth, but their function is to lay the historical or scholarly base for the book's main argument, that the real hero in the rise of English drama is the English people. Not all Englishmen, of course: not the humanists who taught the dramatists how to read and write, introduced them to classical drama, and gave them a practical mastery of the arts of language and thought; nor the noblemen whose interest in, and willingness to stand as patrons of, the companies gave them and the actors legal and social status; nor the dramatists, finally, many of them university-educated, and all of them having a good working knowledge of Latin and considerable respect for classical culture; but *das Volk*. Without the popular tradition, Weimann tells us, 'Shakespeare's drama is unthinkable.' Furthermore, 'the popular stagecraft that Shakespeare incorporated into his unique dramatic method was a popular theatre already developed to its fullest artistic possibilities' (p. xvi) — a hyperbole that begs the question by appropriating as 'popular' an art-form which had a much wider genesis. The wordplay in the popular morality supposedly has 'a meaning and a dramatic function that is, in its way, superior to anything found' in the Senecan tradition or humanist drama (p. 135) — not that Weimann analyses either of those genres. He claims that Queen Elizabeth I condescended to prefer 'plebeian drama' (to 'court art' (p. 172), a statement which quite distorts the issue (the actors who performed at court were the normal professional London companies), and conveniently ignores the fact that she could also enjoy Latin academic drama, and critically evaluate orations and disputations in Latin. In the drama 'humanism' (which Weimann never defines and does not seem to understand, opposing it at one point (p. 179) to 'neo-classical poetics'), 'was greatest when closest to the people', which explains why Marlowe's greatest play is so indebted to 'a popular source *par excellence* — the *Volksbuch*' (p. 180). The fact that Marlowe's play also draws on learned traditions in both philosophy and magic is beneath Weimann's notice. To him the people can do no wrong, nor could Elizabethan society until 'nascent capitalism', acquisitiveness, and the Puritan ethos destroyed its communal existence. (That would have been surprising news to them.) It is important to note that 'popular' and 'plebeian' are not neutral words to Weimann, but terms of praise. Over Shakespeare's critical, often disapproving treatment of mobs he remains silent, referring only once to Jack Cade's 'Saturnalia' (p. 240) — a myth-and-ritual reference which glosses over the brutality and specifically anti-intellectual nature of that rebellion. Just one out-of-the-way footnote (p. 292 n. 26) records Weimann's agreement with other Marxist critics that Shakespeare is 'no partisan of popular rule.'

Weimann's work obviously belongs to naïve Marxism, with its explicit preference for literature that endorses the correct views about the proletariat or the bourgeoisie, about class-consciousness and class-struggle. We are still far away from the highly abstract theoretical models of Althusser, Macherey and Godelier that were being produced in Paris while Weimann was writing this book, and of which no notice was taken in its revised version published in America at the end of the 1970s. This book was already an anachronism when it was published, judged by Marxist standards, and it must be an increasing embarrassment to more sophisticated and politically aware readers today. It is valuable evidence, though, of how ideological expectations can distort historical, social, and aesthetic categories. Weimann uses the inappropriate Marxist categories of 'plebeian' and 'bourgeoisie' to describe what he takes to be the two main groups in Elizabethan London, the latter supposedly attempting 'to suppress stage plays altogether' (p. 99) — where does he think the audience came from? Real historical evidence about the social composition of the audience, which has produced a controversy in our time,[22] is easily available, but Weimann ignores it in favour of a pious Marxist hope for a 'social unity' beyond the class struggle. This in turn distorts his conception of the theatrical profession, since his ideal of a theatre where all the participants come from the same social structure imagines that 'as long as no class divisions separate actor and audience, the spectator remains a potential actor and the actor a potential spectator' (p. 7). In modern society, of course, this situation can happen seldom, and only in closed social groups (schools, prisons). But in any case the social status is irrelevant. What matters is the willingness of one side to act, to adopt a role implying competence in performance, and the readiness of the other side to fill the complementary role of audience, and to pay the performers. (The whole economic side of the Elizabethan theatre, for which profuse documentation exists, is neglected — surprisingly enough in a Marxist critic — in favour of outdated anthropology.) Throughout, Weimann ignores the knowledge we have of the increasing professionalism of Elizabethan actors, their struggle to be accepted as craftsmen, members of a serious professional institution — all topics that have been illuminated by Muriel Bradbrook and by other writers known to Weimann.[23] What poses as objective scholarship is a pre-formed political attitude that ignores all evidence that would call it in question.

Weimann then elevates his simple two-part social model into an aesthetic category. Opportunistically invoking Hegel on the desirable 'identity of the subject and object of comedy' (p. 8), he claims that the 'indivisibility of play and audience' (p. 9) can be seen, or re-created in direct audience-address. According to him this technique achieves 'direct actor-audience contact' (p. 7). He seems blind to the fact that the actor does not actually speak in *propria persona*, but is *pretending* to 'speak to the audience' (uttering lines set down by the author for him to speak at this point), and in that sense is 'manipulating' the audience just as much as (according to Weimann) the other characters do who are pretending to speak to each other. Weimann in fact thinks that the best drama contains the least illusion, and that direct 'audience-contact' is made most properly by the Vice or Fool, who represents a subversive intent with which necessarily *all levels* of the audience (!) identify. It seems to have escaped him that the vice figure is often meant to be rejected, and that in Shakespeare's two great applications of that convention, for the characters of Richard III and Iago, we can hardly do anything but loathe them. Weimann's curious blend of old anthropology and old Marxism results in some very odd aesthetic and critical positions, which are interrelated in ways that the innocent or casual reader may not notice.

Take for instance the Marxist category of 'realism' or 'the real', again, like 'plebeian' not a neutral but a laudatory concept. S.L. Bethell's 'important book' on Shakespeare and the popular dramatic tradition[24] — a work that did much to clarify the use of theatrical convention in Elizabethan drama — is praised but also rejected for its 'unveiled hostility towards realism' (p. xx). In ancient Greece, we are told, 'the dramatic representation of reality found its characteristic art form not in the stylized festival theater but in the popular *mimus*,' which broke away from religion to become 'modern and entirely secular' (two more praise-words), and in which the popular player renounced buskin and mask to become 'a describer of reality' direct, as it were (p. 41). Most of Greek drama, we realise, is thus dispensed with, in favour of a minor and tenuously-documented form. In *As You Like It* Touchstone, that marvellously varied court fool, is praised for introducing 'images of real rural living' (p. 46; 'I remember the kissing of her batler, and the cow's dugs that her pretty chopt hands had milk'd . . .'). Weimann suggests that Lear's lines 'Thou rascal beadle' are meant to be spoken to 'an individual in the audience singled out by an icy stare or accusing finger', so that Lear can engage the audience 'effectively' with issues that are

> experienced realistically as the role dissolves and the man behind the actor speaks directly to his fellow man in the audience. In the final analysis Shakespeare not only strengthens a realistic approach to the world, but to the world of art as well. (p. 220)

In all these instances Weimann, either unaware of or ignoring what philosophy since Nietzsche has taught us about the questionable concept of reality, or indeed of the language in which we discuss reality, assumes that reality is a known and fixed category that we all understand in the same way (perhaps older Marxists did). He privileges it still further by opposing it to 'the ideal' on the one hand, with depressingly predictable results (e.g., p. 5), and to illusion, on the other, with another disastrous mixture of pseudo-anthropology and aesthetic theory.

The historical argument, that the original drama was based on 'cultic, non-illusionary elements', and that even the Attic scene was 'not an illusionary locality' (pp. 4–9) — as if Medea's chariots, or Oedipus' blinding were 'real', not represented events — can be dismissed as fictitious. As for the pseudo-anthropological argument, it rests on a crushingly simple dichotomy. Ritual miming, in the good old days, was an embodiment of action; it was non-representational, non-symbolic; it was the thing itself; it was effective. Imitation, on the other hand, the product of mental activity, art, language, cooperation, the skills of writer and actor and artist, is all of the following negative things: it is 'disenchanting; referential; representational; symbolic; empirical; affective'; and of course, it is illusionary (see pp. 4, 17, 22, 36, 41, 65ff, 77). By an irony of cultural history, Weimann's old-Marxist attack on imitation found a similar target to post-structuralist aesthetics, partly explaining why his book has been hailed by critics who otherwise pride themselves on their theoretical sophistication. Weimann's position, however, is much cruder: the 'dramatic illusion of verisimilitude' signalled an absolute decline of drama, a second fall of man, and we can only regain that prelapsarian unity of actor and audience with the help of the Fool, who can 'break through the "fourth wall" . . . and again conjure and renew the old audience contact' (p. 12). Yet of course we then get only the illusion of breaking the illusion.

What Weimann's assumptions and mental categories offer us is a simple endorsement of 'the people' and 'realism' in drama as against 'the rulers' and 'illusionism'. These binary models are then applied to theatre architecture, to the audience, and to the play as an experience. The polar categories from theatre architecture are the *platea* and the *locus* of the medieval stage. To anyone who has figured out Weimann's social attitudes the resulting configuration is predictable. He opposes the *platea*'s 'platform-like acting area' or 'unlocalized place' to the 'scaffold, be it a *domus*, *sedes*, or throne (the *locus*)' (p. 74), to make a distinction as inevitable as that between mountain and plain in Elizabethan satire, or velvet and cloth breeches. This opposition apparently represents the 'continuing tension between realistic imitation and ritual embodiment' (p. 77), with the *platea* (for *das Volk*) characterised by 'neutrality' and realism, the *locus* (for the bourgeoisie) displaying its 'symbolic' nature and conventionalism (pp. 84, 89, 212, 221), a dichotomy which somehow also involves a distinction between representational and non-representational acting. Scholars of medieval drama will have their views on this distinction: to me it seems both rigid and fictitious. When applied to literary texts it results in the equation of Hamlet's passages of direct address with 'the *platea* tradition of the Vice', which is non-representational; whereas Rosencrantz and Guildenstern, in the same scene (3.2), are said to 'move on the level of the purely representational *loca*', so that the two sides 'operate on different levels' (pp. 131ff). This is to split a play, within one scene, into two illusory levels, in order to correlate it with an illusory dichotomy in society and in theatre architecture. The division does not help the play, and it signally fails to deal with the other instances of direct address. When Hamlet speaks to us in verse, is he then a Vice or a Prince? Socially, Claudius clearly belongs on the *locus*; but do his two passages of direct address shift him to the *platea*? And if so, does he thereby break down dramatic illusion, and recreate the primitive *Ur-einheit* of audience and actor?

These deductions about theatre-architecture and dramatic convention are all the product of an *a priori* belief in the superiority of people over rulers, realism over illusion, expressing a pre-formed ideology which is then used as a critical category to be reproduced in the commentary on drama. The circularity of this process, protected from criticism on either historical or ideological grounds, validating itself by not questioning any of its postulates, has a predictable effect on the literary material it deals with. The 'plebeian' proverb, that verbal resource cultivated and collected at great length by humanists and rhetoricians from Erasmus downwards, is casually appropriated for the people and equated with 'popular idiom' (p. 10), with 'nonaristocratic standards' (p. 130). Hamlet, assigned — partly — to the *platea* position, in speaking 71 of the 140 proverbs in the play, is said to draw on 'rural and plebeian experience' and 'the background of the common worker' (p. 130). Shakespeare supposedly uses proverbs, together with 'nonliterary syntax' and 'colloquial forms', to re-create 'practical life' and 'the common man's concrete world of objects and ideas' (p. 206). But of course Shakespeare used the proverb for characters from all walks, or levels, of life. It is only the critical model that is too narrow to do justice to his range. Not that Shakespeare is ever belittled, quite the opposite.

Indeed Weimann praises his universality and seizes every chance to draw parallels between 'folk drama' and that of the great bard. Thus an instance of 'topsy-turvydom' in the Weston Mummers' Play of 1864 — 'I met a bark and he dogged at me' — seems to the author to suggest not only Lear's 'Thou hast seen a farmer's dog bark at a beggar?' but also Portia's 'Which is the merchant here, and which the Jew?' and even Bottom's 'The eye of man hath not heard . . .'. There is no mention of St. Paul for this last instance, nor of the rhetoric books' discussion of this figure (*hypallage*), nor of the commonness of such forms in all types of language. Weimann claims that such feeble and naïve parallels demonstrate 'the usefulness of such a comparative method' (pp. 39ff), but in fact they only parody it.

Once again we face the issue of what constitutes evidence in a literary argument. Here, as elsewhere, Weimann is completely uncritical, unaware of the circularity of his method, the speculative and tendentious nature of the historical and anthropological evidence on which his case rests. To give one last example of the kind of historical material cited to substantiate his claims for some ritual connections with drama, Weimann takes as literal fact what he describes as 'the new Puritan morality' which 'thundered against the "Dionysian" freedoms characteristic of popular custom'. Weimann knows that Philip Stubbes was a Puritan, and violent, especially given to 'sexual repression', so he ought to have taken Stubbes's diatribes as something other than historical evidence. Stubbes's account of May and Whitsun pastorals, with the lasses and lads dancing around a May-pole ('this stinking Ydol') drawn by oxen, his belief that these pastimes should be led by Satan, and result in some mass orgy (pp. 162ff) — such attitudes may reveal the prurient and self-repressed imagination of a Pentheus in *The Bacchae*, but are in no way reliable historical testimony. Yet, because Stubbes refers to the devil, Weimann is prepared to endorse his manic account, since the 'devilry' could refer back 'to the late ritual heritage,' whatever that means (p. 171; the documentation, p. 285 n. 19, is exceptionally vague). One has the impression that Weimann would be quite glad to find that the Devil existed, since he might be able to link him with ritual drama.

Weimann's book has been praised by critics belonging to the New Historicist and Cultural Materialist groups, and it is easy to see that their dilute form of Marxism would react favourably to his account of a clown in a fragment of the Oxyrhynchos papyri who mocks the onstage action, thus having 'a kind of subversive function' (p. 13), and they no doubt approve of the term 'subversive' becoming an automatic plus-concept, to be equated with Misrule, Utopia, the Roman Saturnalia and Maygames, all representing the blessed state of inversion and topsy-turvydom (pp. 20ff, 94, 121, 158ff). Weimann's automatic endorsement of the subversive, whatever form it takes, and whatever the contextual evidence for its ethical status, comes out most crudely in his treatment of the vice figure. In the morality play *Mankind* Weimann sides with what he takes to be the representative of the people, the vice Myscheff, in his mangling of Latin (pp. 116ff), which supposedly makes us laugh at his opponent Mercy, since the vice is 'subversive' (p. 119) and 'criticizes from the audience's point of view' (p. 153). The vice Hickscorner, too, represents both Utopia and topsy-turvydom (p. 121); it is Saturnalian and even Lollard (p. 126). Similar judgments are made about the vice Sedycyon in *King Johan* (p. 144), and the vice Iniquytie in *King Darius* (p. 146). It never seems to have occurred to Weimann that some members of the audience, if asked to choose one of the two, might have sided with Mercy. He has not noticed that to introduce a comic character mangling Latin presupposes an audience capable of telling the difference between right and wrong usage. Nor has he reflected on the other ways in which such scenes work in drama, let alone the moral significance of the vice to the dramatists.

However pleased some critics may be at Weimann praising subversion or attacking imitation, no-one who takes Marxist thought seriously can be long satisfied with his naïve combination of a sentimentalised proletariat and an ahistorical pseudo-anthropology.

III

The deficiencies of naïve Marxism were most evident to Marxists themselves, as the development of critical theory from Lukács to Adorno, Goldmann, Althusser and others shows all too well. (I think particularly of Adorno's attack on Lukács.) The nature of Marxist literary and aesthetic theory since the 1930s is a vast subject, but several useful surveys exist.[25] The phase that most concerns Shakespeare criticism in the 1980s and 90s is, once again, a product of Paris in the 1960s, the work of Louis Althusser and his associates. Like the other iconoclasts of that place and time, Althusser wished to wipe the slate clean of all existing work in his field, making a total rejection of previous interpretations of Marx, and giving rise to the very strange situation, as a group of English Marxist sociologists put it, that his theory —

which rejects the entire history of marxism as a chronicle of errors, . . . which rejects as irrelevant the experience of the working-class movement within which marxism has developed, and which finds the secret of marxism in various avant-garde (and often very esoteric) versions of psychoanalysis and philosophy of science

— should have been so rapidly accepted by its followers as the new 'marxist orthodoxy' (Clarke *et al.* 1980, p. 6). Yet some of the most prominent Marxist intellectuals vigorously attacked Althusser's theories from the outset,[26] and over the last twenty-five years an impressive body of Marxist writing — which cannot be dismissed as bourgeois reactionism — has described the theories of Althusser as having in fact perverted Marx's legacy, and 'discarded from his work almost all that is of value' (McDonnell and Robins 1980, p. 168). The charge against Althusser is that he expunged 'the revolutionary theoretical, philosophical and political content of marxism in favour of bourgeois sociology, idealist philosophy and stalinist politics' (Clarke 1980, p. 73).[27]

The polemical technique that Althusser developed, similar in many ways to that of Lévi-Strauss, Lacan, Foucault, and Derrida, was to stigmatise various concepts attached to the parties being attacked by what Simon Clarke describes as an act of 'intellectual terrorism. Three terms, "historicism", "empiricism" and "humanism" are drafted in to sweep away all possible opposition. To be labelled by such a term is to be labelled a class enemy, an intellectual saboteur' (ibid.). (This technique is still being used by New Historicist and Cultural Materialist critics to stigmatise their rivals or opponents, a by now threadbare response.) Althusser took over from Lévi-Strauss the structuralist attack on historicism and its polemic against the subject, but like so many of the Paris maîtres à penser had to reintroduce the subject in another guise.[28] But in appropriating the structuralist polemic for his rewriting of Marx Althusser violated some of the fundamental principles of Marxism. As the contributors to a volume called One-Dimensional Marxism. Althusser and the Politics of Culture put it, all the terms he stigmatised are essential to the Marxist critique of capitalist society, which conceives of its eventual transformation by human agency. Humanism is the 'belief in the creative potential of human beings, . . . stunted and alienated under capitalism'; empiricism is the 'belief that there is no higher basis for knowledge than experience', especially that of an oppressed and exploited segment of society; while historicism is 'the belief that knowledge, being based on socially mediated experience and being validated through social practice, is necessarily the product of social conditions at a particular time and which can be changed by those who live under them' (Clarke et al. 1980, p. 5). Althusser, expressing the 'dogmatic marxism' of the French Communist Party in its attempt at de-Stalinisation, by stigmatising these concepts, tried to 'abstract marxism from the historical experience from which it derives', claiming for it 'an absolute authority as source of a knowledge of history that is inaccessible to those who live and make that history' (ibid.).

The detail of the Marxist critiques of Althusser, which seem to me unanswerable, can be left in good hands. But an outline of Althusser's system is needed if we are to understand the recent course of literary theory. Many emphases in his work will be familiar after my earlier discussion of Lacan and Foucault, with both of whom he had close links. He was at one time a patient of Lacan, and his essay on 'Freud and Lacan' did much to promote an alliance between Marxism and psychoanalysis (LaCapra 1982, pp. 91–5; Merquior 1986b, pp. 148–9). This essay also displays affinities with Derrida in its praise of Freud for showing that 'the human subject is de-centred, constituted by a structure which has no "centre" either, except in the imaginary misrecognitions of the "ego"...' (*cit.* McDonnell and Robins 1980, p. 198). Althusser's masters as a philosophy student included Bachelard, from whom he took the notion of historical 'ruptures' which was to have such an influence on Foucault, and he himself taught Foucault (Crews 1986, p. 145; Merquior 1986b, pp. 147–8). Althusser's eclecticism synthesised the already generalised individual components of his models at a still higher, more abstract level of discourse.

In two books published in 1965, *Pour Marx* (English tr. 1969), and *Lire le Capital* (a composite volume; English tr. 1970), Althusser proposed a return to the text of Marx as if he were going back to the true sources, neglected by everyone else. But in fact Althusser deployed the Freudian-Lacanian trick of 'symptomatic reading', looking for significant absences in Marx's text, on which he could base a new interpretation. As Sebastiano Timpanaro, a Marxist classical philologist commented, by adopting this method Althusser licensed a 'theoreticist forcing of texts', distorting them in 'a subjectivist direction', claiming to recreate Marx but in a wholly arbitrary way (Timpanaro 1975, pp. 194, 232). The result was an almost complete distortion of the fundamental elements in Marxist thought. Althusser's strategy in denouncing historicism was, like so many of the self-interested, aggressive acts of 60s intellectuals, intended 'to establish the autonomy of theory and the authority of the theorist' (Clarke 1980, p. 14). The parallel attack on empiricism had a similar self-advancing goal, protecting theory and the theorist from any appeal to historical evidence. As the doyen of English Marxist historians, E.P. Thompson showed in a classic essay, 'The Poverty of Theory or An Orrery of Errors' (Thompson 1978, pp. 1–210), Althusser's attack on empiricism is designed to discredit the whole possibility of historical knowledge, 'since "real" history is unknowable and cannot be said to exist' (p. 2). This is a strategically important move (recalling Lacan and Derrida), for 'by asserting the unknowability of the real, he confiscates reality of its determinant properties, thus reducing the real to Theory' (pp. 22–3). But in breaking with reality, and setting up theory alone as self-verifying, Althusser forfeits the chance of entering into any dialectical or developmental process in which our conceptions can be sharpened and refined by a dialogue with reality (a process well described here from Engels: pp. 52–4; similarly Clarke 1980, pp. 40–43). As Thompson points out, 'since Theory disallows any active appropriation of the external world in the only way possible (by active engagement or dialogue with its evidence) then *this whole world must be assumed*' (pp. 35–6). Just like Freudianism, as Ernest Gellner showed, which preserved an unproblematic notion of external reality, a 'naïve realism' and 'naïve mentalism' (Gellner 1985, pp. 90–91, 99, 104–105), Althusser's programmatic goal of 'theoretical practice' is a form of idealism which, 'since it prohibits any actual empirical engagements with social reality', in fact embraces 'the most vulgar empiricism', assuming the world to be '"what everyone knows"', with all its unexamined assumptions (p. 124).

Althusser's self-enclosure within theory had damaging effects on his philosophy, and produces similar effects, I shall argue, on the literary criticism modelled on him. Several forces in Current Literary Theory, as we have seen, reject all notion of evidence, empirical appeal to the text and its meanings. In 'a mature intellectual discipline', Thompson argues, procedures exist which can evaluate facts or evidence by some external criteria. But in 'a merely-ideological formation (theology, astrology . . . orthodox Stalinist-Marxism)' — we can add Freudianism — the object of knowledge consists 'only in ideological "facts" elaborated by that discipline's own procedures', so denying the very possibility of falsification. Like so many of the systems favoured since the 1960s — Derrida, Lacan, Foucault, and always already Freud — Althusser's system is 'self-confirming', his special concept of 'theoretical practice' being 'a sealed system within which concepts endlessly circulate, recognise and interrogate each other, and the intensity of its repetitious introversial life is mistaken for a "science"' (p. 12).[29] Although professedly Marxist, and therefore materialist, Althusser's system turns out to be an 'idealism', a 'self-generating conceptual universe which imposes its own ideality upon the phenomena of material and social existence, rather than engaging in continual dialogue with these. . . . The category has attained to a primacy over its material referent; the conceptual structure hangs above and dominates social being' (p. 13). Literary criticism based on Althusser has the same overpowering effect on literary texts (its users speak in terms of a 'master code', which implies that the text is its slave). Literary criticism modelled on Althusser also reproduces his emptying out of human behaviour, the denial of human agency, the reduction of men and women to mere *Träger* 'or vectors of ulterior structural determinations' — scientistic language matching Foucault (pp. 2, 122, 147). As Thompson puts it at the end of a superb paragraph describing the depersonalisation produced by theory,[30] denied access to an outer world 'theory is for ever collapsing back into ulterior theory. In disallowing empirical enquiry, the mind is confined for ever within the compound of the mind' (p. 167).

Althusser is a damaging model for literary critics in other respects, notably in his misreading of texts. Claiming that historians have entirely misunderstood Marx, Althusser asserted that 'history features in *Capital* as an object of theory, . . . as an "abstract" (conceptual) object', and that when Marx mentions 'the concrete situation in England' he does so only 'in order to "illustrate" his (abstract) theory of the capitalist mode of production' (p. 23). Anyone who can claim Marx to be an abstract social theorist has truly allowed his own 'de-socialised and de-historicised' categories (p. 95) to impose themselves on the text. Althusser's persistent 'separation of thought and reality', which transformed Marxist historical-dialectical categories into 'fixed, eternal, and so ideal, categories' (Clarke 1980, pp. 40–41), resulted in what many of his critics regard as a fatally abstract concept of ideology. In an essay called 'Marxist Cultural Theory: the Althusserian Smokescreen', two English Marxist sociologists comment on *Lire Capital*, showing that

> Althusser's concept of the whole is premised on the existence of three levels of the social formation — the economic, the political and the ideological, each having a 'relative autonomy' from the others. . . . Althusser's whole is a syncretic one, composed of parts that are defined as external to each other. The parts are theorised *before* the totality, and they take precedence over the totality. (McDonnell and Robins 1980, pp. 158–9)

— an emphasis contrary to Marx's thought.

Althusser's division of society into separate levels, the authors point out, reproduces Marx's 1859 'base/superstructure metaphor', with all its limitations, grasping surface appearances only in its presentation of economy and politics as separate entities (*ibid.*, p. 159), that 'static and mechanical analogy', as E.P. Thompson describes it (Thompson 1978, pp. 84, 157). Having singled ideology out as a separate — non-political, non-economic — factor in society, Althusser gave it a further abstract dimension in an essay in *Lénine et la philosophie* (1969; English tr. 1971), labelling a whole group of institutions — the educational system, the church, the family, political parties, trade unions and the mass media — as 'Ideological State Apparatuses' (ISAs), organs by which the state ensures its hegemony over its subjects. This thesis has been severely criticised by professional sociologists,[31] but has proved most attractive to Foucault-inspired New Historicists and Cultural Materialists, who like to believe that the subject is created by discursive systems and ideology, and is in that process subjected to forces beyond its control.

To Marxists, however, and to others who think it absurd and degrading to reduce 'men and women, in their mental life, in their determinate relationships, in their experience of these, and in their self-consciousness of this experience' to 'instances' and 'levels' (Thompson 1978, pp. 90–97), this theory is wholly unacceptable. As two Marxist critics point out, Althusser's anti-empiricism removes ideology from actual social relations, reducing it to ' "the imaginary relationship of individuals to the real conditions of existence" ' (McDonnell and Robins 1980, p. 165) — an event in the mind. Althusser's anti-historicism, further, makes him assert that ' "ideology is eternal . . . omnipresent, transhistorical and therefore immutable in form through the extent of history" ' (*ibid.*), another thesis absolutely inimical to Marx's vision of social change. Althusser's formulations, they write, are '*a priori* and deductive', not derived from the examination of any ideology at work in any historical society, but setting up 'his own abstract and inflexible theoretical principles' as an interpretation of historical and social reality (ibid., p. 166). Further, by equating 'ideology with the whole symbolic or cultural order', Althusser ended up in a position strikingly close to the sociology of Comte or Durkheim, in which 'ideology is characterised as maintaining social cohesion. This functionalist conception regards ideology, like culture, as *something* to which we are passively subjected'. (Compare Foucault.) Althusser's quietist disbelief that the subject could 'transform ideological consciousness' stands in total contrast to Marxist thought, in which ideology is 'to be negated through (practical) critique' (ibid.). Finally, Althusser's Freudian-Lacanian bent made him claim ideology to be an unconscious process, a theory which would obviously 'make class consciousness impossible'. But the fact is that ideology does not permeate people's minds below the level of awareness: 'the working class does not find it impossible to unmask the ideological mystification of capitalist society' (ibid., pp. 167–8).

Looking at Althusser's work through the eyes of his Marxist critics, with the added benefit of some distance in time from its heyday, it is something of a joke that anyone should have ever accepted his work as an informed exposition of Marxism. E.P. Thompson, writing at the high point of his celebrity, took the uncritical acceptance of Althusser's work as proof of 'a very severe and general intellectual crisis' (Thompson 1978, p. 169). Marxist historians and sociologists have by now completed the demotion of Althusser, but many literary critics still invoke him as a serious intellectual figure, as if literary criticism must always reach outside itself for some higher authority, some fully-formed system on which it can model itself, otherwise unsure of what it should be doing. (If so, then it too is in a permanent state of intellectual crisis.) Althusser's major acknowledged disciples among literary critics have been the Frenchman Pierre Macherey and the American Fredric Jameson. I shall briefly discuss one work by each.

In *Pour une théorie de la production littéraire* (1966; English tr. 1978), Macherey reproduced many of the attitudes shared by that generation of Paris intellectuals. He, too, wanted to wipe the slate clean of all previous work, announcing that in his 'radical departure from all the active tendencies of previous criticism, a new critical question is proposed: What are the laws of literary production?' Exuding self-confidence, like his fellow-iconoclasts, he announced that 'a large price must be paid for returning criticism to the sphere of rationality: it must be given *a new object*. Unless criticism . . . can break definitely with its past', it will merely elaborate public taste (Macherey 1978, p. 12). All criticism hitherto, he affirmed (like Derrida and Barthes), has only tried to 'reproduce and imitate' the work of art (p. 13), 'merely reproducing the work by a factitious and intrusive commentary' (p. 27). The cause of this false direction in all criticism since Aristotle, Macherey writes, echoing Althusser, is the 'fallacy of empiricism', which treats the work of literature 'as factually given' (p. 13), whereas in reality 'the objects of any rational investigation have no prior existence but are thought into being' (p. 5). This attack on empiricism, repeatedly using the formula 'not A but B', is a series of *a priori* assertions which are at best half-truths. Having denied the ontological existence of a literary work, Macherey followed the fashion of his times in attacking humanism, with its 'profoundly reactionary' belief that 'the writer or artist is a creator' (pp. 66–7). Macherey claimed that 'the various "theories" of creation all ignore the process of making; they omit any account of production' (p. 68), a statement that is so untrue about extant literary criticism, theoretical and practical, as to make one charitably suppose that he must have meant something quite idiosyncratic by 'production'. Apparently the mistaken belief in the writer as creator goes along with a belief in the unity of the literary work, which must also *now be denounced*: the work is not *created* by an intention (objective or subjective): it is *produced* under determinate conditions' (p. 78). If you ask what a 'condition' is, Macherey explains that it 'is not . . . a cause in the empirical sense; it is the principle of rationality which makes the work accessible to thought' (p. 49), a vaguely abstract reply which tells you very little.

Despite his trenchant-seeming formulations, much of Macherey's argument is vague and confused. It is oppositional criticism, like the other 1960s products, which simply asserts the opposite of what it takes to be the tradition, in a confident take-it-or-leave-it manner. From henceforth the act of criticism will be one in which 'the critic, employing a new language, brings out a *difference* within the work by demonstrating that it is *other than it is*' (p. 7). For, 'The work is not what it appears to be' (p. 20). Original and self-assertive though these pronouncements seem, they merely apply to literary theory, categorically and without illustration, a principle in Lacan's psychoanalytical theory, which (as we saw in Chapter 1) declared that the operation of language forces the subject to signify 'something entirely different from what it says'. Continuing in the Parisian adversarial mode, Macherey asserts that criticism so far, with its 'arbitrary assumption of the unity and independence of the text, has been grounded in a radical misunderstanding of the nature of the writer's work' (p. 53). 'Interpretive criticism' — a stigmatising term — 'rests on a certain number of fallacies', presupposing 'the active presence of a single meaning around which the work is diversely articulated' (p. 76). Critics in future 'must stress that determinate insufficiency, that incompleteness which actually shapes the work'. This apparent contradiction ('incompleteness . . . shapes') is avoided by postulating the critic's task as being to generate a 'confrontation of separate meanings', which will give the work 'its actual decentred-ness' (p. 79) — as if this should be produced by the critic, not the author! All these pronouncements are obviously just as arbitrary as the fictional windmills that Macherey is attacking (who ever claimed that a literary work had 'a single meaning'?). Their roots in sixties iconoclasm are all too obvious, the parallels with Foucault, Derrida, and Barthes proving once again the homogeneity of that intellectual tradition ('the activity of the writer . . . constitutes and is constituted by a discourse, it has nothing extrinsic': p. 58; 'literary discourse [is] a contestation of language rather than a representation of reality': p. 61).

Macherey is most clearly a child of his times in coming to Marx through Freud and Lacan, that is, by developing his putatively Marxist analysis of ideology with concepts derived from psychoanalysis. The book 'is not self-sufficient', Macherey declared, 'it is necessarily accompanied by a *certain absence*', for, 'in order to say anything, there are other things *which must not be said*. Freud relegated this *absence of certain words* to . . . the unconscious' (p. 85). 'Discourse implies the absence of its object, and inhabits the space vacated by the banishment of what is spoken' (p. 59). The book, again, 'circles about the absence of that which it cannot say, haunted by the absence of certain repressed words which make their return' (p. 80). But, we must object, if these words indeed 'make their return' then they cannot be 'absent'. The psychoanalytic analogy conveniently gives the iconoclastic critic infinite licence to evoke whatever he wishes from a text and even to ignore it, for 'speech eventually has nothing more to tell us: we investigate the silence, for it is the silence that is doing the speaking' (p. 86). — How does one actually investigate silence? How much of one's own speaking does one bring to it ? — To the Freudian Macherey, 'What is important in the work is what it does not say' (p. 87), for 'the work exists above all by its determinate [how does one determine them?] absences, by what it does not say, in relation to what is not'. The absent meaning is not concealed or 'buried' by the work (now seen in anthropomorphic terms), 'it is not in the work but by its side . . .' (p. 154), and so on. This tactic, like Althusser's rejection of historicism, gives the theorist both autonomy and omniscience. As Alan Sinfield wryly remarked of Macherey's conception of a contradiction between what is said and not said, it 'conveniently renders the theory unfalsifiable: if contradictions are present Macherey is right and if they are absent he is again right' (Sinfield 1981, p. 191).

In a syncretist move typifying the homogeneity of French sixties thought, Macherey blends his Foucault-Barthes theory of the indeterminacy and incompleteness of the text with the Freudian-Lacanian notion of significant absences and contradiction, and then applies the compound to the analysis of ideology. His inspiring figure here is less Marx than Lenin, in particular his critique of Tolstoy (pp. 105–35), but Althusser's influence is also acknowledged. The resulting synthesis, however, is anything but coherent. Macherey believed that 'we always eventually find, at the edge of the text, the language of ideology, momentarily hidden, but eloquent by its very absence' (p. 60): but if you have found it, how can it be absent? Perhaps even finding it is illusory, though, because 'ideology is always *elsewhere*; consequently it cannot be totally subdued, diminished or dispelled' (p. 64). An ideology 'is always in some sense incomplete', it seems (p. 116), yet Macherey could still polarise it to achieve the desired

Foucault-Derrida self-contradiction, for 'at the same time as it establishes an ideological content the book presents the contradiction of that content: this content only exists enveloped in the form of a contestation' (p. 129). A later passage, however, contradicts this contestation model by declaring that 'In fact there is no such thing as an ideological contradiction: the inexact character of an ideology *excludes* contradiction' (pp. 193–4). Ideology, Macherey continues, is 'in its way coherent, a coherence which is indefinite if not imprecise . . .'. But it seems that 'an ideology can be *put into contradiction*: it is futile to denounce the presence of a contradiction in ideology' (p. 194), indeed 'no ideology is sufficiently consistent to survive the test of figuration' (p. 195).

It is difficult to extract any coherent sense from Macherey's thought, circling around these abstractions, quite divorced from any contact with society or literature. A later passage in this same essay on Jules Verne declares that bourgeois ideology has its limits, 'but this ideology is emphatically not internally contradictory . . .' (p. 237). Having so often said that ideology is incomplete, however, Macherey must somehow rescue this point, and does so with an almost scholastic piece of hair-splitting: in bourgeois ideology 'it is precisely its insufficiencies, its incompleteness, which guarantee its flawed coherence' (p. 238). Admirers and disciples of Macherey naturally never submit his work to an immanent critique, which would be devastating. Reading past the incoherences, so to speak, what they take from him is a model of incoherence to be found in every poem, play, or novel. 'The finished literary work . . . *reveals* the gaps in ideology' (p. 60). The unity of Verne's work, 'a unity borrowed from a certain ideological coherence, or incoherence' (either way, all eventualities are covered), 'reveals the *limits* . . . of this ideological coherence, which is necessarily built upon a discord in the historical reality . . .' (p. 238). It follows that the

> order which [a work] professes is merely an imagined order, projected on to disorder, the fictive resolution of ideological conflicts, a resolution so precarious that it is obvious in the very letter of the text where incoherence and incompleteness burst forth. (p. 155)

What is important, finally, 'is that the operation of a fictional system ultimately produces an ideological effect (confusion)'. This 'ideological surge denotes the presence of a gap, a defect in the work, a complexity which makes it *meaningful*' (p. 296). It is not, however, a single meaning, for the critic must be prepared to find a 'double explanation which establishes simultaneously two meanings and the gap between them' (pp. 296–7). Incoherence rules.

*   *   *

There is not much Marx in Macherey, it would seem. His theory has obvious affinities with the Freudian-Lacanian-Foucauldian-Derridian reservoir of oppositional postures, undermining and fissuring whatever totality anyone else has ever suggested (the work of literature, Macherey declared, 'is fissured, unmade even in its making': p. 155). Whether we call him a Marxist or a post-modernist is irrelevant, I suppose, provided we recognise that the kind of reading he encourages is disruptive, disintegrating, closest of all, perhaps, to French Freudianism. In the most self-consciously Marxist of Fredric Jameson's books, *The Political Unconscious* (1981), the title immediately proclaims an allegiance with psychoanalysis. Two decades after the Franco-Freudian fissures, Jameson is breaking to American readers the news that 'new' criticism should in future reject the concepts of 'organic form', or 'a work of art as an ordered whole'. Instead it should look for 'rifts and discontinuities within the work', treating 'the former "work of art" as a heterogeneous and (to use the most dramatic recent slogan) a schizophrenic text'. Thus, Jameson writes, with no apparent sense of incongruity in using the terms 'structural', or 'interpretation',

> The aim of a properly structural interpretation or exegesis thus becomes the explosion of the seemingly unified text into a host of clashing and contradictory elements. (Jameson 1981, p. 56)

This is all familiar stuff from post-structuralism, Jameson admits, as in Barthes's *S/Z*, which 'shatters a Balzac novella into a random operation of multiple codes' (or, as he puts it elsewhere, rewrites Balzac as if he were Philippe Sollers). What is different about Althusserian exegesis is that it puts all the pieces back together again — not in the same order, of course (that would be too simple), but by seeing in the disunity, or multiplicity of the text 'the objectification of the ideological by the work of aesthetic production'. In other words,

> the Althusserian / Marxist conception of culture requires this multiplicity to be reunified, *if not at the level of the work itself*, then at the level of its process of production. . . . (p. 56; my italics)

The phrase I have italicised shows that Althusserian exegesis can claim to be as radical as any other post-structuralism, adding a new 'coherent functional operation' which 'requires' (compulsion is the new critical process) 'the fragments, the incommensurable levels . . . of the text to be once again related . . .' (*ibid.*). Only, according to a new scheme of things.

Sharing the post-structuralist belief in the 'discontinuity' of the text, which licenses critics to do violence to it in order to bring out its 'heterogeneous impulses' (*ibid.*), Jameson takes the logical next step of recognising that this new 'coherent functional operation' amounts to a rewriting of the text. In this book, he tells us, 'interpretation is . . . construed as an essentially allegorical act, which consists in rewriting a given text in terms of a particular interpretive master code' (p. 10). Jameson envisages the creation of a vast interpretive allegory in which a sequence of historical events or texts and artifacts is rewritten in terms of some deeper, underlying, and more 'fundamental' narrative, . . . the allegorical key or figural content of the first sequence of empirical materials. (p. 28, similarly pp. 33, 58)

What system can best provide this allegorical key? Did we ever doubt it?

Only Marxism can give us an adequate account of the essential *mystery* of the cultural past. . . . This mystery can be reenacted only if the human adventure is one. . . . These matters can recover their original urgency for us only if they are retold within the unity of a single great collective story; only if, in however disguised and symbolic form, they are seen as sharing a single fundamental theme — for Marxism, the collective struggle to wrest a realm of Freedom from a realm of Necessity; only if they are grasped as vital episodes in a single vast unfinished plot. . . . (pp. 19–20)

Freedom and Necessity come from *Capital*, vol. III, and the plot, outlined in the *Communist Manifesto*, is the '"history of class struggles . . . — in a word, oppressor and oppressed . . ."' (p. 20). An obvious but unavoidable objection must be that to imagine that the 'cultural past', in all its multiplicity, can *only* be understood by being rewritten in terms of one story, is to be naïvely unaware that that monopoly would be totalitarian, denying all other explanations.

Jameson's reference to the Marxist 'collective struggle' may seem to open the door to historical reality, kept remote from Macherey's hermetically sealed theorising. But it is only an illusion. In fact Jameson fully reproduces all of Althusser's abstractionism, placing on the agenda of future 'Marxist cultural criticism . . . *ideological analysis*', which must become 'what Althusser has demanded of the practice of Marxist philosophy proper, namely "class struggle within theory"' (p. 12). These critics will be concerned with words not deeds, discourse, indeed 'class discourse', to be analyzed into '*ideologemes*' (p. 87), such as opinions or prejudices. For Jameson, as for Althusser, ideology implies nothing so coarse as a programme for action, being merely 'a representational structure which allows the individual subject[32] to conceive or imagine his or her lived relationship to transpersonal realities such as the social structure or the collective logic of history' (p. 30) — history being only accessible to us 'in textual form', through its 'textualization, its narrativization' (p. 35). A critic who can empty out the notions of class struggle and historical reality, and who can invoke Althusser's most abstract concept of society in terms of levels, instances, and homology (pp. 39, 45), has no problem in reducing 'the cultural past' to a 'collective plot', a mere narrative detached from any relation to actual events. Interpretation, then, becomes a kind of abstracting or allegorising activity which 'rewrites' a literary text to show it as 'the rewriting or restructuration of a prior historical or ideological *subtext*' (p. 81). Since history and ideology are only texts, the most expedient way to perform this rewriting is to resort to allegory, and Jameson, publishing in the 1980s, seriously recommended the adoption of the four-fold system of allegory practiced in medieval biblical exegesis (see note 3 above), that 'striking and elaborate hermeneutic' (p. 29), that 'great patristic and medieval system', since which 'the only really new and original hermeneutic' has been psychoanalysis (p. 61).[33] As that collocation shows, Jameson overlays twentieth-century concepts on his medieval frame, the Anagogical level being now equated with 'political reading (collective "meaning" of history)', the Moral with 'psychological reading (individual subject)', the Allegorical with 'allegorical key or interpretive code', the Literal with 'historical or textual referent' (p. 31) — next to Gregory and the Victorines stand Althusser, Lacan, Barthes. But Jameson's free-flowing eclecticism was more than a magpie-like accumulation of attractive systems. It, too, like the original Paris anti-systems, was quite consciously designed to give the interpreter absolute freedom of manoeuvre to make whatever 'reductions' and 'generations' within or without the text that he or she should wish. The great advantage of four-level analysis, Jameson writes, is that it performs a 'reduction . . . which then permits the gener- ation of two further interpretive levels, and it is precisely in these that the individual believer is able to "insert" himself or herself (to use the Althusserian formula) . . .' (p. 30 — or was it Foucault's?). Such terms as 'reduction' and 'generation' turn literary criticism into a form of chemical or mathematical activity, another version of sixties scientism.

Although Jameson proposed at one point a four-level division of the traditional Marxist theory (p. 32), he perhaps recognized that the patristic method is not naturally applicable to modern literature. At all events, when it came to discussing ideology he reverted to a two-level one, arguing that in Marxism 'the ultimate (or ideal) form of class relationship and class struggle is always dichotomous. The constitutive form of class relationships is always that between a dominant and a laboring class: and it is only in terms of this axis that class fractions (for example, the petty bour- geoisie) . . . are positioned' (pp. 83–4). Traditional though this two-part model may be in Marxist thought, it is now something of an embarrass- ment. A hundred and fifty years on, Marx's basic social categories — ruling class, bourgeoisie, proletariat — no longer seem adequate. The working class has merged into the bourgeoisie, capitalism is furthered by everyone who owns shares or invests in a savings bank, and a fluid social organ- isation has replaced Marx's rigid stratification. Jameson rejects 'the con- ventional sociological analysis of society into strata, subgroups, professional elites and the like' (p. 84), which is surely a more accurate theoretical model, in favour of the — idealised, mythical, antiquated — Marxist model which sees the 'values' of a class ideology as always situated

  with respect to the opposing class, and defined against the latter: normally, a ruling class ideology will explore various strategies of the *legitimation* of its own power position, while an oppositional culture or ideology will, often in covert and disguised strategies, seek to contest and to undermine the dominant 'value system'. (*ibid.*)

This is the two-part model which, we now know, animates much of New Historicist writing on Shakespeare and will be seen (in a coarser form) in Cultural Materialism. But from the iconoclastic sixties we have now reached the eclectic eighties, so Jameson rewrites the Althusserian-Marxist-Foucauldian position by grafting on to it Bakhtin's concept of the dialogical, converted from an aesthetic into a political concept. Restated then, 'the normal form of the dialogical is essentially an *antagonistic* one', and thus 'the dialogue of class struggle is one in which two opposing discourses fight it out within the general unity of a shared code' (*ibid.*). The intellectualisation or abstractionism is now complete: instead of actual classes locked in hand-to-hand combat, as in Marx's original vision, oppressor against oppressed, we have a 'fight' between 'discourses . . . within . . . a shared code'. We have come a long way from Weimann's naïve Marxism with the proletariat as the initiator and arbiter of all good things. We have lost the sentimentalisation, but we have also lost the human beings.

This abstract model of 'a dominant versus a subordinate ideology' can then be directly applied to literature in the eclectic idiom of the eighties, drawing on decentred subjects, sites of discourse, strategies of containment, and other current notions. Literature is still reduced to language, only now depersonalised and politicised. Yet, it must be said, this two-level model is inadequate to deal with either society or literature. It places all virtue on one side, all vice on the other, whereas a more open-minded model would be able to distinguish the strengths and weaknesses of both sides, and indeed of other groups. This social model can only work with the idea of society functioning at the beck and call of a set of people having complete power, whereas many elements in the social process take place on different levels and with other forms of agency, outside the control of any interest group. The polarisation of society involved (the haves and have nots; the centre and the margin), then reifies the oppressor into a threatening but vague entity, which can be variously defined, as in Althusser's all-embracing Ideological State Apparatuses. Those critical schools who profess to find satisfaction in the notion of a state which both creates and subjects them to 'instances', ideological configurations,[34] and 'paths of discourse', will obviously identify themselves with the oppressed and marginalised. They will endorse any work of literature, or any character(s) within it, who oppose the system, attack others that seem to accept it.

IV

How does all of this affect Shakespeare? In two main ways, I think: neo-Marxist, post-Althusserian criticism either exposes the workings of ideology in Shakespeare; or it finds Shakespeare's plays, as performed and interpreted by later generations, guilty of collusion with the ISAs, aiding the hegemony of the ruling classes. It is not always easy to separate the two, but characteristically the first approach takes some neo-Marxist theoretical pronouncements and confronts them with one or more plays to show how they prove the theory. The second approach outlines a phase of history — the British Empire is favourite — and argues that Shakespeare has been used to forward the dominant ideology. This second approach is sometimes called 'reception' criticism, but in my view incorrectly, for whereas study of a play's reception by a theatre or reading public may well include a political element, Althusserian critics are only interested in ideology. It deserves to be called, like the first type, ideological criticism: the one is internal to the plays, the other external.

As an example of the first I take the essay by James H. Kavanagh, 'Shakespeare in ideology' (1985). The theoretical pronouncements here mostly come from a brief essay by two French Althusserians (in itself unexceptionably orthodox, albeit horribly jargon-ridden), which is quoted extensively, often as 'last instance', to close a discussion on a note of unimpeachable authority.[35] The historical element comes largely from two books I commented on earlier, Weimann 1978 (which shows 'excellent understanding'), bolstered by Siegel 1957 ('too frequently overlooked'), an alliance with naïve Marxism that causes Kavanagh to retail some dreadfully stale history. Shakespeare was apparently 'caught in an ideological space between modified absolutism and insurgent Puritanism' (Kavanagh 1985, p. 150). The medieval 'image of the warrior-Lord' was weakening under the impact of a 'rising bourgeoisie', whose 'proto-scientific reasoning in the form of technical innovation' gained them power, while 'the nascent, potentially egalitarian individualism of the merchants and artisans . . . took the form of Puritan and Calvinist dissidence' (ibid.), so prefiguring the Civil War. Shakespeare, meanwhile, had to not only 'avoid the censure of the London authorities, whose Puritanism militated against any dramatic production', but also satisfy the Queen and her court, keeping favour with his 'patron' (Southampton), while simultaneously entertaining an audience drawn from the 'mercantile, artisanal and working classes' which was 'hungry for concrete, even sensationalistic, representations that could not help but touch on politically sensitive subjects' (p. 150). Yet another 'historian' has to downgrade or stereotype the London theatre audience to make it fit his thesis. As history, this is lamentable.

Let us come to the plays, and to a play within a play, put on by the artisans in A Midsummer Night's Dream. Whereas most readers and playgoers have seen these would-be actors as amusingly trapped by the elementary problems of dramatic illusion in performance (how can the audience tell a real lion from a 'pretend' one?), Kavanagh gives them a solemnly portentous political motivation. Their problem is said to be that of 'producing an *appropriate* — that is, class-appropriate, and therefore politically acceptable — dramatic representation', fulfilling 'the related exigencies of ideology, social class and political power' (p. 153). This premiss has already begged the question by introducing its own politicised criteria. Kavanagh attempts to prove his diagnosis by quoting two passages, first Bottom's desire to play the lion and so 'roar, that I will do any man's heart good to hear me', with Quince objecting that this might 'fright the Duchess and the ladies; and that were enough to hang us all' (1.2.66–78). On which our Althusserian comments:

> This dialogue functions as a kind of internal commentary on Shakespeare's ideological practice. The problematic of proto-professional production denied autonomous political weight in a society struggling to preserve the hegemony of an aristocratic class-ideology is here displayed in order to be ridiculed. Shakespeare's artisans pose the issue quite clearly in their discussion: for *us* to assert an effective ability to manipulate *their* sense of reality . . . would be an unacceptable usurpation of ideological power, possibly punishable by death. . . . (p. 154)

The discrepancy between the text and the critical commentary here is enormous, almost comical, taking with literal, indeed deadly seriousness the mechanicals' amusingly naïve belief in their own histrionic powers to overcome theatrical illusion. As Timpanaro said of Althusser, he had obviously lost all 'sense of the ridiculous' (Timpanaro 1975, p. 195). Here the ideological categories of Macherey and Balibar suffocate the comedy. (I shan't pause to discuss the claim that Shakespeare's society was 'struggling to preserve the hegemony of an aristocratic class-ideology'. No evidence is proposed, in any case.)

Kavanagh's second quotation is from the later scene (3.1.28–44) where Bottom advises his fellows to have the actor playing the lion announce that he is not really a lion but Snug the joiner. Kavanagh comments:

> These workers attempt to solve their problem by inventing a strategy that will break the illusion of transparency, and display the conditions of active ideological production, in a first version of the estrangement-effect. [Quotation] This strategy, of course, is actually an inversion of the Brechtian alienation aesthetic, displaying the conditions of ideological production . . . to enable this workers' troupe to *escape* the political power of a ruling class. (pp. 154–5)

The high level of abstraction, the imposing of an ideological analysis on Bottom's transparently silly and unnecessary suggestion (as if Snug weren't totally visibly himself), shows a complete lack of proportion, or decorum on the critic's part, who cannot decide whether the *Verfremdungseffekt* is made or inverted (how would that work?).

King Lear might seem more suitable to Kavanagh's approach, but his discussion turns into an uneasy melange of trivialising psychoanalysis ('Edmund's symbolic castration of Gloucester', p. 157: the glib Freudian symbolism avoids direct confrontation with the real horrors of blinding), stale thematic reading ('Lear is crushed between the two . . . opposed "Natures"': *ibid.* — J.F. Danby argued this in 1949), and a politicisation that misdefines its targets and misrepresents the play. The indiscriminate politicisation somehow identifies 'an individualist ideology . . . of calculation, self-gratification and perverse desire' (p. 156) with either 'feudal ideology' or 'a bourgeois ethic' (p. 157: the context is unclear), or both. But it does not describe either. The destructiveness of appetites that know no compunction in achieving their desires belongs equally to Goneril and Regan, two royal princesses, and Edmund, a bastard son of an earl: neither feudalism nor the bourgeoisie is responsible. Kavanagh cannot get either the issues or the play straight. This becomes very clear when he cites Lear's plea to Regan, to be allowed his complement of retainers — 'O! reason not the need; our basest beggars / Are in the poorest things superfluous' (2.4.266–72), a passage where, as everyone can see, Lear is still concerned with his own ego. In Kavanagh's cumbersome ideological terminology, this speech shows the play's 'discursive strategy of ideological reconciliation through domination', that is, preserving the 'privileges of a ruling class' instead of 'relating the aspirations of all social subjects to the given level of material and cultural development . . .' (pp. 158–9). It is regrettable that Kavanagh, emulating Macherey and wishing to indict the play as a whole for not resolving its 'opposed ideological elements', fails to quote the speech that precisely expresses those aspirations, Lear's 'Poor naked wretches . . . O, I have ta'en / Too little care of this!' (3.4.28ff). But for me to make such an objection is to be guilty of what one neo-Althusserian contemptuously dismissed as 'the positivistic conception of philological accuracy' (Jameson 1981, p. 13) — that is, reference to the text as evidence.

All forms of ideological criticism, we can now see, risk distorting the plays they deal with, since the dramatist's concern to create a unified structure which will release conflicting human desires yet bring them to a resolution inevitably creates sequences of action that do not correspond to anything in the ideology. Bold critics like Jameson can rewrite the play; others fragment it by picking out only those elements that can be squared with the ideology. Given the ubiquity of the 'dominant ideology' model, one possible approach is to concentrate on the oppressed part of society, since 'ideological commitment', as Jameson describes it, quite properly involves 'the taking of sides in a struggle between embattled groups' (*ibid.*, p. 290). This 'taking of sides', innocent though it may seem, can damage both the play's structure and its historical meaning. For the first failing consider *Measure for Measure* and Jonathan Dollimore's oft-recycled argument that the 'social crisis is displaced onto the prostitutes of the play', who 'are made ... "symbolically central" even while remaining utterly marginal'. The fact that 'not one of the prostitutes speaks', according to this critic, reveals 'their powerlessness and exploitation' (Dollimore 1990b, pp. 474–5; Dollimore 1985, pp. 85–6; Dollimore 1990a, p. 418). This is truly to imitate Macherey in reading significance out of silence, scoring points as an act of sympathy for the marginalised, perhaps, but not as literary criticism. If Shakespeare had needed the prostitutes for his conception of the play, he would have given them a voice, as he did with Doll Tearsheet.

Sympathy with the low-life characters in *Measure for Measure* is extended by David Margolies to Lucio: 'A whoremaster and liar, he has a warmth of friendship that is not elsewhere shown in the play ...' (Margolies 1988, p. 48). This is to overlook the Duke's careful plot to vindicate Mariana and Claudio — but Margolies has nothing good to say about the Duke, whom he finds 'self-important, irresponsible and pompous' (*ibid.*, pp. 48–9). The fact that Lucio, not knowing that the Friar he is talking to is in fact the Duke in disguise, makes a series of malicious slanders of the Duke, means to Margolies that although 'in conventional terms [Lucio] is a liar', he 'may speak what is *essentially* true' (p. 49). This is a sophistic distinction to justify a prejudice against authority-figures. Margolies is happy to see the 'serious image of justice' being 'given a send-up', but his conventional liking for the subversive elements blinds him to the fact that Lucio is shown as a callous and selfish cynic, a mocker of all, a man who (in a plot-parallel to Angelo and Claudio) got 'Mistress Kate Keepdown ... with child ... promis'd her marriage' (3.2.194ff), but abandoned her. Margolies mentions neither point, nor the fact that at the end of the play Lucio (like Angelo) will be made to marry the woman he deceived, despite his protests — 'Marrying a punk, my lord, is pressing to death, whipping, and hanging' — 'Slandering a prince deserves it' (5.1.512ff). In any case, Lucio is a character in a play, having several different functions in the plot. To pick him out for approving comment on the grounds of him being against authority is to treat the play as if it were a plum-pie, with the critic as little Jack Horner.

The witches in *Macbeth* are even more complex figures in a dramatic structure, both natural and supernatural agents, to whom Shakespeare gave many of the destructive features attributed to such creatures, from classical antiquity and the Bible up to the witchcraft craze which reached a peak in England in the late sixteenth century. A large body of knowledge emphasised the destructiveness of witches, but it is instantly visible to anyone who sees or reads the play for the first time. In modern ideological criticism, however, 'taking sides in a struggle between embattled groups' deprives the witches of all their traditional attributes and puts them — since there are only two choices, it is easy to guess where — in the role of 'subverting the dominant ideology'. Dollimore, assigned the task of surveying recent 'Critical Developments' for a widely sold 'bibliographical guide to Shakespeare', recommends to his readers Terry Eagleton's Althusserian-Freudian-Lacanian-Derridian account of the witches in *Macbeth*. As Eagleton sees them,

> The witches are the heroines of the piece [who] . . . by releasing ambitious thoughts in Macbeth, expose [the] hierarchical social order for what it is . . . the pious self-deception of a society based on routine oppression and incessant warfare. . . . Their riddling, ambiguous speech . . . promises to subvert this structure: their teasing word-play infiltrates and undermines Macbeth from within, revealing in him a lack which hollows his being into desire. (*cit.* Dollimore 1990a, p. 408)

Like a high-speed food blender, Eagleton folds into his mixture a bit more deconstruction (the witches 'signify a realm of non-meaning and poetic play which hovers at the work's margins'), a bit more Lacanised Freud (they are 'the "unconscious" of the drama, . . . exiled . . . repressed . . . return'), a touch of New Historicism (they 'inhabit an anarchic, richly ambiguous zone both in and out of official society'), crowning it all with Althusser and Derrida: 'Foulness — a political order which thrives on bloodshed — believes itself fair, whereas the witches do not so much invert this opposition as deconstruct it' (*ibid.*).

That seems to me a glib and opportunistic recycling of current clichés which just drapes itself over Shakespeare's tragedy, distorting it in its own image. In making the witches 'the heroines' of the play it destroys the distinction between good and evil on the supernatural plane, on which the action turns, as does much of Renaissance ethical and religious thought. They are not 'symbols of evil', as one critic put it, but its embodiment. By identifying the 'hierarchical social order' with Macbeth's egoistic, murderous selfishness Eagleton destroys the distinction between good and evil on the natural plane, as well as in Renaissance political thought. An 'ideological analysis' which cannot distinguish between on the one side Macbeth and Lady Macbeth, regicides and murderers who destroy not just Duncan, but also Banquo, Macduff's wife and children, and an untold number of other victims, as that affecting scene between Malcolm and Macduff tells us ('Each new morn / New widows howl, new orphans cry . . .' — 'our country sinks beneath the yoke; / It weeps, it bleeds': 4.3.1–45, 156–240) — and on the other side innocent people murdered in their beds, but has to lump them all together under the rubric of 'official society', is not so much a critical theory as a new form of illiteracy. Eagleton attacks 'official society' for presenting 'its radical "other" as chaos rather than creativity', but the terms are inappropriate (what is creative about the witches?), and the Althusserian ideology blinds him to the play, where time and again deeds, words, and spectacle associate the witches and their magic with death, destructiveness, all forms of malice, any 'deed without a name' (4.1). They are opposed not to official society but to all forms of human existence, individual *and* social. Lady Macbeth voluntarily aligns herself with their form of chaos, exchanging her real feminine creativity for 'direst cruelty', rejecting all 'compunctious visitings of nature' for her 'fell purpose' (1.5.38–53), willingly contemplating destroying 'the babe that milks me' rather than pass up a plot to murder the king so as to gain the crown (1.7.48–60). To any critic who cannot distinguish these savagely anti-human forces from 'official society' we can only say, 'get thee new spectacles'!

Dollimore, however, sees 'something rather important' in Eagleton's account, namely 'a concern with the subordinate, the marginal, and the displaced. In the new work these individuals, groups, or sub-cultures' are seen as important evidence of 'aspects of our past which literary criticism and official history have ignored or repressed'. These minorities can help us to understand the society that 'rendered them marginal (for example, the dominant is understood in terms of its deviants . . .)', and are in any case of great interest in post-Foucault-Althusser-Macherey circles as forces that 'subvert the social order which demonizes them' (Dollimore 1990a, p. 409). Once again the ideological template induces tunnel vision or partial black-out in the critic. In the play, of course, the witches subvert not the social order but the anti-social Macbeth, whose ambitions for the crown are encouraged by them — not released, as Eagleton claims, since we know that Macbeth had them before he met the witches (see 1.3). They also subvert Lady Macbeth, if we can take her invocation to 'you spirits / That tend on mortal thoughts' to be addressed to them. Macbeth and his wife are perfectly capable of subverting the social order without the witches, and pay a terrible price for doing so, he a form of living death and she nightmares and madness. One powerful point demonstrated by the play (no doubt a form of moralistic deterrent in the anti-demonic literature) is that the witches may encourage the forces of chaos in human society, but only to destroy them. In the words that Shakespeare gives to Banquo: 'oftentimes, to win us to our harm, / The instruments of Darkness tell us truths . . . to betray's / In deepest consequence' (1.3.122ff). This much belief we must give to the witches in the play if it is to have any meaning, that they are capable of all kinds of harm, especially to those who use their services. Far from being aspects of our past that have been 'repressed', either, a vast literature on witchcraft and demonology existed then, mostly accepting the Biblical texts which asserted not only that witches exist but that witchcraft is an abomination, to be guarded against with violence if necessary.[36] Dollimore approaches the witches in the well-meaning terms of an activist for marginalised figures in our society, but he fails to see that, being profoundly evil and destructive, they belong outside all social order. Althusserian Marxism turns out to be an all too crude instrument, unable to deal with ethical issues.[37]

When we turn, finally, from ideology in Shakespeare to Shakespeare in ideology, we experience a strange reversal. Dealing with the plays, neo-Althusserians enthuse over the characters who are 'fascinatingly deviant', as Dollimore puts it, subverting the dominant ideology. Dealing with Shakespeare's plays in history, however, since they only have the two categories to choose from, the neo-Althusserians perforce see the plays as exploited by the dominant ideology, joining other Ideological State Apparatuses. As David Margolies confidently puts it,

> Shakespeare, as a central exponent of British culture, has inevitably been incorporated into the dominant ideology and made an instrument of hegemony. The plays are used in a deeply ideological fashion, to propagate and 'naturalise' a whole social perspective. They are filtered, and sometimes quite transformed, to represent a class position that accords with an elitist notion of culture and a ruling-class view of the world. (Margolies 1988, p. 43)

The word 'hegemony' there, which frequently occurs in neo-Althusserian texts, was appropriated by Althusser from the Italian Marxist Antonio Gramsci, for whom it originally referred to '*bourgeois* hegemony over the masses', and was located within 'civil society, in contradistinction to the state' (Merquior 1966b, pp. 100–104). Most of the 'Cultural Materialists'[38] are English, and well aware that our educational system is divided between state schools and private, fee-paying ones, yet the same 'upper-class bias' is said to apply in both (Margolies 1988, p. 43). They no longer distinguish civil society from the state.

Claims such as those made by Gramsci, Althusser, and Foucault, that structures of power and ideological indoctrination surround us, visible or not, are designed to negate criticism. Whoever denies them is simply described as naïvely unaware that ideology, as one feminist in this line of descent puts it, is 'unconscious, unexamined, invisible', something that 'pervades every aspect of our thought and defines our imaginative horizons — "a kind of vast membrane enveloping everything . . ."' (Greene 1992, p. 23). That is a good example of arguments that try to put an issue beyond discussion: but they must be rejected if we are to preserve any independence of thought. The argument is obviously untrue, since — to develop a point made in my critique of Althusser — the mere fact that we can discuss ideologies in the plural means that we can submit any system of belief to rational analysis. As for our own ideology, that is not an activity of the unconscious mind but a more-or-less organised body of ideas and attitudes that we have formed over a period of time, which are subject both to reflection and self-criticism. Greene believes that to see 'ideology as unconscious is quite different from viewing it as a consciously-held belief that can be put on and put off at will' (*ibid.*). But we do not (unless we are insecure, or schizophrenic), put off our beliefs at will: we hold them consistently, and we hope, at least, that we can give a coherent account of why we hold them. I deny the claim that ideology is unconscious and invisible.

I would also deny that Shakespeare has been the property of the ruling ideology, were it not so evident that the argument is circular. None of the critics I have read has attempted to define the ideologies of the various social groups that exist in Britain at any one time, using independent, non-Althusserian criteria; none has shown how the subordinate one was formed (or should it be 'extinguished'?) by the dominant one, let alone the role played by *As You Like It* or *Richard III* in this process. These critics simply assert their claims with varying degrees of sarcasm for the school teachers or examination system involved, all lackeys of the Ideological State Apparatuses. A fairly typical example indicting the teaching of Shakespeare as a form of complicity in a system designed to advance 'capitalism and patriarchy' is Alan Sinfield's claim that Shakespeare has been used in schools to 'adjust young people to an unjust social order', having been 'made to speak mainly for the right' (Sinfield 1985, p. 135) — politically right, presumably. Despite the more socially inclusive nature of comprehensive schooling in Britain since the 1960s, the teaching in literature, he asserts, still 'privileges' some sections of the school, not in terms of innate ability, interest in literature or language, response to imaginative work (the criteria by which 'streaming' used to take place within these schools), but according to 'gender, class and ethnic origins' (p. 136). Girls are disadvantaged by being made to study texts that 'reinforce the gender stereotyping which leads girls to these texts — "women are portrayed as being passive and ineffectual, and taking action only for personal or destructive reasons"', as one feminist puts it (pp. 136–7). Shakespeare thus becomes 'a crucial stage in the justification of elitism' (p. 137), and the whole system, the author observes with distaste, 'seems perfectly adapted for the fastest-growing class fraction, the new petty bourgeoisie working in finance, advertising, the civil service, teaching, the health service, the social services and clerical occupations' (p. 142). These unfortunate people, apparently pursuing socially useful work, are in fact to be regarded with suspicion and contempt, for 'the new petty bourgeoisie (unlike the old, of artisans and small shopkeepers) is constituted not by family but through education' (p. 142).

Despite this Neo-Marxist nostalgia for a society based on family links, everyone knows that education as a means of social advance has been a constant in English life since the Middle Ages. It is a notorious fact that gentlemen's sons felt no need to acquire an education, so that the Medieval-Renaissance schools were soon occupied by a quickly-expanding middle class. (As C.S. Lewis once observed, 'the middle class has always been rising'.) In a society that rewards intellectual abilities and cognitive skills over manual labour it is inevitable that those with a better education will be given tasks carrying a greater responsibility, and may even, notwithstanding the unjust distribution of rewards in most societies, be paid according to their qualifications. Sinfield is at perfect liberty to dislike this system, but as a university teacher himself (to Althusser therefore a member of the petty bourgeoisie)[39] he has been both advanced and disadvantaged by it (compared to bankers and lawyers, say, who carry far more financial clout). He is also free to dislike the petty bourgeoisie as our 'fastest-growing class fraction' (a singularly unpleasant term), but he needs better arguments if he really wants to align Shakespeare with repressive social tendencies. Shakespeare can hardly be accused of reinforcing female stereotypes, since it is obvious to anyone who has studied the place of women in Elizabethan society that his heroines enjoy a degree of independence and a mastery of language and eloquence that are totally untypical of his age. Admittedly, the goal of these resourceful women — Rosalind, Portia, Viola, Helena, Imogen, Cleopatra — is always love and marriage, but that remains the goal of many men and women, even today, and unless heterosexual bonding is to be rejected as a stereotype it is hard to find Shakespeare guilty of unthinkingly accepting social norms. If his women act for 'personal or destructive reasons' so do his men, at times; both sexes also act out of generosity or belief in some personal ideal. Sinfield claims that a teaching emphasis on the ' "continuity between past and present" ' in 'classical humanism' (that post-structuralist bogey-word) is 'an approach designed to train an elite' (p. 143). But to regard history in terms of continuity rather than rupture was the norm for everyone before Bachelard and Foucault, and it remains the view of millions of people who surely constitute no elite. As for Sinfield making the schools teaching Shakespeare responsible for oppressing 'working-class children' (p. 146), it seems to me (if I may use an *ab homine* argument), having started life in a miner's cottage in South Wales and owing my entire education to the enlightened reforms of the 1944 Butler Education Act, that Shakespeare transcends class-divisions, and that a 'materialist analysis' of his work is likely to reduce it to the property of yet another self-constituted and self-righteous group.

Since my concern is with what happens to Shakespeare's plays when subjected to some current critical systems, I shall not pursue this line of argument any farther. If Cultural Materialists wish to see the School Certificate or G.C.E. examinations as part of some vast conspiracy, or indict older Shakespeare critics for expressing patriotic or Cold War attitudes (hating Germans or Communists), they may do so, and demonstrate their own political correctness by so doing. But when this form of ideological analysis in the process distorts Shakespeare, I feel more like intervening. Margolies, for instance, claims that 'the hegemonic use of Shakespeare' in schools takes such forms as 'the enumeration of anti-popular attitudes or explicit statements of reactionary sentiment in the plays, such as the bitter scorn the noble Coriolanus displays towards the populace . . .' (Margolies 1988, p. 51). Like so many of these indictments, full of righteous indignation and vague hints of responsibility, Margolies does not say who enumerates these 'anti-popular attitudes' or why. It is perfectly possible, of course, that reactionary teachers exist, and that they might appropriate aspects of the play as supporting their views, just as neo-Althusserians do for theirs, and just as naïve patriots do in times of national danger.[40] In which case, though, if my experience of class-rooms is at all typical, they are soon likely to find intelligent and independent pupils objecting that this side of Coriolanus is shown in the play itself to be highly unsympathetic. For what Margolies conveniently overlooks is the fact that Shakespeare nowhere invites us to endorse Coriolanus' scorn of the people, that this is shown to be common to the patrician class as a whole but developed in his case with an intensity that embarrasses them (a negative aspect of character), while his initial refusal to temporise on the grounds of political expediency is a sign of integrity (a positive aspect) that challenges the values of the rest of his class and cuts across family loyalties, too, since Volumnia takes it on herself to impress the patrician values on him and does so at the cost of a victory to Rome but death to her son, Rome being revealed in the process to be in a sorry state, the patricians having prestige but no power, the tribunes (representatives of the people) having power but no integrity, expressing nothing but contempt for the people, while the plebs are shown to be confused, manipulated by all parties without having a mind or voice of their own . . . and so on. The play is a far more complex structure of alliances and divisions within social classes and within the family than the crude Althusserian two-part model could ever do justice to.

Attacks on the dominant ideology, I conclude, use the plays for modern political purposes, and distort them in order to fulfil their own ideological agenda. To end with a Cultural Materialist reading of The Tempest (Barker and Hulme 1985) is to see an elevation of Caliban to a heroic position similar to that made by Greenblatt's New Historicism (Chapter 4 above), if more heavily ideological. Parading the usual phalanx of authorities (Balibar, Macherey, Bakhtin, Foucault), with a numbingly abstract vocabulary ('We have chosen here to concentrate specifically on the figure of usurpation as the nodal point of the play's imbrication into this discourse of colonialism': p. 198), the authors claim that literary critics have deliberately closed down the play's 'historical and political signification . . . by a continual process of occlusion' (p. 195). Critics have occluded Caliban's 'political claims', in particular, 'by installing him at the very centre of the play, but only as the ground of a nature/art confrontation' which is here exposed as one of 'the early humanizing forms of incipient bourgeois hegemony' (ibid.). In his 'New Arden' edition of 1954, Frank Kermode did indeed argue that 'Caliban is the core of the play', representing '(at present we must over-simplify) nature without benefit of nurture; Nature, opposed to an Art which is man's power over the created world and over himself; nature divorced from grace, or the senses without the mind'. This 'simple diagram of an exquisitely complex structure', which Kermode subsequently

elaborated in a detailed reading of the play (pp. xxxiv–lix), obviously runs
the risk of abstraction, but the dichotomy of art and nature was important
in Renaissance thought and in Shakespeare (witness *The Winter's Tale*). I
would place the emphasis differently, but it is a perfectly coherent interpretation of the play, and only an Althusserian could see this a-political,
philosophico-aesthetic concept as the tool of 'incipient bourgeois hegemony'. This lumbering and pompous phrase has become an automatic
reflex, a substitute for thought. In fact, a large proportion of any Cultural
Materialist essay on Shakespeare is spent setting out the approved terminology, as if that in itself constituted an argument. This is another
case where, as a critic of Althusser drily observed, the 'terminological
acquisitions are far more numerous than actual conceptual advances'
(Timpanaro 1975, p. 193).

The ideological agenda is predictable, and the play dutifully conforms to
it. Prospero's laconic 'Here in this island we arrived' (1.2.171) is said
to describe 'the relationship between the Europeans and the island's inhabitants' (p. 199) — that is, all two Europeans, Prospero and the infant
Miranda, over and against Caliban (Ariel lives in the elements). Prospero's
'arbitrary rule . . . over the island and its inhabitants' (plural again) is an
'act of usurpation' (pp. 199–200). Not content with exploiting him,
Prospero has a fiendishly clever strategy which 'reduces Caliban to a role in
the supporting sub-plot, as instigator of a mutiny that is programmed to
fail, thereby forging an equivalence between Antonio's initial *putsch* and
Caliban's revolt' (p. 201). Our authors never notice that the revolt is
entirely Caliban's idea, and that, far from being Prospero's doing, it sur-
prises and angers him. Nor do they observe that the plot of Caliban,
Stephano and Trinculo against Prospero functions in the play as a parallel
to the *new* plot of the usurping Duke Antonio and Sebastian against
Sebastian's brother Alonso, King of Naples. Instead, they conclude that
Shakespeare manipulated Caliban into this position so that 'the playing out
of the colonialist narrative is thereby completed: Caliban's attempt —
tarred with the brush of Antonio's supposedly self-evident viciousness — is
produced as final and irrevocable confirmation of the natural treachery of
savages' (*ibid.*). But Shakespeare nowhere makes such general affirmations,
whether about savages or anyone else. Antonio's viciousness is more than
'supposedly self-evident': it is extremely evident to anyone who is actually
seeing or reading the play with a clear and open mind. The fact that
Barker and Hulme end by attributing to *the play* an 'anxiety' about its
ending, the play itself somehow bringing about a 'comic closure' as a means
of 'quelling . . . a fundamental disquiet concerning its own functions within
the projects of colonialist discourse' (pp. 203–4), shows, I think, the
extent to which an ideology can rewrite a play in its own image.

The strong master narrative has won again, as it always will, if we let it.
The play cannot resist; we can.

Epilogue: Masters and Demons

I wish to emphasize from the very beginning that the attitude taken here is of a very personal character. I do not believe that there is any single approach to the history of science which could not be replaced by very different methods of attack; only trivialities permit but one interpretation.   Otto Neugebauer[1]

Looking back through this book, and reflecting on the very diverse range of material it has dealt with, one common element stands out, the degree to which critics pick up the ideas of a 'Modern Master' and model their accounts of literature on the patterns he provides. Whether Freud, Derrida, Lacan, Foucault, Althusser, whether feminist or Christian, one thought-system is taken over as setting the standards by which Shakespeare should be read. Critics derive their assumptions about language and literature, their methodology (in some cases the renunciation of method), their attitudes to life even, from a law-giving individual or system. Adoption of the system usually seems to deprive them of the power to criticise it, or even to reflect on it critically. It is to be absorbed entire, demonstrated or validated through being imposed on this or that play. On the one side the master, on the other his pupils or slaves. The destructive effects of such allegiance were clearly shown by Francis Bacon in 1605:

> And as for the overmuch credit that hath been given unto authors in sciences, in making them dictators, that their words should stand, and not counsels to give advice; the damage is infinite that sciences have received thereby, as the principal cause that hath kept them low, at a stay without growth or advancement.

In the mechanical arts, Bacon saw, a constant process of improvement and development takes place, but in philosophy all too often attention has been captured by the system of one thinker, which loyal exegetes 'have rather depraved than illustrated. For as water will not ascend higher than the level of the first spring-head from whence it descendeth, so knowledge derived from Aristotle, and exempted from the liberty of examination, will not rise again higher than the knowledge of Aristotle'. Bacon's conclusion is that 'disciples do owe unto masters only a temporary belief and a suspension of their own judgment until they be fully instructed, and not an absolute resignation or perpetual captivity . . .'.[2] All too often today, it seems to me, the 'absolute resignation' to a master system, 'exempted from the liberty of examination' not only fails to advance thought but makes it shrink, as lesser wits 'deprave' the original system by a mechanical and unimaginative reproduction of it.

The too loyal follower, passive and uncritical, seems to be imprisoned by the system he has adopted. To Bacon the bad effect of inquiry being restricted to a single system was shown by the medieval scholastics, whose

> wits being shut up in the cells of a few authors (chiefly Aristotle their dictator) as their persons were shut up in the cells of monasteries and colleges . . . did out of no great quantity of matter and infinite agitation of wit, spin out unto us those laborious webs of learning which are extant in their books. (*Works*, 3.285)

The same metaphor occurred to Edward Said in the 1980s to describe Foucault's concept of the ubiquity of power-structures making political engagement pointless: 'Foucault's theory has drawn a circle around itself, constituting a unique territory in which Foucault has imprisoned himself and others with him' (Said 1983, p. 245). At much the same time E.P. Thompson used a variant of the metaphor to convey his feeling of being 'invited to enter the Althusserian theatre', where once inside 'we find there are no exits' (Thompson 1978, p. 32). 'Men imprison themselves within systems of their own creation' also, Thompson writes, 'because they are *self-mystified*' (ibid., p. 165). Certainly their disciples are. I could wish for Shakespeare criticism in future more of the sturdy independence proclaimed by the American composer Virgil Thomson: 'I follow no leaders, lead no followers'.[3]

New perhaps in literary studies, the phenomenon of willing slavehood in the history of thought is ancient. Plato, Aristotle, Aquinas, Descartes, Hegel — many thinkers have attracted disciples, who have loyally expounded their works and re-interpreted contemporary issues in the same terms. In those cases a body of thought existed which was argued through, sometimes polemically and unfairly (Plato against the Sophists, say), but generally with due regard for evidence, accurate citation of instances, and the avoidance of self-contradiction. Not all of our current masters measure up to, or even accept these standards. Freud's work is notoriously speculative, a vast theoretical edifice elaborated with a mere pretence of corroboration, citing 'clinical observations' which turn out to be false, with contrary evidence suppressed, data manipulated, building up over a forty-year period a self-obscuring, self-protective mythology. The system of Derrida, although disavowing systematicity, is based on several unproven theses about the nature of language which are supported by a vast expanding web of idiosyncratic terminology, setting up an autohermeneutical process which disguises the absence of proof or evidence adequate to meet external criteria. Lacan's system, even more vastly elaborated, is surrounded by another series of devices evading accountability, while Althusser's system has been judged 'wholly self-confirming. It moves

within the circle not only of its own problematic but of its own self-
perpetuating and self-elaborating procedures' (Thompson 1978, p. 12). As
for Foucault, Thomas Pavel has acutely described his evasiveness on these
issues as an ' "empirico-transcendental sidestepping", which consists in
conducting arguments on two levels at the same time without a system of
transitions. If historical proof is missing in such a demonstration, the
author will borrow from the language of metaphysics; when philosophical
coherence is wanting, he will claim that the subject matter is only history'
(Pavel 1989, p. 85). Foucault places himself beyond criticism with his non-
empirical concepts of discursive formations and epistemes, but, as Pavel
observes, this 'transcendental discourse surreptitiously takes charge of an
empirical domain. The excessive indetermination inherent in the quasi-
transcendental leads to mistreatment of facts, which because they
are innumerable and precise need completely different types of categories'
(pp. 93–4).

One common element in these new masters is the confidence with
which they proclaim their ideas, untouched by doubt, or else (Derrida,
Foucault) absorbing scepticism into a system that remains, all the same,
dogmatic. Perry Anderson observed that Althusser's 'assertions of the
scientific supremacy of Marxism had been more overweening and categorical' than anyone else's (Anderson 1983, pp. 29–30), and E.P.
Thompson asked with English bluntness, 'how does Althusser have the
neck?' (Thompson 1978, p. 122). Such dogmatism, as Gellner observed of
Freud, although intellectually speaking deplorable, can be effective with
credulous and uncritical readers: 'bare, brazen, unnegotiated assertion, if
skilfully presented, can have a kind of stark authority' (Gellner 1985,
pp. 42–3). It is a primitive rhetoric, of course, based on massive egotism,
with a disdain for the petty details of argument and evidence, and to those
aware of the great range of rational persuasion it is disappointing to see
how successful mere assertion can be. Perhaps these system-builders had
accepted B.F. Skinner's belief — devastated by Chomsky — that 'that
proposition is most true which is enunciated most loudly and most often by
most people'.[4]

Frederick Crews, one of the shrewdest observers of contemporary
culture, describes 'the Grand Academy of Theory' that has arisen since the
1960s as marked by 'a new peremptoriness of intellectual style, embolden-
ing thinkers to make up their own rules of inquiry or simply to turn their
whim into law. Such liberation from the empirical ethos', he observes,
easily promotes 'a relativism that dismisses the whole idea of seeking
truth' (Crews 1986, p. 163). Crews diagnoses in this period a growth of
'apriorism — a willingness to settle issues by theoretical decree, without
even a pretense of evidential appeal' (p. 164). In 1960, he argues, most
people would have agreed with R.S. Crane that an essential attribute of
'the good scholar is "a habitual distrust of the a priori; that is to say, of all
ways of arriving at particular conclusions which assume the relevance and

authority, prior to the concrete evidence, of theoretical doctrines or other general propositions".[5] (Many writers in many fields still share that distrust.) In the fashionable world of self-proclaimed new theory today, by contrast, participants practise '*theoreticism* — frank recourse to unsubstantiated theory, not just as a tool of investigation but as anti-empirical knowledge in its own right.' By empiricism Crews means (like E.P. Thompson) 'simply a regard for evidence', choosing between rival ideas on the basis of observed phenomena, or an appeal to the text, a process in which the individual necessarily acknowledges the judgment of the scientific community. The basic justification for empiricism, he believes, 'consists of active participation in a community of informed people who themselves care about evidence and who can be counted on for unsparing criticism' (p. 164), what he elsewhere calls 'the principle of intersubjective skepticism' (p. 169).

In place of those principles — which to me constitute a genuine link between the humanities and the natural sciences, so different in other respects — Crews documents the presence of 'wilful assertion' in modern theory (p. 165), the unique combination of 'antinomian rebellion and self-indulgence' that 'comes down to us from the later Sixties', that 'dogmatism of intellectual style' so evident in the work of 'Lévi-Strauss, Barthes, Lacan, Althusser, Foucault, and Derrida' (p. 168). One quality these 'gurus of theoreticism' share is that 'all of them neglect or openly dismiss the principle of intersubjective skepticism' (p. 169). Althusser and Lacan were both 'absolutists' who, under the guise of returning to their founding fathers, Marx and Freud, arbitrarily selected those elements that suited them and by 'brazen decree' or *fiat*, with an explicit 'disdain for corroboration', launched their own systems (*ibid.*). In their hands, as Crews perceptively observes, Marxism and psychoanalysis

> exchange an adaptive materialism for allegory. There is no point at which they unambiguously intersect experience and therefore no point where one of their contentions could be modified by behavioral data. They have become, not critiques of inhumane arrangements or guidelines for practical intervention, but master transcoding devices which will sort any text or problem into sets of formally opposed categories. (p. 170)

That dematerialisation of a discipline, reducing it from reality to language, so to speak, is something that I have commented on several times in my discussion of these trends (Chapters 1, 2, 5, 7). The 'poststructural cynicism' of Derrida and Foucault, as Crews describes it, deliberately distanced itself from the concepts of empiricism, evidence, and the notion of a community to whom interpretations are referred. 'Derrida's judgment that "there is nothing outside the text" (Derrida 1976, p. 158) automatically precludes recourse to evidence', while in Foucault's historical works, although 'portentous significance' is attached 'to certain developments and details, his epistemological pronouncements appear to rule out the very concept of a fact' (p. 171). This description echoes Thomas Pavel's analysis, just quoted, with remarkable accuracy. E.P. Thompson has documented a similar slipperiness in Althusser, who 'simplifies his own polemics by caricaturing . . . "empiricism", and ascribing to it, indiscriminately and erroneously, "essentialist" procedures of abstraction', making a 'continuous, wilful and theoretically crucial confusion between "empiricism" (that is, philosophical positivism and all its kin) and the empirical mode of intellectual practice' (Thompson 1978, pp. 6, 10). Rejecting any notion of positivism as privileging the natural sciences and their (once upon a time!) claim to objective certainties, I stand by the 'empirical mode of intellectual practice', which appeals to the experience of reading in order to ground an argument by citing evidence from a (usually) printed text, available to all, subject to interpretation and open discussion. This principle maligned, the theoreticist is free to make whatever assertions he wishes.

The general effect of this absolutism among the Masters of the New Paradigm is to produce what Crews calls an 'appetite for unquestioning belief' on the part of followers matched by, or deriving from, the theorist's 'refusal to credit one's audience with the right to challenge one's ideas on dispassionate grounds' (p. 172). The theorist displays a 'scorn for independent criteria of judgment' that — 'as we ought to have learned by now from the larger political realm' — 'is ultimately a means, not of fostering spontaneity and liberation, but of guaranteeing that entrenched leaders will not be contradicted . . .' (p. 118). The result is the depressing state reached in the 1980s, where

> Sectarian zeal, which now appears stronger than ever in the academy, provides all the guidance required to tell which tenets should be discarded or updated to match the latest political wisdom. (pp. 172–3)

A state of 'fierce parochialism' exists within the university, which would astonish the outsider (perhaps imagining that we are still dedicated to discovering 'the best that has been thought and said'), a combative situation where one 'pugnacious clique' fights another, each group refusing to adapt its method 'to the intellectual problem at hand' (p. 173). As Edward Said independently observed, where once a critical consensus existed that at least disagreement could be confined within certain agreed limits, now there is 'a babel of arguments for the limitlessness of all interpretation; . . . for all systems that in asserting their capacity to perform essentially self-confirming tasks allow for no counterfactual evidence' (Said 1983, p. 230). If you have the system, what else do you need?

The 1960s iconoclasts quite consciously tried to guarantee a *carte blanche* for their own system-building by destroying the criteria of objectivity, empirical practice, evidence. Barthes was reporting on an established change of direction when he announced in 1963 the good news that

the human sciences are losing some of their positivist obsession: structuralism, psychoanalysis, even Marxism prevail by the coherence of their
system rather than by the 'proof' of their details: we are endeavouring to
construct a science which includes itself within its object, and it is this
infinite 'reflexiveness' which constitutes, facing us, art itself: science and
art both acknowledge an original relativity of object and inquiry.
(Barthes 1972, pp. 277–8)

Barthes was accurate in putting structuralism in first place. As the sociologist Simon Clarke showed in his penetrating study of that movement,
Lévi-Strauss's first major work, *Les Structures Elémentaires de la Parenté*
(1949; English tr. 1969) offered a theory of kinship which was prophetic in
having 'no significant empirical content'. To have an empirical content a
theory 'must tell us something about the world', both what it is like and
what it is not like; that is, such a theory must be falsifiable. However,
Clark argues, 'Lévi-Strauss's theory of kinship is not falsifiable because it is
consistent with any possible set of data'. Rather than telling us 'anything
about the form or the operation of the kinship systems that we can find in
actually existing societies', Lévi-Strauss's theories simply reduced 'these
systems to abstract models that are supposedly located in the unconscious',
determining all observable structures (Clarke 1981, p. 54).

The epistemology of structuralism, which took the object of any science
to be an ideal object, not any particular empirical object (p. 102), meant
that it espoused a relativism which simply dismissed any evaluation of
theories by reference to reality. The result, as Clarke puts it, was that
structuralism adopted

the rationalist slogan 'save the theory' as a counter to the old empiricist
slogan 'save the appearances': the task of the scientist is . . . to create a
closed logical theory of an ideal object and not to worry about the
correspondence between this object and a mythical reality. (p. 103)

The task of science, according to structuralism, is 'not to create a view of
the world that is true', but to find a theory which offers 'a coherent and
logical framework for discourse. . . . Thus positivism is preserved by turning
into a form of rationalism' (*ibid.*) — Barthes's pronouncement of the death
of positivism was premature. The structuralist methodological separation of
the ideal object from reality, although preferable to older and cruder
positivism, Clarke judges, had 'serious dangers'. It allowed its users to
preserve theories which could not be falsified by empirical evidence,
however overwhelmingly opposed, such as Lévi-Strauss's kinship theories
(pp. 103–104). Other followers protected their models by claiming that
they existed 'undetected and undetectable in the unconscious'. This
happened, as we saw, with Althusser's 'symptomatic' reading of Marx, and
his relegation of ideology to the unconscious, and it happened with
Foucault's 'epistemes', the construct of a 'system of thought that is an ideal

object, . . . only inadequately and incompletely expressed in the work of a particular thinker'. (Foucault's theory can never be refuted by appeal to the evidence of a particular thinker's not corresponding to the episteme, for this merely shows that the thinker 'had inadequately expressed it'.) Throughout structuralism, Clarke concludes, 'the rationalist development of positivism is the basis on which it is the theory that is made the judge of the evidence and not vice versa' (p. 104).

This, I argue, is exactly the point at which Current Literary Theory has stuck. As — to use Barthes's words — 'a science which includes itself within its object', it is self-contained and endlessly reflexive, not concerned with empirical enquiry into the make-up of the literary work, the complementary roles of writer and reader, the nature of genres, the possibilities of style, or the conventions of representing reality and human behaviour. It pursues the 'closed logical theory of an ideal object', ignoring any 'correspondence between this object and a mythical reality'. Attractive though this option may be to those who believe that Pure Theory is a superior object of study, it is very dubious that it could ever constitute a theory of literature. To begin with, any theory is already a selection from the phenomena to be discussed. No theory can explain everything, so some selection must be made in advance: 'every theory is a theory about a part of the whole that is the world that we daily confront' (p. 130). Current Literary Theory gets along, as I have pointed out several times, by simply ignoring large areas in linguistics, philosophy of language, and rival literary theories. The 'part of the world' that is confronts is truly tiny. But what, in fact, is it a theory of? One basic principle of intellectual enquiry is that

> If a theory is to have any explanatory value it must be possible, in principle, to falsify the claims made by that theory empirically. Such falsification can only be achieved within the terms of the theory, and so can never be absolute. However if it is to be possible at all the theory must define its object independently of its explanations. (*ibid.*)

As we have seen, that is precisely what the systems of Lacan, Althusser, Foucault and Derrida were designed not to do. As Clarke rightly observes, purely formal systems which refuse to define their object independently of their explanations can only be assessed 'in relation to one another on formal grounds: the best theory is that which is simplest, most elegant', or whatever (p. 137). On this basis the literary theory of Thomas Rymer might be judged superior to that of Coleridge, or Henry James. The corollary of a purely formal system, however, is that 'the isolation of the theory from the world of observation means that the theory has no purchase on reality' (*ibid.*).

The unsatisfying nature of Current Literary Theory, I conclude, is that while being an *a priori* construct, largely made up of the negations of other theories, and while continuing to parrot the 60s iconoclasts in scorning empiricism, it still claims to be telling us something about the world.

What the theorists' pronouncements about decentred discourses, expelled subjects, absent presence, or non-referential sign-systems are in fact proving is the accuracy of an observation made by W.G. Runciman, both a theoretical and practising sociologist, namely that 'there is in practice no escape for either the natural or the social scientist from a correspondence conception of truth', for to assert that any proposition is true (or not) 'is to presuppose a relation of some kind between observation-statements and the state of the world', and therefore to employ a concept of truth (Runciman 1983, p. 8). This condition holds for all the assertions of Derrida, Foucault and their followers, despite their attempts to evade accountability, about the nature of language, the incoherence of works of literature, and every other position either excoriated or recommended. Despite their attacks on objectivity, that concept remains inescapable in the human sciences, provided that it is properly understood. A.D. Nuttall recently wrote of the criterion of 'objective truth', that if it is taken to mean ' "truth which . . . states itself, without regard to the nature and interests of the perceiver" ', then we could rightly reject it as superseded.

If, on the other hand, 'objective truth' means 'truth which is founded on some characteristic of the material and is not invented by the perceiver', there is no reason whatever to say that [it] has been super-seded. Indeed its supersession would mean the end of all human discourse, not just Newtonian physics but even *Tel Quel*. Objective atomism is dead but objectivity is unrefuted. (Nuttall 1983, p. 12)

Or, as Francis Bacon put it, 'God forgive that we should give out a dream of our own imagination for a pattern of the world' (*Works*, 4. 32–3).

Following through the history of the iconoclastic movement and its opponents since the 1960s it is heartening to see so much agreement between critics of very different training and background on its attempt to offload any notion of empiricism. To the Marxist classicist Sebastiano Timpanaro, the system-breakers, from Bachelard and Lévi-Strauss to Foucault and Derrida, merely managed 'to blur together under the pejorative label of "empirical" both "lived experience" in the irrationalist sense and the "experimental" '. They made an *a priori* definition of science 'as anti-empiricism, as pure theory', ignoring its function as 'knowledge related to action through a process of reciprocal verification' (Timpanaro 1975, p. 186), a fundamental mistake. Another Marxist critic, Perry Anderson, has commented on the way Derrida and Foucault took up 'the philosophical legacy of the late Nietzsche, in its relentless denunciation of the illusion of truth and the fixity of meaning', trying to escape from 'the tyranny of the veridical' towards 'a free-wheeling nescience' (Anderson 1983, pp. 46–7), glorying in a state beyond meaning or verification. Yet, he responds, 'without untruth truth ceases to be such', indeed 'the *distinction* between the true and the false is the uneliminable premise of any rational knowledge. Its central site is evidence', a related concept disdained by structuralism and its successors, which claimed the licence to indulge in 'a play of signification beyond truth and falsehood' (p. 48). Evidence is particularly important in the historical sciences, however: as E.D. Hirsch points out, in their domain 'decisive, falsifying data cannot be generated at will', as in the natural sciences, so that the interpreter is often faced with the choice between two hypotheses, each having some evidence to support it (Hirsch 1967, p. 181).

*   *   *

For works of literature, to return to our main interest, the evidence cited derives from the text, which needs to have been accurately edited — a supposedly 'factual' scholarly procedure, but which depends on all kind of interpretive hypotheses, including ideological ones (but that is another story). Secondly, citations from the text need to respect its overall meaning, and to reproduce the author's argument reliably. As I showed in Chapter 4, Greenblatt regularly misrepresents the texts he cites, in order (I surmised) to justify a New Historicist *ressentiment*. Although literary criticism has its own procedures, it shares with other subjects in the humanities a responsibility to describe the objects it studies accurately, as the first stage of interpretation. W.G. Runciman's outstanding study of social theory has identified some recurring instances of 'misdescription' which can be used to sum up several of the failings I have documented in current Shakespeare criticism. Runciman divides misdescription into 'misapprehension', involving 'incompleteness, oversimplification and ahistoricity'; and 'mystification', involving 'suppression, exaggeration, and ethnocentricity' (Runciman 1983, pp. 244–9). *Incompleteness* arises from an observer neglecting 'an aspect of the institutions and practices of the society he is studying which is only peripheral to his own theoretical interests but is of much closer significance to "them"'. *Oversimplification* is seen when the researcher fails to realise that 'the beliefs and practices connected with the behaviour' he describes 'are more complex than his account of it' would suggest. Social anthropology guards against this failing by developing 'systematic participant-observation as the basic technique'. *Ahistoricity* arises when the researcher forgets that a report on 'the behaviour of the members of an earlier society' may be accurate but 'will be a misdescription if so presented as to imply that they were capable of conceptualizing their own experiences to themselves in the idiom of a later one'.

These were instances of 'misapprehension'. The first mode of 'mystification' is *suppression*, the researcher's deliberately failing to 'include reports which would make the description which he presents less favourable to his chosen cause'. *Exaggeration*, likewise, 'typically arises when the researcher overstates a description to make a case for purposes of his own'. *Ethnocentricity*, finally, 'arises where the assumptions of the observer's own period or milieu are read into the experience of the members of another in which they do not in fact have any place'. This is particularly likely when the description concerns that earlier society's values, when, for instance, the modern historian applies to them his 'own taken-for-granted distinction between the natural and the supernatural' — or, we can add, a modern notion of witches as marginalised and therefore admirable people. Without going into detail, I think the reader will recall instances of all six of Runciman's categories of misdescription in the Shakespeare critics I have discussed. Less specific, but rather similar criteria for interpretation, as we have seen, were suggested by E.D. Hirsch (legitimacy, correspondence, generic appropriateness, coherence), and S.M. Olsen (completeness, correctness, comprehensiveness, consistence, and discrimination).

Although the literary critic is dealing not with societies, past or present, but with literary works, the same criteria apply, in particular the need to recognise the specificity or individuality of a play or novel, the fact that it has a unique dynamic structure, a growth, complication and resolution of conflicting forces that is different from every other work (unless they belong to the type of *Trivialliteratur* written to a formula, when a description can be made of the genre as a whole). Given the potential uniqueness, at least, of every literary work, it follows that interpretation should begin at the beginning. Not in the sense that the critic's written account must always start with Act One, scene one, but that his reading should begin there, and the resulting interpretation should recognise the fact that every action has its consequences, and that to understand these it is necessary first to understand the action, the motives behind it, whether or not it was an initiating act or one in reply to, or in retaliation for, some preceding act. Drama, like life as Kierkegaard once defined it, is lived forwards but understood backwards, in retrospect. Plays certainly need to be experienced forwards, as evolving out of clearly-defined human desires and their fulfilment or frustration. The first scene of *King Lear*, the first scene of *Othello*, are decisive for the subsequent events and their outcome. For a critic to *start* her account of the latter play with Iago's hypocritical words to Othello, 'I am your own forever' (3.3.476), or for another to base a reading of *Coriolanus* on two brief passages taken out of context is to forfeit any chance of understanding it properly.

Equally, the evidence that a critic draws on concerning the play's individual structure involves him in reliably registering the various levels of plot, and how they interact. In *A Midsummer Night's Dream*, for instance, Shakespeare organises four layers of plot in parallel. First, the impending marriage of Theseus and Hippolyta, 'four happy days' off when the play begins (1.1.2). Secondly, the dispute between Egeus and his daughter Hermia, supposed to marry Demetrius but in love with Lysander. (Fortunately Helena loves Demetrius, and after various comic mistakes both couples achieve their desires.) Thirdly, the dispute between the King and Queen of the fairies, which Oberon resolves to his advantage with the help of a herb that makes Titania fall in love with Bottom. Fourthly, the company of artisans rehearsing their play of Pyramus and Thisbe, duly performed before the concluding nuptials (5.1). The artisans' role is to entertain the court, and in rehearsing their play (1.2; 3.1; 4.2) they certainly entertain the audience (some Cultural Materialists apart). Their leading performer is Bottom, the only (human) character to figure in more than two plot-levels (the fairy Puck takes part in all four), in those touchingly comic but gentle love-scenes with Titania and the fairies (3.1; 4.1). Any attentive reader can see how skilfully Shakespeare sustains these four plot-elements in parallel, bringing them all to a happy resolution in Acts 4 and 5. As we know from the studies of G.K. Hunter and David P. Young, among others, by a process of analysis and synthesis Shakespeare fused a number of disparate elements together to form an admirably balanced unity.[6]

For some recent politically minded critics, however, the truly significant element in the play is that involving the artisans — not for its connection with the illusion basic to theatrical performance (which Theseus discusses in a famous speech), but for its relevance to immediate social unrest. In a recent book, *Shakespeare and the Popular Voice* (Oxford, 1989), Annabel Patterson has argued that the play should be interpreted in the light of the Oxfordshire Rising of 1596 and the midsummer disturbances in London of 1595, which some sources claim to have involved up to a thousand rioters, a mixture of artisans and apprentices. Terence Hawkes reviewed Patterson's book favourably,[7] endorsing her notion that the artisans in the *Dream* offered to Shakespeare's audience 'the worrying potential of the presence on the stage of a number of such persons', Bottom's 'sexual triumph with Titania' constituting 'an enactment in fantasy of upper-class fears regarding the potency of the lower elements both of society and the body'. The artisans' play is now 'thrust into new prominence', as Hawkes puts it, for their 'mocking and sharply focused performance — capable of making its aristocratic audience as uncomfortable as the performance of "The Mousetrap" does in *Hamlet* — takes up virtually the whole of the Fifth Act of the play, and the rehearsals for it resonate in the rest of the action to such a degree that they drown out much of the rather tedious framing plot'.

This may be a demonstration of turning the margin into the centre, but it certainly distorts the play. There is no evidence that the grievances of some working men in 1595–6 are echoed in this or any other play by Shakespeare. His presentations of social unrest (2 Henry VI, *Julius Caesar*, *Coriolanus*) derive from historical sources, and are never keyed to contemporary events. Far from airing their grievances, these craftsmen are entirely preoccupied with their play and with the aesthetics of illusion, only lamenting Bottom's loss of a royal pension by his apparent disappearance ('An' the Duke had not given him sixpence a day for playing Pyramus, I'll be hanged': 4.2.19ff). Bottom's 'sexual triumph with Titania' is a figment in the minds of some post-Kottian critics, and fails to register the comic incongruity of the love-scenes themselves, with Titania oozing love-poetry over Bottom, while he remains, *semper idem*, imperturbable in prose. The performance of *Pyramus and Thisbe* can hardly be described as 'sharply focused', either, given the hilarious series of mishaps that befall it, compounded by the actors' artless commentary. Their play becomes even funnier if we accept, as Thomas Clayton recently suggested, that a whole series of unconscious *sous-entendres* are perpetrated by Wall.[8] If we imagine that Wall presents his 'crannied hole or chink' not, as is customary, with outstretched fingers, but with parted legs, so that the lovers have to exchange kisses between his legs, then a completely coherent series of bawdy jokes emerges ('And this the cranny is, right and sinister, / Through which the fearful lovers are to whisper'; 'O wicked wall, through whom I see no bliss! / Curs'd be thy stones for thus deceiving me!'; 'My cherry lips have often kiss'd thy stones, / Thy stones with lime and hair knot up in thee'; 'O kiss me through the hole of this vile wall!' — 'I kiss the wall's hole, not your lips at all': 5.1.153ff). The gain in comic incongruity by that interpretation (giving meaning to some lines which otherwise seemed pointless) is so great that it would be a pity to ignore it.

Whether or not readers and producers come to accept that new reading, it is obvious that the artisans' play is by every other criterion comic, a parody of outdated verse style, absurd diction, and wooden dramaturgy. Hawkes's parallel with 'The Mousetrap' in *Hamlet* could hardly be less appropriate, if we recall the subject-matter of that play, 'the image of a murder done in Vienna . . . a knavish piece of work', and its intended (and successful) effect on Claudius. Far from being made 'uncomfortable' by the playlet, Theseus and his courtiers keep up a rapid-fire series of deflating comments which are sometimes amusing. The crowning gesture in Hawkes's attempt to appropriate the play for a political reading, his claim that the artisans' rehearsals 'resonate' so strongly that 'they drown out much of the rather tedious framing plot', is another example of the ruthlessness involved in ideological interpretation these days, the seizing of that part of the play which fits your preoccupation and the contemptuous disposal of the rest. I should once like to see a performance of *A Midsummer Night's Dream* either with an audience comprised wholly of Cultural Materialists (if a theatre large enough could be found), and with normal actors, or else one with the Cultural Materialists playing the main roles, and with a normal audience — to see which group could make the other laugh in the way that the play intends. Although I fear that this misinterpretation would be the death of its comedy, perhaps Hawkes as Bottom could show us how this reading could make sense in the play. ('No offence, Hal, no offence'.) Patterson believes that the play's audience is faced with the dilemma of whether or not to join with the aristocrats in their mockery of the artisans. But I wonder how else one could respond, for instance, to Thisby's lamenting *blason* of Pyramus: 'These lily lips, / This

cherry nose, / These yellow cowslip cheeks, / Are gone, are gone! / . . . His
eyes were green as leeks' (5.1.321ff). As Horace put it, *spectatum admissi
risum teneatis, amici?*: 'if you were asked to see such a thing, could you help
laughing, my friends?' (*Ars poetica*, 5). This partial reading of the play,
trying to appropriate it for a politico-social ideology, exemplifies all the
vices of misdescription that our sociologist identified: incompleteness,
oversimplification, ahistoricity, suppression, exaggeration, and ethnocentricity. Ethnocentricity and ahistoricity are also, as we have abundantly
seen, the defining marks of Freudian and (old-style) feminist criticism,
from which the other faults soon follow.

*   *   *

Shakespeare criticism needs to take stock of the ideologies and systems to
which it passively attaches itself: that much, I hope, has become clear. It
has taken over elements from the general intellectual upheaval dating from
the 1960s without reflecting on the methodological consequences of
following Foucault, Althusser, or whoever. In absorbing their polemical
attitudes to previous philosophies or systems, each group of literary critics
today finds itself in opposition not just to all past Shakespeare critics but
also to every other group working now. The result, as several experienced
commentators have noticed, is an atmosphere of fragmentation and rivalry.
The historian Gertrude Himmelfarb observes that, 'for all of the brave talk
about interdisciplinary studies, scholarship has never been as factional and
parochial as it is today' (Himmelfarb 1987, p. 100). The critic and historian of criticism, Denis Donoghue, adapting a phrase from Wallace
Stevens ('the lunatic of one idea'), writes that 'literary critics of our time
are lunatics of one idea, and . . . are celebrated in the degree of the ferocity
with which they enforce it' (Donoghue 1981, pp. 205–6). Donoghue
chooses Kenneth Burke rather than Derrida, for instance, 'because I prefer
to live in conditions as far as possible free, unprescribed, undogmatic.
Burke would let me practice a mind of my own; Derrida would not' (p.
206). Derrida forces a choice on us, Donoghue writes,

> because he has a quarrel on his hands; he feels alien to the whole
> tradition of metaphysics. So he has driven himself into a corner, the
> fanatic of one idea. So far as he has encouraged other critics to join him
> there, turning an attitude into an institution, he has ignored the fact
> that, as Blackmur has said, 'the hysteria of institutions is more dreadful
> than that of individuals'. So is the fanaticism. What we make, thus
> driven, is an ideology, the more desperate because it can only suppress
> what it opposes; or try to suppress it. (p. 207)

A younger commentator on recent developments in literary criticism sees
them as a series of 'competing orientations, each claiming to produce a
more radical break with past conventions than the others'. This struggle to

get out in front of the field has established irritable disagreement as the norm: 'the peevishness of critical debate in literary studies today can sometimes seem absurdly out of proportion to what is finally at stake' (Wayne 1987, p. 57). What is at stake, though, is a whole range of cultural goods: egos, careers, identities, the supremacy of one's group.

The basic problem in current criticism, as I see it, is that many critics cannot experience — or at any rate, professionally discuss — a play or novel 'direct', in itself. They have to impose between themselves and it a template, an interpretive model, some kind of 'enchanted glass', in Bacon's striking phrase. But what that yields, once the reading has been performed, is not the play but the template, illustrated or validated by the play. All that such readings prove, as Crews puts it, 'is that any thematic stencil will make its own pattern stand out' (Crews 1986, p. 173). This felt need for a guide or model can be found in much criticism over the last fifty years. What is new is the desire for collective templates, each group wanting its own magic glass to screen out material irrelevant to its own concerns and give back a reduced, but still clearly discernible mirror of itself, which other users can then reproduce in still smaller forms (the technique known as the 'mise en abyme', a term from heraldry, as Hillis Miller points out).[9] Each group appropriates that part of the work that echoes its own interests, and discards the rest. As Wendell Harris recently observed, in a quite matter-of-fact way, critical groups naturally select those works that can best exhibit 'the power of their approach'. Deconstructionists like texts that can be 'pried open to suggest gaping contradictions', neo-Marxists and New Historicists like texts that 'can be shown to reveal unsuspected workings of political power. Practiced New Critics, deconstructionists, and Marxists', he added, with no sense of impropriety or incongruity, 'can, of course, *read almost any text in a way that supports their own allegiances . . .*' (Harris 1991, p. 116; my italics). To one critic that's just how things are; to others it could signify the denial of literary criticism. Edward Said asserts the contrary principle that

> criticism modified in advance by labels like 'Marxism' or 'liberalism' is, in my view, an oxymoron. The history of thought, to say nothing of political movements, is extravagantly illustrative of how the dictum 'solidarity before criticism' means the end of criticism. (Said 1983, p. 28)

Recent developments in the world of letters certainly bear out that verdict.

One result of the politicisation of literary criticism is that readers now cannot afford to be unaware of the groupings, and the polemical techniques that each uses to advance its own cause and frustrate its enemies'. (A knowledge of rhetoric is useful.) One popular ploy has been to pronounce a critical approach or methodology that you disapprove of 'dead', or 'finished'. As Thomas Pavel has shrewdly observed, 'The Rhetoric of the End' is a metaphor recently 'much used and abused' to declare that its user 'is in a position — or at least a posture — of power' (Pavel 1989, p. 9). In claiming that an era is over, such narratives perform an aggressive act, for to 'conceptualize the end' of a period — or 'the entire metaphysical tradition — amounts to inflicting an ontological degradation on the sequence supposedly ended, relegating it, through rhetorical artifice, to the level of passive narrative material . . .'. If used 'from within history and about history, the notion of an end points less to a *fact* than to a *desire*; far from achieving a real closure, it instead opens a polemic' (*ibid.*). In simple vernacular terms it means 'drop dead! Make room for me.' A variant of this ploy was Lévi-Strauss's appropriating Saussure's notion of the arbitrariness of the linguistic sign for structuralist anthropology and relegating every-thing pre-Saussure to a 'pre-scientific limbo' (p. 10). The first of the categorically assertive Modern Masters, Lévi-Strauss (as Pavel records) never subjected 'the validity of the models adopted . . . to doubt or to systematic research' (p. 11), simply asserting their necessity in what Frederick Crews describes as 'the Parisian manner of stating the most high-handed claims as if they were self-evident' (Crews 1986, p. 149). This assertive technique can be seen very clearly in all the work of de Man.

Despite their claim to modernity, contemporaneity, or whatever, these polemical strategies hark back to a much older and cruder thought-world. As Pavel brings out, 'for Lévi-Strauss to label his adversaries "pre-scientific" was tantamount to pronouncing a symbolic death-sentence, to marking out their narrative end' and the advent of his new regime in anthropology (Pavel 1989, p. 11). This was not so much a scientific gesture, however, as a magical or religious one,

> such is the force of excommunicative utterances. To proclaim the end of other groups and systems exorcizes the fear of having to confront them. . . . When the rhetoricians of scientific salvation announce the end of the infidels, they disguise the desire to annihilate the adversary and ensure complete mastery. . . . (pp. 11, 13)

Thus Derrida's placing of Rousseau in 'ethnocentric Western ontotheo-logy', another commentator observes, 'amounted to an impeachment, for Derrida's bracketing is the equivalent of a casting out or a death sentence' (McFadden 1981, p. 339). The primitive nature of such expulsions is well described in Ernest Gellner's comment that in 'pre-scientific societies' — this is now an ethnographic description, not a dismissal —

> Truth is manifested for the approved members of the society, and the question of its validation is not posed, or posed in a blatantly circular manner (the theory itself singles out the fount of authority, which then blesses the theory). Those who deviate, on the other hand, are *possessed* by evil forces, and they need to be exorcized rather than refuted. (Gellner 1985, p. 120)

It is only in modern 'technological/industrial society', Gellner adds, 'the only society ever to be based on sustained cognitive growth, that this kind of procedure has become unacceptable' (*ibid.*).

Unacceptable indeed, but disturbingly prevalent in Current Literary Theory, which has developed a distinctly authoritarian streak. As S.M. Olsen has shown, such theory now 'represents a form of theoretical imperialism', in that 'conflicts between theories, or more often conflicts between sceptical critics with no supporters of some special theory' turn into an 'ideological struggle' between incompatible value-systems.

If one rejects conclusions yielded by a Marxist or psychoanalytic theory of literature one is blinded by a bourgeois ideology or by psychological defence mechanisms which will not permit one to recognize things as they really are. Protesting against the unreasonableness of deconstructionist readings, one is accused of being a liberal humanist who feels his individuality threatened. (Olsen 1987, p. 203)

In this respect, then, Current Literary Theory 'is authoritarian in a way that theories of the natural sciences are not' (*ibid.*). E.P. Thompson described Stalinism as a doctrine which 'blocks all exits from its system by defining in advance any possible exit as "bourgeois"' (Thompson 1978, p. 133), and several Marxist critics produced many examples of Althusser using this ploy. Demonisation (the first stage to exorcism) of the adversary is now a cliché of literary polemics. For A.D. Nuttall 'the most typical vice' of twentieth-century ideological criticism is the abuse of 'undercutting' explanations, setting down an opponent's weaknesses as being determined by psychological or social factors, hoping to neutralise the opposition 'by ascribing to such explanations an absolute, exhaustive efficacy' (Nuttall 1983, p. 7). True enough, when Nuttall's book was mentioned by one Cultural Materialist he described it as 'espous[ing] a positivistic conservative materialism which rejects the specificity of history . . .' (Drakakis 1985, p. 16). Or, in the vulgar, 'he's not for us, so we are against him'. Such ritual labelling of the adversary risks creating its own version of those despised attributes of a previous generation, 'essentialism' (Graff 1989, p. 174), and 'totalization' (Thomas 1989, p. 200). They become, that is, mechanical gestures of abuse.

Abuse and defamation are, however, things that commentators on the cultural scene nowadays must learn to live with. The republic of letters, or the academy, is now leased out — I write pronouncing it — to a host of competing groups, engaged in the old practices of epideictic rhetoric, *laus* and *vituperatio*: praise for oneself, scorn for the others. One exponent of literary theory asserts that in the coming age it will 'play the central role' in literary studies (*cit.* Merquior 1986a, p. 246). J. Hillis Miller, then President of the Modern Language Association of America, was more insistent. Celebrating 'the triumph of theory' with a hypnotic repetition of that phrase, and engaging the rival Marxists in close-quarter combat, Miller asserted that 'the future of literary studies depends on maintaining and developing . . . "deconstruction"' (Miller 1987, p. 289). For deconstruction and literary theory are the only way to respond to the actual conditions — cultural, economic, institutional, and technological — within which literary study is carried out today. . . . Theory is essential to going forward in humanistic study today. (p. 250)

And so on through many more 'onlys'. But of course the Marxists have a different version. For Fredric Jameson, as we have seen, 'only Marxism' can offer what we need, since the Marxist perspective 'is the absolute horizon of all reading and all interpretation', and constitutes 'something like an ultimate *semantic* precondition for the intelligibility of literary and cultural texts' (Jameson 1981, pp. 17, 75). None of these advocates is lacking in self-confidence.

Which of them shall we believe? Each makes a claim for our attention — no, for our total and absorbing involvement in their discipline before, or indeed to the exclusion of, all others. For Norman N. Holland, veteran Freudian campaigner,

the fantasy psychoanalysis discovers at the core of a literary work has a special status in our mental life that moral, medieval, or Marxist ideas do not. These are conscious and adult and intellectual. Fantasies are unconscious, infantile, and fraught with emotion. Fantasies are what make us grab somebody by the lapels. Ideas do so only if they are the later representatives of fantasy. The crucial point, then, . . . is: the psychoanalytic meaning underlies all the others. (*cit.* Olsen 1987, p. 204)

In other words, fantasies are the first and best, moreover the source from which all other forms of thought develop. Close your Marx, open your Freud. In the struggle to gain, and keep our attention what matters is less logical argument than force of utterance, insistence, emphasis. On behalf of the feminists hear Ann Thompson:

It is important for feminist critics to intervene in every way in the reading and interpretation of Shakespeare and to establish, even more securely than they have already done, that their approach is not just another choice among a plurality of modes of reading, not something that can be relegated to an all-woman ghetto, but a major new perspective that must eventually inform *all* readings. (Thompson 1988, p. 84)

*   *   *

Given such intense jockeying for attention, each group trying to gain and retain that portion of the intellectual space that seems theirs by right, quarrels are inevitable. The feminists, for instance, have fallen out with the New Historicists. The burden of their complaint might be summed up in that line from Browning's 'Lost Leader': 'Just for a handful of silver he

left us'. Whereas American feminists had hoped for an alliance with this
new wave, their one-time allies in the fight against the establishment soon
turned out to be making a new establishment, and furthermore a male
enclave of their own. Peter Erickson, writing in 1987, reported — and it is
a revealing comment on the febrile intensity with which cultural-political
movements are discussed in American universities that he could write the
chronicle of a three-year time-span — that 'by the mid-nineteen-eighties
both feminist criticism and new historicism had . . . entered a transitional
stage marked by uncertainty, growing pains, internal disagreement, and
reassessment' (Erickson 1987, p. 330). At a seminar on 'Gender and
Power' in the 1985 meeting of the World Shakespeare Conference (in
West Berlin), apparently, 'the notion of collaboration quickly broke
down', an 'impasse' emerging over the relative importance of gender.
Feminists attacked the New Historicists for being 'more interested in power
relations between men than between the sexes', and for not acknowledging
the 'absolutely central' position of gender (p. 329). The dispute is a
political one — in the current sense of 'cultural politics' as the activity of
self-constituted critical groups — and is rather parochial, if extremely
bitter. Erickson accuses New Historicism of abusing its 'capacity to confer
legitimacy', sacrificing 'intellectual integrity' to its 'territorial imperative'
(p. 329). Another feminist, Lynda E. Boose, has complained that New
Historicists are exclusively involved with 'the absolutist court and its
strategies of male power' (Boose 1987, p. 731), choosing cultural texts 'to
privilege over the literary one[s]' that are all the same, 'male-authored —
hierarchical — patriarchal' (p. 732). A feminist colleague, Carol Neely,
accuses them of 're-producing patriarchy' and dooming women to silence
(Neely 1988, p. 7 — few readers will have noticed much silence in
American feminism). The New Historicists' desire for mastery, Neely
alleges, can be seen in their continuing 'focus on the single and most
visible center of power, the monarch', a choice that may attempt to
conceal but in fact reveals 'the widespread cultural anxiety about marriage,
women, female sexuality and power engendered by the women's movement
and feminist criticism' (p. 15). — 'To the court of King James!' then
becomes the password for a male group fleeing the women up in arms.

The New Historicists have defended themselves, of course, or proclaimed their innocence.[10] To some readers these group-disputes will seem
tedious, and they may feel like exclaiming, with Mercutio, 'a plague on
both your houses!' But anyone concerned with the present, and more
important, the future of Shakespeare criticism must take note of them. The
danger is that collective animus can reach the point where a group 'targets'
anyone who evaluates their work by independent criteria as an enemy, a
person of no worth or merit, whose motives can only be of the most
dubious kind. Such enemies are obviously '*possessed* by evil forces', as
Gellner describes the opponents stigmatised in pre-scientific societies, and
'need to be exorcized rather than refuted'. That my diagnosis is actual, not

hypothetical, nor hysterical, can be seen from the reaction to Richard
Levin's essay on 'Feminist Thematics and Shakespearean Tragedy', which I
drew on in Chapter 6 (above, pp. 366ff). This is a challenging but fair and
properly documented analysis of a dozen or so recent books and essays, in
which Levin showed that some feminists tend to impose their own beliefs
about gender on to the tragedies, indicting the main male characters as
patriarchal misogynists whose (usually insecure) masculinity is the source of
the tragic catastrophe. Levin's essay appeared in *PMLA* for March, 1988.
A correspondent in the October issue complained that the readings offered
by Levin (and by the feminists) were 'partial', that is, both 'incomplete'
and 'partial in the sense of taking a position on one side of the gender
divide' (p. 818).[11] (This is a new, and I feel, disastrous use of the word: if
we are all doomed to be stuck on 'one side of the gender divide' rational
debate becomes impossible.) The correspondent concluded that 'masculinity is a malady. It is the gender, not the sex, that is the problem'
(*ibid.*). In reply Levin objected to the feminists' claim to possess 'a key to
all human behaviour', in which the 'cause of the masculine malady' is
located in men's 'infantile experience with mothering', or even (in a recent
feminist reading of *Coriolanus*), in 'their fetal tissue' (!). The problem,
then, 'may be sex and not gender after all, and biology can once more
become destiny, but this time only for the men' — a sad prospect, many
would feel. Levin ended by congratulating *PMLA* (which has given much
space to feminist criticism in recent years) for having published his article
in the first place.

But that amicable conclusion was short-lived, for the issue of January
1989 included a truly virulent letter signed by no less than twenty-four
feminists.[12] Rather than applauding *PMLA*, the writers indignantly queried
why it had 'chosen to print a tired, muddled, unsophisticated essay that is
blind at once to the assumptions of feminist criticism of Shakespeare and
to its own' (p. 78). From pure abuse the writers moved on to *ad hominem*
arguments, professing to be 'puzzled and disturbed that Richard Levin has
made a successful academic career by using the reductive techniques of this
essay to bring the same predictable charges indiscriminately against all
varieties of contemporary criticism'. Such indiscriminate smears debase
themselves, of course, but for the record, Levin's work includes many
studies of Renaissance drama besides his analyses of the distorting and
deadening effects of some unexamined assumptions in contemporary
literary criticism. The validity of such analyses is unquestionable, and I
would sturdily support him in the words of Dr. Johnson: 'he who refines the
public taste is a public benefactor'.

Rather than advancing the debate, the twenty-four signatories of this
letter simply repeat the strategy I noted above (p. 359) of saying that
in attacking women men are merely attacking their own weaknesses.
Only instead of Shakespeare's men being guilty of this it is now Richard
Levin, whose critique 'embodies precisely those terms it falsely accuses

feminist critics of: arbitrary selectivity, reductive thematizing, misplaced causality. . . . Accusing us of his own flaws, Levin paternally tries to preempt our strengths . . .'. The writers claim that Levin focussed on 'early work' by feminists: but the essays and books he analyses range from 1975 to 1986; they accuse him of ignoring or mislabelling the work of seven critics: but five of those are in his bibliography; and they claim he 'privileges his favored genre, tragedy', where he merely set out to discuss feminist readings of Shakespearian tragedy, of which there are now a great many (so who's privileging what?).

The writers' indignation shows that they are really concerned with the contemporary political issue, expressing 'the serious concerns about inequality and justice that have engendered feminist analyses of literature'. What they seem unable to realise is that other women, and other men, may share those concerns but still feel that their polemical expression in literary criticism can only produce a distorted reading of literature from the past, which is held up to blame for the ills of the present. There is no sign in this letter of that self-examination or re-thinking of premises and assumptions which Levin's essay could have provoked. These feminist apologists still denounce (in 1989) 'the strategies, structures, psychologies, and oppressiveness of the domination that particular male characters [in Shakespeare] enact'. Their critical work, they claim, has analysed the behaviour of tragic heroes', whose 'abnormal behavior in crisis' still represents 'the values and contradictions of their societies', and who 'often fantasize "a very serious provocation by a woman" when there is none . . .' (pp. 77–8). The quoted remark is Levin's comment on how some of Shakespeare's male characters (he cites Hamlet, Othello, Lear, and Antony) express 'misogynist feelings at certain times, but always in situations of crisis and always in response to what they view as a very serious provocation by a woman'. By omitting Levin's careful delimitation of his statement, and by adding on the qualification *when there is none*', the four-and-twenty signatories of this letter falsify both the critic and the plays, and merely repeat the distortion to which Levin originally referred, the imposition of misogyny as a standard personality trait which is not only untrue to the characters concerned but erodes their individuality, giving them all 'the same stereotypical male sickness'. It is the men, the men who are to blame. (It is time that some feminists caught up with recent theoretical advances in their discipline.)

* * *

There is no need to summarise Levin's reply, which is in the public domain. The one point I pick out is his observation that the writers of the letter evidently want *PMLA* 'to deny publication to any criticism of them that they disapprove of' (p. 79). Any right-minded reader will agree with Levin that a journal which thinks of itself as being open to debate cannot be 'subject to the veto of any group'. That would be to close off critical exchange, and human dialogue, from the outset. Not that Levin expects (any more than I do) to

> convince the signers or others who share their feelings. For them, critiques of feminist criticism are permissible from within the fold . . . , but not from 'a cultural other'. (*ibid.*)

This is surely the most depressing aspect of the current situation, the belief that no outsider has the right to criticise the group, that this right belongs exclusively to members of the group — who would risk, however, being expelled from it. . . . That way lies chauvinism, wars of religion, persecution.

Levin's reply did not, of course, settle the issue, which raged on in the press, on panel meetings at further conferences, and in print.[13] In the next instalment, delivered at another MLA meeting in January 1990 and recently published, Levin and various critics exchanged further arguments (Kamps 1992, pp. 15–60). Addressing the dilemma of the politicisation in literary studies that so many commentators have been deploring, where 'each approach is confined to its own hermeneutically sealed-off discursive space, and adherents of different approaches can only discourse with each other about the politics of their respective ideologies' (*ibid.*, p. 19), Levin proposed a peace treaty based on the triple principles of objectivism, rationalism, and pluralism. By objectivism he means the ability to attain knowledge of a literary text without the resulting interpretation being 'always determined by the interpreter's ideology' (p. 16). By rationalism he means the possibility that 'rival ideologists in their attempt to persuade can invoke rational standards that are themselves not ideological' (p. 20) — otherwise, one would imagine, the automatic rejection of the other group's arguments on the ground of ideology would result in a true *dialogue des sourds*. And by pluralism Levin means the belief that various critical approaches can attain knowledge valid in their own terms, not positing 'a necessary connection between these approaches and political ideologies', yet allowing us 'to live together and talk to each other because we can understand and respect our different approaches' (p. 18). Pluralism 'can be suppressed in favor of monism, which is its only alternative' (p. 20), but modern political history makes us all too aware of how damaging that would be.

I personally welcome Levin's suggestions as moderate, lucidly argued, not attempting to appropriate a larger or better furnished space in the contemporary scene. But in the present climate all peace treaties seem doomed. As Levin shows, Marxists reject pluralism as a 'formalist fallacy' since 'they are not seeking peace but victory. They do not want Marxism to be regarded as one among several valid approaches; they want it to be the *only* valid approach, as can be seen in their frequent references to it as "scientific" (which means all other approaches are unscientific) . . .'

(pp. 18–19). Both Marxists and feminists attack reason and rationality as the *ignes fatui* of previous unenlightened generations, but they also denounce 'self-contradiction' and 'irrationality', which shows they do apply rational standards still, perhaps without knowing it (pp. 20, 52–3). Both groups display what Levin calls

> the genetic fallacy, which claims that our views of the world are caused by our race, gender, class, and similar factors, and that they therefore must be judged on the basis of those causes. But both of these claims are false. Our views may often be influenced by such factors, but are not necessarily determined by them. If they were, there would be no male feminists, or female anti-feminists, no bourgeois radicals or proletarian reactionaries. . . . (p. 54)

The diversity of human temperaments and persuasions is far greater than these deterministic models would allow. But 'even if our views were caused by these factors', Levin adds, 'it does not follow that they must be judged on that basis' (*ibid.*): this would simply divide the world into the lowest common denominators of gender, class, age, and judge their products accordingly. The principle at issue here is one emphasised by a number of the writers with whom I am happy to be aligned — Ernest Gellner, E.P. Thompson, Frederick Crews, W.G. Runciman, Simon Clarke, Edward Said — that in all intellectual debates there must be reference points independent of the participants' biographical situation or ideological adherence. If there are no criteria for evaluating methodology, the use of evidence, procedures of argument, the truth or falsity of the conclusions, then intellectual pursuits become impossible, and unnecessary. Truth will simply be handed down from those in power, while the rest of us acquiesce in its dissemination. Who would want to live in such a world?

The politicisation of discourse means that disagreements are regularly reduced, as A.D. Nuttall and Sten Olsen observed, to some putative underlying motive, psychological (the critic reveals his own 'anxiety'), or political. In his original essay, as he recalls, Levin criticised those feminists' formalist readings of Shakespeare's tragedies because 'some of them ignored parts of the text that did not fit their thesis' (p. 55). The relevant response would have been for them, whether as a group or as individuals, to show either that they did not ignore the part in question or that it really did fit the thesis. Instead, as we have seen, a whole battery of bitter *ad hominem* arguments were ranged against Levin, and continue to be: one respondent argued that his article should have been denied publication because he 'failed to understand the feminist cause'.[14] Levin retorts that he does in fact support feminism but that 'a just cause cannot justify interpretive faults' (*ibid.*). The larger issue is this new tendency in ideology-dominated discourse, the 'defensive move from criticism to politics'. Whoever takes the new ideologues to task for some unsatisfactory critical interpretation is instantly accused of sexist bias, or any of the other demonised labels (essentialist-liberal-humanist-bourgeois...). But this self-protective tactic has damaging effects: 'Marxists and feminists seem to claim a special privilege for their approaches, on political grounds, that grants immunity from the kind of scrutiny to which other approaches are subjected and so would amount to a denial of pluralism', which would mean in turn that only members of a group could criticise other members (pp. 55–6). And the result of this intra-group disagreement, as one feminist complains, is that that movement is now 'split into factions' (p. 57).

These are the depressing but predictable results of the slogan that Edward Said excoriated, 'solidarity before criticism'. The survival of any intellectual discipline depends on there being some external terms of reference by which it can be judged, a language which is comprehensible to those outside the group, a community at large that can evaluate achievements. The alternative is already visible around us, the inbreeding of Derridians, Lacanians, Foucauldians, Althusserians, unable and unwilling to understand any one else's language or concerns. It can be seen in so many places in current Shakespeare criticism, as groups align themselves and polarise the scene into an us/them division. The last instance of polarisation that I shall cite, which also expresses a satisfied feeling of group-consensus, having rejected alternative views as pre-scientific, imperialistic ('add demons here', as one of the ancient magical recipes would say), is Howard Felperin's recent description of the new, or 'current' view of *The Tempest*. Felperin describes the change as having taken place since the mid-1970s, when 'anti-authoritarian, anti-elitist, and anti-aesthetic doctrines were in the wind in a recently politicized academia'. The resulting change to our perception of this play, as he phrases it in a series of (I take it, ironic) rhetorical questions, is absolute, canonical:

> What Shakespearean now would be oblivious or audacious enough to discuss *The Tempest*... from any critical standpoint other than a historicist or feminist, or more specifically, a post-colonial position? Would anyone be so foolhardy as to concentrate on the so-called 'aesthetic dimension' of the play? To dote thus on such luggage would be to risk being demonized as 'idealist' or 'aestheticist' or 'essentialist' by a critical community increasingly determined to regard itself as 'materialist' and 'historicist'. (Felperin 1990, p. 171)

Whether Felperin is making fun of the new orthodoxy or endorsing it is not immediately clear from his text, but others certainly use those 'scare quotes' to demonise their collective enemies. When I read such attempts at stigmatisation, I must admit, a certain stubborn independence rises in me, and I feel tempted to retort: 'Go ahead then! Demonise me! See if I care!' (But that reads like the caption to a James Thurber cartoon.) In more sober language, I would have to say that the 'luggage' so contemptuously rejected[15] is essential accompaniment for a critic, or reader, the ability to receive a play or novel as an experience in itself, over and above our current, ephemeral, and limited concerns. Felperin describes the views of 'a critical community', but it is only one of many, although it may believe it possesses the exclusive source of knowledge. All schools, however, no matter how self-assured or polemical, would do well to accept that other approaches have a validity, and that no-one has a monopoly over truth. '*Patet omnibus veritas*', Ben Jonson wrote (adapting Vives), 'Truth lyes open to all; it is no mans *severall*'.[16] No-one is about to grant New Historicists, materialists, me, or anyone else an immunity to criticism, an exclusive licence to practice the one true mode of interpretation and outlaw all the others. Peace would be desirable, perhaps, but only if all parties grant each other the right to read Shakespeare as they wish, and be taken to task if they distort him.

*   *   *

This has been a book about the practice of Shakespeare criticism, and the effect on it of some current theories. I would like to end with some words from Edward Said's book *The World, the Text, and the Critic*, where he argues that 'criticism is reducible neither to doctrine nor to a political position on a particular question', literary or otherwise.

> In its suspicion of totalizing concepts, in its discontent with reified objects, in its impatience with guilds, special interests, imperialized fiefdoms, and orthodox habits of mind, criticism is most itself, and . . . most unlike itself at the moment it starts turning into organized dogma. (Said 1983, p. 29)

Criticism, Said believes, should be 'constitutively opposed to every form of tyranny, domination, and abuse; its social goals are noncoercive knowledge produced in the interests of human freedom', for 'the moment anything acquires the status of a cultural idol or a commodity, it ceases to be interesting' (pp. 29–30). While recognising that all readings derive from a theoretical standpoint, conscious or not, Said urges that we avoid using dehumanising abstractions:

> it is the critic's job to provide resistances to theory, to open it up toward historical reality, toward society, toward human needs and interests, to point up those concrete instances drawn from everyday reality that lie outside or just beyond the interpretive area necessarily designated in advance and thereafter circumscribed by every theory. (p. 242)

The danger, as we see around us, is that literary theory can 'easily become critical dogma', acquire 'the status of authority within the cultural group' or guild, for 'left to its own specialists and acolytes, so to speak, theory tends to have walls erected around itself . . .' (p. 247). A necessary counter to that tendency is for us 'to move skeptically in the broader political world', to 'record the encounter of theory with resistances to it', and, among other things, 'to preserve some modest (perhaps shrinking) belief in noncoercive human community'. These would not be imperatives, Said remarks, but 'they do at least seem to be attractive alternatives. And what is critical consciousness at bottom if not an unstoppable predilection for alternatives?'

Notes

Preface

1 Descombes 1986, p. 139. Works frequently cited are referred to in this abbreviated form. Full references are given in the Bibliography, p. 491.

2 'In Their Masters' Steps', *Times Literary Supplement*, 16–22 December 1988, p. 1399.

3 Vincent B. Leitch, *American Literary Criticism From the 30s to the 80s* (New York, 1988). For commentary see Donoghue (note 2 above) and Kermode 1989, pp. 39ff.

4 Announcement by Bedford Books (St. Martin's Press) in *PMLA* 105 (1990): p. 1449.

5 In working on Greek tragedy in the late 60s and early 70s (see *Towards Greek Tragedy*: London, 1973) I followed new developments in structuralism and semiology with interest. In the book that emerged, however, I had to reject Lévi-Strauss's structuralist analyses of Greek myth as arbitrary and idiosyncratic (a judgment borne out by the subsequent detailed studies of Pettit 1975, Sperber 1979, and Clarke 1981). By contrast — since it derived from empirical analysis, and did not abandon the concept of individual narratives, or episodes within them, having meaning as a structure of interacting human behaviour — I found the narratological system of Vladimir Propp most helpful in analysing what I discovered to be a coherent pattern in Greek myth of injunctions and prohibitions, ethical, social and religious (see Vickers 1973, pp. 165–267).

6 Greimas' career was marked by a seriousness completely lacking in the self-publicity of the iconoclasts. His scholarly work, sober and even ascetic in tone, developed outwards from *Sémantique structurale* (Paris, 1966; English tr. 1983) in one direction in semiotics, poetics and narrative: *Du sens. Essais sémiotiques* (Paris, 1970; English tr. 1987); *Essais de sémiotique poétique* (Paris, 1971); *Sémiotique: dictionnaire raisonné de la théorie du langage* (Paris, 1979; English tr. 1983; supplement, 1986); *Maupassant: la sémiotique du texte, exercices pratiques* (Paris, 1976; English tr. 1988); *Du sens 02* (Paris, 1983). It also took in mythology, as in *Des dieux et des hommes: études de mythologie lithuanienne* (Paris, 1985), and moved out towards sociology in *Sémiotique et sciences sociales* (Paris, 1976; English tr. 1990); and (with others) *Introduction à l'analyse du discours en sciences sociales* (Paris, 1979). In his teaching at the Ecole des Hautes Etudes en Sciences Sociales, as Jacques Geninasca recorded in his obituary of Greimas (*Neue Zürcher Zeitung*, 14–15 March 1992, p. 27), he 'showed a remarkable consistency in developing his semiotic theory', moving on from the reformulation of Propp's narratology to 'lay the basis for a theory of action and manipulation, studying in turn the phenomena of authorisation or qualification, value-objects, and the passions, insofar as these provide the basis for every kind of human interaction'. The coherence of his development is in impressive contrast to the dissolution of Barthes'.

7 Although I share some of Jackson's criticisms of post-structuralist literary

theory, especially its incoherence as an adversarial system, designed to negate, not to build afresh (Jackson 1991, pp. 1, 3, 13–14, 59, 119, 152, 157, 161, 199), I cannot warm to the alternatives he proposes. He generally endorses Chomsky (while ignoring his many critics: see Clarke 1981 and Meulen 1988), believes in a great future for computer linguistics and 'Artificial Intelligence', happily describing himself as a 'positivist materialist' (see, e.g., pp. 94, 95, 103, 112, 121, 225). Such spurious scientism is hardly an advance on Lévi-Strauss.

8   Anyone wishing to follow up these issues is warmly recommended to use Simon Blackburn's admirable introduction: Blackburn 1988.

9   See below, for Jameson on Althusser, Chapter 7 note 26; for Bowie on Lacan, Epilogue, note 14.

10   My first reaction appeared in the *Times Literary Supplement* for 26 August 1988, pp. 933–5.

Chapter One: The Diminution of Language

1   *Problèmes de linguistique générale, vol. 2* (Paris, 1974), p. 97.

2   For the continuity between these two 'schools' (featuring several of the same actors) see, e.g., Timpanaro 1975, pp. 135–219; Anderson 1983, pp. 32–55; Dews 1987; Frank 1989.

3   The text published in 1916 was edited by Charles Bally and Albert Séchehaye, close associates of Saussure. The liberties they took with the students' notes to which they had access were first revealed by Robert Godel in *Les sources manuscrites du Cours de linguistique générale de F. de Saussure* (Geneva, 1957), especially pp. 95–129. Godel also published further students' notes which were not available to the first editors: 'Cours de linguistique générale, IIe Cours (1908–09)', in *Cahiers Ferdinand de Saussure* 15 (1957): pp. 3–103. In his invaluable

but misleadingly titled *Cours de linguistique générale. Edition critique* (Wiesbaden, 1967–1974), Rudolf Engler reprinted all the manuscript material, juxtaposing it with the printed text, but following, unfortunately, the sequence of the printed edition, not that of Saussure's lectures. Engler's would be more accurately described as a 'source-edition', since it merely sets out all the material in six parallel columns, and in no way edits Saussure's text. Godel offered a specimen of a critical edition in *Les sources manuscrites*, pp. 121–9, but did not pursue the task: a new edition would be very welcome. Godel also added an outline 'Lexique de la Terminologie' (*ibid.*, pp. 252–81), which has been superseded (not wholly satisfactorily) by Rudolf Engler, *Lexique de la Terminologie Saussurienne* (Utrecht, 1968). The most useful edition remains another so-called 'édition critique', by Tullio de Mauro (Paris, 1972; repr. 1985, with postface by L.-J. Calvet: 'Lire Saussure Aujourd' hui', pp. 505–13). This reprints the text of the 1916 edition, without any fresh editorial work, but adds some 200 pages of notes, at least drawing on the manuscript material and on the extensive secondary literature up to 1970. My quotations, in the form *CLG*, are to the French text, in my translation. The English translation by Wade Baskin (New York, 1959) unfortunately does not use the manuscript material and is not always accurate.

4   See the letter to Antoine Meillet of 4 January 1894, when Saussure was studying Baltic intonation: '. . . je vois de plus en plus l'immensité . . . du travail qu'il faudrait pour montrer au linguistique *ce qu'il fait*; . . . . Sans cesse l'ineptie absolue de la terminologie courante, la nécessité de la réformer, et de montrer pour cela quelle espèce d'objet est la langue en général, vient gâter mon plaisir historique. . . . Cela finira malgré moi

par un livre où, sans enthousiasme ni passion, j'expliquerai pourquoi il n'y a pas un seul terme employé en linguistique auquel j'accorde un sens quelconque' (reprinted in Benveniste 1966, pp. 36–7). This essay by Benveniste, 'Saussure après un demi-siècle', quotes other illuminating passages from the correspondence.

5 See Godel 1957, pp.95–129, and de Mauro's note, CLG, p. 406 n. 12. For helpful comments on the editors' treatment, see Calvet 1975, pp. 17–31, and Holdcroft 1991, pp. 13–16, 162–3.

6 CLG, p. 317 and de Mauro's note, pp. 476–7, n. 305; Godel 1957, pp. 119, 181. Harris 1987, pp. 191–2 disputes that this is such an alien addition, on the grounds that the opening sentence of the book included the phrase 'véritable et unique objet' (CLG, p. 13).

7 See Engler's 'Edition Critique', op. cit. in note 3, pp. 168–9, on institutions.

8 As David Holdcroft points out, a signifier 'does have a meaning, since it is associated with a signified', and so signifiers have more than a purely differentiating role: they have values (Holdcroft 1991, pp. 57, 132–3). Neither can signifieds be 'purely negative and differential entities' (pp. 126–30). To take this 'dubious' principle, as structuralists and post-structuralists have done, as the basis for further argument, is to 'build on one of the most opaque parts of Saussure's theory' (p. 130).

9 Ernest Renan, for instance, in his essay 'De l'Origine du langage' (1848), stated that 'la liaison du sens et du mot n'est jamais nécessaire, jamais arbitraire; toujours elle est motivée': cit. Plotkin 1989, pp. 31, 162. No concept in Saussure has provoked more discussion than the arbitrariness of the sign. In his 'Théorie et critique d'un principe saussurien: l'arbitraire du signe' (Cahiers Ferdinand de Saussure 19 (1962): 5–66), Rudolf Engler could already list and discuss over 70 (in

some cases widely diverging) interpretations. Most often cited is the 1939 essay of Emile Benveniste, 'Nature du signe linguistique' (reprinted in Benveniste 1966, pp. 49–55), which argued that the link between the signified and signifier was not arbitrary but necessary, and that arbitrariness actually characterised the link between the sign and the part of reality to which it is applied. For the second point, given the lengths to which Saussure went to present language as a self-contained system that could not have been his meaning, although we might well prefer it. For the first, the fact that the link between the concept 'boeuf' and the acoustic image 'böf' already existed, and that Benveniste claimed that he acquired it in learning to speak ('Ensemble les deux ont été imprimés dans mon esprit': p. 51), means only that the association had been accepted into the langue by the social group into which he was born, not that its original formation was not arbitrary. In this sense, retaining Saussure's point about the arbitrariness of the sign as originally formed or accepted by the linguistic community, I would agree with Lévi-Strauss that 'the linguistic sign is arbitrary a priori but ceases to be arbitrary a posteriori' (Lévi-Strauss 1963, p. 91). For critical comment on Benveniste's essay see, e.g., Descombes 1983, pp. 216–18, and Ellis 1989, pp. 47–8. See also Hans Aarsleff, From Locke to Saussure; Essays On the Study of Language and Intellectual History (Minneapolis, Mn., 1982), pp. 356–71, 382–98.

10 Roy Harris (Harris 1987) indicts Saussure for inconsistency (pp. 58, 199, 225, 230); obscurity and confusion (pp. 61, 81, 89, 95, 119–20, 128, 132, 139, 146, 148, 149, 153, 156, 158, 159, 165, 184, 192, 211, 230, 231, 235); and misleading or inadequately developed analogies (pp. 92–4, 100–102, 121–34). David Holdcroft (Holdcroft 1991)

finds Saussure guilty of vagueness (pp. 32, 63, 65, 97); confusion (pp. 56, 59, 129, 136, 139); contradiction (pp. 60–1, 157); and misleading or inadequately developed analogies (pp. 34, 77–80, 107, 112–15, 119, 131, 132).

11 For illuminating, but often extremely critical accounts of Lévi-Strauss, see Pettit 1975, pp. 37–9, 68–97; Timpanaro 1975, pp. 171–98; Anderson 1983, pp. 37–55; Merquior 1986a, pp. 34–106; Pavel 1989, pp. 9–11, 23–37, 104–6, 138–40. The best account in English is Clarke 1981.

12 See CLG, pp. 100–101, 106–107, 110–11 with note 157; R. Godel, 'Notes Inédites de Ferdinand de Saussure', in Cahiers Ferdinand de Saussure 12 (1954), pp. 60, 62–4.

13 Bacon, Works X, p. 85.

14 Lacan's most notorious attack on Saussure juxtaposed a diagram of a tree, under which the word 'Arbor' is written (Lacan's own invention: no such diagram appears in Saussure), with another of two identical doors, marked 'Hommes–Dames' in order to argue (it is not always clear what, since the prose-style is coyly self-indulgent) that 'in fact the signifier intrudes into the signified' (Lacan 1966, pp. 498–501). My instant objection on reading this essay was that Lacan's diagram is an ellipsis, with the word 'toilet' understood, such conveniences being subdivided at the entry point, and having other structural differences inside. Vincent Descombes now makes the more telling objection that in this 'farcical variation' on Saussure, Lacan has silently changed ground in moving from the singular (Arbor) to the plural (Ladies, Gentlemen), where the drawing in any case might have represented two groups, men and women. 'The "signifiers" in Lacan's example are in the plural because grammar dictates the plural for this particular use. Thus the example does not associate Saussurean signifiers and signifieds but illustrates

a context for using the notices "Ladies" and "Gentlemen". They are statements', not signifiers, in the form 'this door is exclusively for...' (Descombes 1986, p. 180). That example is typical for the slippery way in which Lacan used his terms.

15 Several critics have objected to this distortion: Marc Angenot states that Lacan's references to Saussure constitute 'a simple absorption, literally extravagant, of Saussure's terminology into his own reflection, a reflection not only alien to Saussure's thought but also... diametrically opposed' to it (Angenot 1984, p. 157). Manfred Frank observes that the expression 'signifier' in Lacan's text 'is undoubtedly incorrectly chosen, for... a signifier is itself an ideality, essentially defined by and constituted in view of the signified. It would therefore be self-contradictory to believe that the signified could slide under the signifier, for, as Saussure repeatedly emphasized, the sign can only change as a whole' (Frank 1989, pp. 427–8): even Derrida objected to Lacan's misuse of Saussure. Merquior 1986a, p. 155, comments that to speak of 'an alleged "incessant sliding of the signified under the signifier"... is to assert the primacy of the signifier in a spirit utterly foreign to Saussure's sober polarity: with Lacan, the signified goes overboard and the polarity is destroyed. Thus ultimately the unconscious is no language — it is just... obscurely endowed with a dense, dim margin of symbolic meaning'.

16 In L'Homme Nu (1971), Lévi-Strauss wrote: 'We don't feel at all indulgent towards that sleight-of-hand which switches the left hand with the right, to give back to the worst philosophy beneath the table what it claims to have taken from it above; which, simply replacing the self by the Other and slipping a metaphysic of desire beneath the concept, pulls the foundation from under the latter. Because, in replacing the self on

the one hand with an anonymous Other, and on the other with an individualized desire (even if it designates nothing), there is no way in which one can hinder the fact that one need only stick them together again and turn the whole thing round to rediscover on the other side that self whose abolition one has proclaimed with such a fuss' (p. 563; tr. Clarke 1981, pp. 215–16).

17 See Ferry and Renaut 1985, pp. 259–60 for a terrifying account of the practice encouraged by Lacan of the analyst remaining absolutely silent, refusing any response until the frantic patient realises '"the *betrayals* of his own language"' and begins the '"analytical regression"' that will lead him back from the *moi* to the subject. This practice is apparently in line with Lacan's theory of the 'Other' as 'a reified *moi*', an object that we can treat as we like, since he does not understand his own meaning. The authors comment that here Lacan committed the error 'common to the logic of "all or nothing" that characterizes contemporary anti-humanism, according to which the *real* autonomy of the subject being manifestly illusory, the very *idea* of autonomy has lost all meaning as a guide to practice' (p. 261). This is what I call the coercive dichotomy, or the leap across extremes.

18 As Perry Anderson observes, such analogies 'give way on the smallest critical inspection. . . . Far from the unconscious being structured like a language, or coinciding with it, Freud's construction of it as the object of psychoanalytic enquiry precisely defines it as *in*capable of the generative grammar which, for a post-Saussurian linguistics, comprises the deep structures of language: that is, the competence to form sentences and carry out correctly the rules of their transformations. The Freudian unconscious, innocent even of negation, is a stranger to all syntax'

(Anderson 1983, p. 43). In an essay of 1956, 'Remarques sur la fonction du langage dans la découverte freudienne', Emile Benveniste made a devastating critique of analogies drawn by psychoanalysis between language and the unconscious, demolishing Freud's attempts at linguistics, and making three concise objections: the symbol-system that constitutes language is acquired by a learning process, unlike that of the unconscious; the linguistic sign is unmotivated, Freudian symbols are by definition motivated; and if the unconscious is universal, as Freud claimed, language, by contrast, is divided into differing national languages: Benveniste 1966, p. 75–87.

19 Elizabeth Wright, summarising Samuel Weber's book, *Return to Freud. Jacques Lacan's Dislocation of Psychoanalysis*, in *Times Literary Supplement* 28 February 1992, p. 26.

20 See Stephen Heath, *Le vertige du déplacement* (Paris, 1974), p. 57.

21 Several recent independent studies agree that semiological analyses never cohered as a system (Pettit 1975, pp. 61–4, 106–17), and that the current state of semiology is 'one of simultaneous institutional success and bankruptcy' (Sperber and Wilson 1986, pp. 7–8). Although the 1970s developments gave it a place in university departments, 'no semiotic law of any significance was ever discovered, let alone applied to linguistics' (*ibid.*). Semiotics, another commentator writes, did not realise the truth of Saussure's original contention that language is *sui generis*, cannot simply be lumped with other sign-systems, which lack the ability language has of being 'part of productive systems', capable of generating indefinitely many utterances (Holdcroft 1991, p. 156). Twenty years older, and wiser, we can now see that the question of meaning can no longer be ignored. Courtesy formulas may constitute a sign-system, as Saussure proposed,

and it may well be possible to discover how their rules specify who should use them, and when: but the crucial issue is to discover the rules that define their content and meaning (*ibid.*, p. 157).

22 Vincent Descombes points out that semiology's comparison between human language and a communication code ignores 'one obvious difference: a code is constructed, while a language is not. To construct a code, we require a language'. A natural language is not a code about which, at some primordial time, its speakers 'reached an agreement prior to all conversation with the sole intention of exchanging information' (p. 102). Furthermore, 'a language does not have the univocity of a code, in which the semantic value of each symbol is fixed by decree' (*ibid.*). Languages evolve haphazardly, usages in semantics, grammar, and syntax changing according to local conditions and outside influences, the diachronic element constantly affecting the synchronic. And although set up on a different plane from language, 'the construction of the code is always carried out in the natural language' (p. 103). A code, then, is an artificial construct having properties that make it preferable to language for certain purposes, but it would be a naïve capitulation to the assumed 'rigour' or certainty of science to erect it as the norm for methodology in the humanities. To Descombes the paradox of structuralism is that it attacked the traditional philosophy of human consciousness by claiming that the signifier is not at the service of the subject, and that man is subjected to signifying systems. Yet in downgrading human importance it based itself on cybernetics, the name describing a science intended 'to invest human beings with total control by means of better communications techniques' (p. 103). The Greek work *kybernêtês* means, after all, a steersman. On the de-

ficiencies of communication conceived in terms of a code see also Sperber and Wilson 1986.

23 Only a decade later Barthes consciously rejected the scientistic aspirations of semiotics. Looking back on his career in 1975 he could write of this phase that 'the goal of a semiological science is replaced by the (often very grim) science of the semiologists; hence, one [= Barthes] must sever oneself from that, must introduce into this rational image-repertoire the texture of desire, the claims of the body: this, then, is the Text . . .' (Barthes 1977, p. 71). His career might be described as 'from scientism to hedonism', but even in his latest phase Saussure's categories could be redeployed to serve the present purpose. In *Le Plaisir du texte* (1973) Barthes described one effect of *jouissance* as being that it ' "lifts" the signified, so that all value goes to the "sumptuous plane of the signifier" ' (*cit.* Merquior 1986a, p. 157).

24 In 1961 Barthes used similarly extreme terms in declaring that 'each time men speak about the world, they enter into a relation of exclusion, even when they speak in order to denounce it: a metalanguage is always terrorist' (Barthes 1972, p. 170).

25 The inspiration here is undoubtedly Foucault, present in the audience, and whom Barthes acknowledged as a tutelary spirit (Barthes 1982, p. 458). Compare Foucault's inaugural lecture in the same amphitheatre, six years previously: 'in every society the production of discourse is at once controlled, selected, organised and redistributed according to a certain number of procedures, whose role is to avert its powers and its dangers . . .' (Foucault 1972, p. 216). No agency is named, either here or in other comments on the 'appropriation' of discourse (*ibid.*, pp. 68, 105, 120, 227). The Oxford philosopher Galen Strawson, reviewing Didier Eribon's biography of

Foucault recently, reports that it shows very clearly how 'Foucault was a casualty of the windy and self-indulgent intellectual culture in which he was raised, and of its sad, trashy relation to language'. *The Independent on Sunday Review*, 16 August 1992, p. 17.

26   Foucault's concept of the *episteme* has been criticised both in logical terms, as arbitrary and idiosyncratic, by Jean Piaget, *Structuralism*, tr. C. Maschler (London, 1971), pp. 128–35; and in historical terms, as being completely invalid for the sixteenth century, by George Huppert in '*Divinatio et eruditio*: Thoughts On Foucault', *History and Theory* 13 (1974): pp. 191–207. See also Merquior 1985, pp. 56–75.

27   On Derrida's characteristic practice of borrowing from but heavily criticising German philosophy, see Ferry and Renaut 1985, pp. 46–9, 54–7, 164–97; Dews 1987, pp. 19–24; Frank 1989, pp. 59–61, 195–201, 221–53, 258–61, 262–88, 410–26, 430–8, 442–8; Merquior 1986a, pp. 217–27.

28   See, e.g., Searle 1983, pp. 75–6; Searle 1984, p. 48; Tallis 1988, pp. 87–93, 167–71, 181–5, 211–14; Ellis 1989, pp. 19–21, 45–60, 63–6; Jackson 1991, pp. 63, 105, 186–7 ('Derrida's distortion of Saussure's original intention [accusing him of a completely fictive "phonocentrism"] is very great here, and I think quite inexcusable. It amounts to a big lie, which is believed [by literary critics who have not read Saussure] because no one can imagine why it should have been told.' — Obviously, in order to dispose of a rival eminence). I add another example, Derrida's claim that in Saussure 'the play of differences, which . . . is the condition for the possibility and functioning of every sign, is in itself a silent play. Inaudible is the difference between two phonemes which alone permits them to be and to operate as such' (Derrida 1982, p. 51). This is the

first of many occasions where Derrida takes what Saussure says about the constituent parts of the sign and applies it to the whole. What Saussure actually wrote concerned 'ce qu'il y a de systématique dans ce jeu de différences *phoniques*' (CLG, p. 163; my italics). Saussure was talking about the signifier, the acoustic image, part of the 'material aspect of language' (chapter-title), and it is perfectly clear from the examples given that he conceived of an actual spoken sound. It is quite wrong for Derrida to describe it as 'silent play', and he compounds the error by saying that 'the difference between two phonemes is inaudible'. It is obvious from Saussure's text that although he conceived the phoneme elsewhere in abstract terms, he used the term here in the concrete sense of 'éléments phoniques . . . sons' (sense *b* in Engler 1968, s.v.). Derrida's claim that there is, in the special sense he means, 'no phonetic writing' therefore collapses.

29   A three-card trick is one in which a card-sharper shows three cards, of which one is the point-scorer (the queen, say), and invites bystanders to identify it after he has shuffled all three. For one instance of this technique in Derrida see the first paragraphs of his 1966 lecture, 'Structure, Sign and Play . . .': Derrida 1978, pp. 278–300.

30   On these various misrepresentations: for Lévi-Strauss, see Timpanaro 1975, pp. 177–8; for Foucault, see Plotkin 1989, pp. 13–14, 28–35, 159 note 26; for Althusser, see Thompson 1978, and Chapter 7 below.

31   For more detailed discussions of Husserl and Derrida see, e.g., Tallis 1988, pp. 189–209; Frank 1989, pp. 222–257.

32   See, e.g., Abrams 1979, p. 274, for the judgment that Derrida 'remains committed to absolutism' although he claims to have 'dismantled the traditional absolutes', and Merquior 1986a, pp. 232–4, for the view

that 'radical scepticism, about meaning as about almost everything else, is at bottom just a disappointed absolutism'.

33 See, e.g., Searle 1977, pp. 199–203; Searle 1983, pp. 75–8; Ellis 1989, pp. 18–66; Tallis 1988, pp. 164–233; Merquior 1986a, pp. 215–17; Jackson 1991, pp. 182–91.

34 Dissatisfaction with Derrida's mode of argument has often been expressed: 'Derrida has a distressing penchant for saying things that are obviously false' (Searle 1977, p. 203); 'Derrida's reasons for denying presence, or self-presence to the speaker are invariably badly presented. It is often unclear where he is putting forward an argument and where he is making an assumption. Presuppositions, premises and conclusions are mixed together in the seamless muddle of his prose. Often one does not know when he is presenting his own views and when he is presenting (or misrepresenting) the views of others' (Tallis 1988, p. 181). J.G. Merquior comments critically on Derrida's 'irrationalist philosophy', with 'its blatant non-sequiturs' and 'logical jumps'. He judges that in most of Derrida's later essays 'oracular assertion by dint of jocular or half-jocular pun-juggling has come to replace argument almost completely' (Merquior 1986a, pp. 226, 227, 228).

35 Descombes also commented that 'too evident confusion surrounds the concept of language' in French thought since the 60s: 'the signifier co-opted into the list of determining elements may be a language, or it may be a statement. . . . Sometimes the determining signifier is Saussurean', at others 'it is a message' (Descombes 1986, p. 188).

36 Luce Irigaray, 'Le schizophrène et la question du signe', *Recherches* 16 (1974), pp. 34, 37.

37 *Philosophical Investigations*, tr. G.E.M. Anscombe (Oxford, 1953, 1958), §132.

38 See Tallis 1988, pp. 58, 65–96, for a

truly embarrassing documentation of careless or simply ignorant versions of Saussure put about by the cutting edge of English avant-garde theory, such as Terry Eagleton's claim (in 1983) that Saussure made 'the relation between sign and referent' arbitrary, so that 'literary studies . . . are a question of the signifier, not of the signified'; or Terence Hawkes's announcement (in 1977) that 'since writers use words . . . their art must in the end be composed of signifiers without signifieds', and the critic must respond to 'literature's essential nature in which signifiers are prised utterly free of signifieds' ('prised' suggests an act of violence that you might perform on a recalcitrant dog, or a corpse: so must the post-structuralist critic impose himself on language); or Catherine Belsey's reasoning (in 1980) that 'words seem to be symbols for things because things are inconceivable outside the system of differences which constitute the language', and that 'if discourses articulate concepts through a system of signs which signify by means of their relationship to each other rather than to entities in the word, and if literature is a signifying practice, all it can reflect is the order inscribed in particular discourses, not the nature of the world'. For similar exposures of glaring errors in the exposition of Saussure's ideas in two other English books produced in 1977, see Jackson 1991, pp. 237–41 on Tony Bennett's *Formalism and Marxism*, and pp. 248–53 on the textbook by Rosalind Coward and John Ellis (not to be confused with John M. Ellis, author of *Against Deconstruction*), *Language and Materialism*, which is apparently on the syllabuses of at least twenty institutions of higher education in Britain. All this shows is that our theorists have simply absorbed the clinker or rubble of Derrida *et Cie.* without thinking for themselves. *Quis custodiet?*

39 Blackburn's argument is corroborated

independently by the psychologist H.S. Terrace: see his article, 'In the Beginning Was the "Name", *American Psychologist* 40 (1985): pp. 1011–28, and 'Apes and Us: An Exchange', *New York Review of Books*, 10 October 1991, pp. 53–4, where he argues, against Chomsky's theory of the primacy of a genetically determined capacity for syntax, that 'the cognitive leap to language' must have 'occurred in two stages: first, developing the lexical competence to use arbitrary symbols to refer to particular objects and events, and then the syntactic competence to combine and inflect those symbols systematically so as to create new meanings'. In reply Solly Zuckerman agrees that 'in all logic, rules of grammar and syntax would have been adaptively meaningless had their emergence preceded that of the lexical component of language, of individual words with referential meanings'. Both scholars agree that grammar and syntax developed 'because of the additional adaptive value of joining lexical items in ways that multiplied the meanings that they conveyed' beyond the limits of single words (p. 53).

40 For other useful studies of language acquisition see Roger Brown, *A First Language. The Early Stages* (London, 1973); Elizabeth Bates, *The Emergence of Symbols. Cognition and Communication in Infancy* (New York, 1979); and P. Fletcher and M. Garman (eds.), *Language Acquisition. Studies in First Language Development* (Cambridge, 1986).

41 Benveniste 1966, pp. 225–36: 'Structure des relations de personne dans le verbe' (1946); pp. 251–7: 'La nature des pronoms' (1956); and pp. 258–66: 'De la subjectivité dans le langage' (1958).

42 On the significance of pronouns in Shakespeare see, e.g., Sister St. Geraldine Byrne, *Shakespeare's Use of the Pronoun of Address* (Washington, D.C., 1936); Roger Brown and Albert Gilman, 'The pronouns of

power and solidarity', in T.A. Sebeok (ed.), *Style in Language* (Cambridge, Mass., 1960), pp. 253–76; T. Finkenstaedt, *You and Thou: Studien zur Anrede im Englischen* (Berlin, 1963); V. Salmon and E. Burness (eds.), *A Reader in the Language of Shakespearean Drama* (Amsterdam and Philadelphia, 1987), especially the essays by Joan Mulholland (pp. 153–61) and Charles Barber (pp. 163–79); and my essay '"Mutual render": *I* and *Thou* in the *Sonnets*', Vickers 1989, pp. 41–88. I regret my ignorance of Benveniste's work when I wrote this essay (although one of the linguists I cited, John Lyons, evidently did know it).

43 For many years only parts of Grice's lectures were available, the best known being: H.P. Grice, 'Logic and Conversation', in P. Cole and J.L. Morgan (eds.), *Syntax and Semantics 3: Speech Acts* (New York, 1975), pp. 41–58, and 'Further Notes on Logic and Conversation', in P. Cole (ed.), *Syntax and Semantics 9: Pragmatics* (New York, 1970), pp. 113–28. The full text, together with many other essays, appeared in Grice 1989. In *Towards a Speech Act Theory of Literary Discourse* (Bloomington, Ind., 1977), Mary L. Pratt was able to use the ms. of Grice's lectures as preserved at Harvard. For a guide to commentary on Grice see the two volumes edited by P. Cole, and Horn 1988.

44 Cit. E.A.J. Honigmann, *Myriad-Minded Shakespeare* (London, 1989), p. 60. J.G. Merquior, commenting on Roman Jakobson's literary theory, clarifies the point at issue: 'From the fact that literature is made of language it does not follow that literary meaning (let alone value) is something reducible to language. . . . It is a matter of not mistaking the function of a product, or goal of an activity, for what one needs in order to produce the former or perform the latter': Merquior 1986a, p. 31.

45 See Vickers 1973, pp. 362–7, and

Olsen 1987, pp. 121–37.

46 See my essay on 'Shakespeare's Hypocrites', Vickers 1989, pp. 89–134 (on *Othello*, pp. 110–23).

47 See Bertrand Evans, *Shakespeare's Comedies* (Oxford, 1962).

48 See Vickers 1989, *op.cit.* note 46, 'Shakespeare's Hypocrites', p. 111.

49 *A Short History of Ethics* (London, 1967).

50 See Vickers 1988, pp. 336–7 and note 57.

51 'A general pattern for the working out of a conversational implicature might be given as follows: "He has said that *p*; there is no reason to suppose that he is not observing the maxims, or at least the Cooperative Principle; he could not be doing this unless he thought that *q*; he knows (and knows that I know he knows) that I can see that the supposition that he thinks that *q* IS required; he has done nothing to stop me thinking that *q*; he intends me to think, or is at least willing to allow me to think, that *q*; and so he has implicated that *q*"' (Grice 1989, p. 31).

52 Some philosophers have criticised Gricean speech-act theory for failing to consider language users' attempts at deception and concealment: see Blackburn 1984, p. 114, who also makes the necessary caveat that to read Grice as if he were arguing that meaning could be understood solely 'in terms of some amalgam of intentions, conventions, or beliefs . . . ignores or distorts the compositional nature of language', and fails to consider 'how it is established that a sentence or word means any particular thing' (p. 127).

53 Personal communication, commenting on an earlier draft of this chapter.

Chapter Two: Creator and Interpreters

1 Wittgenstein 1958, Part I, §524.

2 See Thomas Pavel, *Fictional Worlds* (Cambridge, Mass., 1986).

3 See Morse Peckham, *Man's Rage for Chaos* (New York, 1967), for the argument that the function of art is to disturb, not placate us.

4 Nietzsche, *Nachgelassene Fragmente*, November 1887–March 1888, in Nietzsche, *Sämtliche Werke. Kritische Studienausgabe in 15 Bänden*, ed. G. Colli and M. Montinari, Vol. 13 (Berlin, 1980), p. 45: 'Der philosophische Nihilist ist der Ueberzeugung, dass alles Geschehen sinnlos und umsonstig ist; und es sollte kein sinnloses und umsonstiges Sein geben.' The translation is by Walter Kaufmann and R.J. Hollingdale from the work put together by Nietzsche's sister and erroneously known as *The Will to Power* (New York, 1967), p. 23.

5 *The First Anniversarie*, lines 205–214, in C.A. Patrides (ed.) *The Complete English Poems of John Donne* (London, 1985), p. 335.

6 'The Essential Tension: Tradition and Innovation in Scientific Research', in *The Essential Tension. Selected Studies in Scientific Tradition and Change* (Chicago, 1977), pp. 225–39; page-references incorporated in the text.

7 'Editor's Foreword', *Modern Philology* 89:1 (August 1991), p. 3.

8 Eliot's two essays on Milton are conveniently reprinted in F. Kermode (ed.) *Selected Prose of T.S. Eliot* (London, 1975): the 1936 piece is given complete (pp. 258–64), the 1947 one slightly shortened (pp. 265–74). For Leavis, see *Revaluations* (London, 1936; 1959), p. 42.

9 'The Garden of Love', *Songs of Experience*.

10 C. Perelman and L. Olbrechts-Tyteca, *Traité de l'argumentation. La Nouvelle rhétorique* (Paris, 1958; 3rd ed. Brussels, 1976), paras. 90–96, 556–609. Quoted from the translation by J. Wilkinson and P. Weaver, *The New Rhetoric. A Treatise On Argumentation* (Notre Dame, Ind., 1969); page-references incorporated in the text. See also

Brian Vickers, 'The Dangers of Dichotomy', *Journal of the History of Ideas* 51 (1990): pp. 148–59.

11 See, e.g., Graff 1980, pp. 418–19; Altieri 1981, pp. 225–9; Fischer 1985, p. 40; Harris 1988, pp. 162–3.

12 See, e.g., de Man 1979, pp. 10, 31, 32, 47, 49, 50, 54, 76, 147, 160, 161, 162, 173, 187, 196, 197, 203, 205, 207, 208, 209, 212, 234, 240, 245, 269, 292, 293, 294, 299.

13 Horn 1988, pp. 116–17. See also, e.g., Lyons 1968, pp. 275–81; Lyons 1977, pp. 275–80.

14 See, e.g., Searle 1969; Cole and Morgan 1975 (especially the essays by Grice, Searle, Gordon and Lakoff, Davison, Fraser, Schmerling, Cole, Garner, and Wright).

15 On the deficiencies of Foucault's historiography see Merquior 1985 and the many critiques reviewed there, especially those by Klaus Doerner, Jon Elster, George Huppert, Jacques Léonard, H.C. Erik Midelfort, Jan Miel, G.S. Rousseau, Peter Sedgwick, Peter Spierenberg and Karel Williams.

16 *Tristes Tropiques* (Paris, 1955); English tr. by J. Russell (London, 1976), p. 71.

17 *La Pensée sauvage* (Paris, 1962), p. 326; in the anonymous English translation *The Savage Mind* (London, 1972), p. 247. See Merquior 1986, pp. 70–2, for a penetrating analysis of the ruling mood of anti-humanism in French intellectual circles at this time, which amounted to 'an *anti-anthropocentrism*, sometimes verging on *anthropoclasm*, a general demotion of man from his King-of-Creation throne'; also Nuttall 1983, pp. 22–4.

18 Ferry and Renaut 1985, especially 'L'Anti-humanisme de la Pensée 68' (pp. 18–25), 'Le Procès du Sujet' (pp. 41–53), 'Le Sujet en Appel' (pp. 53–61), 'Mai 68 et la Mort du Sujet' (pp. 98–103), the chapters on Foucault, Derrida, Althusser and Lacan, *passim* (pp. 105–261), and 'Retour au Sujet' (pp. 264–85). For other comments on the return of the subject in Foucault see Merquior 1985, pp. 33, 106; Dews 1987, p. xvii, and Frank 1989, p. 386. See also Manfred Frank's searching analysis of the issue of subjectivity in French thought from Lévi-Strauss to Deleuze, lectures 12–24 of *What is Neostructuralism?* (Frank 1989, pp. 183–391, and index s.v. 'Subject' and 'Subjectivity'). There are pertinent comments also in Merquior 1985, pp. 13, 17–18, 49, 77, 80–82, 111, 116–18, and Dews 1987, pp. 70–77.

19 The English translation (by Rupert Swyer) omits the last four words in the French text, which I have added ('régularité, aléa, dépendance, transformation'). They are all terms used in mathematics.

20 On the return or recoil of rejected concepts see Merquior 1986a, pp. 233–4; Dews 1987, pp. 37, 40; Pavel 1989, pp. 51, 88–92; Frank 1989, pp. 21, 96, 397; Burke 1992. For Lyotard's critique of this movement in French thought see Dews 1987, pp. 111–17, 128–33.

21 See Burke 1992, an admirably searching study which appeared too late for me to use; but see Additional note 2.

22 Letter to William Blackwood, 31 May 1902; *The Collected Letters of Joseph Conrad*, ed. F.R. Karl and L. Davies, vol. 2 (Cambridge, 1986), p. 418.

23 See Leavis, 'Literary Criticism and Philosophy', reprinted in *The Common Pursuit* (London, 1952), pp. 211–22, a reply to Wellek's comments on *Revaluation* in *Scrutiny*, 1937.

24 See 'Diabolic Intellect and the Noble Hero', repr. in Leavis 1952, pp. 136–59, especially p. 144 (for Leavis's claim that 'Othello's mind undoes him, not Iago's: the text is plain enough'), and p. 153 ('If we ask the believers in Iago's intellect where they find it, they can hardly point to anything immediately present in the text...'). The appropriate comment is that 'all

textual examples are themselves interpretive problems rather than "brute givens"' (Hirsch 1967, p. x).

25 As Olsen says, the author's 'literary intentions are expressed in the work', which is 'autonomous in the sense that the understanding of it is independent of the author's interpretation of his own production'. The author's account of his work's meaning has no special authority, is open to verification like any other (Olsen 1978, p. 118). For an account of the so-called 'intentional fallacy' diagnosed by W.K. Wimsatt and C. Brooks (which had nothing to do with 'intention' as used here) see Olsen 1987, pp. 27–36, and for the wider importance of intentionality in contemporary approaches to the humanities see Quentin Skinner, 'Motives, Intentions and the Interpretation of Texts' (1976), in Skinner 1988, pp. 68–78, together with 'A Reply to My Critics', ibid., pp. 231–88 (especially pp. 268–85), and John Searle, *Intentionality. An essay in the philosophy of mind* (Cambridge, 1983).

26 Thus Barbara Herrnstein Smith, in *Contingencies of Value: Alternative Perspectives for Critical Theory*, (Cambridge, Mass., 1988), p. 34: 'Since there are no functions performed by artworks that may be specified as generically unique and also no way to distinguish the "rewards" provided by art-related experiences or behavior from those provided by innumerable other kinds of experience and behavior, any distinctions drawn between "aesthetic" and "nonaesthetic" (or "extra-aesthetic") value must be regarded as fundamentally problematic'. This crass denial of the unique properties of art works, individually shaped by their creators, proves the truth of Richard Wollheim's diagnosis that the upshot of an aesthetic which bases itself on the spectator alone (and this is Smith's aesthetic, consciously or not) is 'that works of art will emerge as on an equal footing with works of nature, in that both are looked upon to provide the spectator with a sensuous array of colours, forms, sounds, movements, to which he may variously respond'. Denying the artefact means denying the artist, who 'ends up by dropping out of the picture altogether' (Wollheim 1980, p. 228). As Hamlet says, 'this was sometime a paradox, but now the time gives it proof'.

27 See, e.g., Gerald Else, *Aristotle's Poetics: The Argument* (Cambridge, Mass., 1957), especially pp. 224–32, 423–50, and Vickers 1973, Appendix I (pp. 609–15).

28 *Shakespeare: The Critical Heritage, Vol. 5: 1765–1774* (London and Boston, 1979), p. 165.

29 This essay (cited as Barthes 1982) appeared in *Communications*, no. 11, an issue devoted to 'Vraisemblance'. For similar assertions by Michael Riffaterre see the discussion in Butler 1984, pp. 47–53.

30 Alter refers to Genette's essay, 'Vraisemblance et Motivation', in *Figures III* (Paris, 1969), pp. 71–99.

31 A.D. Nuttall has exposed the obvious fallacies in some arguments made by Terence Hawkes in *Structuralism and Semiotics* (1977), such as the claim that 'The world consists not of things but of relationships', commenting: 'Something is obviously badly wrong' with this theorem, for 'the notion of a relationship presupposes the notion of things which are related. A world consisting of pure relationship, that is, a world in which there are no things, is *ex hypothesi* a world in which no thing is related to any other and in which there could therefore be no relationship. The proposition is thus fundamentally incoherent...' (Nuttall 1983, pp. 8–9). Similarly with Hawkes's pronouncement that 'A wholly objective perception of individual entities is not possible: any observer is bound to *create* something of what he observes. Accordingly the *relationship* between observer and

observed . . . becomes the only thing that *can* be observed. It becomes the stuff of reality itself', on which Nuttall comments that a 'flat contradiction' exists between the first sentence and the second: the observer is not watching relationships, so the deduction at 'accordingly' merely 'denotes inconsequence. What is implied is nothing less than a collective cultural solipsism. This is at first sight horrifying but at second glance absurd since it can advance no claim upon our assent. The monster has no teeth' (*ibid.*, p. 11). See pp. 43-4 for another Hawkes clanger.

32 As Madeleine Doran succinctly put it, that 'Aristotle did not understand [*mimêsis*] in any literally representational or naturalistic sense . . . is clear (1) from his idea of universal truth (poetry representing not what has happened, but what might happen, therefore more "philosophical" than history); (2) from his preference in the shaping of tragic plots for a probable impossibility to an improbable possibility; (3) from his theory of selection and emphasis, tragedy representing men as better than they are, comedy as worse; (4) from his remarks on propriety in character; and (5) from his prescription that tragedy should be written in verse and in an embellished style': Doran 1954, p. 72.

33 I quote from Margaret Hubbard's excellent translation of the *Poetics* in *Ancient Literary Criticism*, ed. D.A. Russell and M. Winterbottom (Oxford, 1972), p. 100.

34 See Bernard Weinberg, *A History of Literary Criticism in the Italian Renaissance*, 2 vols. (Chicago, 1961).

35 I quote from the outstanding edition by Geoffrey Shepherd, Sidney's *An Apology for Poetry* (London, 1965); page-references incorporated in the text.

36 On the repeated criticism of Shakespeare for having failed to observe the neoclassic system of rules, see, e.g., Brian Vickers (ed.)

Shakespeare: The Critical Heritage, 6 vols. (London and Boston, 1974-1981), vol. 1, pp. 4-10, 14-18; vol. 2, pp. 1-12; vol. 3, pp. 1-10; vol. 4, pp. 1-24, 31-8; vol. 5, pp. 1-12, 23-32, 43; vol. 6, pp. 6-42.

37 *Ibid.*, vol. 2, pp. 28-9.

38 See, e.g., Gildon's pointed defence of Shakespeare (in 1694) against Rymer's racist critique; *ibid.*, pp. 72-9.

39 London, 1960.

40 Alter's account of *Tristram Shandy* as the paradigmatic self-conscious novel is worth quoting: 'It continually evinces a three-tiered attitude toward the representation of reality in fiction: to begin with, a hyperconsciousness of the sheer arbitrariness of all literary means, from typography and chapter divisions to character and plot; at the same time a paradoxical demonstration, perhaps especially manifest in Sterne's brilliant stylistic improvisations, of the illusionist power of fictional representations of reality; and, finally, a constant implication of the reader in the arbitrary structure-making functions of the mind, which themselves, as our intimately familiar mental experience, become part of the reality represented in the novel. It will be seen that the third tier is only the mimetic obverse of the critical exposure of mimesis observable on the first tier' (Alter 1978, pp. 239-40). Yet, although it is perhaps only in the late twentieth century that readers can for the first time appreciate 'all the cunning convolutions of Sterne's fictional self-consciousness', Alter notes that the novel remained popular 'throughout the age of realism of the nineteenth century . . . because of the convincing mimesis it produces through its maze of flaunted artifice', the vivid images of domestic and provincial life, the varied characters of 'the two Shandy brothers, Trim's tender sensibilities', and so on (p. 240). For a fuller study see Alter,

Partial Magic: The Novel As a Self-Conscious Genre (Berkeley and Los Angeles, Cal., 1975). This is virtually the only point in Kendall Walton's valuable defence of mimesis where I would take issue with him, the claim that works of literature (he cites *Vanity Fair* and Calvino's *If on a Winter's Night*) 'sometimes discourage participation... by prominently declaring or displaying their fictionality, betraying their own pretense' (Walton 1990, p. 225). But this does not discourage participation, it merely enlarges it to include the narrator with his reminders that we are reading a fiction. The narrator complicates, enriches the fiction of which he is a part.

41   M.C. Bradbrook, *Themes & Conventions of Elizabethan Tragedy* (Cambridge, 1935; 1960), p. 4. See also E.E. Stoll, *Art and Artifice in Shakespeare: A Study in Dramatic Contrast and Illusion* (Cambridge, 1933); A.C. Sprague, *Shakespeare and the Audience. A Study in the Technique of Exposition* (Cambridge, Mass., 1935), pp. 59–96: 'Some Conventions'; S.L. Bethell, *Shakespeare and the Popular Dramatic Tradition* (London, 1944). A valuable recent study, emphasising conventions in performance, is Alan D. Dessen, *Elizabethan Stage Conventions and Modern Interpreters* (Cambridge, 1984).

42   *Henslowe's Diary*, ed. R.A. Foakes and R.T. Rickert (Cambridge, 1961), pp. 317–25.

43   For a useful survey, see Doran 1954, pp. 218–58.

44   See, e.g., Ian Maclean, *The Renaissance Notion of Woman. A study in the fortunes of scholasticism and medical science in European intellectual life* (Cambridge, 1980).

45   See, e.g., Leonardo Bruni, in *De studiis et literis* (c. 1405), addressed to Baptista di Montefeltro, arguing that 'the great and complex art of Rhetoric' is of no use to a woman: 'To her neither the intricacies of debate nor the oratorical artifices of

action and delivery are of the least practical use, if indeed they are not positively unbecoming': tr. W.H. Woodward, *Vittorino da Feltre and other Humanist Educators* (Cambridge, 1897, 1912), p. 126.

46   Similarly Thomas Hardy, in his essay 'The Dorsetshire Labourer' (1883), describing the custom by which agricultural workers moved from one tied cottage to another on quarter-days, when their contracts were terminated or transferred, depicted the removal process as a light-hearted affair: 'the day of removal, if fine, wears an aspect of jollity, and the whole proceeding is a blithe one' (*Thomas Hardy's Personal Writings*, ed. H. Orel (London, 1967), p. 179). But in *Tess of the D'Urbervilles* (1891), chapter LI, the move of Tess's family is portrayed — in line with the tragic intention of the whole novel — as an experience of failure and defeat.

47   Cambridge, Mass., 1990. Page-references incorporated in the text.

48   'Reading the *Oresteia* makes one afraid for one's life': Vickers 1973, p. 425.

49   The only review that I have seen so far (by Sebastian Gardner in the *TLS* for 26 April 1991, p. 14), observes that 'so many demands are loaded on to Walton's notion of make-believe that this highly stretched term loses its natural plasticity, and becomes effectively equivalent to "imagines in some way"....'. So 'it is the more specific forms of imaginative life and notions of representation — of... discerning the content of a painting, making up a story, and so on — that do the real explanatory work, and feed Walton's notion of make-believe with meaning, rather than vice versa.' Instead of 'a single, across-the-board concept', then, we should consider 'a plurality of local concepts'. Gardner nevertheless praises Walton's book as providing 'a superb canonical framework' for the analysis of artistic representation, his theory of make-believe making it 'a strong

50 In Borges, *Labyrinths. Selected Stories & Other Writings*, ed. D.A. Yates and J.E. Irby, 2nd ed. (New York, 1964), p. 248.

51 'Life of Milton', in *Lives of Poets*, World's Classics edition, 2 vols. (London, 1952), Vol. 1, p. 88.

52 *The Road to Xanadu. A Study in the Ways of the Imagination* (Boston and New York, 1927; rev.ed., 1930).

53 See A.T. Kitchel, *Quarry for Middlemarch*, supplement to *Nineteenth-Century Fiction* 4 (1950).

54 See, e.g., Don Gifford, *'Ulysses' Annotated*, 2nd ed. (Berkeley, Cal., 1988).

55 See E. Magee, *Richard Wagner and the Nibelungs* (Oxford, 1991).

56 Letter of 13 December 1898, cit. Norman Sherry, *Conrad's Eastern World* (Cambridge, 1966), pp. 139–40.

57 See, e.g., H. Levin, *The Gates of Horn. A Study of Five French Realists* (New York, 1966), pp. 292–301; and A.J. Krailsheimer's excellent Penguin translation, *Bouvard and Pécuchet* (Harmondsworth, 1976).

58 See, e.g., L.M. Bernucci, *Historia de un Malentendido. Un Estudio Transtextual de 'La Guerra del Fin del Mundo'* (New York, 1989). I owe this reference to Sabine Köllmann.

59 See the classic study by T.W. Baldwin, *Shakspere's 'Small Latine and Lesse Greeke'*, 2 vols. (Urbana, Ill., 1944, 1966).

60 See, e.g., J.W. Lever, 'Shakespeare's French Fruits', *Shakespeare Survey* 6 (1953): pp. 79–90.

61 See, e.g., A.S. Cairncross, 'Shakespeare and Ariosto: *Much Ado About Nothing, King Lear,* and *Othello*', *Renaissance Quarterly* 29 (1976): pp. 176–82.

62 8 volumes, London and Boston, 1957–1975.

63 *Feeling and Form. A Theory of Art* (New York, 1953), p. 364.

64 See Weinberg, *op.cit.* in note 34; also Brian Vickers, 'Rhetoric and Poetics', in *The Cambridge History of Renaissance Philosophy*, ed. C.B. Schmitt and Q. Skinner (Cambridge, 1988), pp. 715–45.

65 See Weinberg, *op.cit.* in note 34, and B. Hathaway, *The Age of Criticism* (Ithaca, N.Y., 1962).

66 See Leo Salingar, *Shakespeare and the Traditions of Comedy* (Cambridge, 1974).

67 On academic drama see F.S. Boas, *University Drama in the Tudor Age* (Oxford, 1914); G.C. Moore Smith, *College Plays Performed in the University of Cambridge* (Cambridge, 1923).

68 Binns, *Intellectual Culture in Elizabethan and Jacobean England. The Latin Writings of the Age* (Leeds, 1990).

69 On collaboration see Bentley 1986, pp. 197–234, and Chillington 1980 (although her argument that 'Hand D' in the ms. of *Sir Thomas More* is the writing of Webster, not Shakespeare, has received very little support: see G.R. Proudfoot in Wells 1990, p. 390). For the plausible arguments of Roger Holdsworth that Shakespeare and Middleton collaborated in *Timon of Athens* see S. Wells and G. Taylor, *William Shakespeare. A Textual Companion* (Oxford, 1987), pp. 127–8, 501–7, which I welcomed in *Review of English Studies* 40 (1989), pp. 406–7.

70 For a basic list of books on Renaissance literary and dramatic theory see Brian Vickers, Bibliographical Appendix to *The Age of Shakespeare*, ed. Boris Ford (Harmondsworth, rev.ed. 1991), pp. 499–576, at pp. 522–4, especially the works by Smith, Spingarn, Herrick, Klein, Stroup, and Weinberg.

71 See M.W. Black, 'The Sources of Shakespeare's *Richard II*', in J.G. McManaway *et al.* (edd.) *Joseph Quincy Adams Memorial Studies* (Washington, D.C., 1948), pp. 199–216, at pp. 212–13 ('Shakespeare looked first at the marginal notes'). See also the stimulating discussion of 'Shakespeare At Work: Preparing, Writing, Rewriting' by

E.A.J. Honigmann, *Myriad-Minded Shakespeare* (London, 1989), pp. 188–221, and other comments on the sources elsewhere (subject to some reservations I made in *Modern Philology* 89 (1991): pp. 106–109).

72 Max Bluestone, *From Story to Stage: The Dramatic Adaptation of Prose Fiction in the Period of Shakespeare and His Contemporaries* (The Hague, 1974).

73 See Muriel Bradbrook, 'What Shakespeare did to Chaucer's *Troilus and Criseyde*', repr. in Bradbrook, *The Artist and Society in Shakespeare's England* (Brighton, 1982), pp. 133–43.

74 See A. Harbage, *As They Liked It: A Study of Shakespeare's Moral Artistry* (New York, 1947), p. xiii.

75 See R. Levin, *The Multiple Plot in English Renaissance Drama* (Chicago, 1971), with an Appendix on 'The Double Plot in Roman Comedy', pp. 225–45.

76 See, e.g., Salingar, *op.cit.* in note 66, pp. 65–7, 207–208, 253–6, 307–309.

77 *John Lyly. The Humanist As Courtier* (London, 1962), ch.vi: 'Lyly and Shakespeare', pp. 298–349.

78 Bullough VII: 299. See *ibid.*, pp. 414–20, for some excerpts from Harsnett. He is also discussed in Muir 1961, pp. 147–61.

79 For his use of Pliny's *Natural History* and the self-defence by C. Furius Cresius, see Muir 1961, pp. 127–8; Bullough VII: 211.

80 Bullough VII: 216, 230; and Ned B. Allen, 'The Two Parts of *Othello*', *Shakespeare Survey* 21 (1968): pp. 13–29.

Chapter Three: Deconstruction

1 *Deconstructive Criticism* (New York, 1983), p. ix; cit. Ellis 1989, p. 88.

2 *Signs of the Times. Deconstruction and the Fall of Paul de Man* (New York, 1991), especially pp. 131–268. Louis Menand, reviewing it for the *New York Review* (21 Nov. 1991, pp. 39–44), did not approve of Lehman's analysis of deconstruction but had to agree with his diagnosis of the deplorable reaction of American deconstructionists to the revelation of de Man's collaborationist journalism, showing that the deconstructive method was not 'the slightest help to its practitioners and defenders' either to establish what de Man had actually meant in these writings (which they distorted to give the most favourable picture), or to make an ethical judgement of them.

3 See, in my bibliography, Abrams 1977, Abrams 1979, and Abrams 1986, all collected in, and cited from Abrams 1989.

4 See, in the bibliography, Graff 1979, Graff 1980, and Graff 1981.

5 See Donoghue 1980, Donoghue 1981.

6 See Searle 1977, a critique of Derrida's essay in the same volume of *Glyph* (Derrida 1977), to which Derrida replied a year later in an article called 'Limited Inc a b c...', *Glyph* 2 (1978): pp. 162–254, a bloated and inspissated self-defence which reminds one of the squid, when injured, emitting a cloud of black ink. Searle discussed Derrida again in the *New York Review* (Searle 1983; with a reply: Searle 1984). I remember being in America when this review-essay appeared, and hearing it described by colleagues teaching literature as an underhand piece of work, written out of personal malice, just to 'get even with Derrida'. These are, all too often, the terms in which supporters of deconstruction describe its critics. So Said imagines that Foucault's criticisms of Derrida derive from 'personal animus' (Said 1983, pp. 212–13). Searle's essay is balanced, critical, and quite lacking in personal animus. All the more regrettable, then, that neither his 1977 nor 1983 evaluations of Derrida are cited by later critics, such as Graff, Abrams, and Said. On Derrida's deplorably

violent response to those who criticised his attempt to exculpate de Man for his anti-Semitic journalism, a self-justifying exercise which simply heaped abuse on those who disagreed with him, see Lehmann 1991, pp. 234–9, 252–8.

7   See Butler 1984.

8   See Lentricchia 1980, pp. 72–9, 122–3, 159–77 for enthusiastic endorsements of Derrida, and pp. 188–210 for even warmer words on Foucault. But see pp. 121, 177–88 for critical comments on the Yale Derridians, especially pp. 281–317 for a highly ambivalent evaluation of de Man. The ambivalence soon yielded to unequivocal condemnation of the 'insidious effect' of de Man's work in producing 'the paralysis of praxis itself': see Lentricchia 1983, pp. 38–52. The new hero is Kenneth Burke.

9   Said wrote a largely favourable survey of the new Paris critics, 'Abecedarium Culturae: Absence, Writing, Statement, Discourse, Archeology, Structuralism', in TriQuarterly 20 (1971), pp. 33–71, reprinted in Said 1975, pp. 277–343. But in his later collection, The World, the Text, and the Critic (Said 1983), it is instructive to follow the growing disillusionment through four essays, 'Roads Taken and Not Taken in Contemporary Criticism' (pp. 140–57; originally in Contemporary Literature, 1976); 'Reflections on American "Left" Literary Criticism' (pp. 158–77; originally in Boundary, 1979); 'Criticism Between Culture and System' (pp. 178–225); originally in Critical Inquiry 4 (1978) as 'The Problem of Textuality: Two Exemplary Positions'); and 'Traveling Theory' (pp. 226–47; originally in Raritan, 1982), and from there to the Introduction (pp. 1–30). Written for this collection in 1983, this essay on 'Secular Criticism' reveals a major loss of sympathy, especially with 'textuality' as a concept outside history, outside political engagement in the real world (pp. 3–5), and

with critical systems that have hardened into dogma (pp. 28–30).

10 See Fischer 1985 (together with Altieri 1979, Scholes 1988); Harris 1988; Tallis 1988 (a wide-ranging book with detailed critiques of Derrida and Lacan, which unfortunately lapses at times into sarcastic dismissal); and Ellis 1989, a lucid and penetrating study, which deserves to become required reading on all courses teaching contemporary literary theory.

11 See Timpanaro 1975; Anderson 1983.

12 See Descombes 1980; Descombes 1986.

13 See Clarke 1981; Merquior 1986a; Merquior 1985.

14 See Frank 1989.

15 See Dews 1987.

16 See Pavel 1989.

17 For an (at this point in his reading) sympathetic account of Derrida's concept of écriture double, see Said 1983, pp. 185–207.

18 See, e.g., J. Schäfer, Documentation in the O.E.D.: Shakespeare and Nashe as Test Cases (Oxford, 1980); Early Modern English Lexicography, 2 vols. (Oxford, 1990).

19 See, e.g., Skinner 1988, pp. 114–16 and 119–32, a devastating review (1979) of Raymond Williams's Keywords (1976), which resulted in its second edition (1983) being largely rewritten (p. 312, n. 1); Brian Vickers, 'Leisure and idleness in the Renaissance: the ambivalence of otium', Renaissance Studies 4 (1990): pp. 1–37 and 107–54.

20 See, e.g., Graff 1980, p. 419; Butler 1984, pp. 79–80; Ellis 1989, p. 126.

21 Pavel 1989, p. 15.

22 See Lentricchia 1980, pp. 76–7 and passim; Cain 1979, pp. 381–2; Fischer 1985, pp. xi–xiii, 83–109. Lentricchia 1983, p. 38, states that de Man's two collections of essays, Blindness & Insight (1971) and Allegories of Reading (1979), 'provided a reading-machine for his disciples: the models of deconstructive strategy, the terminology, the

23 See, e.g., Graff 1979, pp. 173–5; Graff 1980, pp. 405, 409; Lentricchia 1980, p. 301; Ellis 1989, p. 65 ('For since meaning is an aspect of a sign, can it mean anything to say that sign and meaning do not coincide?').

24 See, e.g., Donoghue 1980, pp. 38–9; Graff 1980, pp. 413–15; Fischer 1985, pp. 65–76, a collective documentation of omissions and misreadings that will surprise readers who have heard of deconstruction's reputation for close textual scrutiny. The gap between normal critics and the hagiography applied to de Man by other deconstructionists is enormous. Hillis Miller has judged that 'the millennium would come, if all men and women became good readers in de Man's sense': *Ethics of Reading* (New York, 1986), p. 58.

25 As Denis Donoghue wittily observed, 'Derrida seems to get as much vigor from a state of suspicion as naïve people get from a state of certitude. Rendering certain places of the mind uninhabitable, he derives satisfaction from the integrity of achieving this result. De Man's mind is so ascetic that it thrives without joy, it finds no pleasure in the suspicion which is as near Derrida comes to a principle' (Donoghue 1981, p. 185). Many of de Man's essays gain, as Donoghue puts it, a purely Pyrrhic victory (*ibid.*), attaining no more than what de Man himself calls a 'state of suspended ignorance' (de Man 1979a, p. 19).

26 Denis Donoghue bluntly commented: 'I don't understand this. De Man, implacable in denying to the poet any active power, is evidently willing to ascribe an "act" to "language"; he apparently does this merely for the satisfaction of reporting that the "acts" of language are mechanical, arbitrary, and repetitive' (Donoghue 1980, p. 38).

27 See, e.g., Donoghue 1980, pp. 172–86; Jeffrey Barnouw, reviewing *Allegories of Reading, Comparative Literature Studies* 19 (1982): pp. 459–63; Butler 1984, pp. 68–70.

28 *New York Review of Books*, 1 March 1990, p. 40. See also that journal, 24 June 1989, pp. 32–7, for a review-essay by Denis Donoghue, 'The Strange Case of Paul de Man', suggesting some links between his anti-Semitic journalism and his later criticism. A more pointed connection was made by Stanley Corngold in a letter to the *TLS*, 26 August 1988, p. 931. For further commentary on the violent oppositions in de Man's thought, see Corngold, 'Error in Paul de Man', *Critical Inquiry* 8 (1982): pp. 489–507, and my essay, 'Deconstruction's Designs on Rhetoric', in W.B. Horner and M. Leff (edd.), *A Festschrift for J.J. Murphy* (forthcoming).

29 See, e.g., *The World as Will and Representation*, tr. E.J. Payne, 2 vols. (London, 1958; New York, 1966) I, pp. 275, 279, 352–3, 409–12 (the last word of the main text is 'nothing'); II, pp. 198, 288, 463–4, 474–7, 487, 497, 501, 508, 580, 612.

30 Miller's Presidential lecture, 'The Triumph of Theory, the Resistance to Reading, and the Question of the Material Base' appeared in *PMLA* 102 (1987): pp. 281–91. Another address delivered to university English departments pleading on behalf of deconstruction to be introduced in the teaching of English (misleadingly equated with 'rhetoric', as if the prestige of the older subject could legitimise the new by association), 'The Function of Rhetorical Study at the Present Time', is reprinted in J. Engell and D. Perkins (edd.) *Teaching Literature* (Cambridge, Mass., 1988), pp. 87–109. For a brief critique of Miller's proposal to make deconstruction a part of both undergraduate and graduate curricula, see Abrams 1986, pp. 328–32.

31 *The Arte of English Poesie*, ed. G.D. Willcock and A. Walker

(Cambridge, 1936, 1970), pp. 191–2.

32 See, e.g., *Charles Dickens: The World of His Novels* (Cambridge, Mass., 1958); *The Disappearance of God: Five Nineteenth-Century Writers* (Cambridge, Mass., 1963).

33 For Miller's Wordsworth interpretation see his essay, 'On Edge: The Crossways of Contemporary Criticism' (1979), reprinted in *Romanticism and Contemporary Criticism*, ed. M. Eaves and M. Fischer (Ithaca, N.Y., 1986), pp. 96–110. The most thorough (and devastating) discussion of this essay is in Abrams 1986, pp. 314–28. Miller's essay on Pater (Miller 1976b) has been given extended analysis by Wendell Harris (Harris 1988, pp. 171–9), who shows how Miller endorses Derrida's theory of language's indeterminacy by using two interpretive strategies. The first is a wilful manipulation of Pater's text, involving an 'arbitrary truncation of lines of thought' in Pater to produce the desired result: 'the aporia at which Miller arrives is created in part by choosing to ignore links that can easily be made between various of Pater's key concepts'. The other trick (much used in Miller's Wordsworth essay) is to import 'analogues, parallels, or associations unauthorized by anything in the text, in effect denying that the structure of the text constitutes an internal context that limits possible meanings and relationships'. This move is intended to shatter the unity of the text under analysis in order to 'deny that unity and coherence are guiding principles for the interpretation' of any text: a circular argument, obviously enough, but if such a strategy persuades the writer it will no doubt persuade many of his readers.

34 See, e.g., Cain 1979, pp. 371–81; Ellis 1989, p. 79 note.

35 Descombes 1981, p. 79; Lehman 1991, p. 23.

36 See *Orlando Furioso*, Book XV, stanzas 14, 38, 53; XX, 88; XXII, 10–31; XXXIII, 125; XLIV, 25, etc.

I quote from the excellent prose version by Guido Waldman (Oxford, 1974), pp. 239, 257–8.

37 On deconstruction as power-play see Donoghue 1980, p. 41; Searle 1983, p. 77; and Scholes 1988, pp. 284–5. The burden of other complaints, however, has been that while deconstruction seeks (and gains) power in the academy, it is oblivious to the wider political situations that confront us all. For one example of this criticism I choose Wendell Harris, discussing the degree to which 'consciousness of the interpretive process can help one towards the critical analysis of political significances'. Deconstruction, he shows, gives no help at all, for 'the same deconstructive techniques that one uses to undermine an assumption or argument can be used to undermine the deconstructive manoeuvre one has just employed. Precisely because deconstruction denies the possibility of closure, it can lead down the garden path of an infinite series of reversals. The more serious one's interest in the political significance of a text, the more readily will deconstruction prove a betrayer' (Harris 1988, p. 29).

38 Hawkes, 'Shakespeare and New Critical Approaches', in S. Wells (ed.) *The Cambridge Companion to Shakespeare Studies* (Cambridge, 1985, 1991), pp. 287–302; page-references incorporated in the text. The comparable chapter in *Shakespeare. A Bibliographical Guide*, also ed. S. Wells (Oxford, rev. ed. 1990), pp. 405–28, by Jonathan Dollimore, is an in-group puff for 'Cultural Materialism', Gender studies (especially of the marginalised), and 'New Historicism'. See my notice in *Review of English Studies* 54 (May 1993).

39 From this collection (Drakakis 1985) I shall discuss the essay listed in my bibliography as Evans 1985.

40 From this collection (Atkins and Bergeron 1988) I shall discuss the essays listed in my bibliography as Atkins 1988, Waller 1988, Kopper

41 I quote directly from this collection (Felperin 1990). Felperin earlier published *Beyond Deconstruction. Uses and Abuses of Literary Theory* (Oxford, 1985), to which, strangely enough, he never refers in this latest study.

1988, de Sousa 1988, and Goldberg 1988. This seems to me the weakest of these volumes, as if the critical theory it represented were already exhausted.

42 '*Aporia*: state of indeterminate boundaries in French North America. Population: shifting. Capital: Derridon. Industry: deconstruction. Applications for visas: Mise en Abyme, 47 Boulevard de Man'.

43 Clough to Emerson in 1848: see R.K. Biswas, *Arthur Hughes Clough. Towards a Reconsideration* (Oxford, 1972), p. 151.

44 On Hawkes's misreading of Saussure see Tallis 1988, pp. 65, 70–79, 86–7 (on 'the insistent authority typical of all his sweeping statements', including a 'startling volte-face'), 96, 99, 126–7; and Ellis 1989, pp. 19, 63–4 (showing 'the depths of conceptual confusion', a 'misconception so fundamental as to be disabling').

45 See Brian Vickers, 'Rhetoric and Feeling in Shakespeare's *Sonnets*', in K. Elam (ed.) *Shakespeare Today: Directions and Methods of Research* (Florence, 1984), pp. 53–98.

46 For a perceptive analysis of this speech by Edward Capell in 1780 see Brian Vickers (ed.) *Shakespeare: The Critical Heritage, vol. 6, 1774–1801* (London and Boston, 1981), pp. 246–7. Capell writes that Troilus calls the '"*discourse*" of his reason, passing inwardly, and setting up arguments (*causes*) with and against itself . . . "*madness*" and a "*bifold* (two-fold) authority"; and then proceeds to lay down (explain it is not) wherein this *bi-foldness* lay, in this strange manner: "*where reason can revolt / without perdition* . . ."'. At this point Capell gives up the attempt ('*Davus sum, non Oedipus*'), but returns to define the '*inseparate*

thing' of line 152 as 'the speaker's union with Cressida, which he thought was inseparable, but finds now, by a fight commenc'd in his soul, that there is *division* made in it which is' both vast and imperceptible. 'This enigma he solves by calling for *instances*; and finds one in his heart which tells him that Cressida is still his, and so no separation; another in his remembrance of what had but just pass'd, that contradicts his heart and makes division unmeasurable. Passion, labouring to express itself strongly, is the cause of this intricacy, and withal of that beautiful pleonasm at the speech's conclusion, which sets Diomed's conquest in a light so disgustful.'

47 On Arachne's woof see Ovid, *Metamorphoses* VI, 1–145.

48 Aristotle on hyperbole: *Rhetoric*, 1413a28ff.

49 On the unreliability of witches see, e.g., Reginald Scot, *The Discoverie of Witchcraft* (1584), Book XIII, ch. 15: 'How men have been abused with words of equivocation . . .', and *Macbeth*, 1.3.130ff, with editorial annotations.

50 See, e.g., Joseph Fontenrose, *The Delphic Oracle; Its Responses and Operations* (Berkeley, Cal., 1978); M.P. Nilsson, *Cults, Myths, Oracles and Politics in Ancient Greece* (Lund, 1951); H.W. Parke and D.E.W. Wormell, *The Delphic Oracle*, 2nd ed. (Oxford, 1956).

51 See Vickers 1973, pp. 328–36.

52 A cipher is a zero, which increases the value of the figures preceding it, as the Chorus says in *Henry V*:

And let us, ciphers to this great
　accompt,
On your imaginary forces work.
　　　　　　　　(*Prol.* 17)

The Riverside edition glosses Polixenes' 'cipher' as 'i.e. having no value in itself, yet capable of multiplying the value of the numbers that stand before it'.

53 For commentary on the affected style of this scene see Vickers 1968, pp. 422–5.

54 These are the annotations in the Riverside edition of G.B. Evans (Boston, 1974). More detail in the New Arden edition of J.H. Pafford (London, 1963).

55 See Brian Vickers, 'Analogy Versus Identity: The Rejection of Occult Symbolism, 1580–1680', in B. Vickers (ed.) *Occult and Scientific Mentalities in the Renaissance* (Cambridge, 1984), pp. 95–163.

56 *William Shakspere's Small Latine & Lesse Greeke*, 2 vols. (Urbana, Ill., 1944, 1966), especially Vol. II, chs. 38–41, pp. 239–416; page-references incorporated in the text. It is disappointing that neither of the full-length editions of *Love's Labour's Lost* so far published, by R.W. David for the New Arden edition (1951) and G.R. Hibbard for the New Oxford edition (1990) makes use of Baldwin, a mine of information on Elizabethan grammar schools and the teaching of Latin, logic, and rhetoric.

57 See, e.g., the influential Spanish humanist Vives, in *De tradendis disciplinis* (1531), Book IV, ch. iv, describing *imitatio* as 'the fashioning of a certain thing in accordance with a proposed model'. Vives lays down several cautions: 'what is imitated always remains behind the original', so 'the more models we have and the less likeness there is between them, the greater is the progress of eloquence'. To 'attain good imitation there is need of a quick and keen judgment, as well as a certain natural and hidden dexterity'. Successful imitation reveals 'the goodness of the natural disposition', unimaginative copying shows 'slowness of judgment', while too close imitation results in theft. The crucial point is that by imitating other authors, a writer develops his own style. This whole chapter expresses an important part of Renaissance literary theory, pedantically invoked by Holofernes: *Vives on Education*, tr. Foster Watson (Cambridge, 1913), pp. 189–200.

58 Jonson, *Works* (ed. cit.), Vol. VIII, pp. 635–40. On the two senses of imitation in the Renaissance see, e.g., B. Weinberg, *A History of Literary Criticism in the Italian Renaissance*, 2 vols. (Chicago, 1961): the Platonic–Aristotelian concept involves *mimesis* of an object or event in the external world (vol. 1, pp. 24–6, 51, 60–62, 117, etc.), and the 'Ciceronian' or 'Horatian' one involves *imitatio* of a literary model (vol. 1, pp. 60–62, 91, 100–104, 117, 146–7, etc.).

59 See, e.g., Sister Miriam Joseph, *Shakespeare's Use of the Arts of Language* (New York, 1947), on 'Vices of Language', pp. 64–78, 299–304.

60 Evans cites in a note here Derrida's claim that writing precedes thought as an '"arche-writing . . . which I continue to call writing only because it essentially communicates with the vulgar concept of writing"' (p. 228, n. 4). — 'O base and obscure vulgar!', as Armado scornfully exclaims (*Love's Labour's Lost*, 4.1.67).

Chapter Four: New Historicism

1 *Of the Laws of Ecclesiastical Polity*, I.i, in, e.g., abridged ed. A.S. McGrade and Brian Vickers (London, 1975) pp. 107–108.

2 Louis Montrose accords the priority to Michael McCanles in an essay for *Diacritics* in 1980: Montrose 1989, p. 32 n. 6.

3 See, e.g., Donald Kelley, *Foundations of Modern Historical Scholarhip. Language, Law, and History in the French Renaissance* (New York, 1970), pp. 4–8.

4 I have read, and shall probably refer to, the following works (for full titles see the bibliography): Montrose 1986; Howard 1986; Cohen 1987; Pechter 1987; Fowler 1988; Lentricchia 1988; Veeser 1989 — incorporating the essays designated in the bibliography

as Lentricchia 1989 (reprinting Lentricchia 1988), Montrose 1989, Gallagher 1989, Fineman 1989, Newton 1989, Graff 1989, Thomas 1989, Pecora 1989; Spivak 1989, White 1989; Felperin 1990; Barton 1991.

5 Montrose 1986, pp. 7 (n. 4), 11; Montrose 1989, pp. 18, 25: substituting 'commodified' for 'future-oriented'. Perhaps 'futures' in the stock exchange sense would be more appropriate? New Historicism, Deconstruction, Cultural Materialism, could be quoted alongside 'forward trading' in copper, gold, pork bellies.

6 See Barzun 1974. Other writers have commented on New Historicism as 'one merchandisable rubric amongst others in the not so free marketplace of academic ideas...' (Fineman 1989, p. 51), or as 'the latest fad. . . . (At least it is not advertised as tasting great or being less filling.)': Thomas 1989, p. 187.

7 Frank Lentricchia has over-trumped that move, finding Greenblatt to have the same basic attitude to literature as Hippolyte Taine (Lentricchia 1988, pp. 86–90), as if to say 'New Presbyter is but old priest writ large'.

8 This charge has been made by Howard Felperin, a deconstructionist (Felperin 1990, pp. 183, 188–9), and by any number of embittered feminists: see my Epilogue below, pp. 433ff).

9 So Montrose concedes that 'recent theories of textuality have argued persuasively that the referent of a linguistic sign cannot be fixed; that the meaning of a text cannot be stabilized. At the same time', he defensively adds, 'writing and reading are always historically and socially determinate events, performed *in* the world and *upon* the world by gendered individual and collective human agents'. Unconcerned by the incompatibility of these two positions, he summarises: 'We may simultaneously acknowledge the

theoretical indeterminacy of the signifying process and the historical specificity of discursive practices — acts of speaking, writing, and interpreting': Montrose 1989, p. 23. But what if all the 'gendered individuals' you study, apart from the recent few who have read and believed Derrida, regard their discursive practices as in fact determinate, reliably able to communicate meaning and purpose? And what if they have good reasons for thinking so? For a similar attempt to reconcile divergent positions see Felperin 1990, pp. vi–xii.

10 See, e.g., Fowler 1988, p. 968; Gallagher 1989, p. 43: 'in the mid-seventies... Michel Foucault's work appeared [in English], addressing exactly the issues that preoccupied us'. Victoria Kahn has commented on the New Historicist 'obligatory citations' of Foucault as 'establishing a shared sense of obligatory critical reading as well as a store-house of commonly accepted conclusions. (Hence a reference to Foucault is taken to be sufficient to establish the existence of specifically modern "techniques of the subject" or of a specifically bourgeois form of subjectivity)': review in *Shakespeare Quarterly* 38 (1987): p. 527. Later she describes 'the ambiguities of some New Historical work' as being 'due in part to the overwhelming authority of Foucault', the 'historical fuzziness' produced by his thesis about 'the death of the author' resulting in a 'dehistoricized' view of the past (p. 530).

11 See, e.g., Montrose, 'Gifts and Reasons: The Context of Peele's *Araygnment of Paris*', ELH 47 (1980): pp. 433–61, and '"Eliza, Queene of Shepheardes", and the Pastoral of Power', *English Literary Renaissance* 10 (1980): pp. 153–82.

12 See, e.g., Said 1983, p. 221, on Foucault taking 'a curiously passive and sterile view... of how and why power is gained, used, and held onto', a criticism developed further

on pp. 244–6; and Lentricchia 1988, pp. 30–31, 67–70, 74–86, especially p. 69: 'Foucault's theory of power, because it gives power to anyone, everywhere, at all times, and to no one, nowhere, no time, provided a means of resistance but no real goals for resistance . . . making resistance ever-possible and ever-meaningless', a theory that 'courts a monolithic determinism' and hence 'despair' (p. 70). It is significant that Lentricchia repeatedly applies the term 'paranoid' (pp. 31, 68, 92), and judges Foucault's system 'the most thoroughgoing argument that I have read against Marx's hope for radical social change' (p. 86), a 'depressing message' (p. 92). Cf. also Frederick Crews on Foucault's switch, after 1968, to 'more drastic Nietzschean "genealogies" reducing all truth claims to exercises of power. The attractive new ingredient in Foucault's thought was Sixties paranoia toward the all-hidden, all-powerful oppressors whom he never attempted to identify': Crews 1986, p. 177 n. 11.

13   See the confrontation (in 1971) between Foucault and Noam Chomsky for a Dutch TV series on contemporary philosophy, in Fons Elders (ed.), Reflexive Water. The Basic Concerns of Mankind (London, 1974): 'Human Nature: Justice versus Power', pp. 135–197, especially pp. 174–188, and Said 1983, pp. 245–6.

14   Veeser thinks, for instance, that 'humanists' have aspired to 'the norm of disembodied objectivity' (Veeser 1989, p. ix), an unrecognisable claim; that 'conventional scholars' have built up a 'profoundly anti-intellectualist ethos', and that New Historicism is 'the first successful counterattack in decades' on 'this quasi-monastic order. In response, the platoons of traditionalists have predictably rushed to their guns' (the first we have heard of armed monasteries); and that those who comment on the 'note found among Nietzsche's papers to the effect that

"I have lost my umbrella"' — that is, Derrida — can be included among New Historicists (p. xi). Veeser, master of the muddled metaphor, describes the notions of 'autonomous self and text' as 'mere holograms, effects that intersecting institutions produce' (p. xiii); speculates on 'the degree to which a text successfully erases its practical social function' (p. xi) — so how would you know? and reports that 'New Historicism . . . has had to plunge ahead just to keep itself erect' (ibid.). Veeser is not in a strong position to criticise journalists (p. x).

15   See, e.g., J. Goldberg, James I and the Politics of Literature (Baltimore, Md., 1983); S. Orgel, 'The Royal Theatre and the Role of King', in G.F. Lytle and S. Orgel (edd.), Patronage in the Renaissance (Princeton, N.J., 1981), pp. 261–73, and 'Making Greatness Familiar' in D.M. Bergeron (ed.), Pageantry in the Shakespearean Theater (Athens, Ga., 1985), pp. 22–23.

16   Joseph Conrad, Under Western Eyes, ed. J. Hawthorn (Oxford, 1983), p. 294.

17   One of the few critics to have commented on the anachronisms in New Historicist (and Cultural Materialist) literary theory is Richard Levin. See Levin 1990b, a concise account of five such fallacies, totalising claims that Elizabethan dramatists did not use characters as foils; that the Renaissance did not have a concept of theatrical illusion, had no category of literature, did not connect gender with biology, and had no conception of the self as autonomous and unified. These are transparent examples of projecting late twentieth-century categories backwards.

18   The sub-title of Greenblatt's latest collection of essays (Greenblatt 1990) is 'Essays in Early Modern Culture'. To some readers 'early modern' might seem just a neutral historiographical term, but for others it already carries an ideological significance. Derek Attridge recently

commented approvingly on a book he was reviewing that in its title 'the term "Renaissance" is displaced by "Early Modern Europe"', implying a tension between an encomiastic and an objective approach, between . . . a Eurocentric and a global perspective, and between a cyclical and a linear view of history. In spite of the parturitive metaphor, "Renaissance" points, with a few notable exceptions, to male achievements within the dominant social and economic class; "early modern" opens up a much wider, and less immediately glamorous, field': *Renaissance Quarterly* 40 (1987), pp. 810–11. This distinction is ideologically, rather than rationally motivated. I know of no serious scholar who uses the term 'Renaissance' with encomiastic, Eurocentric, cyclical, patriarchal, or glamorous connotations, but I look forward to new historical work embodying all the opposite qualities.

19 In his first paragraph Burckhardt writes that he is 'treating of a civilization which is the mother of our own, and whose influence is still at work on us': *The Civilization of the Renaissance in Italy*, tr. S.G.C. Middlemore (London, 1965), p. 1. For critiques of Burckhardt see, e.g., Johan Huizinga, 'The Problem of the Renaissance' in *Men and Ideas. History, the Middle Ages, the Renaissance*, tr. J.S. Home and H. van Marle (New York, 1959), pp. 243–287; E.H. Gombrich, *In Search of Cultural History* (Oxford, 1969); and Robert Klein, 'Burckhardt's Civilization of the Renaissance Today' in *Form and Meaning. Essays on the Renaissance and Modern Art*, tr. M. Jay and L. Wieseltier (New York, 1979), pp. 25–42.

20 But perhaps this is just a consequence of the Foucauldian influence rooting New Historicism inescapably in the present. Perhaps the New Historicist medievalist sees the Middle Ages rather as the source of the problems of the modern world, while the New Historicist working on the eighteenth century attaches blame to the Augustans. . . .

21 See Pecora 1989, also A. Biersack, 'Local Knowledge, Local History: Geertz and Beyond', in Lynn Hunt (ed.), *The New Cultural History* (Berkeley, Cal., 1989), pp. 72–96.

22 Yet, surprisingly enough, Geertz goes on to deny cultural interpretation any integrative or cumulative dimension: 'Rather than following a rising curve of cumulative findings, cultural analysis breaks up into a disconnected yet coherent sequence of bolder and bolder sorties . . .' (p. 25). This strange abandoning of cultural analysis as being 'inherently incomplete', producing only more precise disagreement, has not been taken up by the New Historicists, so I shall not discuss it further, only recording my disagreement with it.

23 In a recent essay Greenblatt quotes this remark by Cohen and finds it 'fascinating . . . that concerns like these should have come to seem bizarre . . .' (Greenblatt 1990, p. 169). But he does not answer Cohen's critique of the uses to which such material is put.

24 Review in *Shakespeare Quarterly*, 38 (1987): pp. 249–53, at p. 251.

25 Bourdieu, *Outline of a Theory of Practice*, tr. R. Nice (Cambridge, 1977), p. 195. See also Bourdieu's essay 'Symbolic Capital', *Critique of Anthropology* 4 (1979): pp. 77–85. Two French commentators note that 'Bourdieu désigne par "capital symbolique" les propriétés matérielles lorsqu'elles sont perçues et appropriées comme des propriétés de distinction (l'appartenance à tel club de golf, etc.)': Ferry and Renaut 1985, p. 213 note.

26 See G.G. Smith (ed.), *Elizabethan Critical Essays*, 2 vols. (Oxford, 1904, 1964), 1. p. 201 and 2. p. 148, which gives the correct reference to Aristotle's *Rhetoric*: 3.11.2, not 33.2.2., as Greenblatt has it.

27 Sidney 1965, pp. 137–8 and note

p. 226, defining it as 'the power of representing the subject matter clearly', and referring 'not to the words used in presenting the subject but to the vivid mental apprehension of things themselves'. For Scaliger, see *Poetices Libri Septem* (Lyon, 1561; facs.ed., Stuttgart, 1987), iii, 27; p. 116.

28 See L.G. Salingar, '*King Lear*, Montaigne and Harsnett', in Salingar, *Dramatic Form in Shakespeare and the Jacobeans* (Cambridge, 1986), p. 114.

29 See Greenblatt 1988, pp. 133–4, and 138, where the Duke in *Measure for Measure*, fusing 'strategies of statecraft and religion', is said to be an emblem of Shakespeare.

30 See N.J. Rigaud, 'L'homosexualité féminine dans *A mad couple . . .*', *Bulletin de la société d'études anglo-américaines des XVIIe et XVIIIe siècles* 20 (1985): pp. 23–36. I thank Ian Maclean for drawing my attention to this essay. See also his stimulating study of Michel de Pure's *La Prétieuse*, 'La voix des précieuses et les détours de l'expression', in *Présences Féminines. Littérature et Société au XVIIe Siècle Français*, ed. I. Richmond and C. Venesoen (Paris–Seattle–Tübingen, 1987), pp. 41–71. Brome's play is available in *Six Caroline Plays*, ed. A.S. Knowland (London, 1962).

31 *Women and the English Renaissance. Literature and the Nature of Womankind, 1540–1620* (Urbana, Ill., and Brighton, 1984). One critic rightly hails this book for collecting 'an extraordinary range of materials that are coherently assembled, especially in relation to the central problematic of female transvestism' (Cohen 1987, pp. 25–6). By the same token, its complete absence from Jean Howard's study of cross-dressing in the Renaissance (Howard 1988), seems like an act of disapproving feminist censorship.

32 Greenblatt cites Ian Maclean's outstandingly well-informed and lucid study, *The Renaissance Notion of Woman* (Cambridge, 1980) for the claim that sixteenth- and seventeenth-century physicians 'agreed that male and female sexual organs were fully homologous', so that the clitoris could be aligned with the penis (pp. 79, 83). However, reference to the passage in Maclean's book cited (p. 33) shows him in fact reporting that the difficulties experienced by Falloppio's attempt to make a one-to-one comparison were so great that, 'by the end of the sixteenth century, most anatomists abandon this parallelism'. *Caveat lector Greenblatti!*

33 Maclean, *op.cit.*, p. 32.

34 So Fineman 1989 complains that 'it seems clear that it is Shakespeare's literary text that controls Greenblatt's reading of the history of medicine, and that, correlatively, it is not the case that the history of medicine opens up, on this reading, a novel way to read Shakespeare' (p. 75).

35 See *Shakespeare: The Critical Heritage, Vol. 2, 1693–1733* (London and Boston, 1974), pp. 458, 507–508: Theobald got his knowledge from Warburton, whose copy he borrowed. The most accessible modern presentation of the echoes from Harsnett is in Kenneth Muir's New Arden edition of *King Lear* (London, 1963 ed.), pp. 253–6; also Muir 1961, pp. 147–161.

36 Muir's list includes 'bo-peep', 'neather-stocks' (once elsewhere in Shakespeare), '*hysterica passio*', 'vaunt-courier', 'the prince of darkness', 'star-blasting', 'pue', 'Frateretto' and the other devil's names, 'propinquity', 'auricular', 'gaster', 'asquint', and much else: Muir 1961, pp. 147–161.

37 *New York Review of Books*, 21 November 1991, p. 17. In a footnote Wills cites 'comic references to exorcism in *King Lear*, as in *The Taming of the Shrew* and *Twelfth Night*', observing that 'Greenblatt does not notice that "exorcism" in Shakespeare does not always refer to dispossession. It can mean

"conjuration" (*All's Well*, 5.3.304–6, *2 Henry VI* 1.4.4., *Julius Caesar* 2.1.323–4)'.

38 One essay comments on a sermon in which Hugh Latimer records how he once comforted a pregnant woman who had been sentenced to death for killing one of her children. The woman became apprehensive that she 'would die without being "churched" — that is', Greenblatt glosses, 'without the Catholic rite of purification . . . after child-birth (or menstruation) to cleanse the woman of the stain associated with any blood or discharge' (Greenblatt 1988, pp. 129–30). Greenblatt describes this as a Catholic rite; to Latimer it was 'a doctrinal error': but the Church of England went its own way, including in the Book of Common Prayer a service for the churching of women which exists to this day. Subsequently (p. 132) Greenblatt mistakenly links this practice with Hermione's complaint (in *The Winter's Tale*, 3.2.103–4), that Leontes has denied her 'the child-bed privilege'. Elsewhere Greenblatt refers to the fact that 'between 1560 and 1620 torture was regularly used in the interrogation of Catholics accused of treason' (Greenblatt 1990, p. 13): alas, not only catholics.

39 See Brian Vickers, '"The Power of Persuasion": Images of the Orator, Elyot to Shakespeare', in J.J. Murphy (ed.), *Renaissance Eloquence* (Berkeley, Cal., 1983), pp. 411–35.

40 See, e.g., Vickers 1968, pp. 426–7.

41 See the classic essay by R.S. Crane, 'The Houyhnhnms, the Yahoos, and the History of Ideas', in J.A. Mazzeo (ed.), *Reason and the Imagination* (London, 1962), pp. 231–53.

42 Notes *ad loc.* in *The Complete Works of Shakespeare*, ed. David Bevington, 3rd ed. (Glenview, Ill., 1980), p. 1512, from Charles Frey, 'The Tempest and the New World', *Shakespeare Quarterly* 30 (1979): pp. 29–41, at p. 34.

43 Review *cit.* in note 23 above, p. 250.

44 In Kinney (ed.), *Rogues, Vagabonds & Sturdy Beggars. A New Gallery of Tudor and Early Stuart Rogue Literature*, 2nd ed. (Amherst, Mass., 1990), p. 1.

45 D.B. Quinn (ed.), *The Roanoke Voyages, 1584–1590*, 2 vols. (London, 1955). Harriot's *True Report* is in Vol. I, pp. 314–87: page-references incorporated into the text, prefixed by 'H.' I have modernised u/v and i/j spellings. The *Report* is also found in editions of Hakluyt's *Voyages*, such as the old 'Everyman' edition, 8 vols. (London, n.d.) VI, pp. 164–96.

46 I quote, as Greenblatt does, from Machiavelli, *The Prince and the Discourses*, intro. M. Lerner (New York, 1950), reprinting the Detmold translation, p. 146; subsequent page-references incorporated into the text.

47 See Livy, I.xviii–xxi: in the translation by Aubrey de Sélincourt, *The Early History of Rome* (Harmondsworth, 1960), pp. 37–40. According to Livy, Numa gave Rome 'a second beginning, this time on the solid basis of law and religious observance', since war 'was no civilizing influence, and the proud spirit of his people could be tamed only if they learned to lay aside their swords'. The most effective way of dealing with such a 'rough and ignorant mob' was 'to inspire them with the fear of the gods', and to facilitate this he invented the story that 'he was in the habit of meeting the goddess Egeria by night, and that it was her authority which guided him' in establishing rites, priests, a cult, and an ethos of oath-keeping and peacefulness. The result was an exemplary period of law and order. Note that Livy, no less than Machiavelli, says nothing about this forming the origin of religion. Does Greenblatt seriously think that classical and Renaissance authors know no better than this?

48 *Francesco Guicciardini: The Historian's Craft* (Toronto, 1977), pp. 82–5. Phillips is quoting his 'Considerazioni sulle Discorsi di Machiavelli'.

49 See, e.g., Richard Westfall, 'Scientific Patronage: Galileo and the Telescope', *Isis* 76 (1985): pp. 18–22; Robert S. Westman, 'The Astronomer's Role in the Sixteenth Century: A Preliminary Study', *History of Science* 18 (1980): pp. 105–47; Mario Biagioli, 'Galileo's system of patronage', *History of Science* 28 (1990): pp. 1–62.

50 For a useful and well-illustrated survey, see Helen Wallis, *Raleigh & Roanoke. The First English Colony in America, 1544–1590* (Raleigh, NC., 1988), the catalogue of a joint exhibition organised by the British Library and the North Carolina Museum of History, March 8–June 6, 1985. For White's graphic work, including many drawings and a remarkably accurate map of Virginia, see pp. 49–73; for Harriot's work in geography and navigation, pp. 74–81.

51 John W. Shirley, *Thomas Harriot: A Biography* (Oxford, 1983): page-references incorporated into the text. Professor Shirley had earlier edited *Thomas Harriot. Renaissance Scientist* (Oxford, 1974), in which seven writers make good Harriot's claim to be among the outstanding Renaissance scientists in mathematics, astronomy, and navigation.

52 Greenblatt records that his parents were 'first-generation Americans born in Boston to poor Jewish immigrants from Lithuania' (Greenblatt 1990, p. 6). My ancestors were originally Scottish, who emigrated to Ireland looking for work, but arrived during the great potato famine. Moving on to Wales, they were in time to help open up the coalmines which made so much profit for the lucky few. Where does either of us really belong, 'by right'?

53 Levin 1979, pp. 85–102.

54 See, e.g., G. Bullough (ed.), *Narrative and Dramatic Sources of Shakespeare*, Vol. 4 (London, 1962), pp. 155–432, or the 'New Arden' edition by A.R. Humphreys.

55 *The Boke Named the Governour*, ed. H.H.S. Croft, 2 vols. (London, 1883), II. 406–408. An early (and somewhat bizarre) instance of the disguised ruler moving among his people is Saturninus in *Titus Andronicus*, 4.4.73–7.

56 Dr. Johnson recorded that 'many readers lament to see Falstaff so hardly used by his old friend. But if it be considered that the fat knight has never uttered one sentiment of generosity, and with all his power of exciting mirth has nothing in him that can be esteemed, no great pain will be suffered from the reflection that he is compelled to live honestly, and maintained by the king with a promise of advancement when he shall deserve it'. *Shakespeare: The Critical Heritage, vol. 5: 1765–1774* (London 1979), p. 122. See also ibid. pp. 123–5 for Johnson's marvellous valedictory note on Falstaff, expressing warm affection while preserving clear-headed moral judgment.

57 This is surely a commonplace in *Henry IV* criticism; but see, e.g., Vickers 1968, pp. 113–9.

58 Bradley's essay, 'The Rejection of Falstaff' is collected in his *Oxford Lectures on Poetry* (London, 1909). For Morgann's *Essay on the Dramatic Character of Sir John Falstaff* (1777) and some extremely able refutations of it, see *Shakespeare: The Critical Heritage*, Vol. 6, 1774–1801 (London, 1981), pp. 21–3, 164–80, 326–7, 440–6, 469–79, 490–9. On the continuing trend to see Hal as a 'killjoy' in rejecting Falstaff, see Richard Dutton's excellent survey of modern criticism on 'The Second Tetralogy' in Wells 1990, pp. 337–80, at p. 359; and *ibid.*, pp. 361–2, for anti-militarist reactions to *Henry V* following the first world war.

59 In an essay written about ten years afterwards Greenblatt reaffirms his belief that 'the sites of resistance in Shakespeare's second tetralogy are *coopted* in the plays' ironic affirmation' of kingship (Greenblatt 1990, p. 165; my italics). 'Shakespeare', he

claims, 'shows that the triumph rests upon a claustrophobic narrowing of pleasure, a hypocritical manipulation of appearances, and a systematic betrayal of friendship . . .'. These 'subversive perceptions', however, 'remain within the structure of the play', are thus 'contained', 'indeed serve to heighten a power they would appear to question' (*ibid.*). A decade has only strengthened his sense of the rightness of his interpretation. — The word I have italicised, 'coopted', has taken on a new meaning in some critical circles. As Gerald Graff observes, it was 'in the 1960s that the word "co-opt" in the derogatory sense of neutralize or disarm first entered the language', where it now means ' "to take over; secure for oneself" ', as in the assimilation of ' "an independent minority . . . into an established group or culture . . . *forced to adopt its standards*" ': Graff 1989, pp. 169–70. This will be a valuable addition to New Historicist vocabulary.

60 Lentricchia, for instance, has pointed out that in Greenblatt's essay on 'Marlowe, Marx, and Anti-Semitism' (reprinted in Greenblatt 1990, pp. 40–58), 'even if you've read no Marx at all you see, in the very passages that Greenblatt deploys to make his political point, that Marx is saying something else. The Jew is not a "universal phenomenon", to cite Greenblatt's curtailment of Marx' — the passage Greenblatt quotes omitting this key point — 'but a "universal *anti-social* element". And he is a "universal *anti-social* element" not for all time but for the "*present time*", the time of capital and Christianity which he represents. What is historically specific in Marx' and 'always clear . . . — the antisocial is the undesirable condition of society', is generalised and blurred by Greenblatt to make his Foucauldian case. See Lentricchia 1988, p. 99; 1989, p. 240, with further details of Greenblatt's misreading of Marx's *Eighteenth Brumaire*. Anne Barton,

having shown how Greenblatt distorts *The Tempest* so as to indict it of colonialism, has commented that in the Introduction to *Learning to Curse* (Greenblatt 1990, pp. 11–15) 'a similar distortion of the evidence in order to convict an imperialist can be seen'. Quoting Edmund Scott's *Exact Discourse of . . . the East Indians* (1606) from the Hakluyt Society edition of 1943, Greenblatt reproduces a horrific passage describing how Scott and his men tortured and finally killed a Chinese goldsmith. Greenblatt denounces the editor for having praised Scott's endurance in the face of a long and violent attack by the Chinese, their commercial rivals in Java — 'the moral stupidity of this drivel', Greenblatt proposes, 'obviously reflects the blind patriotism of a nation besieged' (*sc.*, I suppose, England, in 1943) — and says that he 'makes no direct comment on this passage' (Greenblatt 1990, p. 12). Yet, as Barton shows, the Hakluyt Society editor 'does in fact deplore "these barbarous proceedings" in a note appended to the passage itself. More important, however, is the fact that by severing the episode from its context, and also using an old, inaccurate edition instead of the widely available facsimile (1973), Greenblatt has turned Scott into a "sadist" without trying to investigate what might impel a man who was not a psychopath to countenance . . . an act of such appalling cruelty. What Scott and the other employees of the East India Company in Java did to their Chinese prisoner was inexcusable. It is not, however, once returned to its place in Scott's narrative, inexplicable' (Barton 1991, p. 52). As she shows, this act is the climax to a horrific siege, and an explicit retaliation by the English party on the Chinese for having burned most of their men alive — a passage omitted by the Hakluyt editor, and so by Greenblatt. The revenge thus had a 'horrible symmetry', and (another detail omitted by Greenblatt, ever willing to indict Europeans) it was 'overseen and in part directed by officers of the Javan king' (*ibid.*). For her account of 'dubious tactics' in other historical essays by Greenblatt see *ibid.*, pp. 51–4. Finally, for the distortions (due to an *a priori* Foucauldian conception of the self rather than, as here, manipulation of a historical document) in Greenblatt's essay 'Psychoanalysis and Renaissance Culture' (reprinted in Greenblatt 1990, pp. 131–145), see Levin 1990b, pp. 436–7, 442–4, 468–9. Readers of these essays must be on their guard.

61 *Ressentiment*, tr. W.W. Woldheim (from 'Das Ressentiment im Aufbau der Moral', in *Gesammelte Abhandlungen und Aufsätze*, Leipzig, 1915), ed. L.A. Coser (New York, 1961); page-references incorporated in the text.

Chapter Five   Psychocriticism

1 *Against the Self-Images of the Age* (London, 1971), pp. 7–8.
2 Walton 1990, p. 156.
3 See, e.g., MacIntyre 1971, p. 35; Crews 1986, pp. 21, 79–80; Gellner 1985, pp. 10, 130–1, 157–67, 197–9; Hans Eysenck, *Decline and Fall of the Freudian Empire* (New York, 1985); and Sulloway 1991, p. 261.
4 See Vickers 1989, p. 236. To sum up: in 1824 Hamlet and Ophelia were diagnosed as suffering from mania, melancholia and craziness; in 1829, Lear and Edgar: mania and demonia; 1880, Othello: epilepsy; 1917, Hamlet: hysteria; 1920, Lady Macbeth: hysteria; 1921, Shylock: anal eroticism; 1934, Timon: syphilis; 1942, Hamlet: the Ganser state; 1944, Lear: narcissism; 1960, Viola: hermaphroditism; Cordelia: incest; etc.
5 For Jones's essay see the *American Journal of Psychology* 2 (1910): pp. 72ff; for the book, see *Hamlet and*

Oedipus (London, 1949). Avi Erlich, in *Hamlet's Absent Father* (Princeton, N.J., 1978), challenged both Freud and Jones.
6 'Morose Ben Jonson', in *The Triple Thinkers* (New York, 1938).
7 For bibliographies of psychoanalytical Shakespeare criticism see Norman N. Holland, *Psychoanalysis and Shakespeare* (New York, 1964); David Willbern, 'William Shakespeare: A Bibliography of Psychoanalytic and Psychological Criticism, 1964–1975', *International Review of Psycho-Analysis* 5 (1978): pp. 361–72, reprinted and updated to 1978 in Murray Schwarz and Coppélia Kahn (edd.), *Representing Shakespeare: New Psychoanalytic Essays* (Baltimore, Md., 1980), pp. 264–86.
8 Ruth Nevo, *Shakespeare's Other Language* (London: Methuen, 1987); Kay Stockholder, *Dream Works. Lovers and Families in Shakespeare's Plays* (Toronto: Toronto University Press, 1987); Marjorie Garber, *Shakespeare's Ghost Writers. Literature as Uncanny Causality* (London: Methuen, 1987); Stanley Cavell, *Disowning Knowledge in Six Plays of Shakespeare* (Cambridge: Cambridge University Press, 1987).
9 'Freud and the Idea of a Pseudo-Science', in R. Borger and F. Cioffi (eds.), *Explanation in the Behavioural Sciences* (Cambridge, 1970), pp. 471–99.
10 See Cioffi's review of Sulloway's book, 'Freud — New Myths to Replace the Old', *New Society* 50 (1979): pp. 503–504; and F.C. Crews, 'Beyond Sulloway's *Freud*: Psychoanalysis Minus the Myth of the Hero', in P.J. Clark and C. Wright (eds.), *Philosophy, Science and Psychoanalysis* (Oxford, 1986), repr. in, and quoted from, Crews 1986, pp. 88–111.
11 *Isis* 82 (1991): pp. 245–75. I am grateful to Professor Sulloway for sending me the typescript of his essay before publication.
12 Ellenberger 1970, pp. 480–4, and 'The Story of "Anna O.": A Critical

Review with New Data', *Journal of the History of the Behavioral Sciences* 8 (1972): pp. 267–79. As more material about Freud comes to light, his behaviour seems less and less like that of a man of science. The recently published *Clinical Diary of Sandor Ferenczi*, one of Freud's closest disciples, records his horror at Freud's disclosure in 1926 that 'he was uninterested in curing patients whom he regarded as "riffraff" (*Gesindel*)'. Freud's 'candid admission that he considered neurotics to be a rabble only good for supporting analysts financially was a blow from which Ferenczi never recovered'. Disillusioned, he came to see Freud's vanity, hypocrisy, insecurity, concluding in 1923 that 'if he had not been so bedazzled by Freud he would have realized that Freud's brilliant ideas were usually based only on a single case'. See Phyllis Grosskurth's review essay in the *New York Review of Books* for 8 December 1988, pp. 45–7.

13 Wilden, *System and Structure. Essays in Communication and Exchange* (London, 1972), pp. 289–301; Porter, *A Social History of Madness. Stories of the Insane* (London, 1987), pp. 146–66: 'Daniel Schreber: Madness, Sex and the Family', acknowledging his debt to the recent literature on Schreber's case (pp. 246–8), especially Morton Schatzman, *Soul Murder: Persecution in the Family* (London, 1973). Elsewhere Porter gives brief but penetrating evaluations of some other Freudian case-histories, notably 'Dora' (pp. 113–18), 'Little Hans' (p. 163), Freud's own psychoneurosis (pp. 214–22), and the 'Wolf Man' (pp. 223–8). His account of how Freud relentlessly seized on explanations in terms of the patient's infantile sexual neuroses, ignoring the family context (Little Hans's parents threatened to cut his penis off if he misbehaved; Dora was the pawn in an adultery exchange, her disgust being categorised as an 'unhealthy' reaction which actually showed her unconscious desire for the man; and so on) — all this more than justifies Porter's description of Freud as 'an extremely bad listener. He was totally selective, and his appropriation of his patients' stories for his own theoretical purposes was arguably more aggressive and insensitive than the stone-deafness of his predecessors' (p. 35).

14 See, e.g., C. Bernheimer and C. Kahane (eds.), *In Dora's Case* (New York, 1985, 1990; M. Sprengnether, *The Spectral Mother: Freud, Feminism, and Psychoanalysis* (Ithaca, N.Y., 1991); H.S. Decker, *Freud, Dora, and Vienna 1900* (New York, 1991).

15 As Crews records, he had previously been a Freudian, taken in by the 'self-validating doctrines' of 'a seductive dogma that had promised quick, deep knowledge', but which he came to see as 'a faith like any other', a 'doctrine that compels irrational loyalty' (pp. xi–xii). This collection of essays, dating from 1975 to 1985, Crews declares, is intended 'to spare students and others the intellectual befuddlement that I myself endured in my Freudian period. As a member of a society steeped in Freudian platitudes, I would like people to know that the guilt dispensed by psychoanalytic theorists to striving women and to the parents of homosexuals, "neurotics", and psychotics can be plausibly declined' (p. 41). To that guilt-stricken list we can now add, according to some psychoanalysts, cancer patients, who are responsible for their own ailment.

16 *The Freudian Slip. Psychoanalysis and Textual Criticism*, tr. K. Soper (Atlantic Highlands, N.J., 1976): see Grünbaum 1984, pp. 194–206.

17 'The Theory of Your Dreams', in R.S. Cohen and L. Landau (eds.), *Physics, Philosophy, and Psychoanalysis* (Dordrecht and Boston, 1983), pp. 51–71, at p. 69.

18 After a searching evaluation of the case against Freud made by Habermas, Ricoeur, Popper and

NOTES TO PAGES 278-284

others, Grünbaum examines in turn 'The Clinical Method of Psycho-analytic Investigation' (pp. 95–171) and 'The Cornerstone of the Psycho-analytic Edifice: Is the Freudian Theory of Repression Well Founded?' (pp. 173–266), with a synthesising 'Epilogue' (pp. 269–85). Crews judges that after Grünbaum's book 'psychoanalysis . . . stands irremedi-ably exposed as a speculative cult', and 'the wholesale debunking of Freudian claims, both therapeutic and theoretic, will be not just think-able but inescapable' (Crews 1986, p. 81).

19 On psychoanalysis as a self-perpetuating guild see Gellner 1985, pp. 9, 75–9, 94, 127–8; also Paul Roazen, *Freud and His Followers* (New York, 1975), and Janet Malcolm, *Psychoanalysis: The Impossible Profession* (New York, 1981).

20 On psychoanalysis as a belief-system offering salvation, with priests hav-ing pastoral duties, see Gellner 1985, pp. 25–6, 35, 37–43, 62, 109, 131–2, and Crews 1986, pp. 60, 75, 107. On its tendency to split into sects, with rival dogmas, see Crews 1986, p. 78 ('having been founded more on ecclesiastic than on scientific principles, Freud's movement has inevitably splintered into dogmatic sects . . .'), and Georg Weisz, 'Scientists and Sectarians: The Case of Psychoanalysis', *Journal of the History of the Behavioral Sciences* 11 (1975): pp. 350–64.

21 'Victims of Psychiatry', *New York Review of Books*, 23 January 1975, p. 17.

22 *Gulliver's Travels*, Preface; in *Works*, ed. H. Davis, vol. 11 (Oxford, 1959), pp. 6–7.

23 Karen Horney was a German–American doctor who, in the 1930s, expressed doubts about the male assumption behind psychoanalytical dogma: 'She challenged the formid-able phalanx of male analysts to provide convincing evidence to support central doctrines . . . as penis envy and the castration complex. Worse, she pointed out that even if penis envy were to be found to be inordinately prevalent among women it might simply be because the reality was that in the harsh, external world women were at a disadvantage, a social, cultural, economic and polit-ical disadvantage, when compared with men.' This introduction of socio-economic reality into the 'pure psychology' that Freud so often proclaimed (blind, perhaps, to the biogenetic basis of his theories: Sulloway 1983, pp. 425–6, 437–44, 487–8, 495) was not well received. Horney's call for psychoanalysis to be grounded on evidence, take greater account of reality, and 'accept the possibility that neurosis could occur without there being an unresolved Oedipal complex', these positive appeals were regarded as a threat to the discipline's very existence. She was denounced, accused of 'indulging in pathological narcissism', releas-ing her 'repressed anger' at male authority figures, and punished by being 'stripped of her status as a training analyst' at the New York Psychoanalytic Institute. This depressing story shows the dogmatic tendency in Freudianism, its intoler-ance of rival explanatory models. See Anthony Clare's review of Susan Quinn's book, *A Mind of Her Own: The Life of Karen Horney* (London, 1988), in *Times Literary Supplement*, 29 April 1988, p. 465.

24 A defence of Freud against charges of misogyny was provided by Juliet Mitchell, *Psychoanalysis and Feminism* (New York, 1974), but many fem-inists rejected her apologia. Among the influential works taking an op-posed view are Dorothy Dinnerstein, *The Mermaid and the Minotaur* (New York, 1976); Nancy Chodorow, *The Reproduction of Mothering* (Berkeley, Cal., 1982); Daniel Stern, *The First Relationship — Infant and Mother* (Cambridge, Mass., 1977), and *The Interpersonal World of the Infant* (New York, 1985). I am indebted here to Grosskurth 1991.

25　Nevo quotes from *Metaphor: A Psychoanalytic View* (Berkeley and Los Angeles, 1978).

26　I think in particular of *The Diall of Virtue. A Study of Poems on Affairs of State in the Seventeenth Century* (Princeton, N.J., 1963).

27　On the vogue for Greek romance in the Renaissance, and its use by Shakespeare, see, e.g., S.L. Wolff, *The Greek Romances in Elizabethan Prose Fiction* (New York, 1912; 1961); E.C. Pettet, *Shakespeare and the Romance Tradition* (London, 1949; 1970); Carol Gesner, *Shakespeare and the Greek Romance: A Study of Origins* (Lexington, Ky., 1970). Thomas Hägg, *The Novel in Antiquity* (Oxford, 1983) is the best modern introduction to the romance as a narrative genre (subject to some reservations expressed in my review for *Times Literary Supplement*, 20 April 1984, p. 427).

28　Critics continually apply this mode of enquiry to Shakespeare without any misgivings, although sometimes with bizarre results. In *As You Like It* Orlando, having triumphed in the wrestling, is so overwhelmed by Rosalind's beauty that he declares:

　　My better parts
　Are all thrown down, and that
　　which here stands up
　Is but a quintain, a mere lifeless
　　block.　　　　(1.2.238ff)

A quintain was a post, sometimes holding out a shield on a hinged arm, at which riders practising tilting directed their lances. According to Barbara Parker, however, the reference is to be understood as 'symbolically alluding to the "first death" in sin bequeathed to man in Eden. The block that "stands up" is a phallic pun affirming the sensual basis of [Orlando's] infatuation': *A Precious Seeing. Love and Reason in Shakespeare's Plays* (New York, 1987), p. 105. Unfortunately the critic has insinuated an allusion into the text without reading the rest of the line, where a 'mere lifeless block' would be a singularly inappropriate

description of a penis. (Not to mention original sin!)

29　Barzun 1974, p. 78; Crews 1986, p. 98.

30　Green, cit. Nevo 1987, p. 36.

31　Green, cit. *ibid.*, p. 56.

32　Credit for creating other characters in drama is freely given: thus Hamlet is said to have generated the Ghost (p. 46), and also created Ophelia (p. 49): an instance of bisexual creativity, perhaps.

33　Compare Nevo's comment on the dénouement in *Cymbeline*, when Posthumus' anguished lament on realising how much he has wronged Imogen is interrupted by a page-boy (Imogen in disguise, as we know and he doesn't) whom he strikes. This blow, to Nevo, is a 'therapeutic . . . acting out of aggression . . . an uninhibited action, . . . passionate, and this is a capacity that his masculinity needs as much as her femininity desires' (p. 90). The blow clears the air, 'defusing unconscious resentments which could fester and obstruct, functioning to liberate him from his fear of sexual inadequacy, her from her fear of sexual surrender' (p. 91). That explanation might seem to constitute an apology for wife-beating and a suggestion of sado-masochism, confusing sexuality and violence, but it is surprisingly blind to the dramatic context, in which Posthumus can have no idea that the page-boy is Imogen. It is depressing to note that Jung's concepts of Animus and Anima similarly posited a distinction between masculine and feminine in which men are characterised by *logos*, highly developed, and *eros*, less highly, while women are the reverse. But when *eros* possesses Animus, as Jung put it, ' "in vielen Fällen hat der Mann das Gefühl (und hat nicht ganz unrecht damit), dass einzig Verführung oder Verprügelung oder Vergewaltigung noch die nötige Ueberzeugungskraft hätten" ': *cit.* Ursula Baumgardt, *König Drosselbart und C.G. Jungs Frauenbild. Kritische*

Gedanken zu Anima und Animus (Olten, 1987), pp. 60–1. I feel sympathy for generations of women who have had to put up with the chauvinism of the founding fathers of psychoanalysis.

34 As a Renaissance scholar, Garber ought to have recorded that serious objections have been made to Freud's account of Leonardo, notably by Meyer Schapiro, 'Leonardo and Freud: An Art-Historical Study', *Journal of the History of Ideas* 7 (1956): pp. 147–78, reprinted in, and quoted from, P.O. Kristeller and P.P. Wiener (eds.), *Renaissance Essays* (New York, 1968). Freud analysed a dream of Leonardo's in which, as a baby lying in his cradle, a bird ('*nibbio*' in the Italian) inserted its tail in his mouth and struck him inside the lips. According to the German translation Freud was using, the bird was a vulture, and he interpreted its tail as a phallic symbol replacing the mother's breast, the whole forming a fantasy typical of passive homosexuals. The Egyptian hieroglyphic writing for 'mother', moreover, is a vulture; the vulture-headed goddess Mut is sometimes represented with a phallus; and for Freud the resemblance of 'Mut' and 'Mutter' could hardly be accidental (pp. 304–7) — to German speakers, at least. Unfortunately, Schapiro shows that '*nibbio*' actually means 'kite', not vulture; that Leonardo's interest in the kite bird derived from his scientific observations of natural mechanisms for flight; and that the motif of a child being kissed by bees, say, or having honey placed on its mouth, was an ancient aetiology for inspiration or excellence in some future career (pp. 308–15). As for Freud's speculations about Leonardo's childhood, Schapiro shows how several other alternative explanations 'were ignored by Freud because of his certitude about the vulture and its legend' (p. 314). Freud's theories about the significance of Saint Anne as a surrogate mother were disproved

by Schapiro, drawing on church history and art-history (pp. 315–36). Schapiro's judgment that Freud 'ignored the social and the historical where they are most pertinent' (p. 316) may stand as a valid comment on psychocriticism today, which also shares the 'weaknesses . . . found in other works by psychoanalysts in the cultural fields: the habit of building explanations of complex phenomena on a single datum and the too little attention given to history and the social situation' (p. 335). See also A.C. Elms, 'Freud as Leonardo: Why the First Psychobiography Went Wrong', *Journal of Personality* 56 (1988): pp. 19–40.

35 Johnson, *Observations on Macbeth* (1745), in *Shakespeare: The Critical Heritage, Vol. 3, 1733–1752* (London and Boston, 1975), p. 179; Scot, *Discoverie of Witchcraft* (1584), Book III, chs. 2, 9, ed. M. Summers (London, 1930; New York, 1972), pp. 25, 31; Burke, 'Witchcraft and Magic in Renaissance Italy', in Sydney Anglo (ed.), *The Damned Art. Essays in the Literature of Witchcraft* (London, 1970), pp. 32–52, at 37, 40, 49; *Hamlet*, 3.2.351.

36 First published in *Yale French Studies* 55–56 (1977): pp. 11–52; reprinted in *Literature and Psychoanalysis*, ed. Shoshana Felman (Baltimore, Md., 1982). Stockholder 1987, p. 245, quotes an interpreter of Lacan who sees Hamlet as 'liberated in death from "narcissistic attachment to the phallus", which subjects him to the other's desires': 'liberated' is nice.

37 I have not thought it worth while recapitulating large amounts of Lacanian theory to gloss Garber's text. For relatively comprehensible accounts see Wilden 1972, pp. 20–26, 260–94, 483–4; Bowie 1979, and Bowie, *Freud, Proust and Lacan. Theory As Fiction* (Cambridge, 1987), pp. 99–163; also Dews 1987, Frank 1989.

38 See, e.g., Stephen Heath, *The Sexual Fix* (London, 1982), commenting

on the cult of the penis-phallus in contemporary French sexological psychoanalysis (p. 81). One Lacanian describes '"the concept phallus [as] that from which is supported the desire of *both* the man *and* the woman"', both sexes focussing on it because of '"its possible erection, that is to say, to a visible manifestation of desire"' (p. 108). Heath sceptically comments that Lacanian psychoanalysts insist 'that the phallus is not the same as the penis (which nevertheless, as in the passage just cited, seems always to be popping up and giving the lie to such oily double talk . . .)' (*ibid.*). According to Wilden 1972 (pp. 20, 23, 268–9, 284, 286, 292), Lacan always insisted that he was referring to a symbolic, not a real object, but in some of the passages Wilden quotes it is hard to tell the difference, as when he defines the phallus as '"a signifier, the signifier of desire. . . . The phallus represents the intrusion of vital thrusting or growth as such . . ."' (p. 284). Wilden ultimately finds Lacan guilty of Freudian chauvinism (pp. 282, 290), indulging a 'metaphysics of the phallus' and making it a 'privileged object' (pp. 288, 287), so encouraging 'a new justification of patrocentrism and phallocentrism in France' (p. 281).

39 For an up-to-date idea of the actual philosophical preoccupations of Shakespeare's culture, which will confirm the vast distance between the public theatres and the philosophy schools, see *The Cambridge History of Renaissance Philosophy*, ed. Charles B. Schmitt and Quentin Skinner (Cambridge, 1988).

40 See R.H. Popkin, *The History of Scepticism from Erasmus to Spinoza* (rev. ed., Berkeley and Los Angeles, 1979); C.B. Schmitt, *Cicero Scepticus: A Study of the Influence of the 'Academica' in the Renaissance* (The Hague, 1972).

41 Scepticism is identified at various times with an impulse to 'annihilation', to a 'self-consuming disappointment that seeks world-consuming revenge' (p. 6), a 'fear of anxiety of inexpressiveness' (p. 9), a 'disgust with language' (p. 12), a 'refusal of the world in disgust' (p. 15). It is 'a male business', oddly enough, 'not a female business' (p. 16). It is an intimation of 'world catastrophe' first glimpsed in *Antony and Cleopatra*, and involving the rise of the new science, the 'attenuation or displacement of God', the 'attenuation' of Divine Right, and 'the shift from politically arranged to romantically desired marriage' (pp. 20–21), all these things. Scepticism offers the threat of being 'unknowable from outside' (p. 29), the power to 'excommunicate oneself from the community in whose agreement . . . words exist' (*ibid.*). Wittgenstein's notion of a private language is invoked to define scepticism as 'a form of narcissism . . . a kind of denial of an existence shared with others' (p. 143), which is subsequently identified with 'cannibalism' (p. 152). Scepticism can also be connected with fanaticism (p. 206), and nihilism (p. 208). This seems to me a purely private series of associations, lacking either coherence or a basis in the canon of sceptical texts.

42 See Margaret Loftus Ranald, *Shakespeare & His Social Context* (New York, 1987), pp. 5, 37.

43 Some critics are becoming extremely concerned with what might have happened on Othello's wedding night. A recent French study of feasts and festivity in Shakespeare alludes in passing to a theory that Othello's wedding night was interrupted three times, thus inducing in him sexual impotence, for which he compensates with the emotional equivalent of orgasm, the spasm of hysteria which makes him collapse 'en syncope'. See François Laroque, *Shakespeare et la Fête* (Paris, 1988), p. 254, citing J.-M. Maguin, *La nuit dans le théâtre de Shakespeare et de ses prédécesseurs* (Lille, 1988), Vol. I, p. 531, and P. Janton, 'Othello's

"weak function" ', *Cahiers élisabéthains* 7 (1975): pp. 47–50. See also M. Pryse, 'Lust for Audience: An Interpretation of *Othello*', *ELH* 46 (1976): pp. 461–78; T.G.A. Nelson and Charles Haines, 'Othello's unconsummated marriage', *Essays in Criticism* 33 (1983): pp. 1–18. So Iago's grudge, his wish to destroy Othello and Desdemona, his ruthless plotting, working on Othello until he begins to doubt his own sanity — all this was pure irrelevance on Shakespeare's part. Sufficient sexual motivation already existed to bring about Othello's crisis, and it only needs the right technical knowledge to identify the illness from which he suffers.

44   *Shakespeare: The Critical Heritage, Volume 2: 1693–1733*, ed. Brian Vickers (London, 1974), p. 28. Cavell's suggestion that Desdemona must mean by her wedding-sheets those stained with hymenal blood was anticipated by Lynda E. Boose, 'Othello's Handkerchief: "The Recognizance and Pledge of Love"', *English Literary Renaissance* 5 (1975): pp. 360–74, while his idea that Othello's murdering Desdemona was an attempt to undo his act of defloration was paralleled by Edward Snow, 'Sexual Anxiety and the Male Order of Things in *Othello*', *ibid.*, 9 (1980): 384–412. I am not accusing Cavell of plagiarism: the same Freudian approach inevitably results in massive repetition of the available interpretations.

45   Rymer, *op. cit.* in note 44, p. 54.

46   A feminist makes a more perceptive comment on Iago: 'With his power evaporated, philosophy repudiated, and guilt revealed, he has no reason to talk and nothing to say . . .': Neely 1980, p. 232.

47   Neely is again a better guide to Desdemona: 'Her healthy, casual acceptance of sexuality is evident in her banter with Iago (II.i. 109–64) and with the clown (III.iv.1–18), in her affirmation that she "did love the Moor, to live with him" (I.iii.248), and in her refusal to postpone consummation of "the rites for which I love him" (I.iii.257)': *ibid.*, p. 220.

48   Rymer, *op. cit.* in note 44, p. 37.

49   R.W. Dixon, writing to Gerard Manley Hopkins on 11 October 1881, commented on *The Ring and the Book* as marking 'a failure in Browning's power, which manifests itself in these ways. 1. Loss of form, with every kind of monstrosity. 2. The impotent remarking of particulars: as when he observes that the names of Wiseman, Newman, and Manning all contain the word man. 3. Preaching instead of teaching.' See C.C. Abbott (ed.), *The Correspondence of Gerard Manley Hopkins and Richard Watson Dixon* (London, rev. ed. 1955), p. 70.

50   In his chapter on *Coriolanus* (Cavell 1987, pp. 143–78) Cavell draws on earlier work (Adelman, 1978), to give a reading of the play largely in terms of Coriolanus' relationship with his mother (I discuss one aspect of his reading in chapter 7 below). For a corrective to this approach see my essay 'Coriolanus and the demons of politics', in Vickers 1989, pp. 135–93.

51   A useful starting point would be Himmelfarb 1987, especially ch. 2, 'Clio and the New History', pp. 33–46, and ch. 6, 'Case Studies in Psychohistory', pp. 107–20 (reviewing Isaac Kramnick, *The Rage of Edmund Burke* and Bruce Mazlish, *James and John Stuart Mill*). See also Barzun 1974, and David E. Stannard, *Shrinking History: On Freud and the Failure of Psychohistory* (New York and Oxford, 1980).

52   *Patterns of Intention. On the Historical Explanation of Pictures* (London, 1985), pp. 12–13. See also Grünbaum 1984, pp. 2–3. The categories were originally proposed by Wilhelm Windelband.

53   *Shakespearean Criticism*, ed. T.M. Raysor, 2 vols. (London, 1960), I, p. 198.

Chapter Six: Feminist Stereotypes

1   *Morality and Conflict* (Oxford, 1983), p. 7.

2   Elizabeth H. Hageman, Preface to 'Women in the Renaissance II', *English Literary Renaissance* 18 (1988): p. 3.

3   Bibliographies can be found in Lenz et al. 1980, pp. 314–36 and in the two special issues of *English Literary Renaissance*: 14 (1984): pp. 409–25 and 18 (1988): pp. 138–67. See now Philip C. Kolin, *Shakespeare and Feminist Criticism. An Annotated Bibliography and Commentary* (New York, 1991), which gives detailed summaries but avoids any form of evaluation.

4   See, e.g., the critical review by Anne Barton, *TLS* 24 Oct. 1975, p. 1295, and comments by Greene in Greene 1981, p. 42 n. 9. One recent writer finds it 'still inspiring' (Dollimore 1990, p. 416). See also Barton's review of books by Marilyn French and Coppélia Kahn, 'Was Shakespeare a Chauvinist?', *New York Review of Books*, 11 June 1981, pp. 20–22.

5   Novy's argument that 'we must demythologize [the] stereotypes' of Shakespeare as 'the uncritical adherent of the most conservative views of his time', together with its polar opposite of him 'as the universal genius who totally transcends all historical and psychological limitations' (p. 17) is well taken.

6   *The Crisis of the Aristocracy 1558–1641* (London, 1967; the abridged edition), p. 271.

7   The most penetrating review of Stone's book on the family was by Alan Macfarlane, in *History and Theory* 18 (1979): pp. 103–26. Other reviews made briefer, but collectively devastating criticisms: see E.P. Thompson, 'Happy Families', *New Society* 8 Sept. 1977, pp. 499–501; Keith Thomas, 'The Changing Family', *TLS* 21 Oct. 1977, pp.

1226–7; David Berkowitz, *Renaissance Quarterly* 32 (1979): pp. 396–403; Randolph Trumbach, *Journal of Social History* 13 (1979): pp. 131–42; Richard Vann, *Journal of Family History* 4 (1979): pp. 308–14.

8   The best single corrective to Stone is the admirably balanced synthesis by Keith Wrightson, *English Society. 1580–1680* (London, 1982). Important qualifications of Stone's thesis can be found in R.B. Outhwaite (ed.), *Marriage and Society. Studies in the Social History of Marriage* (London, 1981), especially the contributions by Outhwaite, Kathleen Davies, and Vivien Brodsky Elliott. A major source wilfully neglected by Stone (since it would have disproved his argument) is Alan Macfarlane, *The Family Life of Ralph Josselin, a Seventeenth-Century Clergyman. An Essay in Historical Anthropology* (Cambridge, 1970). See also Martin Ingram, *Church Courts, Sex and Marriage in England, 1570–1640* (Cambridge, 1987), pp. 30, 137–8, 141–4, 149, 160, 179 for explicit criticisms of Stone's thesis, and Ralph Houlbrooke, *The English Family, 1450–1700* (London, 1984), chapter eight.

9   See my essay, 'Lawrence Stone and the Myth of the Patriarch', forthcoming.

10   C.L. Powell, *English Domestic Relations 1487–1653. A Study of Matrimony and Family Life in Theory and Practice As Revealed By the Literature, Law, and History of the Period* (New York, 1917; repr. 1972); Kathleen M. Davies, 'The Sacred Condition of Equality — How Original Were Puritan Doctrines of Marriage?', *Social History* 5 (1977): pp. 563–80, reprinted in a slightly revised form (including a critique of Stone) as 'Continuity and Change in Literary Advice on Marriage', in Outhwaite 1981, pp. 58–80. Although she followed Powell in attributing these more enlightened attitudes to the Puritans, Juliet

Dusinberre gave ample evidence of attitudes to marriage in sixteenth- and seventeenth-century England which were nonpatriarchal, emphasising equality and partnership: see Dusinberre 1975, pp. 24, 41–4, 74–5, 82–4, 87, 90, 97–8, 100–102, 109–10, 127, 135. For other feminists aware of more positive Renaissance attitudes to the family see, e.g., Novy 1984, pp. 4–5, 61; Jardine 1983, pp. 42–3; Dreher 1986, pp. 29–35; Bean 1980, pp. 67ff.

11 Margaret J.M. Ezell, *The Patriarch's Wife. Literary Evidence and the History of the Family* (Chapel Hill, N.C., 1987).

12 P. Gartenberg and N.T. Whittemore, 'A Checklist of English Women in Print, 1475–1640', *Bulletin of Bibliography and Magazine Notes 34* (1977): pp. 1–13, could only list 62 women authors, while Patricia Crawford, 'Women's Published Writings 1600–1700', in Mary Prior (ed.), *Women in English Society 1500–1800* (London, 1985), pp. 211–82, identified nearly 300.

13 I was obviously too sanguine about feminists agreeing that Shakespeare presented rape as abhorrent. Catharine R. Stimpson, at least, argues that Lavinia in *Titus Andronicus*, like Lucrece in his narrative poem, represents a disapproving male attitude to '"the raped woman who must be punished"' (*cit.* R.S. White in Wells 1990, p. 188).

14 See, e.g., Vickers 1968, pp. 256–8.

15 Brian Vickers (ed.), *Shakespeare: The Critical Heritage*, vol. 5, p. 108.

16 As Howard delicately puts it, 'Sodomy haunts the fringes of Stubbes's text' (Howard 1988, p. 424). His *Anatomy of Abuses* (1583) is a hysterical fantasy on moralist traditions from the Church Fathers to the Reformation, in no way representative. For the Puritan diatribe see J.W. Binns, 'Women or Transvestites on the Elizabethan Stage?: An Oxford Controversy', in *Sixteenth Century Journal 2* (1974):

pp. 95–120. As for feminist critics (such as Jardine 1983, pp. 9–36) who argue that it was homoerotic passion that the boy actors aroused in their male audience, I am glad to agree with Jean Howard and Kathleen McLuskie that 'boy actors playing women must simply have been accepted in performance as a convention. Otherwise, audience involvement with dramatic narratives premised on heterosexual love and masculine / feminine difference would have been minimal': Howard 1988, pp. 419 note, 435.

17 For further comments on the risk of feminist Shakespeare criticism 'introducing reductive, allegorizing, binary oppositions', see Cohen 1987, p. 25. Another example of a simple dichotomising is Jacqueline Rose's essay on sexuality in *Hamlet* (Rose 1985), which takes T.S. Eliot to task for making Gertrude guilty of 'too much sexuality', supposedly writing a critique 'of *Hamlet* for its aesthetic failure and of Gertrude for being its cause' (pp. 95–103). But of course Eliot described the play as 'dealing with the effect of a mother's guilt upon her son' ('Hamlet', *Selected Essays* (London, 1951), pp. 143, 144), which, however, lacked 'an "objective correlative"'. His point was that 'Hamlet (the man) is dominated by an emotion which is . . . in *excess* of the facts as they appear', namely that 'his disgust is occasioned by his mother, but that his mother is not an adequate equivalent for it . . .' (p. 145). Eliot never accuses Gertrude of excessive sexuality, and Rose merely puts these words in his mouth. Nor does she observe that Hamlet's disgust is also directed against Claudius, 'the bloat king' with his 'reechy kisses, . . . paddling in your neck with his damn'd fingers'. Instead of a balanced assessment Rose reduces the whole play to a misogynistic fable, in which over and over, 'the woman is the cause', 'it is the woman who provokes a crisis', 'the woman becomes both scapegoat

and cause of the dearth or breakdown of (Oedipal) resolution...'. I am disappointed that some feminist critics need to scapegoat women in the plays then as a way of scape-goating men now.

18 This is an old-fashioned character study, isolating one personage from the play and following their appearance scene by scene. Surely modern Shakespeare criticism is capable of more complex analyses?

19 Citing Edith Williams, 'In Defense of Lady Macbeth', *Shakespeare Quarterly* 24 (1973): pp. 221–3.

20 Theodore Roszak, *cit.* Park 1980, p. 115.

21 The occasion which gave rise to this saying was a performance of the play at a provincial theatre in 1775 when the actor Cubit, due to play Hamlet, 'being seized with a sudden and serious illness in the dressing-room just before the play was going to begin', the manager asked the company 'to go through the play omitting the character of Hamlet; which being complied with it was afterwards considered by the bulk of the audience to be a great improvement!' (Frederick Harker, *TLS* 3 June 1939, p. 327, citing W.T. Parke's *Musical Memoirs* (1830).) A feminist-instigated performance of *Othello* without Iago 'were a tedious difficulty', but could no doubt be arranged.

22 *Reappraisals in History* (London, 1961), pp. 194–5.

23 Linda Bamber has questioned the appropriateness of this metaphor, 'whether or not Emilia is the fulcrum of the play, the point of view from which everything assumes its proper shape', commenting rather that 'Emilia is to *Othello* only what Macduff is to *Macbeth*: a glimpse of sanity from the horrid fascination of our madness. Neely's reading implies that we are to center the play on sanity, on Emilia, on the feminine. If we do, Othello is exasperating, his story tedious, and his death good riddance to bad rubbish'. But *Othello* 'does not balance on the emotional

clarity of its women, as the romantic comedies do. It is about confusion, not clarity; the interest is in the ignorant, erring, angry male, not in the knowing, right-feeling woman' (Bamber 1982, p. 13). For her pains Bamber has been accused by other feminists of having 'the dubious distinction of representing the acceptable face of feminist criticism for a number of male Shakespeareans': Thompson 1988, p. 84.

24 For an analysis of the epistemological manipulation by which Iago makes Othello see the opposite of the truth, see Vickers 1989, chapter 3, 'Shakespeare's Hypocrites', especially pp. 114–23.

25 Against Freud: Gohlke 1980, pp. 162f, 165f, 168f; Boose 1987, pp. 714–16, 720, 736. See also chapter 5, note 24.

26 Aristotle, *On the Generation of Animals*, 767b 9ff, 775a 15.

27 Levin 1988: a most searching article, which deals with several issues that I have not touched on.

Chapter Seven: Christians and Marxists

1 'Lay Sermons, I', from *The Statesman's Manual* (1816); in *Samuel Taylor Coleridge*, ed. H.J. Jackson (London, 1985), p. 661. Coleridge's contrast is between allegory and the symbol, which is 'characterized by a translucence of the special in the individual or of the general in the especial or of the universal in the general.... It always partakes of the reality which it renders intelligible; and while it enunciates the whole, abides itself as a living part in that unity of which it is representative.' Allegories, meanwhile, 'are but empty echoes which the fancy arbitrarily associates with apparitions of matter...' (*ibid.*). See also Coleridge's *Aids to Reflection* (*ibid.*, pp. 671–3).

2 *Shakespeare's Biblical Knowledge and*

Use of the Book of Common Prayer (London, 1935).

3 See, e.g., Beryl Smalley, *The Study of the Bible in the Middle Ages*, 2nd ed. (Oxford, 1952); H. Lubac, S.J., *Exégèse médiévale (Les quatre sens de l'Ecriture)*, 4 vols. (Paris, 1959–1964).

4 *The Poetry of Edmund Spenser* (New York, 1963), pp. 127–46.

5 See, e.g., Jacques Chomarat, *Grammaire et Rhétorique chez Erasme*, 2 vols. (Paris, 1981), Vol. 1 pp. 568–79, especially p. 570 n.: 'Erasme a voulu effectuer une rupture [avec le Moyen Age] et effectivement il inaugure (après Valla) l'exégèse moderne . . .'.

6 In his New Cambridge edition of *Othello* (Cambridge, 1984), pp. 191–2, Norman Sanders summarises seven arguments for reading 'Judean', and rejects them all. The 'Old' Cambridge edition by Alice Walker (1957) and the New Arden edition by M.R. Ridley (1958) concur.

7 *Othello. An Annotated Bibliography*, compiled by Margaret Lael Mikesell and Virginia Mason Vaughan (New York and London, 1990). References will be included in the text, giving the item-number (#123).

8 *Hyppolyta's View: Some Christian Aspects of Shakespeare's Plays* (Lexington, Ky., 1961), pp. 140–41. In Bryant's reading of *The Winter's Tale* (ibid., pp. 209–16), Leontes represents the Jew whom St. Paul desired to see saved; Paulina is the St. Paul who helps him; 'Mamillius, who dies, suggests the Jewish Church'; 'Perdita, . . . consistently referred to as the *heir* in the play, suggests the true Church'; while Hermione's "correspondence to the incarnation of divine grace, Jesus Christ", means that her progress through the play re-enacts 'the familiar career of Jesus from Gethsemane to Golgotha'. See Frye 1963, pp. 37–9, for comment.

9 'Some Limitations of a Christian Approach to Shakespeare', originally in *English Literary History* 22 (1955),

repr. in and quoted from Rabkin 1964, pp. 217–29, at p. 222.

10 In addition to Frye and Barnet see Levin 1979, pp. 212–26, 244–5. A fundamental study, widely researched and soberly argued, rejecting the view that *King Lear* is an optimistically Christian drama, is William R. Elton, *King Lear and the Gods* (San Marino, Cal., 1966; 2nd ed., Lexington, Ky., 1988). In the new edition Elton surveys criticism of the play between 1967 and 1987 (pp. 339–45), including further Christian allegorising. For other examples, see a bibliographical guide to recent criticism (Wells 1990) which includes an account of *Measure for Measure* in which Isabella is the target of Protestant anti-monastic satire, and the Duke acts in a way analogous to God (pp. 150–1); also another that sees Timon of Athens performing 'a literal imitation of Christ' (p. 309).

11 See Vickers 1989, pp. 135–93.

12 Some feminist critics, at least, see Volumnia as the domineering mother, instilling her values into Coriolanus, using emotional blackmail when he disagrees with her: e.g., Woodbridge 1984, p. 220 note 12. Bamber 1982 equates Volumnia with Lady Macbeth: 'each urges the hero beyond the limits of decency in his struggle for power' in the world (p. 91). 'By the end of the play', she writes — although the remark is valid much earlier — 'the plot has separated Volumnia and Coriolanus; indeed, they are finally mortal antagonists' (p. 92).

13 Cf. those passages in *Jubilate Agno* on the alphabet, where English letters are given an individual significance (like that ascribed to Hebrew characters by the Cabbalists), such as 'For A is the beginning of learning and the door of heaven', 'For E is eternity — such is the power of the English letters taken singly', or 'For M is musick and therefore he is God': *The Poetical Works of Christopher Smart, I: Jubilate Agno*, ed. Karina

Williamson (Oxford, 1980), pp. 76–8, 91.

14 *Shakespeare Quarterly* 32 (1981): p. 404.

15 In this latest book Siegel repeatedly claims that his earlier study (Siegel 1957) was Marxist (e.g., pp. 15, 30). Even with the wisdom of hindsight I find few traces of Marxism there, and I would hardly describe John F. Danby as 'Marxist influenced' (p. 143, note 34). Equally vague, in my opinion, is the claim embodied in the title of Elliott Krieger's book, *A Marxist Study of Shakespeare's Comedies* (London, 1979). The book never mentions Marx, Engels, Lukács, or Althusser; the one reference to Fredric Jameson is to an early, non-Marxist book. In fact, Krieger's essay — like some other self-proclaimed 'Marxist' readings — is more Freudian, as in its account of Rosalind's 'feigned homosexual courtship of Orlando', which 'precisely reverses the process of paranoid delusional formation that Freud describes': pp. 81–3. The main ideas or analytic models for Krieger's book, which is disappointing in every respect, are the two articles he lists on p. 171, note 1 (Hawkins) and 3 (Berger). The dilution of Marxism in America has reached the point where one recent commentator can observe that 'in American universities critical affiliations like . . . Marxism are not linked to systematic thought. (They are like our political parties, confusing to Europeans because they are important but ideologically evasive and inconsistent.) It is possible in the United States to describe oneself and be perceived as a Marxist literary critic without believing in the class struggle as the principal motor force in history; without believing in the theory of surplus value; without believing in the determining power of economic base over ideological superstructure; without believing in the inevitability, let alone the imminence, of capitalism's collapse' (Greenblatt 1990, p. 3). The 'affilia-tion' is almost meaningless, then.

16 Weimann 1978, revised, updated and translated by Robert Schwartz from Weimann, *Shakespeare und die Tradition des Volkstheaters* (Berlin, 1967). For favourable comments by the Cultural Materialist school of critics, see, e.g., Drakakis 1985, pp. 15–16 (Weimann is said to have reconstructed 'the material historical conditions of performance, representation and reception, all of which are shown to be related dialectically to each other'); Evans 1985, p. 76 ('really is, by a long stretch, the best book . . . on the Comedies . . . fills the historical gap between the Bakhtinian carnival and the Elizabethan and Jacobean stage') and p. 77 (accepting the *locus / platea* distinction as one between 'sealed illusion' and 'utopian levelling'); Rose 1985, p. 117 (also accepting 'the Renaissance division between non-representational and illusionistic stage space'); Kavanagh 1985, p. 232, note 2 (Weimann 'gives an excellent understanding of the disparate sources that nourished Shakespeare's work'); 'arguably the most penetrating analysis of the problem to date': Drakakis, in Holderness 1988, p. 36. For a more extensive critique, including comments on Weimann's ideologically-derived distortions of Greek, medieval, and Tudor drama, see my review in *Shakespeare Quarterly* 32 (1981): pp. 107–18.

17 These include such extraordinarily outdated studies as Hermann Reich on *Der Mimus: Ein litterarentwicklungsgeschichtlicher Versuch* (Berlin, 1903) and *Der Mann mit dem Eselskopf* (Weimar, 1904); Robert Petsch, *Das deutsche Volksrätsel* (Strassburg, 1917); L.W. Cushman, *The Devil and the Vice in the English Dramatic Literature before Shakespeare* (Halle, 1900), Otto Ludwig, *Werke* (Berlin, 1908).

18 I.M. Lewis, *Ecstatic Religion. An Anthropological Study of Spirit Possession and Shamanism* (Harmonds-

worth, 1971), p. 12. On the deficiencies of Frazer and Gilbert Murray see E.E. Evans-Pritchard, *Theories of Primitive Religion* (Oxford, 1965); Joseph Fontenrose, *The Ritual Theory of Myth* (Berkeley and Los Angeles, 1966); G.S. Kirk, *Myth* (Cambridge, 1970), pp. 1–31; and Vickers 1973, pp. 3–51. The definitive exposure of the 'ritual origins' theory of drama remains Sir Arthur Pickard-Cambridge, *Dithyramb, Tragedy and Comedy* (Oxford, 1927) — but not in the sadly emasculated second edition by T.B.L. Webster (Oxford, 1962). See also Gerald Else, *The Origin and Early Form of Greek Tragedy* (Cambridge, Mass., 1965).

19 Margaret Murray's thesis that witches were adherents of a surviving pagan religion has been unanimously demolished by the leading modern authorities: see Alan Macfarlane, *Witchcraft in Tudor and Stuart England* (London, 1970), p. 10; Keith Thomas, *Religion and the Decline of Magic* (Harmondsworth, 1973), pp. 518 note, 614–15, 627; and Max Marwick (ed.), *Witchcraft and Sorcery* (Harmondsworth, 1982), for quite devastating comments on the inadequacy of her work by a number of scholars: Norman Cohn (pp. 146–52, listing 6 other researchers in this field who have dismissed it as worthless: p. 149); Marwick himself (p. 231); Macfarlane (pp. 233–4: from his Oxford D.Phil. thesis); and pp. 327–9 (M.J. Kephart). It is hard to convey to anyone not familiar with recent scholarly work on witchcraft how utterly and completely Murray's work has been discredited.

20 In the introduction and elsewhere Weimann accepts Gilbert Murray, but pours scorn on the American critics Francis Fergusson (p. xx, 128) and O.B. Hardison, Jr. (p. 271 note 23) for using ideas which simply derive from Murray. Margaret Murray's 'anthropological' speculations on Robin Hood are referred

to seriously in the text (p. 28), but a footnote cites a modern anthropologist's evaluation of Murray's belief in 'vegetation-magic' surviving in witch-cults as 'totally false' (p. 268 note 38). Weimann attacks Northrop Frye's work but indulges in the same kinds of post-Frazerian speculations himself. Indeed Frazer's misguided concepts of homoeopathic magic survive in Weimann's account of the folk play as supposedly bringing 'sympathetic' luck (p. 19), or disguise as having a 'sympathetic magical function' (p. 47). There are far too many opportunistic attacks on modern American critics: the traditions that formed Weimann were also political, namely the Cold War and the Berlin wall. Weimann did after all rise to a high post in the Akademie der Wissenschaften of the DDR, and it would be naïve to imagine that he could do so without conforming to the governing ideology.

21 Few readers of the Weston-sub-Edge Mummers' Play will see any connection with the 'magical' or ritual origins of drama when the fool confronts St. George with this Victorian nonsense verse:

> You lash me and smash me
>   small as Flys,
> Send me to Jamaica to
>   make Mince Pies.

True to his liking for unprovable speculations about 'primitive tradition', Weimann suggests that the dragon slain by St. George may be linked with such incarnations of 'the vital powers of life-giving' as 'the Northern Wildhug, the guardian of a well', so that 'the context of a fertility ritual does not seem too far-fetched' (p. 38). Killing such a 'beneficent creature', however, would make St. George an eternal villain, not a British hero.

22 Alfred Harbage's thesis, in *Shakespeare's Audience* (New York, 1941), that Shakespeare wrote for a middle and working class audience, was criticised by Ann Jellalie Cook

in *Shakespeare Studies* (1974) for relying on fragile demographic evidence. In her later book, however, *The Privileged Playgoers of Shakespeare's London, 1576–1642* (Princeton, N.J., 1981), Cook switched track, arguing that the average playgoer belonged to an elite or 'privileged' audience. For some counter-evidence see Andrew Gurr, *Playgoing in Shakespeare's London* (Cambridge, 1987), and further studies cited on p. 252, notes 5ff.

23 See Bradbrook, *The Rise of the Common Player* (London, 1962), and her collected papers, Vol. 1: *Artist and Society in Shakespeare's England* (Brighton, 1982).

24 *Shakespeare & The Popular Dramatic Tradition*, with an Introduction by T.S. Eliot (London, 1944).

25 See, e.g., Peter Demetz, *Marx, Engels and the Poets*, tr. J.L. Sammons (Chicago, 1967: from *Marx, Engels und die Dichter*, 1959); D.W. Fokkema, 'Marxist Theories of Literature', in Fokkema and E. Kunne-Ibisch, *Theories of Literature in the Twentieth Century* (London, 1977), pp. 81–135; David Forgacs, 'Marxist Literary Theories', in A. Jefferson and D. Robey (eds.), *Modern Literary Theory. A Comparative Introduction*, 2nd ed. (London, 1986), pp. 166–203; Butler 1984; Merquior 1986b; Dews 1987; etc. For a penetrating evaluation of the uncomfortable mixture of Althusser, semiotics, and so-called cultural materialism in the work of Raymond Williams and Terry Eagleton, see Catherine Gallagher, 'The New Materialism in Marxist Aesthetics', *Theory and Society* 9 (1980): pp. 633–46.

26 Ferry and Renaut 1985, pp. 205–6, summarise the bitter attacks that Pierre Bourdieu launched on Althusser between 1975 and 1980, including a sharp denunciation of his concept of history as a 'process without a subject' for 'simply substituting for the "creative subject" of subjectivism an automaton sub-

jugated by the dead laws of a history of nature'. Althusser thus created an 'emanationist vision which makes structure, capital, or the mode of production into an entelechy developing itself in a process of auto-realization, and reduces historical agents to the role of "supports" (*Träger*) of the structure, their actions being seen as mere epiphenomenal manifestations of the power belonging to that structure . . .' (my translation, from *Le sens pratique*, 1980). See also Timpanaro 1976, with additional references to Marxist critiques of Althusser by Nicola Badaloni, Lucio Colletti, Lucien Sève, Henri Lefebvre, Jean Fallot, Ernest Mandel, and Eric Hobsbawm (pp. 65 n., 77, 194 n., 251 n.); Thompson 1978, with additional references to Marxist critiques by Derek Sayer, Simon Clarke, Paul Piccone (pp. 194, nn. 13 and 19, 202 n. 134), and Jacques Rancière's important study, *La leçon d'Althusser* (Paris, 1974); Clarke *et al.* 1980; Anderson 1983. Neo-Althusserian literary critics have either never heard of any attacks on the master, or avoid citing them. This is particularly deplorable in the case of Fredric Jameson, who surely knew but simply ignored all these critiques, and while briefly referring to Thompson's *The Poverty of Theory* (Jameson 1981, pp. 39 n., 83 n.) never informed his readers that it constitutes the most devastating evaluation of Althusser imaginable. What should we think of a school that suppresses its critics?

27 On Althusser's apologias for Stalinism see Timpanaro 1975, p. 244 n.; Ferry and Renaut 1985, p. 22; Merquior 1986b, pp. 153–4; and Thompson 1978, pp. 78–80, 122–42, 182–92, e.g., p. 130: 'we can see the emergence of Althusserianism as a manifestation of a general police action within ideology, as the attempt to reconstruct Stalinism at the level of theory'. Thompson's description of Stalinism as 'one of

the ultimate disasters of the human mind and conscience, a terminus of the spirit, a disaster area in which every socialist profession of "good faith" was blasted and burned up' (p. 139), must be borne in mind when we read Fredric Jameson's unconvincing claims that Althusser was actually 'against Stalinism' (Jameson 1981, pp. 27 n., 37), an obviously touchy issue which he then attempts to dismiss: 'It would be frivolous to try to choose between these antithetical evaluations of the Althusserian operation (anti-Stalinist or Stalinist); rather, they mark out a space in which that operation is objectively and functionally ambiguous' (p. 39). Sophisticatedly formulated, that nevertheless seems to me an unethical cop-out.

28 See, e.g., Anderson 1983, p. 37; Ferry and Renaut 1985, pp. 55–6; Merquior 1986a, pp. 233–4; and Frank 1989, p. 96: 'subjectivity, which was repressed in the position of the individual, returns as subjectivity of the reflecting and actively transforming structure — return of the repressed.'

29 Thompson's summary of its self-constituting manoeuvres shows its identity with other theoretical structures of that group. Althusser's is another 'a-historical theoreticism' (p. 4), which 'simplifies [its] own polemics by caricaturing' its opponents (p. 6). It, too, is based on a union of 'highly-specialised disciplines', the main influence being not structuralist linguistics but philosophy, 'a particular Cartesian tradition of logical exegesis . . . modified by the monism of Spinoza', and aspiring towards mathematics, a liking for 'self-enclosed and self-replicating' systems which encourage 'theoretical imperialism' (pp. 9–10, 16). Like the other sixties systems in its slippery methodology, Althusser's also uses pat antitheses, artificially weighted to an extreme either/or choice, excluding a large middle ground (p. 15); it makes 'densely-textured . . . assertions' that turn out

to be truisms (pp. 15–16); it misuses logic, loading the terms of an epigram 'to trick us into a false conclusion' (p. 31); it thrives on spurious questions, pseudo-oppositions (p. 55); it claims to be 'liberating' its subject, but in fact fixes it in a static system (p. 91); it makes 'the only possible alternative' to its programme 'the most crude caricature' (p. 94); and so on. These are all familiar tactics by which a sixties theorist develops his system with self-validating procedures that evade accountability to other criteria. The result is another closed system.

30 'A cloud no bigger than a man's hand crosses the English Channel from Paris, and then, in an instant, the trees, the orchard, the hedgerows, the field of wheat, are black with locusts. When at length they rise to fly on to the next parish, the boughs are bared of all culture, the fields have been stripped of every green blade of human aspiration: and in those skeletal forms and that blackened landscape, theoretical practice announces its "discovery": the mode of production. Not only substantive knowledge, but also the very vocabularies of the human project — compassion, greed, love, pride, self-sacrifice, loyalty, treason, calumny — have been eaten down to the circuits of capital. These locusts are very learned platonists: if they settled on The Republic they would leave it picked clean of all but the idea of a contradiction between a philosopher and a slave. However elaborated the inner mechanisms, torsions, and autonomies, theoretical practice [Althusser's system] constitutes the ultimate in reductionism: a reduction, not of "religion" or "politics" to "economics", but of the disciplines of knowledge to one kind of "basic" Theory only': Thompson 1978, pp. 166–7.

31 See, e.g., Nicholas Abercrombie et al., The Dominant Ideology Thesis (London, 1980).

32 Although we see that Jameson (being

also a Lacanian) has silently dropped Althusser's attack on the subject, he continues to endorse that notorious concept of history as ' "a process without a *telos* or a subject" ' (p. 29), and he believes that 'the Althusserian school' has 'effectively discredited the Marxian version of a properly teleological history . . .' (p. 33). Many historians, Marxist and otherwise, would bitterly dispute that point.

33 Despite Jameson's laudatory epithets, I am bemused that he should be recommending allegory as an 'advance', or method of the future. Most modern readers would regard it as an archaic form of reading, a throwback to a far removed age whose problems with the interpretation of sacred texts can be reconstructed by historical scholarship, but hardly seem an applicable model for us, given the views expressed by Coleridge in my epigraph, and widely shared in modern criticism. Does this desperate remedy mean that Marxist theory finds itself in a cul-de-sac? As if the medieval allegorists did not offer a sufficiently schematic approach, Jameson then warmly endorses the system of Northrop Frye (pp. 68–74, 110–19), that 'fearful symmetry' as it has been not unjustly called.

34 What is the state? Who controls it? If we all suffer from the same ideological indoctrination, then why do so many of us object to the manifest injustices of (say) the British government in the 1980s, its erosion of civil liberties, its 'sale' of nationalised industries in order to popularise capitalism, its militarism, corruption, discrimination, and so much else? My concern is with literary criticism, but as someone living in a society which has also produced Amnesty International, Greenpeace, Charter 88, anti-apartheid campaigns, and many brave workers for human rights, I can only express surprise that the ISAs have been so ineffective. Or is it because the concept was formulated

by Althusser having observed totalitarian states, such as the Soviet bloc? It would fit these, and some Islamic states, but it seems to me irrelevant for Western democracies — despite all their faults.

35 P. Macherey and E. Balibar, 'Literature As an Ideological Form: Some Marxist hypotheses', *Praxis* 5 (1980): pp. 43–58.

36 See, e.g., Deuteronomy 13:10–12; Gal. 5:20; Exod. 22:18, and Skinner 1988, pp. 242–3 for a demonstration of how the distinguished historian Le Roy Ladurie failed to grasp the historical reality of witchcraft beliefs in Languedoc.

37 Jameson, indeed, scornfully rejects the traditional ethical categories of good and evil: Jameson 1981, pp. 59–60, 110, 114–17, etc. For this position he cites Nietzsche, but may also have followed Althusser, who believed that morality ' "would disappear with the abolition of class antagonisms" '. See Thompson 1978, pp. 178–80, for a devastating analysis of how 'any "naturalistic" morality' legitimises destructive egotism: 'The reasons of Reason, uncumbered by the moral consciousness, become, very soon, the reasons of interest, and then the reasons of State, and thence, in an uncontested progression, the rationalisations of opportunism, brutality, and crime'.

38 Their Shakespeare criticism can be conveniently sampled in three collections: Drakakis 1985; Dollimore and Sinfield 1985; Holderness 1988. For critical evaluation of their work I recommend several essays by Richard Levin: Levin 1989 ('Bashing the bourgeois subject'), Levin 1988 ('Leaking Relativism'), Levin 1990 ('Bardicide'), Levin 1992 ('Ideological Criticism and Pluralism').

39 See Ferry and Renaut 1985, pp. 40, 42–3.

40 See e.g., Vickers 1989, pp. 236–7, and 'Something rocking in Denmark. Writing music for Shakespeare', *Times Literary Supplement*, 30 August 1991, pp. 14–15.

Epilogue

1 'The History of Ancient Astronomy: Problems and Methods', *Journal of Near Eastern Studies* 4 (1945): pp. 1–38, at p. 2 (repr. in Neugebauer, *Astronomy and History. Selected Essays* (New York, 1983).

2 Francis Bacon, *Works*, ed. J. Spedding *et al.*, 14 vols. (London, 1857–1874), Vol. 3, pp. 289–90.

3 Letter of 11 November 1977, in *Selected Letters of Virgil Thomson*, ed. T. and V.W. Page (New York, 1988), p. 363.

4 Nuttall 1983, p. 10, citing Chomsky's review of Skinner's *Verbal Behaviour* in *Language* 35 (1959): pp. 25–58.

5 'Criticism as Inquiry; or, The Perils of the "High Priori Road"', in Crane, *The Idea of the Humanities and Other Essays*, 2 vols. (Chicago, 1967), II. pp. 25–44.

6 See G.K. Hunter, *John Lyly: The Humanist As Courtier* (London, 1962), ch. vi: 'Lyly and Shakespeare' (pp. 298–349), for one of the best accounts of Shakespeare's comedies yet written (pp. 318–30 on *MND*), and David P. Young's full study of the play, *Something of Great Constancy* (New Haven, CT, 1966).

7 'Bardbiz', *London Review of Books*, 22 February 1990, pp. 11–13. This review gave rise to a long-running correspondence, in which the virtues and faults of Cultural Materialist Shakespeare criticism were freely debated. Some of the most cogent observations came from James Wood: see, e.g., his letters of 22 March, 25 April, 24 May, and 16 August 1990.

8 '"Fie What a Question's That If You Were Near a Lewd Interpreter": The Wall Scene in *A Midsummer Night's Dream*', *Shakespeare Studies* 7 (1974): pp. 101–13. See also Wolfgang Franke, 'The Logic of *Double Entendre* in *A Midsummer Night's Dream*', *Philological Quarterly* 58 (1979): pp. 282–97.

9 '*Mise en abyme* is a term in heraldry meaning a shield which has in its center (*abyme*) a smaller image of the same shield, and so, by implication, ad infinitum, with ever smaller and smaller shields receding toward the central point': Miller 1976a, p. 11. Readers of Russell Hoban will recall the can of 'BONZO Dog Food' on the label of which 'was a picture of a little black-and-white spotted dog, walking on his hind legs and wearing a chef's cap and an apron. The dog carried a tray on which there was another can of BONZO Dog Food, on the label of which another little black-and-white spotted dog, exactly the same but much smaller, was . . . carrying a tray . . . and so on until the dogs became too small for the eye to follow': *The Mouse and his Child* (1967; Puffin Books ed., Harmondsworth, 1976), p. 30.

10 See, e.g., Goldberg 1988.

11 *PMLA* 103 (1988): pp. 817–18, from Alberto Cacicedo, with Levin's reply at pp. 818–19. One feminist *topos* in Cacicedo's letter that I object to is his assertion that in *Othello* Emilia is 'marginalized, objectified, literally utilized by her husband', made to keep quiet 'despite her mistress's anguish'. While accepting that analysis as far as the three scenes involving Emilia and Desdemona are concerned (see Chapter 2, p. 160, above), I was disconcerted by his further claim, that Emilia's speaking out against Iago at the end of the play is now not a sign of her 'courage' but 'a reflex of the power that her husband has had over her speech in the middle of the play' (p. 818). I do not understand this. What is a 'reflex'? Is her courage merely a delayed but automatic response, as when a doctor taps us on the knee? If so, this comment destroys the meaning of Emilia's ethical behaviour, in order to indict patriarchy again. As for the comedies, Cacicedo complains, characters such as Hero or Beatrice say little in the final scenes, a silence which 'bodes ill' for women, such problematic endings implying that

'profound problems' persist for all the characters. But it is unreal to expect that all the characters, male and female, will be able to have their say in the final scene, letting us know exactly what they feel about the situation. This is to apply yet again the standards of nineteenth-century naturalism, or modern egalitarianism, to matters governed by theatrical exigencies (the need to bring the play to a clearly-articulated conclusion; in some cases — not forgetting Cleopatra — the relatively light stature of the boy actors). To demand that writers give women 'an equal say' is to impose political demands on creative activity.

12 *PMLA* 104 (1989): pp. 77–8, with Levin's reply at pp. 78–9. I must express regret that at least two of the signatories agreed to do so, their work being notable (so far, at least) for its historical depth and absence of vindictiveness.

13 See, e.g., 'A Traditionalist Takes on Feminists Over Shakespeare', *New York Times*, 1 March 1990, pp. C17–C18. As the reporter says, 'the debate will no doubt continue. New schools of feminist criticism are emerging frequently...'. The appetite for debate and controversy in the United States these days seems insatiable. The unwary writer who submits an essay to a journal is likely to find it appearing in print with critical replies already attached to it. Such instant polemics may be good for arousing and maintaining heated debate, but they are not good for truth.

14 This tactic is used by other defenders of exclusive systems. As Frederick Crews says of Derrida's selective borrowings from Freud, 'he encourages the theoreticist habit of treating one's own system as received truth while dividing all other tenets into those that miss one's point (owing, perhaps, to 'repression') and those that can be borrowed to adorn it': Crews 1986, p. 176 n. 9. An example of this practice comes from Malcolm Bowie, a loyal exponent of Lacan, who dismisses all criticism of the master by declaring that 'most published [hostile] responses to which his thought gives rise ... are trivial and written by self-righteous bystanders who have tried and failed, or simply failed to read what Lacan writes'. Of the criticism by Sebastiano Timpanaro (a distinguished classical philologist) that '"in Lacan's writings charlatanry and exhibitionism largely prevail over any ideas of comprehensible, even if debatable nature"', revealing '"an erroneous and confused knowledge"' of linguistics, Bowie merely retorts that 'Timpanaro's remarks show signs of a limited knowledge of Lacan and premature judgement' (Bowie 1979, p. 147). This is to make life too easy for yourself. For demonstration of Lacan's ignorance and misuse of linguistics see, e.g., Georges Mounin, *Clefs pour la linguistique* (Paris, 1968), p. 13, and Descombes 1986, pp. 177–87.

15 Frank Kermode's edition of *The Tempest* is similarly demonised, a by-now ritual gesture in some quarters, for having such subheadings in its introduction as 'pastoral tragi-comedy', 'art and nature', and 'masque elements'. Summarising the course of 'Shakespeare criticism' as 'having recognized itself over the past decade ... to be at one of those moments ... when a "return to history" is on the agenda', Felperin describes the current mood among new historicists and cultural materialists (he himself, we recall, professes to be a deconstructionist although expressing admiration for the latter, English-based group, for having a commitment to changing the world: Felperin 1990, pp. ix, 157 — as if Althusserian–Machereyans could ever engage with social reality) as being one which 'is not about to linger before such aesthetic luggage ... without historicizing [it] anew' (p. 172). I find it strange that just the dimension being mocked

here is the history of literature, genres, and conventions. What crimes are perpetrated in the name of history!

16 *Timber*, in Jonson's *Works*, ed. C.H. Herford and P. and E.M. Simpson, 11 vols. (Oxford, 1925–1952), Vol. VIII, p. 567.

ADDITIONAL NOTES

While this book was being edited and printed a number of studies appeared which add valuable detail.

1 Preface and Chapter One: The Iconoclasts

My argument that the 'profound transformation of intellectual practice' celebrated by some Current Literary Theorists merely transmitted the iconoclastic ideas of a tiny, homogeneous group of Paris intellectuals has been strengthened by the recent publication of biographical material which will undoubtedly affect evaluation of their significance. As Mark Lilla wrote in September 1992, reviewing Althusser's autobiography *L'Avenir dure longtemps suivi de Les Faits* (Paris, 1992), it permits 'a rare glimpse into the backrooms of post-war French intellectual life. And like a number of recent biographies and memoirs, [it confirms] that the radical French philosophies of the period had less to do with grand history or our "postmodern" condition than with the shared obsessions of a small group of thinkers working in the highly centralized French context' (Lilla 1992, p. 3). Althusser's autobiography is of great value, Lilla finds, in documenting 'the biographical sources of a philosopher's thought', yet with its account of the deviousness in his political and academic career, and the violence in his private life, it is also significant as 'another morbid episode in the dénouement of *la pensée 68*' (*ibid.*). *L'Avenir dure longtemps*, Gilbert Adair records, 'is only the latest in a series of texts which have had the effect of demystifying the Parisian intelligentsia of the past two decades. . . . François Weyer-

gans' best-selling novel, *Le Pitre*, was a cruel debunking portrait of Lacan. Barthes's posthumous *Incidents* was a melancholy little volume in which he wrote of his loveless frequentation of rent boys. Hervé Guilbert's *A l'ami qui ne m'a pas sauvé la vie* recounted the violent sex life of his friend Michel Foucault, the first celebrity publicly known to have died of Aids. Julia Kristeva's *Les Samouraïs* was a transparent *roman-à-clef* in which all of the above were shown to have had feet of clay': Adair, 'Sex, murder and philosophy', the *Independent*, 2 July 1992.

Setting aside mere scandal, these writings show, in particular, 'what a profoundly intimate meaning the philosophical flight from subjectivity and the attack on humanism' had for Foucault and Althusser (Lilla 1992, p. 4). Althusser invoked both an 'anti-humanistic Marx' and 'an anti-humanistic Freud to make the same moral point: man is not his own subject'. As Lilla points out, this was certainly true of Althusser, who 'was not the subject of himself. He was possessed by something he could not control, a demon that tormented him for over forty years and drove him to kill the only person he loved' — his wife Hélène, whom he strangled in November 1980, in an insane fit. Now that we know what possessed him for so long and so disastrously, Lilla asks, must we endorse his obsessions: 'are we all so possessed? Althusser's work today appears as one extended effort to make us share his condition, to persuade us not only that modern capitalism mesmerizes through the "Ideological Apparatuses of the State", but, as he later puts it in his last memoir, that "the most terrible, unbearable, and frightening of all Ideological Apparatuses of the State is the family"'. Once we have realised the highly personal motivation of these violent attacks on the individual human subject in Althusser and Foucault, Lilla suggests, we may feel less compelled to assent to their arguments. But 'Why their quest for self-erasure then found resonance among an entire generation of Western intellectuals is a puzzle which historians must confront when they come to write about the time in which we live' (*ibid.*). Similar links can be made in Foucault between sadomasochism and his concepts of language, the *episteme*, and power as involving oppression and submission, above all the single-mindedness with which he developed these ideas.

2 *Chapter Two*: The Death of the Author

Seán Burke's admirable study, *The Death & Return of the Author* (Burke 1992), includes penetrating evaluations of de Man (pp. 1–7), Barthes (pp. 20–61), Foucault (pp. 62–99), Lacan (pp. 99–104), and Derrida (pp. 116–53). While urging anyone concerned with modern literary theories to read it carefully, I pick out a few passages for particular emphasis. Burke links Barthes' 'Death of the Author' with Nietzsche's 'Death of God', showing how Barthes had to create an '"Author-God" ... worthy of the killing', a polemical over-statement which resulted in 'an apotheosis of authorship that vastly outpaces anything to be found' in the tradition he opposed (pp. 22–7). The next stage of rehabilitating the author came in *Sade, Fourier, Loyola* (1971; Engl. tr. 1977), where Barthes was forced to allow what he called an '"amicable return of the author"' with an argument that Burke judges 'flatly contradictory' (p. 30). Barthes praised those three writers as 'logothetes', creators of an 'autarkic' language, 'closed and oblivious to anything outside itself', involving 'a voiding of the linguistic past and present' (pp. 33–6). But this amazing apotheosis was achieved only by denying to his 'founders' of language 'any representational significance in their discourses, any content:

Sade without evil, Fourier without socialism, Loyola without God, these are the postulates' from which Barthes begins (p. 41). The linguistic 'voiding', then (a concept soon picked up by de Man), was a completely circular manoeuvre performed so that Barthes could once again cut language off from reality, but at the price of extraordinarily specious and incoherent arguments (e.g., pp. 37–41). Particularly telling is Burke's concluding demonstration of fundamental and 'insurmountable inconsistencies' in Barthes' treatment of the author-question (pp. 41–61).

As for Foucault, Burke's analysis of *Les Mots et les choses* (1966; Engl. tr. 1970) shows that in arguing his case for the disappearance of subjectivity Foucault wilfully misrepresented Descartes (pp. 66–71), Husserl (pp. 72–4), and Nietzsche (pp. 82–7, 94–5). Having documented the rigidity of Foucault's system, which either bent texts and historical periods to fit, or rejected them altogether (pp. 74–6), Burke brings out the irony (as I have observed in Foucault's later writings) that his work 'does contain a subject in the traditional sense, a subject to whom, moreover, is accredited a sovereignty rare in any history of modern thought' (p. 78), namely Foucault himself (pp. 96–9). Burke's account of Derrida's attack on the author demonstrates a remarkable amount of 'contradiction, ambivalence, unease' (e.g., pp. 121–3, 126–8, 145–6). In all three writers, he concludes, the 'death of the author emerges as a blind-spot', producing 'a massive disjunction' between their 'theoretical statement of authorial disappearance and the project of reading without the author', who remains an active presence. 'Direct resistance *to* the author demonstrates little so much as the resistance *of* the author' (p. 154): another dead-end in Current Literary Theory.

3 *Chapter Three*: Deconstruction

My doubts about the durability of deconstruction seem to be justified. An article by Jeffrey T. Nealon in the current issue of *PMLA*, entitled 'The Discipline of

Deconstruction' (107:5, October, 1992, pp. 1266–79), begins: 'Deconstruction, it seems, is dead in literature departments today. . . . [Its] heyday has apparently passed: precious few critics would identify themselves any longer as deconstructionists; the topic does not dominate MLA convention panels any more; in the summer of 1992, at the School of Criticism and Theory, Barbara Johnson spoke on "the wake of deconstruction" . . .' (p. 1266). Nealon records that 'Deconstruction's death is usually attributed either to suicide — to its falling back into the dead-end formalism it was supposed to remedy — or to murder at the hands of the new historicists . . .' (ibid.). His own diagnosis, however, is that the pure spirit of Derrida has been debased by such 'commodifiers' as Paul de Man and J. Hillis Miller, who turned it into a totalising system (pp. 1268–76). While willing to indict these vulgarisers of the true light, it is sadly typical of the protective devices used to surround the gurus of literary theory that Nealon can list 22 works by Derrida in his bibliography while excluding all his critics.

4   Chapter Three: de Man

The critical consensus documenting de Man's misrepresentation of the authors he interpreted grows steadily. In a collection edited by Luc Herman, Kris Humbeek and Geert Lernout, (Dis)continuities: Essays on Paul de Man (Amsterdam, 1989; 'Postmodern Studies' 2), Ortwin de Graef shows that at a crucial point in his essay on Rousseau's Confessions de Man quoted Rousseau in French but inserted a 'ne' in square brackets, thus adding a negation that is nowhere to be found in Rousseau, the resulting translation giving 'the exact opposite of Rousseau's phrase'. This 'illegitimate' inversion cannot be accidental, de Graef judges (p. 61), adding other instances 'of "dubious translation" or twisted paraphrase' in de Man, warning readers 'to trace de Man's quotes to their supposed sources' (p. 72 n. 18). In the same volume Philip Buyck shows how de Man both mistranslated and misrepresented Nietzsche's work on rhetoric, by which he made 'Nietzsche say exactly the opposite of what he actually says' (p. 156). I have given some more details of these misrepresentations in 'De Man's distortions of Nietzsche: Rhetoric against itself', in Josef Kopperschmidt and Helmut Schanze (eds.), Nietzsche: oder die Sprache ist Rhetorik (Munich: Fink, forthcoming).

5   Chapter Seven: Althusser

Future evaluations of Althusser will be adversely affected by the self-revelations of his autobiography, especially his surprising admission of having had but a slender knowledge of philosophy. As one reviewer reports, 'he was not even particularly conversant with Marx, having read only his early works when he came to write his own seminal texts'. Althusser's skill in extrapolating ideas from commentaries or casual conversations enabled him to bluff his way to success as a Marx expert (his Marxist critics, as we have seen, were not deceived), but he apparently 'lived out his whole life in the terror that his inadequacy as a thinker, his fraudulence (the word he himself uses), would sooner or later be exposed' (Gilbert Adair, in the Independent, 2 July 1992). In the end he exposed himself: as another reviewer puts it, L'Avenir dure longtemps is 'a public disrobing, in which Althusser presents himself as an intellectual faker who had read little Marx, less Freud, and no Nietzsche' (Lilla 1992, p. 3). Lilla's interim verdict typifies the disenchanted evaluation that many informed commentators would now share: 'Althusserian Marxism was an ephemeral philosophical development unimaginable — indeed inexplicable — outside the petit monde of Paris in the 1960s and that unique intellectual Petri dish, the Ecole Normale Supérieure' (ibid., p. 4).

Bibliography

Abrams, M.H. (1989), *Doing Things with Texts. Essays in Criticism and Critical Theory*, ed. Michael Fischer, New York and London.

—— (1977), 'The Deconstructive Angel', *Critical Inquiry* 3: pp. 423–38; repr. in and quoted from Abrams 1989, pp. 237–52.

—— (1979), 'How to Do Things with Texts', *Partisan Review* 46: pp. 566–88; repr. in and quoted from Abrams 1989, pp. 269–96.

—— (1986), 'Construing and Deconstructing', in *Romanticism and Contemporary Criticism*, pp. 127–57. Ithaca, N.Y., 1986; repr. in and quoted from Abrams 1989, pp. 297–332.

Adelman, Janet (1978), '"Anger's My Meat": Feeding, Dependency, and Aggression in *Coriolanus*', in D. Bevington and J.L. Halio (eds.), *Shakespeare, Pattern of Excelling Nature. Shakespeare Criticism in Honor of America's Bicentennial*, Cranbury, N.J., pp. 108–24.

Alter, Robert (1978), 'Mimesis and the Motive for Fiction', *TriQuarterly* 42: pp. 228–49.

Altieri, Charles (1979), 'Presence and Reference in a Literary Text: The Example of Williams' "This Is Just To Say"', *Critical Inquiry* 5: pp. 489–509.

—— (1981), *Act and Quality. A Theory of Literary Meaning and Humanistic Understanding*, Amherst, Mass.

Anderson, Perry (1983), *In the Tracks of Historical Materialism*, London.

Angenot, Marc (1984), 'Structuralism and Syncretism: Institutional Distortions of Saussure', in John Fekete (ed.) *The Structural Allegory. Reconstructive Encounters with the New French Thought*, Manchester, pp. 150–63.

Aron, Raymond (1957), *The Opium of the Intellectuals*, tr. T. Kilmartin, London.

Atkins, G.D. and D.M. Bergeron (eds.) (1988), *Shakespeare and Deconstruction*, New York.

Atkins, G.D. (1988), 'Introduction' to Atkins and Bergeron 1988, pp. 1–19.

Bamber, Linda (1982), *Comic Women, Tragic Men. A Study of Gender and Genre in Shakespeare*, Stanford, Ca.

Barker and Hulme 1985 = Francis Barker and Peter Hulme, '"Nymphs and reapers heavily vanish": the discursive contexts of *The Tempest*', in Drakakis 1985, pp. 191–205.

Barroll, J. Leeds (1988), 'A New History for Shakespeare and His Time', *Shakespeare Quarterly* 39: pp. 441–64.

Barthes, Roland (1957), *Mythologies*, Paris.

—— (1967), *Elements of Semiology*, tr. A. Lavers and C. Smith (from *Eléments de sémiologie*, Paris 1964), London.

—— (1968a), 'The Death of the Author', in *Image-Music-Text*, Essays selected and translated by Stephen Heath (London, 1977), pp. 142–8.

—— (1968b), 'The reality effect', tr. R. Carter (from 'L'Effet du réel', *Communications* 11: pp. 84–9), in T. Todorov (ed.) *French literary Theory Today: A Reader* (Cambridge, 1982), pp. 11–17.

—— (1971), 'From Work to Text' in *Image-Music-Text* (see above), pp. 155–64.

———— (1972), *Critical Essays*, tr. R. Howard (from *Essais critiques*, Paris 1964), Evanston, Ill.

———— (1974), *S/Z*, tr. R. Miller (from *S/Z*, Paris, 1970), London.

———— (1977), *Roland Barthes by Roland Barthes*, tr. R. Howard (from *Roland Barthes par Roland Barthes*, Paris 1975), London.

———— (1982), *A Barthes Reader*, ed. Susan Sontag, London.

Barton, Anne (1991), 'Perils of Historicism', rev. of Stephen Greenblatt, *Learning to Curse*, in *New York Review of Books*, 28 March, pp. 51–4.

Barzun, Jacques (1974), *Clio and the Doctors. Psycho-History, Quanto-History, and History*, Chicago.

Battenhouse, Roy W. (1957), 'Shakespearean Tragedy: A Christian Approach', in Rabkin 1964, pp. 203–16.

Bean, John C. (1980), 'Comic Structure and the Humanizing of Kate in *The Taming of the Shrew*', in Lenz *et al.* 1980, pp. 65–78.

Belsey, Catherine (1985), 'Disrupting Sexual Difference: Meaning and Gender in the Comedies', in Drakakis 1985, pp. 166–90.

Bentley, Gerald Eaves (1986), *The Professions of Dramatist and Player in Shakespeare's Time, 1590–1642*, Princeton, N.J.

Benveniste, Emile (1966), *Problèmes de linguistique générale*, Vol. 1, Paris.

———— (1974), *Problèmes de linguistique générale*, Vol. 2, Paris.

Berggren, Paula S. (1980), 'The Woman's Part: Female Sexuality as Power in Shakespeare's Plays', in Lenz *et al.* 1980, pp. 17–34.

Bevington, David (ed.) (1980), *The Complete Works of Shakespeare*, 3rd ed., Glenview, Ill.

Blackburn, Simon (1984), *Spreading the Word. Groundings in the Philosophy of Language*, Oxford.

Boose, Lynda E. (1987), 'The Family in Shakespeare Studies; or — Studies in the Family of Shakespeareans; or — The Politics of Politics', *Renaissance Quarterly* 40: pp. 707–42.

Bowie, Malcolm (1979), 'Jacques Lacan', in Sturrock 1979, pp. 116–53.

Bullough, Geoffrey (ed.) (1962), *Narrative and Dramatic Sources of Shakespeare*. Vol. 4, *Later English History Plays*, London.

———— (ed.) (1973), Vol. 7, *Major Tragedies*, London.

Burke, Seán (1992), *The Death & Return of the Author. Criticism and Subjectivity in Barthes, Foucault, and Derrida*, Edinburgh.

Butler, Christopher (1984), *Interpretation, Deconstruction, and Ideology. An Introduction to Some Current Issues in Literary Theory*, Oxford.

Cain, William E. (1979), 'Deconstruction in America: The Recent Literary Criticism of J. Hillis Miller', *College English* 41: pp. 367–82.

Calvet, Louis-Jean (1975), *Pour et contre Saussure*, Paris.

Cavell, Stanley (1987), *Disowning Knowledge in Six Plays of Shakespeare*, Cambridge.

Chillington, C.A. (1980), 'Playwrights at Work: Henslowe's, Not Shakespeare's *Book of Sir Thomas More*', *English Literary Renaissance* 10: pp. 439–79.

Chomsky, Noam (1964), *Current Issues in Linguistic Theory*, The Hague.

———— (1972), *Language and Mind*. Enlarged edition, New York; 1st ed. 1968.

Cioffi, Frank (1979), 'Freud — New Myths to Replace the Old', *New Society* 50: pp. 471–99.

Clarke, Simon *et al.* (1980), *One-Dimensional Marxism. Althusser and the Politics of Culture*, London and New York.

Clarke, Simon (1980), 'Althusserian Marxism', in Clarke *et al.* 1980, pp. 7–101.

—— (1981), *The Foundations of Structuralism. A Critique of Lévi-Strauss and the Structuralist Movement*, Brighton.

Cohen, Walter (1987), 'Political Criticism of Shakespeare', in Howard and O'Connor 1987, pp. 18–46.

Cole and Morgan 1975 = Peter Cole and Jerry L. Morgan (eds.), *Syntax and Semantics. Vol. 3: Speech Acts*, New York, San Francisco, London.

Cole, Peter (ed.) (1978), *Syntax and Semantics. Vol. 9: Pragmatics*, New York, San Francisco, London.

Crews, Frederick C. (1986), *Skeptical Engagements*, New York.

De Man, Paul (1971), *Blindness and Insight. Essays in the Rhetoric of Contemporary Criticism*, New York.

—— (1979a), *Allegories of Reading. Figural Language in Rousseau, Nietzsche, Rilke, and Proust*, New Haven and London.

—— (1979b), 'Shelley Disfigured', in Geoffrey Hartman (ed.), *Deconstruction and Criticism*, New York, pp. 39–73.

—— (1986), *The Resistance to Theory*, Minneapolis.

Derrida, Jacques (1976), *Of Grammatology*, tr. G.C. Spivak (from *De la Grammatologie*, Paris 1967), Baltimore and London.

—— (1977), 'Signature Event Context', *Glyph* 1: pp. 172–97.

—— (1978), *Writing and Difference*, tr. A. Bass (from *L'Ecriture et la différence*, Paris 1967), Chicago.

—— (1980), *Positions*, tr. A. Bass (from *Positions*, Paris 1972), Chicago.

—— (1982), *Margins of Philosophy*, tr. A. Bass (from *Marges de la philosophie*, Paris 1972), Chicago.

Descombes, Vincent (1981), *Modern French Philosophy*, tr. L. Scott-Fox and J.M. Harding (from *Le Même et l'autre: quarante-cinq ans de philosophie française 1933–1978*, Paris 1979), Cambridge.

—— (1986), *Objects of All Sorts. A Philosophical Grammar*, tr. L. Scott-Fox and J.M. Harding (from *Grammaire d'objets en tous genres*, Paris 1983), Oxford.

De Sousa, Geraldo U. (1988), 'Semiotics of Kinship in *Richard II*', in Atkins and Bergeron 1988, pp. 173–91.

Dews, Peter (1987), *Logics of Disintegration. Post-structuralist Thought and the Claims of Critical Theory*, London.

Dollimore, Jonathan (1990a), 'Shakespeare, Cultural Materialism, Feminism, and Marxist Humanism', *New Literary History* 21: pp. 471–93.

—— (1990b), 'Critical Developments. Cultural Materialism, Feminism and Gender Critique, and New Historicism', in Stanley Wells (ed.), *Shakespeare. A Bibliographical Guide*, Oxford, pp. 405–28.

Dollimore and Sinfield 1985 = Dollimore, Jonathan and Alan Sinfield (eds.), *Political Shakespeare. New Essays in Cultural Materialism*, Manchester.

Donoghue, Denis (1980), 'Deconstructing Deconstruction', *New York Review of Books*, 12 June 1980, pp. 37–41.

—— (1981), *Ferocious Alphabets*, London and Boston.

Doran, Madeleine (1954), *Endeavors of Art. A Study of Form in Elizabethan Drama*, Madison, Wis.

Drakakis, John (ed.) (1985), *Alternative Shakespeares*, London.

Dreher, Diane Elizabeth (1986), *Domination and Defiance. Fathers and Daughters in Shakespeare*, Lexington, Ky.

Dusinberre, Juliet (1975), *Shakespeare and the Nature of Women*, London.

Ellenberger, Henri F. (1970), *The Discovery of the Unconscious. The History and Evolution of Dynamic Psychiatry*, New York.

Ellis, John M. (1974), *The Theory of Literary Criticism. A Logical Analysis*, Berkeley and Los Angeles.

—— (1989), *Against Deconstruction*, Princeton, N.J.

Engler, Rudolf (1968), *Lexique de la Terminologie Saussurienne*, Utrecht.

Erickson, Peter B. (1981), 'The Failure of Relationship Between Men and Women in *Love's Labour's Lost*', in Greene and Swift 1981, pp. 65–81.

—— (1987), 'Rewriting the Renaissance, Rewriting Ourselves', *Shakespeare Quarterly* 38: pp. 327–37.

Evans, Malcolm (1985), 'Deconstructing Shakespeare's Comedies', in Drakakis 1985, pp. 67–94.

Eysenck, Hans (1985), *Decline and Fall of the Freudian Empire*, New York.

Ezell, Margaret J.M. (1987), *The Patriarch's Wife. Literary Evidence and the History of the Family*, Chapel Hill, N.C.

Felperin, Howard (1990), *The Uses of the Canon. Elizabethan Literature and Contemporary Theory*, Oxford.

Ferry, Luc and Alain Renaut (1985), *La pensée 68. Essai sur l'anti-humanisme contemporain*, Paris.

Fineman, Joel (1989), 'The History of the Anecdote: Fiction and Fiction', in Veeser 1989, pp. 49–76.

Fischer, Michael (1985), *Does Deconstruction Make Any Difference? Post-structuralism and the Defense of Poetry in Modern Criticism*, Bloomington, Ind.

Foucault, Michel (1972), *The Archaeology of Knowledge*, tr. A.M. Sheridan Smith, and *The Discourse of Language*, tr. R. Swyer (from *L'Archéologie du savoir*, Paris 1969, and *L'Ordre du discours*, Paris, 1971), New York.

Fowler, Alastair (1988), 'Bids For Power' (rev. of Greenblatt, ed. *Representing the English Renaissance*), *Times Literary Supplement*, 2–8 September, pp. 967–8.

Fox-Genovese, Elizabeth (1989), 'Literary Criticism and the Politics of the New Historicism', in Veeser 1989, pp. 213–24.

—— (1991), *Feminism Without Illusion. A Critique of Individualism*, Chapel Hill, N.C.

Frank, Manfred (1989), *What is Neo-structuralism?*, tr. S. Wilke and R. Gray (from *Was ist Neostrukturalismus?*, Frankfurt 1984), Minneapolis, Minnesota.

French, Marilyn (1982), *Shakespeare's Division of Experience*, London.

Frey, Charles (1980), '"O sacred, shadowy, cold, and constant queen": Shakespeare's Imperiled and Chastening Daughters', in Lenz *et al.* 1980, pp. 295–313.

Frye, R.M. (1963), *Shakespeare and Christian Doctrine*, Princeton, N.J.

Gallagher, Catherine (1989), 'Marxism and the New Historicism', in Veeser 1989, pp. 37–48.

Garber, Marjorie (1987), *Shakespeare's Ghost Writers. Literature as Uncanny Causality*, London.

Geertz, Clifford (1973), *The Interpretation of Cultures. Selected Essays*, New York.

Gellner, Ernest (1985), *The Psychoanalytic Movement. Or, The Coming of Unreason*, London.

Godel, Robert (1957), *Les sources manuscrites du Cours de linguistique générale de F. de Saussure*, Geneva.

Gohlke, Madelon (1980), '"I wooed thee with my sword": Shakespeare's Tragic Paradigms', in Lenz *et al.* 1980, pp. 150–70.

—— (1981), '"All that is spoke is marred': Language and Consciousness in *Othello*', in Greene and Swift 1981, pp. 157–76.

Goldberg, Jonathan (1987), 'Speculations: *Macbeth* and Source', in Howard and O'Connor 1987, pp. 242–64.

—— (1988), 'Perspectives: Dover Cliff and the Conditions of Representation', in Atkins and Bergeron 1988, pp. 245–66.

Goodman, Nelson (1976), *Languages of Art. An Approach To a Theory of Symbols*, Indianapolis, Ind.

Graff, Gerald (1979), *Literature Against Itself. Literary Ideas in Modern Society*, Chicago and London.

—— (1980), 'Deconstruction as Dogma, or, "Come Back to the Raft Ag'in, Strether Honey!"', *Georgia Review* 34: pp. 404–21.

—— (1989), 'Co-optation', in Veeser 1989, pp. 168–81.

Greenblatt, Stephen (1988), *Shakespearean Negotiations*, Oxford.

—— (1990), *Learning to Curse. Essays in Modern Culture*, New York and London.

Greene and Swift 1981 = Greene, Gayle and Carolyn Ruth Swift (eds.), 'Feminist Criticism of Shakespeare', *Women's Studies*, Vol. 9 nos. 1 and 2: pp. 1–201 (Special Issue).

Greene, Gayle (1981), 'Feminist and Marxist Criticism: An Argument for Alliances', in Greene and Swift 1981, pp. 29–45.

—— (1992), 'The Myth of Neutrality, Again?', in Kamps 1992, pp. 23–9.

Greer, Germaine (1988), 'The Proper Study of Womankind', *Times Literary Supplement*, 3 June, pp. 616 and 629.

Grice, Paul (1989), *Studies in the Way of Words*, Cambridge, Mass.

Grosskurth, Phyllis (1991), 'The New Psychology of Women', *New York Review of Books*, 24 October, pp. 25–31.

Grünbaum, Adolf (1984), *The Foundations of Psychoanalysis. A Philosophical Critique*, Berkeley and Los Angeles.

Halliday, M.A.K. (1970), 'Language Structure and Language Function', in John Lyons (ed.) *New Horizons in Linguistics*, Harmondsworth, pp. 140–65.

—— (1975), *Learning How to Mean. Explorations in the Development of Language*, London.

Hampshire, Stuart (1959), *Thought and Action. A New Approach to Moral Philosophy and to the Problem of Freedom of the Will*, New York (repr. 1969).

Harris, Roy (1987), *Reading Saussure. A Critical Commentary on the 'Cours de linguistique générale'*, Oxford.

Harris, Wendell V. (1988), *Interpretive Acts. In Search of Meaning*, Oxford.

—— (1991), 'Canonicity', *PMLA* 106: pp. 110–21.

Hawkes, Terence (1985), 'Shakespeare and New Critical Approaches', in S. Wells (ed.) *The Cambridge Companion to Shakespeare Studies*, Cambridge (repr. 1991), pp. 287–302.

Hayles, Nancy K. (1979), 'Sexual Disguise in *As You Like It* and *Twelfth Night*', *Shakespeare Survey* 32: pp. 63–72.

Hays, Janice (1980), 'Those "soft and delicate desires": *Much Ado* and the Distrust of Women', in Lenz *et al.* 1980, pp. 79–99.

Himmelfarb, Gertrude (1987), *The New History and the Old*, Cambridge, Mass.

Hirsch, E.D., Jr. (1967), *Validity in Interpretation*, New Haven, Conn.

Holdcroft, David (1991), *Saussure, Signs, System, and Arbitrariness*, Cambridge.

Holderness, Graham (ed.) (1988), *The Shakespeare Myth*, Manchester.

Horn, Laurence R. (1988), 'Pragmatic Theory', in Newmeyer 1988, pp. 113–45.

Howard, Jean E. (1986), 'The New Historicism in Renaissance Studies', *English Literary Renaissance* 16: pp. 13–43.

—— (1988), 'Crossdressing, The Theatre, and Gender Struggle in Early Modern England', *Shakespeare Quarterly* 39: pp. 418–40.

Howard and O'Connor 1987 = Howard, Jean E. and Marion F. O'Connor (1987), *Shakespeare Reproduced. The Text in History and Ideology*, London.

Jackson, Leonard (1991), *The Poverty of Structuralism. Literature and Stucturalist Theory*, London and New York.

Jameson, Fredric (1972), *The Prison-House of Language. A Critical Account of Structuralism and Russian Formalism*, Princeton, N.J.

—— (1981), *The Political Unconscious. Narrative as a Socially Symbolic Act*, London.

Jardine, Lisa (1983), *Still Harping on Daughters. Women and Drama in the Age of Shakespeare*, Brighton.

Kahn, Coppélia (1980), 'Coming of Age in Verona', in Lenz et al. 1980, pp. 171–93.

Kamps, Ivo (ed.) (1992), *Shakespeare Left and Right*, London.

Kavanagh, James H. (1985), 'Shakespeare in Ideology', in Drakakis 1985, pp. 144–65.

Kermode, Frank (1989), *An Appetite for Poetry. Essays in Literary Interpretation*, London.

Klein, Joan Larsen (1980), 'Lady Macbeth: "Infirm of Purpose"', in Lenz et al. 1980, pp. 240–55.

Kopper, John M. (1988), 'Troilus at Pluto's Gates: Subjectivity and Duplicity of Discourse in Shakespeare's *Troilus and Cressida*', in Atkins and Bergeron 1988, pp. 149–71.

Lacan, Jacques (1966), *Ecrits*, Paris.

LaCapra, Dominick (1982), review of Fredric Jameson, *The Political Unconscious*, in *History and Theory* 21: pp. 83–106.

Ladusaw, William A. (1988), 'Semantic Theory', in Newmeyer 1988, pp. 89–112.

Lamarque, Peter (1990), 'The Death of the Author: An Analytical Autopsy', *British Journal of Aesthetics* 30: pp. 319–31.

Lehman, David (1991), *Signs of the Times. Deconstruction and the Fall of Paul de Man*, New York.

Lentricchia, Frank (1980), *After the New Criticism*, London.

—— (1983), *Criticism and Social Change*, Chicago and London.

—— (1988), *Ariel and the Police. Michel Foucault, William James, Wallace Stevens*, Madison, Wisc.

—— (1989), 'Foucault's Legacy: A New Historicism?', in Veeser 1989, pp. 231–42.

Lenz et al. 1980 = Lenz, Carolyn Ruth Swift, with Gayle Greene and Carol Thomas Neely (eds.), *The Woman's Part. Feminist Criticism of Shakespeare*, Urbana, Ill.

Lévi-Strauss, Claude (1950), Introduction to Marcel Mauss, *Sociologie et Anthropologie*, Paris.

—— (1963), *Structural Anthropology* tr. C. Jacobson and B.G. Schoepf (from *Anthropologie structurale*, Paris 1958), New York.

Levin, Richard (1979), *New Readings vs. Old Plays. Recent Trends in the Reinterpretation of English Renaissance Drama*, Chicago.

—— (1988a), 'Feminist Thematics and Shakespearean Tragedy', *PMLA* 103: pp. 125–38; Reply to letters: pp. 819ff.

—— (1988b), 'Leaking Relativism', *Essays in Criticism* 38: pp. 267–77.

—— (1989a), Reply to letter, *PMLA* 104: pp. 78–9.

—— (1989b), 'Unthinkable Thoughts in the New Historicizing of English Renaissance Drama', *New Literary History* 21: pp. 433–47.

—— (1989c), 'Reply to Catherine Belsey and Jonathan Goldberg', *New Literary History* 21: pp. 463–70.

—— (1990), 'The Poetics and Politics of Bardicide', *PMLA* 105: pp. 491–504.

—— (1992), 'Ideological Criticism and Pluralism', in Kamps 1992, pp. 15–21, and reply, pp. 47–60.

Lilla, Mark (1992), 'Marx and Murder. Althusser's demon and the flight from subjectivity', *Times Literary Supplement*, 25 September 1992, pp. 3–4.

Lodge, David (ed.) (1988), *Modern Criticism and Theory*, London and New York, 3rd repr. 1989.

Lyons, John (1968), *Introduction to Theoretical Linguistics*, Cambridge, repr. 1971.

—— (1977), *Semantics*, 2 vols., Cambridge, repr. 1989.

McDonnell and Robins 1980 = Kevin McDonnell and Kevin Robins, 'Marxist Cultural Theory: The Althusserian Smokescreen', in Clarke *et al.* 1980, pp. 157–231.

McFadden, George (1981), Review of Paul de Man, *Allegories of Reading*, *Journal of Aesthetics and Art Criticism* 39: pp. 337–41.

Macherey, Pierre (1978), *A Theory of Literary Production* (tr. from *Pour une théorie de la production littéraire*, Paris, 1966), London.

MacIntyre, Alasdair (1971), *Against the Self-Images of the Age*, London.

Maclean, Ian (1980), *The Renaissance Notion of Women. A Study in the fortunes of scholasticism and medical science in European intellectual life*, Cambridge.

McLuskie, Kathleen (1985), 'The Patriarchal Bard: Feminist Criticism and Shakespeare: *King Lear* and *Measure for Measure*', in Dollimore and Sinfield 1985, pp. 88–108, at pp. 89–91.

Margolies, David (1988), 'Teaching the Handsaw to Fly: Shakespeare as a Hegemonic Instrument', in Holderness 1988, pp. 42–53.

Merquior, J.G. (1985), *Foucault*, Berkeley and Los Angeles.

—— (1986a), *From Prague to Paris. A Critique of Structuralist and Post-structuralist Thought*, London.

—— (1986b), *Western Marxism*, London.

Meulen, Alice ter (1988), 'Linguistics and the Philosophy of Language', in Newmeyer 1988, pp. 430–46.

Miller, J. Hillis (1975), 'Deconstructing the Deconstructors', *Diacritics* 5: 24–31.

—— (1976a), 'Stevens' Rock and Criticism as Cure', *Georgia Review* 30: pp. 5–31.

—— (1976b), 'Stevens' Rock and Criticism as Cure: II', *ibid.*: pp. 330–48.

—— (1976c), 'Walter Pater: A Partial Portrait', *Daedalus* 105: pp. 97–113.

—— (1977), 'Ariachne's Broken Woof', *Georgia Review* 31: pp. 44–60.

—— (1979), 'The Critic As Host', in H. Bloom *et al.*, *Deconstruction and Criticism*, New York, pp. 217–53.

—— (1987), 'The Triumph of Theory, the Resistance to Reading, and the Question of the Material Base', *PMLA* 102: pp. 281–91.

Miner, Madonne M. (1980), '"Neither mother, wife, nor England's queen": The Roles of Women in *Richard III*', in Lenz *et al.* 1980, pp. 35–55.

Montrose, Louis (1986), 'Renaissance Literary Studies and the Subject of History', *English Literary Renaissance* 16: pp. 5–12.

—— (1989), 'Professing the Renaissance: The Poetics and Politics of Culture', in Veeser 1989, pp. 15–36.

Muir, Kenneth (1961), *Shakespeare's Sources*, London.

Neely, Carol Thomas (1980), 'Women and Men in *Othello*: "What should such a fool / Do with so good a woman?"', in Lenz *et al.* 1980, pp. 211–39.

—— (1981), 'Feminist Modes of Shakespearean Criticism: Compensatory, Justificatory, Transformational', in Greene and Swift 1981, pp. 3–15.

—— (1988), 'Constructing the Subject: Feminist Practice and the New Renaissance Discourses', *English Literary Renaissance* 18: pp. 5–18.

Nehamas, Alexander (1987), 'Writer, Text, Work, Author', in A.J. Cascardi (ed.) *Literature and the Question of Philosophy*, Baltimore and London, pp. 267–91.

Nevo, Ruth (1987), *Shakespeare's Other Language*, London.

Newman, Karen (1987), '"And wash the Ethiop white": femininity and the monstrous in *Othello*', in Howard and O'Connor 1987, pp. 143–62.

Newmeyer, Frederick J. (ed.) (1988), *Linguistics: The Cambridge Survey. Volume I, Linguistic Theory: Foundations*, Cambridge.

Newton, Judith Lowder (1989), 'History as Usual? Feminism and the "New Historicism"', in Veeser 1989, pp. 152–67.

Novy, Marianne (1981), 'Demythologizing Shakespeare', in Greene and Swift 1981, pp. 17–27.

—— (1984), *Gender Relations in Shakespeare*, Chapel Hill, N.C.

Nuttall, A.D. (1983), *A New Mimesis. Shakespeare and the Representation of Reality*, London.

Olsen, S.H. (1978), *The Structure of Literary Understanding*, Cambridge.

—— (1987), *The End of Literary Theory*, Cambridge.

Outhwaite, R.B. (ed.) (1981), *Marriage and Society. Studies in the Social History of Marriage*, London.

Park, Clara Claiborne (1980), 'As We Like It: How a Girl Can Be Smart and Still Popular', in Lenz *et al.* 1980, pp. 100–16.

Parker 1985 = Parker, Patricia and Geoffrey Hartman (eds.) (1985), *Shakespeare and the Question of Theory*, New York and London.

Pavel, Thomas (1989), *The Feud of Language. A History of Structuralist Thought*, tr. L. Jordan and T. Pavel (from *Le mirage linguistique*, Paris 1988), Oxford.

Pechter, Edward (1987), 'The New Historicism and Its Discontents. Politicizing Renaissance Drama', *PMLA* 102: pp. 292–303.

Pecora, Vincent P. (1989), 'The Limits of Local Knowledge', in Veeser 1989, pp. 243–76.

Pettit, Philip (1975), *The Concept of Structuralism: A Critical Analysis*, Berkeley and Los Angeles.

Plotkin, Cary H. (1989), *The Tenth Muse. Victorian Philology and the Genesis of the Poetic Language of Gerard Manley Hopkins*, Carbondale, Ill.

Porter, Roy (1987), *A Social History of Madness. Stories of the Insane*, London.

Rabkin, Norman (ed.) (1964), *Approaches to Shakespeare*, New York.

Ranald, Margaret Loftus (1987), *Shakespeare & His Social Context*, New York.

Rose, Jacqueline (1985), 'Sexuality in the Reading of Shakespeare: *Hamlet* and *Measure for Measure*', in Drakakis 1985, pp. 95–118.

Runciman, W.G. (1983), *A Treatise on Social Theory. Volume I: The Methodology of Social Theory*, Cambridge.

Said, Edward W. (1975), *Beginnings. Intention and Method*, New York.

—— (1983), *The World, the Text, and the Critic*, Boston.

Saussure, Ferdinand de (1972), *Cours de linguistique générale*, ed. Tullio de Mauro, Paris; repr. 1985.

Scholes, Robert (1988), 'Deconstruction and Communication', *Critical Inquiry* 14: pp. 278–95.

Searle, John R. (1969), *Speech Acts. An Essay in the Philosophy of Language*, Cambridge.

—— (1977), 'Reiterating the Differences: A Reply to Derrida', *Glyph* 1: pp. 198–208.

—— (1983), 'The Word Turned Upside Down', Review essay of Jonathan Culler's *On Deconstruction*, in *New York Review of Books*, 27 October 1983, pp. 74–9.

—— (1984), 'An Exchange on Deconstruction', *New York Review of Books*, 2 February 1984, pp. 47–8.

Shirley, John W. (1983), *Thomas Harriot. A Biography*, Oxford.

Sidney, Sir Philip (1965), *An Apology for Poetry*, ed. G.K. Shepherd, London.

Siegel, Paul N. (1957), *Shakespearean Tragedy and the Elizabethan Compromise*, New York.

—— (1986), *Shakespeare's English and Roman History Plays. A Marxist Approach*, Rutherford and Madison.

Simpson, David (1988), 'Literary Criticism and the Return to "History"', *Critical Inquiry* 14: pp. 721–47.

Sinfield, Alan (1981), 'Against Appropriation', *Essays in Criticism* 31: pp. 181–95.

—— (1985), 'Give An Account of Shakespeare and Education...', in Dollimore and Sinfield 1985, pp. 134–57.

Smith, Rebecca (1980), 'A Heart Cleft in Twain: The Dilemma of Shakespeare's Gertrude', in Lenz *et al.* 1980, pp. 194–210.

Sperber, Dan (1975), *Rethinking Symbolism*, tr. A.L. Morton (from *Le Symbolisme en général*, Paris 1974), Cambridge.

—— (1979), 'Claude Lévi-Strauss', in Sturrock 1979, pp. 19–51.

Sperber and Wilson 1986 = Sperber, Dan and Deirdre Wilson, *Relevance. Communication and Cognition*, Oxford.

Spivak, G.C. (1976), 'Translator's Preface', in Derrida 1976, pp. ix–lxxxvii.

—— (1989), 'The New Historicism: Political Commitment and the Postmodern Critic', in Veeser 1989, pp. 277–92.

Stockholder, Kay (1987), *Dream Works. Lovers and Families in Shakespeare's Plays*, Toronto.

Sturrock, John, ed. (1979), *Structuralism and Since. From Lévi-Strauss to Derrida*, Oxford.

Sulloway, Frank J. (1983), *Freud, Biologist of the Mind. Beyond the Psychoanalytic Legend*, New York, rev. ed.

—— (1991), 'Reassessing Freud's Case Histories. The Social Construction of Psychoanalysis', *Isis* 82: pp. 245–75.

Sundelson, David (1981), 'Misogyny and Rule in *Measure for Measure*', in Greene and Swift 1981, pp. 83–91.

Tallis, Raymond (1988), *Not Saussure. A Critique of Post-Saussurean Literary Theory*, London.

Thomas, Brook (1989), 'The New Historicism and Other Old-Fashioned Topics', in Veeser 1989, pp. 182–203.

Thompson, Ann (1988), '"The Warrant of Womanhood": Shakespeare and Feminist Criticism', in Holderness 1988, pp. 74–88.

Thompson, E.P. (1978), *The Poverty of Theory & Other Essays*, New York and London.

Timpanaro, Sebastiano (1975), *On Materialism*, tr. L. Garner, London.

Veeser, H. Aram (ed.) (1989), *The New Historicism*, New York and London.

Vendler, Helen (1990), 'Feminism and Literature', *New York Review of Books*, 31 May, pp. 19–25.

Vickers, Brian (1968), *The Artistry of Shakespeare's Prose*, London.

—— (1973), *Towards Greek Tragedy*, London.

—— (1988), *In Defence of Rhetoric*, Oxford.

—— (1989), *Returning to Shakespeare*, London.

—— (ed.) (1974–1981), *Shakespeare: The Critical Heritage*, 6 vols., London and Boston: Vol. 1: *1623–1692* (1974); Vol. 2: *1693–1733* (1974); Vol. 3: *1733–1752* (1975); Vol. 4: *1753–1765* (1976); Vol. 5: *1765–1774* (1979); Vol. 6: *1774–1801* (1981).

Waller, Gary (1988), 'Decentering the Bard: The Dissemination of the Shakespearean Text', in Atkins and Bergeron 1988, pp. 21–45.

Walton, Kendall (1990), *Mimesis as Make-Believe*, Cambridge, Mass.

Wayne, Don E. (1987), 'Power, Politics, and the Shakespearean Text: Recent Criticism in England and the United States', in Howard and O'Connor 1987, pp. 47–67.

Weimann, Robert (1978), *Shakespeare and the Popular Tradition in the Theatre: Studies in the Social Dimension of Dramatic Form and Function*, tr. and ed. Robert Schwartz (from *Shakespeare und die Tradition des Volkstheaters*, Berlin 1967), Baltimore, Md.

White, Hayden (1979), 'Michel Foucault', in Sturrock 1979, pp. 81–115.

—— (1989), 'New Historicism: A Comment', in Veeser 1989, pp. 293–302.

Wilden, Anthony (1972), *System and Structure*, London.

Williamson, Marilyn L. (1981), 'Doubling, Women's Anger, and Genre', in Greene and Swift 1981, pp. 107–19.

Wittgenstein, Ludwig (1958), *Philosophical Investigations*, tr. G.E.M. Anscombe, Oxford, repr. 1989.

Wollheim, Richard (1980), *Art and Its Objects*, rev. ed., Cambridge (1st ed. New York, 1968).

Woodbridge, Linda (1984), *Women and the English Renaissance. Literature and the Nature of Womankind, 1540–1620*, Brighton.

Index